BRUTAL BATTLES OF
VIETNAM
AMERICA'S DEADLIEST DAYS
1965-1972

RICHARD K. KOLB, **EDITOR**

IN RECOGNITION OF THE 50th ANNIVERSARY OF THE VIETNAM WAR

NO ONE DOES MORE FOR VETERANS.

PUBLISHER: Veterans of Foreign Wars

EDITOR: Richard K. Kolb

BOOK DESIGN AND PRODUCTION:
Robert Widener

EDITORIAL ASSISTANCE: Tim Dyhouse, Janie Dyhouse, Kelly Gibson, Kelly Von Lunen and Julie Nonnemaker (graphics assistance).

PUBLISHED BY:
Veterans of Foreign Wars
406 W. 34th Street
Kansas City, Missouri 64111

ISBN: 978-0-9743643-4-6
Library of Congress Catalog Card Number: 2017943415

Printed and bound in USA
by Quad Graphics, West Allis, Wis., and Versailles, Ky.
First printing July 2017

COVER PHOTO: A paratrooper of the 503rd Infantry Regiment, 173rd Airborne Brigade, dashes for cover while under fire on Hill 875 during the Battle of Dak To in November 1967. The regiment's 2nd and 4th battalions sustained 131 KIA in taking the hill between Nov. 18-23. Some 72 died on Nov. 20 alone.
PHOTO BY FONDATION GILLES CARON/GAMMA-RAPHO VIA GETTY IMAGES

TITLE PAGE: Members of C Co., 2nd Bn., 35th Inf., 25th Inf. Div., are pinned down by hostile fire as a radio operator calls for air support five miles north of Duc Pho during *Operation Baker* on May 10, 1967.
NATIONAL ARCHIVES PHOTO

RIGHT: Infantrymen of B Co. 2nd Bn., 14th Inf. Regt., 25th Inf. Div., search a deserted hooch near Cu Chi in May 1966. NATIONAL ARCHIVES PHOTO

DEDICATED TO THE
58,275 AMERICANS
WHO SACRIFICED
THEIR LIVES IN
THE VIETNAM WAR

CONTENTS

CONTENTS

DEDICATION

Brutal Battles of Vietnam: America's Deadliest Days, 1965-1972 is about, as famed war correspondent Ernie Pyle once put it, "the men up there doing the dying" in war. Its objective is simple: to commemorate sacrifice. Based on *VFW* magazine's award-winning series, the book is one-of-a-kind: the first and only to offer a comprehensive U.S. battle history of Vietnam in a single volume. It is geared toward the popular reader. But it is not intended for the uninitiated into the basics of the war—it is not Vietnam War 101. *Brutal Battles* is an unapologetic, straightforward, specifically targeted combat history unencumbered by politics, diplomacy, happenings on the home front, grand strategy, generalship or in-depth analysis of tactics.

For the most part, this book is simply concerned with the experiences of the trigger-pullers. In Vietnam parlance that means men with a military occupational specialty designated 11B in the Army and 0311 in the Marines. Engagements are told from the grunt's point of view by those who were actually there through hundreds of letters and interviews. Perhaps 12% of those who served in Vietnam were infantrymen. Yet in the Army, 70% of GIs killed by enemy action were "beating the bush." They were members of a special fraternity, ultimately holders of the highly coveted Combat Infantryman Badge.

This is certainly not to say that others did not make immense sacrifices. The grunts' fellow travelers—medics/corpsmen and artillery forward observers—immediately come to mind. When all members of the Army combat arms—helicopter crews, field artillerymen, combat medics, armor crewmen and combat engineers—are included they account for 87% of that service's hostile deaths in Vietnam. The

percentage was similar for the Marine Corps. And no one discounts the invaluable support provided by logistical units, the Navy, Air Force and Coast Guard. Because these services did not normally lose men in large numbers in single engagements, special chapters are devoted to them when they did.

In making the book length manageable, it was necessary to be highly subjective. In defining the "deadliest" battles for the purposes of this book, a casualty cut-off count was created by time period. For battles fought from 1965 through 1968, that number was generally 30. Starting in 1969 and running through 1972, it was roughly 20. Many significant firefights not covered in the chapters are listed in the *GI's Combat Chronology*.

Chapters in the book cover distinguishable battles—not ongoing operations or offensives. The official practice of not naming battles doomed them to obscurity. As military historian S.L.A. Marshall said in 1966: "It's the Madison Avenue approach to making bloodshed more acceptable. The net result is a scrambling of history. Battles are not called such and remain unidentified by their place names." Ask the public to name more than one Vietnam battle and you are likely to get a blank stare. Time—hours involved and occasionally days—was a key factor in determining inclusion. Two categories of major exceptions were made. Because the invasions of Cambodia (1970) and Laos (1971) were unique, they are included. Also, the goal was to make sure every infantry division, independent brigade and separate regiment was represented. So in some chapters, the casualty count does not conform to the criteria established for the entire book.

Furthermore, our intent was to emphasize the forgotten and largely unknown battles. Hence, the more famous battles that are already well written about do not proportionately receive as

Members of 1st Battalion, 7th Marines, board amtracs during *Operation Yazoo* in 1967.

Continued on next page

Cavalrymen of B Troop, 1st Reconnaissance Squadron, 9th Cavalry, jump from a UH-1D helicopter during *Operation Oregon* on April 24, 1967.

U.S. ARMY HERITAGE AND EDUCATION CENTER, CARLISLE, PA

much coverage. A perfect case in point: Khe Sanh. At least 10 books have been published about the siege. In other cases, single, definitive histories have been published. Example: Battle of the Ia Drang Valley. For readers who are interested in delving deeper into the actions presented, we have provided a detailed list of book titles in *Further Reading*.

A quick note on format. Although the book chapters appear chronologically, they can be read in any order. Battles fought in Vietnam seldom had any relation to one another. They were waged mostly in isolation. So the reader can initially select accounts based on personal interest. The chapters were designed to stand alone, and not intended as part of one seamless narrative. An added value of the contents are its contributions from a variety of writers. Using multiple authors provided different perspectives and writing styles to the benefit of the reader.

Readers will see two themes continually cropping up in each chapter. First, the individual courage of men in combat. Despite the title of the book *War Without Heroes* and the assertions of certain historians, Vietnam was replete with examples of heroism. The significant number of Medals of Honor, Distinguished Service Crosses, Navy Crosses, Air Forces Crosses and Silver Stars earned attest to this fact, as do the countless examples of unrecognized acts of personal valor.

The second major theme revolves around the specific circumstances of the casualties. Loss of life should be treated as more than a mere statistic. How many men died by unit, how they died and how they came to be in the war zone are essential elements to humanizing their sacrifices. Tracing the evolution of Army manpower sources is vital to this end.

The role of the draft is central to showing how the Army met its manpower needs. To this day, both sides of the divide distort the respective contributions of draftees and volunteers. When you have two former secretaries of defense

degrading the service of draftees, the need for setting the record straight is obvious. On the other hand, when media pundits question the IQ of anyone who actually volunteered, that need becomes even clearer.

Here are the facts: 648,500 draftees served in Vietnam, constituting 25% of the total of 2.6 million troops stationed within its borders. Contrary to popular perception, the Marine Corps did draft—to the tune of 42,633 men. Some 15,485 draftees were killed in action, equaling 32.5% of all hostile deaths. An additional 2,207 draftees died from non-hostile causes. Even among enlisted men only, the ratio of draftee to volunteer killed in action was virtually 50/50. About 5% of Marine enlisted men KIA were draftees. The bottom line: draftees and volunteers were equally patriotic and courageous, and efforts to divide them are most often politically motivated. As the war progressed, the source of military manpower evolved along with public attitudes.

"There is a great silent majority of Vietnam veterans," James R. Ebert wrote in *A Life in a Year: The American Infantryman in Vietnam, 1965-1972,* "who did not see themselves as being particularly special then or now. Theirs is a modesty typical of combat veterans." This book is dedicated to their memories, but especially to the 58,275 Americans who lost their lives.

Joe Galloway, the best-known Vietnam War correspondent, said of those who fought that "they were noble, good people who stood up and served when their country called them." But even more to the point, he stressed: "We are supposed to remember as long as any one of us is alive to remember. It's our job to remember." On this 50th anniversary of the Vietnam War, Galloway's admonition is more appropriate than ever. His words convey the very essence of the purpose of publishing VFW's *Brutal Battles of Vietnam.* It is a tribute committed to remembering, respecting and honoring.

RICHARD K. KOLB, EDITOR
PUBLISHER & EDITOR-IN-CHIEF
VFW MAGAZINE (1989-2016)

FOREWORD

I am proud to say I served as an M-79 grenadier in 1st Platoon, C Company, 4th Battalion, 31st Infantry, 196th Light Infantry Brigade of the Americal Division. I was a specialist 4 humping a 50-pound rucksack and 60 grenades in the searing heat and humidity of the Hiep Duc Valley. That is until I was hit on "Million Dollar Hill" on Aug. 20, 1969. My platoon's mission that day was to recover the bodies of men killed in a sister company. I was wounded twice, and four infantrymen in Charlie Company (my outfit) made the ultimate sacrifice.

My discharge from the Army came on Sept. 11, 1970. It was after three weeks in a Tokyo hospital followed by nine months in a Fort Riley (Kansas) hospital. Rehabilitation in these medical facilities was as sobering an experience as being in a firefight. Such experiences pull soldiers together in combat and afterward. It's this comradeship that sticks with you forever. Taking care of each other, covering the backs of those next to you creates life-long memories.

The military infused me with some lessons that you can't learn as quickly anywhere else. You were thrown together with people from such different backgrounds that it was an eye-opener for everybody—for kids from the South, from farm families in the Midwest, from big cities such as New York and Chicago. What most of us had in common were roots in the lower-middle and working-class. We inherited the work ethic of the blue-collar world.

While in Vietnam you ultimately had to find a reason to be there, a core reason you were doing what you were doing, so if you were going to die there you would know why. For me, it was helping impoverished Vietnamese families. That notion gave me something to grasp on to.

When I played for the Pittsburgh Steelers, I felt I was representing the best of my generation who served in uniform. I was symbolizing our successful readjustment story. Serving in Vietnam shaped my life as it did many of my fellow veterans, reinforcing essential values.

Those values are genuinely reflected in *Brutal Battles of Vietnam: America's Deadliest Days, 1965-1972*. This is a book you can share with family and friends to give them a better idea of what you personally experienced. The essence of combat clearly comes through in the carefully selected battles portrayed. Although the emotionally gripping accounts can resurrect painful memories, they also provide long overdue memorialization of those you served with.

Every American who sacrificed something in Vietnam deserves to be remembered with dignity. Memories of what you did must be preserved as our legacy to future generations. And this single, sweeping chronicle does so masterfully.

Brutal Battles of Vietnam is a monumental work beaming with recognition of and respect for those who fought and died. VFW is to be congratulated for producing such a glowing 50th anniversary tribute to the 3.4 million Americans who served in Southeast Asia during those trying years.

—Rocky Bleier

1st Platoon, C Company,
4th Battalion, 31st Infantry,
196th Light Infantry Brigade,
Americal Division

Wounded Aug. 20, 1969

Member of VFW Post 5756
in Sewickley, Pa.

Recipient of VFW's Hall of Fame
Award, 1975

ROCKY BLEIER

ACKNOWLEDGMENTS

Pfc. Robert L. Fuqua, Jr., 2nd Plt., D Co., 2nd Bn., 28th Inf., 1st Inf. Div., was one of 59 men killed in action on Oct. 17, 1967, during the Battle of Ong Thanh.

First and foremost, the Veterans of Foreign Wars must be congratulated for sponsoring this outstanding recognition of Vietnam veterans. It was in keeping with tradition that the organization made such a gesture on the war's 50th anniversary. After all, between 40% and 50% of VFW members served during the Vietnam War. And 23 of the men who led VFW in the past 33 years are veterans of Vietnam. So it was with great enthusiasm that VFW leaders endorsed this commemorative tribute to all 3.4 million Americans who served in the war.

First-person contributions from members and non-members alike made the book what it is—their personal experiences injected life into the battle accounts and gave them meaning. For more than a decade, while the Vietnam series was running in the magazine, actual veterans of the actions granted interviews and provided priceless letters detailing their life-and-death struggles. No other editor has had such a vast reservoir of firsthand knowledge to draw from. Consequently, in the end, veterans themselves told the history of the war's deadliest battles.

Brutal Battles of Vietnam would barely have been possible without the Coffelt Database. The precise casualty data contained in the book is available nowhere else. The database grew from an effort launched by Richard Coffelt (who died in 2012), a Cold War-era Army vet, in 1980. With the dedicated perseverance of David Argabright, Dick Arnold and Ken Davis this one-of-a-kind archive blossomed into a researcher's dream come true. Without the work of these Vietnam vets and their associates, the absolute accuracy of unit killed-in-action statistics would have been impossible to achieve.

Other vets also have done pioneering research. Gary Roush and Robert Sage, who created and maintain the Vietnam Helicopter Pilots Association database, provide an invaluable resource on helicopter data. They, too, are part of the research team at the Coffelt Database.

Many unit association historians made this project possible, among them Dan Gillotti, Larry Grzywinski, Les Hines, Gary Noller and Keith Short. Paul Herbert, Andrew Wood and Eric Gillespie of the First Division Museum at Cantigny and the Congressional Medal of Honor Society also provided valuable information. Individual vets—too many to name here—have given generously of their time.

Another research pioneer is Doug Sterner, founder of the Military Times Hall of Valor. A fantastic, unique archive, the Hall of Valor details the individual military awards of countless war veterans. Sterner's monumental database offers documentation of medals, as well as descriptive citations all in one place. With this remarkable resource it was possible to relate the heroism of countless Vietnam servicemen whose bravery otherwise would have been lost to history. Moreover, the Vietnam Veterans Memorial Fund's *Wall of Faces* was a vital photo source.

Seldom has one individual author done so much to tell the stories of Vietnam veterans. While there are many top-notch writers of Vietnam history, Keith W. Nolan holds a special place in the pantheon of this war's chroniclers. He was called "the grunt's historian" for good reason. Nolan, who died far too young of cancer at 44 in 2009, produced 13 histories of campaigns and battles. Some of which would have been confined to the dustbin of history if not for his talents. A word of thanks, too, to the publisher of most of Nolan's books—Presidio Press (independent until 2002), then based in Novato, Calif. Its president Richard Kane recognized the value of Vietnam combat history early in the 1980s.

Finally, thank you to current *VFW* magazine staff members Tim and Janie Dyhouse, and former writers Kelly Von Lunen and Kelly Gibson. And a special thanks goes to first-rate proofreader Betty Melin.

VIETNAM: A BEGINNING AND AN END

From a fighting standpoint, America's war in Vietnam (as opposed to the *Vietnamese* war), had three distinct phases. In a nutshell, it began and ended as an advisory war. But in between, the fighting constituted full-fledged warfare against a highly motivated, well-armed and fully uniformed conventional force. Despite notions of an irregular war with a band of pajama-clad guerillas, Communist North Vietnam fielded an army as deadly as any that GIs ever faced.

U.S. career soldiers and Marines who had fought the Japanese in WWII and the Communist Chinese and North Koreans during the Korean War, sometimes rated the fighting ability of the North Vietnamese Army (NVA) as equal or superior. At its wartime peak, the NVA had 685,000 regulars in uniform organized into 24 divisions and 75 separate regiments. Even the Viet Cong, the military wing of the National Liberation Front in the South, could put 200,000 troops (many of them Main Force) on the battlefield, before they were decimated in 1968.

Officially, the U.S. Army's advisory campaign lasted from 1962 through mid-1965. During that period, perhaps 50,000 Americans served in South Vietnam. By the end of 1964, 267 GIs had been killed by enemy action. American military involvement deepened and escalated after Congress's *Gulf of Tonkin Resolution* of August 1964 gave the administration of President Lyndon Johnson a blank check to pursue the war as it saw fit.

In short order, Marine infantry battalions landed at Da Nang in March 1965. They were followed by the Army's 173rd Airborne Brigade in May. U.S. troops were authorized to engage directly in combat that June, launching their first offensive operation by month's end. U.S. troop strength in-country peaked at 543,482 on April 30, 1969. America's ground war persisted until early 1971. American actions by then were designed almost exclusively to back up the Army of South Vietnam (ARVN)—a policy known as "Vietnamization." But before it was all over, 2.6 million GIs had set foot on South Vietnamese soil and a total of 3.4 million, when including the entire Southeast Asia Theater, which encompassed the South China Sea.

The Nixon Administration began withdrawing major U.S. infantry units from South Vietnam on July 7, 1969. Officials proclaimed the end of American offensive ground operations after May 1, 1971, with a "defensive" role becoming set in concrete starting that November. Indeed, U.S. casualties declined tremendously until the last grunts were pulled out of the field in August 1972. By then, the war had reverted, for Americans, to the third phase—advisory again supported by air power. (U.S. air support would continue in Laos until April 17 and over Cambodia until Aug. 15, 1973).

In December 1972, U.S. bombers hit Hanoi—North Vietnam's nerve center—directly. Within a month, on Jan. 27, 1973, the Paris Peace Accords paved the way for America's extrication from the war between North and South Vietnam. All—not just "combat"—American troops were gone by March 29, 1973. America's war in Vietnam was over.

As Col. William Le Gro, intelligence chief of the Defense Attaché Office, said at the time: "The war belonged to the Vietnamese, and they were going to fight it ... [This marked] the end of the Second Indochina War and the beginning of the third." When the Third Indochina War—the *Vietnamese* war—ended on April 30, 1975, American troops had been absent from their soil for two full years. An independent South Vietnam had fallen to the Communist juggernaut.

Pfc. Bill Henry, an M-60 machine gunner with 1st Plt., C Co., 503rd Inf., 173rd Airborne Brigade, was awarded a Silver Star for his actions in the Battle of Hill 65, on Nov. 8, 1965.

PHOTO COURTESY BILL HENRY

BRUTAL BATTLES OF VIETNAM
1965

CHU LAI
HILL 65
AP NHA MAT
IA DRANG VALLEY
KIM SON VALLEY
MY CANH
CHAU NGAI
DAU TIENG
LZ BIRD
SUOI TRE
KHE SANH
VINH HUY
RACH NUI
DAK TO
CON THIEN
DONG SON
ONG THANH
TAM QUAN

IA DRANG VALLEY

THON THAM KHE
QUE SON VALLEY
HIEP DUC VALLEY
HOC MON
HILL 689
DAI DO
SAIGON
KHAM DUC
GO NOI ISLAND
AP TRANG DAU
RUSSELL AND NEVILLE
PLEI TRAP VALLEY
LIBERTY BRIDGE
HILL 996
FSB HENDERSON
CAMBODIA INCURSION
FSB RIPCORD
FSB MARY ANN

BY RICHARD K. KOLB

QUI NHON, 1965:
TERRORISM TAKES A TOLL

"A series of events," occurring in February 1965, "for the first time in the three years since U.S. troops went to Vietnam in force shocked the American people into some sense of being at war," proclaimed *Newsweek* late in that month.

Indeed, Radio Hanoi had exhorted the Viet Cong (VC) to "strike hard, very hard, at the enemy on all battlefields." In response, the National Liberation Front's Liberation Radio vowed GIs would soon "pay more blood debts." That threat was realized on Feb. 10, 1965, in the coastal city of Qui Nhon.

The target: the bachelor's enlisted men's quarters. It was billed as the Viet Cuong ("Strength of Vietnam") Hotel. But structurally the newly constructed four-story building was anything but that. With no reinforced concrete or reinforcing bars, it mostly was made of hollow red bricks held together by mortar and plaster.

Nevertheless, the U.S. government leased the billet for a helicopter maintenance unit. The 140th Transportation Detachment (Cargo Helicopter Field Maintenance), nicknamed the "Phantom Regulators," serviced the aircraft of the 117th Aviation Company (Assault Helicopter). Its 273 men in 1964 were based at the city's airfield.

The 117th's commanding officer, retired colonel James E. Rogers, was against placing the detachment in the hotel. "For both safety and security reasons, I voiced opposition to this arrangement," he said in an October 2014 interview.

CONFRONTING THE VC

At the time of the bombing, 43 men were in their rooms or in a bar on the ground floor. Coordinated attacks on the city began at 8:05 p.m. Two VC killed the South Vietnamese guards posted outside the building while two other VC planted two satchel charges at the main door. A 100-pound plastic charge destroyed the central staircase supporting the hotel.

Four stories were immediately reduced to one as the building crumbled into a pile of rubble more than 30 feet high. Alex Brassert was a U.S. adviser who happened to be in Qui Nhon at the time. "There was a loud explosion, then a second; the lights went out in the whole town," he said. "I saw red flashes in a back window that I think was near the stairwell. Then the Viet Cuong Hotel sank out of my field of vision."

Rescue operations began the day following the Feb. 10, 1965, Viet Cong attack on the Viet Cuong Hotel. Twenty-two men of the 140th Transportation Detachment plus one Green Beret died in the blast.

It was the deadliest single terrorist attack against GIs in the Vietnam War. But the Viet Cong bombing of an Army barracks in this port city is virtually unknown today.

FEBRUARY 1965

> "When we arrived at the hotel, I couldn't believe the devastation. We could hear men yelling for help. We dug for eight straight hours. Men cried out for their mothers, as some of us cried searching for them." —SPEC. 4 RAUL D. SERRANO

> "I discovered that one of his legs was mangled and I was able to free him. I assisted a Korean doctor to amputate his leg where he crawled out of a hole."
>
> —SPEC. 5 JOHN F. HUSKE, SILVER STAR RECIPIENT

117th vet Carl Vogel recalled: "I was in a guard tower that night. At first, I heard what I thought to be machine gun fire from the downtown area. The next thing I heard was an explosion; looked again and saw the hotel that housed the 140th lift into the air and settle to the ground. It was the worst night of my life."

Just before the attack, Spec. 5 Robert K. Marshall was alerted by VC gunfire. He quickly took up a firing position at the drainage port on the balcony. "I fired at them, and as I did, two more figures jumped from behind a newsstand 30 feet to my left and fired at me with submachine guns," Marshall said. "I shoved another clip into my rifle and emptied it, and one more, into them. I hit them both and saw them fall." Some 60 rounds of ammo assured that. "Then the hotel simply disintegrated beneath me," Marshall recalled.

Marshall was not the only American to engage the communists that evening. Special Forces Staff Sgt. Merle O. Van Alstine, a rotational replacement on his third tour, was in the bar that night. According to a vet nicknamed "Iggy" in an account given to Ray Bows in *Vietnam Military Lore*, Van Alstine pulled his sidearm. "Merle nailed them [two VC on a motorbike]. He fired his last six rounds split seconds before the blast. It took them six days to find Merle. His was the last body they found."

RESCUING SURVIVORS, RETRIEVING THE DEAD

Rescue operations were delayed until dawn because the VC took out the local power station, causing a blackout. On duty in the flight operations center when the explosion occurred, Spec. 4 Raul D. Serrano participated in the rescue and recovery.

"When we arrived at the hotel, I couldn't believe the devastation," he says. "We could hear men yelling for help. Digging out was very slow because we did not have proper equipment. We dug for eight straight hours. Men cried out for their mothers, as some of us cried searching for them."

Rummaging through the rubble required nerve, and it was displayed by John F. Huske. His Silver Star citation says that he "immediately, and without regard for his own safety, set about the task of crawling through the twisted wreckage searching for survivors. Throughout the night and early hours of the following day [he] continued rescuing survivors from the shifting and settling wreckage."

Today, says Huske, "I have tried to put those events behind me all these years, but these

Army personnel search through the debris of the Viet Cuong Hotel for survivors of the blast. Twenty-three Americans died in the terrorist attack.

events should be brought to light. I was one of the first responders as part of a quasi-search and rescue team. I spent over 12 hours digging to a man trapped under tons of debris. When I reached him, I discovered that one of his legs was mangled and I was able to free him. I assisted a Korean doctor to amputate his leg where he crawled out of a hole."

Arthur Abendschein was the last American taken out of the hotel alive after 35 hours being trapped. As quoted in *Vietnam Military Lore,* he related: "The big blast inside the hotel blew out all of the windows in my room and made the walls shake and start to crumble. The rubble tumbled around me. It was just liked riding a fast elevator."

That the experience left a permanent psychological impact on the survivors is beyond doubt. "It was very traumatic and had a profound effect on those who offered immediate assistance to the injured in the collapsed building," said Rogers. Lasting more than a week, "the task was very difficult and emotional for those involved in the recovery effort."

TALLYING THE TOLL

Indeed, it was. The detachment had to be reconstituted from scratch. "At the memorial service, I counted 22 pairs of empty boots," Serrano sadly remembers. "It is something that has stuck with me for 50 years."

No Viet Cong terrorist attack took a greater toll in American lives during the Vietnam War than the Viet Cuong Hotel tragedy. A total of 23 GIs died that night: All but one belonged to the 140th Transportation Detachment. The other was a Green Beret.

In addition, seven South Vietnamese women and children in the area of the explosion were killed, too. All 21 of the surviving 140th members were so badly wounded that they required evacuation stateside.

At this stage of the war, U.S. troops in country were mostly regulars. Of the 22 140th members killed, 19 had enlisted; just three were drafted. They ranged in age from 18 to 39; 55% were married.

But Qui Nhon was only a harbinger of things to come. At the funeral of Special Forces soldier Van Alstine in February 1965, one of the pallbearers was most prophetic. "It's a seven-day-a-week, 24-hour-a-day war going on over there, although a lot of people don't seem to be aware of it yet," Master Sgt. Laurel Ward said. "I am afraid the American people are going to see a lot more funerals before it's settled." ✪

THE TOLL

U.S. KIA:
23

U.S. WIA:
21

BY RICHARD K. KOLB

'REMEMBER DONG XOAI!'

"I am using my last battery for the radio and there is no more ammunition; we are all wounded, some of the more serious are holding grenades with the safety pins already pulled. The VC are attacking in human waves. The last wave has been defeated, but we are expecting the next wave now."

This urgent message relayed most likely by Staff Sgt. Harold Crowe from the Dong Xoai Special Forces Camp underscored just how dire the straights were for survivors of a full-scale enemy attack on June 10, 1965.

The camp was located more than 3 miles north of Dong Xoai, district capital of Phuoc Long province in War Zone D. The nearest big city was Bien Hoa, 44 miles to the south. The camp and capital lay astride a Viet Cong (VC) supply route from Cambodia at the intersection of a crossroads. The VC wanted to undermine the strategic hamlet concept and destroy a large Army of South Vietnam (ARVN) force. Dong Xoai made the perfect target.

BREACHING THE PERIMETER

Defending the camp were 11 Green Berets of Detachment A-342, 5th Special Forces (SF) Group, and nine Seabees of Team 1104, Naval Mobile Construction Battalion 11. The Seabees were there to construct a runway. The SF team had just arrived May 25. Some 435 Cambodians and South Vietnamese formed the indigenous force guarding the unfinished perimeter.

At 11:30 p.m. on June 9 the opening barrage began with 400 rounds of 60mm mortar fire. Two SF members were KIA by mortar fragments in the early hours of the 10th. SF Sgt. Donald Dedmon continued to fire his recoilless rifle even after being severely wounded by a grenade until his ammo ran out. While attempting to secure more ammo, he was mortally wounded. Dedmon was awarded a posthumous Silver Star.

VC demolitions and flamethrower teams made up the vanguard of 1,500 men of the 762nd and 763rd VC regiments attacking the camp. An SF sergeant recalled: "The VC would mass, come over the walls with grenades and flamethrowers, then reassemble, mass and come at us again. Just before each assault they'd start yelling and screaming like crazy people. Once they'd gotten inside, there was a lot of confusion."

Within three hours, at 2:30 a.m., the communists had breached the wall, forcing the defenders back to the district headquarters building. SF Spec. 4 Don McLaughlin (later evacuated to the 3rd Field Hospital) told MACV *Daily News Briefs:* "We were trying to fight them off, but they came swarming over the walls. There were eight of us along one wall, and we were trying to fight them off. We moved back into one of the houses in the

On June 10, 1965, Americans engaged in their deadliest battle of the early advisory phase of the Vietnam War. Sustaining 19 KIA, a handful of Green Berets and Seabees aided by helicopter crews made an epic 14-hour last stand at this besieged Special Forces camp.

JUNE 1965

Evidence of the intense firefight is seen in this rear view of the district headquarters. Green Berets made their way to the building but were quickly surrounded, withstanding flame-throwers, machine guns, recoilless rifle and small-arms fire. Medal of Honor recipients 2nd Lt. Charles Williams and CM3 Marvin Shields moved outside the headquarters' defenses and destroyed a VC machine gun position. Shields, however, was mortally wounded in the attack.

MEDAL OF
HONOR

CONGRESSIONAL MEDAL OF HONOR SOCIETY

**CM3
MARVIN G. SHIELDS**
(POSTHUMOUS)

CONGRESSIONAL MEDAL OF HONOR SOCIETY

**2ND LT. CHARLES
Q. WILLIAMS**

compound; the windows were open, and we were hitting the VC with everything we had."

As the fighting raged, acts of courage were commonplace. SF 2nd Lt. Charles Q. Williams, wounded five times, exhibited incredible bravery. One of the Americans on scene observed that Williams "was the calmest man there. He constantly exposed himself to enemy fire without any regard for his own life." Pinned down by a VC machine gun, he fired a 3.5-inch rocket launcher while Seabee Marvin G. Shields loaded it.

"Shields exposed himself to heavy enemy fire many times to aid the wounded and resupply others with ammunition," said a witness, "even after he had been shot in the face." He carried a critically wounded man to safety and was wounded three times. Shields' final act of valor was helping take out that machine gun. On the way back to supposed safety, he was mortally wounded and died aboard a helicopter.

A round fired by Shields and Williams had taken out the VC machine gun, slowing the attack and perhaps ultimately sparing the survivors a fatal fate.

Both Williams and Shields were awarded the Medal of Honor. Three more Green Berets eventually received the Distinguished Service Cross (DSC). Sgt. 1st Class Dallas W. Johnson, though suffering painful shrapnel wounds, killed a VC, evacuated a fellow soldier and personally carried another to relative safety. Sgt. 1st Class James T. Taylor, Jr., a medic, saved the life of his commander. While wounded, he treated the other wounded and fought off attackers all day. Pfc. Michael J. Hand also received the DSC (his actions are not publicly recorded).

Meanwhile, a MACV adviser outside the camp and attached to the 1st Bn., 7th ARVN Regt., went down with its entire helicopter lift after it was wiped out in a rubber field. One other American adviser also perished alongside South Vietnamese troops.

TO THE RESCUE

When the call went out for assistance, among the first to arrive were three members of MACV Special Detachment 5891. Airlifted from Tan Son Nhut Air Base by the 118th Assault Helicopter Company, their UH-1B (*Blue Tail 1*, 2nd Flight Platoon) was quickly targeted.

"[It] had a mortar round explode just outside the cockpit causing it to roll over immediately on its side," wrote James "Pete" Booth in *Returning Fire In the Beginning*. "A split second later, it exploded in a ball of fire. The entire [four-man] crew was killed [as well as two advisers]."

But one of the advisers apparently got off the helicopter when it landed and survived long enough to make a final radio transmission to a circling helicopter pilot. Capt. Bruce Johnson told the pilot his position was taking mortar fire and then the radio went silent.

None of the remains of the men from *Blue Tail 1* were ever recovered or even located. Rumor had it that the VC may have placed their bodies in a well. Their true fate, however, remains unknown.

Tragically, another helicopter was shot down by .51-caliber machine-gun fire at the soccer field. The UH-1D from A Co., 82nd Avn. Bn., was hit on descent at about 500 feet, exploded and burned. All four crewmen were killed. Detached from the 82nd Airborne Division (then serving on the Dominican Republic), the "Cowboys" were based at Vung Tau.

Both A Company and the 118th ("Thunderbirds") were assigned to the 145th Aviation Battalion. It consisted of eight aviation companies and 18 detachments. Pilots and crew from the 145th soon demonstrated flying abilities and aeronautical feats that would become the stuff of legend.

Shortly after noon, the VC captured the district command building, forcing American survivors into the two howitzer pits.

Maj. Harvey E. Stewart, CO of the 118th and a Korean War veteran, led three unarmed rescue helicopters to their position. Capt. William F. Fraker, a UH-1B gunship pilot with the

197th Armed Helicopter Company, escorted the rescue aircraft. Stewart evacuated most of the Americans. But when two were left behind, Fraker swooped down and picked one up, escaping in a hail of VC gunfire. Both Fraker and Stewart received the Distinguished Service Cross.

For the aviators of Stewart's company, June 10 was a powerful motivator. For years, the battle cry of the 118th was "Remember Dong Xoai!"

The 145th continued to perform rescues and medical evacuations of South Vietnamese troops under withering fire through June 11 and beyond. All told, unit aircraft flew 2,700 sorties and airlifted or repositioned 3,500 allied troops. That amazing feat earned the 145th the prestigious Presidential Unit Citation.

On June 13, Special Forces A-Team 311 arrived to rebuild the camp outside of Dong Xoai.

Little known is the fact that Dong Xoai almost became America's first major battle in Vietnam. Because the situation was so dire for the ARVN, Gen. William Westmoreland, commander of U.S forces, decided to commit GIs to combat there.

Some 738 men of the 1st Bn., 503rd Inf., 173rd Abn. Bde., along with elements of the 3rd Bn., 319th Field Artillery, were flown to Phuoc Vinh. They waited there for five days before returning to base on June 18. By then, the VC had withdrawn from Dong Xoai. But it was, according to MACV, "a tactical and psychological victory for the VC."

U.S. Army adviser Maj. James Sterling and soldiers of the ARVN 52nd Ranger Battalion look over the wreckage of a downed U.S. helicopter at Dong Xoai on June 10, 1965.

COUNTING CASUALTIES

Indeed, the communists had inflicted at least 416 KIA on the ARVN in the vicinity of Dong Xoai. To boot, 150 civilians were massacred, many when the VC torched the town with flamethrowers.

Back at the SF compound, the score was decidedly different. Some 134 VC bodies were counted in and around the camp. But that tally was not without a high price. Forty-three of the allied Cambodians and South Vietnamese perished along the perimeter.

Of the 20 Americans based there, five were KIA (three Green Berets and two Seabees) and 14 WIA. Then there were the five MACV advisers and eight helicopter crewmen KIA. A fighter pilot killed brought the final toll to 19.

Maj. Lawrence T. Holland, of the 615th Tactical Fighter Squadron, led a flight of F-100s over Dong Xoai on June 12. Swooping in at a low level, he destroyed a VC gun position but was shot down. Ejecting in time, he became entangled in his parachute and, while dangling from a tree, was shot by VC. Holland was awarded a posthumous Air Force Cross.

MEMORIES NEVER FADE

Fifty years later, the experiences during those days still weigh heavily on the minds of the participants. Jack Grasmeder, then the operations officer of the 118th, along with Ron Hill, flew the lead helicopter on all the assaults on Dong Xoai, including the rescue flight into the compound. He recalls how "everyone in the rescue displayed incredible courage. It is only appropriate that they be remembered today with respect and honor."

Freddy Holder was the crew chief of *Blue Tail 1*. "On the morning of June 10, Platoon Sgt. Joe Compa said to me, 'Holder, you play sergeant today. I'm going flying.' Sgt. Compa took my flight that day and was killed in my place. Their bodies [crew and advisers] have yet to be recovered and returned home," Holder said in March 2015.

In 1995, Holder and VFW member Jim Shield obtained a model H Huey helicopter from Fort Rucker, Ala., to serve as a memorial. Today, it stands in tribute to the seven men lost on *Blue Tail 1*. It is located on the grounds of VFW Post 4252 in Hernando, Fla. ✪

AIR FORCE
CROSS

MAJ. LAWRENCE T. HOLLAND
(POSTHUMOUS)

THE
TOLL

U.S. KIA:
19

A Co., 82nd Avn. Bn. (Detached).....4
MACV SD-5891 5
118th AHC, 145th Avn. Bn..............4
Det. A-342, 5th SFG 3
Seabee Team 1104, NMCB-11.......2
615th Tactical Fighter Squadron 1

U.S. WIA:
119

BY AL HEMINGWAY

VC 'SOUNDLY DEFEATED' AT CHU LAI

Gen. Lewis W. "Silent Lew" Walt, commanding general of the III MAF (Marine Amphibious Force), was in a quandary. Intelligence revealed that the 1st VC (Viet Cong) Regiment was massing for an assault on the airfield at Chu Lai, South Vietnam. Chu Lai, situated on the coast, was located in the southern I Corps region of the country.

Walt discussed his options with his staff and finally decided to strike the enemy in their stronghold on the Van Tuong Peninsula, approximately nine miles south of Chu Lai itself. It was a daring plan since it would leave the airstrip defenses weakened. Walt, however, felt the gamble was worth it.

STARLITE IS BORN

Col. Oscar Peatross, 7th Marine Regiment commander, was in charge of the operation, which was dubbed *Starlite*.

He opted for a two-pronged strike at the VC. He selected the 3rd Bn., 3rd Marines, for the amphibious assault and 2nd Bn., 4th Marines, for the helicopter strike. "The proposed battleground was mostly rolling country," Peatross later wrote, "about three-quarters cultivated, and elsewhere there was thick scrub [spread] from six to 100 feet … and there were few rice paddies. The beaches were sandy, with dunes in some places as far inland as 200 yards."

The 3rd would come ashore on Green Beach just north of the village of An Cuong No. 1; the 4th would be choppered into three landing zones (LZs) named Red, White and Blue.

TERRIFYING MOMENTS

Just after 6 a.m. on Aug. 18, 1965, K Btry., 4th Bn., 12th Marines, fired the opening salvo of the battle for Chu Lai. As the 155mm shells pounded VC positions, the destroyers *USS Orleck* and *Prichett*, and the light guided-missile cruiser *USS Galveston*, let loose a barrage on the enemy. In addition, fighter aircraft from Marine Air Groups (MAG) 11 and 12 dropped 18 tons of ordnance to soften the enemy's bulwarks.

After the preparatory bombardment, the 3rd Bn., 3rd Marines, made its way ashore and quickly moved inland. As the village of An Cuong 1 was secured, I Company set out to take An Cuong 2 and link up with the 2nd Bn., 4th Marines.

The "Magnificent Bastards" of the 2nd Battalion would find the going much tougher than originally thought. E Company soon found itself fighting a well-entrenched enemy

The Main Force Viet Cong were poised for an attack on Chu Lai in August 1965, but their plans were foiled in a "spoiling attack" by Marines in what would be the first major U.S. battle of the Vietnam War.

AUGUST 1965

U.S. MARINE CORPS PHOTO

Marines of E Co., 2nd Bn., 4th Marines, move out of the landing zone near An Cuong on Aug. 18, 1965. The Battle of Chu Lai was the centerpiece of *Operation Starlite*.

NAVY CROSS

CAPT. BRUCE WEBB
(POSTHUMOUS)

LANCE CPL. ERNIE WALLACE

PVT. SAMUEL J. BADNEK

2ND LT. ROBERT FISHEL COCHRAN, JR.
(POSTHUMOUS)

SGT. JAMES E. MULLOY, JR.

LT. COL. JOSEPH EUGENE MUIR

on a ridgeline near the LZ. A forward observer spotted more than 100 VC moving into the open.

He quickly called for a 107mm "Howtar"—a 4.2-inch mortar mounted on a 75mm howitzer frame. The unique weapon was swung into action and within minutes more than 90 VC soldiers were killed.

Meanwhile, UH-34Ds from Helicopter Marine Medium (HMM) Squadrons 261 and 361 began touching down on LZ Blue. As H Company Marines leaped from the aircraft, the enemy hit them with withering fire from atop Hill 43, a small knoll southeast of the LZ.

The first few moments were terrifying. A helicopter door gunner had his jaw torn apart from enemy fire. One Marine was struck in the throat. Another stumbled and fell with a huge wound in his stomach. "You just have to close your eyes and drop down to the deck," said Capt. Howard Henry, a chopper pilot with HMM-361.

'ALL HELL BROKE LOOSE'

Unknown to the Marines, H Company had landed atop the headquarters of the 60th VC Battalion. 1st Lt. Homer Jenkins, company commander, quickly organized his men to assault Hill 43 and eliminate the threat. Skyhawks and Phantoms from Fighter Squadrons 513 and 542 hammered the hilltop as the infantrymen pushed forward. Assisted by M-48 tanks, the Marines soon dislodged the VC from Hill 43.

While Hill 43 was being cleared, I Co., 3rd Bn., was inching its way toward An Cuong 2. The hamlet consisted of 25-30 huts, fighting holes and camouflaged trench lines connected by a system of interlocking tunnels.

As the Leathernecks moved cautiously into the village, a grenade killed Capt. Bruce Webb, the company commander, instantly. He was posthumously awarded the Navy Cross for his extraordinary heroism that day.

"I was there when Capt. Webb got killed," Sgt. Dwight Layman said. "A gook threw a grenade into the command group. It also killed the radio operator. I immediately grabbed an incendiary grenade and tossed it into the spider hole and fried him. I was setting up LZs for the choppers to evacuate the wounded when a round caught me in the back of the neck and went out through my shoulder. That was it for me. My part in *Starlite* was over."

But before the riflemen could secure An Cuong 2, they were told to reinforce K Company, which was engaged in a heavy firefight about 2,000 meters to the northeast.

H Company was moving on An Cuong 2 to meet up with I Company. As they approached the tiny village of Nam Yen 3, it was decided to bypass it and keep going. Without warning, the company was struck with intense automatic weapons fire. An open area between the

Viet Cong prisoners wait in front of a U.S. Marine Corps UH-34D Seahorse helicopter of HMM-161, south of Chu Lai on Aug. 1, 1965.

villages was strewn with spider holes and machine gun nests hidden in grass huts.

"As we came nearer, snipers opened up and then all of a sudden all hell broke loose," remarked Sgt. Victor Nunez of Weapons Platoon. "It seemed a whole damned division of VC was out there waiting for us. Those bastards had us zeroed in [with] machine guns, mortars, recoilless rifles and rocket-propelled grenades. I saw a lot of our guys get hit ... our company Gunny was killed also."

Pfc. Paul Meeters was serving with the Anti-Tank Plt., H & S Co., 3rd. Bn., 7th Marines, when he was called off a helicopter carrier to engage the enemy. He remembers "almost buying the farm" at Van Tang. "We went into the village and received fire from the huts, but as we cleared each hut, fire came from behind us. We later learned the ville was honeycombed with tunnels."

FIERCE FIGHTING

As medevac choppers tried desperately to land, Lance Cpl. Joe Paul, a "baby-faced" 19-year-old fire team leader, positioned himself between the helicopters and the enemy. As he laid down covering fire, wounded Marines were placed aboard the aircraft for evacuation. Unfortunately, Paul was struck several times and died. He was awarded the Medal of Honor posthumously.

The fighting was fierce. Lance Cpl. Ernie Wallace saw enemy soldiers hidden behind hedgerows. He screamed: "Start killing trees!" He began delivering accurate fire at the treeline nearby, killing some 25 VC in the process. His keen observation saved the lives of his fellow Marines. He, too, was awarded a Navy Cross.

Cpl. Robert O'Malley of I Company eliminated an enemy position and was a source of inspiration to his fellow Leathernecks. Although wounded three times, he would not permit himself to be evacuated until all of his squad was aboard the helicopter. He and Paul were the first Marines to be awarded the Medal of Honor for Vietnam. (For Navy Cross recipients, see top of page 24.)

SQUEEZING THE VISE

Soon, elements from the 3rd Bn., 7th Marines, were landing to reinforce the assault battalions. As the additional rifle companies came ashore, the enemy quickly departed the area.

Most VC took off the first night, leaving behind only one company to harass the Leathernecks and to assist with caring for their own casualties. According to author Otto J. Lehrack in *The First Battle*, the VC said they gave up the fight after a day because they "were tired, and the Americans were tired."

Starlite, though, would last another five days as the riflemen combed the area, eliminating VC spider holes they encountered. The Marine units pushed eastward to "squeeze the vise" around the VC and drive them toward the sea.

In the end, 614 VC were confirmed killed in what the communists called the Battle of Van Tuong over the duration of the offensive ending Aug. 24. The Marines also took nine prisoners and confiscated 109 assorted weapons.

All told, American dead numbered 56. On Aug. 18 alone, 49 Marines were KIA— 88% of the total killed (including one Army helicopter pilot). Another 203 were wounded. The breakdown by regiment was 4th Marines (19), 3rd Marines (17) and 7th Marines (9). The hardest hit companies were H Co., 2nd Bn., 4th Marines (15 KIA) and I Co., 3rd Bn., 3rd Marines (14 KIA). The Amtrac (7) and tank (2) companies had nine KIA combined.

By all counts, *Starlite* was a success. The Marines had thwarted a major attack against Chu Lai.

The VC "were, by any objective measure, soundly defeated," found Warren Wilkins in *Grab Their Belts to Fight Them*. And the battle "reassured Marine brass that the latest generation of Leathernecks was cut from the same cloth as their predecessors."

But despite their battering, the tenacious 1st VC Regiment would return to fight another day. ✪

MEDAL OF HONOR

**LANCE CPL.
JOE CALVIN PAUL**
(POSTHUMOUS)

**CPL.
ROBERT O'MALLEY**

THE TOLL

U.S. KIA:
56

U.S. WIA:
203

BY RICHARD K. KOLB

OPERATION HUMP

HELL ON HILL 65

On Nov. 8, 1965, the U.S. Army fought its first big battle in Vietnam. The 173rd Airborne Brigade tangled with a Main Force Viet Cong unit that ended in American victory, but at a steep price in GI lives.

Occurring during *Operation Hump,* the fight for this obscure hill near the junction of the Dong Nai and Song Be rivers took place on Nov. 8, 1965, in the Iron Triangle of War Zone D, about 17½ miles northeast of Bien Hoa. The terrain was unforgiving, consisting of the infamous "wait-a-minute" vines and triple canopy jungle. Trees— teakwood and palmetto—towered over the jungle floor. Some trees reached 250 feet in height and six feet in diameter. Visibility was severely limited.

The 173rd Airborne Brigade, known as "The Herd," has the distinction of waging the Army's first big battle of the Vietnam War. Nicknamed *Tien Bien* ("Sky

Paratroopers of the Weapons Sqd., 1st Plt., C Co., 1st Bn., 503rd Inf., 173rd Abn. Bde., pose for a picture in August 1965 at Bien Hoa.

COURTESY BILL HENRY

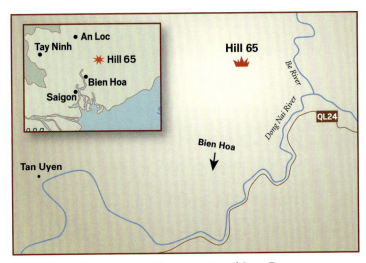

Hill 65 was at the junction of the Dong Nai and Song Be rivers in triple-canopy jungle.

RIGHT: Pfc. Bill Henry, an M-60 gunner with the 1st Platoon of C Company, was awarded the Silver Star for "displaying magnificent fighting spirit" on Hill 65.

SILVER
STAR

Soldiers") by the Nationalist Chinese, the paratroopers had arrived in-country from Okinawa in May. For this round, it was the 1st Battalion of the 503rd Infantry that took the field. Its three rifle companies (A, B and C) were supported by C Btry., 3rd Bn., 319th Field Artillery, as well as the Composite Squad of 2nd Plt., 173rd Eng. Co., and the 1st Team of the 3rd Radio Relay Unit.

Pitted against them was the 3rd Battalion of the 271st Viet Cong Regiment, an elite unit in its own right of the Communist forces. According to Warren Wilkins, author of *Grab Their Belts To Fight Them* (2011), it was led then by Deputy Regiment Commander Bui Thanh Van. The regiment had earned its reputation fighting the South Vietnamese the year before in a pivotal campaign.

BUGLES BLARING, HUMAN WAVES CHARGING

About 8 a.m. the 2nd Platoon of C Company walked into a hornet's nest. The paratroopers were hit with devastating VC .30- and .50-caliber machine-gun fire. "The whole earth seemed to erupt furiously before our eyes," wrote Protestant chaplain Capt. James M. Hutchens in *Beyond Combat* (1968). Hutchens would himself be wounded while attempting to reach the wounded.

2nd Platoon Sgt. Sylvester "Killer" Bryant later described what happened next to the Saigon Press Corps during a briefing. "My platoon was confronted with six automatic machine guns firing directly on us," he said. "We momentarily gained fire superiority over the VC and then ceased fire. And that is where they made their mistake. They started blowing on their bugles and charging us.

"The first charge, I estimated, was about 50 men. They didn't last long. We shot 'em right off the bat every time they started out of their holes. Then, they blew their bugles a second time and they repeated the action. We repeated ours. Things were getting pretty hot on the hill out there, and we were all alone."

Pfc. William Henry was the #1 gunner (M-60 machine gun) for 1st Plt., C Co. "We were on a platoon-sized (86 troopers) recon patrol when ambushed," he recounted in 2015.

MEDAL OF HONOR

SPEC. 5
LAWRENCE JOEL

CONGRESSIONAL MEDAL OF HONOR SOCIETY

"After sustaining severe casualties in the initial two minutes of firing, we pulled into a small perimeter and fought for our lives. We fended off several probes and bugle-blowing human wave attacks for approximately four hours until 2nd Platoon of B Company swung over from its area of operations to help us."

Henry did more than his share to stem the enemy tide. Remaining exposed, he delivered devastating fire on the VC. "His actions in these first critical moments of the battle saved many lives and permitted the formation of a tenable defensive perimeter," according to his Silver Star citation.

Again openly exposed, Henry covered the withdrawal, taking a heavy toll of VC. On two occasions, he crawled forward to retrieve rifles for soldiers whose weapons had malfunctioned. "Displaying magnificent fighting spirit," the citation reads, he "withstood their [VC] most furious barrages and kept his weapon in action" throughout the battle.

Spec. 4 Clarence A. Barto was a grenadier in 2nd Sqd., 2nd Plt., C Co. He likewise had close calls. "The sound of whistles (like referees use) filled the air and then the bugles chimed in as the jungle seemed to jump up running at us," he said. "There were blinking lights in the foliage that were coming on like a wave, a human wave assault. It was like deja vu of Korean War movies I had watched. I fired my M-79 grenade launcher into them, picked up an M-16 and fired until the wave stopped coming. On that hill, the main cause of enemy casualties was small-arms fire."

Later, Barto heard bursts of AK-47 rifle fire. "This obvious execution of our wounded made me angrier than I have ever been," he recalled. "I vowed to myself that even if I had to die I would take as many of the enemy with me as I possibly could. "

Spec. 4 Jerry W. Langston remembered that "the woods seemed to get up and charge at us. The VC had bushes and branches tied to their backs and they started blowing bugles and charged us from three sides. They came down off the hill behind us, from the flank, and across the creek to our front. The fighting was close in, real close. We were really cut off and there didn't look to me much chance left. Each time the VC came at us they blew their bugles. That shook us up at first; then it just made us mad."

Incredible acts of heroism were on display that day. A medic assigned to C Company proved that beyond doubt. Spec. 5 Lawrence Joel, at age 38 a 20-year career man, did not allow a hit to his right leg from machine gun fire to deter his selfless actions. "Completely ignoring the warnings of others," his Medal of Honor citation reads, "and his pain, he continued his search for wounded, exposing himself to hostile fire; and, as bullets dug up the dirt around him, he held plasma bottles high while kneeling completely engrossed in his life-saving mission."

Although hit again, and with a bullet in the thigh, Joel went on to treat 13 more men before running out of medical supplies. Re-stocked, he began tending the wounded once more. He saved one man's life by placing a plastic bag over a severe (sucking) chest wound to congeal the blood.

MIRACLE OF SURVIVAL

Meanwhile, B Company found itself in an equally perilous position. It was committed to secure the right flank of C Company and had to break enemy encirclement twice.

Capt. Lowell D. Bittrich brought 200 men to the fight. "Out of seemingly nowhere came the sounds of three bugles," he recorded in a report. "The enemy came at us shoulder-to-shoulder. It was unreal, like something out of films from the Civil War. Over a short 15-minute period, three desperate reports came from three different NCOs over the company net. Each of them died shortly following their request for help."

Pfc. John Holland was with the 3rd Squad of B Company's 2nd Platoon. Ultimately

COURTESY CLARENCE BARTO

Spec. 4 Clarence A. Barto, a grenadier in 2nd Sqd., 2nd Plt., C Co., takes a break in the field two months after the fighting of *Operation Hump*.

severely wounded, witnessing the first man to die in his unit left an indelible impression. "Even as he laid dead the sons-of-bitches continued to fire into his body, literally tearing it apart," he said. "I've thought of that fight for life many times over the years and to this day don't realize how any of us lived against such odds.

"As long as I live, not one paratrooper who died on that worthless hill will be forgotten. They may have died without cause, but they didn't die in vain because they were part of an elite unit standing well above others."

Elements of A Company had simultaneously attacked the VC's left flank. "We came in on their flank," 1st Sgt. Bill Workman recalled. "The jungle opened up, and we could see almost the entire length of their battle line. Our M-16 and M-60 fire rolled up their line, and took 'em out like ducks in a shooting gallery. The rest of the enemy melted back into the jungle."

As the VC retreated, supporting U.S. fire could be brought fully to bear. Some 117 tactical air strikes, 1,747 helicopter sorties and 5,352 artillery rounds rained on the enemy.

Yet "it was in the highly personal infantry exchanges that American machine-gun, 40mm grenade and rifle fire inflicted the majority of Viet Cong casualties," Warren Wilkins wrote in *Grab Their Belts to Fight Them*. Even bayonets, machetes, axes and entrenching tools were used to deadly effect.

VC attacks began subsiding in the late afternoon. But heavy fire persisted through the night. "The night was pure hell with lots of firing, artillery coming in and the sounds of our wounded in pain," Barto remembered.

After finally hacking out a landing zone on Nov. 9 to evacuate the wounded (Air Force helicopters using Stokes litters could extricate only a few the day before), the entire battalion was off the hill by 7 p.m. Many walked off. "I told my men that we're going to walk out of here like paratroops," Sgt. Bryant said. "That's exactly what happened. We walked out like paratroops and took a lot of VC with us—bodies."

"Our M-16 and M-60 fire rolled up their line, and took 'em out like ducks in a shooting gallery."

—1ST SGT. BILL WORKMAN

PAYING THE PRICE

Indeed, the 173rd had "beat the living hell" out of the VC, as its commander put it. Perhaps Bryant summed up the enemy body count best: "That VC unit we engaged could hold its roll call in a phone booth this morning."

But GIs paid a heavy price, too. In Barto's 10-man squad alone, four were KIA and four WIA. Much to his chagrin, a body was placed in a bag with a tag mistakenly with Barto's name on it. All told, 49 Americans lost their lives in the battle and 83 were wounded. B Company counted 19 KIA, C Company 18 and A Company five. Headquarters Company recorded four deaths, C Battery two and the 173rd Engineer Company one.

Some 88% of the men killed were volunteers; 12% were draftees. Seven were 18 and one, Pfc. Harold Goldman, only 17. After war correspondent Tom Tiede (co-winner of the 1965 Ernie Pyle Award) wrote a story about another 17-year-old, Pfc. Terry Hinson, the reaction stateside was predictable. The 173rd sent all remaining 17-year-olds in Vietnam home.

Brig. Gen. Ellis W. Williamson, brigade commander, summed up Hill 65 most succinctly: "It was not the smartest fight. The enemy had set a trap…" in the hope of luring "us into a battle in an area of his choosing." But as the 173rd's Presidential Unit Citation made clear, "the gallant and determined troops of the 1st Battalion repulsed the Viet Cong and inflicted severe losses upon them … defeating a numerically superior hostile force."

Today, in the annals of Vietnam War history, Hill 65 is overshadowed by later and longer-lasting battles. But to the men who fought there, the memory of the battle will never fade. ✪

THE TOLL

U.S. KIA:
49

U.S. WIA:
83

BY AL HEMINGWAY

BATTLE OF THE IA DRANG VALLEY: 'A TERRIBLE BLOODLETTING'

In late October 1965, North Vietnamese Army (NVA) regulars struck the Special Forces camp at Plei Me, located in the Central Highlands. In response, Gen. William C. Westmoreland, the commander of U.S. forces in Vietnam, chose the newly arrived 1st Cavalry Division (Airmobile) to launch the Pleiku campaign.

LZ X-RAY

Lt. Col. Harold Moore's 1st Bn., 7th Cav, along with B Co., 2nd Bn., was ordered to drive the enemy from the area. On Nov. 14, the 450-man battalion was airlifted into LZ X-Ray in the foot hills of the Chu Pong Mountains. X-Ray appeared flat and unimposing, but the terrain was deceiving.

"Ringed by sparse scrub brush with occasional trees ranging upward to a hundred feet, the landing zone was covered with hazel-colored, willowy elephant grass as high as five feet [actually knee-high]," retired Army colonel John Cash wrote in his article entitled "Fight at Ia Drang," which appeared in *Seven Firefights in Vietnam*. "Interspersed throughout were anthills, some considerably taller than a man, all excellent as crew-served weapons positions."

To the west and northeast, the area was inundated with thick jungle growth, and a dry creek bed ran along the western edge as well.

WANTING TO KILL AMERICANS

The first assault helicopters landed at 10:48 a.m. on Nov. 14 with the fighting at X-Ray finally over by 1 p.m. on Nov. 16.

Soon after landing by helicopter, GIs apprehended an NVA soldier trying to flee. The prisoner was brought before Moore and his Montagnard interpreter, Mr. Nik. Moore quizzed him on the size and whereabouts of his unit. As the captive rattled off his answers in Vietnamese, a "look of apprehension" came over Mr. Nik's face as he turned to Moore. "He says there are three battalions on the mountain who want very much to kill Americans but have not been able to find any," he replied.

That soon changed. As 1st Plt., B Co., pressed forward, it came under intense fire. Capt. John Herren sent Lt. Henry Herrick's 2nd Platoon to assist it. Herrick's men also were pinned down.

Troopers of B Co., 1st Bn., 7th Cav, conduct a sweep forward of the battalion's perimeter at LZ X-Ray on Nov. 16, 1965. B Company's 2nd Platoon fought for its very survival for 26 hours just the day before.

At LZ X-Ray and LZ Albany in mid-November 1965, the 1st Cavalry Division tangled with the North Vietnamese army for the first time. The outcome proved deadly for both sides.

NOVEMBER 1965

MEDAL OF HONOR

CONGRESSIONAL MEDAL OF HONOR SOCIETY PHOTOS

2ND LT. WALTER MARM

MAJ. BRUCE P. CRANDALL

CAPT. ED FREEMAN

"... He was promptly shot in the upper body, 10 feet from me, and I heard the bullet strike human flesh. ... One bullet, one hit, another man down."

—LT. DENNIS DEAL, 3RD PLATOON

Spec. 4 Robert M. Hill began firing his M-79 grenade launcher at the attacking enemy. "We killed a lot of them," he said. "They tried to put a machine gun up on our right and we shot the gunner and two men with him," Hill recounted in Moore's and Joe Galloway's book, *We Were Soldiers Once ... and Young.*

Unfortunately, Herrick and his platoon sergeant were killed as the troopers were engulfed in a murderous crossfire. Swarms of NVA scurried down the hill to join in the firefight. Unknown to Moore, the infantrymen had encountered seasoned soldiers from the 33rd and 66th NVA regiments.

'ANOTHER MAN DOWN'

NVA were attempting to breach the lines between Herrick's platoon and Lt. Dennis Deal's 3rd Platoon. "Suddenly, a lull occurred on the battlefield," Deal recalled in *We Were Soldiers Once ... and Young.* "During that lull one of the men in my platoon got up on his knees. ... He was promptly shot in the upper body, 10 feet from me, and I heard the bullet strike

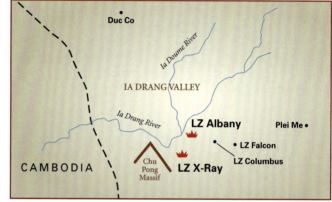

Located in the Central Highlands, the two landing zones proved to be death traps for the 1st Cav Division troopers who took on the communists there in November 1965.

human flesh. It sounded exactly like when you take a canoe paddle and slap it into mud. One bullet, one hit, another man down."

Moore wasted no time in "walking" artillery fire down the mountain. While support fire was helping the troopers, Capt. Ramon A. Nadal, A Company commander, ordered 2nd Lt. Walter Marm's 2nd Platoon to move forward and aid Herren's isolated platoon. Marm's riflemen were soon embroiled in a hot firefight themselves as they tried to reach their comrades.

Suddenly, the NVA intensified their assaults. Enemy soldiers were dug in and hidden in spider holes dotting the thick undergrowth. Marm led his men into the dense jungle as the fighting was now gaining momentum.

Attacking an anthill with a light anti-tank weapon, he ultimately personally killed four NVA. Then by drawing fire to himself, Marm took out additional NVA with grenades. Though severely wounded, he killed the remaining enemy in the position with his rifle only.

The attack stalled, however, when a bullet smashed into Marm's jaw. For his actions, he would receive the Medal of Honor, the first for the division in Vietnam.

Spec. 4 Bill Beck, an assistant machine gunner in A Company, recalled the chaos of the combat: "Men in front of me and beside me were being shot and killed, and dropping. [There was] a lot of havoc. And you were thrown into a position to fight for your life; that's what it came down to. It was do or die."

Pfc. John F. Brennan, a grenadier with A Company, received the Silver Star for taking on an NVA machine gun position until mortally wounded thus saving the lives of men in his squad. 2nd Lt. John L. Geoghegan, another Silver Star recipient, attempted to save the life of Pfc. Willie Godboldt. But he was killed instantly and Godboldt died of his wounds.

CHOPPER PILOTS TO THE RESCUE

Pilots from the 229th Assault Helicopter Battalion flew numerous missions into X-Ray under deadly enemy fire.

Capt. Paul Winkel, a flight leader with B Company, was one of the volunteers to resupply and medevac troops from X-Ray. He was awarded the Silver Star for his gallantry.

Maj. Bruce P. Crandall, flight commander of A Co., 229th Battalion, landed 22 times mostly under intense fire, taking out at least 70 seriously wounded Americans. He finally received his Medal of Honor on Feb. 26, 2007. Modest to the end, Crandall said, "This will probably help veterans be a little prouder of the fact that they did what their country asked and realize that we're still here and being recognized."

Capt. Ed Freeman of A Company volunteered to fly in ammunition, food and water, and take out wounded under a hail of NVA gunfire. Over the next 14 hours, he flew an incredible 14 rescue missions, saving some 30 men. "If I could do anything to prevent my comrades from getting killed, then I would do it," he said. On July 15, 2001, he was awarded the Medal of Honor. Freeman died at 80 in August 2008.

As night fell, the "lost platoon" from B Company was holding on as best it could. Staff Sgt. Clyde E. Savage, a squad leader in 2nd Platoon, could hear enemy soldiers whispering, so he called in artillery fire from nearby LZ Falcon. Spooky (an armed C-47) flew overhead, dropping illumination flares and firing its Gatling guns.

Savage performed some amazing feats of courage as his platoon held out for 26 hours. He started off saving three fellow soldiers by killing three NVA. During the morning of Nov. 15, Savage shot "over 30" NVA, according to his Distinguished Service Cross (DSC) citation.

During that same period, another member of 2nd Platoon also received the DSC for extraordinary valor. Spec. 5 Charles R. Lose, a medic, crawled repeatedly from one wounded man to another, saving numerous lives. Even though wounded in the foot and out of medical supplies, "he demonstrated rare ingenuity and determination by fashioning bandages from C-ration resources," reads his citation. While administering first aid, Lose shielded the wounded with his own body.

As dawn broke, troopers from C Company ventured forward only to be met by a withering wall of NVA automatic weapons fire.

With the tempo of the fighting picking up, Moore radioed for more air support. Soon after, F-4C Phantoms and F-100 jets dropped cluster bombs onto the ranks of NVA preparing for an attack. With late morning, the 2nd Bn., 7th Cav, began landing at X-Ray.

By noon, troopers had finally broken through to the cut-off platoon. The rescuers were met with cheers and "tears of relief." "They were like men who had come back from the dead," Galloway wrote in his book.

One of the heroes of X-Ray was British-born 1st Lt. Rick Rescorla, who commanded 1st Plt., B Co.

Sam Fantino, Rescorla's radio-telephone operator, paid him the ultimate compliment: "His leadership was unbelievable. Rick led his men; he never ordered them, he led them."

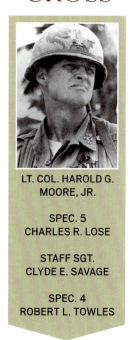

DISTINGUISHED SERVICE CROSS

LT. COL. HAROLD G. MOORE, JR.

SPEC. 5 CHARLES R. LOSE

STAFF SGT. CLYDE E. SAVAGE

SPEC. 4 ROBERT L. TOWLES

"If I could do anything to prevent my comrades from getting killed, then I would do it."
—CAPT. ED FREEMAN

Pfc. Jack Smith

"I crawled over the bodies, all still. The 1st Platoon just didn't exist anymore. One guy had his arm blown off. There was only some shredded skin and a piece of bone sticking out of his sleeve."

—PFC. JACK SMITH, SON OF NOTED ABC NEWS ANCHORMAN HOWARD K. SMITH

PETER ARNETT / AP PHOTO

British-born 1st Lt. Rick Rescorla of 1st Plt., B Co., 2nd Bn., 7th Cav, showed a cool head and determined leadership under fire at LZ X-Ray.

He displayed the same bravery some 36 years later leading employees to safety during the Sept. 11, 2001, Islamist terrorist attack on the World Trade Center. Tragically, he died when the building collapsed.

A rallier of men, he would do the same 36 years later at the World Trade Center where, as Morgan Stanley's security chief, he died saving employees' lives during the Sept. 11, 2001, Islamist attacks.

Despite being outnumbered nearly 10 to 1, the 1st Cav troopers fought like demons. More than 600 enemy corpses were counted on the battlefield.

Of the 81 Americans killed at LZ X-Ray, 69, or 85%, died on Nov. 15. Nearly 70% of the dead were volunteers; the remainder being draftees. Some 83% of the fatal casualties belonged to the 1st Battalion of the 7th Cavalry—more than 60% (41 men) were from C Company alone. But the unit had met and vanquished a determined enemy.

Moore's battalion was relieved, and the 2nd Bn., 5th Cav, began moving to LZ Columbus while the 2nd Bn., 7th Cav, headed toward LZ Albany. Once there, the exhausted infantrymen would be flown to Pleiku.

Moore was later awarded the DSC for demonstrating "superb leadership" while repeatedly exposing himself to enemy fire.

DEADLY DAY AT LZ ALBANY

The 2nd Bn., 7th Cav; 2nd Bn., 5th Cav; and three companies of the 1st Bn., 5th Cav, went into battle on Nov. 17. At 1:15 a.m., a battalion of the 66th and a company of the 33rd NVA regiments sprang an L-shaped ambush. Most of the carnage occurred right off the bat, but sporadic firefights continued into the early evening of the 18th.

As the 7th's 2nd Battalion edged its way to Albany, the terrain worsened; the jungle got thicker and visibility was poor. The column was "obscured in a dim, eerie light." As A Company reached the LZ, the NVA unleashed a firestorm.

"Then the jungle seemed to explode in a crescendo of small arms fire," recalled Lt. Larry Gwin, executive officer of A Company in an interview with *Vietnam Magazine* in 1990. "Mortar rounds started landing in the LZ. The jungle literally opened up with 500 people shooting at each other. We now know that this was the signal for the PAVN [People's Army of Vietnam] to charge."

Enemy snipers were cleverly concealed. Cavalrymen shot wildly at anything they saw or imagined they saw, according to participants.

Pfc. Jack Smith (1st Plt., C Co., 2nd Bn., 7th Cav) son of noted ABC news anchorman Howard K. Smith, watched as 20 soldiers fell all around him in a matter of seconds.

"Just then Wallace [a fellow soldier] let out a 'Huh!'" Smith wrote in an article entitled "Death in the Ia Drang Valley," which appeared in the *Saturday Evening Post* in 1967. "A bullet had creased his upper arm and entered his side. He was bleeding in spurts. I ripped away his shirt with my knife and did him up.

"Then the XO screamed. A bullet had gone through his boot, taking all his toes with it. He was in agony and crying. Wallace was swearing and in shock. I was crying, holding on to the XO's hand to keep him from going crazy."

NVA were now swarming all around the troopers. Smith fired point blank into an NVA soldier's face and watched as his head literally disappeared. Then he heard enemy voices. Smith decided to play dead. The small group began setting up their machine gun; one NVA soldier sat on top of Smith. Suddenly, U.S. M-79 rounds began dropping around him, killing the NVA and wounding Smith. Blood was pouring from his mouth and head.

"I crawled over the bodies, all still," he later wrote. "The 1st Platoon just didn't exist anymore. One guy had his arm blown off. There was only some shredded skin and a piece of bone sticking out of his sleeve."

Miraculously, Smith survived this horrendous ordeal. His C Company was dead center "in the killing zone," sustaining 84% casualties (44 KIA and 50 WIA out of 112 men).

'EVERYBODY IS DEAD'

1st Lt. Henry Dunn, a forward observer with A Company, could hear the moans of the wounded as he lay behind an anthill. He then ran to link up with Gwin and Capt. Joel Sugdinis, A Company commander, who were forming a "last ditch perimeter."

"Sugdinis looked at me and said, 'Everybody is dead,'" Dunn remembered. "He was devastated."

Dunn kept the pressure on the NVA by calling in numerous artillery strikes. "It was hard to call in arty," Dunn explained. "Our people and the NVA were intermingled."

Then the unmistakable roar of a pair of A1-E Skyraiders punctuated the air as they let loose canisters of napalm on the charging NVA. Dunn watched as the fireball quickly consumed fleeing enemy troops. As they became engulfed in flames, he could hear their screams.

Spec. 4 Barry T. Burnite, a machine gunner with 2nd Plt., A Co., was wounded, yet he rallied his squad, provided first aid and redistributed ammo. Employing his machine gun with deadly effect, reads his Silver Star citation, Burnite stayed behind to cover his unit's withdrawal and was mortally wounded.

While artillery and air strikes halted NVA attacks, B Co., 2nd Bn., 7th Cav, landed at dusk. Once again, a brave helicopter crew performed magnificently to keep the troopers supplied.

Capt. Robert L. Stinnet and Capt. Robert Jayne of B Co., 229th Helicopter Assault Bn., flew sorties throughout the night. Their aircraft were riddled with more than a dozen bullet holes as they limped back to Camp Holloway. Each officer would receive the Silver Star.

One soldier's heroism was not fully recognized until 48 years later. In 2013, Spec. 4 Robert L. Towles' Bronze Star was upgraded to a DSC. A member of D Co., 2nd Bn., 7th Cav, he

Soon after arriving at LZ Albany on Nov. 17, 1965, two NVA prisoners were captured and interrogated. The battle there proved to be the single deadliest engagement of the war for Americans.

SILVER STAR

2nd Lt. John L. Geoghegan   Spec. 4 Barry T. Burnite

War correspondent Joe Galloway ultimately gained national fame for his coverage of the battle.

PHOTO COURTESY JOE GALLOWAY

Troopers of the 7th Cav carry the body of a buddy to a Huey on Nov. 15, 1965, at LZ X-Ray. The fighting there claimed the lives of 81 Americans and wounded 129.

THE TOLL

LZ X-RAY:
KIA: 81
WIA: 129

LZ ALBANY:
KIA: 153
WIA: 121

single-handedly destroyed an enemy machine gun and held back the NVA until the wounded could be evacuated.

As the battle drew to a close, the remnants of A and C companies were finally transported to An Khe—there were only 150 men left standing in the battalion.

In just six hours, 153 Americans were KIA at LZ Albany on Nov. 17, most in the opening salvo of the battle. The ratio of volunteer to draftee dead was 60:40. Some 124, or 82%, of those killed belonged to the 2nd Bn., 7th Cav. Hardest hit was C Company with 44 KIA followed by A Company with 35. The 1st Battalion of the 5th Cav lost 23 men.

The Presidential Unit Citation was awarded for an "outstanding performance and extraordinary heroism of the members of the 1st Cavalry Division."

As far as individual valor, Hal Moore would later write in *We Were Soldiers Once…And Young:* "Too many men had died bravely and heroically, while the men who had witnessed their deeds had also been killed… Acts of valor that, on other fields, on other days, would have been rewarded with the Medal of Honor or Distinguished Service Cross or a Silver Star were recognized only with a telegram saying, 'The Secretary of the Army regrets…'"

This deadly valley duel had tremendous historical significance. As the late military historian Harry Summers wrote: "They [NVA] had tipped their hand to their long-range strategic objectives in 1965, but because the United States was so obsessed with the doctrines of counterinsurgency, it could not see that, with the Battle of Ia Drang, the entire nature of the war had changed. The North Vietnamese army, not the Viet Cong, would prove to be the decisive military force of the war."

Joe Galloway, the civilian war correspondent who covered the battle and was awarded a Bronze Star for valor, summarized the aftermath this way: "The battles of Ia Drang in November 1965, although costly to him [NVA Gen. Vo Nguyen Giap] in raw numbers of men, reinforced his confidence. And, while by any standards the American performance there was heroic and tactical air mobility was proven, the cost of such 'victories' was clearly unsustainable, even then."

The Army's official history called it simply a "terrible bloodletting." ✪

BY RICHARD K. KOLB

OPERATION BLOODHOUND/BUSHMASTER II

BUSHWACKED AT AP NHA MAT

The Big Red One's 2nd Infantry Regiment fought its deadliest
battle near the Michelin Rubber Plantation on Dec. 5, 1965.

"I t was a big ambush," 2nd Lt. Stephen Douglas told *Newsweek*. "We lost better than 50% of our company." Though it began that way, the Viet Cong (VC) were ultimately vanquished from the battlefield. But for this infantry battalion, it would be an afternoon imprinted in the memories of its members forever.

A classic search-and-destroy mission, *Operation Bloodhound* (later renamed *Bushmaster II*) penetrated the Long Nguyen Secret Zone. The village of Nha Mat was located five miles west of "Thunder Road" (National Highway 13) and northwest of the Michelin Rubber Plantation. Landing Zone (LZ) Dallas was established inside the plantation to provide fire support.

Originally designed to protect the recently mauled 7th ARVN (Army of South Vietnam) Regiment as it regrouped near Dau Tieng, the mission quickly became one of taking on what was later identified as the 272nd VC Regiment. It comprised four battalions of about 1,200 men.

Tasked with that purpose was the 2nd Bn., 2nd Inf. Regt., 1st Inf. Div. Nicknamed the "Ramrods," the roughly 511 men of A, B and C companies were supported by C Company of the 1st Eng. Bn. and A Btry., 2nd Bn., 33rd Artillery, based at LZ Dallas.

'THEY WERE FIRING FROM EVERYWHERE'

On Dec. 5, 1965, the two forces collided around 12:30 p.m. The Ramrods encountered the VC entrenched in a bunker complex along a forest road. The battlefield was characterized by dense jungle and 3-foot-tall laterite anthills. It was close-quarters combat as the VC resorted to their standard "hugging" tactics to avoid pulverizing U.S. firepower.

B Company launched the attack and was driven across the road. Then the battalion established a defensive perimeter. For two fierce hours, the VC attempted to overrun it. Meanwhile, A and C companies pushed into the bunker complex, eventually securing it.

GIs ran up against crude grenades strung in the trees that were jerked down on top of them. Tree-mounted firing platforms consisting of Chinese-made 12.7mm machine guns raked the jungle floor. "God, they were firing from everywhere," one grunt said. "The .50-caliber was the worst. But they were in the trees, in holes, everywhere. Some even dressed like trees, and we only knew what they were when they fell or fired."

An eerie aura pervaded the battleground because bugle blasts were used by the VC "as a crude command and control mechanism during the battle," according to one historian.

"Around noon, after chasing them, they caught us," recalled Spec. 4 Richard T. Woltman, an M-60 machine gunner with B Company. "We had been moving along an old plantation road in a reverse 'V' formation, one company on each side of the road and a trail company on the road.

"Just as we started to reverse the 'V' formation with one company on the road and the other two still on the sides, all hell broke loose. Rifle fire, machine-gun fire, bells ringing, whistles blowing and the enemy assaulting us."

Yet Woltman kept his cool, helping save the wounded on the field and assisting in their evacuation, for which he was awarded the Bronze Star for valor.

Sgt. 1st Class Juan Santiago was the forward observer

U.S. ARMY PHOTOS COURTESY FIRST DIVISION MUSEUM AT CANTIGNY

Helicopters of the 11th Avn. Bn. drop 2nd Bn., 2nd Inf., 1st Inf. Div., infantrymen into the Michelin Rubber Plantation area to begin a search mission near Ap Nha Mat.

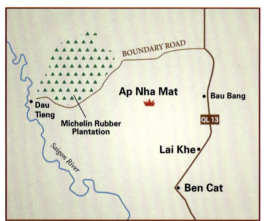

The Michelin Rubber Plantation was the largest in South Vietnam. Its 31,000 acres reportedly served as a communist staging area. It was rumored that the French company paid off the VC to keep it operating.

for an 81mm mortar section and has vivid memories of that day. "When we broke camp the enemy delaying force opened up on us," he said. "We walked on the trail until about 12 p.m. B Company was in the lead with the 3rd Platoon up front. Skyraider A-1 aircraft provided such close air support that the links from their 40mm belts were hitting my legs while I was behind a big tree shooting back at the VC."

Indeed, one anonymous GI would say unequivocally: "It was the Air Force that saved our necks."

In a day marked by courage, Sgt. Oliver J. Fugere, Jr., stood out. A squad leader in B Company, he performed amazing feats of bravery. Setting up a machine gun, his nonstop firing resulted in the "repulsion of three insurgent attacks and approximately 50 Viet Cong casualties," reads his Distinguished Service Cross (DSC) citation.

Then he walked up and down the road to draw fire in order to detect VC positions. In the process, Fugere destroyed sniper and two automatic weapons positions. Not content, the sergeant marked his unit's position with smoke to enable accurate airstrikes. To top it off, he administered emergency first aid to the wounded. So obvious were his selfless sacrifices that Chris Walters, a medic with B Company's 2nd Platoon, launched a one-man crusade in 1996 to unsuccessfully have Fugere's DSC upgraded to a Medal of Honor.

VC attacks against the 2nd Battalion's perimeter were unrelenting. Perilously close, in fact, to succeeding in breaching it. "Our ammunition didn't hold out," Spec. 4 Jerome P. Katcher remembered. "We took more off of the dead bodies, or our own soldiers who were shot … and when the waves stopped, we just went out … A couple of guys would run out and grab the ammunition and just yank it back into us. The wounded who couldn't fire were just loading magazines for the guys who could fire, and we just kept it up."

Close calls with death were too numerous to count but some cannot be forgotten by participants. Staff Sgt. Earle G. Brigham, a team leader in C Company, had one such experience. "It was 12:30 p.m. on Sunday when I smelled their [VC] breath and dropped to the ground as the first shot was fired," he recounted.

"My Bolivar wrist watch, a graduation present from St. Johnsbury Trade School, was shot off my arm as I went down, and my M-14 rifle was hit at the gas cylinder making it a piece of junk. Most of our casualties were hit on the way down in that first burst of fire."

Despite the circumstances, Brigham had the presence of mind to think of his fellow GIs first. According to his Bronze Star citation, he rendered medical assistance while directing fire at the VC. Then he volunteered to lead a clearing party to make way for an evacuation path, saving many lives in the process.

Charles Lindenmayer was an assistant machine gunner in Charlie Company. "Three members of my machine gun team were killed," he said. "Another soldier helping me evacuate the wounded also was killed. When the battle ended, less than half of my platoon was alive."

'ONE HELL OF A FIGHT'

Perhaps 2nd Lt. Douglas summed it up best: "The men put up one hell of a fight. Men assaulted the enemy positions knowing they would die. More died trying to save wounded buddies. There were too many acts of heroism to say any one man was a hero."

The *Vietnam Experience* series, in its brief mention of Ap Nha Mat, placed the valor in another context: "Only the bravery of a few individual soldiers, who repeatedly exposed themselves to hostile fire in order to mark their locations with smoke grenades, spared the battalion from annihilation."

Of course, DSC awardee Fugere and four Silver Star recipients (two posthumous) are among them.

Staff Sgt. John L. Thibeault, while leading a squad from A Company, was mortally wounded. But not before he courageously directed fire against the VC, even though he was severely hit in the opening volley of fire.

His Silver Star, like that of Sgt. 1st Class Willie J. Wright, was awarded posthumously. Wright was killed aiding a wounded squad leader. Platoon Sgt. Honore J. Billy, Jr., and Staff Sgt. Sam Vance lived to receive their Silver Stars.

And the 2nd Battalion as a whole along with A Battery received the Valorous Unit Award (its second in short order; the battalion had been in Vietnam only about 1½ months) for "ignoring withering gunfire and showing indomitable courage as it attacked a numerically superior insurgent force."

Although one officer remarked in the immediate aftermath of the battle that "we got our tails kicked," history's judgment has not been so harsh. Historian Warren Wilkins concluded in *Grab Their Belts to Fight Them*: "Dispirited and suffering heavy casualties, the Dong Xoai Regiment [272nd] finally cracked. Panicked troops fled in disorder to the rear, discarding their weapons and leaving behind wounded comrades. The battle had devolved into a rout."

To be sure, the VC regiment was put out of action for four months. Reportedly, 301 VC bodies were actually counted on the battlefield. Still, it was, as one unnamed sergeant said, "A time of maximum confusion [probably an apt description for virtually all combat] and we paid for that." No doubt, the price was high.

The final tally for the 2nd Battalion and supporting outfits was 43 KIA and 119 WIA. B Company was hit hardest with 21 KIA, or nearly 50% of the total. A Company counted 12 dead (including two medics) and C Company eight. One artillery forward observer and one engineer also were killed. The bodies of three men in 2nd Platoon, B Company, were never recovered. All told, 60% of the men KIA were volunteers; 40% draftees.

But these are cold statistics. Sgt. Santiago humanized them. "I lost a lot of friends that day," he said. "Staff Sgt. James E. Lofgren told me that his wife was going to have a baby on Dec. 5, 1965—the day he died. And Sgt. Leonidas Raisis died of his wounds in a hospital in the Philippines 20 days after the battle on Dec. 25, Christmas."

In spite of all they saw, GIs retained their humanity. Shortly before he was killed, Spec. 4 Julius Roberts, Jr., wrote in a letter to his family: "It is a weird kind of war. There are bodies on the roads that remain for days. It is hot here and it stinks. The only asset this country might possibly have is its people." ✪

DISTINGUISHED SERVICE CROSS

SGT. OLIVER J. FUGERE, JR.

SILVER STAR

SGT. HONORE J. BILLY, JR.

STAFF SGT. JOHN L. THIBEAULT (POSTHUMOUS)

STAFF SGT. SAM VANCE

SGT. 1ST CLASS WILLIE J. WRIGHT

THE TOLL

U.S. KIA: 43

U.S. WIA: 119

BRUTAL BATTLES OF VIETNAM
1966

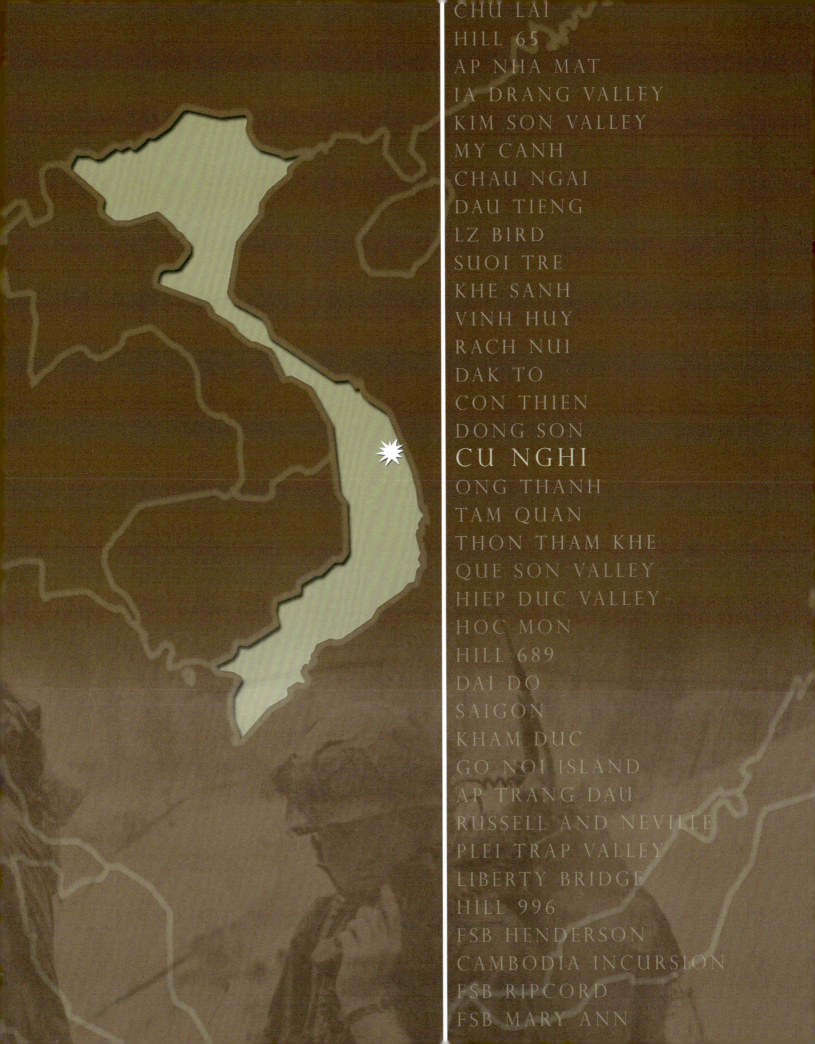

CHU LAI
HILL 65
AP NHA MAT
IA DRANG VALLEY
KIM SON VALLEY
MY CANH
CHAU NGAI
DAU TIENG
LZ BIRD
SUOI TRE
KHE SANH
VINH HUY
RACH NUI
DAK TO
CON THIEN
DONG SON
CU NGHI
ONG THANH
TAM QUAN
THON THAM KHE
QUE SON VALLEY
HIEP DUC VALLEY
HOC MON
HILL 689
DAI DO
SAIGON
KHAM DUC
GO NOI ISLAND
AP TRANG DAU
RUSSELL AND NEVILLE
PLEI TRAP VALLEY
LIBERTY BRIDGE
HILL 996
FSB HENDERSON
CAMBODIA INCURSION
FSB RIPCORD
FSB MARY ANN

BY AL HEMINGWAY

'GRAVEYARD' AT LZ 4: BATTLE OF CU NGHI

As a misty rain fell on the morning of Jan. 28, 1966, the drone of a hundred helicopters, carrying soldiers from the 7th Cavalry into the southern end of the Bong Son Plain, pierced the silent gray skies. This movement was the opening for *Operation Masher* (later continued as *White Wing*), a determined effort to eliminate the enemy presence in the fertile An Lao Valley of South Vietnam's south-central coastal region.

At a meeting held on Jan. 13, top American, South Korean and South Vietnamese commanders had devised a classic hammer and anvil operation to rid southern Quang Ngai province and the northeast quadrant of Binh Dinh province of communists.

Binh Dinh was a hotbed of enemy activity. The South Vietnamese had just about given up on ever pacifying the area. That was the main reason why the joint allied operation was formulated—to gain control of this important region.

On Jan. 25, three days prior to the start of the operation, Col. Harold Moore's 3rd Brigade of the 1st Cav Division (5,700 men) prepared to strike at its objectives. However, tragedy beset the cavalrymen. A C-123 Provider aircraft mysteriously slammed into a mountainside between An Khe and Binh Khe, killing all aboard. All told, 46 men, including the entire crew of the plane, were lost. "The bodies were badly torn," said Lt. Col. Kenneth Mertel. "It was not as bad to get killed on the battlefield, if one had to."

Meanwhile, Moore met with Special Forces Project Delta leader Maj. Charles "Chargin' Charlie" Beckwith to discuss the operation. Beckwith's all-American teams were to patrol northwest of the 1st Cav, in the An Lao Valley.

IN A 'HORNET'S NEST'

On Jan. 28, soon after takeoff, enemy gunfire struck a CH-47 Chinook, causing it to crash at Landing Zone (LZ) Papa. A company from 1st Bn., 7th Cav, responded to protect the downed bird. When it encountered heavy fire, the remainder of the battalion entered the fray.

To the southwest, the 2nd Bn., 7th Cav, was on the move. Two rifle platoons (minus one because of the plane crash a few days earlier) landed at LZ 2 and linked up with C Company, which had been lifted into LZ 4.

LZ 4 was close to the villages of Cu Nghi and Phung Du, which were both surrounded by palm trees, hedgerows, rice paddies and paddy dikes. Also nearby was a cemetery. Numerous mounds dotted the burial ground. Because the LZ was so close to the villages and the cemetery, there was no preparatory artillery fire.

As the first helicopters neared, the enemy let loose automatic weapons fire. The remaining choppers began to land in various locations to avoid being hit. With the company scattered, fire intensified. The cavalrymen had run into elements of the two battalions of the 22nd NVA Regiment.

Firmly entrenched in earthworks, palm groves and bamboo thickets, the NVA had C Company in a murderous crossfire. The unit was so fragmented that soldiers had a difficult time finding each other. Driving rain made air and artillery support impossible.

"We're in a hornet's nest," screamed Capt. John Fesmire on the radio to battalion headquarters.

Indeed they were. With remnants of the company strewn all over the LZ, Fesmire's troopers were cut off. A Company came to the rescue. But the NVA began pouring automatic weapons fire at the troopers as they attempted to cross a rice paddy.

On the Bong Son Plain between Jan. 28–31, 1966, battalions of the 7th and 12th Cavalry, 1st Cav Division, won a hard-fought round with the NVA and VC.

JANUARY 1966

HENRI HUET / AP WIDE WORLD PHOTO

Capt. Joel Sugdinis (squatting in the foreground) of A Co., 2nd Bn., 7th Cav, calls in artillery as his group takes cover in a ditch during *Operation Masher,* Jan. 29, 1966. Intense enemy fire stalled the American assault on LZ 4.

STAFF SGT. LYLE V. BOGGESS/ NATIONAL ARCHIVES #111-CC-33237

A member of B Co., 2nd Bn., 7th Cav Regt., 1st Cav Div., searches a village near Bong Son on Jan. 25, 1966, for Viet Cong after an air strike during *Operation Masher*.

"**Every time you raised your head, it was zap, zap, zap. The dirt really flew.**"

– LT. COL. ROBERT McDADE, 2ND BATTALION, 7TH CAV

THE TOLL

U.S. KIA:
74

U.S. WIA:
220

"Every time you raised your head, it was zap, zap, zap," remembered 2nd Battalion commander Lt. Col. Robert McDade. "The dirt really flew."

A half dozen helicopters attempted to reinforce the beleaguered men. As the birds neared LZ 4, local Viet Cong (VC) concentrated their firepower on the vulnerable choppers. All six sustained hits; only part of one platoon of B Company could land.

As darkness approached, rain fell in torrents. The poor visibility was ideal for the enemy, who tried to infiltrate the perimeter throughout the night. "We captured two VC that night trying to breach our lines," said Pfc. Jim Hackett, A Company medic.

DEADLY DUEL

McDade told his men to consolidate their positions and regroup. "Sgt. Bill Bercaw went out looking for the Charlie Company guys," Hackett remembered. "He went out numerous times to find and bring them back. That was the bravest thing I saw at LZ 4. He was a real hero for doing that." Bercaw would be awarded a Bronze Star with V device for his bravery at Cu Nghi.

Other heroes included Sgt. Marvin L. Lindley of B Co., 2nd Bn., 12th Cav and Capt. Howard E. Phillips of A Co., 5th Avn. Bn., 1st Cav Div., who were awarded posthumous Silver Stars.

The next day, the rain subsided and A1-E Skyraiders and B-57 Canberra bombers struck enemy positions, relieving the pressure on McDade's men. By late morning, Moore, with a company from the 2nd Bn., 12th Cav, arrived on the scene.

As they pressed forward, the infantrymen bogged down in a deadly duel with a Communist machine gun. "My gun is jammed!" hollered Spec. 4 Steve Young. Racing back to the trench under heavy fire, he cannibalized parts from another M-60 machine gun to get his operating again. He then ran back to provide cover for the advancing soldiers.

Napalm eliminated the threat. "When we finally reached the machine gun, we discovered it was a .50-caliber, probably stolen from us or the French," Hackett explained. "Also, the VC manning it was an old man who had been chained to it."

COSTLY VICTORY

Soon, elements from the 1st Bn., 7th Cav, linked up with other 3rd Brigade troops and completed the sweep of the area. Most of the heavy fighting was over.

LZ 4 rated its reputation as the "graveyard": 58 GIs died there alone. The tally for all the Americans killed between Jan. 26 and Feb. 1 came to 74. Another 220 were wounded. Jan. 29 was the deadliest day with 32 KIA. Some 70% of the GIs killed were volunteers; 30% were draftees.

Hardest hit was the 7th Cav with 39 KIAs: 17 from 1st Battalion and 22 from 2nd Battalion. The 2nd's C Company sustained the greatest company losses at 15 men. The 2nd Bn., 12th Cav counted 22 troopers killed. The remaining 17% of fatal casualties were suffered mostly by four aviation units. Three members of Detachment B-52 (Project Delta), HHC, 5th SFG, also lost their lives.

When a mechanical failure in the No. 2 engine of the C-123B Provider brought the transport down in Deo Mang Pass, 42 infantrymen and mortarmen of A Co., 2nd Bn., 7th Cav tragically perished. The four crewmen killed belonged to the 311th Air Commando Squadron. So this short-lived portion of the operation cost 120 Americans.

Maj. Bruce Crandall, commander of A Co., 229th AH Bn., earned a Distinguished Flying Cross at the LZ. His respect for the men he saved was clearly evident. "You always had great confidence in the infantry," he said. (Crandall would later be awarded the Medal of Honor for LZ X-Ray.)

Though the cost was high, the 1st Cavalry Division had driven the VC from the region. Yet as author John Prados wrote in his article "Operation Masher" (*The Veteran*, February/March 2002): "Within a week … intelligence reports mentioned the adversary returning to the sector." ✪

FEBRUARY 1966

BY RICHARD K. KOLB

'EATEN ALIVE' AT MY CANH

Two battalions of the 101st Airborne Division tackled the North Vietnamese WWI-style on Feb. 6-7, 1966, at obscure villages and paid a severe price. Yet they persevered, displaying valor aplenty.

The bombed-out ruins of an inconsequential village called My Canh (2) played host to a little-known yet bitter battle on Feb. 7, 1966. It was one of the many fights in Vietnam remembered by only those who waged it. But it should be known by the entire American public for the sacrifices made there.

It all started as a rather mundane effort to deny the enemy the means of sustaining its troops: food. Phu Yen province on the coastal plain was dotted with rice paddies. The Tuy Hoa Valley, in fact, was known as the "rice bowl." The 810-square-mile valley formed a triangular area with about 22 miles bordering the South China Sea.

Operation Van Buren was a combined allied security campaign to protect local rice crops from marauding Communist troops in II Corps. On this particular day, the enemy confronted was either the heavy weapons company or a reinforced rifle company of the 5th Bn., 95th Regt., 5th North Vietnamese Army (NVA) Div.

Maj. David Hackworth, its opposing commander, heaped lavish praise on his foe. Some 23 years after the battle, Hackworth wrote in his autobiography, *About Face:* "These men were dyed-in-the-wool NVA troops complete with khaki uniforms and armed with AK-47s—upon examination, members of the elite 95th NVA Regiment, the unit known to be operating in this area, whose activities during the [French] Indochina War had

given the bloody Street Without Joy [the stretch of Route 1 from Hue to Quang Tri] its name. They were probably the most formidable enemy fighters in Vietnam."

He continued: "The discipline of this element of the 95th NVA, so skillfully dug in and camouflaged along their hedgerow wall, was iron-tight."

Units of two "Screaming Eagle" battalions would find out just how tight. The 2nd Bn. (A, B and C companies), 502nd Inf., and the 1st Bn. (B Company and the Recon Platoon), 327th Inf., of the 101st Airborne Division encountered heavily reinforced machine gun positions at Canh Tanh (4) and My Canh (2) on those February days.

'WE SHOT UNTIL THEY WERE ALL DOWN'

On Feb. 6, the 502nd's Bravo Company made the opening move when it attacked a hamlet called Canh Tanh (4). Its platoons took up positions around the village and hammered away at the NVA for hours.

Spec. 4 George R. Bassett was a fire team leader in 2nd Squad of the 1st Platoon and was wounded by shrapnel. "We spent upwards of seven hours in that trench," he recalled. "Just on the other side of a very thin bamboo tree line about 18 to 20 enemy combatants appeared out of nowhere. We shot until they were all down. I don't believe that a single round was fired back at us as it was over so quickly."

Leading the 2nd Squad was Sgt. Estevan "Chico" Alvarado. He was severely wounded. "I was shot in my right femur (thighbone)," he said. "The pain was almost

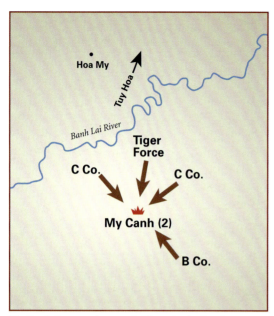

Hoa My

Tuy Hoa

Banh Lai River

Tiger Force

C Co.   **C Co.**

My Canh (2)

B Co.

My Canh 2 was a deserted village in the Tuy Hoa Valley of Phu Yen province. It was the focus of intense combat on Feb. 7, 1966.

COURTESY BENJAMIN CROXTON

The "Tiger Force" was the Recon Platoon of the 1st Bn., 327th Inf. It was awarded the Presidential Unit Citation during the war.

unbearable. I could see the NVA and I engaged them until a bullet entered my left index finger and exited under my thumb. Then I was shot in my left femur. I was shot four times in about 40 minutes. For me, the war was over."

As a brave medic tended Alvarado's wounds, the aid man was shot in his collarbone area. "When he was hit, I saw his collarbone stand up straight through his uniform shirt," the sergeant remembered.

Bravery was in abundant supply on the battlefield. Spec. 4 Duane Olson and 1st Sgt. Alex Vaczi of Bravo were awarded posthumous Silver Stars for their courage in the firefight. Olson's aggressive actions allowed his platoon to maneuver successfully and Vaczi persistently exposed himself by leading from the front. They were among B Company's six KIA in the assault.

Meanwhile, the battalion's C Company, under Capt. Robert Murphy, helped seal off potential escape routes. It came under fire 1.2 miles to the southeast from My Canh, losing one man. Murphy was awarded the Distinguished Service Cross (DSC) for destroying two bunkers and killing six NVA. (Murphy received a Silver Star the next day for leading his company's assault on My Canh.)

'TIGER FORCE' HITS A WALL OF FIRE

Around 9 a.m. on Feb. 7, the NVA pinned down two platoons of C Company near My Canh. They would remain so for four hours. Charlie called for reinforcements. They came in the form of part of the 1st Bn., 327th Inf. (nicknamed "Above the Rest"). Helicopters began depositing the relief force around noon. Commanded by the battalion's executive officer, Maj. Hackworth, it consisted of Bravo Company, led by Capt. Albert E. Hiser, and the Recon Platoon, headed by 1st Lt. James A. Gardner.

Gardner's outfit was a special recon platoon, reinforced to 54 men, dubbed the "Tiger Force." "We got called up as a reaction force and choppered in as a heavy platoon," remembered then-Sgt. Bill Cook. "Just prior to the charge, we were ordered to fix bayonets. Crossing that field was a nasty time. They had two .51-caliber heavy machine guns holding down their corners. One Tiger was hit by the big gun right above the jaw and it took off his head. There were a lot of brave American actions that day."

Cpl. Phil Neel, a machine gunner, experienced some close calls. "We maneuvered so there was a berm between us and the village," he recalled. "I placed my M-60 machine gun on top of the berm and opened up. Enemy bullets passed over my head to within six inches but they never got any lower. Then I heard the cry charge, across open rice paddies! I laid down covering fire. My crew and I then had to run across the same paddy. We made it ok."

The recon men approached the village through what turned out to be thinning elephant grass, which afforded little concealment. Hackworth wrote in his book: "I couldn't believe my eyes. Gardner and his people were walking across the open field between the bridge and [Capt. Robert] Murphy's position [CO of C-2-502] … marching straight across that field in perfect skirmish line, like Pickett's division at Gettysburg … About 20 meters [66 feet] from our position, with one step they walked into a wall of lead."

Despite the circumstances, Gardner was relentless in pursuit of the enemy. The platoon leader, whose tour of duty was up in March, single-handedly destroyed two NVA bunkers with hand grenades. Crawling along a rice paddy dike to reach a third enemy emplacement, he took it out while killing an NVA at six feet away.

Renewing the assault, Gardner blew up yet another bunker. On his way to obliterate still another, he was wounded but managed to silence it with a grenade, falling dead on its rim. He was stitched four times across the chest with NVA machine gun bullets. In 2009, a fellow platoon member remembered him with respect. "He was the kind of leader men wanted to follow," John Hughes said. "Very knowledgeable of his surroundings, he always knew what was going on [in the field]." Gardner's Medal of Honor fully attested to his bravery.

Recon squad leader Sgt. Eldon L. Baker demonstrated similar courage. While crawling across a rice paddy, he was wounded multiple times, including a speech-disabling throat wound. Nonetheless, with his pistol he killed an NVA in a bunker, allowing his men to advance. He refused medical attention and evacuation until all the other wounded were treated first, according to his DSC citation.

'2ND PLATOON NO LONGER EXISTED'

As the Tiger Force fought, B Company also attacked across an open field. Its 2nd Platoon was mowed down. "I was the radio-telephone operator for Capt. Hiser," Tim Zumwalt vividly remembers. "The first contact was huge for 2nd Platoon. To break the stalemate, we started crawling behind a dike that was about 1 foot high and 2 feet thick. Machine gun rounds hit on the other side of the dike, dirt flying into my ears while I was trying to hold down my antennae.

"Crawling again, we came upon the 2nd Platoon lieutenant who was shot through the head. I stared at the hole. We crawled on as the machine gun teared up the dike. I respected Hiser for his bravery and efforts to resolve the stalemated situation. What we didn't know at the time was that 2nd Platoon no longer existed."

Still, Bravo's men persevered in the face adversity as best they could. Many displayed courage in doing so.

When his platoon was pinned down, Spec. 4 Patrick J. Payne assaulted an NVA machine gun and eliminated it with a hand grenade. Two NVA attempted to protect the bunker; he killed them with his rifle. Payne's actions enabled his platoon to move ahead. His valor was recognized with a DSC.

Sgt. 1st Class Ralph J. Bleskan also literally rose to the occasion. Standing up while under fire, he overran the first NVA line of defense. Though wounded in the neck, he went up against a second defensive perimeter. He destroyed it with a round from a LAW (light anti-tank weapon that fires a 66mm rocket). Leading four men across a rice paddy, Bleskan crawled unarmed into a ditch 33 feet from the NVA. From there, he lobbed hand grenades. After being wounded in the leg, he led one more assault. The remaining communist defenders died at his hand in close combat, records his DSC citation.

Hackworth did not remain aloof from the fray. A seasoned combat vet of the Korean War who rose through the ranks, he joined right in. Undertaking a personal recon mission, he "crawled within 20 meters [66 feet] of the enemy position in the face of heavy machine gun fire," reads his DSC narrative. He later "led the attacking force … to a position only 40 meters

MEDAL OF HONOR

1ST LT. JAMES A. GARDNER
(POSTHUMOUS)

Men of B Co., 1st Bn., 327th Inf., 101st Abn. Div., move along a road during *Operation Seward,* September-October 1966. Bravo Company lost 20 KIA in the Battle of My Canh on Feb. 7, 1966.

DISTINGUISHED SERVICE CROSS

MAJ. DAVID H. HACKWORTH

CAPT. ROBERT C. MURPHY

SPEC. 4 PATRICK J. PAYNE

SGT. ELDON L. BAKER

SGT. 1ST CLASS RALPH J. BLESKAN

SILVER
STAR

1ST SGT. ALEX E. VACZI
(POSTHUMOUS)

CAPT. CURTISS BOWERS

SPEC. 4 DUANE OLSON
(POSTHUMOUS)

THE
TOLL

U.S. KIA:
36

[43 yards] from the opposing forces' battle positions." The citation states: "Under fire for approximately six hours," he went on "to rally the attackers and lead them into the NVA positions."

Often time valor is not sufficiently recognized. John Pagel, a vet of B's 1st Platoon, stressed a case in point even 50 years later. "Capt. Curtiss Bowers, our battalion chaplain, was a 'true grunt chaplain,'" he said. "On Feb. 7, he was with the Tiger Force. He pulled 10 to 12 wounded Tigers to safety. His jungle fatigue shirt was shot full of holes yet he was not wounded. Bowers was nominated for the Medal of Honor, instead he was awarded a Silver Star, and he was embarrassed to receive that."

'SUCKED IN AND EATEN ALIVE'

At nightfall, B Company was pulled back into a night defensive position on the outskirts of My Canh. The Tigers and the 502nd's C Company set up a perimeter inside the village. The next morning, remnants of Bravo entered the hamlet. In the darkness, the NVA had faded away. The already-ruined assortment of huts was in American hands.

In his characteristically blunt way, Hackworth described the outcome thusly: "Higher headquarters would describe the battle [as a 'victory'], with the price in U.S. lives only 'moderate.' The fact was we'd been sucked in and eaten alive. We had attacked machine guns as the British and French had in WWI, and I was heartsick at the result."

Indeed, the tally in American lives was grim. A total of 36 GIs died in the combined brawl, if Canh Tanh (4) on Feb. 6 is included. At My Canh (2) alone on the 7th, 30 U.S. lives were lost. All the KIAs were consumed by gunfire, a testament to the lethalness of the NVA machine gun fortifications. The relief force sustained only 28 WIA, a reversal of the usual casualty ratio.

Unit-wise, with 24 KIA the 327th suffered more than two-thirds of the dead. B Company took the biggest hit by far with 20 KIA; the Tiger Force had four. The 2nd Battalion of the 502nd counted 12 fatalities. This early in the war, volunteers—especially in elite Army units—made up the preponderance of personnel. So not surprisingly, almost 90% (32) of the men killed were volunteers.

Phil Neel never forgot the recovery of their bodies in the dark. "I remained in the evacuation area most of the night helping load the dead and wounded onto medevac choppers," he said. "That infantry company [Bravo] had really been shot up by the NVA's .51-caliber machine guns."

Because of enemy fire, helicopter pilots gave the men on the ground only about 15 seconds to load the casualties. "We put the wounded and dead in ponchos and used four men to carry them," Neel continues. "As the aircraft X panel was sliding, we were running and would literally toss the man into the chopper, poncho and all. The crew chief threw himself across the wounded, pinning them to the floor so they would not fall out. We could see enemy tracers converging on the helicopter as it was aloft. Those pilots were the heroes of that night for sure. It is one night I will never forget."

Bill Cook spoke for many My Canh vets when he said, "Not a day goes by for me that some memory of that day does not come to mind. Those who were there understand what I mean." ✪

FEBRUARY 1966

BY AL HEMINGWAY

BATTLE FOR THE KIM SON VALLEY:
CLUTCHED IN THE EAGLE'S CLAW

In the last half of February 1966, the Army's 1st Cavalry Division bested the Viet Cong in Binh Dinh Province. Here is a brief glimpse.

After clashes with North Vietnamese Army (NVA) and Main Force Viet Cong (VC) units in the An Lao Valley, the 1st Cavalry Division was given the unenviable task of driving the enemy from the fertile Kim Son Valley in the third phase of *Operation Masher/White Wing* known as *Eagle's Claw.*

Troopers from the 2nd and 3rd brigades moved into the Crow's Foot area, 15 miles north of Bong Son. Shaped like a crow's foot, the eight ridges "compressed the bottomland into seven valleys which contained numerous streams and a fast flowing river," according to one description. Because of its isolation, the surrounding terrain easily harbored enemy base camps.

On Feb. 15, 1966, B Co., 2nd Bn., 7th Cav, led by Capt. Myron Diduryk, engaged in an intense firefight with soldiers from the 93rd Bn., 2nd Regt., 3rd Div., of

Troopers stay low after dropping by helicopter into a landing zone while under enemy fire on Feb. 11, 1966. The operation was designed to drive the communists from the Kim Son Valley.

BETTMANN / CORBIS PHOTO

DISTINGUISHED SERVICE CROSS

SGT. GARY GORTON
(POSTHUMOUS)

LT. RUFUS STEPHENS

the People's Liberation Army Forces (PLAF).

A combination of artillery fire from Landing Zone (LZ) Bird, Huey gunships and 60mm mortars rained down on the entrenched enemy. A bayonet charge from one of Diduryk's platoons sent the VC scampering from their holes; many were killed as they ran into the open. During the melee, the infantrymen nabbed Vietnamese Lt. Col. Dong Doan, the 93rd Battalion commander.

Meanwhile, the 2nd Bn., 5th Cav, was to establish an LZ and conduct a sweep of the valley. Early on Feb. 17, Capt. Robert McMahon's B Company reached a small clearing named LZ Pete and established a blocking position. Four or five huge bomb craters, created by B-52s, pockmarked the area.

As the company set up its 60mm mortars in one of the depressions, the infantrymen came under fire from the eastern edge of the clearing. McMahon dispatched the 1st Platoon to eliminate the enemy threat. "Go get 'em, Joe!" McMahon screamed to his platoon leader. As the troopers moved forward, they were supported by fire from the mortar section. But the riflemen soon ran into trouble.

"Staff Sgt. Leroy Zubrod radioed in that Lt. Clark had been seriously wounded with four or five bullets in the stomach," McMahon wrote in the after-action report, "and that several others were wounded also."

VC fire from the hills of the Song Bien River Valley on the company's right flank poured down on the GIs. The 2nd Platoon assaulted a hill to the right of the embattled 1st Platoon and quickly secured it. Lt. Charles Johnson led several volunteers from the mortar section to assist them.

HEROISM ON DISPLAY

When a group of Communist soldiers attacked the perimeter, Sgt. Gary Gorton exposed himself to an intense hail of automatic weapons and other fire, throwing grenades and firing his weapon at the advancing Viet Cong.

Gorton personally killed five of the attackers and seized a VC machine gun before he was struck down. He was posthumously awarded a Distinguished Service Cross (DSC).

With the company artillery liaison officer dead and the forward observer from D Company seriously wounded, McMahon told his radio operator, Spec. 4 Estill Frodge, to call in air support on the enemy mortar positions. Within minutes, several "fast movers" delivered a superb pinpoint bombing mission on the VC gun locations.

As the newly arrived 3rd Platoon moved up to reinforce the others, it became embroiled in a firefight with the enemy in an open rice paddy. During the battle, the 3rd Platoon leader's hand was almost shot off at the wrist. McMahon told his executive officer, Lt. Rufus Stephens, to take command.

"Stephens called … and reported his status, and stated that he thought they could break through the Viet Cong to LZ Pete," McMahon recalled. Realizing the men would be burdened by their equipment and the wounded, McMahon ordered Stephens to stay put so the observers in helicopters and fixed-wing aircraft could more easily find them.

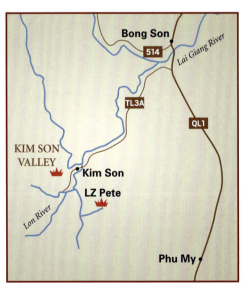

The Kim Son Valley, located about 14 miles southwest of Bong Son, was the scene of bitter fighting in February 1966.

Throughout the battle, Stephens repeatedly stood in the open and directed the medevac choppers into the clearing to assist his wounded men. With this accomplished, he maneuvered through hostile fire to call in artillery and air strikes on the enemy keeping the other platoons pinned down.

But one of the A1E-Skyraiders let loose its ordnance too close, wounding several of Stephens' men. Stephens once again braved VC bullets, calling off the other plane, which was ready to drop its load in the same area. For his extraordinary heroism, Stephens received a DSC.

With half the company on the casualty list (five KIA) and low on supplies and ammunition, McMahon thought the VC might attack en masse and try to overrun their position.

"Then the company commander said those wounded who could move were to get in line and fix bayonets," Pfc. John Martin remembered. "All I thought of was Custer's Last Stand. I thought that was it. That's when I started to get scared. Air support saved the platoon from annihilation. "Skyraiders dropped napalm so close that one white phosphorous bomb hit the edge of the holed-up platoon and one officer threw himself back first into the mud to douse his burning shirt." By late afternoon, supplies and reinforcements from B Co., 2nd Bn., 12th Cav, arrived to relieve the beleaguered outfit.

The following day, A Co., 1st Bn., 5th Cav, was conducting sweeping operations in the Kim Son Valley when it spotted enemy troops.

"The VC quickly let loose a barrage of automatic weapons fire," remembered Pfc. Ralph Mitchell, a medic attached to Alpha Company. "We couldn't see anybody. They were waiting for us. One of our lieutenants went down with a neck wound, and I crawled as fast as I could to reach him." While attempting to get to his downed comrades, Mitchell had his helmet shot off. Troopers were being killed and wounded by the concealed enemy.

"Sgt. Elsie Collins was lying beside me when he took a hit from a .50-caliber bullet," Mitchell said. "Sgt. Walter Terlecki took a hit from the same .50 and fell at my feet behind me. His last word was 'Doc.' Then I got wounded in the back of my right shoulder. Sgt. Dominic Preira got shot the first time and fell, then he got up calling for Sgt. Allison and got hit a second time. He tried to get back up, and they finished him off."

Mitchell faked death in order to survive, managing to crawl away at night to safety. Bodies weren't recovered until the following day.

The heaviest fighting was yet to come—on Feb. 18-19 and Feb. 23. The latter date was the single deadliest of the valley campaign. A, B and C companies of the 1st Battalion, 12th Cav, sustained 21 KIA that day. Alpha Company accounted for 12 of the dead, or 57%. Gunfire was the culprit in all of the deaths. Volunteers contributed more than three-fourths of the fatalities.

'STENCH OF DEATH'

By the time the 2nd Brigade finished fighting in the Kim Son Valley around Feb. 23, "the entire valley floor reeked with the stench of Viet Cong dead," according to one report. The cavalrymen had dealt the enemy a severe blow by repeatedly inflicting heavy casualties on them. However, this advance did not come cheap. 1st Cavalry Division units sustained significant losses.

Casualty figures for this operation are confused at best. Some 40 Americans are clearly identified as being KIA exclusively in the Kim Son Valley. Of those, 16 were killed on Feb. 18-19 and 21 on Feb. 23 alone, accounting for 37 of the 40.

However, additional fatalities are identified with other nearby geographic locations, as described above. For instance, 14 KIA are attributed to the Song Bien River Valley, 10 miles northwest of Phu My City, on Feb. 17. Further complicating counts are the 10 troopers KIA at Tan Thanh (2), nine miles southwest of Bong Son, on Feb. 28, and the 15 deaths four days earlier at Tan Binh, three miles east of Lai Khe.

No matter how the numbers are sliced and diced, the "First Team" underwent some heavy combat during *Operation White Wing (Eagle Claw)*.

As was often the case in Vietnam, success was fleeting. In his book, *Stemming The Tide: May 1965 to October 1966*, John Carland wrote: "Binh Dinh [Province], which was still dotted with fortified villages and mountainous hideouts, was not yet secure." ✪

> ## "Sgt. Walter Terlecki took a hit from the same .50 and fell at my feet behind me. His last word was 'Doc.' "
>
> —PFC. RALPH MITCHELL, A MEDIC ATTACHED TO A COMPANY, 1ST BATTALION, 5TH CAV

THE TOLL

U.S. KIA:
40
Kim Son Valley only

BY RICHARD K. KOLB

'WE HAVE A TIGER BY THE TAIL': CHAU NGAI

"*Operation Utah* was a horror show," wrote Alex Lee, author of *Utter's Battalion,* "one that would have been far less costly had 2nd Battalion, 7th Marines, been allowed to retain the tools [an adequate number of riflemen] needed to fight its way out of trouble."

The Battle of Chau Ngai was the core of *Operation Utah,* essentially a reaction mission in response to a call for help from the 2nd Army of the Republic of Vietnam (ARVN) Division engaged seven miles northeast of Quang Ngai City in I Corps on March 4, 1966.

To the U.S. Marine Corps command, this was an ideal chance to deliver a knockout punch to the 21st Regiment of the 2nd NVA (North Vietnamese Army) Division. Marines would encounter a fierce opponent perfectly capable of counterpunching in this ring.

The village of Chau Ngai was made up of subordinate hamlets identified on the map with numbers. Thus there was Chau Ngai (4) and Chau Ngai (3). The latter was east of Hill 50, the scene of some of the heaviest fighting. Hamlet 4 was about six miles southwest of Binh Son, a base hosting Marine artillery.

Ultimately committed to combat were the 2nd Bn., 7th Marines (approximately 600 men), 1st Marine Div.; 3rd Bn., 1st Marines, 1st Div.; and 2nd Bn., 4th Marines, 3rd Marine Div. B Co., 1st Bn., 7th Marines, was attached to the 4th Marines for this operation. But B Company quickly found itself struggling for survival alone. Batteries K and M of the 4th Bn., 11th Marines (Artillery), provided fire support from Binh Son more than six miles away.

TAKING FIRE FROM ALL SIDES

The landing zone at Chau Ngai (4) was as hot as they get. Twelve of the 30 helicopters that began the airlift were knocked out of operation. 1st Platoon of F Co., 2nd Bn., 7th Marines, was the first of the three assault companies on the ground. Capt. Alex Lee commanded F Company. "Out in the open paddies and manioc fields, it felt as if the incoming fire was almost a wall that had to be penetrated," he later wrote in his book.

Lt. Col. Leon Utter, 2nd Battalion commander, summed

MARINE CORPS PHOTO A186813

A grenadier of F Co., 2nd Bn., 7th Marines, fires his M-79 grenade launcher right after being airlifted to the landing zone at Chau Ngai in March 1966.

In early March 1966, U.S. Marines took on the NVA for the first time in an obscure complex of hamlets, affording Leathernecks an opportunity to knock out a hardcore regiment.

MARCH 1966

MARINE CORPS PHOTO

Lt. Col. Leon Utter's 2nd Bn., 7th Marines, are helo-lifted to engage the 21st NVA Regiment. Before *Operation Utah* was over, 3rd Bn., 1st Marines, and 2nd Bn., 4th Marines, and supporting units as well as ARVN forces, would join in the battle for Chau Ngai.

MARINE CORPS PHOTO A186812

Marines from 2nd Bn., 7th Marines, take cover and return fire as they come under attack during *Operation Utah.* The leathernecks engaged two battalions of the 21st NVA Regiment.

SILVER STAR

Pfc. Gary Rood of F Co., 2nd Bn., 7th Marines, receives the Silver Star for charging and knocking out an NVA machine gun position on March 4, 1966, at Chau Ngai.

up the situation in an after-action report: "We were taking fire from three sides, the front and both flanks, and from an enemy who was literally hugging us so close we couldn't use our supporting arms. We were in a frontal assault, pure and simple, with everything committed from the outset.

"We employed fire and maneuver, taking cover behind rice-paddy dikes, but NVA heavy machine-gun fire was delivered at so close a range it actually destroyed sections of the dikes."

Despite the intensity of the fire, Marines displayed selfless acts of bravery. Sgt. Donnell McMillin of F Company's 2nd Platoon went to the aid of his seriously wounded platoon leader and was mortally wounded. He received the Silver Star. Fellow F Company member Pfc. Gary Rood also was awarded a Silver Star. His citation reads: "He courageously charged through increasingly intense and accurate fire to within 30 feet of an enemy .50-caliber machine gun position. Savagely attacking with hand grenades, he destroyed the enemy gun position."

2nd Battalion corpsman Lawrence Johnson moved a wounded Marine 300 yards under fire to an evacuation point and then was fatally struck down by NVA fire while attempting to reach another hit Marine.

Hospitalman Samuel Orlando of H Company made several daring trips to help evacuate casualties and carried ammo to a machine-gun crew. Orlando "crawled forward in a courageous attempt to render aid, but was mortally wounded," reads his Navy Cross citation.

A much-deserved Navy Cross also went to Lance Cpl. George Norwood, a fire team leader in G Company. Having to assume command of his squad, he assaulted an NVA machine-gun bunker three times, finally neutralizing its fire with a grenade. Though seriously wounded,

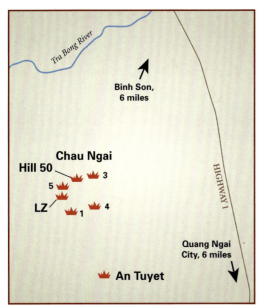

The Battle of Chau Ngai comprised firefights at several small hamlets not far from Quang Ngai City.

he refused evacuation in order to help thwart a counterattack.

Pfc. Richard Bucher with F Company spoke for many when he said, "Right before your eyes with all the chaos a body gets ripped apart, and you say to yourself, 'What the Hell.' You have about three to five seconds to get it together. In a way, I will always be there [Chau Ngai]."

HEADING UP HILL 50

March 5 proved equally as harrowing. The 3rd Bn., 1st Marines, was sent into blocking positions on the high ground some four miles north of the main battle area. Sgt. John Goodwin was wounded that day. "We were flown into the inside of the enemy perimeter," he recalled, "the NVA had dug an underground fortress of interconnected tunnels, bunkers and spider holes on and around Hill 50. The fight continued nonstop for two days. We held our positions, fighting day and night. Before it was over, I was shot in the neck."

One account described the enemy-held Hill 50 as "a large NVA force shielded from sight by bamboo fences and hedgerows, entrenched in an elaborate network of tunnel-connected bunkers and spider-traps, and protected by minefields and booby traps."

Once again, valor was the order of the day with Marines undaunted by the obstacles confronting them. Gunnery Sgt. Talmadge Downing of Weapons Plt., M Co., though wounded in the shoulder, helped other wounded Marines to safety, organized an assault on one objective and then "single-handedly destroyed another enemy position with his pistol and a hand grenade," according to his Navy Cross citation. Out of ammo, Downing picked up an AK-47 rifle and directed a final attack in which he personally silenced the enemy emplacement.

Lance Cpl. James Thiel was in Mike Company's 2nd Platoon. "Of the original 40 men in our platoon only 14 were left," he recalled. "The other men were killed or wounded."

Lance Cpl. Peter Fink, a radio-telephone operator who was the forward observer for the 81mm Mortar Platoon of India Company, reflected on leaving his outfit after being hit: "A bullet took out a piece of bone below my thumb joint and I was medevaced eventually to the hospital ship *Repose*. As it turned out, this was a 'million dollar wound'—I was sent home. There are a lot of mixed emotions about leaving your unit and especially your buddies. But in my case, it probably saved my life. A couple of months later, I learned that my replacement was KIA when my former platoon was overrun."

Fate was crueler to Sgt. William Adams, likewise of I Company. "At Hill 50, I was sent out with two other Marines to retrieve three wounded Marines lying in a rice paddy. The two Marines with me were hit in their chests by AK-47 and machine-gun rounds and fell on top of me screaming in pain. Then another Marine came out to help us and he was hit.

"We were all trapped in the rice paddy. Eventually, we crawled out making our way to the tree line. Two weeks later, March 18, on a different operation, I was wounded. On that same day in 1968 my younger brother was killed in action."

Hill 62 was another hard-fought engagement. Pfc. Rickey Garner, while serving as a

NAVY CROSS

HOSPITALMAN SAMUEL G. ORLANDO (POSTHUMOUS)

CPL. CONRAD A. SIPPLE (POSTHUMOUS)

GUNNERY SGT. TALMADGE R. DOWNING

LANCE CPL. GEORGE O. NORWOOD

runner for 2nd Platoon of L Company, was KIA there. His Silver Star citation describes how he attacked enemy dugouts, including a trench containing a five-man NVA position, which he destroyed while sustaining fatal wounds.

L Company's 3rd Platoon found itself in a difficult position that day, too. Cpl. Jimmy Sanchez was a fire team leader and exposed himself to throw a smoke grenade to cover the evacuation of two wounded Marines and a Navy corpsman, sacrificing his own life for the welfare of platoon members.

FIGHTING FOR SURVIVAL AT AN TUYET

Meanwhile, the 2nd Bn., 4th Marines, had been inserted into the southern area of *Operation Utah.* The battalion ended up fighting around An Tuyet. Cpl. Conrad Sipple was a squad leader with Golf Company. He repeatedly braved enemy fire to assist in evacuating wounded Marines—twice alone. On the fourth sally, he was mortally wounded. His selfless actions earned a Navy Cross.

B Co. (165 men), 1st Bn., 7th Marines, was tasked with guarding a downed helicopter in an LZ near the hamlet of An Tuyet during March 4-5. NVA stormed its perimeter three times during the night. Capt. Robert Prewitt, who received the Silver Star for standing his ground, provided some insight on what that experience was like:

> ## "Under fire for all of March 5, we were bloodied by the enemy for the first time in major combat."
>
> —SILVER STAR RECIPIENT CAPT. ROBERT PREWITT

"Under fire for all of March 5, we were bloodied by the enemy for the first time in major combat. This was the first actual fighting against the NVA in the Marines' combat zone in Vietnam. It is difficult to imagine the so-called 'fog of battle' until actually experienced. Completely surrounded, I ordered 'fix bayonets.' Fortunately, we were re-supplied with ammo, and repulsed the NVA attacks.

"But it had been a grueling and exhausting 48 hours. It was the daring and heroic helicopter delivery of ammunition that turned the tide of the battle and saved us. Miraculously, our casualties were only five killed and 24 wounded."

Among those KIA was Pfc. Gary Sooter. When the NVA attempted to penetrate his platoon's left flank, he exposed himself to mortar and small-arms fire to block the communist troops, saving members of his unit. Sooter sacrificed his life, receiving the Silver Star for putting his platoon first.

'JUST SURVIVORS NOW'

The action at An Tuyet signaled the end of organized NVA resistance. When III Marine Amphibious Force reported "we have a tiger by the tail" it was an apt description of what those three Marine battalions were up against. At the time, *Newsweek* quoted Marine operations officer Maj. E.M. Snyder as saying, "I wouldn't be surprised if it was at least three months before we hear from that [NVA] regiment again. It's just survivors now."

But some 101 Marines died and 278 were wounded in the Battle of Chau Ngai. Most KIAs were split evenly between 3rd Bn., 1st Marines (45) and 2nd Bn., 7th Marines (44), accounting for 88% of total deaths. B and G companies of the 4th Marines counted five and seven KIA, respectively. Broken down by date, the deaths numbered 44 (March 4), 54 (March 5) and three (March 6).

Lt. Col. Utter offered his now-famous assessment of what had become America's mortal enemy in Vietnam: "They're [NVA] not supermen. But they can fight. And they will fight when cornered, or when they think they have you cornered." ✪

THE TOLL

U.S. KIA:
101

U.S. WIA:
278

MARCH 1966

BY RICHARD K. KOLB

HOT PURSUIT IN THE VINH TUY VALLEY

Mid-March 1966 saw three Marine battalions facing off against an equal number of Communist battalions in the vicinity of Chu Lai. The mostly one-day battle bloodied both forces and produced four Navy Cross recipients.

"My God, I can't believe it! They're erupting from the ground. There are hundreds of them," radioed an incredulous UH-1E Huey gunship pilot from Marine Observation Squadron 6. The forward air controller had been observing an enemy-occupied hamlet after undergoing a tremendous bombardment.

This would be an early indicator of what the Marines entering the Vinh Tuy Valley, located about 15 miles southwest of Chu Lai, would encounter. The terrain there was flat and featureless, consisting of a seemingly

Members of 3rd Bn., 1st Marines, are dropped off in Vinh Tuy Valley near the village of Xuan Hoa. The subsequent battle left 22 Marines dead, including 10 in a helicopter shoot-down.

NAVY
CROSS

**GUNNERY SGT.
BILLY HOWARD**
(POSTHUMOUS)

**HOSPITALMAN
2ND CLASS
MARTIN GILLESPIE, JR.**
(POSTHUMOUS)

**CPL. MARWICK
KEMP**

**LANCE CPL.
JAROLD O. BRYANT**

endless dull patchwork of rice paddies. It harbored a determined foe that "had to be killed in his positions by infantry action at close quarters," according to a Marine officer.

That action centered around four hamlets—Phuong Dinh (2), Thach An Noi, Xuan Hoa and Phou Loc (1). Fighting in the valley was prompted by the fall of a South Vietnamese outpost near An Hoa, which was perched atop Hill 141.

When the call came for help, *Operation Texas*—a joint American-Vietnamese initiative to recapture the outpost—was launched in response. Ironically, An Hoa outpost had already been abandoned by the communists when Marines reached it. So the operation effectively became a hot

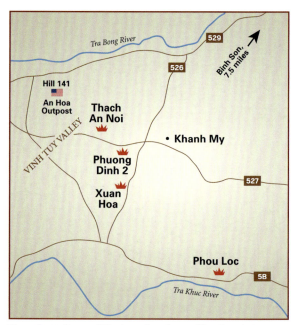

Three battalions of Marines fought a rolling battle in pursuing VC from one village to another in mid-March 1966. Their price in lives was 49 men.

pursuit of the enemy units. Tasked with that mission was 2nd Bn., 4th Marines (D Company from the 1st Battalion was attached), 3rd Marine Div.; 3rd Bn., 7th Marines, 3rd Div.; and 3rd Bn., 1st Marines, 1st Marine Div.

Confronting them were two battalions of the 1st Viet Cong (VC) Regiment and one from the 21st North Vietnamese Army (NVA) Regiment, both part of the 2nd NVA Division. Communist elements occupied the village of Phuong Dinh (2), renamed Tinh Hiep today.

FORTIFIED TO THE HILT

The village was one of the most heavily fortified Marines faced so far in the war. It contained extensive communication trenches, tunnel networks and natural caves. Intense artillery fire from the 3rd Bn., 11th Marines and M Battery of the 4th Battalion along with airstrikes failed to dislodge the VC from the hamlet southeast of the An Hoa outpost.

Consequently, the landing zone at Phuong Dinh (2) was plenty hot when Leathernecks from the 2nd Bn. (nicknamed the "Magnificent Bastards"), 4th Marines, jumped from their helicopters on March 21, 1966. Once on the ground, some life-and-death decisions had to be made quickly. First Lt. Gary Brown, platoon commander in E Company, led the assault on the village. In the heat of battle, he carried wounded to safety. Though shot twice in the arm, Brown remained on the battlefield until his men were in a favorable position. He received the Silver Star.

Another Silver Star recipient (posthumous) was Pfc. Manuel Herrera. After carrying one wounded Marine to safety, he returned for another only to die in a hail of gunfire while attempting to save him.

When E Company became pinned down, Gunnery Sgt. Billy Howard directly supervised evacuation of dead and wounded Americans. And "braving certain death" (according to his Navy Cross citation) rallied his Marines to continue the attack in which Howard was mortally wounded.

Hospitalman 2nd Class Martin Gillespie, Jr., corpsman for the 2nd Platoon of D Company, completely exposed himself to enemy fire to administer aid to a wounded Marine. Sacrificing his own life, Gillespie's reward was saving the life of another along with the Navy Cross.

Bravery was in abundant supply at Phuong Dinh that day. Cpl. Marwick Kemp, a 3.5-

MARINE CORPS PHOTO #A186822

Marines prepare to evacuate killed and wounded from the battle area during *Operation Texas*. Extra ammunition and equipment is taken off the casualties before they are loaded on helicopters.

inch Rocket Squad leader attached to the 3rd Platoon of E Company, risked his life time and again. He personally carried wounded back to safety and oversaw the evacuation of other Marines hit. Kemp was "responsible for the saving of many lives," says his Navy Cross citation, "and directly responsible for over 60 Viet Cong killed by his platoon." (Kemp was killed in action later in the war on Feb. 18, 1969, during his third tour.)

Fighting at Phoung Dinh (2) on March 21-22 took 13 Marine lives—nine from the 2nd Battalion (seven in E Company alone) and four from attached D Company.

Meanwhile, north of the village at Thach An Noi, the 3rd Bn. (known as "The Cutting Edge"), 7th Marines, was ambushed by two Communist companies around 3 p.m. After three hours of fighting, the enemy broke contact. But not before L Company lost six men killed and K Company, one. Among them was Lance Cpl. William Wade, a fire team leader. Crossing open ground, he attempted to aid his wounded squad leader but was fatally shot in the neck, records his Silver Star citation.

BAD DAY AT XUAN HOA

The 3rd Bn. ("Thundering Third"), 1st Marines, until now held in reserve, was committed next with the hamlet objective of Xuan Hoa, situated near Ba Gia and southeast of Phuong Dinh. Things started off badly. A Seahorse from Marine Medium Helicopter Squadron 363 was shot down by .51-caliber machine gun fire at the outset. All four crewmen and six members of Kilo Company were killed.

Sgt. Garrett Randel, a squad leader in 1st Platoon, was originally scheduled to be on that helicopter, but ended up on another thus escaping death. "I have played that fateful day over in my mind too many times to have forgotten the experience," he said, "yet at the same time

The view from a chopper loaded with members of 3rd Bn., 1st Marines, shows smoke rising from a hot LZ near the village of Xuan Hoa. One helicopter was shot down, killing four crewmembers and six Leathernecks of Kilo Company.

PHOTO COURTESY LOU ALBERT

I know that each of us have our own perspective."

Being pinned down by enemy fire was perhaps most unforgettable. "Unless one hugged the village side of the trench, you were shot at," Randel recalled. "Because so many of our people were shot either in the head or upper torso, the enemy most likely had snipers in the trees shooting down on us. Later, one guy in my squad shot into the treetops, and at least one VC fell out of a tree. Shortly thereafter, enemy fire virtually ceased."

Hospitalman 3rd Class Peter Tuttle, 1st Platoon corpsman, can never forget a fellow Navy "Doc" who died. "I relive that terrible day," he said, "questioning if I could have done more for fellow corpsman 'Howdy' Hann. I truly believe it was a no-win situation with that type of wound [head]. I pray Howdy died knowing that I gave him my all. It still hurts me that I lost him."

A rifleman in the 2nd Platoon, Pfc. John Stoddard, says, "I remember most the thirst and inability to stay awake … just exhausted. All night long you could hear Marines moving around and opening canteens looking for water."

Sgt. Edward Bartkoski, leader of 2nd Squad in the 3rd Platoon, has a vivid recollection of Xuan Hoa. "It was still daylight, and I remember the command coming down the line to 'fix bayonets.' We talked about what would happen if we were overrun. We were not going to be taken prisoner and we all would go down together. Neither one [speaking of Lance Cpl. Jim Cooke] of us figured we would make it through the night."

A fire team leader in the 3rd Squad of the 3rd Platoon also was going to make sure he went down fighting. Lance Cpl. Jarold Bryant was caught in a cross-fire yet assisted four wounded. He helped secure the unit objective and in doing so saved lives because he "single-handedly charged through the fury of hostile automatic weapons fire, overrunning a vital position by

> ## "We talked about what would happen if we were overrun. We were not going to be taken prisoner and we all would go down together."
>
> —SGT. EDWARD BARTKOSKI

killing two of the enemy and causing the other to flee," reads Bryant's Navy Cross citation.

Life-saving seemed to be the order of the day. Hospitalman 3rd Class Ronald Kidder alone treated 19 casualties in his platoon, all while under fire. At one point, he silenced a VC machine gun position with an M-79 grenade launcher. From an exposed rice paddy, Kidder carried one Marine 55 yards to administer first aid. His Silver Star was well deserved.

So was the posthumous Silver Star for Cpl. Walter Shortt, a machine gunner in the Weapons Platoon, for his ultimate sacrifice.

Such feats were not uncommon. Cpl. James Weathers, a gunner/team leader in 1st Squad, Rockets Section, Weapons Platoon, also performed a selfless act. "Because we had no targets for our rockets, I started medevacing wounded Marines," he recalls. "One Marine could not walk, so I put him on my back but because of enemy fire I had to crawl approximately 425 yards to the company aid station."

Lou Albert of K Company recalled: "While I was being dropped into the LZ—a very hot one—I took one aerial shot. And also photographed the downed chopper."

All told, 22 Marines—10 in the helicopter shoot-down, 10 in ground combat, a Navy corpsman and an artillery forward observer from G Btry., 3rd Bn., 12th Marines—lost their lives at Xuan Hoa.

All the hardships K Company experienced served only to bring the men closer together. Cpl. Jim Keely, assigned to assist with casualty evacuation, articulated that sentiment best. "Many of the Marines who were killed or wounded that day I had served with since October 1963," he said. "I felt I had someone closer than my own brother. A bond had developed which was unique and difficult to describe to others."

PHOTO COURTESY LOU ALBERT

Lou Albert, K Company, remembers "being dropped into the LZ—a very hot one"—at Xuan Hoa.

TALLYING THE VALLEY TOLL

On March 22, all three battalions secured their original objectives. But the 3rd Bn., 7th Marines, remained locked in combat with Communist troops at the VC stronghold of Phou Loc (1) until after nightfall and into the next day. During that night, the VC slipped out of the hamlet through an elaborate network of tunnels. But not before they had killed three Lima Company Marines, two men of K Company and two Navy corpsmen.

Over the two days of fighting in the Vinh Tuy Valley at the four hamlets connected to retaking the abandoned An Hoa outpost and pursuit of the enemy units responsible, 49 Marines were killed in action. Thirty-nine, or 80%, died on March 21. The 3rd Marines' K Company was hit the hardest with 19 KIA—including six of those killed in the helicopter shoot-down.

Of the 39 Marines killed on the ground, some 80% were lost to small-arms fire in close-quarters combat. The remainder succumbed to multiple fragmentation wounds.

Operation Texas was still early in the war. Marines had been committed to full-scale combat only eight months before. Many deadly days awaited them ahead. ✪

THE TOLL

U.S. KIA:
49

BY RICHARD K. KOLB

'INFERNO on the GROUND':
COURTENAY RUBBER PLANTATION

"You guys are out here alone," Maj. Gen. William DuPuy, commander of the 1st Infantry Division, told C Company officers. "Your chances of getting hit tonight are very good."

Indeed, they were. Charlie Company was being used as bait to lure Vietcong (VC) units into a fight. In the Army's lexicon, this was quaintly known as "creating tempting targets." GIs had another term for it, especially because they had been ordered into a trap.

At this stage of the war, big unit operations were just beginning. One was *Operation Abilene*, a pre-emptive campaign targeting the May Tao Secret Zone in Phuoc Tuy province 40 miles east of Saigon. This search and destroy sweep was relatively uneventful with one exception—the action 10 miles southeast of the village of Xa Cam My.

Mostly north of the hamlet was the Courtenay Rubber Plantation, generally covered by dense vegetation. It was close to this leftover real estate from French colonialism that a relative handful of GIs would literally engage in a life-and-death struggle.

MATCH MADE IN HELL

Sent out on its own, C Co., 2nd Bn., 16th Inf. Regt., 1st Inf. Div., was living up to its nickname—the "Rangers." Vastly under strength and mostly green (known in Vietnam parlance as made up of FNGs), its 134 men under Capt. William Nolen consisted of the standard four platoons. Its only fire support would be the 1st Battalion of the 7th Field Artillery.

An unpleasant surprise awaited the "Rangers." The 274th Regiment of the 5th VC Division was itching to take on the Americans. Its 1st Battalion (D-800) of 400 men would lead the attack, but the other two battalions also committed elements to the upcoming combat. That placed C Company in the unenviable position of being outnumbered at least 3-to-1. The communists called the location of engagement the Tam Bo Stream. Their defenses consisted of trenches 300 yards long and four feet deep.

The 3rd Platoon stumbled into the VC base camps area on April 11, 1966, making contact with snipers at 12:45 p.m. In the initial skirmishing, two GIs were killed and 12 wounded. Before long, Charlie Company was completely surrounded. Tree-bound

2nd Lt. John W. Libs, on a patrol during 1965, played a pivotal role in the battle and later recounted details of the day so it could be reconstructed. He led the 2nd Platoon.

The battle near Xa Cam My on April 11, 1966, saw one U.S. infantry company assaulted by at least a full enemy battalion. Despite the odds, it survived but with some 80% casualties.

APRIL 1966

U.S. ARMY PHOTO BY SPEC. 5 ALLEN K. HOLM

MEDAL OF HONOR

SGT. JAMES W. ROBINSON
(POSTHUMOUS)

AIRMAN 1ST CLASS WILLIAM PITSENBARGER
(POSTHUMOUS)

"Hit twice more in the chest, Robinson nonetheless threw the grenades when he got to within 30 feet of the weapon, destroying the VC position before toppling over dead."

—SGT. JAMES W. ROBINSON'S MEDAL OF HONOR CITATION

Grunts of C Co., 2nd Bn., 16th Inf. Regt., 1st Inf. Div., near the village of Xa Cam My on April 11, 1966. Charlie Company sustained nearly 80% casualties, including 36 KIA, concentrated over about four hours of brutal combat.

VC snipers would prove to be a major problem. Even worse were the 10 machine guns (two of them .50-caliber) that bracketed the quickly formed American perimeter.

At 4 p.m., the VC attacked en force. Before it was over, three assaults would be made. Units from all three 274th battalions contributed to the human waves. 2nd Lt. John W. Libs called it simply an "inferno on the ground." The "Rangers" held their ground, but only with desperately needed artillery support.

'UNSURPASSED HEROISM'

Before long, C Company's perimeter shrank to 40 yards across. "Stretches of porous perimeter were now held only by the dead and dying," Steven E. Clay wrote in his history of the 16th Infantry Regiment, *Blood and Sacrifice* (2000). Tracy Derks, in his account of the battle in *Vietnam* magazine, provided an even more graphic description: "The men listened to the cries of their dying comrades calling out for their mothers, calling out to their deity, calling out to a friend for help; but the living could do nothing for the dying.

The deadly battle of April 11, 1966, took place southeast of the village of Xa Cam My near the Courtenay Rubber Plantation. It was an area harboring Main Force Viet Cong base camps that were well entrenched.

"Along the blood-splattered, tear-gas drenched perimeter, American soldiers began to give up hope."

Each platoon seemed destined for its private hell. 1st Lt. George Steinberg's "4th Platoon fought with heroic abandon, even grappling with the charging Vietcong with bare hands after ammunition ran out," George Wilson wrote in his book, *Mud Soldiers.*

Despite a shattered arm, Steinberg charged a machine gun position, annihilating the crew. Then he withstood two assaults with only 12 men. Charging straight into an oncoming attack, he tossed riot control grenades into the VC. Shot repeatedly, Steinberg threw six grenades, completely disrupting the attack before succumbing to seven wounds, according to his Distinguished Service Cross citation.

Meanwhile, 1st Platoon fire team leader Sgt. James W. Robinson had eerily predicted his fate. In an earlier conversation, he had said: "The first big battle I get into, I will be killed and win the Medal of Honor."

With an M-79 grenade launcher, Robinson started off by eliminating a deadly sniper. Then dragging two wounded GIs to safety, he saved their lives. After collecting weapons from the wounded, he went on to rescue other men. That cost him wounds to the shoulder and leg. But Robinson was just getting started.

Seizing two grenades, he shouted, "I see the .50! I'm going for it. Cover me!"

"In an act of unsurpassed heroism"—to quote his Medal of Honor citation—he charged the machine gun and was hit again in the leg. The VC tracer round set fire to his uniform but that still did not slow him down. Hit twice more in the chest, Robinson nonetheless threw the grenades when he got to within 30 feet of the weapon, destroying the VC position before toppling over dead.

Incredibly, such displays of selfless courage were repeated that day. Charlie Company grunts were in awe of Airman 1st Class William Pitsenbarger, one calling him the "bravest person I've ever known." A member of Detachment 6, 38th Air Rescue & Recovery Squadron, he chose to stay behind after descending 100 feet in his jungle penetrator when the rescue helicopter departed.

"Pitsenbarger exposed himself to almost certain death by staying on the ground, and perished while saving the lives of wounded infantrymen," says his Medal of Honor citation. Immediately tending to the wounded, he saved at least nine lives. When not patching up the grunts, he held off the VC with a rifle and distributed ammo. That was all in the course of being wounded three times.

Pitsenbarger exemplified the motto of the pararescuemen: "That Others May Live!" Killed that night by a sniper, his body was found the next morning with a bullet hole in the forehead. He was the first Air Force enlisted man to be awarded the Medal of Honor since the service was created in 1947. (His action occurred earlier than that of John L. Levitow.)

Staff Sgt. Rolf Schoolman, though wounded, crawled among his men to distribute ammo and then continued the fight. Pfc. Marion Acton, only 18, took out a machine gun crew; he then eliminated several more VC before being killed by a sniper. Staff Sgt. Charles Urconis

DISTINGUISHED SERVICE CROSS

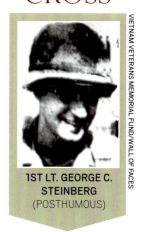

1ST LT. GEORGE C. STEINBERG
(POSTHUMOUS)

SILVER STAR

Maj. Gen. William E. DuPuy pins the Silver Star on Staff Sgt. Charles Urconis at Bearcat Base Camp on April 14, 1966. Urconis killed an entire VC .50-caliber machine gun crew with only a .45 pistol.

PHOTO COURTESY ROGER HARRIS

Pfc. Roger Harris was one of the lucky survivors. He recalled that jaws dropped when other soldiers saw how few of Charlie Company came away physically unscathed.

killed an entire VC .50-caliber machine gun crew with only a pistol and later rescued a wounded officer trapped beyond the perimeter. All three men received the Silver Star.

TERROR OF THE NIGHT

Despite the abundant bravery, things appeared ominous when the sun set. "As darkness enveloped the battlefield," Clay wrote in his history, "VC women began searching the perimeter, stripping the American dead of weapons and ammo, and killing the wounded with a shot to the head."

Sgt. Harold Hunter, of the 4th Platoon, recalled: "I saw the woman bend down to look in his face [of his friend], and then shoot him in the head."

Others barely escaped that fate. Three men of 3rd Platoon, including platoon leader Lt. Martin Kroah, Jr., who had been hit five times, found themselves stranded amidst the communists. They played dead, but one, a medic, panicked while being searched by a female VC and was shot in the head. No wonder the grunts considered them scavenging jackals.

At about the time most of the men thought they were through, a savior came in the form of artillery. Only an artillery curtain of 1,100 rounds saved them from annihilation. Screams from the retreating VC during the night were telltale signs that all was not lost. The VC broke off the battle about 7:30 p.m.

Around 7:15 a.m. on April 12, B Company finally made its way to the beleaguered perimeter. "Ordered to saddle up, we started humping all night until we arrived at the site," recalled Peter Alcala, who was point man for the 1st Squad, 1st Platoon. "It was one bloody mess. Men were receiving last rites, and we started body bagging and matching up body parts. Needless to say, I could not sleep that night."

Charlie Company's living nightmare was over; it was time to leave the dreadful scene. Pfc. Roger Harris, of C Company's 1st Squad, 1st Platoon, wrote years later in his memoirs: "We walked out of the thick jungle into the clearing. Television news cameras filmed us as we walked past 35 body bags without being sure which of our friends were inside them.

"The following morning, Charlie Company was assembled. Some officers and men who had not been on the operation stared at us. Jaws dropped as they saw that there were only 28 of us left standing of the 134 men who had left our base camp at Bearcat" only days earlier.

RESTORING 'PRIDE AND DIGNITY'

No wonder—107 of the men had become casualties for a rate of 80%. Exactly 37 men were KIA, including the Air Force pararescueman. Another 70 were wounded. Some 66% of soldiers killed were volunteers; 33% were draftees. They died in heartbreaking ways. VC executed some of the wounded outside the perimeter. Errant U.S. artillery rounds—"friendly fire"—claimed five lives and mangled 12 more bodies inside the perimeter. Pfc. Edward W. Reilly died in prayer, clutching a St. Christopher's Medal.

Life-long, painful memories and a Valorous Unit Award and streamer embroidered with Courtenay Plantation were all the veterans of Charlie Company would have to remember the showdown at Xa Cam My.

When Gen. DuPuy arrived near the village to assess the situation, Libs had some blunt words for him. "You walked us right into a goddamn holocaust, general," he said. DuPuy's reply: "Yeah, but there's no other way to get a goddamn fight going." That was scant comfort for the young officer.

Some 24 years later when George Wilson skillfully recounted the events of April 11 in his book, Libs could finally derive some relief from the mental anguish he had suffered in the decades following the battle. "After all these years of sometimes debilitating thoughts comes a stranger who somehow has given Johnny Libs his pride and dignity back," he told Wilson. ✪

THE TOLL

U.S. KIA:

37

U.S. WIA:

70

BY RICHARD K. KOLB   *OPERATION CRAZY HORSE*

HILL 766 (ALMOST) LAUNCHES A COSTLY THREE-DAY BATTLE

One company of the 8th Cavalry's 2nd Battalion experienced a hellacious hill fight near the Vinh Thanh Valley on May 17, 1966. When that engagement expanded, the dying and the courage continued unabated.

What started as an attack to relive forces in contact with the enemy turned into a spoiling operation to thwart a major assault on a strategic base. *Operation Crazy Horse* committed GIs to the mountainous jungles between the Vinh Thanh and Suoi valleys in central Binh Dinh province of II Corps. Landing Zone (LZ) Hereford was established as a base of operations. It would become the focus of intense combat.

Maneuvering in the thickly covered hill masses of the valleys proved difficult at best. Identifying terrain features was tricky. So it came as no surprise when an unmapped adjacent hill was climbed thinking it was Hill 766. In fact, it was four-tenths of a mile away. Hence the firefight to come was nicknamed "Almost Hill 766." No matter the name, the battleground was pockmarked with 72 Viet Cong (VC) foxholes and bunkers creating a formidable barrier.

As later intelligence revealed, the 2nd VC Regt., 3rd VC Div., was preparing to assault the Vinh Thanh Special Forces Camp. That regiment fielded the 95th and 97th battalions in the area and could call on the D-26 Local Forces Company for back up.

Over the next three days, May 16-18, 1966, the VC would find themselves up against B Co., 2nd Bn., 8th Cav; 1st Bn. (A and C companies), 12th Cav; elements of the 1st Bn., 5th Cav; and 2nd Bn., 12th Cav of the 1st Cavalry Division. Batteries of the 2nd Bn., 19th Arty and 2nd Bn., 20th Arty provided fire support.

In the evening of May 16, the 8th's Bravo Company linked up with Alpha of the 12th Cav on the slopes of what was thought to be Hill 766 and initiated the engagement with a VC battalion. The two companies formed a night defensive position (NDP). At some point on the 16th, two members of the 12th's Charlie Company, which had secured LZ Hereford, and a Green Beret of Det. A-228, 5th Special Forces Group, were KIA in the area.

'VC HANGING UPSIDE DOWN FROM TREE LIMBS'

The VC launched their attack on the NDP at 6 a.m. on May 17. Bravo Company, with about 92 men, received the brunt of the assault. Sgt. Oscar Harvey, leading the 1st Squad of the 1st Platoon, shouted, "Good God, watch out, here they come!" A VC platoon was less than 100 feet away from their lines.

Sgt. 1st Class Leroy F. Pope, leader of 3rd Platoon, quickly radioed the company command. "I've lost three men," he said. "We're pinned down by rifles and machine guns." Pope was hit three times, twice in the back and once in the nose. Fighting was fast and furious. With ammo rapidly running low, GIs were ordered to fix bayonets.

Casualties were so heavy that Bravo had to be withdrawn. Its 4th (Weapons) Platoon carried the dead

Helicopters offload troops of the 1st Cavalry Division at LZ Hereford. At nearby Hill 766, B Co., 2nd Bn., 8th Cav, fought NVA human wave attacks on May 17, 1966. Bravo Company sustained 23 KIA and was later presented the Valorous Unit Award.

and wounded down the hill to LZ Hereford for evacuation. Sometime after 4 p.m., the remainder of B Company was sent to An Khe after many trying hours on the hill.

The company would later be presented the Valorous Unit Award for "resolutely holding off human wave attacks" and "inflicting heavy casualties on the enemy."

A and C companies of the 12th Cav remained at the LZ. The VC broke off the fight after dark.

Pfc. Robert Roeder was with the Mortar Platoon of Charlie Company of the 12th Cav. His company had been sent to link up with the two companies under siege on the hill. He described the scene: "There were NVA [VC] who had tied themselves in trees who had been shot and killed by the cavalrymen. They were hanging upside down from the tree limbs. The American dead and wounded were lying right off the trail in the midst of the tightly grouped men on top of the mountain."

B Company of the 8th had sustained 23 KIA; A, three; C, one; and C Btry., 2nd Bn., 19th Arty., counted two KIA. American wounded numbered 100.

The battle, however, was not one-sided. The VC suffered far greater losses. Evidence of that was clearly found the next day. "In the woods they [Americans] found nothing but mangled flesh, torn arms and legs and heavy blood trails that carried over the crest and to the eastward," S.L.A. Marshall wrote in *Battles in the Monsoon.*

"All the foxholes and bunkers had been filled with fresh earth. So they started digging. The first hole held the body of an NVA [VC] soldier. They kept at it. By noon, they had uncovered 93 bodies—all buried in the fighting positions by the people who had fled the hill."

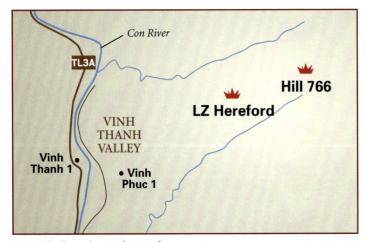

LZ Herford was located east of the Vinh Thanh Valley, and Hill 766 due east of the LZ. These terrain features were situated in central Binh Dinh province of II Corps.

FIGHTING LIKE A 'MAN POSSESSED'

After the relief of the GIs under fire on "Almost Hill 766," the operation expanded to a multi-battalion sweep in pursuit of the 2nd VC Regiment. The 1st Bn., 5th Cav and then 2nd Bn. (a platoon of A and B and C companies), 12th Cav, joined the pursuit later on May 17. The 12th Cav landed east of Hereford at LZ Horse, welcomed by mortars. Bravo and Alpha's platoon were hit by heavy fire from the crest of a ridgeline. They assaulted it and then withdrew.

Fighting continued on May 18. The 12th's B Company was attacked. The platoon from A Company linked up with it at 11 a.m. Later in the afternoon, those two units were stopped in their tracks at a bunker line. Before the day was done, the 12th Cav would lose six KIA and the 5th Cav one man. After dark, the VC departed.

Among the three members of Bravo Company killed was Staff Sgt. Jimmy G. Stewart. Early that morning, B Company was manning a defensive perimeter when it was hit by a reinforced

BLOODSHED CONTINUES ON LZ HEREFORD

Just three days after, on May 21, 1966, the fighting around Hill 766, disaster struck LZ Hereford itself. The Mortar Platoon of C Co., 1st Bn., 12th Cav, was the solitary unit on the LZ that day. It was confined to a small saddle 165 yards long by 45 yards wide and partially covered by elephant grass as tall as five feet. Rugged ridgelines surrounded the LZ.

At about 2:15 p.m., the communists hit with 60mm mortar rounds, rocket-propelled grenades (RPGs) and machine guns. Then the VC swarmed over the base. Twenty-one men were there to defend the perimeter.

Sam Castan, the senior editor of *Look* magazine, was there. He was recognized with a posthumous civilian award for "voluntarily taking up arms ... Thrice wounded, he gave his life in defense of his fellow Americans."

For *Boot to Boot: The Story of Charlie Company,* Doug Warden interviewed survivors and others who were near the LZ then. They related what happened during that terrible time.

"The pilot [of an observation aircraft circling the LZ] reported swarms of attacking enemy soldiers intermingled with our Mortar Platoon and [that he] couldn't fire on the position without killing the defenders," recalled Spec. 4 Bill Martin, a radio-telephone operator (RTO) with Charlie Company. "We stayed in contact with the Mortar Platoon until they were no longer transmitting."

Spec. 4 John Spranza, as the RTO for the Weapons Platoon, was in charge of communications with the company. "I had the long whip antenna on my radio and the gooks apparently saw it and were aiming RPGs at me," he remembered. "I was able to raise the company on the radio and told them we needed gunships and artillery."

Spranza was a miracle survivor. He quickly killed three VC, but was ultimately wounded five times. Initially, he was hit three times in the leg and once in the shoulder by bullets. Then an AK-47 round passed through his face. Convinced he was done for, Spranza urged Staff Sgt. Robert Kirby to leave him behind. Communist soldiers even searched his seemingly lifeless body for valuables.

Spec. 4 Paul J. Harrison put up a last-ditch fight, too. He was at the most forward position of the eastern sector on the LZ. Seeing that the single mortar tube was destroyed, he sprang into action. He inspired others to stand their ground as long as possible. As others were forced to withdraw, Harrison held his position alone. While covering them, he advanced forward. Once his ammo was expended, Harrison used his M-16 as a club and then his fists until he was riddled with bullets. He was awarded the Distinguished Service Cross.

An 'Unbearable Sight'

After receiving the original radio message from Spranza, the remainder of Charlie Company had headed back up the hill to LZ Herford. "We arrived within minutes," said Spec. 4 Jordan Brindley, another company RTO. "All but five members of our Weapons Platoon were killed. The sight was unbearable.

"Dead bodies were everywhere, weapons and bloody equipment were strewn all over the Mortar Platoon position. I found Spranza, he'd been shot a half dozen times. He was barely conscious and in very critical condition. We loaded John and the other survivors on the first available 'dust-off' [helicopter] for medical evacuation to the rear."

Of the 16 GIs killed on LZ Hereford,

DISTINGUISHED SERVICE CROSS

SPEC. 4 PAUL J. HARRISON
(POSTHUMOUS)

VIETNAM VETERANS MEMORIAL FUND/WALL OF FACES

half died by gunfire and half by shrapnel. But all were shot in the head. Sgt. 1st Class Louis Buckley was listed as missing until early 1978 when his remains were identified. Based on survivor accounts, he was assumed tortured to death after being wounded and captured.

Despite their tragic end, Mortar Platoon members had waged a valiant struggle. More than 60 enemy bodies littered the LZ and surroundings.

"I found Spranza, he'd been shot a half dozen times.

He was barely conscious and in very critical condition."

—SPEC. 4 JORDAN BRINDLEY, RTO, C CO., 1ST BN., 12TH CAV

MEDAL OF HONOR

**STAFF SGT.
JIMMY G. STEWART**
(POSTHUMOUS)

> "In the woods they [Americans] found nothing but mangled flesh, torn arms and legs and heavy blood trails that carried over the crest and to the eastward."
>
> —FROM *BATTLES IN THE MONSOON* BY S.L.A. MARSHALL

VC company. Stewart's squad was in the direct path of the onslaught and five of the six squad members were wounded.

So Stewart "became a lone defender of vital terrain—virtually one man against a hostile platoon," reads his Medal of Honor citation. He held his ground to protect the wounded as well as the company perimeter. "He fought like a man possessed," continues the citation, "emptying magazine after magazine at the enemy." VC hurled grenades at him; Stewart threw them back, killing many.

When he ran out of ammo, he retrieved more from his wounded squad members. Exhausted, Stewart held his position for four hours through three assaults while laying waste to the enemy. His actions allowed B Company to be reinforced and to launch a counterattack with the Alpha Company platoon.

Without hesitation, Stewart joined the counterattack. His body was found later in a shallow enemy hole; eight dead VC were scattered around his position. Perhaps 15 others had been dragged away. The wounded he was protecting survived and were evacuated safely to receive medical treatment.

Meanwhile, D Co., 1st Bn., 5th Cav, was providing security for a landing zone. Early in the evening of May 18, the VC struck Delta. When a machine gunner was wounded, Spec. 4 Onsby R. Rose, a radio-telephone operator, took over his M-60. His fire forced the VC to retreat. But not before an enemy grenade landed in his position. Rose threw himself on the grenade, saving the life of the assistant machine gunner while sacrificing his own. Rose received the Distinguished Service Cross.

Overall, fighting around Hill 766 and LZ Hereford had been costly. The total tally was 40 American lives. Some 29, or 73%, were lost on May 17 alone. B Company of the 8th Cav's 2nd Battalion accounted for 23 (58%) of the fatalities by itself. Gunfire killed 28 men (70%) and shrapnel, 10 (25%). Two men died as a result of "friendly fire" when a U.S. artillery round strayed. Some 80%, or 32 men, were volunteers; eight were draftees.

As was often the case, the communists had initiated the battle and withdrawn from the field at a time of their choosing. But they would be back soon. ✪

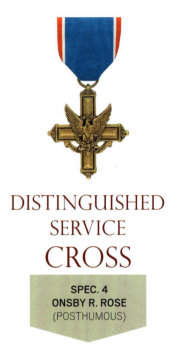

DISTINGUISHED SERVICE CROSS

**SPEC. 4
ONSBY R. ROSE**
(POSTHUMOUS)

THE TOLL

U.S. KIA:
40

U.S. WIA:
110+

BY RICHARD K. KOLB   **OPERATION EL PASO II**

'MEETING' AT THE LOC NINH RUBBER PLANTATION

On June 11, 1966, an infantry battalion of the "Big Red One" collided with a Viet Cong battalion on two hills on a French rubber plantation. The Americans experienced some fatal misfortune during 10 hours of combat.

always felt that the Loc Ninh Rubber Plantation fight of June 11, 1966, was unrecognized for its singularity and importance as a lesson learned," retired Army Col. Richard G. Kurtz said. "The fight was, in reality, a classic stand-up infantry assault on a fortified position [Hill 150] with a VC company plus, dug in along a trench line with overhead cover. I think the relatively heavy casualties the battalion suffered led to the battle being somewhat downplayed and ignored in history."

This overlooked engagement was part of *Operation El Paso II*, a 42-day effort that had begun nine days

Reinforcements for the 2nd Bn., 28th Inf., move to aid fellow "Black Lions" during the Battle of Loc Ninh Plantation on June 11, 1966.

U.S. ARMY PHOTO COURTESY FIRST DIVISION MUSEUM AT CANTIGNY

Three members of C Co., 2nd Bn., 28th Inf., await the order to attack entrenched Viet Cong on Hill 177, one of two hills fought over at Loc Ninh Plantation.

earlier by the 1st Infantry Division and South Vietnam's 5th Division to dislodge the 9th Main Force Viet Cong (VC) Division from Binh Long province. As it turned out, one of its regiments was moving on Loc Ninh. That meant the town, airstrip and nearby Special Forces camp had to be defended.

Charged with sweeping village #10 in the rubber plantation northwest of Loc Ninh were 350 men of the 2nd Bn., 28th Inf. Regt.—the "Black Lions." The Cambodian border was only about a mile away, so that gave the enemy an advantage. Cambodia long served as a sanctuary for Communist forces. Indeed, it was home base for the 9th VC Division. GIs would face off against a battalion of the 273rd VC Regiment.

Here is how the battlefield was described. "Terrain was gently rolling and covered with rubber trees and irrigation ditches," recalled then-Lt. Col. Kyle W. Bowie, commander of the 2nd Battalion. "Fields of fire through the rubber trees there were generally very good. Because the rubber plantation was still being worked, the undergrowth was kept to a minimum. But the rubber trees provided dense overhead cover [for the enemy]."

Well-concealed bunker complexes on two nearby hills, 150 (elliptical in shape) and 177—only 1.2 miles apart—would become the objectives of A, B and C companies, along with the Recon Platoon from the battalion Headquarters Company, that day. It started off as a foggy morning and the fog of battle proved fatal.

ASSAULTING HILL 150

The action began when A Company was opened up on by VC on the southern slope of Hill 150 about 7:30 a.m. Spec. 4 Richard Meadows, the M-60 machine gunner with 1st Squad, 1st Platoon, recounts those early moments in vivid detail.

Now-Capt. Richard Kurtz was the forward observer for A Company on June 11, 1966. This is him two months after the battle in the brigade base camp at Lai Khe.

"Soon, the firing intensified," he said. "We all faced to the right, forming a skirmish line. Immediately, we started taking heavy small-arms and automatic-weapons fire from a hill to our front. The noise was deafening. We took cover behind the rubber trees, which were only about 12 inches in diameter."

Kurtz was then a first lieutenant and forward observer for A Company. "Our battalion

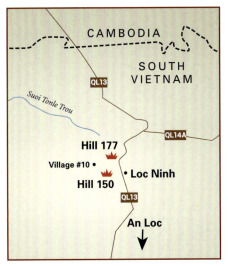

Hills 177 and 150 were 1.2 miles apart. Route 13 ran directly though Loc Ninh City, the intended target of the 273rd VC Regiment in June 1966. The city's close proximity to Cambodia made it a strategic location.

entered the fight against two hills, piecemeal," he remembers. "We conducted a classic, by the book, stand up assault on the hill. We were repulsed by heavy fire from the VC positions. Our lead squads got to within hand grenade-range of the VC, but were stopped cold by accurate machine gun fire.

"Our 81mm mortars were ineffective against the overhead VC fighting positions, and our Civilian Irregular Defense Group (CIDG)—Nung tribesmen in this case—platoon 'left' the battlefield."

Once Kurtz was able to adjust the 105mm artillery fire onto and along the VC trench line, the rounds easily penetrated the VC overhead cover, breaking the coherence of the enemy defense, and sending the communists fleeing from the trenches. Pursuit of the surviving VC company members ended just short of the Cambodian border.

Capt. Raymond V. Blanford, CO of A Company, set the standard for valor. At the base of the hill, he repeatedly exposed himself to intense hostile fire to direct incoming U.S. artillery rounds. Dauntlessly leading his men in an assault on the VC emplacements, Blanford halted the VC attack. Then, among exploding mortar rounds, he initiated a second attack up the hill.

Seriously wounded in the right eye (in which he lost sight), he refused medical evacuation until reinforcements arrived. "When I was hit," he later said, "I felt the blood running off the back of my head. I felt I was going to die." Yet he remained steadfast. Blanford was awarded the Distinguished Service Cross for his bravery.

Meanwhile, B Company, accompanied by Lt. Col. Bowie, had been committed to reinforce A Company. Bravo Company moved past Alpha and preceded by a 16-volley artillery bombardment, took the hill by 4:30 p.m. with the loss of one man. A Company had sustained three KIA earlier in the fight.

> ## "When I was hit, I felt the blood running off the back of my head. I felt I was going to die."
> —CAPT. RAYMOND V. BLANFORD, CO OF A COMPANY

HILL 177: ORDEAL BY FIRE

At 2:30 p.m., C Company and the attached 24-man Recon Platoon stormed nearby Hill 177. Luther Kanter, a recon team member, summed up the action: "C Company assaulted Hill 177 on line from east to west. Recon moved on the VC west along a ridgeline running north. VC opened up with intense automatic rifle fire and grenades. With no cover, the Recon Platoon and part [2nd Platoon] of C Company rushed toward a trench.

"Unknown to the men, the VC had placed a machine gun at one end of the trench. VC fire took a heavy toll on both units. The enemy overran the Recon Platoon." VC ran along the ditch, firing into the wounded, remembered Bowie. Both platoons were decimated.

"But C Company called up its reserve platoon and went on to capture Hill 177" about two hours later at 4:15 p.m., said Kanter.

DISTINGUISHED SERVICE CROSS

CAPT. RAYMOND V. BLANFORD

SILVER STAR

PFC. TIM A NOE (POSTHUMOUS)

SPEC. 4 KENNETH A. BABB (POSTHUMOUS)

"The pucker factor was pretty high while waiting. The artillery rounds landed about 40 yards in front of us, right where they should have been." —LEE HELLE, 2ND PLATOON, C COMPANY

Lee Helle was with C Company's 2nd Platoon. "We were pinned down by the enemy about 30 yards in front of us; they held the high ground," he recalled. "Without the support fire in the correct place, we would have soon joined the rest of the casualties. When you are in thick woods and trying to adjust support fire you are making an educated guess from the start.

"Waiting for that first fire-for-effect support I called in was nerve-wracking. That first spotter round landed to our right front about 100 yards away. The order I gave was left 50 drop 50, fire for effect. The pucker factor was pretty high while waiting. The artillery rounds landed about 40 yards in front of us, right where they should have been."

A genuine hero of Hill 177 was Pfc. Tim A. Noe. Part of a machine gun crew, and already wounded, he stayed with his M-60 to provide covering fire. Suddenly, a grenade landed at the feet of the crew. When everyone else froze, Noe unhesitatingly threw himself on the device, absorbing the full blast of the explosion. For knowingly sacrificing his life, Noe was awarded the Silver Star.

Spec. 4 Kenneth A. Babb also received a posthumous Silver Star. The Recon medic was KIA while administering first aid.

Overall, the artillerymen of the 2nd Bn., 33rd Arty, firing their 105mm howitzers, saved the day, according to most survivors. Some 98 VC bodies were reportedly counted at the end of fighting. And despite its confused origins, this action had interrupted the 273rd VC Regiment's planned attack on Loc Ninh.

A 'MUTUAL SURPRISE'

But things went wrong regardless of the ultimate outcome, as they often do.

"The poor discipline of the U.S. Special Forces Nung CIDG platoon was beyond comprehension," said Kurtz. "The American soldiers fought and suffered valiantly. But as it turned out, in retrospect, they died unnecessarily. We could have finished that fight in the first hour had we known what to expect and had our heavy fire support been pre-planned and on immediate call. The appearance of a full-up, combat-experienced, Mainline VC battalion right in our own backyard was an intelligence failure, par excellence."

Among the GIs who fought on the rubber plantation that day, 34 were KIA and 33 WIA —an unusually high ratio of killed to wounded. The Recon Platoon was hardest hit with 17 KIA, a 71% fatality rate. C Company sustained 13 KIA and A Company three; B Company lost one man. Half of the total deaths resulted from gunfire; 41% died from multiple fragmentation wounds; and 3% from other explosive devices (such as hand grenades). Volunteers (22) made up 65% of the KIA; draftees the other 35%. At this stage of war, at least 50% of infantry companies were still typically composed of regulars.

Kurtz summed up the battle concisely: "In military jargon, Hill 150 [and Hill 177] is classified as a 'meeting engagement.' In plain English, that translates into the unintended collision of two opposing forces. The whole battle was a mutual surprise." ✪

THE TOLL

U.S. KIA:
34

U.S. WIA:
33

SIEGE OF HILL 488

BY CHARLES W. SASSER

When 18 men of the 1st Recon Battalion defended Nui Vu Hill on June 13, 1966, little did they know that they would become perhaps the most highly decorated small unit in the annals of U.S. combat history.

In June 1966, North Vietnamese Army (NVA) and Viet Cong (VC) forces gathered by the thousands in the range of steep mountains and twisting valleys northwest of the American air base at Chu Lai. Then they began moving eastward in platoons and squads. Gen. Lewis W. Walt, commander of III Marine Amphibious Force, placed eight full battalions on alert. He also detailed Lt. Col. Arthur Sullivan's 1st Recon Battalion, 1st Marine Division, to scout the mountains, report on enemy activity, and, when practical, call in artillery and air strikes on enemy movements.

Of the seven Recon teams Sullivan planted around the high rim of Hiep Duc Valley on June 13, Staff Sgt. Jimmie Earl Howard's 1st Platoon of C Company, consisting of 16 Marines and two Navy corpsmen, was assigned the most isolated site. It was deep inside enemy territory on top of a 1,500-foot barren knob called Nui Vu Hill (Hill 488) 4.3 miles northeast of Tien Phuoc. The summit was less than 25 yards across. The only cover was a boulder about the size of a chopped-down VW stuck to the northern edge.

For two days, Howard's unit called in fighter-bombers and artillery on enemy elements. At 7 p.m. on June 15, a U.S. Special Forces detachment reported an NVA battalion and Main Force VC unit heading east toward Nui Vu, less than two miles away. Warned, Howard placed his men on full alert.

Opening Salvo

Two hours later, four Marines manning a listening/observation post on the hill's narrow northern finger detected movement in the dark and shot a VC scout. Its element of surprise sprung, the enemy opened fire with an overwhelming crescendo of automatic weapons. The brief, violent exchange ended as quickly as it began, broken off by the aggressors. One Marine, Lance Cpl. Thomas Powles, was wounded.

Howard pulled his defensive perimeter even tighter. While Marines had the advantage of high ground, the enemy more than made up for it in firepower, superior numbers and the cover of darkness, outnumbering the Leathernecks by at least 25 to 1.

"Pick your targets. Don't shoot at shadows," Howard cautioned. "We don't have an unlimited supply of ammo."

A grenade exploded on the hill's western aspect, killing Pfc. James McKinney. Bamboo sticks began clacking, flowing like a tidal wave to encircle the hilltop in unearthly sound. Then, whistles and a bugle.

"Here they come!"

The din of the breaking battle echoed and reverberated across the valley. Communist machine guns lacerated the hill with bluish-green tracers. Grenades flashed balls of searing light.

> "Pick your targets. Don't shoot at shadows. We don't have an unlimited supply of ammo."
>
> —Staff Sgt. Jimmie Earl Howard

Waves of VC charged, popping up and down in the tall grass as they probed for weak spots. Friendly artillery parachute flares bathed the surrounding draws and saddles in weird yellow light, illuminating hordes of enemy soldiers. Nui Vu resembled an ant hill suddenly ripped open.

Pulled into a tight circle, the Marines defended their tiny perimeter of earth, inflicting heavy casualties.

Deadly Embrace of Combat

"Skipper, get us out of here," Howard pleaded with his battalion command post. "There are too many for my people."

A grenade wounded corpsman HM1 Richard Fitzpatrick. A

LEFT: 1st Plt., 1st Recon Bn., during its early days prior to the siege at Hill 488. Those identifiable are back row, beginning second from left: Sgt. Jimmie Howard, Lance Cpl. Ricardo Binns, Lance Cpl. Ronnie Knowles; fourth from right is Lance Cpl. Hawkins; bottom row, first from left is Lance Cpl. Ray Hildreth, and third, is Lance Cpl. Ralph Victor. Outnumbered 25 to 1, the Leathernecks held out against NVA and VC forces for 12 hours.

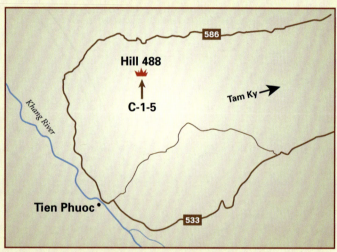

Military history was made by 1st Plt., C Co., 1st Recon Bn., on June 13, 1966, on an obscure knob called Hill 488.

round through the head killed Pfc. Thomas Glawe, followed by another grenade that killed Pfc. Ignatius Carlisi. Lance Cpl. John Adams dispatched two VC with the butt of his rifle before hostile machine gunners cut him down. Lance Cpl. Ray Hildreth then knocked out the machine gunners and a VC mortar tube. 1st Platoon would have been done-for had those weapons survived.

Hands reached out of the grass and grabbed Cpl. Jerrald Thompson. The two men tumbled down the hill locked in a deadly embrace. Thompson buried his knife in his foe's back.

But wounded, he was too weak to crawl back inside the perimeter. Two enemy soldiers dragged him away.

A grenade knocked corpsman HM3 Billy Holmes unconscious. When he revived, a VC was pulling him downhill. He hadn't the strength to resist. Hildreth shot the VC through the head. Holmes dragged himself painfully back to the Big Rock.

Time after time, probing, attacking, the VC threw everything they had at the hill. They expected a quick victory, but it was denied by the fierce defenders. The platoon was taking casualties and burning up ammunition at an alarming rate. The low point of the night came when Howard caught a bullet in his lower back that left him paralyzed.

During a lull, the enemy resorted to psychological warfare in an attempt to demoralize the Marines. "Marines! Marines! You die in one hour!" they said.

Not intimidated, the wounded Marine leader delivered a master stroke in one-upmanship. "All right, Marines!" he called out. "All together now, give 'em the old horse laugh!"

He keyed his radio mike because he wanted the battalion CP to overhear. Col. Sullivan looked stunned. Few moments in the annals of combat compared to that one in sheer audacity. The handful of defenders, outnumbered and hopelessly trapped, seemed to infect each other with a kind of gleeful exhilaration. Their laughter was loud, genuine, rollicking, contagious. Months later, captured VC admitted the ploy had a shattering psychological effect on them.

Since artillery was ineffective with the enemy so close,

MEDAL OF HONOR

STAFF SGT. JIMMIE HOWARD

NAVY CROSS

LANCE CPL. JOHN T. ADAMS (POSTHUMOUS)

MAJ. WILLIAM J. GOODSELL (POSTHUMOUS)

HOSPITALMAN 3RD CLASS BILLIE D. HOLMES

CPL. JERRALD R. THOMPSON (POSTHUMOUS)

CPL. RICARDO C. BINNS

Howard reverted to tactical air support—Huey choppers with rockets and machine guns, followed by A-4 Skyhawks with 250-pound bombs. Smoke and fire writhed like boiling lava a few yards outside the Marines' perimeter.

Pilots fearful of hitting friendlies had to leave a narrow ring untouched around Howard's perimeter. Communist soldiers dug in not 33 yards away and continued savage point-blank fighting so intense that choppers could not get in for a rescue attempt. The Marines would have to hold out until morning.

Only Eight Rounds Left

The platoon soon ran low on ammo. Howard issued one of the most unusual and cunning combat orders of recent history: "Throw rocks. They'll think we still have grenades. Zero 'em when they jump out of the way."

Incredibly, it worked. Attackers instinctively sprang away from the thunk of "grenades," exposing themselves and allowing Marines to make every shot count. It was becoming a crazy fight. The enemy fired automatic weapons; Marines answered with single shots. The enemy hurled grenades; Marines tossed rocks.

After a half-hearted enemy probe during the gray streaks of dawn, Howard pulled off another psyops coup. At precisely 6 a.m., he sounded off with, "Reveille! Reveille! Grab your socks ..."

That did it. Demoralized themselves, enemy forces withdrew under cover of the remaining darkness, dragging their dead and wounded, but still leaving behind more than 40 corpses. The siege of Hill 488 was broken. Howard's battered platoon had a total of eight rounds of live ammunition remaining.

Indeed, the relief force arrived just in the nick of time. Helicopters dropped men of C Co., 1st Bn., 5th Marines, on the south slope of the hill. In fighting their way to the beleaguered platoon, they lost two Marines and a Navy corpsman who died

FINAL MEDAL COUNT

ON THE HILL:

One Medal of Honor

Four Navy Crosses (2 posthumous)

13 Silver Stars (4 posthumous)

AMONG THE RELIEF FORCE:

One Navy Cross (posthumous)

One Silver Star (posthumous)

GRAND TOTAL: **Five Navy Crosses, 14 Silver Stars**

of his wounds five days later.

Maj. William J. Goodsell, tactical air coordinator on one of the helicopters of Marine Observation Squadron 6 (VMO-6), guided the transports to the LZ. He made repeated rocket and machine gun attacks. Then he guided medical evacuation helicopters until shot down. Goodsell was awarded a posthumous Navy Cross. A crewman from VMO-2 also was KIA.

The relief force counted five KIA, bringing total deaths at Hill 488 to 11 and the highest medal count to 19.

Six Marines lay dead of the original 18 defenders. All the rest were wounded. Only three did not have to be carried off the hill on stretchers or in body bags.

Sgt. Jimmie Howard recovered and was awarded the Medal of Honor. Three Marines received the Navy Cross, two of them posthumously, as well as a Navy corpsman. Thirteen others received Silver Stars for valor (four posthumous). And a fifth posthumous Silver Star went to a member of the relief force. The Battle on Nui Vu Hill produced perhaps the most highly decorated small unit in American military history. Someone later remarked that Hill 488 was like the Alamo—with survivors. ✪

TRUNG LUONG: A TRUE TEST OF RESOLVE

BY RICHARD K. KOLB

The 2nd Battalion, 327th Infantry Regiment of the 101st Airborne Division was tested to the maximum over three days in mid-June 1966 in a remote valley of a coastal province. It earned the Presidential Unit Citation.

"I was appalled at the number of casualties the company had suffered," recalled Tom Furgeson, at the time captain of Alpha Company. "I found a secluded area, sat down alone, and cried, and cried, until I couldn't cry anymore." Those casualties were the end result of a three-assault effort to take a seemingly insignificant village.

The Trung Luong Valley is located in coastal Phu Yen province, a part of II Corps during the war. At its center was the abandoned hamlet of Trung Luong 2. It held no strategic value. "We never wanted the village," former Lt. Col. Joseph Wasco, Jr., commander of the 2nd Bn., 327th Inf., told the *Philadelphia Inquirer* 34 years after the battle. "We just wanted them [the enemy]."

The battalion's objective was to investigate North Vietnamese Army (NVA) activity in the valley. This was part of the larger search and destroy mission, known as *Operation Nathan Hale,* to clear the nearby Tuy Hoa Valley. As it turned out, at minimum, the 7th Bn., 18B Regt., 5th NVA Div., was present in the area of operations assigned to the 327th's 2nd Battalion.

Nicknamed the "No Slack" Battalion, the 2nd fielded three companies (A, B, and C) numbering perhaps 400 men on June 20, 1966. Members of the anti-tank and mortar platoons also reinforced Charlie Company. For example, A Company counted 140 men and B Company, 138. A 105mm battery from 2nd Bn., 320th Artillery, provided fire support.

'Fury of Combat Awesome'

A nasty surprise waited A Company when it approached the ville (GI slang for a village) itself. A reinforced NVA company opened fire on Alpha from Trung Luong 2 and then charged the paratroopers. Company members counterattacked, driving the NVA back into the village. But not for long. They were forced to with-

Situated in the coastal province of Phu Yen, the Trung Luong Valley hosted intense combat in June 1966.

draw and establish a defensive position after losing seven KIA.

Meanwhile, Charlie Company was pinned down one-half mile from Hill 258. The hill formed the southern peak of a large hill mass. It was a sparsely jungled saddle shaped like a V and would be a focus of fighting.

In the afternoon, Bravo Company was lifted by helicopter into a hot landing zone (LZ) northwest of the hill. It was quickly pinned down. "The fury of the combat was awesome," remembered 1st Platoon leader 1st Lt. Louis McDonald. "B Company had taken approximately 44 casualties within the first two minutes of the landing. We desperately tried to defend ourselves for the night. We were out of water; what water we had was given to the wounded; and we were low on ammunition." And nine men were dead.

Spec. 4 Philip L. Nichols was a medic with B Company. Before his courageous deeds were done, he had carried or dragged 10 wounded from the killing zone, according to his Distinguished Service Cross (DSC) citation. On his fourth trip under fire, Nichols was shot in the thigh but managed to drag a

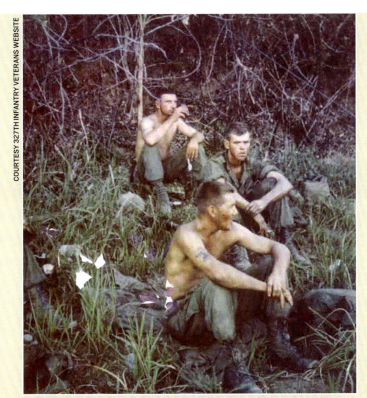

Three members of the 1st Platoon of C Co., 2nd Bn., 327th Inf., 101st Abn. Div., take a break. Charlie Company lost 13 KIA during the Battle of Trung Luong, June 20-22, 1966. The battalion was awarded the prestigious Presidential Unit Citation.

GI to safety. He crawled back for another, and was hit again in the same leg by two more bullets. Although bleeding profusely, he continued to treat wounded. Even while awaiting medical evacuation, Nichols administered first aid.

'Very, Very Terrifying'

The next day, June 21, Bravo assaulted Hill 258, but it was empty of the enemy. The NVA had abandoned their positions during the night.

A and C companies, in the meantime, were busy attacking the hamlet. "It just seemed that the NVA were shooting everything they had in their arsenal at us," remembered then-Capt. Furgeson. He especially recalled the incoming rounds: "All of a sudden there is a deafening explosion. Very, very terrifying. The incoming barrage lasted about 15 to 20 minutes."

The GIs were forced to pull back temporarily. They lost eight KIA and 39 WIA. But after the final of three attempts, they succeeded in taking the village. "One hour before dark, in the village, we numbered 35. A Company had done what was asked of it and we held our positions," said Furgeson.

On the 22nd, Charlie (along with reinforcements from the 1st Bn., 8th Cav) occupied a position dubbed Eagle. It was attacked at 5:40 a.m. by the 2nd Co., 7th NVA Bn. For at least three hours, until about 9 a.m., the forces battled. When the NVA pulled out,

DISTINGUISHED SERVICE
CROSS

LT. COL. JOSEPH WASCO, JR.

SPEC. 4 PHILIP L. NICHOLS

their 2nd Company had been "annihilated." C Company counted five KIA.

2nd Lt. Charles Beegle was with Charlie Company that morning. "The commander of the NVA unit assaulting us was captured during our sweep of the perimeter," he remembered. "We wiped out his entire company. This fighting lasted for over four hours. [It was] two less-than-half-strength platoons against an NVA company."

Lt. Col. Wasco stayed in the thick of things during the full fight. A veteran of both WWII and Korea, he went by the call sign "Wild Gypsy." He led the night defense of besieged companies on the ground twice and directly participated in a daylight counterattack. When it came time to observe the battle from above by helicopter, he did so at a low level. For his role in the entire three-day engagement, Wasco was awarded the DSC.

'Proud of Serving'

Over those three days, 31 paratroopers were killed. Most—18, or 58%—lost their lives on June 20. Gunfire accounted for 94% of KIAs. Two men died from shrapnel wounds. A and B companies each had nine deaths. Charlie sustained 13 KIA, including those from the attached platoons. As an airborne unit, it is not surprising that more than 80% of the KIAs were volunteers. An additional 155 men were WIA.

The 2nd Bn., 327th Inf., had persevered and was rewarded with a much-belated Presidential Unit Citation for Trung Luong 33 years later in 1999. Bruce Masters, a machine gunner with Alpha Company who was wounded on June 21, paid tribute to the men of his unit. "I was and, to this day, still am proud of serving with the guys who I fought beside, bled with and damn near died with on many occasions," he said. "It's [Trung Luong] on my mind every friggin' day. It's never gone away, and it never will," he told the *Philadelphia Inquirer.* ✪

THE TOLL

U.S. KIA:
31

U.S. WIA:
155

BY RICHARD K. KOLB

AMBUSHED AT SROK DONG

The overall mission was to secure the "Big Red One's" (1st Infantry Division) forward base at Quan Loi and the Hon Quan airfield. It was part of an operation dubbed *El Paso II*.

More specifically, it was to carry out a reconnaissance-in-force along portions of National Highway 13 north of the bridge at Cam Le, above An Loc. Because the bridge was largely destroyed, it was necessary to escort engineers to make repairs to the structure. But to the higher command, the overall operation was designed as bait to lure the enemy into a fight.

B Troop of the 1st Sqdn., 4th Cav—nicknamed the "Quarterhorse"—was assigned escort duty on June 30, 1966. Attached was the 1st Platoon of C Company. Ultimately, the troopers would be supported by three full companies (A, B and C) of the 2nd Bn., 18th Inf., known as the "Vanguards."

The terrain along Highway 13 was a mix of dense jungle, tree lines, chest-high grass and rice paddies. Near the hamlet of Srok Dong, due north of An Loc, the Viet Cong (VC) had constructed a bulwark of piled logs. It was close to the intersection of Highway 13 and Route 17, an ideal location for an L-shaped ambush. Indeed, the VC had been ordered to "lay a mobile ambush" of convoys passing by there.

That task was taken up by the 271st VC (Main Force) Regiment of the 9th VC Division. Before the three days of sporadic fighting were over, it would be joined by elements of the 273rd VC Regiment. Both were infused with regulars from the North.

AMBUSH IS SPRUNG

At 9:40 a.m. on June 30, B Troop—led by 1st Lt. James P. Flores—was hit by recoilless-rifle and machine-gun fire while crossing a rice paddy. Within the first 30 minutes, all of its four M-48 Patton tanks were disabled. Accompanying armored personnel carriers (APCs) responded with .50-caliber fire.

"After dismounting the tracks, we were left in an open field," recalled Tutt McCracken, then a lieutenant leading Charlie Company's 1st Platoon. "I had 17 men in my platoon and four were killed in the first few minutes of the fight. By the time we got back to the tracks and started getting back on, I had four wounded. I was down to nine men, and that came down to approximately two per track. We were fighting for

---

A mechanical flame thrower (a "Zippo") from 1st Plt., C Trp., 1st Sqdn., 4th Cav, torches VC emplacements at Srok Dong on June 30, 1966.

For two units of the 1st Infantry Division, combat spread over three days in mid–1966, proved to be a trial by fire. One they survived only with the aid of vital air power.

JUNE 1966

MEDAL OF HONOR

SGT. DONALD R. LONG
(POSTHUMOUS)

SILVER STAR

PFC. CHARLES F. ANDERSON

LT. PETER E. ODENWELLER
(POSTHUMOUS)

our lives. I was hit around noon as our track took a direct hit from a 75mm recoilless rifle."

APCs of C Troop carrying infantrymen atop them arrived quickly, only to be greeted by a rain of mortar shells. Its 1st Platoon countered with a mechanical flamethrower. Not to be deterred, the armored cavalrymen put up a protective shield around B Troop.

Heavy fire support was quick on the scene. B and D batteries of the 8th Bn., 6th Arty, based at Hon Quan, fired 825 rounds over the course of combat. Airplanes, UH-1B Huey helicopters and CH-47 Chinooks ("Guns-A-Go-Go") from the 11th Aviation Battalion provided an aerial arsenal. All told, the aircraft launched 88 close tactical air strikes.

By noon, the remainder of A Company was flown in by helicopter. In hot pursuit of fleeing VC, it was hit. C Company joined the fray. B Company arrived about the time the VC were leaving the battlefield. By 3:30 p.m., the VC had mostly broken off contact. C Troop moved to Checkpoint One and assisted B Troop in evacuating the wounded and suppressing enemy fire.

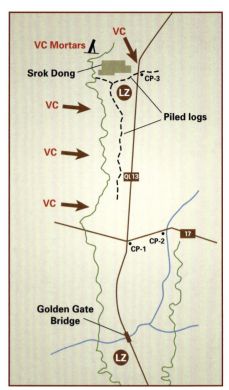

Srok Dong was a village located 10 miles north of An Loc in Binh Long province of southwestern Vietnam.

Pfc. Charles F. Anderson was the only medic available for more than two hours and supervised the evacuation. Under heavy fire, he kept it going until the last wounded man was evacuated. Anderson was later awarded the Silver Star.

One armor recon soldier of C Troop, Sgt. Donald R. Long, especially stood out that day. He carried wounded to the helicopters and provided much-needed supplies under intense fire. Repelling the VC as they attempted to mount his APC, Long helped a severely wounded crew member to safety. When a grenade landed on the carrier deck, "he threw himself over the grenade to absorb the blast and thereby saved the lives of eight of his comrades at the expense of his own life," according to his Medal of Honor citation.

But eight other C Troop armored cavalrymen were KIA along with two from B Troop. The 18th's C Company lost four men killed and Headquarters Company counted one dead. The total tally for June 30 was 16 GIs KIA and 66 WIA.

PURSUIT TO THE CAMBODIAN BORDER

Pursuit of the VC continued into July 1. At sunset, units of the 273rd VC Regiment attacked a reinforced platoon of A Company in its night defensive position near the hamlet of Ta Thiet close to the Cambodian border. C Company and the Recon Platoon, led by 1st Lt. James Magner, came to its relief. Before the VC broke off contact that evening, two A Company infantrymen were KIA, and one man died the same day from C Troop.

On July 2, at 5:45 a.m., the 273rd struck again, hitting the 250 men of A and C companies. Fortunately, they were dug-in in a clearing within a thorny scrub forest 2½ miles from the Cambodian border. And the men were fully alert.

Mortars came first. As one Korean War vet described the situation, "it hailed mortar shells" for two to three minutes.

"The NVA attacked in force at dawn after spending the night before being reinforced by

> # "My guys took everything the enemy threw at them and refused to cave, even at the end when we were out of ammo. We had to throw CS [non-lethal tear] gas when we were not resupplied. It worked." —1ST LT. JAMES MAGNER, RECON PLATOON

other regiments coming across the border, 1½ miles away," said Magner. "Because of heavy fog we couldn't see the attacking units, but we heard them coming. They came right at us, making significant noise through the heavy brush in the dark. Mortars dropped in first. [I was hit and later shot.] They tripped our grenade booby-traps and flares and we set off our Claymores. Then all hell broke loose."

In their sector, Recon Platoon members drove them back with tear gas with winds cooperating. "My guys took everything the enemy threw at them and refused to cave, even at the end when we were out of ammo," Magner said. "We had to throw CS [non-lethal tear] gas when we were not resupplied. It worked."

But one entire infantry squad found their M-16s jammed by sand; ammo and grenades exhausted. Fellow GIs bravely carried ammunition forward to them, some paying with their lives.

The entire action lasted around three hours, claiming the lives of 19 men—nine from A Company, six from C Company and four from the Recon Platoon. But the 273rd retreated, leaving plenty of dead behind. Air power had saved the day. F-100s "laid down so much molten steel that the Viet Cong withdrew shortly after 9 a.m.," according to one account.

'VALIANT WARRIORS'

The 1st Infantry Division commander, Maj. Gen. William E. DuPuy, later concluded: "U.S. forces nearly lost this battle. Air superiority proved to be the deciding factor, inflicting severe losses on the enemy."

Still, GIs paid a dear price in the fighting at and immediately after Srok Dong. The combined nine hours of combat on June 30 and July 2, claimed 92% of American casualties.

Some 38 men were KIA and at least 94 WIA. The 18th Infantry counted 26 dead, or 68% of the total. Alpha Company was hit hardest with 12 KIA. The 4th Cav fatal tally was 12 (75% from C Troop), accounting for the remaining 32%. Volunteers (22) constituted 58% of the deaths; draftees (16) 42%. Most deaths were caused by multiple fragmentation wounds inflicted by grenades and mortar rounds. Gunfire killed one-third of the men.

"As usual, most of the incredible bravery of the young men under fire and crushing pressure from very large units in the thick jungle in heavy fog went unrewarded," the Recon Platoon leader emphasized.

Retired Command Sgt. Maj. Jimmie W. Spencer wrote of the men of the 18th Infantry in general (and equally applicable to all units and time periods): "The important thing is that these valiant warriors performed with dignity and honor. We owe them our respect for their selfless service to the nation. We should honor them for duty faithfully performed." ✪

THE TOLL

U.S. KIA:
38

U.S. WIA:
94

BY RICHARD K. KOLB

DONNYBROOK IN THE BONG TRANG WOODS

"It was the worst battle scene I ever witnessed— the worst day of my life." That's how 1st Brigade commander Col. Sid Berry described the Battle of Bong Trang. He knew firsthand, having assumed command on the ground. And coming from a man who had led a rifle company in Korea and been wounded there in September 1950, this description had genuine credibility.

Bong Trang was the key action of *Operation Amarillo*. A search and destroy mission to clear Inter-Provincial Route 16 from Phuoc Vinh to Di An in two provinces of III Corps, it was initially regarded as a routine clearing of mines for supply convoys. That notion would soon prove not to be the case.

Before the fighting was over, 3,000 GIs from the 1st Bn., 2nd Inf.; 1st Bn., 16th Inf.; 1st Bn., 26th Inf.; 2nd Bn., 28th Inf.; and 1st Sqdn., 4th Cavalry (an armored recon unit) would be committed. They would come up against the Viet Cong (VC)'s Main Force Phu Loi Battalion reinforced by the VC C62 Company, about 500 men in all.

Bong Trang was located about four miles east of Lai Khe, a rubber plantation village and 1st Infantry Division brigade base camp. "The topography and vegetation offered less than ideal operating conditions," recorded the official Army history. "Heavy underbrush cloaked the gently rolling countryside, limiting visibility to little more than 20 meters [66 feet], and trees impeded the movement of armor.

"On the other hand, the landscape offered good cover for enemy soldiers, who maintained myriad trails and fortifications in the area, as well as platforms for observation and sniping."

The tropical hardwood forest, interrupted by occasional clearings covered by short grass, concealed a large network of camouflaged trenches and bunkers. Drainage systems were flanked by abandoned rice paddies.

'UNBELIEVABLE WE WERE STILL ALIVE'

It all started when a 15-man ambush patrol from C Co., 1st Bn., 2nd Inf., got lost. Forced to "coil up" (spend the night) at an unplanned location, the GIs found themselves stranded in the VC Phu Loi Battalion base camp. Making it to a bunker, the men immediately radioed their company commander for help.

"Our objective was to set up an ambush site at a VC water and resupply area," said Pfc. Chuck Mundahl, a member of the so-called "Lost Patrol." "In the morning of Aug. 25, we noticed 20 to 30 VC standing and running around. There were enemy trenches and bunkers next to us that were empty, so we took up positions there, and then it got wild.

"We called in artillery fire on top of us. VC surrounded us. A grenade exploded just above my head. My left shoulder and ankle and inner left thigh were burning, and it felt like I had been kicked in the groin.

"All hell broke loose as the 4th Cav hit the enemy line. The noise was deafening. Those of us who could crawled into a bunker, but the VC tried to finish us off. They must have thought we were dead and/or the rescue force diverted their attention because they moved on past our bunker.

"After the longest night of our lives, two VC went right between us early on Aug. 26. Much to my relief, then I spotted a white star on an armored personnel carrier (APC). When Americans from the relief column reached us, no one could believe we were still alive."

On Aug. 25, 1966, the 1st Brigade of the 1st Infantry Division engaged the Viet Cong Phu Loi Battalion in a lethal free-for-all.

AUGUST 1966

AP PHOTO

Men of the 1st Bn., 16th Inf., are airlifted into a jungle clearing on Aug. 25, 1966. It attacked eastward, encountering yet another Viet Cong base camp. The "Rangers" counted nine KIA in the combat to follow.

B Co., 16th Inf., 1st Div. infantrymen wade through razor-edged elephant grass. The company was seeking a suitable landing zone, as well as tracking withdrawing VC, on Aug. 25, 1966.

C Co., 1st Bn., 2nd Inf., 1st Inf. Div., was a key component of the U.S. force that fought at Bong Trang. Lyle Hewitt, Tommy Freese and Frank Beitzel, members of the Weapons Platoon, were all there on Aug. 25, 1966. Charlie lost 15 KIA.

But before they were finally rescued, a ferocious battle ensued around what became know as The Clearing. "The Clearing, which became the center of the action for the remainder of the day, was the perfect place for an ambush," wrote Army historian John M. Carland in *Stemming the Tide.* "Barely large enough for a single helicopter to land, it was surrounded by tall trees and clogged with thick underbrush and vines, nice cover for the Viet Cong."

The remainder of C Company and 2nd Platoon of C Trp., 1st Sqdn., 4th Cav (nicknamed the "Quarterhorse") came to the rescue riding aboard APCs and arrived about 8 a.m. that morning. They held the ground alone for several hours.

Capt. William J. Mullen III, C Company's commander, praised the men serving with him during the struggle that ensued. "Until 2nd Lt. Bruce Robertson, our forward observer, was evacuated, he called for artillery fires on a continual basis, despite blood spurting from numerous wounds," Mullen recalled.

"My most enduring memory is one of a Charlie Company mortarman … the only man in his platoon not a casualty. As bullets flew all around, Spec. 4 Tommy Freese stood in the open with a 60mm mortar on one shoulder and a sack of ammunition on the other. 'Sir,' he said, 'the 4th Platoon is ready. Where do you want me to shoot?'"

Mullen himself displayed equal courage. He personally resupplied a forward machine gun team with ammo and rescued a soldier trapped by fire after his APC exploded. Then he assured the evacuation of wounded and led an attack that completely overran and destroyed the VC fortifications in his sector. Thus "converting a potentially disastrous situation into a decisive victory," according to his Distinguished Service Cross (DSC) citation.

Lt. James G. Holland III, C Company's 1st Platoon leader, conveyed the intensity of the combat. "When we were about 400 meters [437 yards] from them [the trapped ambush patrol] all hell broke out. We deployed off the cav vehicles and we all returned fire," he remembered.

Later on, when a tank hit a mine, Holland was eight feet away. "The force of the explosion blew both me and my radio-telephone operator out into the rice paddies on the east side of the road. The laterite gravel hits made me feel like I had been wounded numerous times from the bottom of my helmet to the tops of my boots (as it turned out none penetrated)," he said.

Things were just starting to heat up. "The mortars coughed again, this time I took cover in a handy hole, which turned out to be a sump," Holland said. "It reeked, but I stayed. The next rush took us to the VC trench, which we held for the rest of the fight."

Pfc. John H. Johnston, a rifleman in C Company, was part of the initial ambushed rescue force. "It was a bad day burned into my mind: 24 hours of fear, despair and anger," he stresses. "We shifted around all day, trench to trench. I used lots of grenades. There was a continuous roar. Gunpowder and the smell of soured blood. Powder burns on my arms from buddies' weapons. Hot rifle shells going down my collar. Hot. I don't know how we survived."

Desperate straights best describe some situations. Sgt. Wilbur T. Barrow led 2nd Platoon of the 4th Cav's C Troop. "Every time we tried to get out, we were hit by mortars and hand grenades," he recalled. "Privates were taking command of the tracks and calling me for help. My answer to them was pick up their wounded and take salt pills and drink water, and pray, pray, pray! There was no help for anyone."

1st Lt. John R. Johnston, Jr., was a platoon commander in C Troop that day. He reinforced another beleaguered armored cavalry platoon. In doing so, his vehicle was knocked out yet he directed evacuation of the wounded anyway. Then he went on to set up a defensive perimeter under heavy fire. "Throughout the 18 hours" over Aug. 25-26, Johnston's "unimpeachable valor and dynamic leadership inspired his men to resist every hostile attack, finally driving the enemy to retreat into the jungle," records his DSC citation.

Combat during the Battle of Bong Trang, located four miles east of Lai Khe, centered on what was designated The Clearing. The "Big Red One's" 1st Brigade lost 45 men killed after engaging the Viet Cong's Phu Loi Battalion on Aug. 25, 1966.

'LONGEST SUSTAINED COMBAT'

By about 1 p.m., B Company was engaged. It launched three assaults attempting to break through to assist C Company.

Harry L. Guenterberg led the 2nd Squad of 1st Platoon. "I moved my squad to link up with 2nd Platoon on the enemy right," he wrote in a letter years later. "We received fire as soon as we got there. My point man jumped into a trench and I behind him. My machine gun team was knocked out and all were wounded. The enemy had concrete bunkers with some steel trap doors for firing out of while keeping in contact with what was left of my squad. A third Chinese-made grenade wounded me, and I woke up in the rear of the line."

Later, when his platoon of B Company faced annihilation, Pfc. Herbert S. Bechtel put his machine gun to effective use in covering its withdrawal. He especially placed his focus on the wounded being evacuated. Though seriously wounded himself, Bechtel stayed at his machine gun. Wounded once again, he successfully covered the withdrawal but at a steep price. When he was found dead at his M-60, Bechtel's fingers were still on the trigger and all ammo expended.

By this time, the original rescuers had to be rescued. In came the 1st Bn., 26th Inf., and B Trp., 1st Sqdn., 4th Cav. Lew Graff was with the 26th Infantry Scout Dog Platoon. "Contact was heavy and the bullets were flying," as he described the situation. "Overall, that was probably the longest sustained combat that I experienced in Vietnam. We were in early on the 25th and it seemed like we were under almost constant fire for the rest of the day and most of the night. We were pulled out late on the 26th. The presence of the 4th Cav was instrumental in our winning that fight in such a comparative short time."

Steady leadership played a part, too. "Lt. Col. Paul F. Gorman, our battalion commander,

> "Gunpowder and the smell of soured blood. Powder burns on my arms from buddies' weapons. Hot rifle shells going down my collar. Hot. I don't know how we survived."
>
> —PFC. JOHN H. JOHNSTON, C COMPANY RIFLEMAN

DISTINGUISHED SERVICE CROSS

CAPT. PETER S. KNIGHT
(POSTHUMOUS)

CAPT. WILLIAM J. MULLEN III

LT. COL. PAUL F. GORMAN

PFC. HERBERT S. BECHTEL
(POSTHUMOUS)

1ST LT. JOHN R. JOHNSTON, JR.

was a man who really earned the Distinguished Service Cross—he actually acted as the battle coordinator and force commander," Graff firmly believes.

Gorman, a Korean War infantry officer and recipient of the Silver Star in 1952, assumed direct command on the ground of eight companies from three battalions. He repeatedly exposed himself to heavy fire. Gorman was burned when one napalm container was accidentally dropped on his command post while calling in artillery and airstrikes to within 50 meters [55 yards] of his own lines.

Just before noon, the 1st Bn., 16th Inf., was airlifted into the fight. Attacking eastward, it encountered another VC base camp. The "Rangers" of B Company had the objective of securing a landing zone, as well as intercepting the VC. Capt. Quentin L. Seitz, Jr., company commander, recalled, "Most of the units fought all day on Aug. 25, each thinking it was the only one in the battle. It was a day marked by many acts of great leadership and bravery."

A Company entered the fray, too. "We were airlifted by helicopter and jumped off in a rice paddy," said Sgt. Neil Skiles. "The Viet Cong were concealed in trees and hidden bunkers. We were crawling toward the main force when I got hit by shrapnel from a mortar shell above the right eye and in the right arm about three hours after the battle started."

Skiles touched on a problem that would plague the iconic M-16 rifle for years: "Our own M-16 is a wicked weapon if taken care of, but if it isn't, of course, it will jam. The clip for the M-16 is made for 18 shells, but quite a few men overloaded the clip by putting in 20 [rounds], which resulted in about 50% of the jams."

Sgt. William Page recalled, "When my unit was deployed the evening of Aug. 25 until the morning of the 26th, we lost two company commanders. One of them, Capt. Peter S. Knight, was killed and received the Silver Star." Knight's award was upgraded to a DSC. He rushed to the assistance of a stricken platoon, exposing himself to VC fire and was hit. Nevertheless, Knight continued to lead the assault on an entrenched enemy until mortally wounded.

TRAGIC MISHAP INFLICTS CASUALTIES

Infantry units continued to feed into the engagement piecemeal. The 2nd Bn., 28th Inf., was airlifted to a blocking position to the north at 8:45 a.m. on Aug 26. But it never made contact with the VC.

Meanwhile, A Trp., 1st Sqdn., 4th Cav, was ambushed that morning. Hank Stewart was a machine gunner on a tank. "After reaching the main battle area," he said, "we encountered two tracks from C Troop that had been knocked out by rocket-propelled grenade and 57mm recoilless rifle fire. The crews were all dead. Our one tank began firing canister [encased shot] into the VC base camp, and then returned fire with .50-caliber and M-60 machine guns. Soon our tracks were full of the dead and wounded. Then we were ordered to an LZ to have them evacuated."

The "Blue Spaders" of the 26th Infantry were protecting a downed Air Force helicopter that morning. As the VC were breaking out, they hit that unit one last time. But enemy resistance largely ceased by 8:30 a.m.

By then, the four battalions had linked up to encircle the enemy encampment. Demolition teams from the 1st Engineer Battalion destroyed the base fortifications.

Tragically, though, "friendly fire" had inflicted additional casualties. As the VC exited the battlefield, fire continued to be called in on them. Two Air Force F-4 fighter-bombers accidentally dropped napalm on C Co., 1st Bn., 16th Inf., positions and then strafed the unit for five minutes with 20mm cannon fire. Two men were killed and 14 wounded.

"It took five minutes on the radio to get him [the pilot] to quit firing at us," 2nd Lt. Walter Harrison said. "Everything was on fire." Pfc. William Sparks said, "I never saw anything like it.

Pfc. John H. Johnston, David Washington, Gary Wells and Allen Duenas of the 1st Bn., 2nd Inf., received valor awards for Bong Trang. Duenas received a Silver Star, while the other three were awarded Bronze Stars for valor.

A guy in back of me had it [napalm] all over his back." A brave Sgt. 1st Class Fairburn, himself burned but able to assist the wounded, recounted the horror: "It was truly surreal—a blinding flash of light, an intense moment of heat, and a feeling of the air being sucked out of your lungs."

But those deaths were only two of the 45 GIs killed in the day-long plus battle known to those who fought it as simply "August 25." Gunfire claimed 25 men (56%) while shrapnel snuffed out the lives of 18 (40%). "Friendly fire" in the napalm strike killed two. Some 39 (87% of the total) of the KIA occurred on Aug. 25; six early on Aug. 26.

The 1st Bn., 2nd Inf.—nicknamed the "Black Scarf Battalion" in Vietnam—accounted for 47% of the KIA at 21, with C Company alone losing 15 men. Charlie Company of the 2nd's 2nd Battalion lost two men. The 16th Infantry counted nine dead; the 26th Regiment five. C Trp., 1st Sqdn., 4th Cav, sustained seven KIA. One rocket crewman from the 5th Arty was killed. Volunteers amounted to 62% of deaths; draftees, 38%. At least 183 men were wounded.

FIGHTING DOGGEDLY AND BRAVELY

In the end, Lt. Col. Richard Prillaman, commander of the Black Scarf Battalion, concluded that Bong Trang was "essentially a meeting engagement in which neither side was prepared for or really wanted heavy contact." The ambush patrol's entrapment "forced us to fight, and the invasion of their base camp forced the Viet Cong to hold their positions in the face of a strong U.S. effort."

1st Brigade commander, Col. Sid Berry, summed it up this way: "The VC had several advantages, principally well-constructed, heavily fortified positions in jungle terrain they knew intimately. We thrashed our way almost blindly into the enemy's base camp and fought him on his home ground under conditions favorable to him."

Strategic considerations aside, the men on the scene did their jobs. Capt. Dick Kurtz, the artillery fire support coordinator for HQ Co., 1st Bn., 16th Inf., observed years later: "At the tactical level, the vast majority of the U.S. soldiers, NCOs and junior officers performed superbly.

"The fighting men of the 1st Brigade team temporarily destroyed the operational effectiveness of a first-rate VC battalion. The soldiers fought doggedly and bravely against a seasoned VC force, which mounted an aggressive and determined defense on its home turf."

James Holland, who lost five men in his 1st Platoon of C Company, expressed what warriors have feared since time immemorial: "The battle had been ferocious and many of us had believed at various times during the fight this day would be our last. There were too many brave men who died in the Battle of Bong Trang, infantry and armored cavalry alike, for it to fade away as a footnote." ✪

THE TOLL

U.S. KIA:
45

U.S. WIA:
183

BY RICHARD K. KOLB

OPERATION ATTLEBORO

STANDOFF AT DAU TIENG

During 72 hours in early November 1966, five battalions of the 27th Infantry Regiment and 196th Light Infantry Brigade took on the 9th VC Division in War Zone C. The final outcome was costly but once again showed U.S. resolve.

It might have started out as a walk in the sun to locate enemy rice caches, but it quickly turned into a fight for survival. One that pitted a North Vietnamese Army (NVA) unit against a large U.S. force in sustained combat for the first time in III Corps.

That fight was part of *Operation Attleboro*—a search and destroy mission to eliminate all Communist troops west of the Michelin Plantation. One officer later called the specific plan for Nov. 3, 1966, ludicrous. Indeed, it proved to be a complicated maneuver that was illogical and confusing from inception, resulting in units scattered beyond coordination. Yet GIs made the best of the situation.

The intent was to knock out the 9th Viet Cong (VC) Division and its attached 3rd Bn., 101st NVA Regt., in Tay Ninh province. The opposing forces collided 4.3 miles northwest of Dau Tieng. Dau Tieng base camp—home to a brigade of the 25th Infantry Division—was situated along the east bank of the Saigon River midway between the Michelin and Ben Cui rubber plantations.

Combat was confined to a 2.4-square-mile-patch of real estate where the Ba Hao stream flowed into the Saigon River. The battlefield was covered by double-canopy forest with trees reaching 25 feet high. Clusters of elephant grass and clumps of bamboo interspersed the woods.

Military historian S.L.A. Marshall, author of *Ambush: The Battle of Dau Tieng,* wrote: "The area is leopard-spotted with grown-over open spaces, old graveyards, and clusters of huts. The occasional patches of elephant grass in the clearings are anywhere from bull-rush size to twice the height of a man … visibility within the forest for the rifleman averages about 25 to 30 meters [82 to 98 feet], twice the distance of horizon in primary jungle."

'IT HIT THE FAN'

Assigned the task of rooting out the communists was a task force eventually consisting of 11 rifle companies from five battalions. The 25th Infantry Division supplied the 1st and 2nd battalions of the 27th Infantry ("Wolfhounds"). They were on loan to the 196th Light Infantry Brigade, which fielded the 2nd Bn., 1st Inf.; 3rd Bn., 21st Inf.; and 4th Bn., 31st Inf. The 1st Battalion, 8th Artillery (105mm howitzers) provided fire support.

On Nov. 3, the battalions of the 1st and 31st Infantry moved toward the Ba Hao stream while the 27th's 1st Battalion (two companies) was air-assaulted into Landing Zone (LZ) Lima Zulu south of the stream to form blocking positions. Meanwhile, a company each of the 27th and 21st Infantry remained in reserve. Things

ABOVE: Wounded "Wolfhounds" of the 27th Infantry are helped out of the woods to await medical evacuation in early November 1966.

RIGHT: Maj. Guy S. Meloy III (left) is assisted by Capt. Lowell J. Mayone and Maj. Hal Myrah on Nov. 5, 1966. Meloy was awarded the Distinguished Service Cross for taking command of the entire three-day Battle of Dau Tieng and leading his troops, though wounded, with complete composure.

went awry from the start. The six attacking and blocking companies became separated and lost in the forest.

Around 10:30 a.m., contact was made with the VC.

"We were in the first wave off the choppers at about 10 a.m.," recalled John Martinko, a squad leader in 1st Plt., C Co., 1st Bn. "We walked into elephant grass and it hit the fan. I was grazed by a bullet on my left side. Later, I was shot in my right thigh. The bullet went in and out of my leg, detonating a smoke grenade that was on a wounded guy's gear that I had over top of my own. I fell on the smoke grenade, burning my right trunk and right arm.

"Because my M-16 jammed, like so many others, I used a wounded man's M-79 grenade launcher. I thought I was going to die that day. Charlie seemed to have a sight on anybody who got up. The firefight subsided by about 3 p.m., and I was medevaced out around two hours later, spending 10 days in the 25th MASH station at Cu Chi."

Reserve companies were quickly called in. By nightfall, the men had formed two defensive perimeters: five companies on the west and five on the east. Those in the west were led by Maj. Guy S. Meloy III, commander of the 1st Bn., 27th Inf.

B Company of the 1st Infantry (nicknamed "Cold Steel") was among those sent to Meloy's

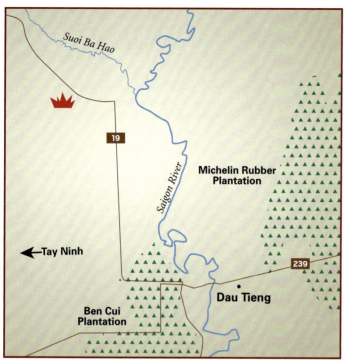

Eleven companies from five U.S. battalions were committed to battle 4.3 miles northwest of Dau Tieng between Nov. 3 and 5, 1966. They engaged the 9th VC Division where the Ba Hao stream flowed into the Saigon River.

AMBUSH BY S.L.A. MARSHALL PHOTO

A Huey helicopter kicks up dust as a group of grunts of the 1st Bn., 27th Inf., attack across a clearing during the Battle of Dau Tieng in November 1966.

aid. On the way, its 2nd Platoon was hit by a command-detonated Chinese-made Claymore mine.

"In one gigantic blast it cut down 24 men," according to one account, killing seven and wounding 17.

"Over a length of 37 meters [121 feet], the trail was a welter of blood," Marshall wrote. "Death had poured out of the mahogany tree. Well-camouflaged within the roots at the front had stood a giant VC Claymore mine. It had been command-detonated … The platoon had been mowed down like dried grass by a scythe."

The company was then ambushed and pinned down. C Company of the 21st (the "Gimlets") was airlifted to join Meloy. By day's end, 13 GIs were dead.

'LIKE A FT. BENNING MAD MINUTE'

Fighting intensified all over the battlefield as Nov. 4 wore on. The NVA's 3rd Bn., 101st Regt., was just waiting for the right moment to strike, when Meloy's units entered the woods.

"Lying in wait a short distance away were the North Vietnamese in mutually supporting bunkers," George L. MacGarrigle wrote in *Taking the Offensive.*

"Some of the bunkers were made of concrete, and all had thick overhead log coverings and bristled with machine-gun emplacements and camouflaged fighting positions. Interconnecting tunnels and trails hidden from the air provided access for rapid reinforcements."

Once the lead GIs had walked into a series of concealed fire lanes extending from the bunkers, the NVA opened fire. "One minute it was quiet," Meloy later said, "and the next instant it was like a Fort Benning 'Mad Minute' [a training demonstration of rapid firepower lasting 60 seconds]."

Marion L. Allard was with B Company. "For six hours, the fire never diminished; we had to shout to be heard over the radio," he remembered. "The battalion fought off numerous suicide attacks by the enemy, who was equipped with automatic weapons, steel helmets, webbed gear and various uniforms."

Meloy committed his other two companies (A-1-27 and C-3-21) over the next hour, but they quickly became pinned down. A Company withstood three attacks, losing 12 KIA, most of the men for that day.

Sgt. Lester Armstrong, a squad leader in C Company of the 21st Infantry, allowed his unit to ultimately advance without further casualties. His platoon was holding fast because of a VC machine gun emplacement and being flanked by six VC. Armstrong "grabbed a machine gun and charged directly into the intense hostile fire," reads his Distinguished Service Cross citation. "Although wounded, he increased his fire and killed the six VC protecting the bunker. He then attacked the machine gun bunker, killing three VC."

Reinforcements began arriving with the first two rescue companies taking casualties

Survivors of C Co., 1st Bn., 27th Inf., 25th ID, after the Battle of Dau Tieng. The 27th "Wolfhound" Regiment lost 36 men KIA in the fighting and demonstrated immense courage.

before reaching the beleaguered units. Three enemy human wave assaults came close to overrunning the Americans.

Lt. Bob Duffey led a platoon of B Co., 2nd Bn., 1st Inf., in attempting to reach Meloy.

"It was physically impossible to move any faster through that jungle," he remembered. "The fighting was too spread out and too sporadic—it wasn't like there were clear-cut lines. You simply had to find the enemy and fight them where they were."

Four hours into the fighting, C Co., 2nd Bn., 27th Inf., landed and attacked enemy positions. But the company was hit hard and became trapped with only 30 to 40 men remaining effective. During the night and near dawn, two rescue attempts were made in which a total of 12 GIs were KIA. Meloy radioed: "We have made two attempts to reach their position and have suffered heavy casualties each time. They are about 150 meters [492 feet] north of my perimeter."

At this stage, Meloy took over the entire battle. He had taken direct command of a trapped company, setting up a night defensive perimeter. The next morning, though wounded by shrapnel, he refused medical evacuation. He organized the defense against VC human wave attacks. During the remaining 36 hours, Meloy continuously exposed himself to fire with complete composure, according to his Distinguished Service Cross citation.

FIGHTING WITHDRAWAL

As Nov. 5 unfolded, the remaining companies of the 27th's 2nd Battalion were flown into the perimeter piecemeal. A Company was among them, playing a major role in rescue attempts.

"I remember very clearly the bodies of the men killed the previous day from C Co., 2nd Bn., the unit we went to assist, as we advanced through the dense foliage," said James L. June. "I made it through only the first two to three hours of the fight. After being wounded, I spent 16 months in Walter Reed Army Medical Center recuperating. My company alone suffered 12 KIA and included two Medal of Honor recipients."

A Company commander Capt. Robert F. Foley seized a machine gun, charged forward and fired as he went. Blown off his feet and wounded by the grenade, he still went on to destroy, single-handedly, three enemy gun emplacements. Pfc. John F. Baker, Jr., at 5 feet 2 inches tall and only 105 lbs., led repeated assaults against VC bunkers. Tossed into the air by a grenade explosion, he persisted. Over a two-hour ordeal, Baker recovered eight wounded GIs, destroyed six enemy bunkers and killed at least 10 communists. Both Baker and Foley

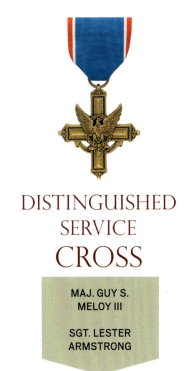

DISTINGUISHED SERVICE CROSS

MAJ. GUY S. MELOY III

SGT. LESTER ARMSTRONG

MEDAL OF
HONOR

CAPT. ROBERT F. FOLEY

PFC. JOHN F. BAKER

THE
TOLL

U.S. KIA:
53

U.S. WIA:
159

received the Medal of Honor.

Three companies from the 4th Bn., 31st Inf., also arrived, bringing the grand total under Meloy to 11.

B Company of the 1st Bn., 27th, led by Capt. Robert B. Garrett, broke through first, reaching the trapped "Wolfhounds" of C Company by noon. Four hours later, Garrett's men and the survivors finally made it to Meloy.

Over the next two hours, Meloy broke contact with the NVA by moving each company to the rear separately for helicopter extraction to Dau Tieng and Tay Ninh West. A and B companies of 3rd Bn., 21st Inf., secured the LZ for extraction of the 27th's 1st and 2nd battalions, which began at 5:10 p.m. The 2nd Bn., 1st Inf., held onto the blood-stained battlefield.

COUNTING THE HUMAN COST

When the tally was complete, 53 GIs were dead and 159 wounded. Thirty-six, or 68%, of the fatalities were sustained by the 27th Infantry; the 196th Light Infantry Brigade had 17 KIA. More than half of the killed (28) came from the Wolfhound's 2nd Battalion. The second highest battalion hit was taken by the 2nd Bn., 1st Inf., at 15—28% of the total. The single largest company loss was that of A Co., 2nd Bn., 27th Inf., with 12 KIA.

Nov. 5 was the deadliest single day with 43% of the U.S. deaths, Nov. 4 at 32%, followed by the opener on Nov. 3 with 25%. Enemy gunfire accounted for 72% of KIAs. Most of the multiple fragmentation deaths were in the single mine explosion early on. As far as component, nearly two-thirds (34 men) were volunteers and draftee KIAs numbered 19.

Medics took a particularly frightful beating in the battle: five KIA (all from HQ Co., 2nd Bn., 27th Inf., on Nov. 5). Philip Webster, a medic with B Co., 2nd Bn., 1st Inf., recorded his memories of those November days in a powerful personal letter two decades later.

"Nov. 3 was a terrifying day spent evacuating casualties," he wrote. "B Company's 2nd Platoon was wiped out by a Chinese Claymore mine mounted to a tree and zap—seven men were KIA and 17 WIA.

"Next day [Nov. 4], the battle would go on for 10 hours. As a medic, I had plenty to do. We lost three medics that day and one to combat exhaustion. While pinned down, I patched a fellow medic's foot with bullets buzzing over my head and ricocheting off trees behind me. I was terrified with my heart pounding and up in my throat. I felt like crying but didn't; just prayed. It was a horrible experience, one which I will never forget—the feeling that I should have been able to save more lives than I did.

"On the third day, we pulled out our dead. Rigor mortis had set in on many corpses and the smell was nauseating. Maggots crawling on open wounds. Equipment had to be cut off bodies. Legs and arms were blown off, which had to be matched up. It was a sickening experience."

Two medics were awarded posthumous Silver Stars. They were among at least nine Silver Star recipients who sacrificed their lives in the 27th Infantry. Two Medals of Honor and two Distinguished Service Crosses topped off the array of valor displayed in the battle.

The official Army history concluded of Dau Tieng: "The three-day engagement was at best a standoff, although the enemy apparently had been hurt the most, suffering upwards of 200 dead." One company of the 3rd Bn., 101st NVA Regt., was mauled on Nov. 5, fleeing the battlefield without orders.

But that did not lessen the pain for the Americans. On Nov. 6, 196th Brigade elements retrieved the remaining bodies. Duffey, of the 1st Infantry, recalled: "The hardest thing I had to do was identify so many of the dead in *Operation Attleboro*. It still gives me a lot of pain to remember their faces, the body bags, the tags tied to toes and all that." ✪

BY RICHARD K. KOLB

TRAPPED ALONG 'THE VALLEY OF A THOUSAND GHOSTS'

For two platoons of one infantry company, late November 1966 along the Cambodian border proved to be a lethal four hours. And it was one of the highest proportional losses for the 1st Cavalry Division in Vietnam.

"We're surrounded—for God's sake bring artillery fire in on us!" pleaded Pfc. John Godfrey, 3rd Platoon radio-telephone operator (RTO). Then radio contact was broken. That was Godfrey's last transmission. He was later found dead with the handset of his radio still in his hand.

A Saigon press bureau dramatically described the battle in which Godfrey made his desperate plea: "A hopelessly outnumbered U.S. Army platoon of 21 men stood off a 400-man North Vietnamese battalion for four hours Monday. In the end, it called in artillery fire on its own positions as the communists engulfed it in human wave assaults."

The official Army history, *Taking the Offensive*, dismissed the fierce fight in a mere four sentences, simply labeling it a "disaster." To the men who waged it, however, the battle had far greater meaning.

On Nov. 21, 1966, C Co., 1st Bn., 5th Cav, 2nd Bde., 1st Cav Div., found itself in a precarious position. Its three rifle platoons were thinly spread that day. The company fielded 110 men: 30 in 1st Platoon, 45 in the 2nd Platoon and command post group and 35 in the 2nd Platoon. But 3rd Platoon was down to 21 men after a 13-man squad was sent back to Landing Zone (LZ) Hawk. Some 46 of the company's infantrymen were recent replacements.

In the field for 72 days straight, Charlie Company was dispatched on a search-and-destroy mission into the Chu Pong foothills along the Ia Drang Valley for three days. This was a commonly known enemy infiltration route. The reconnaissance-in-force was part of *Operation Paul Revere IV,* a continuing screening and surveillance mission along the Cambodian border.

Charlie Company's mission was in the southwest corner of Pleiku province about seven miles southwest of Duc Co. The nearest village was Ph Athena, a stone's throw (4/10 of a mile) across the border in Cambodia. Much to their surprise, the GIs would confront three companies of the 5th Bn., 101C Regt. of the North Vietnamese army (NVA) in their area of operations (AO).

That AO consisted of fairly open scrub brush with patches of bamboo, elephant grass and wait-a-minute vines (entangling bushes). The 2nd and 3rd platoons ended up on low ground next to a creek bed with scattered bushes. It was surrounded on three sides by high ground. As the division historical report put it, "The terrain was not entirely prohibiting, though the heavy forest did restrict routes of movement and limited observation."

LURED INTO A TRAP

Grunts of Charlie Company were airlifted by Huey

A memorial service for the 34 GIs killed in the brutal Chu Pong foothills engagement was held at the 1st Cavalry Division's base camp at An Khe around Dec. 10, 1966.

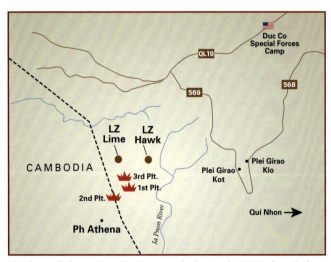

The fierce fight on Nov. 21, 1966, took place only 4/10 of a mile from the Cambodian border just east of the village of Ph Athena. LZ Hawk was about two miles farther east in the southwest corner of the Vietnamese province of Pleiku. Duc Co had a U.S. artillery firebase.

helicopters to beat the bush west of LZ Hawk. It was a pad large enough to accommodate only two helicopters and was situated two miles east of the Cambodian border. First sighting of the NVA on Nov. 21 occurred at 9:30 a.m. Then six NVA lured the 2nd Platoon into a trap west of a trail. Firing commenced a half hour later before the men, as they advanced on a knoll, realized what they had walked into.

"But they had all passed the point of no return and were aware of it," S.L.A. Marshall wrote in his book *West to Cambodia*. "Spread out and separated as they were, with few of them mobile and the great number, if not pinned down, then flattened by fire, it was already impossibly late to order them back away." They had been ambushed by two NVA companies.

Acting platoon Sgt. Julius Durham was one of only two who survived to tell what happened to 3rd Platoon. In June 2016, he recounted the details.

"On the morning of Nov. 21, 2nd and 3rd platoons initially linked up," he said. "3rd Platoon stayed put as 2nd Platoon moved out. When it got about 200 yards away from us, 2nd Platoon made contact with the NVA. The 2nd radioed for help and

GIs of Charlie Company take a break during a search and destroy mission through an old French plantation near Pleiku in the Central Highlands after the battle in December 1966.

Lt. Hector Martinez, Spec. 4 Bill Tuey and 1st Platoon leader Lt. Tim McCarthy pose for a photo at An Khe in November 1966. McCarthy was killed later on Dec. 20. Tuey was awarded the Silver Star for his pivotal role.

when we moved, the NVA hit us. We had no idea we had been surrounded. Fighting lasted a lot longer than reported in the press before we were completely overrun.

"The jungle was thick so we took cover behind trees, and set up a round perimeter. Combat was close-quarters. NVA were running every which way, shooting and throwing hand grenades. It was an individual fight for survival. Because our RTO was killed, we received no fire support at all.

"After the battle was over, four to five GIs and I were still alive. Then the NVA executed all the wounded—guys would scream and you would hear the communists shoot once or twice. I was lying face down and had my M-16 strapped to my arm. An NVA took my steel pot [helmet] off and put his AK-47 barrel to the back of my head. But in a split second he was gone. I will never know why he did not pull the trigger. I laid still until reinforcements arrived.

"Evacuated to Japan, I spent three months in the hospital there. My parents found out I survived in an NBC Huntley-Brinkley Report on the evening news."

Durham feigned death and lay motionless for nearly an hour. His Silver Star citation credits him with "visually directing an air strike from his position on the ground, which caused the North Vietnamese to flee."

In the fall of 2016, Earle Mosely recounted the full story regarding the fate of the 3rd Platoon. "I was the point man in 1st Sqd., 1st Plt., C Co., and led the 1st Platoon back to 2nd Platoon that day," he said. "I know Pfc. Anthony Gray was the last man standing in 3rd Platoon. On Nov. 21, he was the ammo bearer on a three-man M-60 machine-gun crew. Gray

> **"An NVA took my steel pot [helmet] off and put his AK-47 barrel to the back of my head. But in a split second he was gone. I will never know why he did not pull the trigger."**
>
> —SGT. JULIUS DURHAM, SURVIVOR OF 3RD PLATOON

PATRICIA LEE / THE VIETNAM MEMORIAL WALL

Dalton "personally repelled several enemy assaults with his accurate fire. Although wounded twice by the intense hostile fire, he remained steadfast."

—SILVER STAR CITATION

Pfc. John M. Dalton, a machine gunner in the 2nd Platoon, died at his M-60 providing life-saving covering fire for his platoon members. He was awarded a posthumous Silver Star.

SILVER STAR

PFC. JOHN M. DALTON
(POSTHUMOUS)

SGT. JULIUS DURHAM

PFC. ANTHONY GRAY

SPEC. 4
WILLIAM D. TUEY

CAPT.
HAROLD WUNSCH

was awarded the Silver Star in June 1967, courtesy of then-Sen. Hugh Scott of Pennsylvania."

Fifty years later, Anthony Gray spoke of that "life-changing battle." "In fact, I was the last one firing before being overrun," he recalled. "I was critically wounded after being hit by carbine fire and a hand grenade. I lost my right eye and had my jaw broken by the rifle fire along with many other injuries to my face." Gray's ordeal was actually chronicled in Philadelphia's *Sunday Bulletin* on Dec. 25, 1966.

Later, A Company (57 men) under Capt. James W. Drake was the first to arrive on the scene of the platoon's final stand. Drake described the sad sight to Marshall, who provided a graphic description in his book.

"Their [A Company] brief maneuver was only a heart-breaking body count of friends," Marshall wrote. "The corpses were all facedown, and all were pointed in one direction, forward. There were 19 bodies, strung out along the dim trail over a distance of not more than 30 meters [33 yards]. … All the bodies were badly battered and mangled."

REPELLING THE ASSAULTS

After the NVA company wiped out 3rd Platoon, it turned its fury on the besieged 2nd Platoon. For some two hours, all enemy fire was concentrated on these 45 GIs. Many rose to the occasion, including Spec. 4 William D. Tuey. The forward artillery observer (his parent unit was the 1st Battalion, 77th Artillery) for C Company, Tuey also became an acting sergeant for 2nd Platoon at only age 18.

Marshall called him "a superb fighter who is at his best when the pressure breaks other men." Indeed, for his steady courage under fire, Tuey was reportedly recommended for the Distinguished Service Cross but awarded the Silver Star.

"I was totally involved in adjusting artillery fire, adjusting fire from the overhead gunships, bandaging the wounded and informing approaching units of our situation," he said. "I was still able to use my M-16 and observed NVA falling when I would shoot them."

Another Silver Star recipient, this one posthumous, was Pfc. John M. Dalton, a machine gunner with 2nd Platoon. Staying at his M-60 until losing consciousness, he held off the NVA long enough for airstrikes to impact. According to his citation, Dalton "personally repelled several enemy assaults with his accurate fire. Although wounded twice by the intense hostile fire, he remained steadfast." Found still unconscious, Dalton died before he could be medevaced.

Spec. 4 Larry Williams was a grenadier in the 2nd Squad of the 2nd Platoon. He had been in Vietnam for only 31 days. "I had a feeling this would not be a usual patrol, so I filled up on ammo and supplies," he recalled. "I packed 72 rounds for my M-79 grenade launcher. When the fight was over, I had only one shotgun shell and the rounds in my .45 pistol left. Nov. 21 was the most intense firefight I experienced during my entire tour in Vietnam.

"Trapped in a horseshoe ambush, we were about three hours without any fire support. When it did arrive, I started crawling because I could feel the heat from the napalm. I also was grazed by a bullet across the stomach.

"After the airstrikes, the NVA broke contact and B Company arrived. It took the 14 of us remaining four to five hours to hump back to the landing zone."

F-100 Super Sabre jets ultimately broke the attack with horrifying effect. "I could see NVA soldiers running while they were on fire from the fervent heat caused by the napalm explosions," said Tuey.

Retreating NVA were unsuccessfully pursued. Capt. James R. Taylor led B Company on their trail. Before being ordered out, the company had penetrated 383 yards into the enemy's Cambodian sanctuary.

Pfc. Steve Hassett, at An Khe in mid-December 1966, was a fire team leader in the 1st Platoon on Nov. 21. His platoon arrived just after the airstrikes ended. He helped evacuate the dead and wounded Americans.

'BLOOD STREAMED DOWN ON US'

1st Platoon (it had been lost) linked up with 2nd Platoon right after the airstrikes ended. Pfc. Steve Hassett was a fire team leader in the 1st Platoon and had the unenviable job of collecting dog tags from the dead. "Most of the dead GIs were about eight to 10 feet apart," he remembers. "I found two friends of mine—Pfcs. Joe Scicutella and Joe Rabon—lying within a few feet of each other. We had gone through infantry training and jump school together."

Hassett recalls: "A cargo net was dropped from a Chinook helicopter and spread on the ground. The dead of the 2nd Platoon were wrapped in ponchos and stacked in the net— taking them to the rear and an early return home."

That emotionally draining task left an indelible impression on Tuey, too: "We first placed the wounded in baskets lowered from Chinooks hovering overhead. They were hoisted up while blood streamed down on us. Next, we placed the dead bodies in baskets and they were also hoisted out. When this was completed, we were covered in blood and there was no water to wash with."

One thing that always gnawed at Hassett was how much the new weapon issued in Vietnam was a contributing factor to the casualties. "In the fall of 1966, our company probably had only one cleaning kit and rod for every three or four riflemen," he said. "I don't know how many men had jammed M-16s on that day but it is likely that some of them died holding a weapon that couldn't fire."

When the final count was made, 34 men from C Company had been killed: 20 in 3rd Platoon and 14 from 2nd Platoon. At least 11 were wounded. More than 90% died from small-arms fire; the remainder from multiple fragmentation wounds. Thirteen of the KIA had been in Vietnam for a month or less. Volunteers made up 56% of the count; draftees 44%. Pfc. George Turner, an RTO from B Btry., 1st Bn., 77th Artillery, was attached to 2nd Platoon when killed.

They had joined the many communist casualties in what the Vietnamese superstitiously called the supposedly haunted "Valley of a Thousand Ghosts."

The 1st Cavalry Division historical report claimed C Company's sacrifice thwarted the NVA's planned attack on the U.S. artillery base at Duc Co. Its recon-in-force interrupted the 101C Regiment's move, the report asserted, because it forced the enemy to abort the mission once it lost the element of surprise.

Hassett believes otherwise. "That sounds like an after-the-fact excuse to me," he wrote in his personal account of the battle. "We were spread so thin, our presence was so obvious and our noise discipline so bad that the NVA could easily have infiltrated around us if that was their intent. Charlie Company was their target and a damn inviting one at that." ✪

THE TOLL

U.S. KIA:
34

U.S. WIA:
11

BY RICHARD K. KOLB

HEDGEROW COMBAT IN THE HIGHWAY 506 VALLEY

Although 1966 was a year of big battles, this one was perhaps the least known. Virtually ignored in both official and popular reports, it was a fray worthy of recognition because of the sacrifices made. This was especially so considering the fact that an amazing five Distinguished Service Crosses (DSC) were awarded for a single hours-long engagement.

Operation Thayer II was a search and destroy effort aimed at pacifying Binh Dinh province in II Corps. An unintended consequence of the operation was a thrust into Highway 506 Valley, located about 2½ miles southeast of Landing Zone Pony. The valley was situated nine miles south of Bong Son, an area of operations all too familiar to troopers of the famed 1st Cavalry Division.

On Dec. 17, 1966, elements of C Co., 1st Bn., 8th Cav, spotted an enemy squad moving into the Suoi Ca Valley (known as "Happy Valley"), an infiltration route into the Bong Son coastal plains. When Charlie Company pursued, it got more than it bargained for. So it called for back up from the division.

The aero-rifle platoon (known as "Blue") of A Troop, 1st Squadron, 9th Cav, which provided aerial reconnaissance, answered the call. It was air-assaulted to the northeast in what was known as Highway 506 Valley. Encountering heavy resistance, the "Blue" Platoon was followed by a platoon of D Troop (a ground cavalry unit). Then came four companies (A, B, C and D) of the 1st Bn., 12th Cav—nicknamed the "Chargers."

What the cavalrymen had stumbled on was at least the equivalent of a reinforced Communist battalion. The 7th and 9th battalions of the 18th Regiment of the 3rd North Vietnamese Army (NVA) Division were supposedly in the area searching for rice supplies. As it turned out, they were probably preparing for an attack on LZ Bird, which occurred 10 days later.

The goal of the reinforcements was fairly straightforward: encircle the enemy that had already engaged the U.S. unit. But as was common, things did not always go as planned. Well-prepared bunkers and trench lines confronted the men, and they had to fight through hedgerows. Even the palm trees dealt death on this day.

'FIRING FROM THE HIP': COURAGE WAS COMMON

1st Lt. James P. Simons, a team leader, led the UH-1 transport helicopters infiltrating the aero-rifle platoon. Flying at tree-top level on the outskirts of the battle area, he helped prevent an enemy escape. After rearming and refueling, Simons returned

Dec. 17, 1966, saw the 1st Battalion, 12th Cavalry, battle a reinforced enemy battalion in a bloody slugfest near Landing Zone Pony. For the "Chargers," the day was among its worst.

DECEMBER 1966

SSG Henry Trotty SFC James Latham SSG Lamb SGT Johnson Robert O. Smith David W. Osborne Tom Cusick
David Black Ivory Whitaker LeRoy Burgess Lawrence "Doc" Holder Donald Garvin David Rowe Unknown
Lt. John Rudd

3rd Platoon, Charlie Co., 1st BN, 12th Cavalry - Oct. 1966

SGT Daniel Rozzelle PFC James Kelley SP4 Terry Rosario Eddie Fain SP4 Barnes Unknown Gary Lusk Unknown PFC Van Zant Unknown Bill McKoewn

COURTESY JOHN RUDD/ THE STORY OF CHARLIE COMPANY

The 3rd Plt., C Co., 1st Bn., 12th Cav, 1st Cav Div., was air-assaulted into the 506 Valley on Dec. 17, 1966, under withering NVA fire. Charlie Company lost eight KIA in the battle. The platoon is pictured here that October.

to mark hostile positions with smoke grenades. Then he actually hovered his helicopter over NVA bunkers, dropping hand grenades on them. Despite being hit by several rounds, he kept the aircraft hovering to assure safe evacuation of casualties. Simons' concern of his fellow troopers was rewarded with a DSC.

Sgt. Ceasar Bryant was a squad leader in the "Blue" Platoon. He had only three weeks left in-country but was not about to leave his men. Moving to within 15 feet of a

machine gun emplacement, he lobbed grenades at it and then charged. He was about to throw his last grenade when felled. Despite serious wounds, he crawled back for a weapon and attacked again. Just 10 feet shy of the bunker, Bryant was fatally wounded.

"We were in pretty heavy contact with a North Vietnamese regiment," then-Lt. Jim Haslitt recalled years later. "I had flown Sgt. Bryant into many landing zones and he always led his men off the chopper. He was a fine

SILVER STAR

VIETNAM VETERANS MEMORIAL FUND/WALL OF FACES

SGT. ROQUE PERPETUA, JR.
(POSTHUMOUS)

SGT. CEASAR BRYANT
(POSTHUMOUS)

PFC. JOHN E. HORN
(POSTHUMOUS)

PFC. JOHN G. LARSON
(POSTHUMOUS)

The Highway 506 Valley was located nine miles south of Bong Son in Binh Dinh province of II Corps. The Bong Son coastal plains inland from the South China Sea became a familiar stomping ground for GIs.

example of an infantry squad leader. I also flew his body out of his last LZ, and I'll never forget the loss of such a man." Bryant received a posthumous Silver Star, as did fellow A Troop member Pfc. John E. Horn.

The 1st Battalion rifle companies came next and confronted the NVA head-on. The 12th's Delta Company ran into a meat grinder, judging from the casualties it sustained. Before the fighting was done, it incurred 58% of the regiment's KIAs. In fact, it faced off against an NVA bunker line of battalion strength. Machine guns mowed the infantrymen down in a frontal assault.

"Delta Company was the first to go in," said Michael Anderson, a medic with the 3rd Platoon. "Upon arrival, I had an eerie feeling about this place. We jumped off the helicopters and were ordered to line up and sweep the village. Suddenly, we were receiving gunfire from every direction. Before long, everyone around me was dead. Only seven of my platoon remained on the battlefield. The next morning, we collected our dead. I will never forget seeing the casualties aboard that Chinook, its bloody floor was a horrible sight."

After passing through this gauntlet, platoon Sgt. Roque Perpetua engaged the NVA at less than 100 feet. He crawled up and down the lines, and after locating a bunker he charged it. According to his Silver Star citation, Perpetua, though wounded, continued his one-man assault, reaching to within 16 feet of the bunker before being mortally wounded.

Machine gunner Pfc. Roger K. Hattersley ran into fire 43 yards to his front. Still, he held his position to cover wounded. When his ammo ran out, Hattersley picked up another weapon from a wounded man and helped him to withdraw. Then he resumed his attack. "Jumping to his feet firing his weapon from the hip," says his DSC citation, he "fearlessly charged the NVA emplacement."

Although wounded halfway to the bunker, he continued forward. Hattersley was found wounded a second time and lying unconscious next to the NVA bunker with a dead communist inside. "His attack silenced the main enemy firing position and enabled his unit to overcome the NVA," continues the citation.

Meanwhile, a recoilless rifle team from A Company moved to eliminate a machine gun position and ran into a buzz saw of fire. Squad leader Sgt. Sherman G. Fuller provided covering fire for the team. When two of the team were KIA and two WIA, he organized the rescue effort and personally administered first aid to the hit medic. As the NVA continued to rake the area with fire, he covered the medic with his own body and was wounded. Fuller persisted in engaging the communists until forced to be evacuated, records his DSC citation.

DESPERATE FIGHT IN THE PERIMETER

Lt. John Rudd led C Company' 3rd Platoon in the mission to link up with the heavily engaged D Company. The remainder of C Company arrived later under withering fire. It tried to close the gap between D and B companies in the dark, but it underwent its own ordeal by fire in the process.

After two company commanders became casualties, Maj. Leon D. Bieri, battalion operations officer, flew in to take command of Charlie on the ground. He inspired the pinned down company to mount an assault. Then he led a platoon in a flanking maneuver, running into three NVA who had penetrated their perimeter.

"Armed with only a pistol, he killed all three, but suffered a serious shoulder wound," according to his DSC citation. He killed another sniper behind the lines. Not done, he successfully led a squad in a flanking attack and directed aerial attacks. "Major Bieri then supervised evacuation of the wounded until he passed out for loss of blood," says the award narrative.

Charlie Company medic Pfc. Alton R. Kennedy was wounded in the leg while aiding a

DISTINGUISHED SERVICE CROSS

SGT. SHERMAN G. FULLER

FAMILY PHOTO

PFC. ROGER K. HATTERSLEY

MILITARY TIMES HALL OF VALOR

MAJ. LEON D. BIERI

FAMILY PHOTO

PFC. ALTON R. KENNEDY
(POSTHUMOUS)

VIETNAM VETERANS MEMORIAL FUND/VALL OF FACES

1ST LT. JAMES P. SIMONS
(POSTHUMOUS)

soldier. Yet he went on to bandage another man. Kennedy made several trips under heavy fire to carry out more wounded. When another GI was left lying 33 feet from a bunker, he retrieved him and dragged him back to the company perimeter. Returning for more men who had been hit, he was fatally wounded attempting to rescue a GI only feet from a machine gun position. Kennedy received a posthumous DSC.

Another medic, Pfc. John G. Larson, also performed heroic life-saving feats at the cost of his life. NVA concealed in hedgerows unleashed a torrent of fire on C Company men at about 40 yards. As casualties mounted, Larson made numerous trips forward to treat and help evacuate the wounded. After aiding men of his own platoon, he moved to another that had its medic knocked out of action. He moved back and forth between the platoons. When a close friend was wounded, Larson shielded him with his own body. In the midst of trying to revive the man, he was mortally wounded, reveals his Silver Star citation.

TERRIBLE TOLL TAKEN BY GUNFIRE

Bravo Company's helicopter-borne troopers touched down about nightfall. Its objective was to break through NVA lines and link up with C Company. Bravo finally made contact with Charlie's 1st Platoon at 9:30 p.m. "We were getting harassing sniper fire from positions in palm trees all throughout the area as we drove southward," B Company Capt. Roy Benson remembered.

So the GIs put their Starlight scopes to good use. A Starlight is an image magnifier that gathers reflected light from the stars or moon to illuminate targets. "Immediately after knocking one of the NVA snipers out of a palm tree, another NVA would shimmy up to replace the other, and we would wait till he got in position and then knock that NVA out of the tree," Benson said. Apparently, Carlisle Mahto was a deadly shot, killing about 10 NVA snipers strapped in trees overlooking 1st Battalion lines.

Bravo successfully evacuated the wounded of Charlie Company by chopper while withstanding small probing NVA counterattacks.

As darkness had enveloped the battlefield, the NVA escaped the intended encirclement. The 1st Battalion assaults on fortified bunkers hidden by hedgerows had been costly. NVA machine gun and other small-arms fire took its toll. Of the 36 1st Cav Division troopers KIA, a full 94% died by gunfire; only two were killed by shrapnel.

Of the four 1st Battalion rifle companies (they lost a total of 31 men), D Company suffered most with 18 KIA. C Company had eight KIA and A Company, four. The 9th Cav's 1st Squadron sustained five KIA—three from D Troop and two in A Troop. All units combined counted 81 wounded. In 1966, Army combat units were often manned by many volunteers. That was reflected in the KIA tally in the Highway 506 Valley: 23 (64%) of the men were volunteers; 13 (36%) were draftees. No matter how they came into the service, their dedication to their fellow unit members was beyond question, as it would be throughout the war. ✪

THE TOLL

U.S. KIA:
36

U.S. WIA:
81

BY AL HEMINGWAY

STEADY STAND at LZ BIRD

S taff Sgt. Delbert Jennings did not feel good. His stomach pains worsened, and he had trouble sleeping. Besides his illness, he was worried. His undermanned weapons platoon was assigned to defend the northern sector of the perimeter at Landing Zone (LZ) Bird. It was a large area to defend for a mere 22 soldiers, some of whom were new replacements and had seen no action.

LZ Bird was one of several forward artillery bases that provided support for the 1st Cavalry Division in the Kim Son Valley of Binh Dinh province. Many felt Bird was located in an exposed area—"a freak of geography fashioned by the vagaries of a meandering river," according to one description. From the air, it resembled a T-bone steak. It was 820 feet in length and about 262 feet wide and was bordered on the south and west by the Kim Son River.

A dozen howitzer positions spotted the LZ. The 155mm guns of C Btry., 6th Bn., 16th Artillery, were situated at the northern perimeter, and at the southern tip were the 105mm cannons of B Btry., 2nd Bn., 19th Artillery. Interspersed among the gun positions were infantrymen from C Co., 1st Bn., 12th Cav, 1st Cav Div.

'LIKE SITTING DUCKS'

Just before Christmas 1966, both sides called a truce to hostilities. However, at 1 a.m. on Dec. 27, the unmistakable sound of incoming mortar rounds were heard. The chattering of enemy heavy machine guns and 57mm recoilless rifles cracked in the night air. Soon, soldiers from the 22nd North Vietnamese Army (NVA) Regiment— perhaps 1,000 men were in the force—had successfully breached the perimeter.

"The moon was out and between the rain clouds … and you could see hundreds of NVA, most in single file, coming at us," wrote Spec. 4 John McGinn, Jr. "I was on the northeast side. I felt like we were sitting ducks."

Spec. 4 Gary Peasley and Spec. 4 Donald Woods began raking the NVA attackers with M-60 machine gun fire. They stood their ground, enabling Jennings and Staff Sgt. Colmar Johnson to muster a group of GIs to re-establish a secondary perimeter.

As the two NCOs rallied the troops in their sector, 1st Lt. John Piper and 1st Lt. Charles Campanella emerged from their tent to see 40 to 50 NVA soldiers breaching the southeast corner of the perimeter. Both officers began to withdraw to the gun parapets to defend them. They made it safely to the Fire Direction Center and were

A savage assault by North Vietnamese Army regulars was stopped by the combined efforts of artillerymen and infantrymen at LZ Bird during *Operation Thayer II* on Dec. 27, 1966.

DECEMBER 1966

Weary troops rest after the ferocious battle at LZ Bird. Though U.S. casualties totaled 58, the NVA lost 266.

MEDAL OF HONOR

CONGRESSIONAL MEDAL OF HONOR SOCIETY

**STAFF SGT.
DELBERT JENNINGS**

joined by battery commander Capt. Leonard Shlenker, Jr., 1st Lt. Michael Livengood, 1st Lt. John Reike, Staff Sgt. Carroll Crain and radio operator Spec. 4 Clint Houston.

"Some of the NVA jumped over the trench going to another gun position," Houston recalled. "Lt. Livengood fired his M-79 grenade launcher as they jumped over. I fired at one NVA coming up the trench yelling at me. I know two of my tracer rounds hit him."

COURAGE SAVES LIVES

As Shlenker's group was leapfrogging toward No. 1 gun pit, Jennings and Johnson's men fought for their lives. Jennings killed about a dozen NVA, then another three who were attempting to destroy one of the 155mm howitzers.

Jennings' Medal of Honor citation reads: "Observing that some of the defenders were unaware of an enemy force to their rear, he raced through a fire-swept area to warn the men, turn their fire on the enemy, and lead them into the secondary perimeter.

"He personally led a group of volunteers well beyond friendly lines to an area where eight seriously wounded men lay. Braving enemy sniper fire and ignoring the presence of booby traps in the area, they recovered the eight men."

Meanwhile, at the gunpit, desperate measures were necessary.

"I would look to the rear, then move up and rest my back on Livengood's boots," Houston said. "This ditch was only about 2½ to 3 feet deep. Then Lt. Reike got hit in the throat and the bullet traveled down to his stomach.

"We tried to stop the bleeding as best we could, but the NVA were swarming all around us. We gave him a .45 pistol and told him we would try to keep them off of him as we went for more help."

As Reike lay dying, Spec. 4 Charles Tournage arrived on the scene. The young medic had been all over the battlefield, helping wounded soldiers. He was completely naked. When the opening shots were fired, he had no time to get dressed.

After giving first aid to Reike, Tournage raced to find additional medical supplies. In his search, he narrowly escaped death. In the darkness, a charging NVA mistook him for a fellow soldier. "As the Viet swerved off on an oblique, Tournage had time to get off one M-79 round that, armed in just the right split-second, hit the target in the middle of the back and tore the North Vietnamese apart," military historian S.L.A. Marshall wrote in his book *Bird: The Christmas2tide Battle.*

Combat was intense, especially when confined to isolated pockets.

"We fired our M-60 machine gun for three to five minutes … using 800-900 rounds of ammo before we were overrun," McGinn explained. "We played dead. It was no use in trying to fight off any more of them. They kicked me and went through my pockets and took my billfold and watch. I lay there praying, waiting to be shot in the head."

Fortunately, communications had been restored and illumination rounds from LZ Pony bathed Bird in an eerie light, sparing McGinn's life.

Spec. 4 William Dunbar had flown in from LZ Pony just the night before. "It is not an easy task to describe what happened since people were running all over," he recalled, "the loud bursts of weapons, soldiers yelling to each other amidst what looked like a grand finale at a Fourth of July fireworks show."

> # "It was so haunting. It screeched like a million bees. I saw a big hole in their ranks, and then I heard screaming. Those bodies were ripped to shreds."

—SPEC. 4 CLINT HOUSTON, ABOUT THE FIRING OF FLECHETTES INTO THE RANKS OF ATTACKING NVA SOLDIERS

SILVER STAR

CAPT. LEONARD SHLENKER, JR.

SPEC. 4 CHARLES TOURNAGE

1ST LT. CHARLES CAMPANELLA

STAFF SGT. GREGERIO NIETO

SPEC. 4 DAVID OSBORNE

DISTINGUISHED SERVICE CROSS

1ST LT. JOHN PIPER

STAFF SGT. CARROLL CRAIN

'SCREECHING BEES'

Artillerymen were busy doing their jobs, too. Piper and Staff Sgt. Robert Underwood loaded a beehive round into one of the 105mm howitzers. Yelling a warning to get down, Piper yanked the lanyard. Instantly, 8,500 flechettes (tiny metal-shaped arrows) tore into the attacking NVA ranks.

"It was so haunting," Houston remembered. "It screeched like a million bees. I saw a big hole in their ranks, and then I heard screaming. Those bodies were ripped to shreds. Then they fired again with the same results. The assault was stopped dead in its tracks."

With the enemy momentum halted, the troopers began taking back overrun gun pits. A formation of UH-1 helicopters fitted with aerial rocket artillery, and several armed CH-47 Chinook helicopters, hammered NVA positions at Bird.

"The sun came up, and the carnage was everywhere," Houston said. "We loaded our dead and wounded on the arriving choppers. The NVA dead were lined up. Blood was running in the ruts all along the LZ. I remember it was so cold and wet. And I will never forget the smell."

The battle had lasted only an hour. Of the 199 men on LZ Bird that night, 28 were KIA and 67 WIA—a 48% casualty rate. While half the KIAs were infantrymen, nearly 40% were artillerymen. The two artillery batteries lost 11 men; the 12th Cav's C Company counted 14 dead. A few other occupational specialties were in the mix, including two men from the 11th Aviation Group.

Gunfire accounted for about 60% of those killed and multiple fragmentation wounds claimed the remainder. By late 1966, draftees were starting to dominate combat arms units, so they made up 64% of the deaths.

Acts of valor were recognized. Piper and Crain earned the Distinguished Service Cross. The Silver Star went to Shlenker, Campanella, Staff Sgt. Gregerio Nieto, Tournage and Spec. 4 David Osborne. Five of those killed also received Silver Stars.

Besides individual awards, all the units involved were eventually presented the Presidential Unit Citation. Along with the batteries and infantry company mentioned, detachments of the 11th Pathfinders Company and 229th Aviation Battalion, as well as 1st Plt., D Trp., 1st Sqdn., 9th Cav, were included.

S.L.A. Marshall summed up the enemy failure in his book this way: "The NVA failed to deny the defenders the use of the main trench, and in the bunker-to-bunker fighting they were being out-gamed by the few men who stood in their way. The deeper the enemy advanced, the more he was becoming diffused."

Capt. Nguyen Song Phuc, of the 22nd NVA Regiment, agreed: "It was a disastrous defeat for our side." ✪

THE TOLL

U.S. KIA:
28

U.S. WIA:
67

BRUTAL BATTLES OF VIETNAM
1967

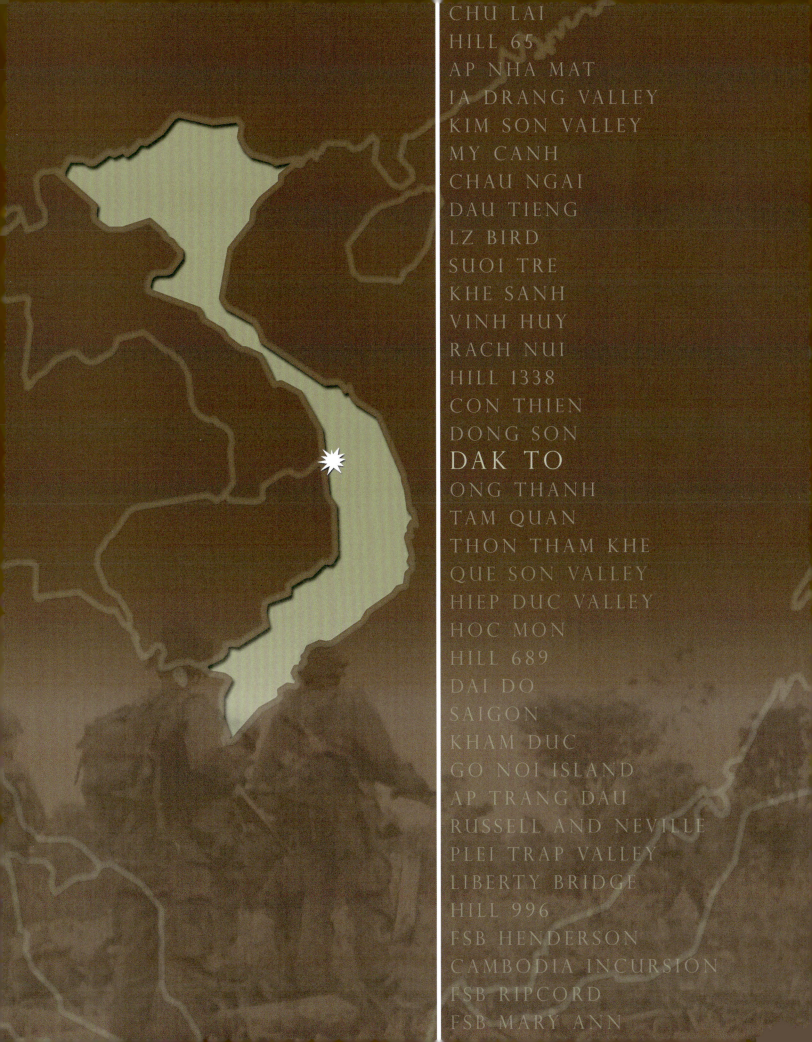

CHU LAI
HILL 65
AP NHA MAT
IA DRANG VALLEY
KIM SON VALLEY
MY CANH
CHAU NGAI
DAU TIENG
LZ BIRD
SUOI TRE
KHE SANH
VINH HUY
RACH NUI
HILL 1338
CON THIEN
DONG SON
DAK TO
ONG THANH
TAM QUAN
THON THAM KHE
QUE SON VALLEY
HIEP DUC VALLEY
HOC MON
HILL 689
DAI DO
SAIGON
KHAM DUC
GO NOI ISLAND
AP TRANG DAU
RUSSELL AND NEVILLE
PLEI TRAP VALLEY
LIBERTY BRIDGE
HILL 996
FSB HENDERSON
CAMBODIA INCURSION
FSB RIPCORD
FSB MARY ANN

BY RICHARD K. KOLB

'FIRST TEAM' TRIES A TRAP AT TRUONG SON

Like so many contacts with the enemy in Vietnam, this battle started with an ambush that produced even more ambushes. And American infantrymen extricated themselves from a bad situation with pure grit and determination.

GIs were on a large-scale clearing and pacification offensive called *Operation Pershing* on the Bong Son coastal plain in Binh Dinh province of II Corps. The 1st Cavalry Division was specifically attempting to trap and destroy the 22nd North Vietnamese Army (NVA) Regiment.

Part of the 3rd NVA Division, the 22nd—supported by a Viet Cong (VC) heavy weapons company—had eluded the Americans far too long. So when the opportunity arose to engage and eliminate it, the "First Team" jumped at the chance. That happened when elements of the division's 1st Brigade made contact with a part of the Communist regiment on March 19, 1967. Fighting began in earnest on the 20th.

Eventually, seven rifle companies from three battalions took casualties in the attempt to seal the enemy inside the hamlet of Truong Son, located about 2½ miles west of Tam Quan. But it was a scattered fight taking place at various locations, ranging from about two to four miles from the hamlet.

Units ultimately involved included the 2nd Bn., 12th Cav ("Chargin' Chargers!"); 1st Bn., 5th Cav ("Black Knights"); and 1st Bn., 8th Cav ("Jumping Mustangs"). Companies of these battalions soon found themselves ambushed and fighting for their own survival. But they were supported by the 2nd Bn., 20th Aerial Artillery and the 1st Bn., 77th Artillery.

SWEEPING AN ISLAND, CROSSING A CEMETERY

"The enemy was well positioned in camouflaged, concrete bunkers on a highly defensible island," according to a 12th Cav report. "He employed machine guns, individual automatic weapons, mortars and recoilless rifles and had snipers tied in the treetops." Alpha Company of the 2nd Battalion faced this firepower head on, counting six KIA before the day was done.

Surrounding rice paddies and incessant sniper fire prevented the 12th's 2nd

GIs of the 1st Cavalry Division wait at an isolated landing zone on the Bong Son Plain for a second wave of helicopters during *Operation Pershing* in 1967. Members of the "First Team" engaged the communists that March 20-21, 1967, sustaining 36 KIA.

Over two days in March 1967, several battalions of three 1st Cavalry Division regiments tangled with an elusive NVA regiment on the Bong Son Plain of central coastal Vietnam.

MARCH 1967

PHOTO BY PATRICK CHRISTIAN/GETTY IMAGES

MEDAL OF
HONOR

SPEC. 4 CHARLES C.
HAGEMEISTER

CONGRESSIONAL MEDAL OF HONOR SOCIETY

Battalion from moving, so reinforcements were called in. The 5th Cav's A Company (1st Battalion) was airlifted to the scene of the action around 6:30 p.m. It maneuvered into an adjacent area to block enemy escape routes, immediately coming under heavy fire from elements of the 7th Bn., 22nd NVA Regt.

Its 1st Platoon hit the ground and within five minutes only five members remained unwounded. GIs were moving through the local graveyard when they were ambushed from three sides by NVA and VC.

"They had dug-in concrete positions, trenches and heavy weapons—.51-caliber machine guns, 57mm recoilless rifles and 81mm mortars," Spec. 4 Charles C. Hagemeister remembered. "It was our 27-man platoon against at least 150 [enemy soldiers]." Combat was close range; NVA got within 10 yards of the defenders positions.

Men sought cover behind gravesites. James Bowen was with the Mortar Platoon. "I was there that night, and thankful that an above ground grave saved me," he recalled. "It was hell!"

Hagemeister took the bull by the horns. Referring to him years later, Spec. 4 Robert Fisher said, "I saw a man do one of the most incredibly brave things that day." As the company medic, Hagemeister had immense responsibilities—saving numerous lives by treating and evacuating casualties. But he truly went above and beyond those duties.

At one point, the medical aid man was compelled to pick up an M-16 and take out the enemy. Sighting in on the muzzle flash, he shot a sniper out of a tree. Then, as they ran toward his flank, the Nebraskan killed three NVA silhouetted against the burning village. Not yet finished—to protect the wounded only a few yard away—he silenced a Communist machine gun. After securing the help of another platoon, he went about rescuing the wounded despite the unceasing fire directed at him.

His "repeated heroic and selfless actions at the risk of his life saved the lives of many of his comrades and inspired their actions in repelling the enemy assault," reads Hagemeister's Medal of Honor citation.

'LIKE THE ROAR OF A RAILROAD TRAIN'

Wayne Seely, part of the three-man forward observer team from the 77th Arty, played a pivotal part in the battle. Fifty years later, he remembered the details vividly. "A Company walked into the V of an ambush that was set at a right angle," he said. "Each leg of the ambush was about 109 yards long and included numerous automatic weapons. There were two 81mm mortars and a 57mm recoilless rifle in the vortex.

"The ambush was not sprung until our lead platoon was eyeball to eyeball with the NVA. The lead platoon leader, Pete Larson, had been promoted to captain that day and chose not to go back to base camp so he could spend a final night with his platoon. He was KIA. What an irony.

"I was able to get artillery support from three batteries, which could not have been in a better position for fire support. The battery off to my left fired along the left flank of the ambush and the one to my right along the right flank. They were both 105mm batteries. With another battery (155mm) behind the vortex, I was able to move rounds closer and closer, trapping the enemy between our company and the artillery.

"The fight started near dusk and lasted until midnight. During that time, I directed the firing of over 1,300 rounds. Our casualties would have been much greater if it had not been for a rise in the terrain between us and then a gentle slope away from the enemy. Also, there were many grave sites that offered protection. In fact, we never got out of that field of graves.

"I can still hear the roar of the 57mm recoilless rifle rounds as they passed over our heads. It was like a railroad track and having a train pass over you. That night I will never forget!"

For the 5th Cav's A Company, the worst of the fighting was over as March 20 ended, after the wounded were secure. "When we got the word to pull back, which was 11:30 p.m. or

Spec. 4 Ray A. Rhodes, age 20, of Moulton, Ala., was among the six KIAs of C Co., 1st Bn., 5th Cav, on March 21, 1967.

12 that night—5½ to 6 hours into the firefight—we were at the point we could disengage and withdraw to the company perimeter," Hagemeister said. Three Alpha troopers had been KIA and 18 WIA. A Company was later recommended for the Presidential Unit Citation.

As March 21 dawned, elements of the 12th Cav then swept the island of NVA.

'JUMPING MUSTANGS' JOIN IN

Meanwhile, A and D companies of the 1st Bn., 8th Cav, also converging on Truong Son, became heavily engaged on the 20th, north of Landing Zone (LZ) Sand (battalion headquarters). Combined, the two companies sustained 13 KIA that day, with eight of the dead from Delta Company alone.

1st Sgt. John "Pappy" Loughran, a 44-year-old Korean War and WWII vet, was there. "Delta was a top-notch company," he recalled years later. "These young men, officers and enlisted, were outstanding. They were the cream of the crop.

"Foremost [among my memories] are those who gave the full measure. At least once a week, I mentally have a roll call of their names. I will never forget them. I often think of the young man who had the feeling that his luck had run out and wrote his 'last letter' on March 19, 1967. The next day he was among those who were KIA."

Although a major portion of the enemy force broke off the evening before, the NVA's 7th Battalion continued to fight on March 21. The 1st Battalion of the 5th Cav suffered seven more men killed, mostly all (six) from C Company, in that combat.

B Co., 1st Bn., 8th Cav, found itself in a major firefight, too, in which it lost seven KIA.

Spec. 5 James Hancock was the head medic with Bravo Company and the only aid man there: "That morning we were several yards out into an open rice paddy outside of LZ Sand when NVA opened up on us with small-arms fire and automatic weapons. Fighting our way back to a nearby village, we were pinned down there for the remainder of the day. Some of us spent the night in a bomb crater.

"Several times during the day I heard screams for medic and managed to get to the wounded and get them to a safer place. Some were medevaced out that afternoon. Next morning, we went back to the village to retrieve our remaining KIAs. As it turned out, well-concealed trenches and tunnels surrounded the entire village."

SLIPPING AWAY AGAIN

Over the two days of combat, 36 Americans were killed. The 8th Cav's 1st Battalion was hardest hit with 20 KIA, or 55% of the total. The 5th Cav counted 10 dead (28%) and A Company of the 12th Cav six. More than 60% (22) of the men lost their lives on March 20 with 14 killed the next day.

Gunfire accounted for the vast majority of KIAs—30, or 83%. Multiple fragmentation wounds, by comparison, claimed only six GIs. With an increasing number of draftees filling the ranks of the combat arms, casualty figures began to reflect that trend. Deaths now tilted toward draftees (19) versus volunteers (17).

As was so often the case in Vietnam, the outcome at Truong Son was inconclusive. Despite the 1st Cav's best efforts to trap the NVA's 22nd Regiment, it once again escaped. "By early April, it was evident that the 22nd had slipped north into the mountains of southern Quang Ngai with only its 8th Battalion remaining in Binh Dinh, shunning combat and well hidden in the An Lao Valley," recorded *Taking the Offensive*, the U.S. Army's official history. ◯

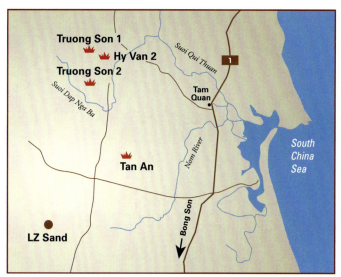

Fighting raged around the hamlet of Truong Son, 2½ miles west of Tam Quan. Units were scattered anywhere from two to four miles from the hamlet, engaging in separate yet tactically related firefights.

THE TOLL

U.S. KIA:
36

BY RICHARD K. KOLB

FIREBASE GOLD REPELS RED ONSLAUGHT

t was "worse than anything I've seen in World War II or Korea," declared Lt. Col. John A. Bender, commander of the 3rd Bn., 22nd Inf., in the aftermath of one of the Vietnam War's bloodiest single battles.

Interchangeably known as the Battle of Suoi Tre or Firebase Gold, this often overlooked engagement occurred during *Operation Junction City II,* a massive search and destroy sweep of War Zone C. Located in III Corps, fighting took place 20 miles northeast of Tay Ninh near the abandoned hamlet of Suoi Tre.

A firebase, dubbed Gold, was carved out of a dry rice paddy area north of the Suoi (Vietnamese for stream) Samat. Egg-shaped, it was 328 by 437 yards. Combat was concentrated in this limited space for more than four hellacious hours. Initially defending the artillery base was the 2nd Bn., 77th Arty (105mm, towed) protected by the 3rd Bn., 22nd Inf. (less C Company). The total force numbered 450 men.

To their aid came the mechanized 2nd Bn. ("Triple Deuce"), 22nd Inf.; 2nd Bn. (less B Company), 34th Armor; and the 2nd Bn., 12th Inf. All these units were part of the 3rd Brigade (called the orphan or bastard brigade), 4th Inf. Div., then under the operational control of the 25th Infantry Division.

Confronting them on March 21, 1967, were 2,500 hardened Communist troops of the 272nd Viet Cong (VC) Main Force Regiment reinforced by two unidentified battalions and supported by the U-80 Artillery Regiment. These six battalions constituted part of the 9th VC Division.

'HOLOCAUST OF FIRE AND SHRAPNEL'

The saga of Firebase Gold began two days earlier on March 19 when the mission to establish it near the Cambodian border got underway. That objective turned deadly almost immediately when the helicopters airlifting the troops touched down unknowingly into a mined landing zone.

The 68th and 118th Assault Helicopter companies (AHC) of the 145th Combat Aviation Battalion had the honors that day. When 118th helicopters came in on the second flights they were hit by command-detonated artillery shells. "My ship was hit by the concussion from exploding mines and choppers," remembered Spec. 4 Harold R. Childress, a door gunner with the 118th. After "the landing zone erupted in a holocaust of fire and flying shrapnel," according to his Bronze Star citation, he and others "remained in the minefield administering first aid to wounded soldiers."

On March 21, 1967, the 3rd Brigade, 4th Infantry Division, achieved a decisive victory in the four-hour Battle of Suoi Tre, earning a Presidential Unit Citation.

MARCH 1967

Fought on March 21, 1967, the Battle of Suoi Tre witnessed human wave attacks by the 272nd VC Regiment. The base claimed 47 American lives, but its defense inflicted 647 killed on the communists, reportedly the single largest enemy toll of the war.

Painting by James Davis Nelson. The artwork, owned by the New York Veterans Affairs Museum in Albany, N.Y., measures 6 feet by 12 feet.

Despite their best efforts, the casualty toll was high. Among the helicopter crews, four perished in crashes (three from the 68th and one in the 118th). Nine men of B Co., 3rd Bn., 22nd Inf., and a mortarman from HQ Company died—three in the crashes and seven from shrapnel on the ground. Fourteen deaths and the battle had yet to begin.

Only one day passed before all hell broke loose. Prematurely triggered by a security patrol beyond the perimeter, the VC attack started shortly after daylight with 500 to 700 rounds from 60mm and 82mm mortars slamming into the base. While the security patrol made it back to base, a four-man listening post from the 1st Platoon of Bravo Company was not so lucky.

Vastly outnumbered, these GIs surrendered. One of the four was wounded and was lying in the bottom of the foxhole. The other three got out, dropped their weapons and raised their arms. VC executed them with bullets to the backs of their heads. One of the dead Americans fell back into the foxhole, covering the wounded soldier. Asked what had happened, the survivor, Pfc. Edward Watson, said, "We apparently had fallen asleep."

Defensive ambush patrols from A Company (15 men) and B Company (12 men) also were hit hard, each taking almost 50% casualties.

Misfortune persisted. At 7:45 a.m., the sole forward air control aircraft, a Cessna 0-1E Bird Dog from the 19th Tactical Air Support Squadron (TASS), was shot down by heavy machine gun fire, crashing into the trees beyond the firebase. Both the pilot and observer were killed.

'HUMAN WAVES, JUST LIKE IN KOREA'

"The actual attack took place about 6:30 a.m.," said Spec. 4 William Blakey, who was caught in the maelstrom. "The VC opened up with numerous automatic weapons and started to charge. They came out of the wood line and swept toward the 105s [artillery pieces]."

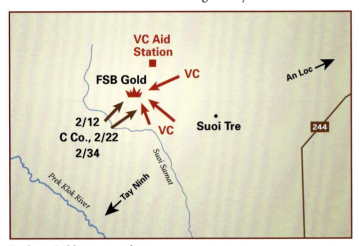

Firebase Gold was carved out of a dry rice paddy area near the abandoned hamlet of Suoi Tre, 20 miles northeast of Tay Ninh, in III Corps not far from Cambodia.

Sgt. Milburn Van Meter remembered, "They were so intent on getting at the guns that a whole pack of them ran right past me. We just turned and picked them off as fast as we could shoot."

The 77th's artillery pieces were indeed the primary target. "They started to push back more and more positions and it looked as though they were going to put the guns out of action," Battery B Capt. John Cartland said. "We leveled our tubes to shoot at point-blank range. My men never left the guns, even when the VC were just feet away."

Sgt. Bill Riggs and his company were caught outside the perimeter because of a sweep the day before. "Our whole company was pinned down," he recalled. "We just dropped to the ground. We were in the open and couldn't move. There was no place to hide. We could hear bugles blowing in the background from the Vietnamese human wave attacks, just like in Korea. Just a mass of people charging.

"We could see the gunners on their artillery pieces holding their M-14s like baseball bats, just swinging at the enemy."

As Gen. William Westmoreland, commander of U.S. forces, later said, "It's rare that an artilleryman has to fight like an infantryman, but you men [of the 2nd Bn., 77th Artillery] did an excellent job."

Shortly before 8 a.m., the perimeter was breached. Quickly, an interim perimeter was set up and the situation became dire. The 77th quick reaction force, made up of cannoneers (those not firing), cooks and clerks and drilled in infantry tactics, joined the fray. And none too soon. Some 26 dead VC were found within 55 yards of the Fire Direction Center.

> ## "As the VC were charging, you would shoot one and see him fall. A little while later, you'd be shooting the same guy, who was all wrapped up [in bandages] ... shot up with opium."
> —KEN GOSLINE

"They [artillerymen] were standing in the open without cover, continuing to load and fire the 105mm howitzers with beehive rounds and HE [high-explosive]. Many fell from wounds," said James D. Holder, a squad leader in A Co., 3rd Bn., 22nd Inf. "They stayed on duty continuing to fire their weapons until they were silenced or ran out of ammo. I came away that day with a newfound pride in the artillery folks."

Fighting was desperate on all sectors of the perimeter. "It's hard to describe that day," recalled grunt Ken Gosline. "It was almost like an out-of-body experience. As the VC were charging, you would shoot one and see him fall. A little while later, you'd be shooting the same guy, who was all wrapped up [in bandages] ... shot up with opium. It was unbelievable."

HEROISM IN ABUNDANCE

Sgt. Jerald W. Wilhelm, a team leader in the 3rd Battalion's Bravo Company, while defending his position alone took out 10 VC with a Claymore mine. He later manned a machine gun with deadly effect. Wilhelm was awarded one of six Distinguished Service Crosses (DSC) earned on Firebase Gold.

Spec. 4 Richard L. Hazel, with the battalion's A Company, fought outside as well as inside the perimeter. Holding his ground, he placed steady M-79 grenade launcher fire on the human waves of attackers, and silenced a recoilless rifle position. Yet he still found time to aid the wounded. Hazel also led an assault to reclaim overrun positions, helping to hold them for four hours until reinforcements arrived, according to his DSC citation.

Four of the DSCs went to "red legs" (artillerymen). Besides directing the artillery defense of the firebase, Lt. Col. John W. Vessey, commander of the 2nd Battalion, assisted as a cannoneer and personally knocked out three VC rocket launchers with an M-79. The future chairman of the Joint Chiefs of Staff would later remark that 105mm rounds were landing "about 75 meters [82 yards] to our front and we couldn't lower the tubes anymore."

Battery B artillerymen alone received three DSCs. Its chief, Sgt. 1st Class Raymond D. Childress, almost single-handedly maintained a steady fire of anti-personnel rounds from his howitzer. He fired 200, some sighted through the tube, inflicting devastating enemy casualties. Although seriously wounded when his howitzer was destroyed by a direct hit, Childress nonetheless continued to move ammo and was hit even more severely. Unable to walk, he still led from a ditch until the fighting ended.

Pfc. Earl C. Haupt III was wounded in the neck and left eye yet continued to help firing his howitzer. He then took out a recoilless rifle with a grenade launcher. Not content, Haupt made repeated trips to the ammo storage area. Hit in the thigh while returning to the perimeter for the fourth time, he assisted short-handed gun crews.

As part of the 2nd Battalion's reaction force, Spec. 4 Samuel W. Townsend reinforced the infantry on the perimeter. He rescued a wounded man accidentally left behind. Later, he destroyed a recoilless rifle/machine gun emplacement with a hand grenade. Townsend eliminated another machine gun before being wounded by shrapnel.

BEEHIVE ROUNDS CUT VC TO PIECES

What sticks in many men's minds was the devastating impact of the firebase artillery. The 77th's 2nd Battalion fired 2,240 rounds of 105 mm, including high-explosive and 40 "beehive" canisters. Each contained more than 8,000 tiny *flechettes* (metal darts) released at the muzzle of the piece. Some likened the howitzer used in this fashion to a "105mm shotgun."

Commenting on the lethal effect of the beehive rounds, Spec. 4 James Morales said,

"They'd [VC] fall down or be chopped to pieces. But more kept on coming. You're so busy you don't know what you're doing. But I prayed, and God was here with us. He came and helped us."

An anonymous GI told a reporter: "The guns shot out a shower of shrapnel with each blast and just cleared a path right through the Viet Cong. The VC got within 25 yards of the guns, but the men stayed right there. Eventually, they had to use small arms. When a mechanized battalion of reinforcements rallied in with armored personnel carriers the guys started jumping up and down."

No doubt, artillery kept the men alive, at least for the time being. In some sectors of the perimeter, GIs had exhausted 90% of their ammo. Some resorted to using captured AK-47s and Chinese Communist carbines.

"It was a tough situation there and we more or less ran out of ammo and everything," recalled Bob Choquette nearly 50 years later. Three members of his gun crew were KIA. "Five more minutes, and we wouldn't have been here [today]. None of us."

A Communist noose tightened around the troops. "Charlie pushed us back into a tight perimeter," said Capt. Jerry Jeffrey, commander of Battery C. "He was fighting for his life and he was fighting damned well, too. Then came the most beautiful sight in the world—APCs and tanks."

Tanker Gary Lapp, C Co., 2nd Bn., 34th Armor, stands on his tank Charlie 3-2, prior to the battle.

'CAVALRY' TO THE RESCUE

When mechanized units arrived, it was reminiscent of a scene from a classic Western movie.

Master Sgt. Andrew Hunter said, "They haven't made the word to describe what we thought when we saw those tanks and armored personnel carriers. It was divine." Capt. George Shoemaker, CO of A Co., 3rd Bn., 22nd Inf., put it most succinctly: "The first thing I saw was two M-48 tanks and I wanted to kiss them."

The relief force got there at 9 a.m. "A Co., 2nd Bn., 12th Inf., was the first to arrive at the battle site, 10 minutes before the 22nd Mech battalion," Bill Comeau points out with pride. "Had we not arrived when we did, the defenders may very well have run out of ammunition and the results might have been very different." Comeau's unit was hit hard by mortars during the approach.

The 22nd's mechanized 2nd Battalion smashed through the VC, effectively breaking the attack. Dwight L. Brenneman was a forward artillery observer with the 3rd Platoon of A Company. "When we broke out of the jungle, it was like a shooting gallery," he said. "The VC were caught in the open between us with nowhere to retreat."

As the VC fled, the 34th Armor swept through the firebase area, killing numerous VC. The Air Force also provided close air support. The 19th Tactical Air Support Squadron flew 14 immediate missions totaling 31 sorties.

SILVER
STAR

Master Sgt. Andrew Hunter earned a Silver Star for his bravery during the battle.

DISTINGUISHED SERVICE
CROSS

RIGHT: In a ceremony following the battle, Gen. William C. Westmoreland, center, awarded Distinguished Service Crosses to men of the 2nd Bn., 77th Arty—Lt. Col. John W. Vessey, Jr., Pfc. Earl C. Haupt III and Spec. 4 Samuel Townsend—as well as Spec. 5 Richard Hazel (second from right).

NOT PICTURED: Also receiving DSCs for Suoi Tre were Sgt. Jerald W. Wilhelm and Sgt. 1st Class Raymond D. Childress.

Lt. Col. John W. Vessey, Jr., commander of the 2nd Bn., 77th Artillery, on Firebase Gold on March 21, 1967, was the best-known of the six soldiers awarded the Distinguished Service Cross for heroism there (upgraded from a Silver Star). Vessey, a tireless champion of MIA accounting, went on to become chairman (1982-85) of the Joint Chiefs of Staff. He died in August 2016.

Then-Lt. Roger W. Frydrychowski, leader of the Recon Platoon of the 2nd Bn., 22nd Inf., provided a graphic description of events: "In a single column, Recon, Charlie Company and 34th Armor entered the edge of the 3rd Battalion's perimeter. The defensive position was smoldering. It gave the appearance of having been flattened. Some VC tried to climb onto our tanks as we moved between the firebase and the main VC attack. Pistols and M-16s kept them off the tanks.

"When the battle ended, there were VC bodies every few feet. The total official body count was 647. I am told that this was the single largest enemy body count of the war. Bulldozers were lifted in and the bodies dumped into huge mass graves."

Sgt. Riggs had the unenviable task of later helping tally that body count. "We had a tank with a bulldozer blade that dug a trench, and we were chucking the bodies into the trench. With the heat and humidity, it didn't take long for the stench to really get to you. There's no way to describe it, just the smell of rotting flesh."

By 9:30 that morning, the original perimeter had been restored. And by 10:45 a.m. the battle area was secured.

Full-fledged tragedy had been narrowly averted. "Years later, I learned that the VC officer in charge of the attacking force at Gold had orders to kill everyone there, then set up an ambush for the troops coming to assist," related John Mersinger, an infantryman with C Co., 2nd Bn. (Mech), 22nd Inf. "No wonder there was an amazing number of rocket-propelled grenades found in the jungle—they were intended for us."

The men who stood so steadfastly at Firebase Gold were recognized with the highest unit award. "Through their fortitude and determination, the personnel of the 3rd Brigade, 4th Infantry Division, and attached units, were able in great measure to cripple a large Viet Cong force," reads the Presidential Unit Citation (PUC). It adds, "Striking the Viet Cong on the flank, the 2nd Battalion, 22nd Infantry, smashed through the enemy with such intensity and ferocity that the enemy attack faltered and broke."

A LETHAL TOLL

But that PUC came at a steep price. Gold claimed the lives of 52 Americans. During the March 19 landing zone insertion, 14 GIs were killed: 10 from B Company, three in the 68th

PHOTO COURTESY GARY LAPP

PHOTO COURTESY CAPT. ED SMITH, A CO., 2ND BN., 12TH INF.
BILL COMEAU/ WWW.ALPHAASSOCIATION.ORG

ABOVE: An M-88 tank recovery vehicle of A Co., 34th Armor, uses its bulldozer blade to dig a mass grave for some of the 647 Viet Cong soldiers killed in the battle.

LEFT: Men of A Co., 2nd Bn., 12th Inf., take a break next to one of two quad-50s (four .50-caliber machine guns mounted as one unit) used to defend FSB Gold. The other quad was destroyed by a point-blank artillery round when the VC attempted to turn it on the Americans.

AHC and one in the 118th AHC. Seven of these men died in the actual helicopter shoot-downs; the remaining seven in booby-trapped artillery shell explosions and from shrapnel.

And early in the assault on the firebase, the two forward air controllers from the 19th TASS were killed.

Of the base defenders, 22 men of the 3rd Bn., 22nd Inf., were KIA; 10 from the 77th Artillery; one GI from the 11th Artillery; and one with the 71st Artillery. The relief force sustained two KIAs: one each in the 12th Infantry and 22nd's mechanized 2nd Battalion. All told, 187 men were wounded—92 of whom required evacuation.

Counting both March 19 and 21, 63% of the KIAs (33) were suffered by the 22nd Infantry—B Company alone accounted for 20 of them. Gunfire (28), shrapnel (14), air losses (9) and "friendly fire" (1) caused the total number of American deaths.

The shift in manpower sources for the Army ground combat arms was clearly evident in the casualty count. Some 90% of the men killed with a ground specialty were draftees. As the 3rd Battalion's Lt. Col. Bender put it, "This was the first big fight these men have engaged in and they were magnificent … There may be something wrong with the draft back in the States, but there's nothing wrong with the draft over here."

Four decades after the battle, Roger Frydrychowski, the Recon officer, paid all the GIs at Gold the greatest tribute. "The men in our whole battalion were individually and collectively outstanding. On that day [March 21, 1967], as on each day of my time in Vietnam, I was most privileged to command and serve with the finest men I will ever know." ✪

THE
TOLL

U.S. KIA:
52

U.S. WIA:
187

BY RICHARD K. KOLB

'SLAUGHTER HOUSE' AT BINH SON

For three companies of the 2nd and 3rd battalions of the 1st Marines, April 21, 1967, was a day of unforgettable carnage in the Que Son Valley.

The Que Son Valley would prove to be one of the deadliest places in Vietnam. Strategically located in that valley was a hill mass called Nui Loc Son (Hill 185). The hilltop was ideal for observing enemy infiltration in the valley below so it rated the stationing of a special unit.

F Co., 2nd Bn., 1st Marines, 1st Marine Div., was double the size of a typical Marine rifle company. With attached units it numbered 300 men. To aggressively pursue the communists, Foxtrot Company dispatched 120 men in the dark hours of April 21, 1967, 2.5 miles northeast of the hill's summit.

This was the opening day of *Operation Union I.* It was a search and destroy mission designed to eliminate the last Viet Cong stronghold between Da Nang and Chu Lai. More specifically, the Que Son Valley.

F Company's destination was a collection of hamlets called Binh Son, 29 miles southwest of Da Nang. Islands of huts were situated on acres of rice paddies in the steep-sided valley. The killing zone was a dry, 44-yard-wide paddy pitted with well-entrenched bunkers and fighting holes. They and other terrain features concealed a battalion of the North Vietnamese Army's (NVA) 31st Regiment, 2nd NVA Division.

After moving off Nui Loc Son, F Company made first contact at 7 a.m. More than two hours later, the unit was hit hard, forcing it to pull back to the tree line. Despite being under heavy fire, the 2nd and 3rd

platoons, covered by 1st Platoon, were ordered to assault Binh Son (1) at 11:15 a.m. It all hit the fan as the Marines actually entered the village; a well-laid NVA ambush stopped them cold in their tracks.

COURAGE AMIDST CHAOS

The ambush was highly efficient, immediately killing 14 and wounding 18 Marines.

"With every round they fired, one of our men would drop," said Pfc. Richard L. Bratton. "We'd take more casualties trying to get a man out. Half the time we didn't know what the hell was happening." At one point, Bratton ended up at a gate to the hamlet. "Three of them [NVA] came around a hut and threw three grenades at me," he said. "They didn't go off. I fired everything I had. Missed."

Ron Stih was with 2nd Platoon. "The order came to assault the village under fire," he said. "Outnumbered many times over, an assault now—to run across an open rice paddy directly at the NVA—seemed like suicide. The captain made the call for us to move out, so we did.

"Rounds were hitting all around me, dirt and water flying all over me. When Lance Cpl. Uvaldo Sanchez was shot in the head, he fell on top of me, blood all over him and me. Every time I moved, NVA would fire on my position. I was afraid to move, knowing any second that the gooks were going to come out of the village and finish us off.

Members of 2nd Bn., 1st Marines, walk through high grass as they approach the village of Binh Son (1) on April 21, 1967. A well-entrenched enemy battalion laid in wait, cutting down Foxtrot Company as it crossed a dry rice paddy.

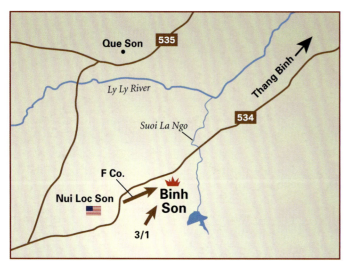

Binh Son (1) was located about three miles southeast of Que Son.

"I prayed a lot, promised to be a better person, everything you could imagine. I laid there for about six hours until it started to get dark. Then I crawled back across the paddy until I was inside the tree line.

"In the morning, we brought in our own dead. Nothing smells like a body that has been in the hot sun all day. I handled a lot of bodies, ours and theirs. But this was so much different. One of ours had a death grip in the ground. I had to pull really hard so we could get his hand loose. It's been 50 years now and not a day goes by that I don't relive that day."

Machine gunner Dieter Maass recalled, "As we approached the village, we started hearing them beating metal on metal and ringing bells. They obviously knew we were coming. When the assault came, I was on the right side. When we got about 50 yards out, the mortars started coming. Some of us ended up behind a dike 30 yards from the tree line. (Maass and others remained pinned down there throughout the afternoon.)

"At about 5:30 p.m., I tried to crawl back to where the attack started. I got less than 10 yards before being shot through the leg just below the knee. Then mortars started falling

"A few minutes after the first airstrikes were over the NVA came on. When 3rd Platoon took off across the rice paddy again, Marines were dropping like flies. 3rd Platoon was being wiped out right in front of us."

—BILL COOPER, 1ST PLT., F CO., 2ND BN.

PHOTO COURTESY BILL COOPER

Bill Cooper and John Holtman, both machine gunners in 1st Plt., F Co., 2nd Bn., 1st Marines, survived the carnage at Binh Son.

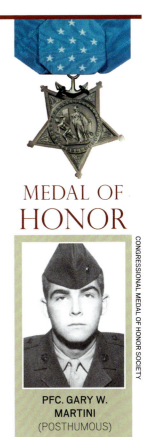

MEDAL OF
HONOR

PFC. GARY W.
MARTINI
(POSTHUMOUS)

CONGRESSIONAL MEDAL OF HONOR SOCIETY

SILVER
STAR

CAPT. GENE DEEGAN

CPL. FLOYD E.
MILLER

SGT. BERNARD E.
TERHORST

MILITARY TIMES HALL OF VALOR

again. I laid in the grass. NVA walked right by me.

"As it got darker, I started crawling again, passing out several times. Doc [Navy corpsman] John Scott and I crawled back together but guys had to come out and get me. About 1 a.m. on April 22, I was evacuated by helicopter. If I had not been, I would have bled to death by morning."

2nd Platoon Navy corpsman John Scott said, "When the mortar hit, I was sure I was dead. For myself and other survivors, the following day was a chopper ride to the Navy hospital in Da Nang (I ended up in the same ward as Dieter Maass) or a flight to the hospital ship just offshore. Only one chopper could make it in to medevac casualties that night, although several tried."

Each Marine seemed to experience his own private hell. Bill Cooper was a machine gunner with 1st Platoon and suffered loss but also heard of enemy compassion. "A few minutes after the first airstrikes were over the NVA came on. When 3rd Platoon took off across the rice paddy again, Marines were dropping like flies. 3rd Platoon was being wiped out right in front of us.

"Then 1st Platoon was ambushed. Explosions started going off all around us. We were taking lots of casualties. Doc Allen Firmneck took two rounds to the face. A 60mm mortar explosion killed Ralph Scheib. He was due to go on R&R [rest and recuperation] to Hawaii the next day to meet his wife and newborn baby that he had never seen and never would.

"We were told that the dead and wounded in the rice paddy were all stripped of their gear. But not one of our wounded had been finished off. In fact, one Marine with a sucking chest wound had been reportedly bandaged by an NVA soldier."

Bill Kelly was a field radio operator assigned to a forward air control team directly supporting F Company. "The enemy force was larger than we were led to believe," he remembered. "I was wounded that morning within the first half hour of calling in airstrikes.

A forward observer and his radio operator of 3rd Bn., 1st Marines, scramble from a CH-46 Sea Knight helicopter in a hot landing zone near Binh Son. They were part of the relief effort to rescue Foxtrot Company.

Sgt. Keith Lamb (holding map), artillery liaison to the 3rd Battalion, was part of the Bald Eagle reaction force.

I spent the rest of the day trying to provide air support and bring in a couple of choppers to get out the more seriously wounded, one of whom was the captain. Later in the afternoon while calling in support, I was wounded a second time by a mortar round. It was the longest 48 hours of my life."

Amidst the chaos of the combat, courage emerged in F Company. Pfc. Gary W. Martini was wounded while rescuing a Marine. Yet he went back for another one only 22 yards in front of the NVA trench line. "Through a final supreme effort, he moved his injured comrade to where he could be pulled to safety, before he fell, succumbing to his wounds," reads his Medal of Honor citation.

Cpl. Floyd E. Miller, a machine gun team leader, also saved lives. Under heavy fire, he retrieved medical supplies and equipment and administered first aid to the wounded. Miller carried two Marines to safety and aided another dangerously exposed Marine.

Sgt. Bernard E. Terhorst, as platoon sergeant, assumed command, reorganizing his unit. He repeatedly exposed himself to intense fire, leading survivors to a tree line and repelling an enemy assault.

Company commander Gene A. Deegan took a bullet to the chest but walked and crawled

55 yards to reestablish his command post. From there, he directed Foxtrot for several hours, refusing evacuation until fighting mostly stopped.

All three Marines were awarded the Silver Star.

'BALD EAGLE' TO THE RESCUE

After F Company was pinned down, a call went out for an emergency reaction force (called "Bald Eagle") from the 3rd Battalion. Cpl. John M. Papcun, a radio operator for the artillery forward observer, took that call at battalion headquarters and went in to the battlefield with Command Group Alpha.

"When we landed, we ran out the rear hatch of the chopper, keeping our heads down and getting low in the elephant grass until the helicopter left," he recalls vividly. "Bullets were flying everywhere and we needed to get to a tree line for cover. We quickly set up a command post (CP)."

A fourth mortar round scored a direct hit on that CP, momentarily knocking out Papcun. Shrapnel sheared off his radio's antenna. "I don't recall much after that," he said. "But we dug in and I laid there all night. I will never forget the sounds of the choppers taking out the dead and wounded Marines."

Sgt. Keith Lamb was the artillery liaison to the 3rd Battalion. His job was made all the more difficult by the utter chaos. "I couldn't call in artillery fire with the helicopters in the way, and they couldn't land with all the firing going on. The place smelled like a slaughter house. Flies covered the wounded, and the ground everywhere was soaked with blood."

Mike Company (about 135 men) of the 3rd Battalion was the "Bald Eagle" unit that day—an outfit held in ready reserve for just such occasions as Foxtrot's predicament. Often overlooked, however, is the role played by an element of India Company.

"India's 1st Platoon hit the hot LZ with the 3rd Battalion Command Group while the rest of I and M companies were diverted to another LZ," said Richard C. Anderson, then the platoon's lieutenant. "Seven India Company Marines and one attached Navy corpsman died in the Battle of Binh Son, all from my platoon. They deserve to be remembered."

M Company was inserted onto the battlefield about 1 p.m. Capt. William M. Wood led the company, and does not pull any punches. "The NVA suckered us out and then hit us hard," he recalls. "The enemy allowed us to land, then we were pinned down by automatic weapons and mortars. But at least we were in the tree line unlike F Company in the rice paddy. We had no artillery support; only the airstrikes saved us. Six to eight hours later and far into the night, the NVA left because they knew we would eventually outman them."

Mike Company had covered only 50 yards in three hours. One of its platoons tried to get into Binh Son but halfway across the paddy the NVA cut it up. "At any open space wider than six feet you had to be moving fast or you would be hit," said Pfc. Mike Denton.

Pfc. Dave Gustafson, a machine gunner in 1st Platoon, said, "We never did advance any further than the tree line bordering the paddy. The day turned into a standoff. Sometime after dark, the enemy sent a final mortar barrage and melted away into the mountains."

Despite the outcome, Gustafson continues, "Acts of selfless courage were commonplace.

Men of Mike Co., 3rd Bn., 1st Marines, slip through a tree line in attempts to rescue F Company's wounded.

> "Dead Marines and NVA still littered the ground, lying in grotesque, macabre positions. Stiff cold hands could be seen raised toward the sky in supplication, asking to be taken to a place of peace." —PFC. DAVE GUSTAFSON, 1ST PLT., M CO.

Many Marines crawled out into the rice paddy under intense fire to rescue the dead and wounded. Some of the stricken Marines had been out there for hours, victims of the initial ambush earlier in the day. More than one Marine was killed or wounded trying to rescue these men [of Foxtrot]. They were men unknown to us in Mike Company, but were fellow Marines who needed help."

One such example was that of Pfc. Floyd H. Perry, Jr., a rifleman. On four separate occasions, he assisted in carrying wounded to safety from an exposed rice paddy. Although he was awarded the Bronze Star, many others went unrecognized for their selfless acts.

PERMEATED BY THE SMELL OF DEATH

The aftermath of battle, as it does in all wars, often leaves the most indelible impression on the men who bear witness. Gustafson eloquently and graphically captures these raw emotions: "The smell of death, cordite, burning houses, feces, putrid fish, jungle rot and fear intermingled, forming an entity as palpable as the enemy himself."

Continuing, he remembered, "Morning dawned bright and sunny. Dead Marines and NVA still littered the ground, lying in grotesque, macabre positions. Stiff cold hands could be seen raised toward the sky in supplication, asking to be taken to a place of peace. The sickeningly sweet smell of death permeated the air. Marines hauled the stiff bodies from where they had fallen and piled them at the command post for evacuation."

Bill Cooper has similar memories. "We got to the command post and saw row after row of dead Marines on ponchos. All of Foxtrot Company dead were there plus more from the 3rd Battalion rescue companies. When a helicopter landed, we carried each Marine aboard, laying the bodies side by side all the way back to the ramp. We were ordered to walk over the top of the bodies so we could start the next row forward. This was repeated. It was the edge of insanity."

Pfc. Joe Wadlow, a rifleman in 2nd Platoon, brought it down to an even more private level. Speaking poignantly of the loss of a personal friend, he lends credence to the axiom that in close-knit units like the infantry it does not pay to become too closely attached. Yet knowing full well that this is virtually impossible.

"I crawled back to the old hooch at the rear of our position and was advised that Fred West was stacked up in a poncho with about 15 other Marines who had been killed," Wadlow recorded. "I think I went into shock as I sat at the entrance of that hooch looking at the stack of dead bodies wrapped in ponchos. I might have even cried.

"My fire team leader, Greg Fassbinder, gave me a bit of advice that turned out to be something I would remember forever. 'Better him than you,' he said. 'You better get used to it

Four of the nine Marines in this photo of 2nd Sqd., 2nd Plt., F Co., 2nd Bn., 1st Marines, were KIA at Binh Son. Those in the picture are: front, Pfc. Christopher Podmaniczky (KIA); middle row, Lance Cpl. Ken Dixon, Pfc. Daisy Clover, Lance Cpl. Jack Waldon and Lance Cpl. Dick Simpson; back row, Lance Cpl. Uvaldo Sanchez (KIA), Pfc. Miller, Pfc. Louis Cerrano (KIA) and Pfc. Edward Egan (KIA); left rear, Sgt. Scarpinato, (WIA).

if you want to survive this place.' It worked for me, but I will never forget Fred West."

After the brunt of the fighting was over, the 1st Battalion of the 1st Marines on the right flank with the 3rd Battalion of the 5th Marines in reserve conducted a sweep of the area. During the battle, B Btry., 1st Bn., 11th Marines, as well as a platoon from the Army's 3rd Bn., 18th FA (175mm), provided support.

Foxtrot had finally returned to Hill 185 about 1 a.m. on April 22. The NVA broke contact with the other units at 4:30 a.m. As veterans of the battle indicated, this deadly engagement was essentially a draw. Elements of the 31st NVA Regiment simply withdrew when the additional Marine battalions started to close in on them.

Marines paid a severe price for coming down off Nui Loc Son in the darkness of April 21. F Co., 2nd Bn., 1st Marines, sustained 69% of the total 48 KIA (including two on April 22). Of its 33 dead, 20 belonged to 2nd Platoon alone. That is out of a company of 120 men who tackled Binh Son. H&S, India and Mike companies of the 3rd Battalion counted 15 KIA, or the remaining 31%. Gunfire claimed the overwhelming majority of the fatal casualties—41 or 85%. At least 145 Marines and corpsmen were wounded.

No matter the final tactical results, the sacrifices made are what count most. As John Scott put it, "The story needs to be told about the battle for the participants' sakes—so many are names on the black granite wall [Vietnam Veterans Memorial]." ✪

THE TOLL

U.S. KIA:
48

U.S. WIA:
145

BY AL HEMINGWAY

STRUGGLE FOR THE HILLS: FIRST BATTLE OF KHE SANH

Khe Sanh, tucked away in the northwest section of South Vietnam, overlooked a major infiltration route during the war. In 1966, the Marines constructed a combat base in its vicinity to patrol Hills 861, 881S and 881N. With no initial hostile contact, it seemed enemy activity had subsided. Early in 1967, however, Leathernecks would discover that the 325C North Vietnamese Army (NVA) Division had returned.

OPENING SHOTS ON 861

On April 24, a platoon from B Co., 1st Bn., 9th Marines, left Khe Sanh Combat Base (KSCB) and established an 81mm mortar position on Hill 700, just south of Hill 861. The mortars were to provide additional support to the remainder of the company searching for caves.

A five-man patrol climbed Hill 861 to establish an observation post. Nearing the top, the NVA ambushed the small party. Only one Marine survived. These were the opening shots of the first battle of Khe Sanh.

Mortars and 105mm howitzers from KSCB pounded NVA positions atop Hill 861. Capt. Michael W. Sayers ordered his remaining platoons to hit the enemy from the rear. As the riflemen moved forward, bullets tore into their right flank.

"My fire team proceeded up 861 when I heard a loud crack," Lance Cpl. Chris Harte said. "I saw the point man reach for his head and crumple to the ground."

Placing a mortar tube between his legs, Lance Cpl. Dana C. Darnell lobbed 60mm rounds at the NVA. On more than one occasion, he braved enemy fire to obtain more shells. He was killed two days later and was posthumously awarded a Navy Cross.

> "I saw the point man reach for his head and crumple to the ground."
> —LANCE CPL. CHRIS HARTE

RING OF STEEL

Casualties mounted as automatic weapons fire poured from cleverly concealed bunkers. As they tried to move forward, shrapnel from an 82mm mortar round wounded Harte and another Marine. "My arm and leg were burning," Harte said. "The Marine to my right had blood pumping out of his mouth."

The cannons of the 12th Marines (an artillery regiment) sent thousands of rounds crashing into the hills to support the infantry. "Artillery put a ring of steel around my

In late April and early May 1967, four battalions of the 3rd and 9th Marines, 3rd Marine Division, clashed with the North Vietnamese Army on Hills 861, 881S and 881N.

APRIL 1967

AP PHOTO

Marines of 2nd Bn., 3rd Marines, cover the advance of riflemen advancing toward the top of Hill 881, on May 2, 1967.

AP PHOTO

> # "The blast destroyed the radio and sent a 9-inch piece of shrapnel into my head and broke my arm in two places."
>
> —PFC. DON HOSSACK, M-3-3RD

NAVY CROSS

LANCE CPL. DANA C. DARNELL
(POSTHUMOUS)

PVT. 1ST CLASS JOHN R. MEUSE
(POSTHUMOUS)

LANCE CPL. FREDERICK G. MONAHAN

CPL. ROBERT J. SCHLEY
(POSTHUMOUS)

defensive position that was so tight we were taking dirt from the impact," Sayers recalled. "No doubt it saved our lives."

Harte remembered, "Night fell and word was passed we were moving out. It was damp and very dark. The moans and cries of the wounded only made it more eerie. A light rain started to fall. We had no water, so I licked the raindrops off my rifle. It gave me some relief."

K Co., 3rd Bn., 9th Marines, arrived later and had the unenviable task of retrieving the casualties scattered on 861. "As gentle and as caring as we could, we helped bring Marines down the face of the hill," Pfc. Larry D. Stevanus wrote in a letter. "Some were in so much pain they screamed if we moved them the wrong way."

Choppers from Marine Medium Helicopter Squadron (HMM) 164 had a difficult time trying to evacuate the wounded and drop off supplies. "We were like magnets," Cpl. Sam Beamon said. "We only had so many seconds on the ground before their mortars would start coming in. They were really accurate, too. Some choppers were riddled with holes."

Hill 861, over three days (April 24-26), cost 1st Bn., 9th Marines (24 lives), 3rd Bn., 3rd Marines (20) and A Co., 3rd Tank Bn. (1) for a total of 45 KIA. Kilo Company accounted for all of the 3rd's fatalities; virtually all were in Bravo Company of the 9th.

On April 28, the 2nd Bn., 3rd Marines, advanced on Hill 861. The mountain was saturated with 250- and 500-pound bombs. When the riflemen reached the crest, however, they discovered the elusive NVA had retreated. Amid the stench of decaying bodies, shattered trees and blackened earth, they found 25 mutually supporting bunkers and more than 400 fighting holes. They were virtually impenetrable to air and artillery strikes.

From April 24 through May 3, 1967, two Marine regiments faced intense fire on three hills. Combined, they lost 125 KIA over those days.

'THEY WERE KILLING US' ON 881S

Attention now shifted to Hill 881S. Shaped like a peanut and running east to west, the hill was "rough going" for the Leathernecks on April 30. Suddenly, "everything went off," and members of M Co., 3rd Bn., 3rd Marines, were fighting for their lives.

"Myself, 2nd Lt. Joe Mitchell and Lance Cpl. Lester Ray Calhoun were taking cover behind a log when an 82mm mortar landed near us," said Pfc. Don Hossack, the company radio operator. "The blast destroyed the radio and sent a 9-inch piece of shrapnel into my head and broke my arm in two places. Thank God for my helmet. It saved my life."

Hossack realized the NVA were attempting to flank his platoon. "They were closing with us," he said. "I heard whistles, and they emerged from their tighter bunkers. A Russian-made RPD machine gun had us pinned down. They were killing us."

Commandeering another radio, Hossack called KSCB for artillery support. "They were right on the money," he said. "The barrage wiped out 30 to 50 NVA."

A short distance away, K and M companies, 3rd Bn., 9th Marines, also were involved in heavy combat. "We finally reached the top and began tossing hand grenades into bunkers," said Lance Cpl. Harry O'Dell of K Company. "Bullets were so close they sounded like cracking whips. A mortar round hit and blew me back into one of their bunkers. I was dazed, and my uniform was soaked in blood."

Lance Cpl. Joe O'Neill and Pfc. Leslie Wyeth of M Company were retrieving the body of a dead Marine when snipers cut them down. "Rounds struck Wyeth in his legs, and one got me in the shoulder and the throat," O'Neill said. "I was gasping for air, and I tried to yell to clear my passageway. Our corpsman, Mike House, came out of nowhere to assist me." House would receive a Silver Star for his gallantry and O'Neill a Bronze Star.

April 30 on Hill 881S resulted in 45 dead Americans. All 26 KIA in the 3rd Bn., 3rd Marines, belonged to M Company. That included Navy Cross recipient Cpl. Robert J. Schley. Virtually all 19 KIA in 3rd Bn., 9th Marines, were members of Kilo Company.

Hill 881S was ultimately secured. The victory, however, was bittersweet. "You can't say we took the hill," O'Dell said. "They just left."

Navy corpsman Vernon Wike, 19, tries in vain to save the life of a wounded Marine during the Battle of Hill 881N on May 3, 1967.

BODIES EVERYWHERE ON 881N

One hill remained in NVA hands—881N. Two companies from the 2nd Bn., 3rd Marines, assaulted it from the south and east on May 2, resulting in five KIA in Golf Company. The enemy let loose with everything they had. Even experienced combat Marines had never known such heavy fire. Late in the afternoon, the Leathernecks consolidated their positions.

Early the next morning, on May 3, hundreds of NVA soldiers struck E Company's lines. Fighting was hand-to-hand as the enemy breached a portion of the perimeter. A composite squad of combat engineers was quickly organized to bolster the weakened defenses. Artillery and 106mm recoilless rifle fire finally stopped the attack.

2nd Lt. James R. Cannon was stunned. In *The Hill Fights: The First Battle of Khe Sanh,* author Edward F. Murphy quotes him: " 'There were bodies everywhere, mostly NVA. About 80 enemy dead littered the ground in front of the 1st and 2nd squads' positions. No doubt others had been dragged away by their comrades. Dead Marines lay there, too. I couldn't tell a black from a white Marine. Four hours in the sun had already badly decomposed the bodies.' "

Cannon was extremely proud of his men. "The actions of Echo Company earned them two Navy Crosses [Lance Cpl. Frederick Monahan and Pfc. John R. Meuse], five Silver Stars, six Bronze Stars with Combat V and 150 Purple Hearts," he later recorded. "We killed 236 NVA."

But Hill 881N came at a heavy price. On May 3, 29 men died. Some 24 of them came from Echo Company, including one Navy corpsman and a radio operator attached from H&S Company. Adding the five men from the day before brings the bill in lives to 34 for what was dubbed *Operation Beacon Star.*

By May 5, Hill 881N was firmly in Marine hands. "The Hill Fights" officially ended on May 12. The NVA's plans to overrun KSCB failed. "But it was the toughest fight we had in Vietnam," Lt. Gen. Victor Krulak reckoned. ✪

THE TOLL

Hill	KIA
861	45
881S	45
881N	34

DESPERATE FIGHT ON A 'HILL OF ANGELS'

BY RICHARD K. KOLB

A determined enemy assault on Con Thien in early May 1967 was thwarted over four hours of combat, but at a terrible price in Marine lives.

Con Thien Combat Base had a well-deserved reputation as a bad place to be stationed. Whether it was "The Hill of Angels" (in Vietnamese) depended upon one's survival experiences. Not in dispute, however, was that Hill 158 (FSB A-4) was strategic but highly vulnerable to enemy fire and attack. That was proven beyond doubt on May 8, 1967.

On this date, the outpost was manned by reinforced A and D companies of the 1st Battalion, 4th Marines. They were backed by a Marine engineer platoon and A Co., 3rd Tank Bn.—three tanks with 12 crewmen. Two Marine amtracs and an Army M-42 Duster (a tracked vehicle with two 40mm anti-aircraft guns) ultimately joined the fray.

The attack came at 2:40 a.m. with 300 artillery and mortar rounds accompanied by sappers. Launched by the North Vietnamese Army (NVA) 4th and 6th battalions, 812th Regt., 324B Div., the onslaught gained full momentum at 4 a.m. Breaching the perimeter wire with Bangalore torpedoes, the sappers paved the way for NVA regulars using flamethrowers to torch bunkers.

The brunt of the attack fell on Delta Company. And its members rose to the occasion. Posthumous Silver Stars were awarded to three of its men: Cpl. Ralph Watington, Pvt. Jesus Limones and Navy corpsman John Laning.

Alpha quickly sent a platoon to assist its sister company. A grenadier in 1st Platoon, Lance Cpl. Michael Finley, fired two M-79 grenades at an NVA machine gun crew beyond two burning amphibious tractors. After taking out that gun and its crew, Finley aided a wounded Marine and was mortally wounded while helping his wounded squad leader. He received a posthumous Navy Cross. Cpl. Gary Kreh, a squad leader in the 1st Platoon, led his men under intense fire and saved lives until felled by Communist fire. His Silver Star was posthumous.

Meanwhile, the tankers were holding down the northern part of the perimeter. Two of them of A Co., 3rd Tank Bn., received the Navy Cross for outstanding heroism. Although severely wounded, Sgt. David Danner grabbed the .30-caliber machine gun from his disabled tank and laid down fire, killing 15 NVA. At the same time, he distributed ammo to riflemen and rescued a wounded man. Lance Cpl. Charles Thatcher did likewise. Wielding the .30-caliber from his tank, he provided covering fire, resupplied fighting holes and assisted wounded companions all while hit himself.

'Human Carnage Shocking'

By daylight, Delta Company and reinforcements had closed the opening in the wire. Mopping up NVA remnants caught within the perimeter continued until about 9 a.m.

Dan McCall was on night ambush with 2nd Platoon of Alpha Company on May 8. "The destruction when viewed the next morning was astounding," he remembered. "Bodies were everywhere. Weapons and NVA TNT bundles were all over the place. Many Marines had dug out from under what was their bunkers. Engineers dug a huge, single grave to bury all the NVA dead."

Even for battle-hardened Marines, the sight was something to behold. "The human carnage was shocking," wrote James P. Coan in Con Thien: The Hill of Angels. "Approximately 200 NVA bodies lay dead inside and outside of the perimeter." Coan noted, "For days afterward, whenever the wind was right, a dead-body stench descended on Con Thien like a putrid fog."

But the American cost in casualties was equally shocking. "By mid-morning," Coan wrote, "all that remained of a once-vibrant group of American boys was a jumbled mass of unrecognizable lumps of charred bodies."

The initial barrage of artillery, rocket and mortar fire had inflicted the most human damage, killing 20 Marines, 43% of the total. Gunfire claimed 18 men and satchel charges and shrapnel eight lives.

The terrible tally: 46 KIA and 110 WIA. A (16) and D (18) companies accounted for nearly 75% of the KIA. H&S Company counted five dead—three mortarmen and two Navy corpsmen. The seven other men killed came from four different units—including two from A Co., 3rd Tank Bn. and two from 4th Plt., B Co., 1st Amtrac Bn. ✪

BY RICHARD K. KOLB

'VICTORS' OF HILL 110

Six Marine rifle companies took on the North Vietnamese in the Que Son Valley in a fierce day-long battle on May 10, 1967. To the Marines, the outcome was a hard-fought win.

"The tropical sun and vermin quickly claimed the dead after a battle—bodies rigid, swarming with flies, ants, and maggots that were oblivious to the violence and single-mindedly taking advantage of this bountiful harvest of corpses; bodies so black and swollen that their living allegiance could only be determined by their uniforms and equipment; bodies encased in a poisonous aura of foul air."

That's how Otto J. Lehrack described the aftermath of the Battle of Hill 110 in his book, *Road of 10,000 Pains.*

Hill 110 was located 2½ miles north of Que Son city in Quang Nam province. Nearby was the hamlet of Nghi Ha and other terrain features such as Nui Nong Ham (Hill 185) and Suoi Cho Dun, a narrow river. Not a large hill, 110's bottom was covered with chest-high elephant grass.

The objective on May 10, 1967, was straightforward: take Hill 110. But taking the hill was easier than holding it because a battalion of North Vietnamese Army (NVA) regulars lay in wait. This was the stomping ground of the 2nd NVA Division, especially the 3rd NVA Regiment.

As part of *Operation Union I*—intended to eliminate the last Communist stronghold in the Que Son Valley—the Marines committed most of two battalions. They were the 1st Bn. (A, C and D companies), 5th Marines, 1st Marine Div. and the Special Landing Force of the 9th Amphibious Brigade—Battalion Landing 1/3 (1st Bn., 3rd Marines) consisting of B, C and D companies.

'I COULD SEE THE END COMING'

The 5th Marine's Charlie Company was moving up the southwestern slope of Hill 110 when it was hit. "Charlie Company was receiving fire in a deafening roar," recalled Russell J. Caswell, captain of the company. "No other company from 1/5 could reach Hill 110, although Delta and Alpha tried. Then things went from bad to worse—the M-16s which they had been forced to accept to replace their dependable M-14s didn't work. McNamara [Defense Secretary Robert] and Westmoreland [Gen. William, commander of U.S. Forces] had issued them rifles which double-fed and jammed."

C Company took the hill, but was then pinned down by fire from a cane field below and caves in the lower slopes of Nui Nong Ham. "As we got near the crest of the hill, all hell broke loose," said Cpl. Bill Pettway, Caswell's radio-telephone operator. "We started receiving intense fire directly in front of us from the fields near the river area."

Cpl. Jim Coxen was the grenadier for his squad in 2nd Platoon. "C Company was the only company on Hill 110," he recalled 50 years later. "There were maybe 80 of us. We were fighting an NVA regiment and held them off for about 12 hours before they quit trying to get at us and left. We had no air support or arty support. There was no cover, nearly no concealment.

"I never heard such a volume of fire like that or that many bullets whizzing around. I shot up all my ammo (grenades). The noise was overwhelming. We were

NAVY CROSS

LANCE CPL. JOHN E. RUSTH

STAFF SERGEANT ELPIDIO ALLEN ARQUERO (POSTHUMOUS)

CPL. THOMAS SANDERS (POSTHUMOUS)

CPL. JOHN M. REID (POSTHUMOUS)

PHOTO COURTESY OTTO LEHRACK

VIETNAM VETERANS MEMORIAL FUND/WALL OF FACES PHOTOS

SILVER STAR

CAPT. RUSSELL JAMES CASWELL

PFC. THOMAS L. FOY (POSTHUMOUS)

CPL. WILLIAM FRANCIS LESHOW

PFC. RUSSELL P. MILLER (POSTHUMOUS)

PFC. JAMES C. RILEY (POSTHUMOUS)

HM3 DONALD PATRICK WATSON

CPL. STERLING S. WOODS (POSTHUMOUS)

SGT. HILLOUS YORK

pretty sure we were all going to be killed if we didn't get some support soon. When the battle was over, we were all exhausted, hot, dehydrated and coming down from a 12-hour adrenalin charge."

Plenty of Marines rose to the occasion. Lance Cpl. John E. Rusth, a fire team leader and his squad's sniper (M-14), led his team to the crest of the northeastern slope. As indicated, fire originated from the hedgerows and sugar cane fields at the base of the hill. So Rusth led a grenade and bayonet assault down the hill, routing the NVA.

On 10 separate occasions, he went back down the hill to assist wounded Marines back up the slope. Already hit in the thigh by a bullet, on his tenth descent he brought the Marine to safety, finally collapsing from the wound and heat exhaustion. His courage was recognized with the Navy Cross.

Sgt. Hillous York, a Tennessean whose great uncle was Sgt. Alvin York of WWI fame, certainly lived up to the family name. Taking over the 3rd Platoon, he organized the rescue of casualties and provided covering fire, personally killing six NVA.

As York related to author Otto Lehrack in *Road of 10,000 Pains*: "The fighting was point-blank. There was just a little strip of grass between the two forces. After the fight started going good, we were nose to nose across the strip of grass that in places was no more than 12 feet across … right up in your face … I could see the end coming."

Both York and Caswell, who oversaw the resupply of water and ammo to his men and organized the evacuation of the wounded, were awarded the Silver Star.

CHARGING INTO THE LION'S DEN

Meanwhile, B and C companies of the 3rd Marines had responded to the call for help. But they were stopped in their tracks. Both companies put up a valiant fight in attempting to assist their fellow Marines on Hill 110.

Cpl. Thomas Sanders, a machine gun squad leader in C Company, placed himself between the enemy and his unit members. NVA got to within 20 feet of his position and he raked the trench line before being killed. His selfless actions allowed nine Marines to gain cover and resume fighting. Sanders received a posthumous Navy Cross.

Cpl. John M. Reid, a rifle squad leader in the company's 3rd Platoon, displayed similar valor. When his platoon was pinned down, he seized an

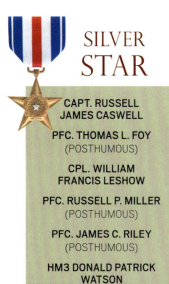

COURTESY HILLOUS YORK/OTTO LEHRACK

Sgt. Hillous York, great-nephew of WWI hero Alvin York, lived up to the family name, earning the Silver Star for his bravery on Hill 110.

available machine gun and laid down cover fire so six members of his squad could find a safe position. While in the rice paddy, Reid ultimately prevented the NVA from overrunning 3rd Platoon. But in doing so, he was wounded in the leg and then hit again fatally, according to his Navy Cross citation.

The 3rd Marine's Bravo Company underwent a trial by fire, too. Staff Sgt. Elpidio Arquero, at the head of its 1st Platoon, directed return fire and coordinated an assault. Repeatedly exposed in rallying the force, he "charged directly into the entrenched enemy positions" and "halted the [NVA] advance" long enough for the men to withdraw and take out the wounded, says his Navy Cross citation. Arquero did so at the cost of his own life.

Such bravery was almost commonplace in Bravo Company. Meeting the enemy head on, inflicting heavy casualties, holding ground and saving lives by selfless acts were the order of the day. Four riflemen sacrificed their lives carrying out all of the above. Posthumous Silver Stars went to Cpl. Sterling S. Woods, Pfc. Thomas L. Foy, Pfc. James C. Riley and Pfc. Russell P. Miller.

VICTORS VERSUS SURVIVORS

When the two companies of the 3rd Marines could not advance, they called for help. But only one platoon of Alpha Company—a "Sparrow Hawk" rapid-reaction force—could reach them. Too much fire was directed at the helicopters to land additional reinforcements.

The 5th Marine's A Company also was called in. While moving on Nghi Ha (3) hamlet on the Suoi Cho Dun—1.2 miles east of Hill 110—Alpha's command post was strafed by F-4 fighter-bombers, killing five Marines and wounding 24. The company was then forced to break off its attack.

Later, the Command Group and D Company of the 5th Marines fought their way to a nearby hill. 1st Battalion mortar men showered the NVA with shrapnel. Then Delta and Charlie companies linked up, driving the enemy to the northwest.

Cpl. Tom Kintner, a member of C Company, recalled: "The next morning they [NVA] were gone, and we went to the bottom of the hill. Gook bodies were just lying on top of each other." One estimate put the number of communists killed at 116.

When the American tally was taken, the total number of dead was 35. The 1st Bn., 3rd Marines, was hit hardest with 20 KIA—more than half in B Company alone. An attached forward observer from A Btry., 1st Bn., 12th Marines also was KIA. The 1st of the 5th (C Company) had nine killed by enemy action, including a Navy corpsman. Five men from Alpha Company were killed by "friendly fire," and one by the NVA. Of the enemy-caused dead (30), 60% were claimed by gunfire; the remaining 40% by shrapnel. Some 135 Marines were wounded.

Russell "Jim" Caswell, Charlie's CO, summed up the feelings of many of his men: "They were victors of the battle for Hill 110. They never referred to themselves as 'survivors'—no enemy soldier ever broke through their lines or enveloped their flank." This was a victory sure enough in a war with so few concrete measurements for decisively winning a battle. ✪

Hill 110 was located 2½ miles north of Que Son city in Quang Nam province. The top of the hill provided little cover or opportunity for concealment.

COURTESY JIM COXEN

C Company grenadier Jim Coxen, Howard Jones (KIA) and Larry Desmond take a break in the Que Son Valley in early May 1967.

THE TOLL

U.S. KIA:
35

U.S. WIA:
135

BY SUSAN KATZ KEATING   *OPERATION FRANCIS MARION*

'FIGHTING 4TH' MAKES ITS MARK AT PLEI DOC

During the 4th Infantry Division's famous "Nine Days in May," one in particular stood out. On May 18, 1967, one platoon of B Co., 1st Bn., 8th Inf., made a desperate last stand.

The soldiers proceeded cautiously through the jungle highlands west of Pleiku, near the Cambodian border, on the morning of May 18, 1967. The men were part of *Operation Francis Marion,* aimed at stopping the North Vietnamese Army (NVA) from seizing the Ia Drang Valley. The Americans belonged to B Co., 1st Bn., 8th Inf., 1st Bde., 4th Inf. Div. Most were young, and many were new to Vietnam. But they all were about to become seasoned warriors, via a series of savage battles known simply as "The Nine Days in May Border Battles." The worst of those battles was this day.

By the end of those nine days, some 2,000 GIs would go up against 1,500-2,000 regulars of the NVA's 32nd and 66th regiments. The enemy would attack in groupings that vastly outnumbered the Americans. Three men from the 4th Infantry Division would earn posthumous Medals of Honor. Another six received the Distinguished Service Cross (DSC), half losing their lives. The 1st Brigade would earn a coveted Presidential Unit Citation for heroically disabling two full enemy regiments and curtailing an entire season's offensive.

ORDEAL OF B COMPANY

As outlined in the after-action report for May 18-26, the five battles can be traced to 10:40 a.m. on the 18th, when a lone NVA soldier appeared before B Company, and then took off along a well-used trail. Additional enemy soldiers popped in and out of view, until the acting company commander, 1st Lt. Cary Allen, dispatched his men into action.

Two platoons quickly organized a perimeter as best they could within the dense jungle, while two others—the 1st and the 4th—set out to investigate. And the 4th Platoon soon sighted another NVA. GIs gave chase.

"It was a decoy," said John Barclay, who was an 18-year-old automatic weapons rifleman assigned to 1st Platoon. "It was a lure meant to draw them into a trap." It worked. The 4th Platoon quickly was surrounded and attacked.

"The rest of us tried to break through to them," Barclay remembered. "But then we came under attack. We fought all afternoon. By around 4 p.m., we knew they weren't coming back. In fact, they were being annihilated."

Platoon Sgt. Bruce Grandstaff, 4th Platoon leader, fought valiantly to save his entrapped men. Time after time, he raced through enemy fire in order to help his wounded men, or to try to pop smoke grenades up through the jungle canopy to mark his position. Wounded first in one leg and then the other, Grandstaff called in increasingly closer artillery strikes.

Bleeding profusely from multiple wounds, he crawled forward until he was able to lob grenades atop an enemy machine gun emplacement. Finally, a desperate Grandstaff called in an artillery strike on his own position.

Ray Harton was then assigned to the 6th Bn., 29th Arty. "I was told the platoon wanted artillery on top of them," he recalled. "I said, 'Are you sure that this is what they want? Yes, put it on top of them.' I immediately made a correction for C Btry., 5th Bn., 16th Arty, and fired many 155mm rounds on top of them."

An enemy rocket took Grandstaff's life. Later, he was awarded a posthumous Medal of Honor.

Only eight men lived through the attack on the 4th Platoon. The survivors then endured a gruesome ordeal, pretending to be dead while NVA kicked and looted American bodies, shooting anyone who showed the barest sign of life. One survivor later reported that an NVA actually sat on his back and shoved a hand down his shirt to see if he was still breathing.

The rest of B Company, meanwhile, continued to fight until it drove off the enemy. Recalled Barclay: "At the end of the day, I was amazed I had survived this horrible battle. It had just begun." Bravo's 4th Platoon was truly annihilated: 26 men were KIA along with a forward observer and medic, as well as two other B Company members. A full 70% of the men were draftees and a majority were killed by gunfire. The 4th Platoon's collective courage was indisputable: one Medal of Honor, three DSCs (all posthumous) and six posthumous Silver Stars.

By the next morning, B Company had been joined by the battalion's A and C companies, plus the Reconnaissance Platoon from HQ Company. Members of A Company found what was left of the 4th Platoon, and spent much of the day helping to care for the casualties.

THREE-WAVE ASSAULT

Action resumed on the 20th, after the 1st Brigade set up a defensive perimeter at a new site. "We had put up a low rock wall between two trees as protection," recalled Kent Combs, who was a 20-year-old with the Recon Platoon. "Sometime after dark we started taking mortar fire, followed by ground attacks."

Earlier that evening, Combs had talked to a friend from C Company, Pfc. Leslie A. Bellrichard: "He was leaning against a tree, reading his Bible." When the attack was in full swing, with the Bible safely stowed away, Bellrichard repeatedly rose from his foxhole to throw

On May 18 and 20, 1967, firefights raged in the Plei Doc District eight miles northwest of Duc Co. The 1st Battalion of the 8th Infantry lost 30 KIA and 16 KIA on those days, respectively.

"By around 4 p.m., we knew they weren't coming back. In fact, they were being annihilated."

—JOHN BARCLAY, 1ST PLT., B CO.

MEDAL OF HONOR

SGT. BRUCE GRANDSTAFF
(POSTHUMOUS)

PFC. LESLIE A. BELLRICHARD
(POSTHUMOUS)

STAFF SGT. FRANKIE Z. MOLNAR
(POSTHUMOUS)

'HUMAN-WAVE' ATTACKS

The 3rd Battalion of the 12th Infantry provided a backstop, preventing the NVA from retreating to its sanctuary in off-limits Cambodia.

A fierce assault hit its night defensive position in the Chu Goungot Mountains southwest of Pleiku City on May 22. The enemy sent human waves against A and B companies. Eight members of B Company and two from Alpha were KIA.

"Heavy close-in fighting raged for four hours until the enemy force finally broke contact and exfiltrated from the battlefield," reads the brigade's Presidential Unit Citation.

A GI of the Recon Plt., 1st Bn., 12th Inf., 4th Div., takes cover during one of the "Nine Days in May" battles in 1967.

grenades into the midst of charging NVA.

During one such attempt, Bellrichard was knocked backward by an exploding mortar round. When his armed grenade slipped out of his hand and into an occupied foxhole, Bellrichard threw himself atop the grenade, using his own body to absorb the explosion. Mortally wounded, he still managed to fire into attacking NVA before succumbing to his wounds. The action cost Bellrichard his life, and also earned him a Medal of Honor.

(Another Medal of Honor was earned that night by Frankie Z. Molnar, a 24-year-old staff sergeant who saved the lives of fellow B Company men when he threw himself on a live enemy grenade.)

The companies fended off the three-wave assault that engulfed their night defensive position. In two hours of fighting, 16 men were KIA and 65 WIA from A, B and C companies.

4th Infantry Division soldiers remove a wounded NVA prisoner to an evacuation helicopter on May 23, 1967.

HOLDING HILL 521

Hard fighting occurred on the 26th, involving C Co., 3rd Bn., 8th Inf., on Hill 521, situated 6.8 miles northwest of Duc Co.

Richard Jackson was a medic assigned to Charlie Company. "Doc" Jackson was on patrol with his unit on May 26 when he stopped for a "nature call." From the corner of his eye, Jackson saw a slight movement—a shadow, perhaps, shifting position. He alerted his unit members. Then, as Jackson described it: "All hell broke loose."

Some 300-500 NVA attacked with B-40 rockets, grenades, intense AK-47 fire and mortars, or possibly artillery. "That firefight was so intense, and the noise so deafening that it made

Members of B Co., 3rd Bn., 8th Inf., 4th Inf. Div.—Sgt. Fink, Spec. 4 Ricardo Lopez, Sgt. Shearer and Spec. 4 Fred Helms—assisted Charlie Company on Hill 521.

DISTINGUISHED SERVICE CROSS

1ST SGT. RICHARD L. CHILDERS

1ST LT. BRANKO B. MARINOVICH

SPEC. 4 JOSEPH M. PEREZ

you strain to keep your senses," Jackson recalled. "Enemy fire was slamming into our position like rainfall."

Jackson immediately went to work. "I was taking care of the wounded and seeing my guys get killed on a scale that was overwhelming," he said. When Jackson himself took a hit, he pressed onward. "I continued to weave my way through the carnage to get to whomever I could."

Jackson recalled hearing his platoon sergeant shout repeatedly for his soldiers to keep the enemy at bay. The Americans did as their sergeant asked. "Our line held," Jackson said. "The Vietnamese finally realized C Company was no slouch." But Charlie Company lost 10 KIA on that hill, four of whom received posthumous Silver Stars. Moreover, three DSCs were awarded for May 26: 1st Sgt. Richard Childers and Spec. 4 Joseph M. Perez of Charlie Company, as well as 1st Lt. Branko B. Marinovich, commander of Bravo.

A squad from the 3rd Battalion's B Company had eagerly jumped into the fight. It had just come in from ambush patrol and was on perimeter guard when it heard C Company being hit at the bottom of the hill. "We took off down the hill and went right into the middle of it," said Spec. 4 Fred Helms. "My friend Spec. 4 Ricardo Lopez was hit immediately one or more times by sniper fire. He rolled downhill screaming for me to help him."

'UNWAVERING COURAGE'

It was that sort of fighting spirit that rated the 4th a Presidential Unit Citation: "The combined fortitude, determination and unwavering courage of the 1st Brigade's personnel rendered two North Vietnamese Army regiments ineffective and totally disrupted the 1967 summer monsoon offensive in the Central Highlands."

A battle survivor added this perspective. "We weren't a high profile group," said Landis Bargatze, who was assigned to A Co., 3rd Bn., 8th Inf. "We weren't Special Forces or Airborne. We were mostly just a bunch of draftee grunts who turned out to be damn good soldiers." ✪

THE TOLL

U.S. KIA:
(May 18 only)
30

BY RICHARD K. KOLB

ENGULFED IN A 'HOLOCAUST OF FIRE' AT SUOI CAT

"Enveloped in a classic Communist ambush," Associated Press correspondent Peter Arnett wrote, an armored column "was destroyed amidst burning and exploding vehicles and dying men" in a "holocaust of rocket and recoilless-rifle fire that stabbed at the column from a distance as close as 15 feet."

It all started as a routine resupply mission for the 1st Plt., K Trp., 3rd Sqdn., 11th Armored Cavalry (ACR). The convoy included seven armored cavalry assault vehicles (ACAVs), commonly known as armored personnel carriers (APCs), the troop's mess truck, a tank from the squadron's M Company and a jeep carrying three men from the 595th Engineer Co., 86th Eng. Bn.

K Troop was providing security for a part of the 595th Engineer Company working the Gia Ray rock quarry; along with the village of Suoi Cat. The carriers were moving along National Route 1 from the quarry to the junction of routes 1 and 2 when they were hit less than a mile west of Suoi Cat on May 21, 1967. The ambush occurred during *Operation Kitty Hawk*, one intended to secure installations and lines of communications in Long Khanh province of III Corps.

'FIGHTING FOR OUR LIVES'

Less than 50 GIs, perhaps only 44, manned the convoy when it was attacked by a reinforced battalion of the 274th Viet Cong (VC) Regiment. The route taken had been cleared for mines earlier. But the VC were concealed in 10-foot-high elephant grass and hidden behind dirt mounds along 1,100 yards of the road. Vietnamese civilians went about their daily business in a surreal setting, simply laying down in a nearby field during the fighting.

The VC unleashed a torrent of anti-armor weapons that included 75mm and 57mm recoilless rifles (lightweight, portable tube artillery), rocket-propelled grenades (RPGs), .50-caliber machine guns and mortars. The lead APC was hit by a 75mm round at about 8:50 a.m., initiating the ambush. It quickly became a fight for survival by single vehicles and individual GIs.

"I was on the lead APC (K-10) that took the first rounds from the enemy—75mm

M-113s and M4SA3 tanks of the 11th ACR deploy down a road between jungle and a rubber plantation during *Operation Cedar Falls* in January 1967. K Troop, 3rd Squadron, was ambushed near Suoi Cat while returning from the Gia Ray rock quarry on May 21, 1967.

In about 30 minutes, one platoon of an armored cavalry convoy along Route 1 suffered nearly 100% casualties at the hands of a Viet Cong battalion on May 21, 1967.

MAY 1967

U.S. ARMY PHOTO

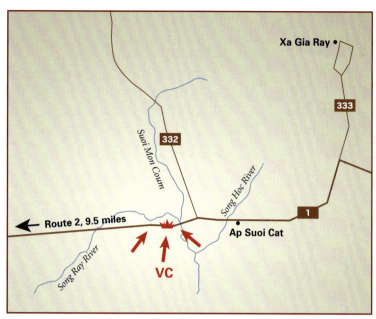

The ambush occurred less than a mile west of Suoi Cat. The convoy was traveling along National Route 1 from the quarry.

Spec. 4 Clair N. Poorman's armored personnel carrier was designated K-16. It was the third track in line and hit numerous times. But K-16 was the only one still running out of seven APCs after the VC sprung the ambush.

and RPGs," recalled then-Pfc. Gaetano "Tony" Puglisi. "My APC was so damaged that we had to abandon the vehicle and take cover on the ground. That was until we were able to climb aboard another APC to continue the fight.

"Anthony Royball was shot in the left temple by small-arms fire. He went down and knocked me down as he fell on top of me, pinning me beneath. I got him off of me and took over the M-60 machine gun. I thought we had them on the run until the track took a fatal hit in the transmission. I fired 900 rounds, watching the barrel turn red and then white before it exploded in my face."

Spec. 4 Clair N. Poorman, Jr., was on the third track in line. "Before the ambush started, we were waving and throwing extra c-rations to the VC who were walking along the road only feet from us," he recalled. "We thought they were the Popular Forces' [militia units] members from the village until they opened up on us only feet away.

"My track [APC, K-16) was the only one that still ran out of seven tracks, a jeep and a 2½-ton truck—all the rest were destroyed. But we took two recoilless rifle hits to the rear and two RPG hits on the left side. I was wounded by RPG fire. The VC were overrunning everything and we were fighting for our lives."

2nd Lt. Ted Hendrickson, an officer from the 595th Engineer Company, was driving Poorman's APC. The regular driver let the engineer take over at the controls. One of the rounds also hit the track's nose. "We halted and a cloud of blue smoke billowed up in front of me," Hendrickson told a reporter. "Then, as it cleared, I saw just in front of us on the highway, about 15 feet away, two Viet Cong gunners setting up a 57mm recoilless rifle."

Hendrickson went head-on after the VC. "One was just about to slam a shell into the breach when he saw me coming," he said. "The other one holding the barrel tried to jump aside. I ground over him first. Then I crunched the weapon. Finally, I ran over the gunner himself."

As Poorman indicated, the APC was hit four more times. Hendrickson and his men were all wounded. Nevertheless, the engineer and his crew pushed on, rescuing 10 other wounded men under intense fire.

The four tracks in the rear of the column took the brunt of the casualties. Pfc. Edward Miller, wounded and the sole survivor of the APC designated K-13, endured a harrowing experience.

"When the first two rounds struck the ACAV, the impact knocked me down inside the track, Miller remembered. "My crewmates were all dead due to massive injuries. All our massive firepower was blown apart from the recoilless rifle rounds hitting the ACAV." So

> ## "As I got nearer, I could see he [a VC] had something in the bag, an explosive, a satchel charge [a canvas bag filled with explosives]. All I had on me was the knife, a hunting knife with a four-inch blade that I'd used to skin rabbits I'd shot back in Maryland."
>
> —SPEC. 4 RICHARD E. FRIEND, JUST BEFORE HE KILLED THE ENEMY SOLDIER

Miller had to resort to firing his M-16 and then throwing hand grenades.

"I threw them all, killing or wounding some of the attackers who were moving in my direction," Miller said. But he was later knocked out by the blast of a VC grenade. As he came to, he recalled, "My arms were behind me and I was being dragged away by the VC. [As relief arrived], the VC dropped my arms, leaving me there."

Meanwhile, the single tank in the column was taking a beating, ultimately sustaining 14 hits from recoilless rifle rounds. Its commander, a Sgt. David Wright, took out a VC 57mm recoilless rifle crew. The tank loader, however, died of his wounds.

PHOTO COURTESY EDWARD MILLER

Pfc. Edward Miller was the sole survivor of the APC designated K-13. All his fellow crewmembers were killed. Eventually knocked out by a VC grenade blast, he was actually captured by a VC but dropped when relief arrived just in time.

FEATS OF SURVIVAL

Both smaller vehicles were targeted, too. The mess truck was disabled and the driver, Pfc. Frank Gregory, attempted to play dead. But a VC turned him over on his back and fired two shots into his left side. A VC actually sat on his face while going through Gregory's pockets. Fortunately, he passed out and was later rescued by the relief force.

Engineers in the jeep underwent an equally death-defying experience. A recoilless rifle round hit the jeep, spinning the vehicle into a ditch and killing the driver. Spec. 4 Richard E. Friend, a bulldozer driver who was manning the M-60, lost his M-16 in the crash.

"I ran past three Viet Cong lying in a hole," he said at the time. "I bent my head down instinctively. I told myself that this was the end. I wasn't armed. All I had was my knife. But incredibly, they didn't fire at me. Maybe they were only ammo bearers."

But later, a bullet hit his chest. The ammo clip in the pocket of his flak jacket, however, prevented him from being wounded. "As I got nearer, I could see he [a VC] had something in the bag, an explosive, a satchel charge [a canvas bag filled with explosives]," Friend said. "All I had on me was the knife, a hunting knife with a four-inch blade that I'd used to skin rabbits I'd shot back in Maryland."

Grabbing the VC by his collar, Friend plunged the knife into his body. But there is more to the story, as his Distinguished Service Cross (DSC) citation makes clear.

He had spotted the VC with the satchel charge approaching an APC 300 yards away. "Friend stood up in the withering barrage and dashed to the carrier under a hail of bullets,"

DISTINGUISHED SERVICE CROSS

SPEC. 4
RICHARD E. FRIEND

STAFF SGT.
HOMER L. PITTMAN

according to his citation. "Armed only with a knife, he leaped on the insurgent and fought a fierce hand-to-hand battle with the enemy soldier, killing him before he could destroy the carrier. His action … was responsible for saving the lives of several comrades in the carrier."

PREPARING FOR A LAST STAND

Heroism was widespread during that half-hour. Combat continued to swirl around the lead APC. Staff Sgt. Homer L. Pittman was its vehicle commander and acting platoon sergeant. After evacuating his men from the track, he then covered them by hurling grenades at the VC.

Taking command of another APC, he evacuated the wounded, as well as ammo from the burning vehicle. "Once on the ground, he exposed himself to the enemy fire time after time to carry the ammunition to the perimeter he had set up," reads his DSC citation. "For 20 minutes, Sgt. Pittman directed the fire of his men to repel the assaults … saving the lives of many of his men."

In doing so, he may have taken out as many as 10 VC, despite "bullets flying everywhere," as Pittman described it.

RELIEF ARRIVES IN THE NICK OF TIME

At 9:10 a.m., K Troop's other two platoons were committed to the fray as a relief force. By then, the fight had been going on for about 20 minutes.

"I wasn't involved in the ambush, but I was literally the first relief on the scene," remembered Darrell Zipp, a private first class with 2nd Platoon, 50 years earlier. "At full throttle, we arrived in about five minutes. The sight was something out of hell.

"Three vertical columns of black smoke were three burning tracks. Sgt. Homer Pittman was in the commander hatch of another track, still pumping away on the .50-caliber machine gun. I pulled up to about 50 yards from him and with an arm movement he indicated where the VC went. All 2nd Platoon tracks turned 45 degrees right and opened up with everything they had."

Tony Puglisi remembered: "Air cavalry appeared, engaging the enemy with rocket- and machine-gun fire. Soon after, a jet fighter also came screaming into the battle along with the K Troop reaction force. The enemy broke contact and ran."

1st Lt. Chuck Burr, executive officer of K Troop, was to the point in his assessment of the ambush. "3rd Squadron and K Troop were very well trained and prepared," he said. "It was the lack of communications with 1st Platoon that caused the death of the troopers." Indeed, the platoon was plagued by radio problems from the very start.

Gary Carlson and Darrell Zipp, 2nd Plt., K Trp., take time for chow in the Suoi Cat area in 1967. Zipp drove the first track in the rescue column.

When the ambush's tally was taken, 18 GIs were dead. Sixteen were from K Troop's 1st Platoon, one from the tank company (M) and the equipment operator/driver from the 595th Engineer Company. Two of the tracks had four men each KIA. Multiple fragmentation

PHOTO COURTESY DARRELL ZIPP

M-113s of 2nd Plt., K Trp., 3rd Sqdn., plow through the thick jungle near Suoi Cat, 1967. Armor played a unique role in the Vietnam War, and the 11th Armored Cavalry Regiment ("Blackhorse Regiment") was always at the tip of the spear.

wounds and burns claimed most lives. KIAs were split evenly between draftees and volunteers, a ratio soon to change in future battles.

According to one count, 28 men were WIA, leaving only Pittman—who was in the center of the firestorm—unwounded. Another account says three GIs were not hit. No matter how you look at it, the casualty rate for this convoy was extreme.

In a blow-by-blow chronicle of the Suoi Cat fight, Bob Hersey, a vet of K Troop (1968-69) who maintains the unit's website, concluded: "The ambush itself was thoroughly planned and devastatingly executed by the VC. Against a single cavalry platoon, [initially] unsupported by either air, artillery or friendly ground forces, the result was a foregone conclusion. That as many men survived as did is a tribute to the courage [besides the two DSC's, five Silver Stars were awarded] and initiative of the individual American soldier." ✪

THE TOLL

U.S. KIA:
18

U.S. WIA:
28

BY RICHARD K. KOLB

EAGLE LANDING PUTS NVA ON THE RUN

The 3rd Battalion, 5th Marines, experienced a treacherous landing zone in late May 1967 when it hit the ground in the valley as deadly as a flytrap.

The mission, part of *Operation Union II*, started as an attempt to destroy the remnants of one North Vietnamese Army (NVA) regiment. It ended confronting an entirely different unit.

On May 26, 1967, companies L, M and I of the 3rd Bn., 5th Marines, 1st Marine Div., alighted at a spot designated Landing Zone (LZ) Eagle, near the hamlet of Cam La (1) in the Que Son Valley of Quang Tin province. They were not far off of Route 534.

Before the day was done, the Marines would tangle with a battalion (about 1,000 men) of the 3rd NVA Regiment. A flat rice paddy, about 1,100 yards across, surrounded the LZ. So the men of the 5th established a perimeter around the paddy. Over the next seven hours or so, they would go toe-to-toe there with the seasoned Communist regulars.

LIMA IN THE LIMELIGHT
The first helicopters touched down at about 9:40 a.m.

MARINE CORPS PHOTO #A421853

Men of the 3rd Bn., 5th Marines, 1st Marine Div., head for rice paddy dikes after a helicopter landing at LZ Eagle. Combat was close up and lethal over some seven hours.

L Company encountered mostly sniper fire. But heavy fire awaited M Company and the battalion command group that followed. I Company landed at noon.

A half hour before, however, L Company assaulted a tree line. Then and throughout the fighting, Lima's men put it all on the line. Capt. Harold D. Pettengill, commanding officer, was hit by shrapnel. It wounded the muscles in his neck and caused a hearing loss. Yet he refused medical evacuation. He went on to direct air and artillery fire to assure a safe landing for the remainder of the battalion.

Navy corpsman John E. Schon repeatedly exposed himself to enemy fire to render first aid and evacuate casualties. He did so until mortally wounded. Cpl. Benjamin Richardson sprinted across a paddy field four times to rescue the wounded. On the fourth trip, Richardson was mortally wounded.

Cpl. Lowell R. Lloyd, a fire team leader in 2nd Platoon, was wounded in the stomach but carried another Marine 50 yards toward cover. Temporarily stopped by a shot in the leg, he was hit a third time after getting up. Lloyd died during his fourth attempt to bring the man to safety.

All four of these acts of bravery were recognized with a Silver Star.

'UP CLOSE AND PERSONAL'

With L and M companies attacking, I Company enveloped the enemy flank.

Cpl. Tim Hanley, of I Company, recounted in Otto J. Lehrack's *Road of 10,000 Pains:* "We assaulted through this tree line and got the gooks on the run, and it was a Marine's dream come true … There were 30, 40 bodies by the time we finished."

M Company, supported by a platoon from I Company, swept a nearby village around 2 p.m. "A hedge row stopped the whole company," Capt. Jim McElroy was quoted in *Road of 10,000 Pains*. "There was firing everywhere … The enemy was just waiting. That was pretty nasty because it was up close and personal."

Pfc. Fred Riddle, a mortar man (60mm section) with M Company, could testify to that firsthand. "It was my first time being shot at, and the feeling can't be explained unless it has happened to you. Heavy ground fire and mortar fire was everywhere. Two 82mm mortar rounds landed right in the middle of our group and Marines went down everywhere." Riddle was among the wounded, hit by shrapnel in the right shoulder.

"Because all the mortar section was either KIA or WIA, it didn't exist any longer," he said. "I was all that was left, so I was put in 3rd Platoon and assigned to the perimeter. I remember going into the night; my thoughts of whether it was going to be my last day or not because we were heavily outnumbered. "

Close-quarters combat failed to deter Cpl. Roger V. Inscore, a machine gun squad leader in 1st Platoon. While his unit was seizing a tree line, he moved from gun to gun directing suppressive fire. He also attempted to save a dying Marine. After returning to his squad, he was killed by a sniper. Inscore was awarded the Silver Star posthumously.

By 4:30 p.m., the Marines had overrun the last NVA positions. This turned out to be a deadly affray, especially for Lima Company. It counted 19 KIA, 46% of the total. M and Headquarters & Service companies each had eight men killed; I Company, four. The 1st Shore Party Battalion counted two dead, including a Navy corpsman. Of the 41 KIA, 32 (78%) were lost to gunfire and nine to shrapnel. NVA soldiers executed two of the former. Some 82 Marines were wounded. ✪

LZ Eagle was located south of Route 534 in the Que Son Valley. Fighting there claimed the lives of 41 Marines and Navy corpsmen on May 26, 1967.

SILVER STAR

CPL. ROGER V. INSCORE
(POSTHUMOUS)

CPL. LOWELL R. LLOYD
(POSTHUMOUS)

CAPT. HAROLD D. PETTENGILL

CPL. BENJAMIN RICHARDSON
(POSTHUMOUS)

HM2 JOHN E. SCHON
(POSTHUMOUS)

THE TOLL

U.S. KIA:
41

U.S. WIA:
82

BY AL HEMINGWAY

VICIOUS AMBUSH AT VINH HUY

"I had a bad feeling about this one," recalled Lance Cpl. George Schneider of D Co., 1st Bn., 7th Marines. "Whenever they give you cold beer before going out, you know the stuff is going to hit the fan."

Schneider's words would prove prophetic. After arriving in South Vietnam, the III Marine Amphibious Force (MAF) kept a watchful eye on the fertile and populous Que Son Basin. Straddling Quang Nam and Quang Tin provinces, the area was one of the "keys to control the five northern provinces of Vietnam." The enemy realized the importance of the region as well. Without this rice-rich countryside, and the support of the people, the North Vietnamese Army (NVA) could not conduct combat operations in the coastal lowlands of I Corps.

BLOODY SHOOTING GALLERY

The morning of June 2 had D Co., 1st Bn., 5th Marines, and F Co., 2nd Bn., 5th Marines, moving toward Objective Foxtrot, near the village of Vinh Huy. By midday, F Company approached a 1,000-yard "horseshoe-shaped" rice paddy flanked by low hill masses called Hill A and Hill B, both of which were covered by thick underbrush. Due to the dense foliage, both companies had lost visual contact with each other.

"It was just too quiet, too serene," Pat Haley wrote in an article entitled "Ambush at Union II" in the November 1989 issue of *Marine Corps Gazette*. "You could almost smell the presence of the enemy."

When three platoons and the headquarters group were well within the massive paddy, the 3rd NVA Regiment sprung its trap. "All hell broke loose as the incoming NVA projectiles turned the rice paddy … into a bloody shooting gallery," Haley wrote.

> "All hell broke loose as the incoming NVA projectiles turned the rice paddy … into a bloody shooting gallery."
>
> —PAT HALEY

'YELLING FOR A CORPSMAN'

Enemy machine gun fire from hills A and B sliced into the infantrymen. Also, the NVA had dug in on the northern and eastern edges of the paddy, delivering deadly automatic weapons fire. Men dove for cover behind the smaller dikes to protect themselves. Luckily, the enemy's aim was slightly low. Moreover, their fields of fire did not include the 3rd Platoon, located in the rear of the column.

Three battalions of the 5th Marines lived up to their fighting reputation on June 2-3, 1967. Two companies in particular paid a severe price.

JUNE 1967

Leathernecks of F Co., 2nd Bn., 5th Marines, bolt from a helicopter during *Operation Union II* on May 29, 1967. The 2nd Battalion lost 33 KIA—44% of the total—over the two-day battle.

NATIONAL ARCHIVES #127-N-A372953

MEDAL OF HONOR

CAPT. JAMES A. GRAHAM
(POSTHUMOUS)

Low on ammunition, Graham said in his last radio transmission that he was being assaulted by 25 NVA soldiers. He was killed while attempting to repulse the attackers.

NAVY CROSS

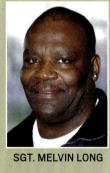

SGT. MELVIN LONG

GUNNERY SGT. JOHN S. GREEN

CPL. LLOYD WOODS

The 1st and 2nd platoons, however, were being cut to pieces. Several rocket-propelled grenade (RPG) rounds slammed into one area, lifting a sergeant "straight up in the air." The concussion of the blast rendered him speechless and deaf.

"The 2nd Platoon radioman was hit through his helmet and a chunk was missing from the top of his head," Cpl. Tom Searfoss recalled. "A gunner was firing—I don't recall his name. Someone yelled and I looked, and the lower part of his jaw was missing."

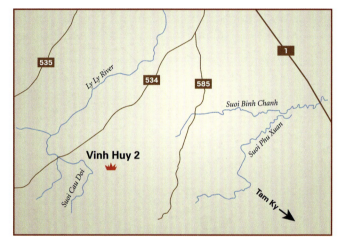

Vinh Huy was located in the Nui Loc Son Basin five miles southeast of Que Son in Quang Tri province.

Remembered Lance Cpl. R. Dean Johnson: "Our ammo man for our M-60 machine gun team was hit in the shoulder. I don't know how long we were pinned down—it seemed like forever. I had run out of water, and I drank a little brown rice paddy water to wet my mouth. Everyone was yelling for a corpsman."

INCREDIBLE HEROISM

Capt. James A. Graham, F Company commander, was everywhere on the battlefield, directing his unit's defenses. He took charge of his hastily organized headquarters group. It attacked straight through 2nd Platoon's position to eliminate several NVA machine gun nests.

Silencing one of the guns, the beleaguered Leathernecks were able to move some of their wounded to a safer area in the paddy. Although wounded twice by this time, Graham refused to leave, ordering everyone to the rear while he remained with a wounded Marine.

Low on ammunition, Graham said in his last radio transmission that he was being assaulted by 25 NVA soldiers. He was killed while attempting to repulse the attackers. He received a posthumous Medal of Honor.

"We felt Graham was the best possible commander," said Cpl. Brent MacKinnon, Graham's radio operator. "He gave his all in the face of certain death."

Meanwhile, Sgt. Melvin Long and his squad moved against Hill A. Long successfully maneuvered his men atop the rise and poured fire into enemy automatic-weapon emplacements.

"It was a beautiful sight to behold," Haley wrote. "Long was wounded during his exposure, but was really psyched up. He was on a roll; ignoring his wounds, he continued firing his weapon, inserting new magazines two or three times. He was like a wind-whipped flame, unquenchable." Long would receive the Navy Cross.

An unsung hero of the day was the company's Kit Carson Scout (an enemy soldier who defected) named Kinh. He personally killed between 25 and 30 NVA hiding in spider holes, which were covered by straw mats.

Meanwhile, D Co., 1st Bn., 5th Marines, also was in the thick of things. "Pinned down in the paddies," Sgt. Chuck Jenkins related, "we were taking heavy casualties. From my company alone there were 18 KIA and 23 WIA."

A Marine from K Co., 3rd Bn., 5th Marines, lends a helping hand to a fellow Leatherneck during *Operation Union II*. The 3rd Battalion lost 13 KIA in the fighting around Vinh Huy.

HEART-BREAKING CASUALTIES

D Co., 1st Bn., 7th Marines, began to arrive by late afternoon as reinforcements. "I crossed a board over a small stream," Lance Cpl. Schneider said. "We were in a cemetery when 82mm mortars started dropping in on us. They [NVA] had trenches all over the place. Our mortarman, Wallace Leonard, was great. He kept moving around and lobbing those 60mm rounds right on top of them. He was something to see." The 7th's Delta Company was fortunate in suffering only one KIA.

After additional U.S. air support and ground troops arrived, the NVA broke off contact. A temporary truce was called the next day. "For the rest of June 3," Edward F. Murphy wrote in *Semper Fi*, "in one of the most bizarre incidents of the war, the two foes worked side by side as they searched the tall grass for the bodies of their fallen comrades." Quickly reorganizing, the NVA retrieved their casualties and escaped.

The Leathernecks suffered 75 killed and 139 wounded during the struggle in the Vinh Huy complex. June 2 claimed 40 Marine lives; June 3, 35. The deaths were overwhelmingly (97%) the result of gunfire. Of the three 5th Marines' battalions, the 2nd counted 33 KIA, the 1st had 25 and the 3rd lost 13 KIA. Foxtrot Company of the 2nd accounted for at least 25 of the men and 32 if those attached from H&S Company are included (two Navy corpsmen among them). Delta Company in the 1st Battalion had the second greatest company loss with 18 KIA.

Besides Graham's Medal of Honor, three Navy Crosses were awarded to members of F Company—Gunnery Sgt. John Green, Sgt. Melvin Long and Cpl. Lloyd Woods. Six posthumous Silver Stars were awarded to Marines and a Navy corpsman. The 5th Marines had lived up to the highest traditions of the Corps. ✪

THE TOLL

U.S. KIA:
75

U.S. WIA:
139

BY RICHARD K. KOLB

XOM BO II TESTS THE LIMITS OF ENDURANCE

This turned out to be far more than a typical "walk in the sun." About 500 GIs made a grueling march to a landing zone (LZ) and in one afternoon sustained 37% casualties. It would be a day few would or could ever forget.

Operation Billings, undertaken in about the last two weeks of June 1967, was planned as a spoiling attack, a preemptive assault. The objective was to search for and destroy the 271st Viet Cong (VC) Regiment of the 9th VC Division, a familiar foe in War Zone D, III Corps.

But the enemy knew the Americans were coming, so they arranged an unpleasant welcome. At least four companies of the 1st and 2nd battalions of the 271st were well prepared. Each company was equipped with three 60mm mortars and a heavy Chinese machine gun. The 2nd Battalion had 30 to 50 North Vietnamese regulars assigned to it.

The communists waited eagerly near the village of Xom Bo, located 10 miles north of Phuoc Vinh in Phuoc Long province. Their ambush site was a 15-acre, oval-shaped clearing in the jungle. Surrounded by triple-canopy forest made up of tall trees, thick bamboo and elephant grass, visibility was limited to 50 to 66 feet. Clusters of bamboo and anthills ultimately provided the primary means of concealment.

GIs called the clearing LZ X-Ray. On June 17, grunts of the 1st Infantry Division's 3rd Brigade tripped the trap. They had marched about two miles north from LZ Rufe. A and B companies, as well as the Recon Platoon, of the 1st Bn., 16th Inf. (the "Rangers") and A and B companies of the 2nd Bn., 28th Inf. ("Black Lions"), eventually entered the killing zone. Fortunately, they could count on quick-response fire support from the 2nd Bn., 33rd Arty. (105mm howitzers) and other artillery.

'GOD HELP US, THERE ARE HUNDREDS OF THEM'

"We moved into an area where there was a clearing," recalled James Mauchline, then a private in the Headquarters Company's Security Squad for the 1st Bn., 16th Inf. "We just started to dig inside the tree line and got ambushed." That was about 1 p.m.

Greg Murry was with A Co., 1st Bn., 16th Inf. A weapons squad leader in 2nd Platoon, he was on the northeast portion of the perimeter. "Alpha Company led

Men of A Co., 1st Bn., 16th Inf., deploy in the northern sector of LZ X-Ray on June 17, 1967. Xom Bo II, the largest battle of *Operation Billings,* was fought by the 1st Bn. 16th Inf., and the 2nd Bn., 28th Inf.

Four rifle companies of the "Big Red One" got more than they bargained for mostly in one crowded hour of combat at LZ X–Ray on June 17, 1967.

JUNE 1967

U.S. ARMY PHOTO COURTESY FIRST DIVISION MUSEUM AT CANTIGNY

> ## "Squad leader Sgt. Frank Romo and his men got cut off. I'll never forget his name and always remember his last words, 'God help us; there are hundreds of them!' Then the radio went silent." —SPEC. 4 FRANK J. LIMIERO, 3RD PLT., A CO., 1ST BN.

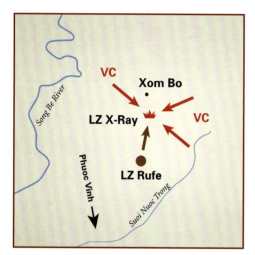

Combat took place at LZ X-Ray near the village of Xom Bo, 10 miles north of Phuoc Vinh in Phuoc Long province. An engagement had taken place in the same location earlier in June 1967. Hence the name Battle of Xom Bo II. GIs marched some two grueling miles from LZ Rufe to reach the landing zone.

the way in securing LZ X-Ray," he said. "We arrived at the north end of the LZ after a four-hour march. We had walked in but the VC were expecting to ambush us when we flew in by helicopter. When a resupply helicopter approached, the VC ran forward into groups of us and the battle began."

Two groups of 60 to 70 VC slammed against 3rd Plt., A Co., 1st Bn., 16th Inf. Reportedly, they used tear gas during the assault. Spec. 4 Frank J. Limiero, a radio-telephone operator (RTO) with Alpha Company's 3rd Platoon, remembered that day vividly.

"After an all-morning, exhausting march, we prepared our defensive position, which the enemy probed. Then they began a ground assault. Squad leader Sgt. Frank Romo and his men got cut off. I'll never forget his name and always remember his last words, 'God help us; there are hundreds of them!' Then the radio went silent."

Limiero played a pivotal part in the battle. Taking charge when others became incapacitated, he exposed himself to heavy fire and assured his fellow soldiers were supplied with ammo. Limiero "moved forward of his defensive line to a position from which he called for and adjusted artillery fire with devastating accuracy upon the enemy until the insurgents were forced to withdraw." So reads his Silver Star citation. Then he helped evacuate casualties.

Meanwhile, B Co., 2nd Bn., 28th Inf., came under intense fire. One of its positions was overrun and the bodies of dead Americans were used as shields. "The VC had two .50-caliber machine guns ready for us, so they would have us in a crossfire," recalled Don Koch of Bravo Company.

Undeterred by the odds, Pfc. Ben Walker assumed control of his squad in the 1st Platoon of B Company, moving it into heavy contact with the enemy. An RTO, he directed fire onto the two VC who had taken over a U.S. position. Exposing himself to communist fire, he adjusted mortar fire to drive off the VC. He was awarded the Silver Star.

A second assault hit the 16th's A Company at 1:30. VC got to within 50 feet of the 2nd and 3rd Platoon lines. Pfc. Daniel J. Phelps of the 3rd Platoon and another GI killed 10 of the enemy in two minutes. After the soldier with him was killed, Phelps manned his position alone through the entire battle. He, too, received the Silver Star.

"A storm of enemy fire came into our positions from very close range," Murry said. "It shredded the vegetation just above our heads. Most of the 1st Platoon in front of us was overrun and either killed or wounded. The 2nd Platoon formed a line with some of the survivors of the 1st. Our machine gunners never received the recognition they deserved for the brave fight they put up that day."

Elements of A Co., 2nd Bn., 28th Inf., entered LZ X-Ray at 12:15 p.m. on June 17, and moved north along the positions held by B Company. Thirty minutes later, the Battle of Xom Bo II started.

SILVER STAR

SPEC. 4
FRANK J. LIMIERO

LT.
DOUGLAS A. LOGAN

PFC.
DANIEL J. PHELPS

PFC.
JOHN J. RIECK, JR.

PFC. BEN WALKER

At the same time, the Recon Platoon, on the southeast part of the perimeter, was attacked along a 130-foot front. Its M-60 machine gun position was quickly overrun. Everyone at the command post was killed, yet Recon waged an epic struggle. But it was probably over in 15 minutes. Recon Platoon leader Lt. Douglas A. Logan radioed the commander of the 1st Battalion: "We're stacking them like cordwood," he said. By then, they had killed 30 VC.

Logan's bravery was rewarded with a Silver Star. "I was at the brigade aid station the day he died and have thought of him many times since our days in Vietnam," remembered James C. Hardin, then the executive officer of C Company (it was not in the battle). "Doug was an excellent leader. He knew and took care of his men. Moreover, he had the quiet courage to always be out front and to lead by example."

"Most of the 1st Platoon in front of us was overrun and either killed or wounded. The 2nd Platoon formed a line with some of the survivors of the 1st."

—GREG MURRY, WEAPONS SQUAD LEADER, A CO., 1ST BN., 16TH INF.

CARNAGE CAUSED BY ARTILLERY

Virtually all veterans of the battle agree that artillery saved them by thwarting the second assault, which ended 15 minutes after it started. The 33rd Artillery fired 8,250 rounds in support of the beleaguered infantrymen.

A medic from the 1st Bn., 16th Inf., scans the sky for a medevac helicopter to evacuate a wounded GI from LZ X-Ray on June 17, 1967.

Pfc. Douglas Wallin was among the nine members of the Recon Platoon killed in the epic defense of their sector of the LZ X-Ray perimeter. Wallin died of his wounds more than two months after the battle.

Capt. George E. Creighton, Jr., author of the after-action report, wrote: "The U.S. artillery barrage was so close to the perimeter that occasional pieces of shrapnel reached the friendly positions through the trees. Still hot after filtering through the umbrella of bamboo, the shrapnel sizzled on the men's wet clothes. It was largely a result of this massive, close-in artillery support that the VC were unable to reach the U.S. positions."

Tactical air strikes, 43 in all, also had a decisive role. Indeed, many of the men's most searing memories deal with these lethal sorties. Pfc. Fred Hill of B Co., 2nd Bn., 28th Inf., recalled, "The air support was so close on our left flank that the smoke completely enveloped us as we laid on the ground."

U.S. jets dropped napalm (a highly incendiary fluid) on the VC. "We could feel the tremendous heat as a flaming fireball landed on positions that hid numerous VC," said Frank Limiero of A Co., 16th Inf. "Their screams lasted only seconds as they became engulfed in sticky flames. This slowed the VC advance. Whistles began to blow and they broke contact. But not before 15 minutes of mortaring.

"A thick, choking smoke lingered about two feet along the forest floor from the massive amounts of ordnance that had been fired. Equipment and bodies lay all over, where men had fought to the death on both sides. We survivors finally retreated farther behind the lines as new troops took our places."

Don Koch of Bravo Company (2-28) was struck with how the land was physically denuded: "In the morning after a long night, we went out to patrol the area where the airstrikes and artillery hit. It looked like a tornado went through the jungle. A person could stand and look all around. Nothing [vegetation] in that area was over five feet high. I had heard that the VC were sliding bodies over the bank into the river and putting some in bomb craters so we could not get a body count."

While the frontal assault stalled, VC automatic weapons fire and 60mm mortar rounds continued to harass the GIs. Ceasing for a period, a mortar barrage hit again at 3:30 p.m. and continued sporadically until 5 p.m. "We got the dead and wounded out and started digging in," Fred Hill recalled. "We were still taking fire at various points around the perimeter. It was starting to get dark. We got hit with mortars and a .50-caliber machine gun."

'COMBAT INEFFECTIVE'

Expectedly, many men could never forget the losses. Murry said, "About 43 men from the 2nd Platoon (A-1-16) walked into LZ X-Ray. I was one of eight who flew out unscathed." Fred Hill remembered, "The next day we were told that B Company (2-28) was combat ineffective because of the number of casualties sustained." Limiero remarked: "Of my company's (A-1-16) original 100 or so men, only seven walked away that day."

The casualties affected even the replacements who came after the battle. "After being decimated, the rest of 3rd Platoon (B-2-28) was re-staffed with brand-new replacements known as 'twinks.' I was one of them," John McCoy said. "I have extremely strong memories of the bloody web gear laying on the ground in front of the supply hooch."

The final tally was 37 KIA and 150 WIA. The 16th Infantry was hardest hit with 26 of the KIA (70% of the total): A Company, 15; Recon Platoon, nine; and B Company, two. The 28th Infantry had 11 KIA—10 in B Company with most from its 3rd Platoon and one in A Company. An additional two artillerymen died accidentally when a 175mm gun blew up at a supporting firebase near An Loc.

Casualties are transported from LZ X-Ray to a staging area for evacuation by helicopter.
Some 150 "Big Red One" grunts were wounded in the Battle of Xom Bo II on June 17, 1967.
Thirty-seven soldiers were killed in action.

Shrapnel wounds accounted for 22 (59%) of the dead and gunfire 15 (41%). Manpower
sources for the Army's combat arms by mid-1967 had largely switched from the war's earlier
volunteers. Draftees among the KIAs numbered 30, or 81% of the total dead.

"We had lived through a nightmarish plunge into a bloody and masochistic battle that tested
us all," wrote David Hearne, author of *June 17, 1967: Battle of Xom Bo II*. "We had survived the
harshest conditions and the grueling intensity of pitiless violence." Yet the end result was less
than desired, found Hearne, who was an artillery forward observer from B Btry., 2nd Bn., 33rd
Arty, assigned to the Black Lions. "Xom Bo II could be likened to a couple of pugilists beating
one another up so badly that they both end up in the intensive care ward. At Xom Bo II, there
were no real winners, just a bunch of dead and wounded on both sides." ✪

THE TOLL

U.S. KIA:
37

U.S. WIA:
150

BY SHANNON HANSON

RIVERINE WARFARE ON THE RACH NUI

AP PHOTO

In early 1967, the Army's 2nd Brigade, 9th Infantry Division, joined forces with the Navy's River Assault Flotilla One to form the Mobile Riverine Force (MRF), a joint force in which the Navy provided the mobility, and the Army provided the ground troops. It operated in the Mekong Delta, and was about to enter a swampy no-man's land ideal for the communists.

The MRF's first major operation, code-named *Operation Concordia I*, was launched June 19, 1967. Its objective was to capture a large enemy redoubt that provided local forces with rest and training camps in the Can Giuoc district, 17 miles south of Saigon, and 5.6 miles northeast of Can Duoc village in Long An province.

That morning, the 2nd Brigade's 4th Bn., 47th Inf. Regt., landed north and east of the objective, while two companies of the 3rd Bn., 47th Inf., landed north and west. Both battalions were to sweep the northern area, then assemble and move south together. During the troop movements, a call came in that the Viet Cong's (VC) 5th Nha Be Battalion had been sighted in the southeast section of the redoubt. C Co., 4th Bn., and C Co., 3rd Bn., secured the site, but found no VC.

The final phase of the operation had A Co., 4th Bn., linking up with C Co., 4th Bn., several miles to the south. Instead of hacking through the vegetation along the banks of the Rach Nui River, A Company chose to wade across the rice paddies. Several hours of trudging through 10-inch deep water and thick mud wore on the soldiers.

Sam Castellano, a radio-telephone operator with Alpha, recalls vividly what unfolded. "We were crossing a dry rice paddy just before noon when we got the call to hit the deck," he said. "We were in no way bunched up; we were spread out so far that we covered several rice paddies."

Unbeknownst to the soldiers, VC were hidden in well-camouflaged bunkers and spider holes in the area. They had organized an L-shaped ambush within the tree line of spiny green mangrove palms. A Company neared the cluster of thatched huts that sat at the elbow of the L around noon, and the VC opened up, catching the soldiers in a vicious crossfire near the hamlet of Ap Bac.

"Just before noon, as we walked across the rice paddies, all hell broke loose. We had walked into an L-shaped ambush, and our guys were falling fast," said Jim Henke, a

As one member of the 9th Infantry Division fires his M-16, another tries to clear his jammed weapon during a battle near Dong Tam on May 3, 1967. Only weeks later in June, elements of the division got baptized in the art of riverine combat.

June 19, 1967, was seared in the memories of men from the 4th Battalion of the 47th Infantry like no other date. The Battle of Ap Bac in the watery graveyard of the Mekong Delta was among the 9th Division's deadliest.

JUNE 1967

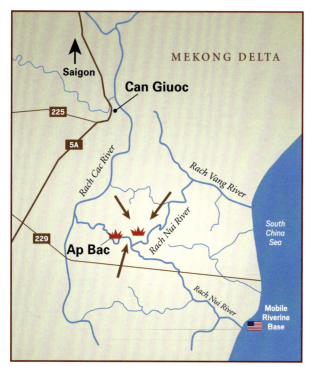

MEKONG DELTA

Saigon

Can Giuoc

Rach Cac River

Rach Vang River

Rach Nui River

Ap Bac

Rach Nui River

South China Sea

Mobile Riverine Base

Fierce combat took place on June 19, 1967, about a mile east of the village of Ap Bac on the north bank of Rach Nui Creek. It turned out to be an aquatic deathtrap for the 4th Bn., 47th Inf., 9th Div.

member of Alpha Company. "To watch this ate at you because you could not get to them."

'NOWHERE TO GO'

Chaplain Lt. Raymond "Padre" Johnson, watching the advancing GIs from the medical aid boat, saw the ambush unfold: "Suddenly, the VC opened up from an L-shaped tree line with machine guns and recoilless rifles—unbelievably accurate fire … just too unreal to grasp. I had had first-hand experience with the fury of action, but nothing like this."

In his book, *Brown Water, Black Berets,* Lt. Cmdr. Thomas J. Cutler wrote: "In horror he [Johnson] saw men thrown down before him, lacerated by enemy fire. Falling bullets and bodies turned the usually calm pools of paddy water into miniature storm-wracked seas."

Pfc. Frederick Haag recalled, "We had nowhere to go. We just dove into the water." The soldiers tried to stay down, but they had to keep their heads above water to breathe. Snipers began picking them off, one-by-one.

Conditions continued to worsen: Soon the tide came in, immersing the men in neck-deep water. Casualties quickly mounted. "I had approximately 50 men wounded," A Company commander Capt. Robert L. Reeves said. "Some of them died almost instantly."

When reinforcements arrived, B Company came up behind A Company to evacuate the wounded. Medical evacuation helicopters made valiant rescue efforts, losing four choppers shot down by nightfall. "I was pinned down in the mud for four hours until we were able to get back to the waterway after dark," recalled Sgt. Jerry Mathesis of the 4th's B Company. In his diary of June 20, he recorded: "We started to sweep the open rice paddy and found all kinds of dead bodies from A Company out there."

The MRF boats maneuvered in to block enemy escape routes. They unleashed 20mm and 40mm cannon fire, as well as .30-caliber and .50-caliber rounds into VC positions. Hand-held weapons were fired from all quarters, aircraft dropped ordnance and Army artillery pounded relentlessly.

Airstrikes, helicopter gunships and artillery unleashed immense firepower. "It was so close that the bombs just lifted us off our stomachs, and the shrapnel from the artillery fell on us," said Capt. Herbert Lind, CO of the 4th's Charlie Company. "I got hit several times but it had lost its 'steam' each time."

Men of C Company attacked mid-afternoon, but were forced to back off. They joined a two-company attack when the rest of the 4th Battalion arrived, but failed. Bill Reynolds, who was with the 2nd Platoon of the 4th Battalion's C Company, had an amazing close call. "I was firing my M-79 grenade launcher toward a tree line when a bullet blasted right through my barrel, narrowly missing me," he said.

Clarence Shires led 1st Platoon of the 4th's Charlie Company and witnessed a heart-wrenching scene. "Our hearts dropped as we looked out across an open area and saw the dead of A Company all over the place," he wrote in a letter to his parents three days after the battle. "Eighty percent of the company was dead or wounded." After nightfall, they attacked a third time, penetrating the complex, but had to pull back once again.

Chaplain Johnson watched an already wounded soldier get hit again by enemy fire. He ran out onto the paddy to bring the man to safety. "Padre, they're bleeding to death," the young man panted. "Medics are all dead." So Johnson and two others grabbed stretchers and went out to bring the wounded men back to the medical aid boat.

Indeed, a tremendous toll was taken on the medics. "Our medics ran from one wounded soldier to the next," Henke remembered, "exposing themselves until they were hit."

Later, after additional rescue parties were operating, Johnson tended to GIs on the paddy. Twice, the men he was helping were hit by fire.

MONITORS SAVE THE DAY

The only thing that prevented a complete disaster was the arrival of converted WWII landing ships the GIs called "monitors" (after the Civil War vessel). Then described by *Time* as gunboats "that can slither along like water moccasins in shallow inlets and stand up to direct hits from recoilless rifles," they came in behind the VC position, using 40mm cannon and 81mm mortars to chop the camouflaging trees down and expose the enemy.

"The monitors came right in on top of them," Reeves said. "Their firepower saved us. It was pretty bad." Navy Lt. Augustine Marana, aboard one of the ships, recalled, "We kept laying the fire in, and just chopped the trees down."

Though battle would last into the night, the monitors' arrival turned the tide for the Americans. By morning, the remaining VC were gone; an off-site Navy decision to pull back the gunboats before nightfall allowed them to escape across the Rach Nui River. Regardless, according to Cutler, "The Viet Cong were rendered ineffective in Long An Province for more than a year."

Chaplain Johnson, who was awarded the Silver Star for his actions, described June 19 as "the longest day of my life." He was not the only hero that day. Spec. 4 Noel T. West was posthumously awarded the Silver Star, as was medic Daniel Sandstedt, also KIA.

West, according to his citation, completely disregarded his own safety: "As bullets pounded the ground and filled the air around him, West dashed from casualty to casualty, rendering aid that in several cases proved to be of a life-saving nature. Hostile machine-gun fire sprayed the rice paddy, and West, while aiding yet another wounded soldier, was hit and mortally wounded. West gave his life in order that others might live."

John C. Schuh was point man for 2nd Sqd., A Co., 4th Bn., that day. "The VC cut us to pieces—I was hit three times," he said. "The water all around us was red with blood. After I became isolated, I eventually had to swim to a boat. Starting to go down, someone jumped in and saved my life. Someday I would like to thank whoever that was. June 19 will live in my memory forever."

The final GI toll: 47 KIA and 150 WIA. The vast majority (41 or 87%) of those killed were from the 4th Battalion. Two-thirds (27, including the six medics) of them belonged to Alpha Company. Charlie Company counted 11 dead; Bravo, three. B and C companies of the 3rd Battalion lost five men combined. Shrapnel wounds caused 72% of all fatalities. A full 85% of the KIA were draftees: the 9th Division was heavily manned through the Selective Service.

The ferocious battle along the Rach Nui is sometimes referred to as the Battle of Ap Bac. But as vet Lynn Hunt put it: "We just call it 19 June." ✪

Two Viet Cong prisoners are interrogated aboard a Riverine Monitor, or Assault Support Patrol Boat. Wielding 40mm and 80mm guns and 81mm direct fire mortars, the monitors came in behind the VC force. Their immense firepower turned the tide of the battle.

THE TOLL

U.S. KIA:
47

U.S. WIA:
150

BY TIM DYHOUSE

BATTLING ON THE SLOPES OF THE CENTRAL HIGHLANDS

little less than two miles separated the men from their objective that morning. That's all the distance the 137 grunts from A Co., 2nd Bn., 503rd Abn. Inf., 173rd Abn. Bde., had to cover on June 22, 1967, to reach a Special Forces camp in Vietnam's Central Highlands. They were looking forward to clean clothes, hot meals and the relatively easy guard duty they would be assigned.

But by the end of that fateful day, 76 men from Alpha Company would be KIA in one of the bloodiest firefights—dubbed the "Battle of the Slopes" by the Americans because of the steep terrain—any U.S. infantry unit waged in the war. It would also prove to be the scene of one of the most infamous atrocities committed by North Vietnamese Army (NVA) troops against Americans.

'BODIES CLEAVED LENGTHWISE'

The battalion's A and C companies had spent June 18-21 patrolling around Hill 1338, just south of the Special Forces camp at Dak To, which had been hit by a mortar attack from the mountaintop a few days earlier. Up until June 22, their search-and-destroy mission had been fairly uneventful.

"We moved through the hills of Dak To, not keeping track of time," recalled Spec. 4 John L. Leppelman of C Company. "It was an endless search for Charlie and occasionally taking sniper fire with no head-on contact. These hills were actually mountains—steep, muddy and leech-infested. We were usually under triple canopy jungles, which made it appear dark and dreary."

During the mission, grunts from C Company found the bodies of two Green Berets who had been killed the week before just southwest of the Dak To camp. It was a particularly gruesome discovery.

"Their bodies had been cleaved lengthwise, cut wide open from groin to head," according to Edward F. Murphy in *Dak To: America's Sky Soldiers in South Vietnam's Central Highlands*. "Their insides were as clearly exposed as a cross-section drawing in an anatomy textbook. [Battalion surgeon Capt. Joseph X.] Grosso wondered just what kind of an enemy they were facing in the Central Highlands."

Soldiers of C Co., 2nd Bn., 503rd Abn. Inf., 173rd Abn. Bde., stand ready at a landing zone to be airlifted as helicopters approach in the distance on June 11, 1967. Eleven days later, they would be sent in as relief for A Company, which was mauled in the Battle of the Slopes near Dak To.

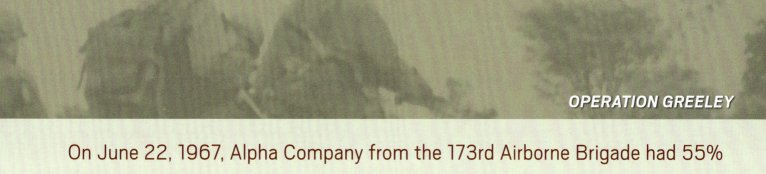

On June 22, 1967, Alpha Company from the 173rd Airborne Brigade had 55% of its men killed in a matter of minutes near Dak To. Most of the KIAs occurred when North Vietnamese Army troops summarily executed 43 wounded GIs.

JUNE 1967

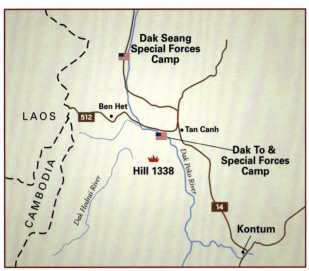

The slopes of Hill 1338, 4.3 miles southwest of Dak To, were covered with the blood of 76 GIs on June 22, 1967.

DISTINGUISHED SERVICE CROSS

SGT. 1ST CLASS ROBERT R. LITWIN
(POSTHUMOUS)

VIETNAM VETERANS MEMORIAL FUND/WALL OF FACES

'WE'RE BRACING FOR AN ALL-OUT ATTACK'

Early on June 22, 2nd Platoon led A Company off Hill 1338. The plan was to have the company's four platoons back at the base camp by 3 p.m. C Company, which had spent the night less than a mile up the hill from A Company, was to continue the search-and-destroy mission.

A Company's 3rd Platoon, followed by the Weapons and 1st platoons, fell in behind 2nd Platoon. At 6:58 a.m., the first shots rang out when the lead squad ran into what was later determined to be the flank of the 6th NVA Battalion, 24th NVA Regiment, an elite, 800-strong unit.

Third Platoon hurried to help the 2nd, and the two units quickly formed a V-shaped perimeter in a small clearing down the steep, narrow jungle path. At 8:10 a.m., the NVA launched its first of three frontal attacks on the paratroopers.

Commanders at Dak To were close enough to hear AK-47 and M-16 fire. But because of the dense jungle and mountainous terrain, they could see nothing, even from helicopters above the battle site. When A Company commander Capt. David H. Milton radioed the enemy contact to Dak To, battalion commander Maj. H. Glenn Watson told him to "develop the fight and keep us informed," as he called in artillery from 3rd Bn., 319th Arty, to help the pinned-down platoons.

The artillery fire was largely ineffective for two reasons: Many of the shells exploded in the tops of the huge trees, and the NVA knew that the closer they hugged the Americans' perimeter the safer they were, as the shells that did penetrate the jungle fell harmlessly behind them.

Then-173rd commander Brig. Gen. John R. Deane, Jr., called in air strikes, pummeling the NVA. Huey gunships arrived for close-in support. Still, the NVA prepared for a second assault.

"Six, we're bracing for an all-out attack," radioed 1st Lt. Donald R. Judd, 2nd Platoon's leader, back up the hill to Milton. "We're laid out well. About a hundred gooks are getting ready to hit us." (Judd received a posthumous Silver Star for saving two men while severely wounded and leading his men until killed.)

The Americans repulsed the attack, but still the NVA had surrounded 2nd and 3rd platoons. Milton ordered 1st Platoon to help, but it couldn't reach the scene of battle. C Company was ordered to abandon its mission and assist.

Before long, both 2nd and 3rd platoons' leaders were dead, and all platoon sergeants were wounded. Soon after, Milton permanently lost radio contact with his forward elements.

When Sgt. 1st Class Robert Litwin saw his platoon leader killed, he immediately took charge. Wounded an incredible four times in saving platoon members, he was hit yet again while covering their withdrawal. The fifth wound claimed his life. Litwin was awarded a posthumous Distinguished Service Cross.

'SMELL OF DEATH HUNG HEAVILY'

At the first sounds of battle, A Company's senior medic, Spec. 5 Richard E. Patterson, made his way toward the firefight. By the time Milton ordered survivors back up the hill to his command post, Patterson had been shot in the hand, and an enemy grenade had shattered his ankle and torn his Achilles' tendon.

"Finally, one of the paratroopers threw Patterson over his shoulder and started uphill," according to Murphy. "Behind him, Patterson could hear the wounded screaming for mercy as the NVA walked among them, executing those paratroopers still alive."

Only three members of A Company's most forward platoons survived the slaughter. One was a man Patterson had seen changing a red-hot M-60 barrel with his bare hands. Another had been shot three times in the back. And another had his ring finger cut off by a machete-wielding NVA while he played dead.

That night at Dak To, A Company formed up for a headcount. "There was one man left to each of the three squads in my platoon," recalled Pfc. Clarence Johnson of 1st Squad, 2nd Platoon, which had first encountered the NVA that morning. "There were 33 men standing in formation June 22, 1967."

The next day, C Company policed the battlefield. William Parks was 1st sergeant of Charlie Company. "All my unit could find was dead men from A Company," he said.

Murphy wrote: "No one could comprehend the horrible scene. Dozens upon dozens of American bodies lay sprawled in death's grotesque grip. A heavy veil of black flies swarmed over the swollen corpses and the thick pools of blood and gore. The smell of death hung so heavily in the jungle that many of Charlie's paratroopers were unable to control their stomachs. They staggered behind trees to vomit."

It was clear from exit wounds in their faces that many of the men had been executed, and a large number of the bodies had been mutilated.

NATIONAL ARCHIVES PHOTO #III-SC-64I3I3

Members of C Co., 2nd Bn., 503rd Abn. Inf., 173rd Abn. Bde., charge from their UH-1D helicopter toward a treeline during a heliborne assault on June 11, 1967. Just 11 days later, these troops would come upon the gruesome fate of A Company.

'NO WORDS TO DESCRIBE THE BRAVERY'

The final toll for Alpha Company (137 men): 76 KIA; 23 WIA. Of the dead, 43 suffered close-range head wounds. Overall, gunfire killed 48 men (63% of the total); shrapnel caused 28 of the deaths. Volunteers made up 80% of the KIA tally; draftee dead numbered 15. Being an airborne unit, the 173rd was largely composed of volunteers.

Paratroopers estimated the number of NVA killed between 50 and 75, based on remains they pulled from shallow graves.

One of the few survivors of A Company's forward platoons summed up the hellacious fight he and his fellow "Sky Soldiers" faced that day. "We were outnumbered, outgunned and faced a near solid wall of small-arms fire by the NVA regiment," Pfc. Clarence Johnson remembered. "We fought and remained engaged until there was no position left to defend. In reality, the only defensible position was behind the barrel of the weapons we held in our hands. And on that day, it wasn't enough. There are no words to describe the bravery of the men fighting this battle." ✪

THE TOLL

U.S. KIA:
76

U.S. WIA:
23

BY AL HEMINGWAY

MAYHEM IN THE 'MARKETPLACE'

Located just two miles from Vietnam's Demilitarized Zone (DMZ), Con Thien was a small remote firebase. To keep the pressure off Con Thien, the Marines initiated *Operation Buffalo* in the summer of 1967. Two companies of infantry intended to establish forward operating bases north of the Trace—a 660-yard swath of land situated between Con Thien and Gio Linh. Then they would sweep the area separating the bases.

Oppressive heat and humidity greeted the Leathernecks on the morning of July 2, 1967. A Co., 1st Bn., 9th Marines, headed north, while the battalion's B Company proceeded southeast. Everything went smoothly until B Company reached an area called the "Marketplace"—a road junction near the place indicated on Marine maps as "Market"—and started receiving enemy machine gun fire.

CHAOS REIGNS

As the riflemen assaulted, they soon discovered they had encountered two battalions from the North Vietnamese Army's (NVA) elite 90th Regt., 324B Div. The communists had constructed fighting holes and were using the 7-foot-high elephant grass and dense thickets of bamboo to their advantage.

The outnumbered Marines from 3rd Platoon had become disoriented in the attack and were fighting in small isolated pockets. NVA soldiers wearing Marine flak jackets and helmets were hollering in English, further confusing the infantrymen. Things got even worse. As the Marines' AR-15 rifles jammed, the enemy overran them.

Capt. Sterling K. Coates, B Company commander, tried to maneuver his 2nd Platoon to outflank the enemy. The intense automatic weapons fire, however, prevented this. He then instructed two squads from 1st and 2nd platoons to advance against a tree line.

Author James P. Coan described the horrific scene in his book *Con Thien: The Hill of Angels:* "Snipers up in trees fired down on the pinned-down Marines, picking off anyone with a radio or anyone who made a hand signal. The survivors tried to withdraw, but most were shot down. Few made it back alive. Several NVA ran across the road between 2nd and 3rd platoons, taking the Marines under fire from both sides of the road. To make matters worse, mortars and artillery began crashing down,

Members of K Co., 3rd Bn., 9th Marines, recovered the bodies of Leathernecks from B Co., 1st Bn., 9th Marines, who were killed two days earlier on July 2, 1967.

Route 561, two miles northeast of Con Thien, became a death trap for the men of the 1st Bn., 9th Marines—especially Bravo Company— on July 2, 1967. Yet "The Walking Dead" persevered.

JULY 1967

NATIONAL ARCHIVES #127-N-A188874

Members of K Co., 3rd Bn., 9th Marines, move behind one of their attached tanks from the 3rd Tank Battalion as it skirts a large bomb crater during *Operation Buffalo.* This tank-infantry combination, aided by artillery and air strikes, destroyed an NVA defensive position near Con Thien on July 4, 1967.

further cutting off the 3rd Platoon and the command group from 2nd and 3rd platoons. Bravo was getting murdered."

Meanwhile, Capt. Albert C. Slater, leader of A Company, was trying desperately to link up with Bravo Company. Mortars started falling amongst his men, and he told the 3rd Platoon to remain behind and form a perimeter to protect the helicopters attempting to ferry the wounded to safety. After the main force departed, the NVA overran the 3rd Platoon. Casualties mounted.

"I held a wounded Navy corpsman and took the battle dressing off his web gear," Cpl. Tom Evans from Alpha Company said. "He was sliced by shrapnel so badly from head to foot I didn't recognize him. I couldn't figure out where to apply the bandage that would do any good. He began gurgling. I yelled 'Breathe, you bastard! Breathe!' Then he died. I'll never forget his eyes, pleading for help, but there was nothing I could do."

A few survivors managed to make their way back to the company.

The 1st Battalion of the 9th Marines was ambushed along Route 561 on July 2, 1967. It lost 90 men KIA.

'WE ARE BEING OVERRUN'

Back at the Marketplace, Bravo Company was making a last stand. The NVA had used flamethrowers to set the elephant grass and hedgerows ablaze. As the Leathernecks ran to escape the flames, waiting NVA snipers killed them. Those who chose not to run were burnt alive in the inferno.

Staff Sgt. Leon Burns, 1st Platoon commander, was everywhere on the battlefield. In his book *Operation Buffalo, USMC Fight For The DMZ,* author Keith William Nolan wrote: "The NVA [soldier] came over the embankment with bush hat, ammo vest and automatic weapon, and Staff Sgt. Burns stood up again from his cover. This time the shotgun barked with lethality. In fact, the 12-gauge blew away most of the man's head." For his outstanding leadership and

NAVY
CROSS

STAFF SGT.
LEON BURNS

heroism, Burns would be awarded the Navy Cross.

The company command group learned a relief force was on its way. The help, unfortunately, did not arrive in time for them. Capt. Warren O. Keneipp, the air liaison officer, uttered these last words on the radio: "I don't think I'll be talking to you again. We are being overrun."

Capt. Henry J.M. Radcliffe was leading a platoon-size force, plus four M-48 tanks from B Co., 3rd Tank Bn., to assist the beleaguered infantrymen. As the column raced toward the Marketplace, it came upon "dazed and wounded Marines struggling back."

Radcliffe's men fought off several attempts by NVA soldiers trying to outflank them. Helicopter gunships and C Company arrived to augment the small group as it pressed forward. As the unit proceeded, it encountered remnants of the 1st Platoon. Radcliffe asked the platoon leader, Burns, where the remainder of the company was. He answered: "Sir, this is the company, or what's left of it."

Lt. Gatlin Howell, former platoon commander with Bravo Company, was stunned at the carnage. He became "a man possessed," looking everywhere for any survivors of the ambush. Together with Cpl. Charles A. Thompson, Gatlin managed to save more than two-dozen wounded Marines.

"There were bodies all over the place, and the NVA artillery was killing us," Pfc. Bruce Horton of C Company recalled. "I saw a Marine propped up against a tree. His legs and arms were shattered. He looked just like a living skeleton."

SHOCKING TOLL

Every available truck was commandeered by the battalion executive officer, Maj. D. Curtis Danielson, to pick up the survivors as they trickled back to Con Thien.

As evening approached, Leathernecks from the 3rd Bn., 9th Marines, landed at the Marketplace to relieve the battered companies.

Marine casualties at day's end were shocking: 92 killed and 190 wounded. Bravo Company suffered an appalling 52 KIA—57% of all Americans killed in the ambush. Some of the 16 dead from H&S Company were attached to B Company, so Bravo's toll was actually higher. Only 27 men from B Company escaped physically unharmed.

The KIAs from H&S included eight Navy corpsmen, four radio operators and four men with other specialties. A Company lost 15 men and C Company, 4. Two artillery forward observers from D Btry., 2nd Bn., 12th Arty, along with a two-man crew from Marine Fighter Attack Squadron 542 shot down, also died in action.

Gunfire claimed 43 lives and shrapnel took another 38. The cause of death for the remainder was either not reported (four), an explosive device (four), perishing in the crash (two) or in one case, burns.

Nolan wrote in *Operation Buffalo* that the ambush on July 2, 1967, "was the worst single disaster to befall a Marine Corps rifle company during the entire Vietnam War."

There was no accurate body count of enemy dead, but the communists did not escape the ferocity of the artillery and air strikes. But as James Coan wrote: "Still, the battlefield belonged to the NVA at the end of the day, and by anyone's definition, that meant it was their victory." ✪

OPERATION BUFFALO

Despite its appalling start, *Operation Buffalo* was deemed a success when it ended on July 14, 1967. The enemy lost many men. The Marines sustained 159 dead and 345 wounded. Although short in duration, the large-scale Communist offensive was "considerably more vicious" than anything the Leathernecks had experienced thus far in northern I Corps.

The awful memory of the Marketplace battle would haunt the 1st Bn., 9th Marines. In the fall, the unit returned and conducted patrols in the area. There was still an eerie feeling in the air where so much death had occurred a few months earlier.

"It was like walking through a cemetery," Nolan wrote. "No one in the sweep stopped, no one said a word."

"I saw a Marine propped up against a tree. His legs and arms were shattered. He looked just like a living skeleton."

—PFC. BRUCE HORTON OF C COMPANY

THE TOLL

U.S. KIA:
92

U.S. WIA:
190

BY RICHARD K. KOLB

BRAVO COMPANY'S LAST STAND IN THE IA PNON VALLEY

"I think they are after us," Spec. 4 Charles Laing recorded in his diary entry of July 11. The radio-telephone operator (RTO)'s—a member of the Weapons Platoon of C Company operating alongside Bravo—fears were soon realized. Upon entering the Ia Drang Valley, the GIs became the hunted, with deadly consequences.

"In just an hour-and-a-half, elements of the 7th Battalion, 66th NVA Regiment, have all but destroyed Bravo Company. Third Platoon is wiped out," Roger Hill wrote in *Red Warriors*, a 2008 report on the battle. For the men of the company, this day would be seared in their memories for life.

What brought the "Red Warriors" (the nickname for the 1st Battalion, 12th Infantry) to this point was *Operation Francis Marion.* A typical search and destroy effort, it was designed to prevent the North Vietnamese Army (NVA) from infiltrating the Ia Drang River Valley. The specific mission of the 1st Battalion companies on July 12, 1967, was bomb damage assessment. Two B-52 bomb strikes had been made and higher ups wanted to know the results.

The dreaded Ia Drang is located in the Central Highlands of Pleiku province. When the clash of arms came it was 3½ miles east of the Cambodian border and about 8½ miles south of Duc Co. It actually occurred in the Ia Pnon River Valley. Bravo's battlefield was rolling hills covered by tall grass, thinly dispersed trees and some thickets of heavier forest. Rain and dense fog blanketed the wooded hills.

B and C companies of the 12th Infantry, 4th Division, took the field. Both were vastly understrength. C Company counted 84 men. B Company consisted of 68 men, with four medics from Headquarters Company; four engineers from 1st Plt., B Co., 4th Engineers; and a three-man forward observer team from B Btry., 4th Bn., 42nd Artillery, attached. B's 3rd Platoon, for example, had only 18 men.

The two companies were up against the 7th Bn., 66th NVA Regt., 1st NVA Div. That amounted to more than 1,000 regulars, fresh from their sanctuary in Cambodia.

'MY GOD, WE ARE SURROUNDED!'

Each company established a perimeter about two-thirds of a mile apart. C Company was moving when it spotted NVA about 8:30 a.m. C Company's 2nd Platoon patrol was soon surrounded. B Company sent a platoon to guide C's patrol to safety, but it was hit,

Members of B Co., 1st Bn., 12th Inf, 4th Inf. Div., stand by as a Huey lands. Bravo Company underwent an ordeal by fire on July 12, 1967, losing 34 KIA in the Central Highlands battle.

On July 12, 1967, in the Ia Drang Valley Hills, B Company of the 1st Bn., 12th Inf., 4th Inf. Div., was assaulted by a full North Vietnamese battalion. It proved to be the regiment's single deadliest engagement of the war.

JULY 1967

DISTINGUISHED SERVICE CROSS

2ND LT. GARY V. RASSER

1ST LT. FRED BRAGG
(POSTHUMOUS)

SPEC. 4 BYRON W. THOMPSON

too. At about 11 p.m., the NVA closed the trap around C's 2nd Platoon and B's 3rd Platoon. Both companies were then ordered to support their respective platoons. B came under heavy attack within the next 45 minutes.

1st Lt. Lister L. Sells was an artillery forward observer attached to C Company. He had 11 days left in Vietnam. "C and B companies were maybe 55 yards apart," he recalled. "At early daybreak, the jungle erupted into a firefight. I was simultaneously calling in artillery on our flank as it was apparent that we were in trouble. I heard someone say on the radio, 'My God, we are surrounded!' I heard 1st Lt. Fred Bragg directing artillery fire, but I had my job, doing the same to protect the brave men of Charlie Company.

"As the firefight raged, I heard the radio mike keyed one last time and for a moment the mike was open and I heard NVA chatter. The communication went dead. We knew B Company was in real trouble. We were pinned down also as I took over calling in artillery for both B and C companies."

At that time, B's command group was struck by mortars, killing the commanding officer. So 1st Lt. Fred Bragg, the FO from Battery B, took command. Though seriously wounded, he continued to direct artillery strikes on the NVA until a mortar round destroyed his only remaining radio. "Staying in the open, he poured round and after round of deadly fire into the advancing enemy force," reads his Distinguished Service Cross (DSC) citation. But Bragg was ultimately killed.

Pfc. LeRoy H. Charboneau was an RTO on B Battery's forward observer team. While securing another radio from a wounded GI, he was wounded. Then his second radio was destroyed. Isolated, he fired his rifle until the magazine was empty and then he resorted to using a .45 pistol, until mortally wounded, says his Silver Star citation. Nineteen rounds penetrated his lower extremities and a 20th his chest. A final round was found in his forehead. He died at Bragg's side.

By 11:40, all of B Company was pinned down. B's 3rd Platoon was quickly whittled down to a few men and was out of ammo. It made a virtual last stand. The company was without artillery support for 30 minutes.

Sgt. Rockwell G. Jamison, a squad leader in the company, stayed back to cover his men. "He was so close to the enemy that often he did not have time to reload his rifle, but instead had to drive them off in hand-to-hand combat," according to his Silver Star citation. Jamison led his men, distributed ammo and helped the wounded until mortally wounded.

Pfc. Gary L. Waguespack was an ammo bearer in a machine gun team. He also remained behind to provide cover, helping to throw back several NVA assaults. Sticking to his position until the bitter end, he was killed while attempting to move a machine gun in place to continue the fight. Waguespack received the Silver Star, too.

PLIGHT OF 2ND PLATOON

2nd Lt. Gary V. Rasser led Bravo's 2nd Platoon. "Things really started when 3rd Platoon became pinned down by 'Charlie' [short for Viet Cong, but these were NVA regulars] during a sweep," he told *The Ivy Leaf,* the 4th Infantry Division newspaper. "The rest of the company moved up on line to aid the platoon, but Charlie began mortaring us and throwing out heavy small-arms fire.

SILVER STAR

SGT. ROCKWELL G. JAMISON
(POSTHUMOUS)

PFC. LEROY H. CHARBONEAU
(POSTHUMOUS)

PFC. GARY L. WAGUESPACK
(POSTHUMOUS)

"There was a line of NVA in front of us, so we fought our way through that and reached what was left of the 2nd Platoon. We began to pull everyone back to the patrol base and discovered another line of Charlies."

Rasser elaborated to the Associated Press: "My three machine-gunners were killed in the first half hour by North Vietnamese who had us completely surrounded to within 50 yards. Seven of my men were dead. The other six were nowhere around. We decided to fight our way home. We just kept moving on and on. We lost all track of time and were deafened by all the shooting. But somehow we made it and managed to scramble back into the base we had started from five hours earlier."

A fellow platoon member, Pfc. Tom Garty, witnessed Rasser's courage: "The lieutenant went through four M-16s and one machine gun. When it seemed we had nowhere else to go he would be up and charging straight for Charlie. I don't know how we made it out alive. There were Charlies all over the place."

Rasser's leadership under fire did not go unnoticed. His DSC citation described how he fired until running out of ammo. Then he picked up an M-16 from a fallen soldier, then a grenade launcher and finally a machine gun. Though personally inflicting heavy casualties on the NVA, he was unable to stop the attack. So "he led his men in a fierce charge through the enemy lines to a safer position."

Garty was a 2nd Platoon RTO and wounded like so many others. "Where we were at, the ground was so rocky and hard we could not dig in the way you should at night," he recounted.

"My platoon was sent out to see how bad it was for the 3rd Platoon. When we were on a small hill, I think the only one with cover to hide in, we spotted a great number of NVA together. We were told not to fire on them. To this day, I don't understand why. When we went back with the rest of the company all hell broke loose.

"NVA were everywhere, even in the trees. They mortared the heck out of us and came at us in waves. We ran out of rounds and had to fight hand-to-hand with no air or artillery support. Things happened that day that I could never have imagined and still to this day can't talk about. You had to just lie on the ground and pray you had something in front of you for cover.

"When my radio and leg were hit with shrapnel, I had to change radios with a dead RTO. I was medevac'd to the 71st Evacuation Hospital in Pleiku."

Spec. 4 Mel Perttunen carried an M-79 grenade launcher and remembered "green tracers all over the place, B-40s screaming in, and mortars dropping everywhere. Bullets and shrapnel were hitting the rocks all the time. (I kept getting rock fragments out of my face for years afterward when I shaved.)." Tragically, on Jan. 14, 1968, Perttunen was in a truck when it hit a mine, and he lost both legs. He died at age 50 in 1997.

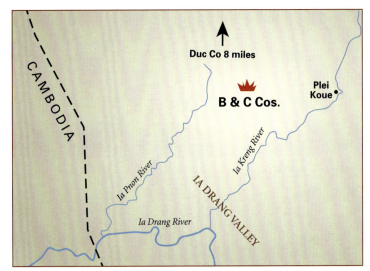

The "Red Warriors" fought one of their defining battles of the war in the Ia Pnon River Valley, about eight miles south of Duc Co.

Pfc. Tom Garty and a Montagnard woman are captured on film in the Central Highlands. The "Mountain People" were staunch U.S. allies, affectionately called "Yards" by GIs.

THREE OF B COMPANY'S KIAs

PHOTOS COURTESY RALPH E. PRICE

Pfc. Robert Echols

Spec. 4 Charles Mark Judge, Jr.

From left: Johnny West, John Hackett, Robert Strange (KIA) and Thudus Clayton.

Fighting was ferocious in every sector. Spec. 4 Byron Thompson, a squad leader, was on point for 2nd Platoon. Though wounded, he refused medical aid and continued fighting. Even more seriously wounded in a grenade explosion, he stayed in the fight. After running out of ammo, Thompson was rushed by three NVA. He "killed two of the attackers with his knife and the third in a furious hand-to-hand battle," reads his DSC citation.

"Before reaching safety, he killed 30 North Vietnamese soldiers with deadly rifle fire and close-in fighting." Overall, Thompson's actions helped enable B Company to withdraw to a secure position.

Spec. 4 Alberto Lopez-Rodriquez led a machine gun squad in 2nd Platoon. "B Company was short because of the scarcity of replacements," he said. "I think that the NVA commander had knowledge of that fact. The assault was rapid and devastating. We began to have casualties very quickly. The Chinese 82mm mortar projectiles were too much for our soldiers in an open field without overhead cover. All my squad members were KIA or WIA, including myself. I am thankful for the artillery covering our withdrawal, especially the low-flying helicopters that shot rockets into the NVA troops, stopping the attack."

Sgt. Lloyd Hahn was an FO with the 81mm mortar section of Weapons Platoon. "When the call came to move out, Weapons Platoon brought up the rear," he said. "As we got to the base of a small hill, mortar rounds began to land all around us. Ending up alone, I eventually made it back to our perimeter."

THE TOLL

U.S. KIA:
34

U.S. WIA:
42

POW:
7
(2 died of wounds)

NVA FADE BACK INTO CAMBODIA

Meanwhile, C Company rescued its isolated platoon and withdrew to its original defensive position around 12:30 p.m. When additional reinforcements arrived, the NVA broke contact and withdrew to their sanctuary in Cambodia. By 1 p.m. or so, the jungle was largely quiet.

C Company then went out to B's rescue. It reached it in time, shortly after 4 p.m., only to recover bodies. "Eventually, we got all the bodies gathered together and picked up," said Lt. Lewis Easterly, company executive officer. "We loaded 32 dead Americans on helicopters that afternoon for transport back to the battalion's fire support base. We didn't have body bags, so we just carried the bodies in ponchos and laid them out in two rows on either side of the landing pad."

B Company counted 25 KIA (plus two more who died of wounds while captive) and 37 WIA. Headquarters Company had four medics KIA; B Battery three forward observers.

ORDEAL OF THE POWs

BESIDES SUFFERING a severe fatality rate, Bravo Company initially counted seven POWs, all of whom were wounded when captured. Two members of 2nd Platoon—Pfc. James Van Bendegom and Spec. 4 James Schiele—died of their wounds shortly after capture. Bendegom perished at an NVA hospital in Cambodia. Schiele died on his way to an NVA field hospital and was buried along a trail. The remaining five GIs survived until released on March 5, 1973.

Sgt. Cordine McMurray, the 3rd's platoon sergeant who had only eight days left in-country, related: "We couldn't shoot our way out. They were everywhere. I got shot up and still have shrapnel in my leg. I got shot in the shoulder and face and I got a hand grenade in my right leg."

Pfc. Nathan Henry was the company RTO in Headquarters Platoon. He was knocked out by mortar fire and woke up to find his hands and feet bound. Two female NVA carried him away suspended from a pole. "A lot of the guys in my company were wounded," he said. They [NVA] tied them to a tree before they shot them. We didn't know if we were going to be killed or what."

Spec. 4 Martin Frank relived the close calls. "A grenade went off close to me and knocked me senseless just as the NVA came over the hill. I thought they'd interrogate and execute us, but they didn't. We crossed into Cambodia and were held in camp for about 11 or 12 months."

The POWs walked 48 days through Cambodia and Laos to get to Hanoi on Christmas Day 1969.

"We were moving in Russian or Chinese-made trucks when our Air Force dropped a couple of 500-pounders and almost got us," Frank said. "In North Vietnam, we moved four times before ending up at the 'Hanoi Hilton' [Hoa Lo Prison]. I was held for five years, seven

Cordine McMurray

James Van Bendegom

Stanley Newell

Nathan Henry

Martin S. Frank

James Schiele

Richard Perricone

months and 26 days."

Pfc. Stanley Newell, like his fellow POWs, was long haunted by his experiences. "Immediately following the battle, I can remember lying on the ground, face down listening to the North Vietnamese talking and moving among the dead and wounded American soldiers," he wrote in his memoirs. "Several times, I heard isolated shouts and single gunshots. They were shooting everyone and I'm next," he thought.

"Over the next 10 days, five more Americans joined me on the trail," Newell continued. "Two would die of their wounds before we reached the first permanent camp. No one ever imagined it would be almost six years before we would be released. Who ever thought the war would last that long."

Then-Pfc. Richard R. Perricone told the *New York Daily News* in 1998: "I got shot in the leg, had shrapnel in my arm, and I got knocked out by a hand grenade. The next thing I knew a guy was shaking me awake; I was already tied up."

At a reunion in 2007, Perricone graphically described the conditions of captivity: "The camp I lived in was 20 miles inside Cambodia. We were allowed to bathe about once a week or every 10 days. There were stocks the whole length of the bed. The stocks were two trunks about five inches in diameter. At night, we put our legs into the stocks."

When a group of the Americans tried to flee their captors, it cost them six months in stocks 24 hours a day. "We tried to escape from there Nov. 6, 1967, but failed and were recaptured," Perricone said. "After the escape attempt, our legs were in the stocks all the time. I spent a little over two years in the jungles of Cambodia. Then I moved to North Vietnam where I stayed until March 5, 1973, the day I was released."

Perricone spent 2,064 days in captivity, enduring physical beatings as well as psychological torment. "They showed us movies of anti-war protesters ... it hurt to see that," he said. "I lost 5½ years of my life ... But I don't regret going."

Besides 34 KIA, five men were held as POWs until the end of the war (see sidebar). C Company sustained five wounded.

Gunfire accounted for the vast majority (94%) of the killed. Some three-fourths of the dead were draftees, reflecting the Army's manpower pool at the time.

Lt. Lister Sells remembered: "When dawn broke and we could tell (we thought) the tremendous firepower of 105s, 8-inch howitzers, 155s and 175s had chased the NVA out of the area. I witnessed NVA brutality firsthand—men had been shot in the forehead at pointblank range and many had their bootlaces tied together." ✪

BY RICHARD K. KOLB

RUNNING THE GAUNTLET
IN THE 'DEAD MAN'S ZONE'

U.S. MARINE CORPS PHOTO #A191240

n military speak, it was called a spoiling attack, a tactical probe into enemy territory. To the Marines charged with the mission, it amounted to a running battle near Thon Cam Son, some three miles from Con Thien, lasting until dark.

This reconnaissance-in-force was part of *Operation Kingfisher,* which was intended to screen North Vietnamese Army (NVA) entry from the Demilitarized Zone (DMZ) into South Vietnam's Quang Tri province. The DMZ was the stomping ground of the NVA 324B and 325C divisions, among other enemy units. A regiment of one of these divisions, or perhaps an independent one, would have a nasty surprise awaiting the Marines.

A 6-mile-wide buffer zone from which both sides agreed to keep their military forces enveloped the 39-mile-long demarcation line. It ran roughly along the 17th parallel, forming the official boundary between North and South Vietnam. A portion of the line followed the course of the Ben Hai River. For the men who fought there, the DMZ became known simply as the "Dead Man's Zone."

For the jaunt into the forbidden zone, the Marines assembled an armored column built around the 2nd Bn., 9th Marines, 3rd Marine Div. The 2nd Battalion consisted of E, F, G, H and Headquarters & Service companies. A platoon of tanks from A Co., 3rd Tank Bn.; three ONTOS (a tracked vehicle armed with 106mm recoilless rifles) from C Co., 3rd Anti-Tank Bn.; three tracked engineer vehicles; and engineers from C Co., 3rd Engineer Bn.

HELL BENT INTO 'INDIAN COUNTRY'

Making no contact with the enemy on July 28, about 10 a.m. the next morning the column headed south from the Ben Hai River. Returning along Provincial Route 606, the order of the column was E Company, Command Group (CG) A, H&S Company, CG B and F, H and G companies.

At 11:15 a.m. on July 29, 1967, the NVA detonated a 250-lb. bomb buried in the road. When Marine engineers exploded a second bomb, the NVA opened fire from strongpoints along the road. Booby traps were strategically placed off the roadside. A torrent of fire engulfed the vehicles.

A Marine armored column, including tanks, moves toward the Ben Hai River in the DMZ on July 28, 1967, a day before the battle. The column contained companies or elements from five battalions of the 9th Marine Regiment.

When the 2nd Battalion, 9th Marines, entered the DMZ on July 29, 1967, it was ambushed by perhaps 1,000 Communist troops near Thon Cam Son, precipitating a battle all the way back to the border.

JULY 1967

PHOTO COURTESY PAT CORVAGLIA

"At a bend in the road, the NVA set off a 250-lb. bomb. Shrapnel from the bomb flew all around me, hitting Marines in front of and behind me. Mortared from the rear, we were being attacked from both flanks."

—LANCE CPL. PAT CORVAGLIA, 2ND SQD., 2ND PLT., E CO.

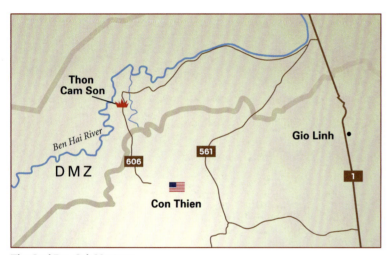

The 2nd Bn., 9th Marines, fought off a North Vietnamese Army regiment near Thon Cam Son in the Demilitarized Zone on July 29, 1967. The Ben Hai River formed a portion of the boundary between North and South Vietnam. Combat occurred about three miles northwest of Con Thien in Quang Tri province.

The NVA units "quickly fragmented the armored column into roughly company-sized segments," records the official Marine Corps history, *Fighting the North Vietnamese, 1967.* "Each isolated segment fought its own way through the gauntlet of fire." Enemy rocket-propelled grenades took a toll on all of the tracked vehicles.

"We had moved north along an old deserted dirt road with flank security on both sides, cutting our way through nasty brush," recalled 1st Lt. Don Bonsper, leader of 1st Platoon in E Company. "July 29 started chaotically. Tanks could not traverse this terrain. As a large force, we were sitting ducks—an enormous target of opportunity. So we returned south along the same road the battalion had used to go north.

"Moving out, Echo Company was the first. 2nd Platoon had the lead, and I was next with 1st Platoon. Within minutes, the enemy-command detonated a 105mm artillery round hanging from a tree. The explosion could be heard for miles. Then came the mortars, exploding all around us. That was just the beginning of an all-afternoon, bloody battle to fight our way back to Con Thien and Cam Lo."

Lance Cpl. Pat Corvaglia was at the very tip of the spear that day and vividly recalls the chain of events. "2nd Squad, 2nd Platoon, Echo Company, was designated the point unit to lead the whole battalion out," he said. "I was about the fifth or sixth man down the column. We also had two engineers with minesweepers up front sweeping for mines. Recon-by-fire drew the NVA out. Once that happened, they lost the element of surprise. But they had us in a perfect ambush so we had to start pushing south toward Con Thien to get the hell out of there.

"At a bend in the road, the NVA set off a 250-lb. bomb. Shrapnel from the bomb flew all around me, hitting Marines in front of and behind me. Mortared from the rear, we were being attacked from both flanks. The two engineers along with two Marines from the first fire team were killed. We were in the battle for quite a while in the hot July sun. We had to move dead Marines off the road because tanks were trying to move out of the ambush. I still have images in my head of how bad those poor Marines were torn up.

KINGFISHER: INTO THE DMZ

Photos courtesy Les Stevenson

1: A tank recovery vehicle destroys an NVA bunker.

2: Cpl. Les Stevenson, 2nd Battalion radio operator, takes a break in front of an NVA structure. The Ben Hai River is just behind the hill.

3: Armored vehicles begin to return back out of the DMZ.

4: Charly Frazier and David Newcomb watch as an air strike provides support just before the NVA ambush.

PHOTO COURTESY KIRK GRANDJEAN

One of the surviving Marine tanks makes it way through the lines on July 30, 1967.

"Suffering from heat exhaustion, I had to be medevac'd out. We had to use tanks and an Amtrac to transport the wounded because choppers couldn't land. Next day at Con Thien, I was told 2nd Squad no longer existed. I believe four of us survived, the rest were dead or wounded."

E Company's Lance Cpl. Michael F. Gaffney was one of many who displayed courage in the face of dire circumstances, earning the Sliver Star posthumously. He was shot in the head by a sniper.

BURNING HEAT OF NAPALM

Lance Cpl. Henry W. Bernard, Jr., likewise was awarded the Silver Star, also paying with his life. A mortar man in H&S Company, he saw that a tank loaded with wounded was in jeopardy. So he repeatedly rushed forward to aid those who could not leave the tank. Bernard did so until shot and killed.

A fellow member of that company, who was placed in the 106mm recoilless rifle platoon, was Cpl. Cordell Price. (Normally a heavy truck driver, Price had less than 30 days left in-country.) He also was designated a stretcher-bearer on a six-man team and became isolated in the chaos of combat.

"Off we went bravely, blindly and dumbly into NVA territory," Price remembered. "We lined up to walk back down the way we came. Then it happened! We started to receive heavy mortar fire. NVA spotting was so good that as we ran toward the stream, the enemy fire over our heads anticipated our direction of travel. Getting as low as possible against a paddy dike, I felt rocks kicking up from the mortars hitting the ground as the rounds were being walked back toward us.

"Phantom jets firing 120mm cannons, and dropping high-explosive rounds along with canisters of napalm to our immediate front and flanks added to the counterattack. The fighting was so intense and close that we could feel the heat from the napalm burning the brush.

"My team of stretcher-bearers loaded up a wounded Marine. We became totally cut-off. Dark came and we were not able to dig foxholes. One could not see five inches in front of one's nose. When morning came we were rescued. But the mechanical mule [a small, motorized platform for carrying a 106mm recoilless rifle but more commonly used to transport weapons and troops] was fully loaded with plastic tarp-like stretchers filled with the bodies of Marines."

STENCH OF DEATH

F Company was tasked with establishing a helicopter landing zone (LZ) to evacuate casualties from H&S and E companies. After the casualty-bearing tanks reached the LZ, the NVA unleashed intense firepower, especially deadly were the mortars. Seven men were KIA and 31 WIA in this firestorm alone. While attacking to close the gap between itself and H&S Company, mortar fire inflicted another two KIA and 12 WIA on Foxtrot Company.

SILVER STAR

**LANCE CPL.
MICHAEL F. GAFFNEY**
(POSTHUMOUS)

**LANCE CPL.
JAMES P. PROCTOR**
(POSTHUMOUS)

VIETNAM VETERANS MEMORIAL FUND/ WALL OF FACES

PFC. BILLY J. BENNETT
(POSTHUMOUS)

**LANCE CPL.
HENRY W. BERNARD, JR.**
(POSTHUMOUS)

**LANCE CPL.
LEONARD LAGRONE, JR.**

CPL. ANTHONY PERINO

CPL. KENNETH L. WALTERS

2ND LT. DAVID H. WILLOUGHBY

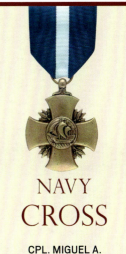

NAVY CROSS

**CPL. MIGUEL A.
RIVERA-SOTOMAYOR**

"This was my first real battle," said then-Lance Cpl. Robert C. Smith of F Company. "The NVA set up three main ambush points for us. We fought, sustaining lots of killed and wounded. KIAs were piled on tanks. I will never forget the stench from the dead caused by the searing heat and from the hot tanks. I lost some friends in this fight. Yet we fought our way out along that hot, humid, dusty road."

A grenadier in the 3rd Platoon of F Company exemplified that determination. Cpl. Miguel A. Rivera-Sotomayor ran out of M-79 grenade launcher ammo. So he instinctively seized an M-60 machine gun and later fired up a magazine from an M-16. Though wounded in the arm, he had to be restrained by a corpsman from going back into action. His actions silenced NVA machine guns, allowing his platoon to free itself from being pinned down. Sotomayor was awarded the Navy Cross.

Fighting at the LZ was fierce. 2nd Lt. David H. Willoughby sprinted 100 yards to save a wounded Marine. Next, he enabled trapped Marines to escape by laying down machine gun fire. Later, returning to the LZ, he and his men engaged the NVA until exhausting their ammo. But they pinned down the enemy long enough to allow another company to make it out of the killing zone.

A rifleman with F Company's 2nd Platoon, Pfc. Billy J. Bennett, sacrificed his life for his unit. He hurled grenades and fired his rifle, ignoring an arm wound. His efforts permitted a separated platoon to rejoin the company. Then low-crawling 100 yards across the LZ, he saved a wounded Marine before dying. Bennett, like Willoughby, was awarded the Silver Star.

Heroism certainly was not in short supply on July 29. Lance Cpl. James P. Proctor, a squad leader in H Company, maneuvered his squad through enemy fire, delivering suppressive fire and evacuating the wounded, located some only 11 yards from NVA positions. "He courageously negotiated the murderous enemy cross fire three times to evacuate wounded Marines to safety, before he fell fatally wounded by machine gun fire," says his Silver Star citation.

Another Silver Star went to Cpl. Anthony Perino, a fire team leader in Hotel Company. He

> "**We fought, sustaining lots of killed and wounded. KIAs were piled on tanks. I will never forget the stench from the dead caused by the searing heat and from the hot tanks."**
>
> —LANCE CPL. ROBERT C. SMITH

U.S. MARINE CORPS PHOTO #A189064

Grunts of the 2nd Bn., 9th Marines, return on July 30, 1967, from a hard-fought battle near Thon Cam Son in the DMZ the day before. The 2nd Battalion and attached units sustained 33 KIA and 251 WIA in an afternoon of fighting.

single-handedly assaulted a fortified bunker, taking it out with rifle fire and hand grenades. Perino's actions saved the lives of numerous Marines.

HIT ON ALL FOUR SIDES

G Company, like all the units in the firefight, suffered its share of the grief. At the rear of the column, it was almost cut in half by an assault. "This was not a good day for us," Lance Cpl. Douglas R. Witcraft said. "They hit us from all four sides. During the battle it got so hectic that we had bad guys running all through our lines. Several times we didn't know which way to shoot. At some point, I got separated from my squad and ended up all by myself. I met up with three other Marines who also were isolated from their squad.

"We carried a dead Marine in a poncho. We walked until almost dark, spending the night in a bomb crater. Several times throughout the night NVA walked past the crater trying to get back to their units. Next morning, after a four-or five-hour walk, we reached Marine tanks, one of which we lifted the dead Marine onto."

Cpl. Kenneth L. Walters, a squad leader in Golf Company, was instrumental in destroying an enemy machine gun position and silencing mortar tubes. While helping wounded Marines, Walters was wounded. Undeterred, he covered his squad members, killing six NVA himself and continuing to aid those in need.

Fellow company member, Lance Cpl. Leonard Lagrone, Jr., put his machine gun to lethal use. Standing his ground and firing from the shoulder, he personally killed 15 NVA and helped prevent his unit from being overrun. Lagrone and Walters both received the Silver Star.

Every veteran has unique memories of a battle, and one thing in particular stuck in 2nd Lt. Russell Ryan's head. He was the leader of 1st Platoon of G Company on that day. "I knew something was up when we got steak and eggs (powdered) for breakfast," he recalled. "We were then off on a 'show of force' patrol into the DMZ. It was eerily quiet on the way in, but not so on the way out. We were ambushed by a reinforced NVA regiment.

"Why we came out the same way we went in is anybody's guess. It made no sense. We took considerable casualties. Our company CO was hit and taken out of action, and I assumed command. Late that night, while slowly trying to reconnect with the main battalion (from which we were separated during the lengthy firefight), we hooked up with others from G Company who were holed up in the bush. They had sustained numerous KIA and WIA.

"My group went back to them and spent a very long night listening to the voices of nearby NVA. Dawn finally broke, medevac choppers came in to take the dead and wounded out and we slowly made our way back to the battalion. I have never eaten steak and eggs for breakfast since that day."

'HELL IN A HELMET'

Later in the afternoon, E Company and Command Group A finally broke through enemy lines. Two squads of E Company remained pinned down. H Company formed a perimeter at 7:30 p.m., soon joined by other elements. G Company established a night defensive position at about 9 p.m. The NVA faded into the jungle.

Yet all the firing did not stop. A lit cigarette caught the attention of a sniper. "At about 3 a.m. on July 30, an NVA sniper crawled to within 15 feet of the fighting hole next to me and shot a Marine of F Company in the back," vividly recalls then-Cpl. Les Stevenson, battalion radio operator. "Three of his buddies also were wounded. No one returned fire because it was too dark to see the enemy and we didn't want to give away our positions. It was very frustrating and eerily quiet. Thirst and hunger took a back seat to fear. It was a night I have never forgotten."

The next day, M Co., 3rd Bn., 4th Marines, which had established a defensive perimeter, linked up with the remainder of 2nd Bn., 9th Marines. All units were out of the DMZ just before noon. Nicknamed "Hell in a Helmet," the 2nd Battalion had experienced just that.

The excursion into the "Dead Marine's Zone" was expensive. A total of 33 Marines lost their lives and 251 were wounded (191 required medical evacuation) on the ground. Gunfire claimed 20 (61%) of the men and shrapnel or booby traps 13 (39%). The 2nd Battalion counted 26 KIA from the following companies: E (9), F (6), G (5), H (3) and H&S (3). Attached units made sacrifices, too: A Co., 3rd Anti-Tank Bn. (3); C Co., 3rd Eng. Bn. (3) and A Co., 3rd Tank Bn. (1). The bodies of two G Company Marines were never recovered.

In addition, four crew members of a CH-46 Chinook from Marine Medium Helicopter Squadron 164 were KIA when the NVA shot their chopper down on July 30. It was on scene to evacuate the dead and wounded. The men's remains were not recovered until 1993.

"After researching this battle for 12 years," Stevenson said, "I am convinced that it is one of the most overlooked of the war. The men who died there deserve better." ✪

> ## "During the battle it got so hectic that we had bad guys running all through our lines. Several times we didn't know which way to shoot."
>
> —LANCE CPL. DOUGLAS R. WITCRAFT

THE TOLL

U.S. KIA:
37

U.S. WIA:
251

BY AL HEMINGWAY

DEADLY DAY AT DONG SON

As 1967 was drawing to a close, the enemy stepped up activity in the fertile Que Son Basin. The U.S. Marines were determined to deny them access to the rice crop and screen the district polling places because of the upcoming elections.

In the pre-dawn hours of Sept. 4, 1967, D Co., 1st Bn., 5th Marines, 1st Marine Div., was ambushed near the village of Dong Son by elements of the 2nd North Vietnamese Army (NVA) Division.

A UH-1E "Huey" gunship arrived to support the Leathernecks, but as soon as a strobe light illuminated the darkness, the enemy pounded their positions. Fighting was intense as the company commander, Capt. Robert F. Morgan, was killed by NVA machine gun fire.

Several helicopters from Helicopter Marine Medium (HMM)-363, and a Huey gunship, were shot down as the communists popped "decoy smoke" to confuse the pilots. B Co., 1st Bn., 5th Marines, was sent in, and it soon secured the eastern portion of Dong Son.

By then Delta Company had sustained 29 KIA, including five attached rear echelon personnel and two Navy corpsmen. Eight B Company riflemen also went down in a hail of gunfire.

'PROTECT THEM WITH AIR STRIKES'

With both companies heavily engaged, K and M companies of 3rd Bn., 5th Marines, were given the order to move out. "We were alerted to the impending conflict," said Lt. Col. Peter L. Hilgartner, 3rd Battalion commanding officer, "when one of our scouts brought in a Chinese-made, magazine-fed, light machine gun which was found teetering back and forth on a large rock."

Hilgartner did not have long to wait for the "impending conflict." Soon after capturing the weapon, his companies came under a broadside of automatic weapons fire from the NVA located in an L-shaped, entrenched position at Chau Lam (1).

Sgt. Lawrence Peters, a squad leader with M Company, was struck in the leg as he stood directing his men to seize a small knoll laced with enemy machine gunners.

Leathernecks of K Co., 3rd Bn., 5th Marines, cross a footbridge only a few weeks prior to the battle at Dong Son. Some 55 Marines were KIA on Sept. 4, 1967, in the brutal combat.

As part of *Operation Swift,* companies of the 5th Marines'
1st and 3rd battalions tackled the NVA near Que Son on Sept. 4, 1967.

SEPTEMBER 1967

NATIONAL ARCHIVES #127-N-A370259

... Capodanno raced to his side and put himself between the wounded man and the enemy machine gun.

He took 27 bullets in the back.

Sept. 4, 1967, proved to be an unforgettable day around Dong Son for the 5th Marines, costing them 55 men.

MEDAL OF HONOR

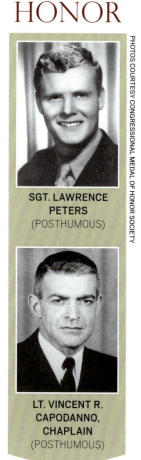

SGT. LAWRENCE PETERS
(POSTHUMOUS)

LT. VINCENT R. CAPODANNO, CHAPLAIN
(POSTHUMOUS)

While rallying his squad, he was wounded again in the face and neck. Wounded several more times, Peters finally passed out from loss of blood and died from his wounds.

His Medal of Honor citation reads in part: "[He] stood erect in the full view of the enemy firing burst after burst forcing them to disclose their camouflaged positions."

1st Lt. Rob Whitlow, a forward air controller (FAC) in a Cessna O-1 Bird Dog, directed air strikes. Whitlow later wrote: "God was with us that evening. I think the reason we were able to extend the time was that we flew such a slow and consistent pattern all night. We never left the orbit over M Company.

"I am sure that [Capt. Robert] Fitzsimmons probably had leaned out the fuel mixture. We never even considered or talked about the decision to stay. There was no decision: Marines on the ground were under heavy attack and our job was to protect them with air strikes."

HEROIC CHAPLAIN

Father Vincent R. Capodanno, the battalion chaplain, was everywhere on the battlefield. Disregarding enemy fire, the "grunt padre," as he was called, knelt by the wounded, saying prayers and assuring them that help was on the way. (Father Daniel L. Mode wrote a book about him entitled *The Grunt Padre.*)

Despite a wound to his hand, he kept going. Then shrapnel from a mortar shell rendered his right arm useless. He refused medical evacuation, remaining with his Marines. One eyewitness later said: "There he was, moving slowly from wounded to dead to wounded, using his left arm to support his right as he gave absolution."

When Navy corpsman Armando Leal, assigned to 2nd Plt., M Co., 3rd Bn., 5th Marines, was struck by NVA fire, Capodanno raced to his side and put himself between the wounded man and the enemy machine gun. He took 27 bullets in the back. Leal was hit numerous times and would receive a posthumous Navy Cross. Capodanno would be awarded a Medal of Honor posthumously.

Today, on Staten Island, N.Y., where he was born, the Father Capodanno Monument stands in tribute at Fort Wadsworth.

NAVY CROSS

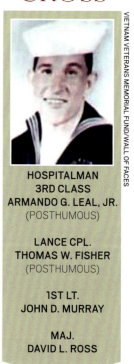

HOSPITALMAN 3RD CLASS ARMANDO G. LEAL, JR.
(POSTHUMOUS)

LANCE CPL. THOMAS W. FISHER
(POSTHUMOUS)

1ST LT. JOHN D. MURRAY

MAJ. DAVID L. ROSS

STRUGGLES AT VINH HUY (3) AND HILL 43

On the afternoon of Sept. 6, 1967, B Co., 1st Bn., 5th Marines, encountered a large enemy force near the village of Vinh Huy (3), seven miles southwest of Thang Bin.

"We looked up and saw many NVA in full uniforms, packs and cartridge belts running across the rice paddy at us," Lance Cpl. Lonnie Henshaw said. "We started shooting and we could see them falling, but they didn't stop, and more and more of them kept coming. Nothing could stop them; it was like they were doped up."

A grenade suddenly fell among the command group but before it could explode, Sgt. Rodney Davis fell upon it, absorbing the blast. For his bravery, Davis received a posthumous Medal of Honor.

Utilizing tear gas to shield their withdrawal, the Marines established a new perimeter. Once the tear gas cleared, however, the NVA hit their lines. Artillery shells from the 2nd Bn., 11th Marines, crashed to within 55 yards of the besieged company. Air strikes hammered the enemy, exploding as close as 109 yards away from friendly lines. The combination of the two soon caused the NVA to retreat. But B Company had lost 18 KIA, including three attached H&S personnel and two Navy corpsmen.

All night long, the enemy attempted to infiltrate the Marine perimeter at Dong Son (1). Communist soldiers crept forward and tossed grenades at the defenders. A few penetrated D Company's lines but were driven back. When it was over, four Marines were dead.

MEDAL OF HONOR

SGT. RODNEY DAVIS
(POSTHUMOUS)

NAVY CROSS

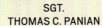

SGT. THOMAS C. PANIAN

2ND LT. DENNIE D. PETERSON
(POSTHUMOUS)

LANCE CPL. THOMAS B. DRISCOLL

Meanwhile, northeast of Vinh Huy, I and K companies of 3rd Bn., 5th Marines, seized Hill 43 after bitter fighting.

Just as the Leathernecks consolidated their perimeter, the NVA attempted to push them off the summit.

"[The enemy is] swarming over the top of this hill, and I've got to get to work," a Huey gunship pilot radioed to headquarters. The chopper's mini guns ripped into the Communist ranks, killing 23 of them.

The Marines repulsed attack after attack in the dark. At times, they were engaged in hand-to-hand combat. Finally, tear gas broke the enemy's last assault, and the remainder of the night remained quiet.

Daylight saw 88 NVA soldiers strewn in front of the perimeter. The Marines lost 29 killed and 109 wounded. With 24 KIA, I Company suffered 83% of the fatalities. Among them was 2nd Lt. Dennie Peterson, the FO who earned the Navy Cross.

Once again, the Marines foiled another attempt by the communists to gain a foothold in the Que Son Basin.

THE TOLL

VINH HUY (3)	HILL 43
U.S. KIA:	**U.S. KIA:**
18	29

COSTLY VICTORY

Fighter jets soon roared overhead and let loose 1,000-pound bombs on the hordes of NVA soldiers trying to surround the infantry. "I'd like to thank the FAC who called it in," remarked Cpl. Joseph Fuller. "I think that is what really saved us." Fighting at Chau Lam cost Mike Company 18 lives, including the chaplain and Navy corpsmen.

All told, 55 Marines and Navy corpsmen were KIA in the vicinity of Dong Son in a single day, and 104 WIA. The following morning, the Leathernecks counted 130 dead enemy soldiers. Besides the two Medal of Honor recipients, four Navy Crosses were earned for the day's actions.

As with all operations conducted in this area, the victory was costly for the Marines in terms of casualties. But despite their losses, the 2nd NVA Division would regroup and return to fight another day. Blood would flow, once again, in the Que Son Basin. ✪

THE TOLL

U.S. KIA:
55

U.S. WIA:
104

BY RICHARD K. KOLB

HILL 48 & THE CHURCHYARD: BATTLES FOR CON THIEN

"It was God awful, but on the other hand one of the proudest events in my life," said Rick Eilert in January 2010. "Yet still I feel a terrible sense of guilt for having survived." In September 1967, Eilert was a 19-year-old private first class with the 2nd Platoon of M Company. He was referring to the deadly battle of Hill 48 on Sept. 10 near Con Thien.

Local missionaries called it the "Hill of Angels"; Marines dubbed it a living hell. Con Thien Combat Base was part of Leatherneck Square, the Marine area of operations (AO) just below Vietnam's demilitarized zone. The helicopter landing zone there became known as "Death Valley."

Nui Ho Khe was an elongated hill (designated Hill 88) located a little more than half a mile southwest of Hill 48, a topographical feature occupied by Marines and situated at the northern apex of a v-shaped valley. As fate would have it, fierce fighting would envelop parts of that valley.

> ## "Yet still I feel a terrible sense of guilt for having survived."
> —PFC. RICK EILERT

In late summer 1967, the 3rd Battalion, 26th Marines, under the operational control of the 3rd Marine Division, took its "time in the barrel," as Leathernecks called duty around Con Thien.

The 3rd Battalion was dispatched to the area to secure the combat base's endangered main supply route (MSR). The MSR ran between Con Thien and Cam Lo, located on Route 9. The battalion consisted of Headquarters & Service, India, Kilo, Lima and Mike companies. An average rifle company had 190 men. Alongside the riflemen were platoons of B Co., 3rd Tank Bn. and A Co., 3rd Anti-Tank Bn.

BAPTISM OF FIRE IN THE CHURCHYARD

Just two days after arriving, on Sept. 7, separate battalion elements were attacked about two miles south of Con Thien in what became known as The Churchyard. They were hit by two NVA battalions from the 812th Regiment, 324B Division. As it turned out, those NVA were based in the heart of the Marine AO. They nearly overran the

Happy to be alive, these Marines are all that remained of a platoon in one company of the 3rd Bn., 26th Marines, at the end of the September 1967 fight along the DMZ.

In early September 1967, the 3rd Battalion, 26th Marines—"The Professionals"—took on an entire NVA regiment in the vicinity of Con Thien, blunting a major ground assault on that combat base.

SEPTEMBER 1967

PHOTO COURTESY DICK CAMP

NAVY CROSS

CAPT. ANDREW DeBONA

STAFF SGT. RUSSELL ARMSTRONG

CPL. JAMES J. BARRETT

SGT. DAVID BROWN (POSTHUMOUS)

LANCE CPL. RANDALL BROWNING

Tanks of the 2nd Plt., B Co., 3rd Tank Bn., joined Kilo Company to rescue ambushed elements of India Company on Sept. 7, 1967.

Marines amidst darkness.

Two platoons of I Company supported by tankers were hit first. During the night, an I Company platoon commander, Staff Sgt. Russell Armstrong, helped save his unit. Though severely wounded in both legs, he refused evacuation and continued to call in artillery strikes, distribute ammunition and care for the wounded. "Unable to walk," says his Navy Cross citation, Armstrong "dragged himself across the hazardous area by the use of his arms alone and resolutely directed his platoon in successfully joining the main body of the company."

Starting around 5:30 p.m., the

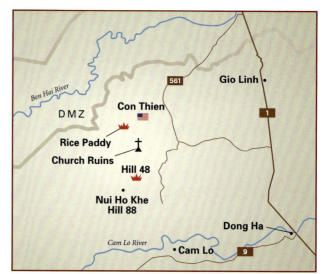

On Sept. 7 and 10, the 26th Marines waged battles at The Churchyard and Hill 48, costing 59 American lives.

battalion perimeter at a deserted churchyard was hit by intense enemy fire. Fighting would persist for five hours. "I was amazed at how calm and collected these young Marines were from start to finish," recalled Eilert. "In my case, I was certain my heart would explode in my chest because I was so frightened."

Throughout the ordeal, Capt. Tom Early, battalion communications officer, remembered how "the NVA dragged away their dead with meat hooks that had ropes attached … I think they also did it to demoralize us." Perhaps 50 NVA were killed.

But the Marines paid a heavy price, too: 21 KIA and some 70 WIA. I and K companies

Pfc. Rick Eilert, 2nd Platoon, M Company, 3rd Battalion, 26th Marines, in the field near Khe Sanh in August 1967. His unit withstood swarms of NVA, some dressed in Marine uniforms, on Sept. 10.

each lost seven men. H&S Company counted four dead, including a Navy corpsman. An engineer and artillery forward observer also died, as well as an M Company member. Lance Cpl. Charles Bennett had to retrieve the dead. "Some of the guys were already decomposing," he said. "They smelled terrible and some were blown all to hell." Mortar and rocket fire accounted for 80% of Marines killed that night.

HILL 48 IN THE BULLS-EYE

The Churchyard was only a prelude of what was to come. Sept. 10 proved to be an even deadlier day. While advancing to a new sector, the 3rd Battalion was attacked by the entire 812th NVA Regiment approximately four miles southwest of Con Thien. Isolated into two separate defensive perimeters, Marines were hit by enemy waves.

The battalion objective that day, according to James Coan, author of *Con Thien: The Hill of Angels,* was Nui Ho Khe—the stronghold of the 812th NVA Regiment on Hill 88. The 26th Marines—"The Professionals" as they were nicknamed—may have spoiled a major enemy attack in the making by engaging the NVA when they did.

The four-hour battle—from 4:15 p.m. to 8:30—began with a barrage of 140mm rocket rounds followed by a coordinated ground assault. At one point, a full NVA battalion rose

DISTINGUISHED SERVICE CROSS

MILITARY TIMES HALL OF VALOR

CAPT. CHARLES L. DEIBERT

up from a rice paddy in unison. It was like a shooting gallery for the Marines. "I thought they were stoned," recalled Bennett. Tanks were awfully handy in these circumstances. Tank machine guns mowed down up to 40 NVA in one instance.

Incredible acts of bravery were displayed. Sgt. David Brown, platoon sergeant of 3rd Plt., L Co., was on his last day in-country. He repeatedly and single-handedly charged enemy positions, disrupting the enemy assault on his unit. While encouraging his men, he was mortally wounded. Brown was nominated for the Medal of Honor, but received the Navy Cross instead.

> He [Sgt. David Brown] repeatedly and single-handedly charged enemy positions, disrupting the enemy assault on his unit.

Cpl. James J. Barrett also was awarded the Navy Cross. A squad leader in I Company, "he rallied his men, reorganized the platoon and led them in an effective counterattack," says the citation. Over the course of this battle, Barrett tended to the wounded and assured their evacuation. No less than five times, he took the initiative of repositioning his men to stop the NVA.

Meanwhile, on Hill 48, M Company, commanded by Capt. Andrew DeBona, faced its own life-and-death struggle. Hit by an enemy assault led by NVA wearing USMC flak jackets and helmets, it repelled the attack. Ontos, Greek for "thing," resembling small tanks armed with six externally mounted 106mm recoilless rifles attached—which mowed rows of NVA "down like they were corn"—were critical to Marine survival.

Lance Cpl. Randall Browning commanded an Ontos of A Co., 3rd Anti-Tank Bn. Despite being seriously wounded, he repulsed NVA charges with various weapons. Browning was instrumental in "thwarting the enemy's attempt to overrun the battalion's position and prevented the capture, injury or possible death of many Marines," according to his Navy Cross citation.

DeBona's actions did not go unrecognized either. His Navy Cross citation reads: "Constantly exposing himself to the enemy while repulsing another enemy assault and concurrently organizing a defensive perimeter, he displayed a tremendous degree of composure and calm, inspiring his Marines by his presence of mind and outstanding courage."

COMBAT IN THE CRATER

That was not all. When 20 Marines became stranded in a bomb crater out front of the lines, DeBona led a reaction force to the rescue. He remained behind to cover the withdrawal, counting 39 NVA bodies in the crater. The captain was the last man to leave that hole in the ground. He was recommended for the Medal of Honor.

In a personal account of the action, DeBona recalled: "A unit was pinned down in a bomb crater about 100 meters in front of 1st Platoon's position. I had never before or since been that afraid even during a second tour with Vietnamese marines during the 1972 Easter Offensive. I knew that if I went into that crater I would be dead. Calm settled over me that I can't describe except that I accepted the inevitable."

The day after the battle, Marines policed the area for NVA corpses. "We found two lines of enemy KIAs connected by meat hooks through their shoulders," DeBona said.

There is more to this story that is seldom told. Cpl. Frank Taggart was point man for 2nd

> ## "I knew that if I went into that crater I would be dead. Calm settled over me that I can't describe except that I accepted the inevitable."
> —CAPT. ANDREW DeBONA COMMANDER, M COMPANY

Squad, 2nd Plt., M Co. and was severely wounded by rocket fire in the crater. "We engaged the enemy dressed in U.S. Marine uniforms, helmets and flak jackets," he said. "Left out is the heroism of two Marines. Cpl. Ron Hickenbottom and Lance Cpl. Vernon McNeese took deliberate aim, shooting and killing a lot of NVA, most of whom were shot in the head. They even tended to the wounded."

Beginning in 1999, Taggart made it his personal crusade to see them recognized. Finally, in 2001, Hickenbottom received the Silver Star. Unfortunately, McNeese had died by then.

Another unsung hero of Sept. 10 was Army Capt. Charles L. Deibert, commander of the 4th Plt., 220th Recon Airplane Co., 212th Combat Support Avn. Bn. Piloting an 0-1 "Bird Dog," call sign Catkiller 4-6, he marked targets for fixed-wing aircraft. "One of his marking rounds was so accurate that it detonated in the center of three North Vietnamese machine gun positions," reads his Distinguished Service Cross citation. Facing a murderous enemy barrage, he "turned a possible defeat into a rout of the enemy and prevented numerous casualties to the Marines."

> ## "However, NVA dressed as Marines made it into our lines. I found one dead NVA so disguised."
> —PFC. RICK EILERT

For all the Marines present, the experience was harrowing. 2nd Platoon of M Company had set up just past a huge bomb crater to the west of the company command post. "Swarms of NVA came directly toward us," Eilert said. "If they got up to our line, we drove them back every time. However, NVA dressed as Marines made it into our lines. I found one dead NVA so disguised.

"When we pulled back to form a tighter perimeter, the area was covered with dead and wounded Marines; they just seemed to be everywhere. Next day, when we went out to retrieve our dead, I came across the bodies of four Marines I knew personally."

EXEMPLARY FIGHTING SPIRIT

More than 140 NVA dead were counted on the battlefield. Yet it had all been at a steep cost in Marines. The 3rd Battalion sustained 38 KIA on Sept. 10: 35 Marines and three Navy corpsmen. K Company alone suffered 17 KIA—46% of the total. Two tankers from B Co., 3rd Tank Bn., were among the total. Once again, artillery, rocket and mortar fire inflicted the greatest casualties, accounting for 79% of the dead. In addition, 192 men were wounded.

Jim Coan, in his excellent 2004 tribute to all Marines who fought at Con Thien, concluded: "The garrison at Con Thien owed a debt of gratitude to the 3rd Battalion, 26th Marines, for their tenacity and fighting spirit." (Coan, incidentally, led a tank platoon of A Co., 3rd Tank Bn., in September 1967.) ✪

THE TOLL

The Churchyard
(Sept. 7)
U.S. KIA: 21
U.S. WIA: 70

Hill 48
(Sept. 10)
U.S. KIA: 38
U.S. WIA: 192

BY SUSAN KATZ KEATING

'BLACK LIONS' PERSEVERE AT ONG THANH

In the fall of 1967, the 1st Infantry Division's 28th Infantry—the famed "Black Lions"—dispatched its 2nd Battalion to participate in *Operation Shenandoah II*. The mission sought to seek and destroy the enemy in numerous locales between Saigon and the Cambodian border, including areas west and northwest of Lai Khe.

In mid-October, *Shenandoah II* turned brutal for the 2nd Battalion, when the unit suffered staggering losses during the grueling battle at Ong Thanh.

On Oct. 8, the 2nd Battalion responded to intelligence reports that an enemy main force regiment was close, near the village of Chon Thanh. Three of the 2nd Battalion's rifle companies—Alpha, Bravo and Delta—departed their base at Lai Khe and air-assaulted to a site about 13 miles to the northwest. The 2nd Battalion's Charlie Company was detached to protect the supporting 15th Field Artillery element.

From Oct. 8-15, the forward-deployed Black Lions made almost daily contact with Viet Cong. On Oct. 16, after moving to a new night defensive position near Ong Thanh Creek, the 2nd Battalion fought against troops from the primary target unit: Col. Vo Minh Triet's 271st Regiment, a crack Communist unit.

"We fought brilliantly," says Clark Welch, who was the lieutenant in charge of D Company. "It was a textbook version of a search-and-destroy mission," with some 20 enemy killed. That night, visiting brass from division headquarters flew into the 2nd Battalion's camp and praised the soldiers, awarding Welch a Silver Star on the spot.

"They told us the next day would be the same," Welch recalls. "We were going to conduct a frontal assault on the enemy. It was going to be a great day for the Black Lions."

OUTNUMBERED 10-TO-1

Some in the 2nd Battalion questioned the frontal assault and other aspects of the plan. Welch tried to convince the 2nd Battalion's commander, Lt. Col. Terry Allen, Jr., that the plan placed the soldiers at excessive risk. Nevertheless, the order stood.

At 8 a.m. on Oct. 17, the Black Lions embarked on their mission. Bravo Company remained in place to guard the night defensive position. Alpha Company moved out in the lead, followed by Delta. Embedded within Delta was a Headquarters Company group of 10 officers, including Allen. Sources place the number of troops who entered the jungle as somewhere between 142-155 men. There is no question, though, that both Alpha and Delta marched at far below full company strength. Perhaps 65 and 73 men, respectively.

The column moved directly south. The men picked their way through dense, thick jungle, advancing only a half-mile in two hours. "We did not see or hear the enemy," says Jim George, the captain in command of Alpha. "But they were all around us."

The unseen enemy consisted of 1,200 members of the Main Force VC 271st, along with about 200 guerrilla fighters. In all, the communists outnumbered the Americans by about a 10-1 ratio.

Some of the enemy were hiding in tall trees, concealed by foliage. Others were lodged inside well-fortified bunkers that first had been used by the Viet Minh in their fight against the French.

Later, it would emerge that Col. Triet had intended

On Oct. 17, 1967, A and D companies of the 2nd Bn., 28th Regt., 1st Inf. Div., engaged in one of the Vietnam War's most ferocious fights. Claiming 59 U.S. lives in just two hours, the battle report was not declassified until 1991.

OCTOBER 1967

PHOTO COURTESY FRED KIRKPATRICK

Men of D Co., 2nd Bn., 28th Inf., wait outside of Lai Khe on Oct. 8, 1967, before being choppered to the base camp on the Ong Thanh River. Just nine days later, many of them would be killed in an ambush by a crack Communist unit.

COURTESY 28TH INFANTRY WEB SITE

A Co.: Staff Sgt. Willie C. Johnson, Jr. (KIA), far left, was shot 100 times.

VERLAND GILBERTSON PHOTO

D Company commander Lt. Clark Welch (far right) describes skirmishing with the enemy on the evening prior to the battle to senior officers Col. George Newman, Lt. Col. Terry Allen, Jr., Maj. Donald Holleder and Brig. Gen. William Coleman. Allen ordered a frontal assault on the enemy base. He was killed in the battle.

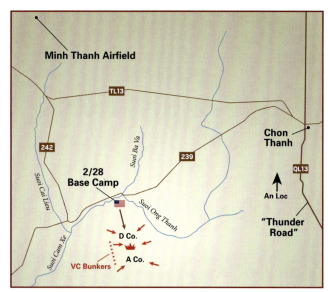

Located about seven miles southeast of Minh Thanh Airfield, Ong Thanh River is in Binh Long province.

3rd Squad, D Co., members are, front row: Fred Kirkpatrick, Emil Megiveron (KIA), Gary G. Lincoln (KIA); back row: Frank McMeel, Donnie Hodges and Reynolds Lonefight.

D Company: Daniel Sikorski (KIA), left, and an unidentified companion fill sandbags.

to pass through the area on the way to points west. But the 271st was out of food, so it stopped at a base camp near the Ong Thanh to await a shipment of rice. The 271st dug in and hid, waiting for the Americans to leave so that the unit could receive its rice. Eventually it became clear that the Americans did not plan to leave.

On the morning of the 17th, the enemy waited in silence as the Black Lions advanced ever closer to the Communist camp.

From time to time, A Company stopped to conduct cloverleaf maneuvers, in which small groups of men fanned out into the jungle, then returned to report what they had found.

Staff Sgt. Willie C. Johnson, Jr., a platoon leader, came back from one of these maneuvers and reported that he had seen footprints. His men saw movement in the trees.

At 10 a.m., the Communist commander gave the prearranged signal: three sharp taps on a block of wood.

'OVERWHELMING ASSAULT'

The enemy opened fire on Alpha Company. At first, some of the soldiers from Delta, as well as the A Company commander, heard what sounded like a firefight. But this was no skirmish.

"It was a sudden, overwhelming and unbelievable assault," Welch says.

The attack included rifle fire and rocket-propelled grenades (RPGs) coming down from the trees, machine gun fire from ground level and explosions from Claymore mines.

Alpha Company's first platoon took the brunt. The point man, Pfc. Clifford Lynn Breeden, took six bullets to the torso. Johnson, the platoon leader, would be hit 100 times. (He died in a hospital in Long Binh.)

Men fell in quick succession. Those who were left standing became a unit of heroes. Tom "Doc" Hinger, a medic, raced under fire, frantically trying to save his wounded fellows. Some scrambled to return fire while pulling others out of the kill zone. George sent in his second platoon as reinforcement. This, too, took heavy casualties. In very short order, key Alpha personnel—the point man, the radio-man, the forward observer—were either dead or wounded.

"A Vietnamese soldier came running toward us with a Claymore in his hand," George says. It killed a number of soldiers, and dealt George a disabling injury. "I started to blow my nose, and I had bone coming out." George, the company commander, was rendered nearly deaf and blind from a serious wound to the face.

Just minutes after the attack began, A Company was annihilated.

The astonished D Company did what it could to help retrieve Alpha's dead and wounded, along with some weapons and ammunition. Delta soon found itself not only protecting the battalion command post, but also caring for A Company's wounded.

BATTLE RAGES

Now D Company came under fire. The assault came from the front and the right, from some 33-66 feet away. "All of a sudden all hell broke loose and we were receiving fire from all directions," recalled Paul D. Scott, radio operator for Lt. Welch. "We had snipers in the trees, RPGs being fired along with heavy machine-gun and small-arms fire."

The VC remained concealed in their dug-in positions. The Americans were fully exposed.

"We had nothing to hide behind," Welch says. "Not even protective gear for our bodies. We just had our T-shirts and fatigues."

Delta could not move. The soldiers were pinned in place.

Bill McGath, a grenadier, was pinned behind a tree by an unseen assailant. The young private first class watched in horror as rounds exploded beside him, over and over again. "He was going to get me, and then he was going to move on to the next man," McGath recalled.

McGath somehow found the presence of mind to use geometry to help locate the sniper. "I used to play a lot of pool back home, so I used an old pool technique to pinpoint the spot," McGath said. The trapped soldier traced with his eyes the intersection of the enemy's firing lines, and lobbed off some M-79 grenade launcher rounds of his own. "After that, he stopped firing," McGath recalled.

Delta's forward observer, 2nd Lt. Harold "Pinky" Durham, Jr., tried to call in desperately needed artillery support. At first, artillery base personnel resisted Durham's request. Only the lead company—in this case, the decimated Alpha—was permitted to call in artillery. Durham argued vehemently, though, that because Alpha Company was gone, Delta now was the lead company.

"He was spectacular," Welch says with a catch in his voice. "Absolutely spectacular. He got the artillery."

Durham continued to work under fire to direct artillery and also to help the wounded. He became seriously wounded himself, first by a Claymore, and then by machine-gun fire. Durham used his own last moments to save another man's life before collapsing in death, his fingers still clutching the radio handset.

The battle raged for two hours of pure nightmare. Men continued to fall. All 10 in the headquarters unit, including Allen, died. Men worked mightily to save one another. Sgt. Lee Price insisted on protecting the desperately wounded George with his own body.

"There were a lot of heroes that day," George says quietly.

At noon, VC Col. Triet abruptly called off the attack. "It just quit," McGath said. "Just like that." Triet later explained during a reunion with Welch that he feared "B-52s," a Vietnamese catch-all term for any form of fire from the sky. Additionally, Triet thought all the GIs were dead.

That wasn't entirely true. But the toll was indeed shocking: 59 Black Lions were killed in action that day. Delta Company lost 26 men and Alpha 22, including their respective forward observers. Headquarters Company dead numbered 10, among them three medics. One soldier from the 121st Signal Battalion was killed, too. More than 70% of those killed succumbed to shrapnel wounds. A bit more than half (54%) of the men were volunteers; 46% were draftees. Most of the surviving troops were wounded—132.

George believes casualties would have been higher if A Company had not performed that final cloverleaf. "We tripped the ambush before it was fully set. They were not ready for us. If we had kept going, we all would have been killed."

A virtual locker full of medals went out to the Black Lions for what they did at Ong Thanh. Durham received the Medal of Honor; Clark Welch, Terry Allen and Don Holleder, the Distinguished Service Cross; "Doc" Hinger and 13 others, the Silver Star; five others, posthumous Bronze Stars for valor.

"Every last one of our men put up a great fight," said Fred Kirkpatrick, a D Company point man who was sent on R&R shortly before the battle began. "To this day, I am awed and humbled at what our guys endured." ✪

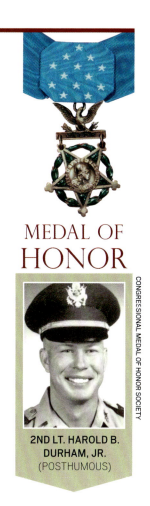

MEDAL OF HONOR

2ND LT. HAROLD B. DURHAM, JR.
(POSTHUMOUS)

DISTINGUISHED SERVICE CROSS

LT. COL. TERRY D. ALLEN, JR.
(POSTHUMOUS)

MAJ. DONALD W. HOLLEDER
(POSTHUMOUS)

1ST LT. ALBERT CLARK WELCH

THE TOLL

U.S. KIA:
59

U.S. WIA:
132

BY TIM DYHOUSE

HILL 875: 'UNPRECEDENTED VICTORY'

I n November 1967, North Vietnamese Army (NVA) units were determined to rid the Central Highlands of American forces. The NVA poured thousands of troops into an area where the borders of Cambodia, Laos and South Vietnam meet. Specifically, they sought to destroy Special Forces camps at Ben Het, about five miles east of the Cambodian border, and at Dak To, some 10 miles east of Ben Het. The U.S. camps represented a major roadblock at the southern end of the Ho Chi Minh Trail.

The Americans reacted to the NVA buildup by launching *Operation MacArthur,* with the 4th Infantry Division assuming operational control over the 173rd Airborne Brigade. It fielded the 1st, 2nd and 4th battalions of the 503rd Infantry Regiment, and supporting units such as the 335th Aviation Company. The 4th Infantry Division's 1st Brigade included the 1st, 2nd and 3rd battalions of the 8th Infantry Regiment; 1st and 3rd battalions of the 12th Infantry Regiment; and the attached 2nd Sqdn., 1st Cav Regiment.

Opposing them at one time or another were the NVA's 24th, 32nd, 66th and 174th regiments, totaling 7,000 men, constituting the NVA 1st Infantry Division. One paratrooper said of the enemy: "They fight like they're all John Waynes, three clips and making every bullet count."

'A MERCILESS LAND'

Combat was brutal, close and fought in the unforgiving terrain of the Central Highlands. "It is a merciless land of steep limestone ridges, some of them exceeding 4,000 feet," wrote Robert Barr Smith in *Vietnam* magazine. "The sharp ridges are covered with double- and sometimes triple-canopy jungle. The draws between the ridges are dreary, tangled places of perpetual twilight. The jungle is laced with vines and thorns, and in it live diverse snakes, a million leeches and about half the mosquitoes in the world." Another historian called the terrain "probably the wildest in South Vietnam if not all Southeast Asia."

The weather, however, during the operation was "excellent," according to F. Clifton Berry, Jr., in *The Illustrated History of Sky Soldiers, The Vietnam War,* with dry conditions and daily high and low temperatures ranging between 91 and 55 degrees.

U.S. paratroopers of the 503rd Inf. Regt., 173rd Abn. Bde., battled an entrenched and virtually invisible enemy on Hill 875 between Nov. 18-23, 1967.

In November 1967, the 173rd Airborne Brigade sent 3,200 paratroopers to the Dak To area of the Central Highlands. The centerpiece of that operation was the ferocious fight for Hill 875.

NOVEMBER 1967

PHOTO BY FOUNDATION GILLES CARON/GAMMA-RAPHO VIA GETTY IMAGES

MEDAL OF HONOR

CONGRESSIONAL MEDAL OF HONOR SOCIETY

PFC. JOHN BARNES
(POSTHUMOUS)

PFC. CARLOS LOZADA
(POSTHUMOUS)

MAJ. CHARLES J. WATTERS, CHAPLAIN
(POSTHUMOUS)

"The noncoms kept shouting, 'Get up the hill, get up the goddamn hill.' But we couldn't. We were surrounded, and we were firing in all directions."

—A 173RD AIRBORNE BRIGADE PARATROOPER

DEADLY PRELUDE

Fighting around Dak To was actually a series of intense clashes culminating in the decisive battle for Hill 875. Leading up to that climactic end, the 173rd Airborne Brigade fought several engagements seven miles southwest of Ben Het.

On Nov. 6, A, B, C and D companies of the 4th Bn., 503rd Inf., fought the NVA for four hours in the Ngok Kam Leat chain of hills and adjacent Hill 823, losing 18 KIA.

Then on Nov. 12, A, C and D companies of the 1st Bn., 503rd Inf., engaged the NVA for eight hours at two separate locations in the vicinity of Hill 823 sustaining 15 KIA.

Pfc. John Barnes of C Company earned a posthumous Medal of Honor on Nov. 12 when he saved the lives of several wounded men by throwing himself on a grenade. Before this heroic act, according to his citation, Barnes "dashed through the bullet-swept area, manned the machine gun [the team had been killed] and killed nine enemy soldiers as they assaulted his position."

The next day, on Nov. 13, A and B companies from the 2nd Bn., 503rd Inf., fought for more than four hours near Fire Support Base 16, located about five miles south of Hill 823. B Company counted 22 KIA after the firefight. All told, three separate days around Hill 823 cost the 503rd Infantry 55 KIA.

'GET UP THE GODDAMN HILL'

On Nov. 18, four members of D Co., 4th Bn., 503rd Inf., were killed by artillery and mortar fire at Hill 875—the first KIA there. By the 19th, the NVA's 174th Regiment, moving south along the Laos/Cambodia border, had covered the retreat of the 66th Regiment. The 174th set up on Hill 875 about 10 miles southwest of Ben Het and around four miles east of Cambodia. The 173rd's 2nd Bn., 503rd Inf., led the assault.

Companies C and D started up the hill at 9:43 a.m., with A Company providing rear security and attempting to cut out a landing zone at the bottom. C and D companies soon found themselves absorbing small-arms fire and grenade attacks from seemingly every direction.

"Jesus, they were all over the place," one paratrooper recalled. "The noncoms kept shouting, 'Get up the hill, get up the goddamn hill.' But we couldn't. We were surrounded, and we were firing in all directions."

Company commanders pulled their troops back and called for more firepower. Artillery from A Bty., 3rd Bn., 319th Artillery Regt., and air strikes started ravaging the hilltop.

Meanwhile, NVA soldiers began a ferocious attack on A Company at the bottom of the hill. Pfc. Carlos Lozada, after receiving orders to retreat back up the hill, provided covering fire, at times walking backward up the hill spraying M-60 machine-gun fire into the brush on either

Members of the 4th Bn., 503rd Inf., 173rd Abn. Bde., remain pinned down by mortar fire during the assault on Hill 875 on Nov. 23, 1967.

side of the trail. When his weapon jammed, an NVA bullet ripped into his head. Lozada's actions garnered him a posthumous Medal of Honor.

The surviving paratroopers of A Company hustled up the slope and into a perimeter formed by the beleaguered C and D companies.

"By 3 p.m.," Terrence Maitland and Peter McInerney wrote in *A Contagion of War,* "the C Company commander reported they were surrounded by 200 to 300 NVA and under attack by mortars, automatic weapons and B-40 rockets."

Six helicopters from the 335th Aviation Company attempting to resupply the pinned-down troopers were shot down during the day. U.S. aircraft hit enemy positions as close as 55 yards to the perimeter as GIs dug in for an NVA night attack.

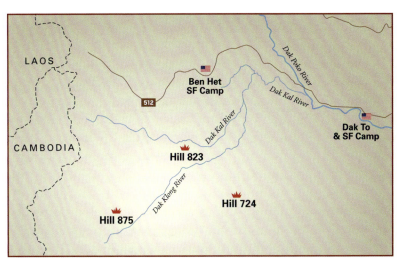

Hill 875, located about four miles from Cambodia in Kontum province, witnessed some of the war's bloodiest combat. That was especially so on Nov. 20, when 72 GIs were KIA.

DISTINGUISHED SERVICE CROSS

**1ST LT.
TRACY H. MURREY**
(POSTHUMOUS)
HILL 875, NOV. 20
C-4-503RD

**SPEC. 5
EDWARD GARCIA**
HILL 875, NOV. 21 & 23
B-4-503RD

**SPEC. 4
JERRY C. KELLEY**
(POSTHUMOUS)
HILL 823, NOV. 12
C-1-503RD

AP PHOTO

U.S. troops move toward the crest of Hill 875 on Nov. 23. Grunts from two companies of the 1st Bn., 12th Inf., were among those to reach the summit of the tortured landscape that day.

'SLEPT WITH CORPSES'

Tragically, one air strike hit too close to the paratroopers. At 6:58 p.m., a Marine Corps fighter-bomber mistakenly dropped two 500-pound bombs on the U.S. position. One hit outside the perimeter, killing 25 NVA troops. The other hit C Company's command post and aid station. At least three men were confirmed killed by the bomb. The actual number is open to dispute but was likely much higher, perhaps a score.

"[There were] heaps of dead after that bomb," a survivor remembered. "You didn't know where to go, you did not know where to hide. You slept with corpses. I slept with Joe. He was dead, but he kept me warm."

One soldier who didn't survive the blast was chaplain Maj. Charles Watters. During the battle, Father Watters had ventured outside the perimeter at least five times, carrying wounded troops back to the aid station. According to survivors, he was on his knees giving last rites to a dying paratrooper when the bombs hit, killing him instantly. Watters received a posthumous Medal of Honor.

The next morning, Nov. 20, 4th Bn., 503rd Inf., set out to relieve the 2nd Battalion paratroopers. NVA snipers made the going slow, but B Company finally reached the perimeter by dusk. Two more companies arrived after dark and provided much-needed food and water to the exhausted troopers.

"Dawn on Tuesday, Nov. 21, revealed a scene on Hill 875 no survivor of that battle could ever forget," Edward F. Murphy wrote in *Dak To: America's Sky Soldiers in South Vietnam's Central Highlands.* "The enormous amounts of ordnance expended by both forces had turned the once-lush tropical jungle into a scarred and torn landscape." Abandoned weapons, helmets, rucksacks, clothing, canteens and empty ration containers littered the battlefield. "The acrid odor of decaying and rotting flesh combined with the smells of vomit, feces, urine, blood, gunpowder and napalm etched itself permanently into the memories of those who were on Hill 875," Murphy wrote.

> ## "The acrid odor of decaying and rotting flesh combined with the smells of vomit, feces, urine, blood, gunpowder and napalm etched itself permanently into the memories of those who were on Hill 875."
>
> —EDWARD F. MURPHY FROM *DAK TO: AMERICA'S SKY SOLDIERS IN SOUTH VIETNAM'S CENTRAL HIGHLANDS*

'EVERY OBJECTIVE WAS TAKEN'

Throughout the day, U.S. airstrikes and artillery continued to pound the top of the hill, as the NVA lobbed mortars at the U.S. perimeter. The 4th Battalion launched an unsuccessful attack at around 3 p.m., and pulled back to defensive positions after dark.

On Nov. 23, the 4th Battalion from the north slope coordinated a final assault on the hilltop with the 1st Bn., 12th Inf., 4th Inf. Div., charging up the south slope. However, neither battalion faced heavy resistance. The NVA had decamped during the night, denying the Americans a chance at some revenge. But the GIs had fulfilled their objective. "To walk away from Hill 875 would have diminished the importance of their sacrifices," Murphy concluded. "The paratroopers' esprit de corps, elitism and personal pride would not permit that."

Though they were severely bloodied, the paratroopers inflicted even heavier losses on the NVA. So heavy, in fact, that the NVA's 32nd, 66th and 174th regiments were unable to participate in the 1968 Tet Offensive.

"In a strictly military sense, the Dak To fighting has been a victory for the allied forces," war correspondent Peter Arnett was forced to admit in an Associated Press report filed after spending 10 days at the scene. "Every objective was taken. The enemy loss in lives was about four times that of the allies." In fact, the 173rd earned the Presidential Unit Citation for its "hard-fought and unprecedented victory."

LETHAL FIRE: ENEMY AND "FRIENDLY"

Over the six days between Nov. 18-23, 131 GIs died on or around Hill 875. Some 55% of the deaths (72) occurred on Nov. 20 alone. Another 31 men (24% of the total) were killed on Nov. 19. With the exception of eight men attached—four members of A Btry., 3rd Bn., 319th Arty; three engineers of the 173rd Engineer Company; and the chaplain—all of those killed in action belonged to the 503rd Infantry Regiment. Its 2nd Battalion lost 89 men—both Alpha and Charlie companies each suffered 29 KIA. The 4th Battalion's fatalities numbered 30, with Bravo Company accounting for 18 of those.

For the medics in the mix, casualties represented far more than statistics. The anguished cries of the wounded are what they remember most. "There is something gut-wrenching about severely wounded men that I will never forget," recalled Earle Jackson, a 173rd medic who served on Hill 875. "It is that most become delirious and almost always cry out for their mothers." ✪

THE TOLL

(Hill 875 only)
U.S. KIA:
131

U.S. WIA:
411
(Evacuated only)

4TH DIVISION'S ROLE OFTEN OVERLOOKED

BY TIM DYHOUSE

While not capturing newspaper headlines like Hill 875, the Ivy Division nonetheless waged crucial struggles for Hills 724 and 1338.

Far too often, the part played by 4th Division GIs around Dak To is glossed over. In the days leading up to the fight for Hill 875, 4th ID units sought out the enemy south of Dak To.

In fact, the first significant contacts were made by its elements on Nov. 3–4 around Hill 1338. "On Nov. 3, A and B companies made a combat assault from Dak To airstrip to a ridge line just below Hill 1338," recalled Alex Cooker, then the platoon leader of 3rd Plt., B Co., 3rd Bn., 12th Inf. "We were ambushed by the NVA a short distance from where we landed. Thus began the Battle of Dak To."

About 5.6 miles to the west of 1338 was Hill 724. According to KIA figures grouped by the Coffelt Database, Hill 724 was the scene of extended combat for most of a week beginning Nov. 4. The heaviest fighting took place over Nov. 10–11. The 8th Infantry lost 23 KIA on the 11th alone. Overall, the 8th counted 47 dead; the 12th Infantry had 12 killed; and two crewmen of the 119th Assault Helicopter Company died for a total of 61 KIA.

A and D companies of 1st Bn., 12th Inf. (the "Red Warriors"), participated in the final assault on Hill 875. Harold B. Birch, battalion commander at the time, recalled that "about 14 Red Warriors were wounded in the attack, some by a misdirected American helicopter gunship."

Division doctors at Dak To kept busy, too, often getting by on only three or four hours of sleep a night. "We treated around 1,200 wounded during the period of the battle," said William J. Shaffer, who served as the executive officer of B Co., 4th Medical Bn. "One thing that we took a great deal of pride in was that every wounded soldier, many in very, very serious condition, reached the 71st Evac Hospital at Pleiku alive."

4th ID commander Maj. Gen. William R. Peers told news cor-

U.S. ARMY PHOTO COURTESY KEN BENDER

COURTESY STEVE EDMUNDS

ABOVE: A GI of D Co., 1st Bn., 12th Inf. Regt., 4th Div., takes a break from heavy fighting during the battle for Dak To in November 1967.
LEFT: 3rd Bn., 8th Inf., members Gary Clark, an RTO with HQ Co., and Steve Edmunds, 2nd Plt., C Co., prepare to leave Hill 724 in November 1967.

respondents, "As far as brutal fighting goes, I would say this is the worst we've had." That was confirmed by the 1st Brigade's Presidential Unit Citation, which was awarded for "severely crippling three enemy regiments" in the Dak To district.

The "Forgotten Fourth's" individual bravery also was validated with the award of four Distinguished Service Crosses for actions at Hills 724 and 1338 from Nov. 3–17.

DECEMBER 1967

BY RICHARD K. KOLB

OPERATION UNIONTOWN/STRIKE

FIGHTING FIERCE AROUND FIREBASE NASHUA

For units of the 199th Light Infantry Brigade, Dec. 6, 1967, would be like no other day of their nearly four years in Vietnam. It was an engagement that supremely tested the men's resolve to persevere.

"It turned out to be the bloodiest single day for the 199th Light Infantry Brigade during its entire time in Vietnam," lamented Bruce Drees, a company commander in the unit 50 years before. "Dec. 6, 1967, provided the most intense action I witnessed during my two tours in Vietnam as a rifle company commander." Yet that action proved the mettle of the men involved beyond dispute.

During the first two weeks of December 1967, the U.S. Army carried out *Operation Uniontown/Strike* to prevent rocket and mortar attacks on the Bien Hoa-Long Binh military complex in War Zone D. For its part in the operation, the 199th Light Infantry Brigade (nicknamed the "Redcatchers"), established Fire Support Base (FSB) Nashua that Dec. 4.

Nashua was located 20 miles north of Bien Hoa near the village of Ku Tru Mat in Bien Hoa province. The clearing on which the firebase was built was surrounded by double- and triple-canopy jungle.

Little did the Americans know that a mere 1¼ miles southeast of their stronghold was an enemy base in the vicinity of Phouc Loc. It was occupied by the D-800 (K1) Battalion of the Dong Nai Regiment. A Main Force Viet Cong unit, the regiment was recently infused with North Vietnamese Army (NVA) regulars. The battalion fielded more than 300 men.

The U.S. firebase was home to the 4th Battalion (the "Warriors") of the 12th Infantry. For fire support, it looked to C Btry., 2nd Bn., 40th Artillery. Before the

Members of B Co., 4th Bn., 12th Inf., 199th LIB, carry a wounded soldier from the field during a firefight in Lhu Duc District on Oct. 14, 1967. Less than two months later, the 4th Battalion endured its bloodiest day in Vietnam.

day was done, the 4th Battalion's A and B companies, platoons of D Trp., 17th Cav (Armored) and A Co., 3rd Bn., 7th Inf., would join the fray. The latter was the brigade's ready-reaction force, based at FSB Concord, on Dec. 6, 1967.

All outfits involved had one thing in common: They were understrength. When the 12th's Alpha Company

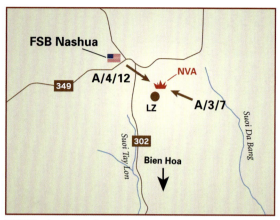

FSB Nashua was the centerpiece of the Dec. 6, 1967, action, which took place 1.2 miles southeast of the firebase.

MEDAL OF HONOR

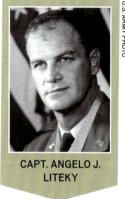

U.S. ARMY PHOTO

CAPT. ANGELO J. LITEKY

left the perimeter, its 2nd and 4th platoons and command post group numbered only 78 men.

AN INVITATION TO FIGHT

Things got started at dawn when the communists fired about 25 rounds of 82mm mortar fire at the base. "The enemy commander made a number of mistakes," recalled Bruce Drees, then captain of A Company. Among them, "he 'invited' us to come to where he was by mortaring us from a position close to his base. That was unbelievably stupid, especially when they really should have moved away from us."

Perhaps, however, the communist commander was cocky precisely because of his position. D-800's base camp was circular, 50 to 65 yards in diameter with zigzag trenches along the perimeter. Roofed bunkers, capable of harboring 15 to 20 Vietnamese, were placed every 33 feet apart. The whole complex was concealed by triple-canopy jungle. The thick vegetation restricted visibility to less than 100 feet.

This is what the A Company platoons unknowingly had to look forward to when they set out to search for the source of the mortar fire. After struggling through thorny bushes and "wait-a-minute" vines for hours, the "Warriors" finally made contact at about 2 p.m. Communist weaponry inflicted heavy casualties immediately. Claymore antipersonnel mines set off at less than 66 feet from the enemy perimeter took a toll.

"The 2nd Platoon advanced on line for about 100 feet and the world seemed to explode," Drees said. "The noise was absolutely deafening. Our two platoons and the headquarters command post were reduced in fighting strength to less than 40 men in the initial minute of contact. 4th Platoon was reduced to squad strength in the first seconds."

Dennis Castaldo was with 4th Platoon. "The firepower of that Vietnamese camp was absolutely incredible … but no one ran. Everyone stood their ground as they were told," he remembered.

A PADRE'S INCREDIBLE COURAGE

In the face of such odds, the feats of courage were astounding. Capt. Angelo J. Liteky, the Catholic chaplain for the 199th LIB, inspired all the men, among whom he was universally revered. "The Padre" dragged two wounded to safety, administered last rites under intense fire and evacuated wounded men. He crawled back with a severely wounded soldier on his chest. Then he rescued another GI from thorny underbrush.

Not content, he directed medevac helicopters. Liteky personally carried more than 20 men to the landing zone for evacuation. This was all done while the chaplain was suffering wounds in the neck and foot. He was not wearing a flak jacket (having given it to someone else) or a helmet.

Testimonials to Liteky's incredible bravery were numerous. Staff Sgt. Robert Moore, a squad leader in the 2nd Platoon, recalled he was "everywhere, carrying stretchers, lugging ammo, handing out water and cigarettes … he was just tremendous and he never would get down …" 1st Lt. Henderson Garnett of Bravo Company said, "That chaplain seemed to be doing everything. There was sporadic fire all over the LZ, but he never stopped caring for the wounded and encouraging the men."

At one point, two GIs had to pull him down and sit on the priest to keep him from trying to get through enemy fire to find a soldier who turned out to be already dead. "We were pinned down, but every time I saw him, he was standing up and walking around," said platoon Sgt. Dan Garrison. "The only time I saw him get down was when he was pulling somebody out. He just wouldn't quit."

> ## "Later, when I was told they were alive, I had trouble believing it … Their faces were just a bloody pulp—nothing but raw open flesh. The concussion of the explosion had virtually ripped their faces off."
> —CAPT. BRUCE DREES

When he was awarded the Distinguished Service Cross (DSC) in Vietnam, Liteky remained characteristically low key. "It was my first heavy contact … suddenly the air was full of sound and flying steel and fury, and many of our men were falling and calling for medics, and there was just no time to be afraid or concerned about oneself with so many needing help," he said.

"There wasn't time to really think. I think that what moves someone to act in an emergency is pride—personal pride—and a concern that we all have for each other in times like that. There were a lot of good men out there." Yet the beloved "Padre" confessed, "I thought if I were going to die, it would be now." After returning stateside, Chaplain Liteky was presented with the Medal of Honor in November 1968. (He died Jan. 20, 2017.)

'BRAVEST MEN I HAVE EVER SEEN'

Such displays of selflessness were not limited to men of God. 1st Lt. Wayne H. Morris, head of A Company's 4th Platoon, led three perilous assaults until ordered to withdraw. He carried wounded to safety, making sure none were left behind. When reinforcements arrived, Morris attacked again. This inspired his men to "overrun and defeat the enemy forces," says his Distinguished Service Cross (DSC) citation.

Spec. 4 Gary G. Hahn was a squad leader in the 4th Platoon. Shot in the arm and struck again by automatic weapons fire, he nonetheless crawled forward, firing as he went. He got to within about 50 feet of an enemy machine gun position, tossing three hand grenades but was hit a third time, fatally. His actions inspired fellow squad members to destroy the bunker and earned Hahn the Silver Star.

Then there is the saga of Pfc. Allen Oakes and Pfc. Jose Arcevedo-Perez, both members of Alpha's 2nd Platoon. Lt. Morris said of them, "I shall never forget the actions of these brave men. They did not hesitate to try and do what had to be done, even though it was so unbelievably dangerous. They are two of the bravest men I shall ever hope to see. Thank God for both of them."

Under a terrible hail of fire, the duo went forward against orders. "Three times during this period, enemy groups of platoon size attempted to assault us," Capt. Drees wrote in their Silver Star recommendations. "Each time they [the VC] were decimated, in part due to the actions of these two men." Then a Claymore mine exploded directly in front of them and Oakes and Arcevedo-Perez were left for dead. Chaplain Liteky even administered last rites.

"Later, when I was told they were alive, I had trouble believing it," Drees said. "Their faces were just a bloody pulp—nothing but raw open flesh. The concussion of the explosion had virtually ripped their faces off."

Both men received the Silver Star. But in Arcevedo-Perez's case, it was 28 years after the fact. His paperwork had been lost all those years.

DISTINGUISHED SERVICE CROSS

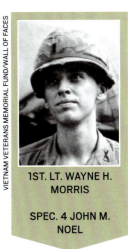

1ST. LT. WAYNE H. MORRIS

SPEC. 4 JOHN M. NOEL

SILVER STAR

SPEC. 4 GARY G. HAHN
(POSTHUMOUS)

CPL. ROBERT A. PRETTY
(POSTHUMOUS)

2ND LT. JOHN SOGNIER
(POSTHUMOUS)

PFC. JOSE ARCEVEDO-PEREZ

2ND LT. GARY R. CLARK
(POSTHUMOUS)

SGT. GUY FINLEY
(POSTHUMOUS)

PFC. ALLEN OAKES

DEVOTION TO THE END

Running out of ammo, the two A Company platoons disengaged to regroup and retrieve the wounded. "The enemy pressure and firepower was so intense that I instructed them [the platoon leaders] to leave the dead and only bring out the wounded," Drees said. "The initial contact lasted between 30 and 50 minutes."

Alpha reorganized and went back to the fight, but this time with reinforcements. Two platoons of the 4th Battalion's B Company, a platoon from D Troop of the 17th Armored Cav and A Co., 3rd Bn., 7th Inf., joined in. The latter unit was airlifted by the 187th Assault Helicopter Company from Firebase Concord to the north of the VC camp to attack on the flank. Bravo Company and Delta Troop made radio contact with Alpha, moving out to renew the attack about 5 p.m.

The 7th Infantry actually attacked at 6:15 p.m. When it did, the VC were ready. The infantrymen were hit by accurate enemy fire in the center of the east side of the base camp.

"We were airlifted around 3:30 p.m.," remembered Daniel Aragaki, who was with the Weapons Platoon of A Co., 3rd Bn., 7th Inf. "When we jumped from the moving chopper five feet off the ground we never saw each other [referring to a fellow soldier] again. I found my platoon as it was forming up on the outskirts of the jungle. One of our gunships was shooting five feet in front of us. Casings were falling on top of us and burning our necks. The gunship finally stopped firing at us.

"Because the jungle was so thick we formed a single file. A few minutes later, Claymores went off and we were in the biggest firefight I had been in. Jerald Peyton, behind me, was hit by a Claymore blast in the face and shot several times. [But he survived.] Rounds were hitting the tree just above my head. We could hear the NVA talking and yelling at each other but could not see them. So we just shot into the jungle in the direction of their voices. Darkness came like a rock dropping out of the sky and the shooting stopped."

For other members of the 7th the shooting proved fatal. Four who fought to the end earned the Silver Star. 2nd Lt. John Sognier was attempting to overrun a bunker when he was KIA. Three other men died together, literally shoulder to shoulder where they fell.

2nd Lt. Gary R. Clark, a platoon leader, and some of his men made it to the center of the enemy base camp. It proved to be their final action. First wounded in the leg, Clark was then hit by a Claymore blast wounding both legs and a thigh. Still, he took on an enemy emplacement. Finally knocked out of action by automatic weapons fire, he ordered his men to leave him and continue the assault. Platoon Sgt. Guy Finley, who assisted the wounded and helped evacuate them, refused the order. So did Clark's radio-telephone operator, Cpl. Robert Pretty. They stuck with him to the end.

COMING TOGETHER AS ONE

Meanwhile, Bravo Company and the armored cav unit engaged the communists. Phil Tolvin, who arrived at the LZ with Bravo, recalled in *Days of Valor,* "As I began to move forward again, all hell broke loose. We were opened up upon with automatic weapons fire. My steel pot was ripped from my head as I hit the dirt with all my strength. All we could do was to keep at a low angle to the earth to prevent ourselves from being riddled by the hail of lead traversing our position from the two forces that straddled us."

Staff Sgt. James A. Pius was the leader of 2nd Platoon in B Company. "We teamed up with an element from D Troop, 17th Cav, and rode in on their armored personnel carriers [APCs] to reinforce Alpha Company," Pius said. "The battle was intense … one of the APCs got hit by a rocket-propelled grenade … A second and much larger explosion came from a tree. I climbed on top of the APC, and could see the NVA moving to flank us on the left. With hand grenades and automatic weapons we were able to take out three enemy positions."

Pius added, "I witnessed many acts of bravery, and men from all units coming together as one. In the end, a relatively small force … gained the edge over a superior force in a well-entrenched fortification."

One of those acts of bravery was performed by Spec. 4 John M. Noel of Delta Troop. When the commander of one of the five APCs was wounded, Noel assumed command without hesitation. A blast severed his arm, and he sustained another severe wound to the abdomen. Still, Noel refused evacuation and fought on until his position was untenable, according to his DSC citation.

'A SCENE FROM DANTE'S INFERNO'

When it was nearly night, the VC broke contact and faded into the jungle darkness. U.S. units established defensive perimeters. By morning, the enemy was gone, averting another bloody encounter. The scene inside the deserted VC camp was horrific.

"The whole place was like a scene out of Dante's Inferno," wrote Robert Tonsetic in his book, *Days of Valor*. "Before they [VC] left, however, they took the time to finish off several wounded Alpha Company soldiers who lay inside their perimeter, a senseless act of cruelty that the Americans would not soon forget."

"Redcatchers" of A Co., 4th Bn., 12th Inf., 199th LIB, take a rest after the fighting in December 1967.

Spec. 4 Cliff Kaylor

Cliff Kaylor was part of the force that entered the camp on Dec. 7. He saw "lots of American bodies lying dead in the trenches … Many were shot between the eyes with a single round, as if executed."

The American tally for the fighting around Firebase Nashua was 26 KIA and 92 WIA. The 4th Battalion's A Company had five KIA along with two medics from Headquarters Company. E Company counted two dead. It had engaged in a firefight north of Nashua. Delta Troop lost three men at the base camp and another two to a command-detonated mine while clearing a road earlier in the day.

A Co., 3rd Bn., 7th Inf., took the biggest hit with 10 KIA. That battalion HQ Company also lost a medic to "friendly fire." In addition, the day before, a member of a long-range patrol from F Co., 51st Inf., was KIA. And the German shepherd scout dog, King, died of his wounds. Gunfire claimed nearly two-thirds (17) of the lives; shrapnel, 8 (31%); and an accident one. Deaths were split evenly between draftees and volunteers.

Every loss of life permanently impacts those who witness it. Bruce Drees has one death indelibly etched in his memory: "I remember seeing one of our men shot through the chest crawling on the road. I realized he was dying and no one was with him. My worst moment of the war was then because I did not dare to stop and comfort him in his last moments of life." He added, "The men who did the suffering and dying need to be remembered."

Drees also took great pride in the men with whom he served. "My opinion is that the individual self-discipline of the men of A Company was the key factor in the outcome of the battle." Then-1st Lt. Wayne Morris agreed wholeheartedly about the esprit de corps of the GIs in the two Alpha platoons. "Our uniforms were filthy and caked with mud and blood … But we moved into a perfect tactical patrol formation and walked into the FSB [Nashua] as a solid and cohesive unit." ✪

THE TOLL

U.S. KIA:
26

U.S. WIA:
92

BY SUSAN KATZ KEATING

GOING TOE-TO-TOE AT TAM QUAN

During the buildup to the infamous Tet Offensive of 1968, Vietnamese communists gave clear signs of impending action on the Bong Son Plain of Binh Din province. American troops stationed in the area had no way of knowing they soon would become embroiled in a ferocious fight that would span the course of two grueling weeks. Clearly, though, a battle was brewing. The only question was, when and how would it begin?

The answer came late on the afternoon of Dec. 6, 1967. Scout helicopters from the 1st Squadron of the 9th Cav's A Troop were flying near the village of Dai Dong, following up on intelligence reports that the 22nd NVA Regiment had moved its headquarters into the area.

From their airborne perch, the scouts spotted a radio antenna outside a hut. Simultaneously, hidden enemy gunners took aim at the helicopters and opened fire. An aerial rifle platoon from A Troop went in to investigate. The platoon immediately came under intense enemy fire and found itself pinned in place. The 9th Cav dispatched D Troop's Red Platoon to assist. This unit also quickly became entrapped.

INTO A HAIL OF BULLETS

The 1st Cavalry Division's 1st Brigade ("All the Way") had entered the lair of the 7th and 8th battalions of the 22nd Regt., 3rd NVA Div. And now, what had started out as an aerial reconnaissance mission had turned into a combat emergency, with two platoons threatened with annihilation.

With darkness approaching, two additional units, from B Co., 1st Bn., 8th Cav, and from A Co., 1st Bn., 50th (Mechanized) Inf., arrived to assist. The 50th served as a general reserve in Vietnam, starting off with the "First Team."

These units, too, encountered instant violence. "We immediately came under fire from the tree line," recalls David James Bowman, a B Company radio-telephone operator (RTO) who stepped off of a Huey utility helicopter and into a hail of bullets.

Bill Martin, a medic from B Company, was with a platoon approaching a downed helicopter when the lead man was shot in the shoulder. The wounded sergeant lay in shock, fully exposed to enemy fire. "We dragged him back for better cover," said Martin, who administered mouth-to-mouth resuscitation in a vain attempt to save the man. Other lives also were lost quickly to NVA fire. Two men of B Company and two from the 9th Cav were KIA on Dec. 6.

As the fight continued into the night, descending flares cast an undulating light over the

The deadliest engagement of *Operation Pershing* occurred between Dec. 6-20, 1967, around a village called Dai Dong. The 1st Cavalry Division's 1st Brigade engaged in a two-week running battle, emerging victorious.

DECEMBER 1967

NATIONAL ARCHIVES PHOTO #IIII-CCV-391-CC41409

A radio-telephone operator and a rifleman, both of D Trp., 1st Sqdn., 9th Cav, 1st Cav Div., stand on a trail watching while a VC hut burns down in Binh Dinh province on July 21, 1967. That same unit drew first fire at Dai Dong five months later.

DISTINGUISHED SERVICE CROSS

PFC. THOMAS D. BOUCHARD

CAPT. DONALD A. ORSINI

VIETNAM VETERANS MEMORIAL FUND/WALL OF FACES

battlefield. The illumination revealed eerie surroundings. Bowman saw that he was lying next to an enemy hand, protruding from the earth. "The dead soldier must have been in an underground bunker that had collapsed from our supporting artillery fire," he recalled.

With the help of the 50th Infantry's fire-blazing armored personnel carriers, the extra forces rescued the entrapped platoons by day's end.

In the morning of Dec. 7, the action resumed. GIs used a combination of blocking fire, artillery and teargas; then they moved in for the fight. The communists were largely concealed inside well-camouflaged bunkers that were protected by an extensive network of trenches. The terrain was interlaced with punji pits and booby traps.

The mech unit managed to move through the intricate defenses, only to become entangled in hand-to-hand combat in the trenches. "This was my first taste of a big battle," says Rigo Ordaz, who rode in with the 1/50th's D Company. "This was my baptism under fire."

SEALING ESCAPE ROUTES

While these GIs slugged it out in the trenches, other units were fully engaged elsewhere. Among them was C Co., 2nd Bn., 8th Cav, which was assigned to help seal off enemy escape routes.

Gerald Saylor was a second lieutenant in charge of a weapons platoon that headed north along the coast. "We started getting sniped at within a half hour of moving out," Saylor said. Eventually, the platoon traversed a rice paddy while heading toward a village. "One hundred meters [109 yards] into the rice paddy, all hell cut loose," Saylor said. He dropped to the earth. His rifle sank beneath his body and into the mud. "My weapon was useless."

Saylor had no option but to stay as low as possible alongside his RTO, Pfc. James Elrod, whose rifle also was gummed up with mud. "I was laying there listening to the rounds cracking overhead, wishing I could cut the buttons off my fatigues so I could get even lower," Saylor recalled.

Elrod briefly removed his helmet, which he always did before speaking. In that instant, he took a direct hit in the head. He fell forward into the water. Saylor and John Gunderson, a chaplain who had just crawled onto the scene, bandaged Elrod as best they could. "We knew he wasn't going to make it," Saylor remembered. "We tried anyway."

Others in the unit continued to fall. Seven members of C Company, including an artillery forward observer and a scout dog handler, died on "Pearl Harbor Day." And so did four of A-1-8th and one from A-1-50th.

An incredible act of bravery was demonstrated by Pfc. Thomas D. Bouchard. Assigned as a cook to HQ Company of the 1st Bn., 8th Cav, he boarded a helicopter and flew to Dai Dong where he quickly reverted to being a rifleman. Besides saving casualties from a hit APC, he personally destroyed several NVA bunkers, in one instance killing three communists at point-blank range. Bouchard received the Distinguished Service Cross (DSC).

Saylor and his able-bodied men took on the overwhelming task of pulling the dead and wounded under fire from the rice paddy and into a drainage ditch. They followed the ditch to a better position and continued the fight from a nearby village.

WITHERING FIRE AT TRUONG LAM

Three days later, on Dec. 10, the 50th's B Company was dispatched northward to clear villages along the coast. As the mechanized column moved near the village of Truong Lam, the first platoon came under heavy fire. Two other platoons went in to relieve the pressure. Before long, all three platoons were intensely engaged.

"We were getting withering fire at close range and didn't have the option of fighting into the opposing force because we were blocked by a ditch," said Richard Guthrie, then the B Company

Though the battle began at Dai Dong, a sweep of other hamlets, like Truong Lam and My An 2, lead to more fights with the NVA.

commander. Guthrie's radio frequency was blocked, preventing him from calling in help. "I told my sergeant to go find out what happened to the radio," Guthrie recalled. "He took three steps and was shot through the chest." Another platoon sergeant limped up and said the unit was being fired on from the trees.

Bravo Company suffered 10 KIA that day near the village. (Only May 5-6, 1968—the firefight at An Bao—claimed more lives (16) from the 50th in Vietnam in a single action than Truong Lam.)

12TH CAV AT MY AN

Within five days, on Dec. 15, D Co., 1st Bn., 12th Cav, was sent to reinforce the 50th near the village of My An (2), not far from Dai Dong. There it came up against elements of the 9th VC Regiment. Spec. 4 Allen J. Lynch, an RTO, spotted three of his fellow soldiers lying wounded on the open battlefield. Lynch raced through the deadly fire zone in order to help the wounded men. For the next several hours, Lynch defended and protected the three soldiers. He labored with such ferocity—repeatedly carrying the wounded men to safer ground, and killing seven enemy soldiers at close range—that he later was awarded the Medal of Honor.

Lynch was certainly not alone in his courageous actions. Capt. Donald A. Orsini, CO of D Company, attempted rescue of wounded troops and successfully continued rescue efforts even though he was seriously wounded. He was awarded the DSC.

By far, the deadliest day of the fight for Tam Quan was Dec. 15. Some 22 men of the 12th Cav's 1st Battalion lost their lives then. Charlie Company sustained the single largest number of KIAs at nine. Three medics from HQ Company died, too, some of whom were likely serving with C Company. One company member, Sgt. Richard Boeshart, received a posthumous Silver Star. Tragically, the only other associated fatalities were three members of C Co., 1st Bn., 8th Cav, killed by "friendly" artillery fire on Dec. 15. Sporadic fighting continued in the area for yet another five days. The battle officially ended on Dec. 20.

The engagements at Dai Dong and My An are collectively known as the Battle of Tam Quan, and to the men as the Battle of Dai Dong. Ironically, as Glenn H. Sheathelm, artillery recon sergeant with 1st Plt., D Co., 1st Bn., 8th Cav, points out, "The second Battle of Tam Quan didn't actually take place there but was more focused on Dai Dong, Binh Phu, An Thai and Thien Chanh."

No matter what its name, though, the horrendous fight left its mark. "This was the first time we encountered a force big enough to stand and fight," Guthrie said. "They didn't leave. They stood fast." The Americans, though, held sway. But they did so at a cost. Three units sustained the lion's share of killed in action: 12th Cav (23), 8th Cav (17) and 50th Infantry (12). Five units accounted for the remaining seven men, including two U.S. advisers attached to the 40th ARVN Regiment. All told, 59 Americans were killed and 250 wounded in the complex fight for Tam Quan.

'UNBEATABLE COMBINATION'

"The importance of the Battle of Tam Quan is that we caught the enemy before they had a chance to attack us on that Tet Offensive," says Ordaz. Indeed, Gen. John Tolson concluded in *Airmobility, 1961-1971* that the Bong Son Plain "was the least affected of any part of South Vietnam during Tet."

This was a direct tribute to the men on the field of battle—to the 1st Brigade. In his wide-ranging after-action report, Col. Donald Rattan, the 1st Brigade commander, wrote that the force molded on the field of battle during those intense days was an "unbeatable combination." The men who served in this battle, Rattan wrote, were "gallant, quick reacting, flexible and tireless." Furthermore, "Their one burning goal—to find and defeat the enemy—became a realization in gaining this important victory." ✪

MEDAL OF HONOR

SPEC. 4 ALLEN JAMES LYNCH

THE TOLL

U.S. KIA:
59

U.S. WIA:
250

BY SHANNON HANSON

SURVIVING THE 'STREET WITHOUT JOY'

As 1967 was drawing to a close, Special Landing Force Bravo had one more commitment to round out the year. In *Operation Badger Tooth*, the 3rd Battalion, 1st Marines, was to conduct search-and-destroy operations through 14 towns and villages in southern Quang Tri province.

Intelligence came through that suspected enemy forces were hiding in the villages of Thon Tham Khe and Thon Trung An in the coastal region east of Route 1, named the "Street Without Joy" by French war correspondent Bernard Fall during the French Indochina War (1946-54). The battalion was instructed to clear the villages, then continue with the original plan.

L Company swept both villages on Dec. 26, with M Company in support, and found nothing. The next morning, both companies set out to sweep the villages one more time before moving on. As 2nd Platoon, the leading platoon of Lima Company, approached the edge of Tham Khe at about 11 a.m., a concealed enemy force opened up with machine guns, rifles and mortars.

When shots first rang out, said Larry Christensen, a grenadier with 2nd Platoon, "we started running to the village. We didn't have much for cover. We would have been sitting ducks where we were."

Marines of K Co., 3rd Bn., 1st Marines, are moved by amphibian tractors during *Operation Badger Tooth* before assaulting the fortified village of Thon Tham Khe. The company lost six men in the battle; 48 were KIA in all on Dec. 27, 1967.

'DEAD MARINES ALL AROUND'

Taken by surprise, casualties mounted quickly.

"We took cover in a creek bed and put down cover fire for our fellow Marines caught in the open," Christensen said. "We tried to get all our wounded and dead into the bed. I remember one of our Marines standing up in the open area, and he kept firing magazine after magazine to try to keep the gooks' heads down so others could recover the dead and wounded."

When word came over the radio that 2nd Platoon had come under fire, 1st and 3rd platoons headed in for support. Cpl. Gene Ward, fire team leader in 1st Platoon, recalled that the area around the village was deep sand, totally open with no cover.

On Dec. 27, 1967, the 3rd Battalion of the 1st Marines was severely tested in the Battle of Thon Tham Khe, sustaining 48 KIA within seven hours.

DECEMBER 1967

U.S. MARINE CORPS PHOTO #A190208

Marines of 3rd Bn., 1st Marines, take cover as they fight to enter the village of Thon Tham Khe on Dec. 27, 1967. Their search of the village the previous day failed to detect the presence of the elaborate but well-camouflaged positions of the 116th NVA Battalion.

PHOTO COURTESY JOHN REGAL

Sgt. John Regina, foreground, and Dennis "Doc" Day, both with 2nd Plt., K Co., 3rd Bn., 1st Marines, wait before assaulting the village of Thon Tham Khe.

The village of Thon Tham Khe was situated southeast of Quang Tri and north of Hue on the Vietnamese coastline of the South China Sea.

The men were soon pinned down with machine gun fire.

Capt. Thomas S. Hubbell called for air strikes and naval gunfire while the company regrouped. He ordered a frontal assault and led the charge himself.

"Out of the corner of my eye, I saw the captain fall like a downed grizzly," Lance Cpl. Randall McGlone wrote in his book, *Guts & Glory.* "He had been shot in the forehead."

With the captain's radioman down as well, Lima Company lost contact with the rest of the battalion. But the assault on the enemy bunkers continued.

"Dead Marines lay all around, and the air was hazy from the smoke of small-arms fire and grenades," McGlone said.

"At some point in time in the battle," said 2nd Platoon radioman Cpl. Mike Freed, "as we were pinned down by enemy fire in the creek bed, and our dead, wounded and equipment were everywhere, I realized that no one was coming—no police, no firemen, no Mom and Dad. All we had was our faith in God and the young Marines to our left or right."

Lt. Col. Max McQuown ordered M Company to join the fight on Lima's left flank, and it immediately came under heavy fire. He then ordered K Company to attack from the south end of Tham Khe, to take the pressure off Lima and Mike companies.

Like Lima, K Company Marines had to cross a sandy area with no natural cover.

"A tree line marked the south edge of the hamlet, and the enemy was dug in and camouflaged," said company commander Capt. John Regal.

Third Platoon commander 1st Lt. Peter Nies recalls that maneuvering was reduced to very short running spurts, due to sporadic but heavy fire. For cover, they pushed and dug sand in front of the bodies of Marines who had already been hit.

"It took us all afternoon to take our objective," Regal said, "and we did so only with the aid of two tanks that finally made it ashore."

SHORT OF THE TREE LINE

Pfc. Jim Snyder and pointman Pfc. Carlos Lozano of 1st Plt., Lima Co., were within a few hundred yards of the tree line when Lozano was shot in the head. Snyder tried to dig a hole in the sand with his hands for cover. When he looked behind him, he saw that the rest of Lima had pulled back, but a corpsman ran out to assist them.

Lozano died a short time later, but Snyder and the corpsman couldn't move. "We were pinned down out there all day with no communication with the rest of the company," Snyder said. "Every time we tried to move from that position they would fire at us. We waited until it was pitch dark before we took Lozano back and found what was left of the company. There weren't many."

"The breaking up of the enemy's front line had erased any danger of our being overrun," McGlone said, "and the destruction of the central bunker had weakened their position to the point that they, like us, were just trying to hold their positions."

Many remained stuck there.

"For the rest of the day we made no appreciable progress," Ward said. "We did not find out the condition of 2nd Platoon until evening, when we were able to advance under cover of darkness. Most had been killed in the initial ambush. We spent the next few hours carrying our dead and wounded to safety. It was the worst night of my life."

Christensen was one of several volunteers to ferry the wounded to a Medevac helicopter. Under heavy fire, the Marines jumped into the helicopter for cover. It took off, but took fire in its hydraulic line and was forced to land. Christensen helped evacuate the wounded men from the helicopter and set up security.

Pfc. F. Reindersma mans the radio as Dennis "Doc" Day, gives medical aid to Pfc. S.S. Kramlich after he sustained a back wound. Day was KIA at Lam Xuan a short time later on Feb. 2, 1968.

"If it wasn't for the rest of Lima Company and other battalion units, I don't think any of us from Lima Two would have survived," Christensen said, "and I salute them."

"The survivors of our charge were tired but unbeaten," McGlone said. "The charge had taken a terrible toll on our company. The majority of our enlisted men (128) were killed or wounded; the captain, two platoon commanders and two staff sergeants were also down. Only one staff sergeant and one lieutenant remained."

VILLAGE SECURE, CASUALTIES HIGH

At 6 p.m., all companies were ordered to pull back and cordon off the village for the night. Both I and K companies were able to tie in with each other, but close enemy contact and the presence of the dead and wounded in front of their positions kept L and M companies from pulling back until nearly midnight.

The next morning, the battalion attacked Tham Khe from the south, met little resistance and had secured the village by noon. They found few enemy bodies—there were 31 known dead, but 100 bodies were later found northwest of the village by ARVN forces—but did discover hidden bunkers and well-constructed, camouflaged fighting holes. Clearly, the village had been properly prepared for a fight by the 116th NVA Battalion.

Nies recalls seeing 10 to 12 dead Marines from Lima Company, including an entire 3.5-inch rocket team killed in place in firing position. In all, 48 Marines were killed *that day*: 26 from Lima, 12 from Mike, six from Kilo, two from H&S Company and two members of C Co., 1st Eng. Bn. Gunfire claimed 96% of all the lives lost. Some 86 men were wounded.

After the battle, McGlone said, "We searched for abandoned weapons and supplies, and then destroyed the entire village."

According to Snyder, McQuown said all the actions taken that day were in the normal line of duty, so no medals would be awarded. But, Snyder says, "Everyone that day deserved a medal." Some awards did follow: McGlone received a Bronze Star for valor; Snyder and Freed each received a Navy Commendation Medal with Combat V. The battalion received two Navy Unit Commendations and a Presidential Unit Citation.

A tragic epilogue was yet to come. Cpl. David O. Kamp of L Company received multiple gunshot wounds during the battle, including one in his neck that left him paralyzed. He died March 19, 1997, as a result of his wounds, making him the battle's 49th fatality. His name was added to the Vietnam Veterans Memorial in Washington, D.C., on Memorial Day 2000. ✪

THE TOLL

U.S. KIA:
49

U.S. WIA:
86

BRUTAL BATTLES OF VIETNAM
1968

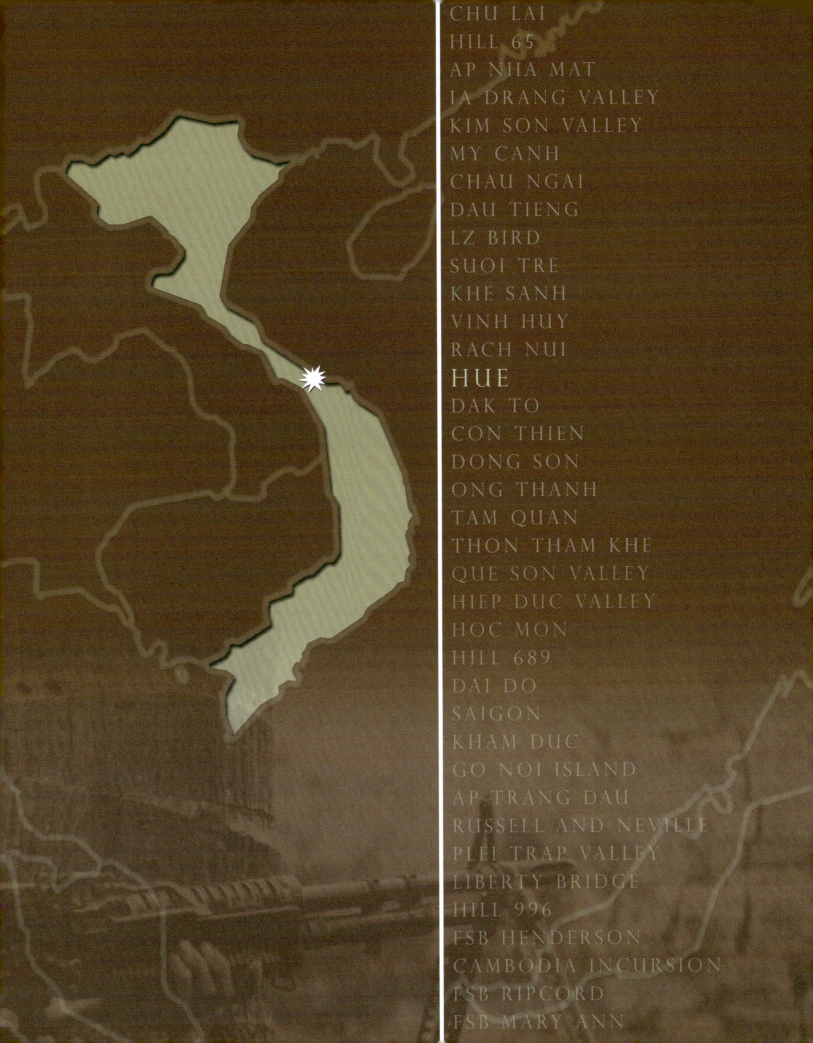

CHU LAI
HILL 65
AP NHA MAT
IA DRANG VALLEY
KIM SON VALLEY
MY CANH
CHAU NGAI
DAU TIENG
LZ BIRD
SUOI TRE
KHE SANH
VINH HUY
RACH NUI
HUE
DAK TO
CON THIEN
DONG SON
ONG THANH
TAM QUAN
THON THAM KHE
QUE SON VALLEY
HIEP DUC VALLEY
HOC MON
HILL 689
DAI DO
SAIGON
KHAM DUC
GO NOI ISLAND
AP TRANG DAU
RUSSELL AND NEVILLE
PLEI TRAP VALLEY
LIBERTY BRIDGE
HILL 996
FSB HENDERSON
CAMBODIA INCURSION
FSB RIPCORD
FSB MARY ANN

BY TIM DYHOUSE

'BAD NEWS' IN THE QUE SON AND HIEP DUC VALLEYS

As New Year's Day 1968 approached, U.S. soldiers in Vietnam's Que Son Valley braced for an attack. GIs and their commanders knew the valley, located in Quang Nam province in the I Corps tactical zone about 20 miles south of Da Nang, was strategic terrain.

What they didn't know was that the enemy viewed it as a natural thoroughfare to funnel troops into Hue for the planned Tet Offensive later in the month. It would be dubbed "Death Valley" by those who survived the combat between Jan. 2-8, 1968.

'INSANITY' AT LZ LESLIE

The first encounter was near LZ (Landing Zone) Ross, property of the 3rd Brigade, 1st Cav Division, in the western part of the valley. On Jan. 2, C Co., 2nd Bn., 12th Cav inadvertently ran into elements of the 2nd NVA (North Vietnamese Army) Division in the western Que Son Mountains during a patrol. The Americans fought well, losing two KIAs while killing 39 NVA troops.

In his book *The Illustrated History of Chargers: The Vietnam War*, F. Clifton Berry, Jr., wrote, "It was the start of a week of continuous unrelenting combat between regiments of the 2nd NVA Division and two U.S. brigades. Neither rain nor darkness saw the fighting abate."

Two NVA prisoners captured in the initial fight confirmed that a full-scale attack on LZ Ross was imminent. At 1:30 a.m. on Jan. 3, three battalions of the 3rd NVA Regiment launched a four-hour attack on Ross and hit LZ Leslie, about three miles southwest of Ross, as well.

A, B and C companies of 2nd Bn., 12th Cav and tanks from B Troop, 1st Sqdn., 1st Armored Cav, defended Ross. The Americans ignored intense mortar and rocket fire that was supposed to keep them hunkered down while NVA sappers infiltrated the perimeter wire. Warned of this tactic, GIs punished the attackers, killing 242 enemy with only one U.S. KIA and 63 WIA. The attack at Ross ended at about 5:30 a.m.

NVA troops did infiltrate the perimeter at LZ Leslie, which some GIs have said "was in a terrible place for an LZ" because it was surrounded by high hills. For a 19-year-old private first class spending his first night in Vietnam, the spot was intimidating.

Troopers of 2nd and 3rd platoons, A Co., 2nd Bn., 12th Cav gather for a photo in October 1967 before their brutal fight in Que Son Valley. Because of its many casualties, 2/12 became known as the "Death Battalion."

Two U.S. brigades fighting during the first week of January 1968 in adjacent valleys in Vietnam's I Corps thwarted an NVA buildup for the upcoming Tet Offensive. But the cost for the 196th LIB and 3rd Bde., 1st Cav Div., was 182 KIA.

JANUARY 1968

"Incoming mortars, rockets, gunfire and a human wave attack began. The machine gunner in my bunker fired until the barrel glowed red and then began to sag from the heat."

—JERRY McNELLY, D CO., 2ND BN., 12TH CAV

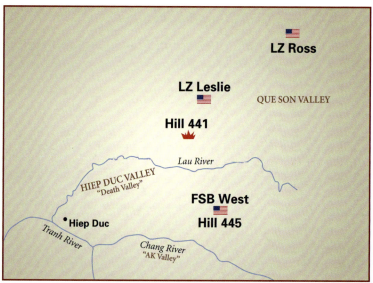

LZ Ross, Leslie and FSB West were at the heart of the NVA attempt to control the Hiep Duc and Que Son valleys in January 1968.

"I had fallen asleep for what seemed to be only a few minutes," recalled Jerry McNelly of D Co., 2nd Bn., 12th Cav, and a VFW life member from Phoenix, Ariz. "Then the insanity started. Incoming mortars, rockets, gunfire and a human wave attack began. The machine gunner in my bunker fired until the barrel glowed red and then began to sag from the heat. As B-40 rockets flew over our bunker, the NVA overran our position."

McNelly saw an NVA soldier with a satchel charge enter an ammo bunker up the hill from his position. "I dove into my bunker as the ammo bunker exploded," he said. "I could not hear anything. I remember I had no ammo and don't remember much after the explosion. I didn't believe I would be able to survive 12 months of this insanity, after all, this was only my first night."

The fighting continued at LZ Leslie all day on Jan. 3. At noon, McNelly and the other defenders received reinforcement from a company of the 1st Bn., 7th Cav. A total of 12 Americans died at Leslie: D Company lost eight men, Alpha (2) and two artillerymen. Some 64 NVA were killed—including 40 inside the perimeter—during the attack.

Meanwhile, A Co., 5th Bn., 7th Cav, engaged NVA troops west of LZ Ross on Hill 62 on Route 536, losing three KIA.

"We could see them firing quad-50s [four .50-caliber machine guns mounted as one unit] from a village across a small stream from LZ Ross," recalled Wayne R. Gibbs, who was a 21-year-old infantryman with 1st Platoon. "The NVA didn't think we would fire back since they were using the village as cover. They were wrong." Gibbs was seriously wounded by a mortar round at about 12:30 p.m. when his platoon was lured into an ambush.

"Our new lieutenant was a little rambunctious, and we got pinned down," he recalled. "The NVA had zeroed in their mortars on a [helicopter] gunship in front of us. One round went long and landed near me. It tore up my spleen pretty bad, and I got a lot of shrapnel in my legs. But our guys took out a lot of their soldiers."

Gibbs said he learned later that captured documents confirmed that the "NVA didn't like to tangle with the 3rd Brigade" (7th Cav's parent outfit in the 1st Cav Division).

'LIKE ANTS STREAMING OUT OF THE HILLS'

During all of this, the 196th Light Infantry Brigade (LIB) had its own fight to the south. Soon after midnight on Jan. 3, NVA troops began dropping mortar rounds on FSB (Fire Support

Base) West, only about three miles south of LZ Leslie but on the other side of the formidable Hill 441 in the Hiep Duc Valley.

Patrolling northwest of FSB West during the day, D Co., 4th Bn., 31st Inf., 196th LIB reported some 60 to 70 NVA troops between them and the firebase. By dusk, D Company had repositioned itself to provide a better defense of FSB West.

"We were laagered down below the north side of Hill 445 [FSB West]," recalled Ron Morenz of D Company's 3rd Platoon. "The NVA had crossed a stream in front of us and hit us from several villages. I don't know how many there were, but another guy who had a better vantage point said they looked like ants streaming out of the hills."

Artillery batteries from 2nd Bn., 20th FA and 3rd Bn., 82nd FA atop West fired at the enemy down below. But Morenz says a small squad-sized NVA unit snuck up the west side of the hill and harassed the artillerymen the entire night of Jan. 3-4 in an effort to keep them occupied. Morenz was wounded around 1 a.m.

"A mortar round hit the command post and woke me up," he said. "I was low crawling when the next one dropped, and I got hit in the leg and back."

For the next 48 hours, NVA sappers, supported by mortar and rocket fire, tried to infiltrate the American bases.

CHAOS IN 'THE TRENCH'

On the evening of Jan. 5, the NVA stepped up its attacks around FSB West in Hiep Duc Valley. A regiment-sized NVA force encircled a night defensive position of C Co., 2nd Bn., 1st Inf., in a low-lying area GIs called "the trench" just to the west of the firebase.

Fire Support Base West, located in the Hiep Duc Valley, was home to elements of the 196th Light Infantry Brigade in January 1968. The firebase dominated the southwestern end of the valley, an ideal place to support the brigade's combat operations.

DISTINGUISHED SERVICE CROSS

**1ST LT.
STEVEN C. DRAKE**
(POSTHUMOUS)
C CO., 2ND BN.,
1ST INF. REGT.,
196TH LIB

**SPEC. 4
GORDON W. GASKIN**
HQ CO., 2ND BN.,
12TH CAV, 1ST CAV DIV.

**1ST LT.
BROMLEY H. GERMAN**
(POSTHUMOUS)
A CO., 3RD BN., 82ND
ARTY, AMERICAL DIV.

PFC. ALLEN B. GLINES
(POSTHUMOUS)
A CO., 5TH BN.,
7TH CAV, 1ST CAV DIV.

**LT. COL.
BOB L. GREGORY**
(POSTHUMOUS)
2ND BN., 12TH CAV,
1ST CAV DIV.

**CAPT.
ROBERT L. HELVEY**
A CO., 2ND BN.,
12TH CAV, 1ST CAV DIV.

**2ND LT.
RICHARD J. SEIBERT**
(POSTHUMOUS)
D CO., 3RD BN.,
21ST INF. REGT.,
196TH LIB

**1ST LT.
JAMES M. STONE**
(POSTHUMOUS)
C CO., 2ND BN.,
12TH CAV, 1ST CAV DIV.

STAFF SGT. JOHN E. DARNELL, JR.
C CO., 2ND BN., 12TH CAV, 1ST CAV DIV.

1ST LT. ROBERT M. LANDRY
D CO., 3RD BN., 21ST INF. REGT., AMERICAL

STAFF SGT. RONALD E. MALACHI
C CO., 2ND BN., 1ST INF. REGT., 196TH LIB

1ST LT. RONALD S. TAYLOR
C CO., 2ND BN., 12TH CAV, 1ST CAV DIV.

PHOTOS COURTESY
VIETNAM VETERANS MEMORIAL FUND/WALL OF FACES
AND MILITARY TIMES HALL OF VALOR

"They caught us when we were vulnerable," said Mike Seniuk, of 1st Sqd., 2nd Plt., C Co. "They broke us up into small groups and tried to finish us off one group at a time. If you moved or fired your weapon, you were dead."

The company commander was wounded and evacuated around 6 p.m. By 8:40 p.m., C Company reported NVA troops were inside its perimeter.

"We could see the muzzle flashes from the enemy," said Capt. Larry Byers, commander of A Co., 4th Bn., 31st Inf., 196th LIB. "I received orders at 2050 [8:50 p.m., Jan. 5] to move A Company to reinforce. We requested 81mm illumination to help us see our way off Hill 445 [FSB West] because there was no moon. Traveling was slow."

The firebase was parallel to C Company's position.

"If it hadn't been for them, we would have been wiped out. They saved us," Seniuk said. "I've since talked with guys from 4/31 who told me they couldn't believe the number of green tracers from NVA AK-47s shooting into us. To come down and help us after seeing all the firing took a lot of guts."

The enemy was estimated to be a reinforced NVA regiment along with Main Force (formal units) Viet Cong, anywhere from 800 to 1,200 troops.

Seniuk says all of C Company's platoon leaders were killed that night, and the unit was in danger of dissolving into chaos. C Company's acting commander, Lt. Steven C. Drake, was killed just after midnight.

1st Lt. Bromley German, who had been directing artillery fire onto the NVA, took charge, but was killed shortly thereafter. German earned a posthumous Distinguished Service Cross (DSC) for calling in strikes extremely close that repulsed the assault.

> ## "There were a lot of heroes that night. Most of them are dead."
>
> — MIKE SENIUK, 1ST SQD., 2ND PLT., C CO.

Seniuk, who was wounded by shrapnel from a mortar round, says the Americans fought back mainly with hand grenades because muzzle flashes would have exposed their positions.

By 12:44 a.m., Jan. 6, Byers' unit had linked up with C Company, which lost nine KIA (including an Army journalist) on Jan. 5. Early on Jan. 6, eight more Charlie Company members were KIA along with two artillerymen from A Btry., 3rd Bn. 82nd Arty.

Ed Latini, who served under Byers in 2nd Sqd., 2nd Plt., said artillery fired from FSB West drove off or killed nearly all the enemy that night. "I think we gathered up 35 or 40 bodies and found about six mortar positions the next morning," said Latini. "I remember piling the bodies up. I think we put a dent in that regiment."

Seniuk recalls the relief of seeing friendly faces after a hellish night. "In the early morning, before dawn, a voice shouted out to us through the fog, 'Don't shoot,'" Seniuk said. "It was a soldier from 4/31. He looked around and said 'Oh my God, what happened.'" Seniuk has the names of all C Company soldiers killed that night, plus two others, tattooed on his arms. "There were a lot of heroes that night," he said. "Most of them are dead."

Spec. 4 Jim Heitz and another soldier walk away from a burning hut while on a search and destroy mission. Heitz was wounded near LZ Ross.

PURSUIT OF THE NVA BEGINS

In the Que Son Valley early on Jan. 7, A and C companies from 2nd Bn., 12th Cav, began search-and-destroy sweeps southwest of LZ Ross to regain control of the area.

Urged on by commanders to move faster, both companies soon found themselves surrounded by NVA troops and were pinned down west of LZ Ross, near Xuan Que (2), for the rest of the day.

"We walked into an ambush, and we had NVA troops in between us and C Company," recalled Jim Heitz, a 20-year-old specialist four with A Company's 3rd Platoon. "I was the fourth man in the formation. Our point man was killed, and the squad leader was shot through the chest but survived. The third man was not wounded. I remember thinking, 'This is it.'"

One platoon from C Company was cut off completely and under attack all night, suffering five KIA. Platoon leader Lt. Ronald S. Taylor earned a DSC for keeping the platoon intact during the night.

B Troop, an armored cavalry unit attached to 3rd Bde., 1st Cav Div., during the Que Son battles, moved in from LZ Ross to help the beleaguered cavalrymen and also find Lt. Col. Robert L. Gregory, 2nd Battalion's commander, whose helicopter had been shot down at 1:12 p.m. while circling over the battle. Gregory, along with Maj. Lawrence M. Malone (2/12's operations officer), Master Sgt. Richard C. Keefe and four helicopter crewmen were killed in the crash. Their bodies weren't recovered until March 1968.

B Troop leader Capt. John Barrevetto was killed while attempting to locate the chopper. Unfortunately, when B Troop's men managed to fight their way to the pinned-down Americans, they mistook A Company for the enemy and opened fire. Some of A Company's wounded may have been killed as they lay in an old bomb crater.

PHOTO COURTESY MIKE OBERG

Soldiers guard enemy prisoners captured during the fighting in the Que Son Valley. Enemy losses were substantial.

"We got caught in the crossfire between B Troop and the NVA," Heitz said. "One guy grabbed a shirt and waved it at B Troop to stop firing. Afterward, they loaded us [the wounded] into an armored personnel carrier. I was right next to Capt. Barrevetto's body."

Fighting in the vicinity of Xuan Que, including the helicopter shoot-down, cost the lives of 24 men: 11 from A Company, seven in the chopper loss, five in Charlie Company and one member of B Troop.

At first light on Jan. 8, a relief force from LZ Ross and tanks from B Troop rescued the pinned-down cavalrymen. Charles A. Krohn wrote in his *The Lost Battalion* that "the extraction was made a little easier by the arrival of B-52 bombers that dropped 500-pounders on the mountain passes to the west." Krohn also credits "the pilots and the crew of the helicopter who flew in late dusk to deliver ammo to the encircled men."

Back in the Hiep Duc Valley on Jan. 9, fighting renewed for the 196th LIB. D Co., 3/21, commanded by Capt. Roland Belcher, patrolled west of FSB West where C Co., 2/1 had been chewed up on Jan. 6. Shortly after noon, Belcher's company walked into a horseshoe-shaped ambush and began taking heavy casualties. By 3 p.m., Belcher had been killed and all radio contact from his unit ceased. Over Jan. 9-10, 14 members of Delta Company—part of Task Force Oscar—were KIA after being surrounded 3.7 miles northeast of Hiep Duc village.

Four companies composing two task forces moved to help Belcher's company. Enemy contact waned in early evening, enabling 58 survivors from D Company to join the reinforcements. Within two days, the NVA had moved out of the area.

In the Que Son Valley, the 2nd Bn., 12th Cav (nicknamed the "Death Battalion") alone sustained 43 KIA and 116 WIA. The 1st Cav's 3rd Brigade as a whole had 116 KIA. The 196th Light Infantry Brigade while operating in the Hiep Duc Valley suffered 64 KIA, 204 WIA and 10 captured. Three of the POWs died in captivity. Combined, the two brigades counted 182 KIA in one week in those valleys. Twelve DSCs (half of them posthumous) attest to the courage of the men who fought in the valleys.

The NVA had been foiled in its attempt to control the region. But for the GIs who survived the fighting, and would later slug it out during the Tet Offensive, the mood was anything but celebratory.

A cavalryman who was wounded in the Que Son Valley said the area was "bad news for the French, it was bad news for us and it was bad news for the Marines who came in after us." ✪

THE
TOLL

U.S. KIA:

182

PAYING 'COMPOUND INTEREST' AT CEMETERY HILL

BY TIM DYHOUSE

When the Tet Offensive was launched at Tuy Hoa, the NVA paid dearly.

They received the call at about 2 a.m. on Jan. 30, 1968, while "out in the bush" conducting ambushes. An American artillery battery at Tuy Hoa, located on the coast of the South China Sea in Phu Yen province, had been overrun by the NVA.

Paratroopers from D Co., 4th Bn., 503rd Inf., 173rd Airborne Bde., and attached units loaded into helicopters and landed at the Tuy Hoa North airstrip at dawn.

The NVA had attacked the U.S. compound during the night because it contained a prison with a large number of Communist inmates, whom they planned to release, arm and use to help take over Tuy Hoa. Because of Delta Company they never got the chance.

"My troops killed all the NVA who had infiltrated the perimeter that night," said Ted Arthurs, 4th Battalion's sergeant major at the time. "I believe there were 18 killed. We piled the bodies near the wire, and the Tuy Hoa villagers came out to inspect the bodies."

Arthurs says the NVA would often come into villages and conscript young men into the army, and their families would never see them again. He believes the villagers were trying to identify the bodies as those of their relatives.

Around noon, with the Americans firmly in control of the compound, 4th Battalion's commander, Lt. Col. James H. Johnson, ordered an attack on the NVA entrenched in Tuy Hoa, some 1,000 yards from the airstrip. To get to the village, the GIs assaulted through an old graveyard atop a slight rise. The fight would become known as the Battle of Cemetery Hill.

One paratrooper remembers the NVA were "well dug in and were everywhere, like a shooting gallery."

"One popped from a hole and shot me in the chest an instant before I could shoot him," 1st Sgt. Robert Brewington recalled.

> One paratrooper remembers the NVA were "well dug in and were everywhere, like a shooting gallery."

"He kept shooting at my head. I lay still and played dead."

Brewington said a young machine gunner rolled him onto his back and dragged him toward a berm. At that instant, the machine gunner was shot in the right elbow.

"He kept dragging me with his left arm, and I was shot again with the bullet creasing my chin and ricocheting off my tooth," Brewington said. "I don't know what happened to the young man who saved me. I did hear that he lost his arm, but I don't know."

After the initial assault, D Company pulled back to allow air strikes on the village, which occurred around 2 p.m. An NVA soldier captured during the battle later said that "most of the battalion staff was killed or wounded by the air strikes."

By 3:30 p.m., 4th Battalion's C Company had joined the fight and was in position with D Company (counting only 44 men) for a fresh assault. Unfortunately, a short 81mm round fired by GIs hit near the D troopers' left flank as they waited, wounding 15 and ultimately rendering Delta Company "combat ineffective," according to the after-action report.

The Americans remained dug in as air strikes pounded the village during the night. The assault, planned for the morning, never occurred. NVA troops not killed or wounded by the air strikes escaped into the mountains during the night. Two battalions from the 47th ARVN Regiment occupied the village in the morning against light opposition.

As a result of the battle, 23 GIs died: eight from D Company, five from HQ Company, four from C Company, three from 3rd Bn., 319th Arty, and three of C Btry., 6th Bn., 32nd Arty. Arthurs, whose 2006 book *Land With No Sun* (Stackpole) details the battle, says the Americans killed 189 NVA and took some 30 as POWs. As Arthurs said in the after-action report, "Charles [NVA troops] paid off with compound interest for every casualty he extracted from us." ✪

BY AL HEMINGWAY

THREE DEADLIEST DAYS
AT KHE SANH

Vietnam's longest and probably most controversial battle also is one of the most written about of the war. Yet relatively little attention has been focused on the highest casualty-producing actions of the siege— those outside the perimeter.

Built on a 300-foot plateau 15 miles south of the DMZ, the Marine base overlooked the Rao Quan River and Route 9, which linked Laos to South Vietnamese coastal cities. Hilltop outposts provided protection. And this is where the deadliest clashes took place.

Some 6,000 Marines defended Khe Sanh Combat Base, including the 5,000-man 26th Marine Regiment. 1st Bn., 9th Marines and 1st Bn., 13th Marines (Artillery) reinforced it. South Vietnam's 37th Ranger Battalion was sent in, too. The Americans faced off against perhaps 15,000 to 20,000 North Vietnamese troops at one time.

DEFENSE OF OUTPOST ALPHA (HILL 64)

Hill 64 was 550 yards west of the 9th Marines' position at the Rock Quarry and manned by 1st Platoon reinforced by Weapons Platoon (bringing the total to 66 men), A Co., 1st Bn., 9th Marines. From its summit, the hill supposedly provided an extra measure of security.

On Feb. 8, under cover of a thick fog, three NVA companies attacked the Marines. Mortars saturated the hilltop, and enemy soldiers rolled over the concertina wire using canvas sheets.

Platoon commander 2nd Lt. Terence Roach was immediately gunned down, and soon the enemy drove the Leathernecks back, seizing a portion of the hill.

"From sheer weight of numbers," Alpha Company vet Randell Widner later wrote in *Proud Warriors*, "the North Vietnamese gradually pushed the Marines back until the enemy owned two-thirds of the outpost."

Widner continued, "Pfc. Michael A. Berry of the 1st Squad was engaged in a furious hand grenade duel with the NVA soldiers, when a Chicom grenade hit him on top of the helmet and landed at his feet. "Pfc. Berry picked it up and drew back to throw it, but the grenade went off in his hand." Luckily, Berry was relatively unscathed when the projectile's "uneven frag

> ## "Pfc. Berry picked it up and drew back to throw it, but the grenade went off in his hand."
>
> —RANDELL WIDNER, A CO., 1ST BN., 9TH MARINES

The siege of Khe Sanh occurred between Jan. 20 and April 14, 1968. During the campaign, three separate actions would stand out in terms of U.S. casualties sustained in short spans of time.

JAN-APR 1968

Two members of B Co., 1st Bn., 26th Marines, take aim at the NVA in February 1968.

MARINE CORPS PHOTO #A190833

MARINE CORPS PHOTO #A801090

Leathernecks of the 1st Bn., 9th Marines, perform perimeter duty west of the Khe Sanh Combat Base in early March 1968. Outposts such as this were dangerously exposed to enemy attack, as a 1st Battalion platoon of A Company found out on Feb. 8 on Hill 64.

pattern" traveled down and away from his body and undoubtedly saved his hand.

The fighting was unmerciful as the Leathernecks put up a desperate stand to hold the hill. Isolated pockets of infantrymen grabbed anything they could get to defend themselves. Marines used entrenching tools and five-gallon water cans as weapons.

"I had the M-79 and was the grenadier," said Pfc. George Einhorn in the book *Voices of Courage: The Battle for Khe Sanh, Vietnam* by Ronald J. Drez and Douglas Brinkley.* "I kept firing it straight up into the air because that's how close they were to us. We kept moving constantly because every time I fired a round, I was getting grenaded. The M-79 made a big flash. It was a dead giveaway."

As the enemy crept ever closer, the survivors withdrew to the southernmost area of the trenchline and piled sandbags to afford themselves some protection. Although the riflemen braced themselves for the inevitable assault, it never came. Instead, the NVA chose to toss grenades at the Marines, causing additional casualties.

Lance Cpl. Arnold Alderette recalled: "We ran short of grenades … just to keep them on their toes and not to be tempted to charging, we would throw rocks. And when they wouldn't go off, then the enemy would come in and rush us again, and that's when we would throw the real grenades."

"We ran short of grenades … just to keep them on their toes and not to be tempted to charging, we would throw rocks."

—LANCE CPL. ARNOLD ALDERETTE

At dawn, Capt. Henry J.M. Radcliffe, company commander, led the remainder of his unit to relieve the embattled Marines defending the hilltop. After fighting to the foot of the hill, Radcliffe called in an air strike.

As the jets pounded the NVA, the infantrymen struck the enemy's lines. The ferocity of the assault drove the NVA from the summit. As the communists scurried down the hill, several 106mm recoilless rifles and 90mm rounds from a tank cut them down.

The Marines from the 1st and Weapons platoons had suffered grievously: 27 dead and another 23 wounded. The lifeless corpses of some 150 NVA soldiers were strewn about the area as well.

In an ironic twist, Col. David E. Lownds, commanding officer of the 26th Marines, ordered the remnants of Alpha Company back to the main base, and Hill 64 was abandoned.

Mike Coonan, the surviving corpsman, said: "It is a story that deserves to be told. The few stories written provide only an incomplete picture and at worst distort the truth and dishonor the dead."

Hill 64 was located outside of Khe Sanh Combat Base, less than one-third mile west of the Rock Quarry.

TRAGEDY OF THE 'GHOST PATROL'

As enemy activity increased around the main base, it was decided to dispatch a patrol to reconnoiter the area outside the wire.

On Feb. 25, the 1st and 3rd squads of 3rd Plt., B Co., 1st Bn., 26th Marines, led by 2nd Lt. Donald Jacques, was handed the tough assignment. These 47 men were to sweep along the wire to find an enemy mortar position. From the outset, Jacques' patrol ran into trouble when it inadvertently left its predetermined course and ran into an enemy ambush.

"I was standing face-to-face with this one NVA, and I wanted to shoot him, but my rifle wouldn't shoot," recalled Pfc. Alexander Tretiakoff. "I took the magazine out and threw it away, and put another one in. To my right was a lance corporal and Pfc. McKenzie, and McKenzie was shot."

Using a captured PRC-25 radio, NVA soldiers confused the situation by sending false messages back to the communications center at the combat base. Supporting fire from mortarmen and tankers attempted to provide a protective shield for the Marines as they withdrew. The pea-soup fog, however, thwarted their efforts.

Withdrawing as rapidly as they could and trying to take as many wounded as possible, the survivors made it to a series of trenches. The NVA poured automatic weapons fire and grenades into the Leathernecks.

"[A] grenade had just gone off, and I was stunned, and Lt. Jacques came by and said, 'We gotta get out of here. Get

"And I just started crawling. ... I looked over and he [Jacques] stood up for some ungodly reason, and that's when he got it."

—LANCE CPL. ARNOLD ALDERETTE

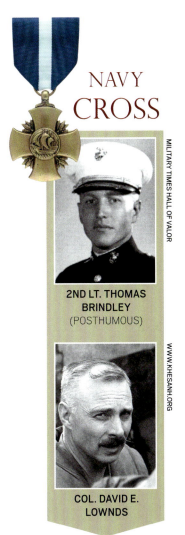

NAVY CROSS

2ND LT. THOMAS BRINDLEY (POSTHUMOUS)

COL. DAVID E. LOWNDS

ABOVE: Marine forward observers of the 26th Marines try to spot NVA mortar positions from the front lines at Khe Sanh in February 1968.

RIGHT: Marine tankers dig in their tanks to form a defensive fire line on the Khe Sanh perimeter on March 2, 1968.

out the best way you can,'" said Navy corpsman Frank Calzia. "And I just started crawling. I left my rifle; I just had my .45 with me. I looked over and he [Jacques] stood up for some ungodly reason, and that's when he got it. I crawled over to him. He'd caught it right across both femoral arteries, and he was dead within minutes."

What began as a routine patrol had evolved into a nightmare. Casualties turned out to be 28 killed and 17 wounded. It would be known as the "ghost patrol" because 25 of the men's bodies could not be recovered. This was on direct orders from Maj. Gen. Rathvon Tompkins, commander of the 3rd Marine Division.

"The ambush of Feb. 25 occurred just east of our location," remembered Recon Marine Raymond A. Milligan. "Marines from Bravo Company went out on what was supposed to be a line-of-sight patrol, but they ran right into an ambush. When B Company Marines ventured out to recover the bodies a month later, we manned their position." (The 3rd Recon Company sustained 10 KIA and nearly 60 WIA during the siege.)

On March 30, B Company fixed bayonets and charged across a road to recover remains of the 25 Marines KIA a month earlier. With vengeance spurring them on, the enraged Leathernecks destroyed the NVA bunkers, killing 115 communists in the process. But 12 Marines died.

"We were on the 'gray sector' of the perimeter around the airstrip during the siege," recalled former B Company rifleman Bill Jayne. "My platoon went out to help but was hit in an ambush. Bravo Company did a lot of damage to the NVA, but we lost a lot of guys, too."

Only two bodies were found that day. Not until April 6 was the recovery operation completed as best it could be by the 1st Battalion's Delta Company.

Ultimately, Marines recovered partial remains of nine men, who were buried in a mass grave at Jefferson Barracks National Cemetery in St. Louis. One was mistakenly identified as Ronald Ridgeway, but he had actually been captured and was released in March 1973.

A U.S. Air Force C-123K transport was hit by enemy fire over Khe Sanh on March 6, 1968, killing 57 Americans.

SHOOTDOWN OF THE C-123 PROVIDER

On March 6, U.S. Air Force Lt. Col. Frederick J. Hampton was on his second approach to land his C-123K Provider aircraft at Khe Sanh airstrip. To avoid a midair collision with an Air America (CIA) plane, Hampton aborted the first landing a mile southeast of the intended runway. Suddenly, enemy gunners struck one of the aircraft's engines and a few moments later the aircraft spiraled into the ground, exploded, and burned in the crash.

It was the single greatest loss of American lives at Khe Sanh: 57. The crash killed 50 Marines (46 of them from the 26th Regiment and including one Navy corpsman); six U.S. Air Force personnel from the 311th Air Commando Squadron, 315th ACW and 15th Aerial Port Squadron; and one civilian, Robert Ellison, a photographer for *Newsweek* magazine. Hardest hit was the 1st Battalion's H&S Company with 15 men killed.

Ellison had spent weeks with B Co., 1st Bn., 26th Marines at Khe Sanh and returned voluntarily to the besieged base. It was a fateful decision. "I don't want to leave until those Marines do," he had said. "I will march out with them."

Due to the hostile environment, the crash victims' bodies were not retrieved and identified until weeks later. Two sets of remains, however, were never recovered: U.S. Air Force Staff Sgt. William F. Anselmo and U.S. Air Force Staff Sgt. Noel L. Rios. Both had been to Khe Sanh before to repair damaged aircraft and a "check of Dong Ha hospital, the mortuary detachments in the area and other bases/outposts was made, but no trace of either man could be found," according to a biography of Anselmo. Their whereabouts, to this day, are still shrouded in mystery.

The siege of Khe Sanh persisted for more than another month. It became legendary. The 26th Marine Regiment would receive the Presidential Unit Citation. But these *three* actions alone that claimed 112 American lives in a matter of mere minutes or hours would soon be forgotten. ✪

Editor's Note: Official casualties for the entire siege of the base itself were 205 KIA and 1,600 WIA. The Army relief effort (Operation Pegasus) by the 1st Cav Division cost 97 KIA and 667 WIA. The Rev. Ray Stubbe, author of Battalion of Kings, *calculates that 402 Americans from all services died around Khe Sanh between Jan. 20 and March 31, 1968.*

*Quotes from Marines Einhorn, Alderette, Tretiakoff and Calzia are all from the same book.

THE TOLL

(Grand total for entire battle)

U.S. KIA:
205

U.S. WIA:
1,600

'OUR FINEST HOUR': MPs BATTLE FOR SAIGON

BY RICHARD K. KOLB

On Jan. 31, 1968, the U.S. Army's Military Police Corps fought its deadliest battle ever. In doing so, the 716th MP Battalion earned the Presidential Unit Citation.

'They're coming in! They're coming in! Help me! Help me!" Spec. 4 Charles Daniel pleaded in his last radio transmission as the Viet Cong breached the Chi Mac Dinh entrance to the U.S. Embassy in Saigon. The Tet Offensive of 1968 had begun and there was only one U.S. force capable of defending key installations in South Vietnam's capital city.

"The MPs were our eyes and ears in the opening stages of the battle for Saigon," said Lt. Col. Richard E. George, provost marshal there on Jan. 31, when the city was engulfed by chaotic combat for nearly 24 hours.

Because of the status of forces agreement, no U.S. combat units were allowed in Saigon. That left security up to the 716th MP Bn., 89th MP Grp., 18th MP Bde. That battalion consisted of four military police companies (A, B, C and attached 527th) with one rifle security company (C had 196 men) from the 52nd Infantry attached. But when the full-scale assault began, only 300 men were immediately available for duty. That number quickly grew to 800 in action by dawn. Reinforcements also came from the 95th MP Battalion, including D Co., 52nd Inf.

One of the MP Corps' missions had always been "to fight as infantry when required." This would be one of those occasions. "We converted from an MP battalion to a tactical infantry battalion in less than three hours and, in essence, we were unassisted for the first 12 to 18 hours," said Lt. Col. Gordon D. Rowe, CO of the 716th. Although not infantry trained and often derided as "Saigon warriors," the MPs would soon prove their mettle in battle.

Their urban battlefield was vast, encompassing four major combat areas within the 50-square-mile Capitol Military District (CMD). It contained 130 military installations. Other U.S. security guard units contributed to the defense. The Air Force's 377th Security Police Squadron (SPS) handled the

PHOTOS COURTESY UNITED STATES ARMY MILITARY POLICE CORPS REGIMENTAL MUSEUM

The MP quick-reaction force (above) led by Lt. Frank Ribich (left) gathers outside of the U.S. Embassy grounds.

5.46-square-mile Tan Son Nhut Air Base on the city's outskirts. C Company of the Marine Security Guard Battalion normally protected the four-acre U.S. Embassy compound. Both outfits would be heavily engaged on Jan. 31.

The U.S. military police/security guard units faced a fanatical foe. Thousands of Viet Cong (VC) infiltrated Saigon on the Lunar New Year. Eleven local VC battalions, spearheaded by the C-10 Sapper Battalion, targeted the CMD. Approximately 23 VC of the latter unit hit the Embassy.

U.S. Embassy Besieged

Spec. 4 Daniel and Pfc. William Sebast of the 527th MP Company put up a valiant fight, killing two VC, but they were gunned down on Embassy grounds at 2:47 a.m. Four hours later, elements of B Co., 716th, launched a counterattack to retake America's diplomatic nerve center.

A ferocious battle raged in an alley near Bachelor Officers' Quarters #3. Military policemen, other soldiers and a South Vietnamese V-100 armored vehicle attempt to rescue survivors from the ambushed convoy that had been carrying an MP quick-reaction force.

Pfc. Paul V. Healey led the assault. Ramming the main gate with a jeep, he resorted to shooting the lock off with a pistol when that failed. Killing eight VC with rifle fire and grenades, he went on to help save a trapped Embassy officer. According to his Distinguished Service Cross citation, Healey "placed fierce fire on the Viet Cong in the building until they were annihilated ..." and was "instrumental in the successful defense of the U.S. Embassy."

Healey later recalled his confrontation with the enemy: "Just me and him, face to face. And I just fired and killed him. Then I reloaded. The two VC had just come from around the corner. There's a good chance there's somebody else there, so I threw a grenade and the grenade exploded. There were three bodies there when we went around the corner. You know, I was very, very lucky. Things just went my way that day." Fighting at the Embassy cost the lives of four members of the 527th MP Company, as well as a Marine security guard.

Standoff at the Phu Tho Racetrack

Meanwhile, at 4:45 a.m., an urgent message came across the radio from Jeep Patrol 95. "The driver caught a slug in the gut and I'm under heavy automatic weapons fire. Can you give me help?" The 6th Binh Tan VC Battalion had attacked in the vicinity of the Phu Tho Racetrack in the city's Cholon section, an ethnic Chinese suburb.

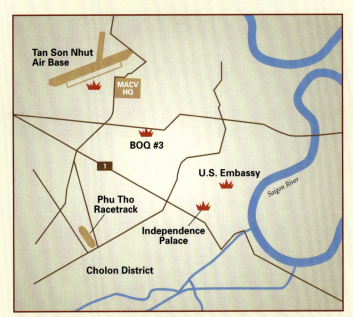

MPs fought fiercely at the U.S. Embassy, near the Phu Tho Racetrack and at BOQ No. 3. Air Force 377th Security Police Squadron members protected Tan Son Nhut Air Base with their lives.

The response to the call for help was immediate. Sgt. Michael Grieve and Pfc. Roland Bowen of A Co., 716th, arrived and provided covering fire. They made a gallant stand with a machine gun, but were killed. Their courage garnered Silver Stars.

Fighting was fierce, with VC using the bodies of their comrades as stepping stones to get at the American airmen. Still, they held out for 24 precious minutes, blocking penetration of Gate 51.

Spec. 4 Max Whitmyer was with the 12-man reaction force that came next. "We got half a block from the corner and we could see bodies lying beside two jeeps there," he told *Detroit News* correspondent Robert L. Pisor. "We found a wounded MP under a truck—he and his buddy had heard 95's call for help and had run into the same ambush. We started back, received fire from the rear, and finally got pinned down in a hotel for the rest of the morning."

A second quick reaction force from C Co., 52nd Inf., got to the scene shortly thereafter. It, too, was ambushed. Pfc. Dennis Darling was among those who went down a side street. "There were bodies all over the place," he said. "There were three dead VC and many puddles of blood. One GI, who had a medical armband on, had been shot in the face with an AK-47 on full automatic. There was a dead ARVN [South Vietnamese soldier] in a jeep and a couple of mama-sans [older females] and their kids and stuff from their houses—all shot in a pile in the street."

Staff Sgt. Herman Holness, of the 52nd's C Company, went into action after the lead vehicle in his patrol was attacked. Reaching the disabled truck with its wounded and trapped GIs, he unleashed relentless fire on the VC until able to drag them to safety. Despite being badly wounded, he refused evacuation. Holness received the Silver Star.

The 52nd "Ready Rifles," as they were nicknamed, paid a steep price for their rescue efforts: eight were killed in action. Besides the 10 members of the 716th KIA (including C-52) near the racetrack, four grunts of the 199th Light Infantry Brigade and two men of the 1st Signal Brigade died there. Quick reaction forces had been quickly assembled from an assortment of service and support units.

Death in an Alley: BOQ No. 3

It was at Bachelor Officers Quarters (BOQ) No. 3, east of Tan Son Nhut Air Base, that the MPs sustained their greatest number of casualties. It started with the two MPs of Unit C9A being killed there at 4:08 a.m.

In response, a 25-man reaction force was sent to the BOQ, located 2½ miles northwest of the Embassy. The men were riding in a 2½-ton truck escorted by two gun jeeps when it was ambushed by a company-size VC force in an alley. Machine gun fire and B-40 rockets rained down on the Americans. The last two vehicles absorbed the full brunt of the attack at less than 10 feet away. VC were concealed in buildings on both sides of the alley, pouring in volley after volley of fire.

"Suddenly, there were two loud explosions and bright flashes of light behind me," MP John R. Van Wagner said. "Automatic weapons fire swept the alley, and we ran for the BOQ. We knew it was bad in there, but we didn't know how bad until almost noon."

The radio traffic revealed the gravity of the situation: "Waco 6-0, that alert force is laying down there in the alleyway. They're pitched up against the wall, if any of them is still alive ..." Another message said, "We tried to go down the alley. They blew up a Claymore [mine] on us. We're going to hold tight right here."

Spec. 4 Charles Miller (B Company) and 1st Lt. Gerald Waltman and Spec. 4 Ronald Kendall of C Company, 716th, were among those who braved the alley. All three assisted the wounded and saved lives, each earning the Silver Star.

At around 5 p.m., after 13 hours of combat, the alley fight ended. But only after a U.S. armor unit cleared the VC out. "We really needed armor at BOQ No. 3," said Lt. Col. George. "We couldn't get the wounded out of that alley for more than 12 hours and there's no question in my mind that men died there who didn't have to." Fifteen men died there, to be precise: 12 from C Co., 716th; one in the 212th MP Company (Sentry Dog); and two from D Co., 52nd Inf. (Rifle Security).

Last Stand at Bunker 51

On Tan Son Nhut airbase itself, the Air Force 377th SPS was undergoing its own special hell. Bunker 51 was located 246 feet south of Gate 51, a focal point of the offensive. A rocket and mortar barrage hit at 3:30 a.m. followed by 600 VC assaulting the old French bunker. It was manned by only five security policemen.

"You could see and hear them as they walked across a rice paddy," recalled Sgt. Alonzo Coggins. "It was scary, very scary." Fighting was fierce, with VC using the bodies of their comrades as stepping stones to get at the American airmen. Still, they held out for 24 precious minutes, blocking penetration of Gate

DISTINGUISHED SERVICE CROSS
PFC. PAUL V. HEALEY

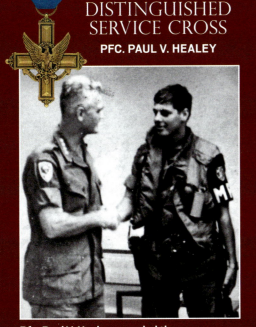

Pfc. Paul V. Healey, awarded the Distinguished Service Cross by Gen. William Westmoreland, led the counterattack on the U.S. Embassy, killing eight Viet Cong and saving American lives.

SILVER STAR

Eight MPs of the 716th MP Battalion were awarded Silver Stars for their role in the battle of Saigon:
Sgt. John Shook (He was with Pfc. Healey)
Pfc. Steven Sears
Spec. 4 Ronald Kendall
Spec. 4 Alvin Troyer
Spec. 4 Charles Miller
Spec. 4 Bruce MacCartney
Spec. 4 Vincent Giovannelli
Sgt. 1st Class James R. Lobato
(Center: Lt. Col. Gordon R. Rowe, battalion commander.)

Other Silver Stars recipients were:

Sgt. Michael Grieve *	Sgt. Alonzo Coggins
Pfc. Roland Bowen *	Sgt. William J. Cyr *
Staff Sgt. Herman Holness	Sgt. Harold L. Fischer *
1st Lt. Gerald Waltman	Sgt. Edward C. Hebron *
Maj. Carl Bender	Sgt. Roger B. Mills *

* Posthumous

51 and buying time for fellow GIs to prepare for the onslaught.

Ultimately, the bunker took 20 direct rocket hits, killing four of the five airmen. The fifth, Coggins, was so badly wounded that he was left for dead by the VC. Then he survived for eight hours, sometimes under intense U.S. artillery and air strikes. "I was the only one who got out alive," Coggins said years later. "God placed angels around me to get out of the hell that I went through."

Coggins finally received his Silver Star in 1999, 31 years after the fact. His four fellow security policemen—Sgt. William J. Cyr, Sgt. Harold L. Fischer, Sgt. Edward C. Hebron and Sgt. Roger B. Mills—received their Silver Stars posthumously at the time. Maj. Carl Bender, 377th SPS operations officer and the one who ordered the fire on enemy-held Bunker 51, received the Silver Star, too. Bender killed eight VC in the Echo Sector near the bunker, but took 54 shrapnel hits in the process.

'Highest Degree of Gallantry'

That the military police and security guard units did their collective duty expertly is beyond doubt. Brig. Gen. Albin Irzyk, Saigon area commander and a hard-bitten WWII veteran, said, "Their [MPs] perfor-

mances as combat troopers can be described in only the most glowing of superlatives."

The very highest echelon of command readily agreed. The 716th MP Battalion and attached units were awarded the Presidential Unit Citation for responding to "enemy activity under extremely difficult and hazardous conditions, displaying the highest degree of gallantry and determination."

That gallantry was costly, though. A total of 35 military policemen and attached security guard riflemen sacrificed their lives on Jan. 31, 1968—most in the first 12 hours—during the battle for Saigon. That tally includes 27 men from the 716th, three from the 95th MP Bn., four of the 377th SPS and one member of the Marine Security Guard Battalion. Shrapnel wounds caused 60% of the deaths; gunfire the remaining 40%. Volunteers constituted 63% of the fatalities; draftees, 37%. The 716th also had 44 WIA.

Lt. Col. George, the provost marshal, said years later, "To have served with men of this caliber has always been a source of pride for me." He perhaps put it best when he remarked, "For this indeed was the Corps' [Military Police] finest hour." ✪

THE TOLL

U.S. KIA:
(MP, SP & SG)
35

U.S. WIA:
44

BY AL HEMINGWAY

HUE: COMBAT FOR THE ANCIENT CAPITAL

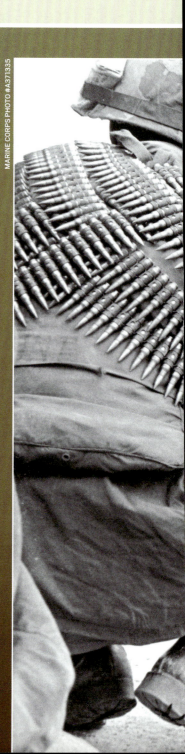

I n preparation for the Tet Offensive, the North Vietnamese Army (NVA) infiltrated the former French colonial capital, digging fighting holes and establishing strong points throughout Hue. Reducing these points became the hallmark of the fighting for Marines during *Operation Hue City*. For the Army, the task was to prevent enemy reinforcements from entering the city, and later from escaping it.

'HELL' AT THE MACV COMPOUND

In the early morning hours of Jan. 31, 1968, the 4th and 6th NVA regiments were poised to strike at Hue City. Enemy forces moved on the MACV (Military Assistance Command, Vietnam) compound, but 200 Americans inside the complex reacted quickly and thwarted their attempt to breach its walls.

MACV clerk-typist Spec. 4 James Mueller recalled: "The explosions, the flares, the small-arms fire, the loud noises, the yelling, the screaming and the chaos seemed to go on forever. We stayed in our bunker, followed the sergeant's orders to defend the corner and prayed that we would survive this hell."

Despite a thick fog and heavy NVA anti-aircraft fire, Chief Warrant Officer Frederick Ferguson of C Co., 227th Aviation Bn., 1st Cav Div., flew down the Perfume River at a low level under a hail of enemy flak to save the crew of a downed helicopter. After an extremely difficult landing in a confined area, his aircraft was badly damaged by mortar fire.

In *And Brave Men, Too*, Tim Lowry interviewed Ferguson: "[The chopper] was shaking so bad you couldn't read the instrument panel. So I pushed it into the Hue-Phu Bai air strip, and when I cleared the fence, I just slid it onto the sand out front. If that barbed-wire fence had been another strand higher, I don't think I'd have made it over." Ferguson was awarded the Medal of Honor for his extraordinary flying skills in saving the lives of five men under a "hail of mortar fire."

Pfc. Dominick Carango, H Co., 2nd Bn., 5th Marines, provides fire support with his M-60 machine gun during the street fighting in Hue in February 1968. His assistant crouches nearby with bandoliers of 7.62mm ammunition rounds wrapped around him. Hue was the deadliest urban combat for the Leathernecks since Seoul during the Korean War.

MARINE CORPS PHOTO #A371335

From Jan. 31 to Feb. 25, 1968, Marines and soldiers slugged it out with the NVA for control of perhaps Vietnam's most symbolic city during the Tet Offensive.

JAN-FEB 1968

Lance Cpl. Robert Wallace (left) of H & S Company along with A Company members, 1st Battalion, 1st Marines, carries a 106mm recoilless rifle during the battle for Hue. This weapon proved deadly effective in blowing holes through walls.

MARINE CORPS PHOTO #A190343

SOUTH BANK OF THE PERFUME RIVER

Task Force X-Ray, consisting of two battalions of the 1st and 5th Marines, was ordered to move out that same day. Boarding trucks, A Co., 1st Bn., 1st Marines and G Co., 2nd Bn., 5th Marines snaked their way up Route 1. Augmented by four M-48 tanks, the column was approaching the outskirts of the city when it was ambushed. Realizing the severity of the situation, additional reinforcements were rushed to Hue.

Hue was two cities in one, a modern and old city (including the Citadel), separated by the Perfume River. It would be house-to-house fighting, down 11 city blocks, to drive the enemy from the modern city. The grunts threw smoke grenades to hide their movements as riflemen rushed into buildings tossing grenades. Other Marines followed close behind, M-16s on full-automatic.

"The first day was terrible," recalled Lance Cpl. Barney Barnes of G Co., 2nd Bn., 5th Marines. "We lost a lot of guys as we ran across the Nguyen Hoang Bridge. You could hear the bullets hitting the girders. It was the longest 400 meters [437 yards] I ever ran.

"The NVA played tricks as well. We were attacking the hospital, and they would lie in the hospital beds and pretend to be corpses and pop up and shoot. Another time our platoon sergeant greeted two nuns in the hallway. When they bowed, he did. He smiled until they pulled a pistol on him. Luckily, it misfired and they took off running. He could see they were men under the habits."

> ## "We were attacking the hospital, and they [NVA] would lie in the hospital beds and pretend to be corpses and pop up and shoot."
>
> —LANCE CPL. BARNEY BARNES, G CO., 2ND BN., 5TH MARINES

OPPOSITE PAGE: Marines seek cover in the rubble of the east gate tower during fighting in the Citadel. It was the heart of the former Imperial Capital of Vietnam.

PHOTO BY ARMY SPC. 4 JOHN OLSON

MEDAL OF
HONOR

SGT. ALFREDO
GONZALEZ
(POSTHUMOUS)

In heavy house-to-house fighting in the Citadel, a C Co., 1st Bn., 5th Marines, machine gunner fires his M-60 machine gun at an enemy position on Feb. 19, 1968.

Cpl. Lester Tully of G Co., 2nd Bn., 5th Marines, remembered: "Our squad was sitting next to a fence when a grenade came flying over at us. Luckily, no one was injured. A Marine with a 3.5-inch rocket launcher saw them running down the canal, and he put a round right between them. What a shot.

"We went through several platoon commanders. One day a new one arrived, Lt. Pete Pace [2005-07 chairman of the Joint Chiefs of Staff]. He called a meeting of the platoon—all 13 of us showed up! That's all we had left. Pete listened to us; he was an exceptional leader."

A Co., 1st Bn., 1st Marines seized the Joan of Arc School, where Marines traded rifle and grenade fire with enemy soldiers across a courtyard.

"We got the bright idea of carrying our 106mm into the room to fire across the courtyard at them," said Cpl. Dave Jones of H & S Co., 1st Bn., 1st Marines. "That back blast nearly killed us all, and the steel beds went flying across the room, but we never received any more enemy fire after that."

Lance Cpl. Robert Wallace (he went on to become a VFW commander-in-chief and executive director of VFW's Washington Office) of H&S Co., 1st Bn., 1st Marines, explained that "the 106mm recoilless rifle was indispensable during the battle. We manhandled that weapon everywhere and blew gaping holes in walls so we could move from structure to structure."

Sgt. Alfredo Gonzalez of A Co., 1st Bn., 1st Marines, was everywhere firing his LAAW (light anti-armor weapon) at the enemy when a B-40 rocket scored a direct hit, killing him instantly. He would be awarded a Medal of Honor posthumously for repeatedly exposing himself to danger to rescue wounded and assault enemy positions between Jan. 31 and Feb. 4.

On Feb. 6, H Co., 2nd Bn., 5th Marines, seized the provincial capitol building. Gunnery Sgt. Frank A. Thomas, assisted by Pfc. Walter R. Kaczmarek and Pfc. Alan V. McDonald, tied the Stars and Stripes to a flagpole and raised it amongst jubilant cheers from the Marines witnessing the event.

This iconic photo of Sgt. P.L. Thompson, 1st Bn., 5th Marines, on the emperor's throne in the Citadel palace was a message to the communists that American troops had retaken Hue.

ABOVE: Soldiers of the 5th Bn., 7th Cav, 1st Cav Div., approach a gap within the bullet-riddled walls of the Citadel.

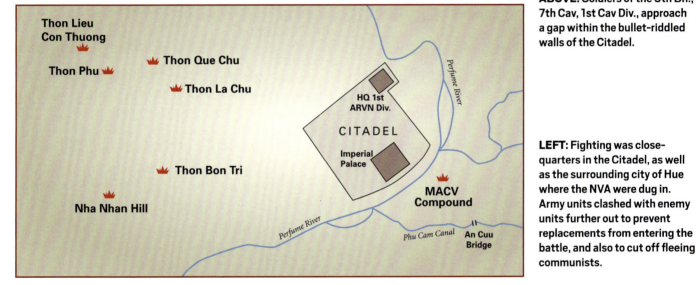

LEFT: Fighting was close-quarters in the Citadel, as well as the surrounding city of Hue where the NVA were dug in. Army units clashed with enemy units further out to prevent replacements from entering the battle, and also to cut off fleeing communists.

By Feb. 9 (though mopping-up would continue for days), the modern city was completely in Marine hands, but only after losing 38 KIA and 320 WIA.

THE CITADEL: IMPERIAL PALACE

The Citadel was a maze of one-story, thick-walled, masonry homes with very narrow streets. Tanks would have a difficult time maneuvering down the restricted passageways, so the infantry had the unenviable task of routing the communists from their lairs.

On Feb. 15, D Co., 1st Bn., 5th Marines, assaulted the Dong Ba Tower (also called the Dong Ba Porch), an observation point overlooking the old city. The infantrymen came under fire from a machine gun situated in its perch, and B-40 rockets sent shrapnel and chunks of concrete flying through the air. A 3.5-inch rocket launcher managed to get off three well-placed rounds and blasted the enemy from the two-story tower above the Dong Ba Gate.

In his book *Phase Line Green: The Battle for Hue, 1968,* then-1st Lt. Nicholas Warr of C Co., 1st Bn., 5th Marines, remembered when a mechanical mule carrying a 106mm recoilless rifle was hit: "The mule driver's left arm was blown off at the shoulder. I remember watching as the corpsman worked on this young man and being amazed when the mule driver realized that it was his left arm that was missing.

MEDAL OF HONOR

CHIEF WARRANT
OFFICER FREDERICK
FERGUSON

STAFF SGT.
CLIFFORD SIMS
(POSTHUMOUS)

STAFF SGT.
JOE HOOPER

"I can remember hearing him ask someone to fetch it, because his wedding ring was on the third finger of the hand of that now useless arm. The arm was found, the swollen ring finger was removed, and the ring was returned to its rightful owner. It seemed to give him some comfort as they carried him away on a wooden door …"

(Phase Line Green was the northern edge of Mai Thuc Loan Street.)

"There was virtually no visibility at all," Maj. Robert H. Thompson, CO of 1/5 said. "If you could find 20 meters [65 feet] of open space you were lucky. Fighting in the Citadel was unlike anything I had ever experienced. We were in such close quarters with the enemy, often just meters away. We had no room to fire and maneuver. In essence, the fighting was an exercise of reducing fortified positions."

Finally, on Feb. 21, the Marines completely seized the northeast wall. Reinforced by L Co., 3rd Bn., 5th Marines, they then turned to the southeast wall. Grenades were pitched through smashed windows and doorways, as fire teams rushed in shooting at anything that moved. Entering the palace throne room, adorned in gold leaf with two thrones atop a raised dais, one sergeant noticed two dead enemy soldiers. He walked over to nudge them with the end of his rifle, making sure they were dead.

The battle for the Citadel was over. The 1st Bn., 5th Marines, alone counted 47 KIA and 240 WIA—24 of their dead were sustained just on Feb. 16-17.

NIGHT MANEUVER AT THON QUE CHU

While the Marines were slugging it out in Hue, U.S. Army units were tapped to close the back door (dubbed *Operation Jeb Stuart*) to NVA reinforcements outside the city. Lt. Col. Richard Sweet's 2nd Bn., 12th Cav, 1st Cav Div., encountered a regimental-size enemy force. The 2nd Battalion made an air assault just outside a South Vietnamese outpost called PK-17 northwest of Hue and then fought at Thon Que Chu on Feb. 3-4.

"It was a disbursement area for troops and supplies going to Hue," remarked Pfc. Phil Wickersham of D Company. "We had no artillery or air support either. There were lots of women enemy soldiers, too. They were good shots. Most of our wounded got hit in the head and chest."

Pfc. Carl Johnson, a sniper with B Co., 2nd Bn., 12th Cav, remembered: "The front of our position was littered with dead and dying NVA. That morning we had around 27 men in our platoon. That evening there were only seven of us left. We were only a small part of the raging battle that day, but our platoon suffered greatly. We had to bury our dead and leave them as we prepared to move out in the dark." Though wounded himself, Johnson assisted other wounded and killed 20 NVA. He earned the Silver Star.

Realizing he was vastly outnumbered and surrounded, Sweet decided on a daring plan: a night march from the hamlet. On the evening of Feb. 4, under cover of a torrential rainstorm, the riflemen quietly began their withdrawal.

Led by point man Pfc. Hector Camacho, the battalion arrived at its destination, the high ground just outside of Hue, overlooking the enemy's MSR (Main Supply Route).

"It was a Herculean effort on everybody's part to get through that night march," remarked Pfc. Jerry McNelly, also of D Company. "We had to hold on to one another, it was so dark. At times, we came within 20 yards of enemy units. I was totally exhausted when we reached our destination. I had two leeches the size of small bananas on my legs when I pulled up my trousers."

Maj. Charles Krohn, battalion intelligence officer, later wrote: "At one point, I was carrying three rifles. Some soldiers, who earlier hid their wounds to avoid being evacuated by one of the few helicopters able to reach us, found themselves at the outer limits of their endurance. But they made it." Krohn earned a Silver Star for repeatedly exposing himself to enemy fire to gather intelligence. He also was at the Pentagon at the time of the Sept. 11, 2001, terrorist attacks.

Sweet's bold maneuver had saved his unit from certain annihilation, but the 2nd Battalion lost 21 KIA and 135 WIA.

BATTLE FOR THE LA CHU WOODS

A few miles north of Hue, the 1st and 5th battalions, 7th Cav; 2nd Bn., 12th Cav; and the 2nd Bde., 101st Airborne Div., met a large NVA force at Thon Que Chu and Thon La Chu. For the next two weeks, repeated attempts were made to overrun the densely wooded area, but the enemy fought tenaciously. The troopers soon dubbed the La Chu Woods T-T for "tough titty."

On Feb. 21 GIs advanced, but the assault soon stalled because of an enemy bunker that kept troops pinned down. Pfc. Albert Rocha and Jake DeBoard of D Co., 5th Bn., 7th Cav, crawled forward with a Bangalore torpedo. They forced the pole-charge through an aperture where it exploded. One lone survivor attempted to escape, but was gunned down by Rocha. After they eliminated the enemy position, the attack gained additional momentum.

Meanwhile, soldiers from the 101st Airborne and the 2nd Bn., 12th Cav, also moved into the woods.

"Our squad was supposed to draw fire," said Spec. 4 Mike Oberg of A Co., 2nd Bn., 12th Cav. "We were so close, one NVA soldier urinated on me. I wrestled him to the ground and shot him. Then all hell broke loose. The bullets sounded like a bunch of weed whackers, there were so many of them."

2nd Lt. Thomas Dobrinska of B Co., 2nd Bn., 12th Cav, continuously exposed himself to hostile fire in leading his men forward and pulling the wounded to safety. While overrunning the last bunker, Dobrinska was struck and killed. He would be presented a posthumous Distinguished Service Cross (DSC) for his exemplary actions.

"Men displayed incredible bravery," remembers George Patterson of the 2nd Battalion. "Around Feb. 15 at Thon Bon Tri, Lt. Jenson had us set up the machine guns and instructed us to start firing as he crawled forward. He blew up four NVA positions with grenades. I always wondered if he received a medal for that."

Under the skilled leadership of Staff Sgt. Clifford Sims from D Co., 2nd Bn., 501st Infantry, 101st Airborne Div., his squad furiously attacked a heavily fortified NVA position, freeing a pinned-down 1st Platoon. Ordered next to assist the 3rd Platoon, Sims was providing covering fire when he "heard the unmistakable noise of a concealed booby trap," and flung himself upon it. The resulting blast killed him instantly. For his sacrifice, Sims received the Medal of Honor posthumously.

Staff Sgt. Joe Hooper, also of D Company, was a one-man army. While attacking an NVA bunker, his squad was pelted with shrapnel from enemy rockets and automatic weapons fire. He charged across the river and destroyed several bunkers. Although wounded, he continued onward, saving several wounded soldiers trapped in the line of fire.

Hooper then assaulted three enemy positions by himself with grenades and killed two NVA soldiers who had shot the chaplain. Next, he became involved in hand-to-hand combat

PHOTO FROM ROBERT L. HELVEY; COURTESY CHARLES KROHN

Two unidentified soldiers of the 2nd Bn., 12th Cav, 1st Cav Div., appear exhausted after their narrow escape from NVA encirclement on Feb. 4, 1968.

Hooper then assaulted three enemy positions by himself with grenades and killed two NVA soldiers who had shot the chaplain.

Corpsman D.R. Howe treats the wounds of Pfc. D.A. Crum, H Co., 2nd Bn., 5th Marines, on Feb. 6, 1968.

with an NVA officer, whom he bayoneted to death.

When his squad reached the final line of enemy resistance, he single-handedly raced down a small trench that ran the length of four NVA fortifications, methodically tossing grenades as he passed each one.

Hooper neutralized three more enemy bunkers before the final pocket of the enemy collapsed. Although weak from blood loss, he refused medical evacuation until the next day. He was awarded the Medal of Honor.

After a bloody confrontation, the woods were finally in American hands. The soldiers were now just three miles from the northwest corner of the Citadel.

VICTORY AT A STEEP PRICE

It took 26 days to recapture Hue, and at a heavy price. In all, 216 Americans were killed and 1,364 were wounded in the battle: 66% of the dead were Marines; 33% soldiers. The 5th Marines (1st and 2nd Battalions) counted 126 KIA and the 1st Cavalry Division, 68, of that total. Valor was clearly evident—four Medals of Honor, 10 Navy Crosses and at least one DSC, not to mention Silver Stars, were awarded. Even three members of the media received Bronze Stars for helping to evacuate wounded.

Besides the 384 South Vietnamese soldiers KIA at Hue, Communist atrocities left 2,810 Vietnamese civilians in shallow graves; another 1,946 were never found.

"The putrid smell of rotting corpses drifted over the city like a thick fog," wrote George W. Smith, author of *The Siege of Hue*. "The bodies, bloated and vermin infested, attracted rats and stray dogs." Smith was describing earlier casualties south of the river, but his description aptly fit the entire aftermath of Hue. ✪

THE TOLL

U.S. KIA:
216

U.S. WIA:
1,364

'WE HAVE TANKS IN OUR WIRE!'

BY TIM DYHOUSE

Special Forces troops make a valiant stand at Lang Vei.

The Green Berets at Lang Vei faced overwhelming odds. Outmanned, outgunned and cut off from ground reinforcements, the 24 Americans comprising Det. A-101, C Co., 5th Special Forces Grp., and Det. B-16 (1st Mobile Strike Force Company) along with about 400 Montagnards, would be on their own in the face of a well-coordinated North Vietnamese Army (NVA) armor assault.

Only a week before, the Tet Offensive had begun, and the camp in Quang Tri province, some five miles west of Khe Sanh, was a prime target during the enemy's rampage. Just after midnight on Feb. 7, 1968, the lead elements of 400 ground troops of the 66th NVA Regiment supported by 11 Soviet-made PT-76 tanks attempted to breach the camp's outer perimeter. With the frantic radio message, "We have tanks in our wire!" Sgt. Nicholas Fragos signaled to detachment commander Capt. Frank Willoughby that the fight had begun.

For the next 11 hours, the Lang Vei defenders would fight heroically—yet unsuccessfully—to defend their camp. They received artillery support from the Marine base at Khe Sanh, as well as air strikes. But when Willoughby requested two rifle companies from the besieged 26th Marines at Khe Sanh, he was turned down twice.

"The Marines declined to send a relief force because they felt that any attempt to reinforce via [Highway 9] would be ambushed," according to the *Battle of Lang Vei* by John A. Crash. "A heliborne assault, they believed, was out of the question because it was dark and the enemy had armor."

Some three hours after the attack began, radio transmissions from the camp ceased. But the fighting raged on.

A group of Green Berets at a smaller outpost less than a mile east of the camp had been calling in air and artillery strikes during the night. At dawn, they attempted to retake the camp. The group was led by Army Sgt. 1st Class Eugene Ashley, Jr., and included Sgt. Richard H. Allen, Spec. 4 Joel Johnson and some 100 Laotian soldiers.

Ashley, who would earn the Medal of Honor posthumously for his actions that fateful day, led five attacks on the NVA troops.

MEDAL OF HONOR

SGT. 1ST CLASS
EUGENE ASHLEY, JR.
(POSTHUMOUS)

VIETNAM VETERANS MEMORIAL FUND/WALL OF FACES

DISTINGUISHED SERVICE CROSS

MAJ. GEORGE QUAMO

LT. COL. DANIEL SCHUNGEL

MILITARY TIMES HALL OF VALOR

"During his fifth and final assault, he adjusted air strikes nearly on top of his assault element, forcing the enemy to withdraw and resulting in friendly control of the summit," according to his MOH citation. "His valiant efforts carved a channel in the overpowering enemy forces and weapons positions through which the survivors of Camp Lang Vei eventually escaped to freedom."

After being seriously wounded by machine gun fire, Ashley was carried off the hill, only to be killed when an enemy artillery shell hit his area. By 5:30 p.m., all known survivors had been evacuated to Khe Sanh.

Of the 24 Americans at Lang Vei, seven were killed, three captured (and repatriated in March 1973) and 11 wounded. More than 200 of the Montagnard troops were killed and 75 wounded. Enemy losses were estimated at 200 KIA. Besides the MOH recipient, Distinguished Service Crosses were awarded to Maj. George Quamo and Lt. Col. Daniel Schungel

In the end, the camp was overrun and destroyed. "Thus did Lang Vei fall, marking the first successful use of armor by the enemy in the Vietnam War," according to Crash. "There were those who believed that the loss would eventually lead to the destruction of Khe Sanh, but those fears never materialized." ✪

BY LARRY JAMES

KILLING ZONE at HOC MON

In perhaps the Vietnam War's deadliest single engagement,
in terms of time and KIAs, 48 men of C Co., 4th Bn., 9th Inf.,
25th Div., were killed by the Viet Cong in just eight minutes on
March 2, 1968, north of Saigon.

A little after 9 a.m. on March 2, 1968, 92 American soldiers began a search-and-destroy mission near Saigon. They were looking for a Viet Cong force of undetermined size that had been firing rockets into Tan Son Nhut Air Base. The operation was expected to last all day.

In less than eight minutes, 48 of those Americans were dead or dying, 28 were wounded and the U.S. Army had suffered one of its most catastrophic losses of the Vietnam War.

The men of the 4th Bn., 9th Inf. (Manchus), 25th Inf. Div., arrived in the canal-riddled Hoc Mon district just north of Saigon on Feb. 25. The area was new to them, but the enemy was not. They had met the VC they knew as the *Go Mon* battalions before, and these encounters had been costly—12 dead and dozens wounded in six days.

The mission on March 2 was much like those that preceded it. Sweep the area, find the enemy and kill him. Battalion commander Lt. Col. John Henchman had drawn up an operations plan and briefed his company commanders. But in late February, brigade headquarters gave him a new mission. To make sure there was no confusion about the change, Henchman arranged an aerial reconnaissance early on the 2nd

for each of his company commanders.

"I elected to let my four company commanders make an aerial reconnaissance of the area in which they were going to conduct the operation," Henchman said later. "And to make a reconnaissance of the route they were going to use for their attack positions. The terrain was very difficult because of the number of treelines, etc., that are in the area."

Capt. Willie Gore's C Company was to lead, but he was late returning from his reconnaissance, and the battalion began to move without him. As his men hurried to catch up, they began to wonder why no one was out on flank security. The concern only grew as the civilians who had been mixed among them suddenly turned around and headed back the way they had come.

Still, C Company hustled along, crossing one bridge after another. Before Gore knew it, he ran into an unsecured area where more than 200 automatic rifles, machine guns, RPGs and command-detonated mines were laying in wait. The VC's signal to trigger the ambush was a burst of machine gun fire aimed at the lead elements of the column.

"Third Platoon was the lead platoon of C Company," recalled Platoon Sgt. Jesse B. Lunsford. "We had just cleared the second bridge when a group

Members of C Co., 4th Bn., 9th Inf., 25th Inf. Div., check civilian IDs on Highway 248 on March 1, 1968, one day prior to the ambush that killed 48 of them.

of 25 or more Vietnamese walked down the middle of the road and through our formation. This was a diversion to make us feel safe. Suddenly, machine gun fire came straight down the road. I was hit in the leg."

DEATH IN THE KILL ZONE

Point man Pfc. Darrell Wheeler was the first to die, killed instantly in that initial burst, which also claimed the life of the man behind him, Pfc. Clifford Stockton.

Spec. 4 Augustine Lugo was third in line. "I was 50 to 70 meters [76.5 yards] behind the point," Lugo told an Army interviewer later. "The first fire came from our right side. ... There was more than one. I heard them all over. When they opened up, everybody hit the ground." Lugo swung his M-79 grenade launcher toward the trees to his right and got off one round before a second enemy burst dumped him unconscious on the edge of the road.

While the men in front still had no real sense of what was happening, automatic rifles opened up from a second position to the right. Then fire began from behind them, no more than a dozen yards off in the small trees on the left side of the road.

There was no going forward, no going back. The VC were on both sides of them with interlocking fields of fire. C Company was trapped inside a quarter-mile-long killing zone.

As Gore raced for cover, radio-telephone operator (RTO) Danny Luster immediately began calling for artillery fire. No sooner had he keyed the push-to-talk switch than a bullet hit his right bicep, knocking the handset away.

MEDAL OF HONOR

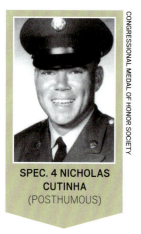

SPEC. 4 NICHOLAS CUTINHA
(POSTHUMOUS)

DISTINGUISHED SERVICE CROSS

PFC. ARISTIDES SOSA
(POSTHUMOUS)

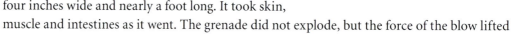

A second round hit him in the head above the right ear. Again, he reached for the handset. Again, it was knocked away by a bullet that shattered his left arm. Then, wham, wham, wham, wham, wham! Five hammer blows in his back and side. His radio took the first three, but two rounds tore through his side just above the liver.

"It seemed like they were after the radio," Luster said years later. "It was busted and useless, and I knew I had to get rid of it." He wriggled out of the radio, bounded to his feet only to fall again as another burst hit him in the right ankle and sent him sprawling on his back.

Then an RPG struck, glancing off his right hipbone, raking his stomach and tearing open a gash four inches wide and nearly a foot long. It took skin, muscle and intestines as it went. The grenade did not explode, but the force of the blow lifted Luster off the ground and flipped him face down.

The next bullet struck him in the chest, collapsed his left lung and fractured his spine. He was again flat on his back, staring up into an almost cloudless sky and bleeding from eight serious wounds. He was still conscious.

From where wounded 3rd Platoon RTO Rudolph Love lay, he could see that somehow 1st Platoon's machine gun crew had moved nearly 219 yards from their original position in the line of march toward the head of the column. "I saw 'Porky' [Spec. 4 Nicholas Cutinha], our machine gunner, with Mathis, his ammo bearer, near a hooch to the north," Love told an interviewer later.

Love said it was almost impossible to understand how Cutinha and Pfc. James Mathis had the nerve to stand up in the face of all that fire. But the volume of fire Cutinha was putting out was welcome.

The next time Love looked up, he could see Cutinha was moving again, trying to get closer to where he could direct fire on what seemed the VC's strongest position. "Porky took off down the ditch and headed for the 3rd Platoon," Love said. "Mathis froze there. I hollered for him to join us, but he didn't come." It was the last time Love saw Cutinha alive. In sacrificing his life, Cutinha had heroically defended the company and ultimately received the Medal of Honor.

SURVIVAL INSTINCTS TAKE OVER

"Manchus" not hit in the initial bursts of fire had instinctively dived for the shallow ditches on each side of the road. As they hit the ground, the ditches erupted in a coordinated series of explosions of command-detonated mines and RPG fire. Many of them took the full force of the explosions from only feet away and were blown apart.

Gore's command group was one of them. "My weapon was cut completely in half and was not operable," Gore said. "I looked around for any other type of weapon. I didn't find any. I noticed one of my RTOs was still alive in a lot of pain. I managed to get him some water and get him in a comfortable position. I couldn't move because another man had fallen across my legs and one of my RTOs was across my legs.

"I was pinned down and we were still under heavy fire. I noticed an enemy machine gun position to my left about 20 meters [66 feet]. We tried to neutralize it, but we couldn't knock it out. I took about six or eight rounds through my bedroll on my back."

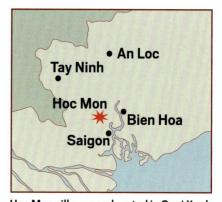

Hoc Mon village was located in Quoi Xuah hamlet about 6.8 miles northwest of Tan Son Nhut Air Base. The Route 248 Bridge was the scene of the action on March 2, 1968, during which 48 GIs were KIA in mere minutes.

"They were all over. They were moving around taking everyone's equipment off them. I just played dead."
— AUGUSTINE LUGO, SPC. 4

ABOVE: Marty Shoemaker was one of the 28 wounded.

BELOW: Alvin Cayson was KIA at Hoc Mon. This photo of Cayson was taken at Firebase Katum in January 1968.

Third Platoon rifleman Pfc. Dan McKinney found himself lying in a pool of his own blood on the exposed surface of the road. Someone was next to him with words of encouragement, and administering a shot of morphine. Then he heard other voices. Was it over? But as he listened, he heard men moaning, then gunshots. No one was coming to help. The VC were killing the wounded.

Augustine Lugo came to only to see a small group of VC walking toward him. "They were all over," he said "They were moving around taking everyone's equipment off them. I just played dead." One picked up his grenade launcher while two others rolled him over, took off his web gear, searched his pockets, then rolled him face down again before hurrying back into concealment.

Others were caught in the ditches, too. Pfc. Aristides Sosa was part of the four-man team from A Co., 65th Eng. Bn., accompanying Charlie Company. Already wounded in an explosion, he immediately rolled on top of a grenade when it threatened a fellow solider. That selfless act saved the soldier, but killed Sosa, who was awarded a posthumous Distinguished Service Cross.

"The firing became more intense with RPGs hitting the road by the dozens," said Lunsford. "This was the killing zone and they just kept killing us. I was wounded in the right arm. After five hours of laying in the middle of that Hell, Delta Company flanked our position and got us out."

Larry Criteser was a grunt in D Company and witnessed the scene of some men clutching small Bibles and photographs. "It was one of the most horrible experiences in my entire life," he remembered.

PERFECTLY EXECUTED AMBUSH

Even though most of C Company's casualties occurred in the first eight minutes of the ambush, it was mid-afternoon before the rest of the battalion reached them and began treating the wounded and recovering the dead.

Forty-eight Americans were KIA at the Route 248 Bridge near Hoc Mon. All but two were members of Charlie Company. One was an engineer in A Co., 65th Eng. Bn.; the other was an artillery forward observer from A Btry., 7th Bn., 11th Arty. More than three-fourths of the men were draftees, and 23% were volunteers. Gunfire claimed over half the lives while shrapnel killed 42% of the "Manchus." The cause of death was undefined for three. Twenty-eight GIs were wounded.

"As an operating room nurse at the 12th Evac Hospital in Cu Chi, the number of casualties from that ambush overwhelmed me," recalled Nancy Overstreet. "Some of the wounded survived the atrocities only by playing dead. Over the years, I have shared this experience with people, and they walk away in disbelief."

An after-action report placed the blame for the disaster on the lack of flank security. But interviews with a VC commander who was there show a meticulously planned and executed ambush that was likely to have succeeded regardless. ✪

THE TOLL

U.S. KIA:
48

U.S. WIA:
28

COURAGE SHINES AT AP NAM PHU

BY RICHARD K. KOLB

For one 82nd Airborne Division company, April 4, 1968, was unforgettable. For the 3rd Brigade as a whole, it was the single deadliest action during its entire 22 months in-country.

The 3rd Brigade (the "Golden Brigade") of the famed 82nd Airborne Division was sent to Vietnam as an emergency response to the Tet Offensive of 1968. Arriving in mid-February 1968, its original mission was to help protect the ancient capital of Hue in I Corps.

Part of that mission was participating in *Operation Carentan II*, a search and destroy sweep of the lowlands of Quang Tri and Thua Thien provinces. The North Vietnamese Army (NVA) 324-B Division and 4th NVA Regiment were known to operate in this region. The exact identification and size of the force encountered this particular day is not known. But the combat experienced was symbolic of the firefights grunts most often fought in Vietnam.

On April 4, 1968, C Co., 1st Bn., 505th Inf., about 70 to 80 men under the command of Capt. Paul Davin, saddled up and set out to establish a blocking position north of the hamlet of Ap Nam Phu. It was located northwest of Hue and near the Song Bo River. The three rifle platoons of Charlie Company were deposited by helicopter into a graveyard east of the village not long before nightfall.

Quickly, the paratroopers were pinned down in an open rice paddy. 1st Platoon was in the lead, with its point squad receiving sniper fire 164 yards from the hamlet. When the rest of the platoon came to assist the wounded inflicted by the snipers, they were hit with a heavy volume of fire. Most casualties occurred in the opening salvo and communications were cut off with no radio contact.

The 505th Infantry of the 82nd Airborne Division, based at Camp Rodriguez, served in Vietnam starting in February 1968. On that April 4, its 1st Battalion's C Company sustained nine KIA at Ap Nam Phu.

A 'Million Dollar Wound'

Sgt. Richard Davidson was a squad leader in 1st Platoon that fateful day. He was a rare commodity in the Army: a Canadian who volunteered to serve. Moreover, he was a French-speaker from Montreal, Quebec. "I joined the U.S. Army to make a better life," Davidson said. "I had only 2½ months left on my three-year enlistment when the orders came for Vietnam, but I wanted to go. I wore a scapular hoping for religious protection."

Davidson barely escaped death, so some would say he was being looked out for. "Everything seemed to happen in about 45 minutes," Davidson remembered. "We jumped off the chopper into a rice paddy. The radio-telephone operator [RTO] and lieutenant in front of me were shot, and I crawled by them. The NVA were in underground firing positions, well protected and at an angle.

"I was pulling soldiers back to safety when I got hit. One guy was shot in the head and died over me. I was on a rice paddy dike when an NVA threw a hand grenade, spraying me with shrapnel. I was also shot in the rear end, had a testicle shot off and was hit in the penis. It was a million dollar wound, but it cost me 6½ months in various hospitals."

Spec. 4 Salome Beltran also was in 1st Platoon. "We landed in a rice paddy about 5 p.m. and were hit immediately with AK-47 sniper fire and then machine guns," he said. "NVA were even in the tops of trees. Most of our casualties were sustained in the opening burst of fire. We had to get to the casualties. So everyone helped gather up the wounded. There was great companionship and love among the men.

"At one point, I crawled into a bomb crater and ended up on top of a wounded guy. He told me to stay there. I did, and it probably saved my life. We remained pinned down until dark; sniper fire lasted until about 9 p.m.

"April 4 was the most difficult day of my time in Vietnam, and one of the hardest days of my life."

C Company headquarters group set up on an earthen berm overlooking the fighting. Spec. 4 Thomas Locastro was the RTO for the company commander. "I was initially located at a gravesite some 82 feet from the battle site," he recalled. "I was sent down to restore communications with the 1st and 2nd platoons. No radios were operating in the creek bed. As I ran across an open field to return to Capt. Davin, I was wounded by a B-40 rocket explosion.

"In the opening crossfire, Sgt. Jerry Shain was captured. We could hear him holler before he was executed. The NVA also kept shooting the dead American bodies. During the night, about 40 of us were back to back with fixed bayonets and ready to fight the anticipated assault that never came."

As night fell, Charlie Company had established a night defensive position in bomb craters.

SILVER STAR

COURTESY SALOME BELTRAN

LEFT: Spec. 4 Salome Beltran was in the 1st Platoon, which took the lead in the advance on Ap Nam Phu. He helped save the lives of fellow GIs and was awarded the Silver Star.

Other Silver Star recipients:

CAPT. PAUL DAVIN

STAFF SGT. JESSIE TABOR

A Long Night on the Perimeter

Charlie's 2nd and 3rd platoons came to their sister platoon's assistance as fast as possible. 2nd Lt. Richard Underwood led the 2nd Platoon. "There was no artillery prep on the landing zone before we arrived," he said. "1st Platoon was already approaching the village when we landed. We headed for the village on the right flank. Members of the 1st Platoon fell just short of the village tree line.

"Then we began taking fire. An earthen berm that ran along the village's perimeter provided cover. NVA had killed or wounded members of 1st Platoon as close as possible to their fighting positions to limit how close we could fire to them, especially with artillery. I had to low crawl to reach Staff Sgt. Jessie Tabor of 1st Platoon.

"Fighting continued into the darkness, most of the night. The wounded had to be evacuated. Gunship pilot Capt. Jerry Frye expended all his ammo, so he came to pick up the wounded. I guided him into the LZ with a flashlight. Next morning, the NVA were gone. We collected our dead and moved them out. Then we moved out toward our next fight, the Lazy W River."

C Company's dead numbered nine. All suffered gunshot wounds. Another 23

A memorial service for the nine 82nd Airborne Division paratroopers KIA on April 4, 1968, and others was held at Camp Rodriguez (later called Eagle), the 3rd Brigade base camp southwest of Hue.
COURTESY RON YORKOVICH, 82ND AIRBORNE DIVISION ASSOCIATION, GOLDEN BRIGADE CHAPTER

men were wounded. One common denominator among both the dead and living was courage. Seven, or 78%, of the KIAs were awarded posthumous Silver Stars. Beltran, Davin and Tabor also were recognized with the Silver Star. Life-saving and attempts to do so were the order of the day on April 4. ✪

BY SHANNON HANSON

'WALKING DEAD' SHOW VALOR ON HILL 689

As the siege of Khe Sanh came to a close in mid-April 1968, elements of the 1st Bn., 9th Marines, held the high ground on Hill 689 a few miles to the west. It appeared that enemy units were returning to the area, as Marines had made contact with remnants of an NVA platoon on April 13 and 15.

On the morning of the 16th, Capt. Henry D. Banks of A Company led two reinforced platoons totaling 85 men on a search-and-clear mission southwest of the perimeter on the hill. At 10 a.m., Banks ordered two squads to search a nearby ridge covered in four-to-six-foot elephant grass. They soon came under small-arms and sniper fire.

The first Marine killed was Cpl. Robert H. Littlefield. David Ford remembered: "The first shot fired went through Littlefield and almost hit me. I thought he was going to live. Toward dark, I saw him still laying there, but by then he was dead."

Banks deployed the company, with 1st Platoon establishing a base of fire and 2nd Platoon, led by 1st Lt. Michael P. Hayden, attacking up the ridge. NVA fired from well-concealed bunkers in a horseshoe shape and drove the Marines to the ground.

"It appeared that when the 2nd Platoon had gotten into position to assault, that they [NVA] were just waiting for them, and just cut them down with small-arms fire," Banks said.

Hayden said their only choice was to attack and take the hill, and under machine-gun cover, he led the charge.

"We didn't move 15 feet when Lt. Hayden got hit and was killed," said Sgt. Paul J. Cogley. "Suddenly, they opened up and everybody hit the ground. We stayed that way for a least an hour."

Banks ordered the 2nd Platoon to fall back, but the dead and wounded were still within 10 feet of the enemy bunkers and could not be extracted. Casualties mounted, and soon 10 Marines had been killed and 20 wounded.

At about noon, Lt. Col. John H. Cahill, commanding officer of 1st Battalion, ordered D Company, under Capt. John W. Cargile, to assist A Company in evacuating the dead and wounded.

Leathernecks of 1st Bn., 9th Marines, aid a downed helicopter during *Operation Scotland II* in the DMZ on Sept. 20, 1968. That April 16, the battalion suffered 42 KIAs on the south slope of Hill 689.

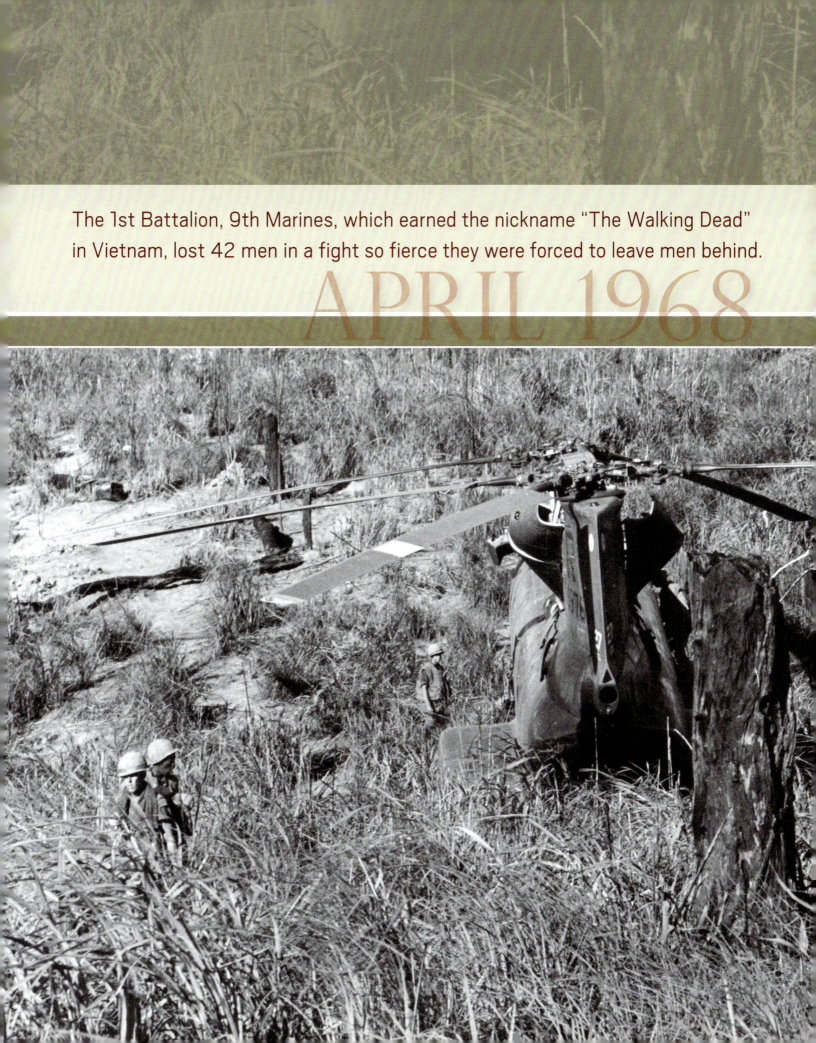

The 1st Battalion, 9th Marines, which earned the nickname "The Walking Dead" in Vietnam, lost 42 men in a fight so fierce they were forced to leave men behind.

APRIL 1968

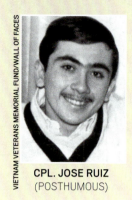

CPL. JOSE RUIZ
(POSTHUMOUS)

"After this, he [Cpl. Jose Ruiz] and his men continued on the assault. There he gave his life by jumping in front of a wounded Marine to save his life."

—CPL. JOHN KOCSIS

SILVER STAR

'BEST MEDICAL CARE' POSSIBLE

Meanwhile, Cahill moved out with two platoons of C Company, led by Capt. Lawrence Himmer, to sweep the bunker complex from the rear and clear out any enemy resistance. 2nd Lt. David O. Carter of 2nd Platoon led the advance up the ridge.

Enemy fire broke out from hidden fortified positions, and Himmer, both platoon commanders and several squad leaders fell wounded.

"We got to the top of the hill—they were everywhere," Carter said. "They were dug in bunkers. I was hit three times. I went up [there with] 32 men, and only eight men didn't get hit. We did one hell of a job up there. I think the only thing that saved us was basic aggressiveness."

Pfc. Eddie R. Pritchett saved Carter's life. Himself wounded, Pritchett knocked Carter down to keep him from being hit, and placed him in a protected place. Pritchett then jumped into an NVA-occupied emplacement and engaged them. He received the Bronze Star.

After Carter and the platoon sergeant were wounded, Cpl. Jose Ruiz took charge of the platoon. He rendered first aid to the wounded, regardless of the danger. "He got down and gave each and every one of them the best medical care he could," Cpl. John Kocsis said. "After this, he and his men continued on the assault. There he gave his life by jumping in front of a wounded Marine to save his life." For his selfless bravery, Ruiz was posthumously awarded the Silver Star.

C Company's valiant assault enabled A Company to extract all of its wounded and most of its dead.

NOT ENOUGH WALKING BODIES

By 3 p.m., A and C companies had suffered high casualties and were nearly immobilized in the elephant grass by enemy fire from the bunker complexes. Cahill ordered D Company to deploy along A Company's right flank and attack across the ridge.

The company advanced, but with the deep grass and enemy fire, progress was slow with casualties mounting. "Our movement in any forward direction was nominal due to intense fire and extremely accurate sniper fire," Capt. Cargile said. "We were receiving sniper fire from two to three directions. Still, we could not pinpoint the source. The snipers were very good. Four out of my five KIAs had been shot in the head."

After learning of D Company's heavy casualties at 5:30 p.m., Cahill ordered the battalion to extract the wounded and any KIAs they could, and pull back. Cahill was unaware that Gen. Rathvon Tompkins had issued a standing order that all KIAs should be evacuated.

"We were forced to do something we had never done before—just leave bodies out, to report people as missing," said 1st Lt. Kenneth L. Harman, executive officer of C Company.

THE RESCUE OF CPL. HUNNICUTT

The morning after the battle, on April 17, Marines heard the voice of Cpl. Hubert H. Hunnicutt III calling across the valley. He was wounded and taking shelter in a bomb crater. Volunteers in two CH-46 helicopters attempted to rescue him, but when they landed, they received heavy fire from NVA and found only decapitated and disembeweled bodies of Marines. A second rescue attempt shortly after yielded not Hunnicutt, but a Pfc. G. Panyaninec.

Hunnicutt, meanwhile, crawled out of the crater and came upon Capt.

Lawrence Himmer, who was still alive. Hunnicutt stayed with Himmer, receiving AK-47 fire in the leg, hand and elbow and playing dead for about five hours. He moved Himmer down the ridge, but they were separated when Hunnicutt fell into a gorge.

The following morning, Hunnicutt

COURTESY HIMMER FAMILY

Capt. Lawrence Himmer

yelled for help again. "About noon, an Army Huey started flying around me," he recalled. "[It] dropped two red smokes on me and scared me to death. I thought they were going to blow me away."

Hunnicutt was rescued and received the Navy Cross for his efforts to save Himmer, whose body was recovered five days later.

Hunnicutt stayed with Himmer, receiving AK-47 fire in the leg, hand and elbow and playing dead for about five hours.

"I don't feel this was through carelessness of the individuals. It was simply that there weren't enough walking bodies left to carry the limp bodies out."

Cahill said he felt that "additional casualties would have resulted if I had chosen to remain on the hill. Plans were formulated by me to recover the KIAs on the 18th, but other plans by higher headquarters had been made, preventing the battalion to do this job."

Elements of 2nd Bn., 3rd Marines, were sent in to recover the bodies on April 21. "This was a fierce fight," said David Brombaugh, who was part of the recovery operation. Seven men of the 2nd Battalion were KIA. "The bodies [from April 16] were in bad shape from the days left there, and many were mutilated. We got all the bodies the morning of the 22nd and walked back to Khe Sanh."

The 1st Bn., 9th Marines, lost 42 killed in action on Hill 689 and 32 wounded. C Company took the biggest hit with 19 KIA (49%), then A Company with 13 (33%) followed by Delta Company at seven killed (18%). Three Navy corpsmen from H&S Company sacrificed their lives aiding the wounded. Explosive devices such as hand grenades accounted for virtually all of the deaths.

Bob O'Bday was a machine gunner with Weapons Plt., C Co., 1st Bn., 9th Marines, that unforgettable April 16. His brief words summed up the *espirit de corps* not only of the "Walking Dead," but of all Marines. "It was an honor to serve with these men," he said. "We fought bravely to protect each other." ✪

THE TOLL

U.S. KIA:
42

U.S. WIA:
32

BY TIM DYHOUSE

'MAGNIFICENT BASTARDS' BATTLE AT DAI DO

I n the darkness of the early morning of April 30, 1968, a U.S. Navy utility boat motored down the Bo Dieu River just south of Vietnam's demilitarized zone. Hidden in dense vegetation along the shoreline, North Vietnamese Army (NVA) troops watched silently.

As the boat neared the convergence with the Cua Viet River, a little more than a mile downstream from Dong Ha in Vietnam's Quang Tri province, the NVA troops unleashed a barrage of rocket-propelled grenades (RPGs), small-arms fire and recoilless rifle rounds.

The attack killed one sailor, wounded six more and heralded the beginning of a three-day fight known as the Battle of Dai Do. Part of the "Mini Tet" offensive launched in May 1968, the battle's objective for the enemy was to destroy the 3rd Marine Division's headquarters located nearby at Dong Ha.

Dai Do was one of five hamlets (along with An Lac, Dinh To, Dong Huan and Thuong Do) clustered on a small peninsula where the Bo Dieu River empties into the Cua Viet River, a major U.S. military water transportation link during the Vietnam War. Supplies flowed up the Cua Viet from the Gulf of Tonkin to Dong Ha, supply hub for the 3rd Marine Division and U.S. troops at Khe Sanh, Camp Carroll, the Rockpile, Con Thien and several fire support bases.

The 3rd Marine Division's Dong Ha Combat Base was about 1½ miles southwest of the peninsula. Two of its units involved in the fight—the 2nd Bn., 4th Marines (dubbed the "Magnificent Bastards" for their fighting prowess in WWII), and the attached B Co., 1st Bn., 3rd Marines—were both based at Mai Xa Chanh about three miles north of the Dai Do village complex.

The peninsula itself was nominally under control of the South Vietnamese 2nd ARVN (Army of the Republic of Vietnam) Regiment.

The enemy consisted of three full regiments (6,000 men) of the 320th NVA Division, heavily outnumbering the Americans.

In the weeks leading up to the attack, NVA troops had infiltrated the area and constructed formidable and well-camouflaged defenses, such as trenches, fighting

Two Marines, including one with three light anti-armor weapons strapped to his back, from the 2nd Bn., 4th Marines, survey the ruins of the hamlet of Dai Do after several days of heavy fighting in May 1968. The battalion's heroic stand at Dai Do prevented the enemy from opening an invasion corridor into South Vietnam.

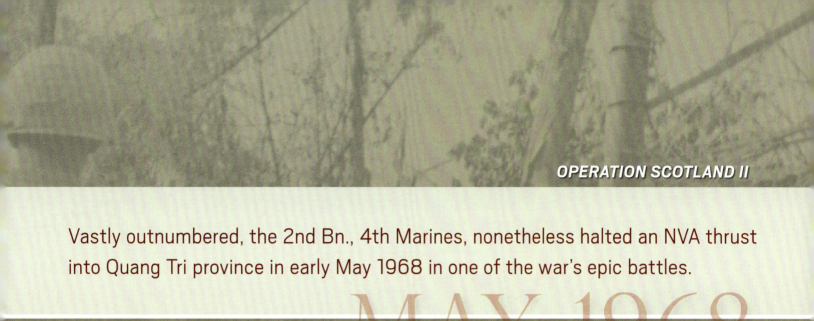

Vastly outnumbered, the 2nd Bn., 4th Marines, nonetheless halted an NVA thrust into Quang Tri province in early May 1968 in one of the war's epic battles.

MAY 1968

MEDAL OF HONOR

CAPT. JAY VARGAS

CAPT. JAMES E. LIVINGSTON

"Dai Do was toe-to-toe, hand-to-hand, house-to-house fighting that took place over an area of some 300 yards for three days."

— HM3 ROBERT CRIDER, E CO., 2ND BN., 4TH MARINES

holes and A-frame bunkers. This was all done under the supposedly watchful eyes of the 2nd ARVN troops.

"They [ARVN troops] were asleep at the switch," recalled Lt. Col. William Weise, commander of 2nd Battalion.

Another Marine believes a local Viet Cong support battalion built the defenses with tacit ARVN approval.

"The ARVN unit responsible for the ground made no effort to interfere with the VC efforts or to even report them," wrote 2nd Lt. Vic Taylor of H Co., 2nd Bn., 4th Marines. "Not surprisingly, the VC commander's brother-in-law was an officer in the ARVN unit."

Dai Do was a hamlet near the Marine supply hub of Dong Ha.

Consequently, once the fighting began, the NVA had effective fields-of-fire and made use of the rice paddies, open areas and hedgerows surrounding the villages.

"Dai Do was toe-to-toe, hand-to-hand, house-to-house fighting that took place over an area of some 300 yards for three days," said Bob Crider, who served as a Navy corpsman with E Co., 2nd Bn., 4th Marines, and became VFW's director of membership. "Prior to that, contact with the enemy had been potshots, ambushes and hit-and-run jungle fighting. At Dai Do, they stood and fought for the first time. It also was the first time I saw an NVA medical officer on the battlefield. I know because we killed him."

SEVEN KILLED IN FIVE MINUTES

After the 3:30 a.m. attack on the Navy utility boat, Weise, from his command post at Mai Xa Chanh, ordered H Company to clear the village of An Lac at the southern end of the peninsula where the attack occurred. Supporting H Company were two platoons on Amtracs (amphibian tractors) from F Company, two M-48 tanks and the 2/4's recon platoon.

As H Company attempted to cross a small stream at the village of Bac Vong to gain a foothold on the peninsula, it was hit with intense fire from the villages of Dong Huan and Dai Do. Weise then called in air strikes on the villages from Navy ships, helicopter gunships, fixed-wing aircraft and artillery.

During the bombardments, H Company commander Capt. James Williams moved his Marines about 400 yards north and crossed over the stream.

Around 2 p.m., as soon as the air strikes ended, H Company—under the cover of white phosphorous and smoke shells fired by 12th Marine artillery batteries—attacked Dong Huan from the west, or the enemy's rear. By 3 p.m., H Company had secured Dong Huan.

Meanwhile, F Company, under command of Capt. James Butler, attacked Dai Do from the north. The four Amtracs on which the Marines were riding were inviting targets for NVA rocket-propelled grenades (RPG), and two were soon knocked out of action. When the Marines were within 100 yards of the village, NVA infantry opened up with AK-47 fire. U.S. artillery strikes allowed F Company to gain a tenuous position on the northeast section of Dai Do.

At the southern end of the peninsula, Weise, now coordinating action from a Monitor gunboat on the Bo Dieu, ordered the 3rd Marines' B Company to attack the original objective, An Lac, from the river. Landing on the shoreline in Amtracs around 4:15 p.m., the Marines faced a withering and unexpected fusillade from NVA troops entrenched in An Lac. Within the first five minutes, seven Marines were killed and 14 wounded. F-4 Phantom air strikes helped the Marines eventually secure the beachhead.

That night, F Company joined H Company in Dong Huan, while B Company held fast at An Lac as artillery and mortar fire kept the enemy at bay. All told, 12 Marines were killed and 107 wounded during the day.

'EVERY TROOPER HAD A CAPTURED AK-47'

As the sun rose May 1, B Company Marines observed 40 to 50 enemy sappers (explosives experts) crawling up a deep crevice toward their position. Firing into them, the Marines left tangled masses of bodies and "a scene even [director Steven] Spielberg couldn't re-create for the movies," according to one.

Around 9:45 a.m., G Company arrived at An Lac by riverboat. The unit took over for the exhausted B Company, which acted as a reserve force, while G Company attempted to take Dai Do. Marine artillery and aircraft, as well as naval gunfire, pounded the entrenched enemy as G Company prepared its assault. Intense, close combat ensued as the Marines neared the village. By 2 p.m., after bypassing some of the enemy bunkers, they had reached the northern part of Dai Do.

"I started out with 123 men, and by the time I got through the village I was down to 41," recalled Capt. Jay Vargas, G Company commander. "Every trooper had a captured AK-47."

The NVA, though, would not give up. Long-range artillery from north of the DMZ, mortars and enemy troops in some of the bypassed bunkers forced G Company back to the eastern edge of the village. F Company attempted to help by attacking Dai Do from Dong Huan, but was stopped short. Around 5 p.m., Weise ordered B Company to fight its way to G Company, but its advance also stalled.

Help arrived in the form of E Company, led by Capt. James E. Livingston. After crossing a stream that marked the west side of the peninsula, E Company made it to An Lac around 5:30 p.m. Livingston and the commander of his recon platoon, 1st Lt. Clyde W. Mutter, helped B Company Marines collect their wounded and withdraw to An Lac. F Company also pulled back to Dong Huan.

U.S. casualties for May 1 were 20 dead and 44 wounded, but the Marines captured two NVA soldiers and killed 91.

A 'PERSONAL TURKEY SHOOT'

During interrogation, one of the enemy prisoners confessed that at least 12 NVA companies were in Dai Do, prompting Weise to plan a predawn attack on May 2. E Company would fight its way to G Company and then both units would clear the village. H Company would

"I started out with 123 men, and by the time I got through the village I was down to 41."

—CAPT. JAY VARGAS

NAVY
CROSS

**LT. COL.
WILLIAM WEISE**

**SGT. RICHARD F.
ABSHIRE**
(POSTHUMOUS)

be in reserve, while F Company held Dong Huan and B Company secured An Lac.

E Company kicked off the assault at 5 a.m., with supporting fire from G Company. Marines hit the more than 100 enemy bunkers with flamethrowers, white phosphorous, grenades, satchel charges and LAAWs (light anti-armor weapons). After intense, hand-to-hand fighting, the two Marine companies secured the village by 9:30 a.m.

At about 1 p.m., H Company moved through Dai Do to attack Dinh To and Thuong Do, located immediately northwest along the peninsula's western stream. The NVA furiously counterattacked and soon surrounded H Company. Without waiting for orders, Capt. Livingston rounded up E Company, which was down to 30 men, and rushed to help as RPGs and 12.7mm machine-gun fire ripped into his Marines.

By this time, H Company's commander had been wounded, and 2nd Lt. Vic Taylor took over. After initial success spurred by E Company's arrival, the assault bogged down in the face of another NVA counterattack. "It dwarfed the fighting that had gone before in intensity and volume," Taylor said. "I recall seeing banana trees and the masonry walls of a hooch cut down by the NVA automatic weapons fire. The bushes to our front seemed to be alive with heavily camouflaged NVA soldiers."

Sgt. James W. Rogers of E Company said Livingston's calm presence kept Marines from panicking. "NVA soldiers were all over," Rogers recalled. "As soon as you shot one, another would pop up in his place. We were receiving a lot of machine gun fire."

Lance Cpl. James O'Neill, a sniper attached to H Company, spotted three NVA 12.7mm machine guns and began eliminating gunners as soon as the enemy replaced them. "In 15 minutes," reported *Leatherneck* magazine, "O'Neill killed approximately 24 of them and wounded another dozen in his personal turkey shoot."

By 2:30 p.m., Weise had moved his command post to Dai Do and ordered E and H companies back to the village. He then coordinated a two-pronged assault. G and F companies would move north along the east bank of the stream that formed the western boundary of the peninsula into Dinh To and then onto Thuong Do. At the same time on the west bank of the stream, 2nd ARVN troops would move north to take the village of Thuong Nghia.

The attack commenced at 4 p.m., and G Company, meeting little resistance, moved easily through Dinh To and into the southern part of Thuong Do. But F Company, to the east, was slowed by artillery and automatic weapons fire. At 5 p.m., G Company started taking fire from west of the stream, where the ARVN troops were supposed to be. It was actually enemy soldiers, and, according to a *Vietnam* magazine article about the battle, there was strong evidence that the 2nd ARVN Regiment had collaborated with the enemy.

During this time, NVA troops had maneuvered in between G and F companies. With the situation worsening, Weise, accompanying G Company, called in artillery "all around and on top of us." During this engagement, he was seriously wounded by AK-47 fire. "Every Marine who was able to shoot, including wounded who could handle a weapon, fired and the fighting was violent and close," Weise recalled later.

G Company fought its way back to F Company's position in Dinh To and, by 6 p.m., the battalion had regrouped at Dai Do. May 2 proved to be the deadliest day of the battle by far: 51 KIAs accounted for 53% of the total. Another 111 Leathernecks were wounded.

TWO MEDALS OF HONOR AWARDED

Throughout the night of May 2, sporadic skirmishing continued, but most of the serious fighting was over. In the morning, 1st Bn., 3rd Marines, advanced on Dinh To and Thoung Do and found the NVA had fled. They had vanished during the night. Victorious, the Marines had secured the peninsula and reopened the vital Cua Viet waterway.

The Marines paid dearly for their victory: 87 KIA and 297 WIA. More than half of the

GIMLETS HOLD THE LINE AT NHI HA

With the outnumbered Marines fully engaged at Dai Do, U.S. commanders knew that fresh NVA troops from north of the DMZ could easily tip the battle's momentum toward the enemy. To prevent reinforcement, they called upon the Army's 3rd Bn., 21st Inf. (known as the "Gimlets"), 196th Light Inf. Bde.

The Gimlets, under control of the 3rd Marines, were ordered to clear the village of Nhi Ha, some five miles north of Dai Do and only three miles below the DMZ, of enemy soldiers. A, B and C companies launched their attack at around 8 a.m. on May 2 following a Marine artillery and mortar bombardment on Nhi Ha. By 1 p.m., C Company had reached the village and was immediately ambushed by elements of 4th Bn., 270th Independent NVA Regiment. That day cost 12 KIA; 14 WIA.

The Gimlets' commander, Lt. Col. William P. Snyder, ordered his reserve D Company and A Company to cover C Company as its men pulled back about 600 yards east of Nhi Ha, where the three companies spent the night as U.S. artillery pounded the NVA. B Company secured Lam Xuan, directly south of Nhi Ha across Jones' Creek.

Despite repeated assaults from A, C and D companies over the next two days, the Americans were unable to dislodge the enemy. Not until May 5, when Air Force jets hit Nhi Ha with 2,000-pound bombs, were all enemy troops eliminated, either having fled or been killed. Some were "propped up in their caved-in trenches with their heads missing," according to *Vietnam* magazine.

The Gimlets took over Nhi Ha, but the enemy counterattacked May 6, with the Americans routing the NVA. In the afternoon, A Company reconnoitered the village of Xom Phuong about a 1.2 miles northwest. Lured into an ambush, A Company lost 12 dead, 19 wounded and one captured (he was released on March 5, 1973).

The Army's duty in Nhi Ha ended May 15, 1968, when the Marines replaced it. Overall, the 21st Infantry lost 28 killed and 130 wounded—86% in the two ambushes. But it had accomplished its objective of preventing NVA reinforcements from reaching Dai Do.

Some [NVA] were "propped up in their caved-in trenches with their heads missing ... "

fatalities were sustained on May 2. Only one death occurred on April 29 and just three on May 3. The 2nd Bn., 4th Marines, counted 66 dead (76% of the total); the 1st Bn., 3rd Marines, 18 killed (21% of the total). The 4th's Foxtrot Company had the most deaths at 22 followed by Golf Company with 19. The 3rd Marines' Bravo Company lost 16 men. H (10), E (9) and H&S (6—including three Navy corpsmen) accounted for most of the remainder. Two men of H Btry., 3rd Bn., 12th Marines; an anti-tank assaultman; and two L Co., 3rd Bn., 3rd Marines, riflemen killed on May 3 made up the difference.

Heroism abounded. Captains Vargas (wounded three times in three days) and Livingston both earned Medals of Honor. Lt. Col. Weise and Sgt. Richard F. Abshire (posthumously) earned Navy Crosses. Four posthumous Silver Stars and a Navy Unit Commendation to 2nd Battalion, 4th Marines, also were awarded.

Though it received little attention in press reports at the time, the Battle of Dai Do was a major strategic victory for the Americans. Besides killing at least 1,568 NVA troops (buried by Marine engineers) and capturing several heavy weapons, the "Magnificent Bastards" had prevented the destruction of 3rd Marine Division headquarters at Dong Ha and a major supply center some six miles south at Quang Tri City. Dai Do would "go down in Marine lore as one of the greatest miracles against all odds in battle," said Blair Underwood, narrator of the 2016 documentary, *The Magnificent Bastards of Dai Do.* ✪

THE TOLL

U.S. KIA:
87

U.S. WIA:
297

BY KEITH W. NOLAN

STREET BATTLE IN SAIGON

On May 6, 1968, C Co., 5th Bn. (Mech.), 60th Inf., rode its armored personnel carriers, better known as tracks, into District 8, a suburb along the southern edge of Saigon. Intelligence indicated that the Viet Cong (VC) planned to strike within the district that very night.

The enemy had already attacked other points in Saigon the day before as part of a nationwide show of strength timed to coincide with the opening of the Paris peace talks. Given the enemy's previous wave of urban attacks during the Tet Offensive, the follow-up campaign was dubbed the Mini Tet Offensive.

In this instance, the intelligence was correct. At 3:45 a.m. on May 7, the 1st Platoon of C Company was attacked while guarding the Y Bridge, which spanned the Doi Canal, linking District 8 with the old colonial heart of Saigon. The platoon held the bridge, then counterattacked at dawn.

On the west side of the district, meanwhile, the 2nd and 3rd platoons rode to the rescue of the local police headquarters, catching the VC in the open as they sprinted forward from a tree line. The hapless guerrillas were pinned behind a dike by M-16 and M-60 fire, then blasted into rags by a Cobra helicopter gunship.

The survivors took shelter in a tin-roofed residential area. A Company, commanded by 1st Lt. Merle James Sharpe and having rushed to the scene from the battalion base camp, cautiously advanced down the main street, only to come under fire from windows and alleys.

Sharpe noted in a letter home that although "we were in [the enemy's] killing zone and had been taken by surprise," his troops responded "with an intense volume of their own [fire]. We moved our tracks up and unloaded on Charlie with .50-caliber machine gun[s]. Due to the buildings on both sides of the street, we could only bring two to three [tracks] up at a time."

Sharpe pulled his men back after two were killed and one of the tracks reduced to a burnt-out hulk by a rocket-propelled grenade. Next, Sharpe called in air strikes, then led two attacks that finally drove the VC back into the rice paddies behind the semi-flattened neighborhood where gunships fell upon them like birds of prey.

Members of B Co., 2nd Bn., 47th Inf., fire on Viet Cong positions south of the "Y" Bridge, May 11, 1968. A wounded Capt. James Craig is carried to safety past Spec. 4 Anthony Midkiff, who peers down from behind the gun shield.

From the rice paddies of the Mekong Delta, battalions of four regiments of the 9th Infantry Division were suddenly plunged into urban combat in Saigon's District 8 during the so-called Mini Tet Offensive of May 1968.

MAY 1968

DISTINGUISHED SERVICE CROSS

SPEC. 4 DENNIS K. JONES
(POSTHUMOUS)

SPEC. 4 GREGORY A. RUSSELL
(POSTHUMOUS)

CAPT. EDMUND B. SCARBOROUGH
(POSTHUMOUS)

1ST LT. MERLE JAMES SHARPE

Infantrymen of B Co., 2nd Bn. (Mech.), 47th Inf., 9th Inf. Div., race down a street to take up positions amid the fighting on May 11, 1968.

Sharpe was twice wounded during the firefight: a fleck of shrapnel in the stomach, and a larger piece that pierced his back above his right shoulder blade, broke the scapula, and disabled his arm. For ignoring his wounds until the enemy had been dislodged, the young company commander would be awarded the Distinguished Service Cross (DSC).

REINFORCEMENTS

On May 8, the 3rd Bn., 39th Inf., commanded by Lt. Col. Anthony P. DeLuca, took up where Sharpe's company had left off and fought its way, west to east, through the housing along the Doi Canal. As night fell, DeLuca established his command post in a Buddhist pagoda at the foot of the Y Bridge.

On May 9, the 2nd Bn. (Mech.), 47th Inf., pushed east to west along the Doi Canal to link up with DeLuca at the Y Bridge. Eight men of B and C companies were killed. "The enemy was right on top of us," recalls Lewis W. Hosler, then the .50-caliber gunner on a track. "You could see them popping up on rooftops to fire down at us. … When it was all over with, the front of my track looked like a porcupine from all the rounds sticking in it. They had embedded right in the aluminum armor."

Enemy resistance was ferocious throughout District 8. The guerrillas dug bunkers inside and between houses, concealing themselves under sheets of corrugated tin and other debris. They knocked holes in adjoining walls so they could flit unseen from building to building.

At one point, Sgt. David B. Leader, a squad leader in B Co., 6th Bn., 31st Inf., attached to DeLuca's battalion, found himself pinned down in an alley with a sniper at either end. The houses from which the snipers were firing were marked with smoke grenades for gunships. Flushed out by the fire, a fleeing VC ran past Leader, who quickly sighted in at a range of 66 feet and squeezed the trigger on his M-16. The shot sent the VC cartwheeling.

At another point in the battle, 1st Lt. Hildebrando Madrigal, a platoon leader in DeLuca's battalion, crawled down a drainage ditch with a small team, and into a rubbled, two-walled house behind enemy lines.

Within minutes, an enemy soldier trotted across a field near the house. One of Madrigal's riflemen knocked the man down with a single shot, then cooly shot two more unwary VC.

The enemy finally took the group under AK-47 fire.

"Chunks of plaster were flying all over," recalls William Bausser, then an artillery forward observer. "Madrigal and I looked at each other, and we both said, 'Let's get out of here!' We retreated. I mean, we ran out of there!"

Given the enemy's tenacity, DeLuca and his fellow battalion commanders were forced in their frustration to flatten entire neighborhoods to eliminate the snipers and machine-gun crews ensconced among the civilians.

"The noise level has been tremendous with a constant stream of air and artillery support," DeLuca wrote home on May 11. "We have gone a total of 800 meters [a half mile]—pushing, taking casualties, and pushing back. So far we have accounted for over 200 VC, but we have paid for it."

An armored personnel carrier from B Co., 2nd Bn. (Mech.), 47th Inf., 9th Inf. Div., moves forward to fire on enemy snipers.

A PYRRHIC VICTORY

Heavy fighting continued through May 12, and then, suddenly, it was all over on May 13. The battered enemy had decamped during the night, leaving behind their dead. "It was all sort of surreal," recalls former platoon leader Nicholas C. Procaccini.

"There was smoke and fire and bodies strewn about, bloated, disgusting. [Civilians] were walking around, looking at their destroyed property. Lot of old people. Lot of crying. It was really sad."

In addition to fighting in the streets of District 8, units of the 9th Division also fought in the rice-paddy country south of Saigon in a successful effort to interdict further enemy infiltration into the capital during Mini Tet. Eight men were killed during this effort.

This included Capt. Edmund B. Scarborough, commander of C Co., 5th Bn. (Mech.), 60th Inf., which rushed from Saigon on May 10 to hit a VC unit besieging an outlying village. He was among three KIA at the Y Bridge. Until fatally wounded, Scarborough led his men in a direct assault that killed 26 VC, according to his DSC citation.

Spec. 4 Gregory A. Russell of 3rd Plt., C Co., 6th Bn., 31st Inf., who lost his life during the pursuit of the retreating VC at Da Phuoc, was posthumously awarded the DSC. The radio-telephone operator provided vital communication until mortally wounded. Another recipient of the DSC, Spec. 4 Dennis Jones, served as an artillery forward observer for B Co., 6th Bn., 31st Inf. Over three days (May 10-12) in the Cholon area of Saigon, he directed strikes amidst house-to-house fighting until KIA.

"The troop morale is high," DeLuca wrote. "There were so many heroes that it makes you want to burst with pride." One of his letters home described how he entered his battalion aid station during the battle. "Everyone was looking glum except one soldier and he smiled as I came up to talk to him; yep, he was the wounded one, with a bad head wound. It tears you up [to see wounded American soldiers], but [their uncomplaining attitude] gives you the charge you need to keep pushing."

Starting May 5 and running through May 12, 38 men of the 9th Infantry Division plus one of the 52nd Infantry (716th MP Battalion) died fighting in District 8 and nearby. Regimental losses were nine (31st), 11 (39th), 10 (47th) and eight (60th). Places like Xom Cau Mat, Xom Ong Doi and the bridge over the Rach Ong Nho became part of the "Octofoil" Division's lore. ✪

"There was smoke and fire and bodies strewn about, bloated, disgusting."

—PLATOON LEADER NICHOLAS C. PROCACCINI

THE TOLL

U.S. KIA:
39

BY TIM DYHOUSE

FIERCE FIGHT AT KHAM DUC

U. S. troops defending a temporary Special Forces campsite near the Laotian border on May 10, 1968, were shocked when NVA forces hit them with artillery and mortar fire in the predawn darkness. Ngok Tavak, an old French fort, and Kham Duc, some five miles north and about 50 miles southwest of Da Nang in northwestern Quang Tin province, represented the last remaining Special Forces presence on the Laotian border in I Corps.

The camp provided a reconnaissance window through which the Americans kept tabs on Communist movements along the Ho Chi Minh Trail. And the GIs knew, following the Tet Offensive and the temporary overrunning of another Special Forces camp at Lang Vei in February 1968, that at some point the NVA would hit Kham Duc. Their concerns were reinforced by reports in March indicating the NVA's 2nd Division, which had been in South Vietnam for several years, was on the move.

Awaiting the enemy at Ngok Tavak was the 113-man 11th Mobile Strike (Mike) Force composed of native Nungs, ethnic Chinese recruited mostly from Cholon, the Chinese section of Saigon.

Three Green Berets, three Australian Training Team advisers, as well as 43 Marines and one Navy corpsman of D Btry., 2nd Bn., 13th Marines, with two 105mm howitzers, also were part of the force.

> "If they [the AC-47 crew] had not arrived, I am quite sure none of us would have survived."
>
> —CAPT. JOHN WHITE, AN AUSTRALIAN ARMY OFFICER WHO COMMANDED THE 11TH MIKE FORCE

NAPALM STRIKES AID ESCAPE EFFORT

A mortar barrage began at 3 a.m. on May 10, and the ground attack commenced some 30 minutes later. But it was the treachery of some of the supposedly allied ethnic lowland Vietnamese of the Civilian Irregular Defense Group (CIDG) from Kham Duc that was most disconcerting.

Before the NVA assault on Ngok Tavak started, a small group of CIDG soldiers (later determined to include Communist sappers) led the initial charge into the Marine section of the isolated outpost. Yelling "Don't shoot! Don't shoot! Friendly! Friendly!" the turncoat CIDG platoon barreled inside the camp and immediately assaulted Marine positions with hand grenades and satchel charges.

MAY 1968

Between May 10–12, 1968, the U.S. Special Forces Camp at Kham Duc and a nearby position, Ngok Tavak, fell to North Vietnamese forces. For Marine artillerymen and Army grunts, 32 of whom were left behind as MIAs, the situation was dire. Then aviators came to the rescue.

DON RICHARDSON PHOTO

Civilian Irregular Defense Group (CIDG) troops line a trench while men of A Co., 70th Eng. Bn., man a machine gun on the Kham Duc base perimeter during a NVA attack.

COURTESY WEST VIRGINIA ARCHIVES AND HISTORY

Leathernecks of D Btry., 2nd Bn., 13th Marines, were among those who defended the temporary base at Ngok Tavak. The artillery outfit earned a unit commendation for valor because of its actions there, losing 13 KIA. Some of the unit members are, first row: an unknown Marine, William McGonigle (KIA), Gene Whisman and James Sargent (KIA). Back row: Roger Mayte, Phillip Dulude, unknown truck driver and Ray Heyne (KIA).

KEN BENWAY PHOTO

Sgt. Ledbetter, Capt. John White, Spec. 4 Kenneth Benway, WO Frank Lucas, Sgt. Blomgren, Sgt. Glenn Miller and WO Don Cameron were based at Ngok Tavak. Australian advisers led the 11th Mobile Strike Force.

Suffering heavy casualties, the defenders killed the infiltrators and stopped the initial assault. But a subsequent three-pronged NVA attack soon overran half the camp. An Air Force AC-47 gunship flying above the base and blasting away at the enemy throughout the night may have been the only thing that saved the defenders.

"If they [the AC-47 crew] had not arrived, I am quite sure none of us would have survived," said Capt. John White, an Australian army officer who commanded the 11th Mike Force.

A counterattack at daybreak allowed the Mike Force to briefly regain control of the fort. But with their water and ammunition nearly exhausted and no firm prospect of aerial reinforcement or evacuation, they knew they had two choices: escape or die.

At 1 p.m., after the Marine artillerymen "spiked," or disabled, the tubes of their howitzers, White led the survivors out of the camp. With the aid of napalm strikes, they marched through dense jungle to a hill east of Ngok Tavak, where they were picked up by four Marine helicopters and flown to Kham Duc.

American losses at Ngok Tavak were 15 KIA and 21 wounded. Of the total KIA, 13 were Marines of D Battery and two Green Berets of Det. A-105, 5th SFG. Twelve bodies were not recovered at that time. A Marine helicopter pilot of HMM-265 also was killed accidentally.

The Marine battery (only 11 men escaped unhurt) earned the Meritorious Unit Commendation with "V" device for the defense of Ngok Tavak. Two artillerymen received the Navy Cross: Cpl. Henry Schunck and Lance Cpl. Richard Conklin. Both were seriously wounded.

Australian Bruce Davies, who served two years with White's unit—Australian Army Training Team-Vietnam—disputes a commonly held belief that 12 Americans supposedly "vanished" while searching for Special Forces Spec. 4 Tom Perry before escaping to Kham Duc.

"It's controversial owing to the number of Marine bodies that were left on the hill, as well as the Special Forces soldier," Davies said. "There was no search party. These men had been killed in action prior to the evacuation of the position."

Davies' book, *The Battle at Ngok Tavak* (2009), delves deeply into the attack. "The battle is a story of tactical intrigue and controversy," Davies said. "It attracted my attention for several reasons. Why were two Marine 105mm howitzers out in the western wilds of I Corps supporting a Special Forces Nung company that was commanded by an Australian? On the surface, it appeared to be a tactically foolish plan that called for further analysis."

Kham Duc and Ngok Tavak, situated near the Laotian border due west of Chu Lai, were prime targets of NVA forces on May 10-12, 1968. The attacks killed 42 Americans.

OUTPOST DUTY NO 'CAKE JOB'

By the time White and the other survivors reached Kham Duc at around 7 p.m., it was already under attack as well. Defending the base itself, which sat in the center of a mile-wide bowl-shaped valley, was a Special Forces "A" team (Det. A-105), as well as elements from the Americal Division: 2nd Bn. (A, B and C companies), 1st Inf., 196th Light Inf. Bde.; 1st Bn. (A Co.), 46th Inf., 198th Light Inf. Bde; 3rd Bn. (A Btry.), 82nd Artillery (with five 105mm howitzers); and 70th Eng. Bn. (A Co.), The 1st Infantry's Delta Company arrived later on May 12, providing ground security for the evacuation.

After reinforcement, total effective strength at Kham Duc on May 11 was some 815 U.S. (730 Americal, 60 engineers and 25 SF) and about 75 reliable CIDG troops. Nearly 300 dependents of the CIDG soldiers from a nearby village also were present. Enemy strength was two reinforced regiments.

"When we were brought in to guard the perimeter it seemed like a cake job, since we had been out in the field for months on end," recalled Tom Grabowski of C Co., 2nd Bn., 1st Inf., in *The Illustrated History of the Chargers* by F. Clifton Berry.

Americal soldiers from E Company, a platoon-sized unit, reinforced CIDG troops at three of the seven observation posts (OPs) in the hills ringing the base. During the day of May 11 and into the night, the enemy rained mortars on the airstrip and camp. On May 12, OP 3 squad members withdrew without casualties. Both OP 1 and 2 were eventually overrun. NVA soldiers had already surrounded Kham Duc.

Four Americans and one Vietnamese, too wounded to leave, remained behind at OP 1 with a radio and continued transmitting into the afternoon. One helicopter was badly damaged in an unsuccessful attempt to rescue them.

Before the enemy could assault OP 3, the 10 Americans there were told to return to Kham Duc. With a large force of NVA between them and the base, they had to fight their way back, not arriving until 2 p.m. on May 12.

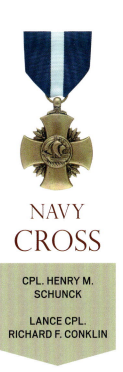

DISTINGUISHED SERVICE CROSS

SPEC. 4 WILLIAM H. BLEDSOE

NAVY CROSS

CPL. HENRY M. SCHUNCK

LANCE CPL. RICHARD F. CONKLIN

AIR FORCE CROSS

MAJ. BERNARD LUDWIG BUCHER
(POSTHUMOUS)

LT. COL. WILLIAM BOYD, JR.

MAJ. JESSE W. CAMPBELL

LT. COL. ALFRED J. JEANOTTE, JR.

PHOTOS COURTESY WWW.VETERANTRIBUTES.ORG

PHOTO COURTESY DENNIS FLORES

Soldiers of the 196th Light Infantry Brigade man a fighting hole while watching an American aircraft land at besieged Kham Duc, May 10-12, 1968.

Soldiers of A Co., 70th Eng. Bn., wait in a ditch beside the runway to be airlifted out during the battle of Kham Duc.

The Americal infantrymen fought desperately at the other two outposts as AC-47 gunships dropped illumination flares and fired on the attackers with their mini-cannons.

According to *After Tet: The Bloodiest Year in Vietnam* by Ronald H. Spector, "As the outposts were overwhelmed, the defenders directed gunship and artillery fire onto their own positions. A few managed to escape into the Kham Duc perimeter, but many died on the hill outposts."

By 9:30 a.m. on May 12, the NVA held nearly all of the high ground surrounding Kham Duc. Most of the Americal men listed as missing after the battle died defending the outposts.

By 10 a.m., the NVA were launching company-sized assaults on Americal positions around the airstrip outside the camp, and then launched a massive attack on the camp's eastern perimeter about 2 p.m.

WESTMORELAND ORDERS EVACUATION

Even before this, Gen. William Westmoreland, commander of all U.S. forces in Vietnam, ordered Kham Duc evacuated beginning at 7:30 a.m. The first helicopter to arrive, a CH-47, was shot down in the middle of the base's 6,000-foot-long runway. The NVA downed two more aircraft before anyone had a chance to escape. In all, 10 aircraft were lost at Kham Duc that day. The 14th Aviation Battalion maneuvered through a "devastating rain of hostile mortar and machine gun fire" to resupply ammo and evacuate troops, according to its Valorous Unit Award citation.

It was apparent that because of the intense ground fire and the large number of people needing to be evacuated, giant C-123s and C-130s from the Air Force's 834th Air Division would be needed for the airlift. By noon, a C-130, a C-123 and a few Army and Marine helicopters managed to evacuate 145 GIs and Vietnamese civilians. Then, the NVA stepped up their attacks, and for the next three hours, the evacuation stalled.

Air Force Maj. Bernard L. Bucher managed to land his C-130 on the debris-strewn runway. CIDG troops and civilians, in a state of panic, swarmed the plane, convinced the Americans intended to leave them behind. Between 150 and 200 managed to crowd onto the plane.

Lt. Col. Joe Jackson's C-123 (at top in the middle) turns around on the airstrip at besieged Kham Duc to pick up Air Force combat controllers left behind. Forward air controllers played a vital role.

MEDAL OF
HONOR

**LT. COL. JOE
JACKSON**

As Bucher lifted off, his plane was hit by heavy machine gun fire, crashing and exploding less than a mile from the runway. All aboard were killed, including the crew of five from the 774th Tactical Airlift Squadron and one Green Beret. Bucher was awarded the Air Force Cross posthumously.

C-130 pilots orbiting Kham Duc watched the tragedy unfold below them, awaiting their turn to dive through ground fire to rescue the defenders. Five more braved the carnage, with one crash-landing after NVA gunners shot away its hydraulic system. Pilots and crew evacuated more than 400 people before Air Force commanders called off the operation because of the high losses.

"I was on a plane out of Kham Duc," said Bill Tidwell, a medic with 4th Plt., C Co., 2nd Bn., 1st Inf., 196th LIB. "Another aircraft that took off was shot down. We were supposed to get on that plane, but the Vietnamese rushed the plane ahead of us. Those two days at Kham Duc always stood out as the scariest of my entire time in Vietnam."

'ALL OF A SUDDEN, WE WERE ALIVE'

Because of the confusion and miscommunication, three Air Force combat controllers ended up stranded at Kham Duc. Convinced they were left behind, they decided to fight rather than be taken prisoner. "We had 11 magazines among us," Air Force Tech. Sgt. Mort Freedman said. "We were going to take as many of them with us as we could."

Thanks to Air Force Lt. Col. Joe Jackson of the 311th Air Commando Wing, the combat controllers had one last chance for escape. Dodging NVA anti-aircraft fire, Jackson flew his "lumbering C-123 like a fighter" toward the now enemy-held Kham Duc airstrip.

With only 2,200 feet of runway available in the center of the landing strip, Jackson slammed on the brakes as he touched down, stopping just short of a demolished helicopter. Enemy fire was ever present. The combat controllers scurried up the C-123's loading ramp, while Jackson turned the plane around. "We were dead," one of the airmen recalled later, "and all of a sudden we were alive."

With mortars and rockets crashing around him, Jackson powered up the throttle for take-off. The men had no time to spare. "We hadn't been out of that spot 10 seconds when

An aid station is set up near the runway at Kham Duc to treat the wounded.

mortars started dropping directly on it," Jackson recalled. "That was a real thriller. I figured they just got zeroed in on us, and the time of flight of the mortar shells was about 10 seconds longer than we sat there taking the men aboard."

Jackson earned the Medal of Honor for his bravery, becoming the only airlifter ever to receive the nation's highest military award in Vietnam.

The next day, some 60 B-52s dropped about 12,000 tons of bombs on the abandoned camp. Unfortunately, some Americans remained at Kham Duc.

LARGEST MIA RECOVERY

Three soldiers who had been at OP 2—Sgt. Ron Sassenberger, Pvt. Wilbert Foreman and John Colonna—were unable to make it back to the base for evacuation. They were able to evade the NVA for three days and were finally picked up by a U.S. helicopter on May 15.

Cpl. Julius W. Long, Jr., of E Co., 2nd Bn., 1st Inf., was the only soldier from OP 1 to successfully make his way back to the camp. When he reached it, he found himself alone. The NVA captured Long on May 16 and transferred him to a POW camp in North Vietnam, from which he was repatriated on March 16, 1973.

(Spec. 4 Bill Wright and squad leader Orlando Vasquez also escaped OP 1, making their way to the airstrip. Both earned Silver Stars.)

The battles at Ngok Tavak and Kham Duc produced more American MIAs than any other engagement in the Vietnam War: 12 at Ngok Tavak and 20 at Kham Duc for a total of 32.

Two years later, U.S. troops returned to Kham Duc to conduct search and recovery operations on July 18-21 and Aug. 17-20, 1970. They recovered five sets of remains: Pfc. Harry Sisk and Pfc. Antonio Guzman-Rios, who had been at OP 1; and Spec. 4 Richard Bowers, Pfc. Randall Lloyd and Sgt. 1st Class Johnnie Carter at OP 2. Of the 10 men at OP 1, five had been killed. At OP 2, only three of the 13-man team survived.

All told, 42 Americans sacrificed their lives at Kham Duc (26) and Ngok Tavak (16)—20 Americal soldiers, 14 Marines, five airmen and three Special Forces members. Except for two, all of the Americal deaths were from the 1st Infantry's 2nd Battalion: the most (eight) were in E Company. Some 85% of the deaths at Kham Duc were incurred on May 12.

Fast forward to August 2005. After 12 years of investigations and three excavations that represented the single largest MIA recovery operation in U.S. history, the remains of 12 Americans who fought at Ngok Tavak were identified. They were buried at Arlington National Cemetery on Oct. 7, 2005. Then in December 2006, the remains of two Americal GIs were identified and brought home for burial.

Though the last remaining Special Forces border camps in northwestern South Vietnam had been destroyed, they were soon replaced by camps farther inland. After leaving Kham Duc, secretive Studies and Observation Group troops set up another launch site at a place with much better weather for helicopter operations.

Heroism was never in short supply at Kham Duc or Ngok Tavak. Besides the Medal of Honor, two Navy Crosses and four Air Force Crosses, medic William Bledsoe received the Distinguished Service Cross (DSC). He saved the lives of other wounded despite being severely hit himself at OP 3. "I witnessed 'Doc' Bledsoe work his magic," remembered E Company vet David Sisk. "He certainly deserved the DSC." ✪

THE TOLL

Kham Duc
U.S. KIA:
26

Ngok Tavak
U.S. KIA:
16

BY TIM DYHOUSE

OPERATION ALLEN BROOK

GOING GETS ROUGH ON GO NOI ISLAND

In mid-May 1968, battalions of the 7th and 27th Marines met fierce enemy resistance at three hamlets strategically located in the Thu Bon River Valley during *Operation Allen Brook.*

Defending Da Nang was priority No. 1 for U.S. commanders following the Tet Offensive in early 1968. They believed the city—the main U.S. port on the China Sea and the most important logistical hub in the northernmost part of South Vietnam—was the target of the enemy's second phase of anticipated attacks, which they called "Mini Tet."

They also believed the North Vietnamese Army (NVA) would launch attacks from Go Noi Island in the Dien Ban district, only 15 miles south of Da Nang. Known as a relatively safe haven for both NVA and Viet Cong (VC) military units, the island and its residents provided strong support for the Communist political and military agendas. Go Noi also was located at the northern foot of the Que Son Mountains, a natural clandestine route into Vietnam for NVA units infiltrating from Laos.

To help protect the city, U.S. commanders launched *Operation*

PHOTO COURTESY COL. TULLIS J. WOODHAM, JR.

Two 3/27 Marines help a heat-stricken Capt. Robert R. Anderson, commander of H&S Company, back from the front line where he was helping remove casualties. For many Marines, the 110-degree heat during the Go Noi battles was as brutal as the enemy.

SOME OF THE 3/27'S CASUALTIES

KIA—
Cpl. Thomas W. Mills

KIA—
Cpl. John E. Hazelwood

WIA—
Cpl. Bob Simonsen

KIA—
Sgt. Jack B. Gorton

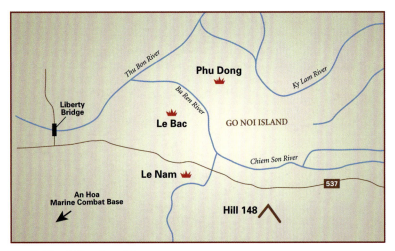

Firefights at three hamlets on Go Noi Island in mid-May 1968 cost the lives of nearly 100 men of the 7th and 27th Marine regiments.

Aug. 24, 1968) as a part of a larger plan to drive the communists out of Go Noi's 7,000-acre area. About five miles east of An Hoa, Go Noi was located in the Thu Bon River Valley, situated at the confluence of the Thu Bon, Ky Lam, Ba Ren and Chiem Son rivers. Seven-foot-high elephant grass covered much of the flat terrain, and for a good part of May 1968 the temperature hovered around a brutally humid 110 degrees.

The American forces facing off against the communists in the Battle of Go Noi Island were from the 3rd Bn., 27th Marines, and the 7th Marines, both 1st Marine Division units. Newly arrived from the States in February 1968, nearly three-fourths of the 27th's 3rd Battalion had non-infantry military occupation specialties, such as cooks, engineers, truck drivers and mechanics.

"These Marines would soon prove the old Marine Corps saying that 'every Marine is a basic rifleman,'" wrote former Cpl. Bob Simonsen, of I Co., 3/27, in his book *Every Marine: 1968 Vietnam, A Battle for Go Noi Island*.

Go Noi was home to three local Viet Cong units: R-20 Battalion, V-25 Battalion and T-3 Sapper Battalion, as well as Group 44, the headquarters for the enemy's operations in Quang Nam province. Marines also suspected that elements of the 2nd NVA Division were trying to reconnect in the sector.

Leathernecks would soon face off against the communists in a deadly series of three back-to-back firefights.

PHU DONG: 'WE HIT A HORNET'S NEST'

From May 4-15, elements of the 7th Marines encountered relatively light yet persistent resistance as they swept from west to east across Go Noi. On May 7, Golf Company lost nine KIA about three miles northeast of Liberty Bridge.

Hoping to flush out 2nd NVA Division units, Marine Lt. Col. Roger H. Barnard, commander of the 3rd Bn., 7th Marines, launched a plan to deceive the enemy. He ordered all Marine units out of Go Noi in the early evening of May 15 as if the operation had been completed.

That night, Barnard's command group, along with A Co., 1st Bn., and G Co., 2nd Bn., from the 7th Marines, as well as I Co., 3/27, snuck back across the Thu Bon River and re-entered Go Noi in a single-file march. Around 9 a.m. on May 16, I Co., 3/27 and G Co., 2/7 approached the village of Phu Dong, surprising NVA troops.

"My first platoon began sweeping on line, firing blindly at first, into the brush, which soon erupted back with heavy rifle and machine-gun fire," Simonsen wrote. He added that a Marine on either side of him was killed before he was wounded himself, taking "a four-round burst, the last bullet striking my helmet and knocking me out."

Barnard recalled that "we hit a hornet's nest," and the NVA machine-gun fire was "like being in the butts at the rifle range."

Artillery and mortar fire failed to dislodge the enemy. Only after some 50 air strikes were the NVA forced out of their bunkers and trenches.

The Marines, who sustained 26 dead and 38 wounded, killed 130 NVA. Two members of the 7th Marines—2nd Lt. Paul F. Cobb of A Co., 1st Bn., and Navy corpsman Petty Officer Robert M. Casey with G Co., 2nd Bn.—earned posthumous Navy Crosses during the fighting. Of the KIAs, 13 belonged to the 2nd Battalion's Golf Company, 11 to Alpha of the 1st Battalion and two were members of I Co., 3rd Bn., 27th Marines.

After the battle, Barnard determined that his Marines had run into an NVA regimental headquarters and extensive supply depot. "When all enemy resistance ceased and the dust had settled, it was clear we had achieved a significant victory," deducted Barnard.

That night, the Marines set up defensive positions several hundred yards west of Phu Dong and just north of the village of Le Bac. In the morning, with I Company in the lead, the Marines set out for the hamlet of Le Nam, directly to the south.

LE NAM: 'IT WAS INCREDIBLY HOT'

"We entered a village just as daylight broke," said Lance Cpl. Allen Ciezki of 3rd Plt., I Co. "I saw movement, and we all opened up. I hit an NVA as he grabbed a heavy pack and tried to run. Suddenly, we were hit by incoming mortar rounds."

Ciezki's sergeant ordered him to stay with the wounded, as the rest of I Company rushed into the tall elephant grass between them and an eight-foot-deep dry riverbed some 50 yards ahead.

As Marines in the lead started across the gulley toward a tree line on the opposite bank, NVA troops sprang an ambush from defenses "of significant width" in the trees.

Ciezki, after being relieved by corpsmen, rushed to "the killing zone" of the dry riverbed where "about three dozen or more Marines were pinned down and exposed" by the Communist fusillade of mortars, rocket-propelled grenades and small-arms fire.

"I spent the rest of the day and night there helping to fight the NVA, rescuing and caring for the wounded, and providing cover for those who went for water," Ciezki said. "All afternoon and into the evening, Marines were being killed trying to rescue the wounded."

One Marine, 18-year-old Pfc. Robert Burke of I Company, a truck mechanic pressed into infantry service, decided something must be done.

NAVY CROSS

**2ND LT.
PAUL F. COBB**
(POSTHUMOUS)

**PETTY OFFICER
ROBERT M. CASEY**
(POSTHUMOUS)

"**All afternoon and into the evening, Marines were being killed trying to rescue the wounded.**"

—LANCE CPL. ALLEN CIEZKI, 3RD PLATOON, I COMPANY

MEDAL OF
HONOR

PFC. ROBERT BURKE
(POSTHUMOUS)

"He darted to the barren sandy cliff and approached the reinforced concrete bunkers one by one, wiping out one enemy machine-gun emplacement after another, all the while being exposed to murderous enemy fire," wrote Cpl. Terry Rigney of H&S Co., 3/27, who served as an intelligence analyst during the fights on Go Noi. "He continued his one-man assault until enemy fire brought his efforts and his short 18 years of life to an end."

Burke's heroism allowed dozens of wounded Marines to be removed from the battlefield. As a result, he became the youngest Medal of Honor recipient of the Vietnam War.

Hearing of I Company's plight, 3/27 commander Lt. Col. Tullis J. Woodham, Jr., ordered the battalion's two remaining companies, K and L (M Company was providing security at Da Nang Air Base), to make an air assault to the south of, or behind, the NVA bunker positions to help relieve the pressure on I Company. The two companies arrived around 3 p.m. about a half-mile from the firefight.

"When our choppers landed, we immediately started receiving incoming fire," said Cpl. Johnny Johnson of K Co., 3/27. "The NVA had laid out their fields of fire, and we were right in it." Johnson said Capt. Joel Parks, K Company's commander, ordered the Marines into the tree line from which the NVA were firing. With the aid of extensive air and artillery support, they broke through the NVA lines and finally connected with the survivors of I Company around 7:30 p.m.

According to Johnson, they secured the area, "aided the wounded as best we could," and occupied the NVA's fighting positions. Four days later, Johnson was wounded. "Published reports later said I was the last surviving member of my platoon to be medevaced," he said.

I Company had sustained 20 KIA and 50 wounded. Total U.S. casualties for the day were 28 Marines dead and 105 wounded. The NVA lost 81 killed.

LE BAC: 'ALL HELL BROKE LOOSE'

During the night of May 17, the 3rd Bn., 7th Marines, left Go Noi and was replaced by the 3rd Bn., 5th Marines, which operated mainly to the east of 3/27 for the rest of the month.

Around 9:30 a.m., May 18, 3/27 Marines began taking sniper fire from Le Bac, some 300 yards to the north. Woodham ordered K and L companies (he had deemed I Company to be "combat ineffective" because of casualties and the "almost total annihilation of their officers and staff NCOs") to clear the area. He also ordered M Company to Go Noi from Da Nang to replace I Company.

Lt. Col. Tullis J. Woodham, Jr. (right) commander of the 3rd Bn., 27th Marines, uses a radio to assess the situation in Le Bac. At left is his operations officer, Maj. Ernest T. Fitzgerald.

As K and L companies moved closer to Le Bac, the NVA unleashed an intense barrage of rifle, machine-gun and sniper fire from a tree line.

"Our point man, Pfc. George Botes, was about 50 feet from the trees when the enemy opened up," said Lance Cpl. Art Riordan of 1st Sqd., 1st Plt., L Co. "I was fourth or fifth in the column and everyone got hit, including a corpsman alongside of me. Of all the sights, sounds, smells and 120-degree heat, one stands out: battalion Sgt. Maj. [Robert] Snyder standing, with grease paint under his eyes, shooting snipers out of the trees."

The lead squads were quickly pinned down. "People were dying, and we couldn't get to them," said Cpl. Charles D. Hukaby, an interpreter with K Company. "At one point, the platoon commander could see people only 25 meters [27 yards] in front of him, but we couldn't get to them." The intense heat prompted Marines to discard their flak jackets and gas masks, as water became a precious commodity.

"The choppers started coming in to medevac the wounded and dead from India, Kilo and Lima," said Sgt. Wesley Love of K Company. "All hell broke loose—RPGs, mortars, machine guns, light arms, everything you could think of was going off all at the same time."

"All hell broke loose—RPGs, mortars, machine guns, light arms, everything you could think of was going off all at the same time."

—SGT. WESLEY LOVE, K COMPANY

PHOTO COURTESY TERRY RIGNEY

Men of 3rd Bn., 27th Marines, re-enter Le Bac on May 26, 1968. Its K and M companies sustained 11 KIA there two days before.

Not long after that, around 3 p.m., more helicopters arrived with M Company replacements. Most of the remaining I Company Marines boarded the helicopters for evacuation to Da Nang. As he saw the members of M Company offloading, Love said he asked them derisively where they had been the whole time. "Someone just glared at me and kept going," he said.

M Company's arrival allowed K Company, which had taken the most casualties, to pull back into a reserve role. Air, artillery and napalm strikes helped from above, while Lance Cpl. Gary Much of L Company provided firepower on the ground. He earned a Silver Star when he blew apart an NVA bunker with what he called "a luck shot" with his 3.5-inch rocket launcher.

"The battle went on most of the day and into the evening," Woodham recalled. "We fired everything that we could get ahold of. We fired up almost all of the artillery ammo that the division had for its allocation. It was incredibly hot, and we lost many Marines to the heat." The NVA withdrew under cover of darkness.

The three costliest days of Go Noi Island for the 3rd Bn., 27th Marines, were May 17, 18 and 24. Some 47% of its deaths (28) occurred on May 17. I Company sustained the greatest loss with 20 KIAs—one third of the total. M Company had 12 KIA, while K and L companies had 10 each. Four Navy corpsmen lost their lives. Only three men were from units other than the 3rd Bn., 27th Marines, on those days. Gunfire caused 85% of the fatalities. Four 3-27th Marines died in bomb explosions.

Besides a Medal of Honor, two Navy Crosses and at least seven Silver Stars (two of them posthumous—Sgt. John Burton and Pfc. Thomas Sharpe), the 1st Marine Division as a whole garnered the prestigious Presidential Unit Citation for Go Noi Island.

"The enemy was totally crushed on Go Noi Island," Simonsen wrote in his book. "They lost 1,017 known killed. [And] American generals have argued that forays such as *Allen Brook* kept the enemy off balance and disrupted his supply system and bases." Generals also credited *Operation Allen Brook* with pre-empting an NVA/VC offensive against Da Nang.

"Given the lack of coordination, staying power and imagination the Communists had repeatedly demonstrated in their attacks on towns and cities, compared with their formidable fighting qualities on the defensive," Ronald H. Spector wrote in *After Tet: The Bloodiest Year in Vietnam*, "one may wonder whether such pre-emptive operations were worth the cost."

Nonetheless, one thing remains crystal clear—the bravery displayed by Marines on Go Noi is undisputed. That in itself is a lasting tribute. ✪

THE TOLL

U.S. KIA:
96

U.S. WIA:
300

BY RICHARD K. KOLB

AMERICA'S ELITE DECIMATE NVA SAPPERS AT FOB-4

The Presidential Unit Citation (PUC) says it all. It contains phrases like "fought officially denied actions" in "unheralded top-secret missions deep behind enemy lines across Southeast Asia." They "inflicted casualties out of all proportions to their own losses" while making "unacknowledged sacrifices."

Awarded on April 4, 2001—not until 28 years after the unit was disbanded—the PUC recognized the remarkable achievements of the highly secretive Studies and Observation Group (SOG). SOG, falling under Military Assistance Command Vietnam, oversaw classified, covert operations. Members signed agreements swearing not to reveal their clandestine missions for 20 years. "When people asked about what we did," remembered Staff Sgt. Patrick J. Watkins, "we said we were in Vietnam" only.

Perhaps 3,000 men served in SOG throughout the war. Although recruits were taken from every service, the majority of personnel were funneled through the 5th Special Forces Group—the famed Green Berets—based in Nha Trang.

Command and Control North (CCN) was the largest of SOG field commands. It was responsible for operations conducted in North Vietnam and Laos. Forward Operating Base 4 (FOB-4) was headquarters for CCN. FOB-4 and the mission launch site were located southeast of Da Nang on the north side of Marble Mountain at its base. The eerie mountain (actually five peaks) was laced with caves and dotted by Buddhist shrines. The eastern front of the compound bordered on the South China Sea with a 300-yard beachside.

IMMORTALIZED IN LEGEND & LORE

One of SOG's many "unacknowledged sacrifices" occurred on Aug. 23, 1968. "It is now part of the Group's [5th SFG] DNA," wrote one Special Forces vet, "and these casualties are

Staff Sgt. Larry Trimble was assistant team leader of "Spike Team" Rattler. His nine-man team manned an outpost on Marble Mountain and was instrumental in preventing far greater casualties in the assault.

A three-hour assault on a headquarters command of the Studies & Observation Group on Aug. 23, 1968, caused the greatest single casualty list in U.S. Army Special Forces history.

AUGUST 1968

COURTESY LARRY TRIMBLE

This photo of "Spike Team" Rattler, including Ed Ames, was taken at FOB-4 before the attack.

immortalized in its legend and lore." John Plaster, a SOG vet and author of *Secret Commandos,* recorded: "On that night at CCN's Da Nang compound, more Green Berets were killed and wounded than in any incident in the history of the U.S. Army Special Forces."

The assault that created this tragic event was definitely an inside job. The North Vietnamese Army (NVA) could count on a cook's helper to provide vital intelligence. For enemy sappers—specially trained infiltrators with demolition expertise—strengths and locations were critical. Perhaps 200 Americans—at least twice the normal number—were present that night because of promotion boards and monthly officer meetings.

With personnel numbers and facility placements, the 100 sappers of the NVA Special Operations Brigade had perfect targets. And they undertook their mission in deadly earnest. The words inscribed on the headbands of dead sappers attested to their fanaticism: "We came here to die."

"These were Hanoi's most elite commandos," three-tour SOG vet Plaster wrote in *Secret Commandos.* "Their bodies greased to squeeze through fences, they wore only loincloths or khaki shorts and carried AKs [rifles], grenades, hand-thrown RPGs [rocket-propelled grenades], and woven baskets containing demolition charges. Each held five pounds of explosives, enough to make toothpicks of a flimsy wooden hooch."

John Stryker Meyer, also a SOG vet and author of *On the Ground: The Secret War in Vietnam,* wrote: "They [sappers] moved quietly through the darkness. They had planned for months and chosen this day, Aug. 23, 1968, and time carefully. Everything was as their informants had said it would be and now all that was left was execution. Various elements broke off to their assigned positions. Machine guns in place and satchel charges at the ready, they waited for the signal."

SAVING AMERICAN LIVES UNDER PRESSURE

Around 2:30 a.m., the NVA sappers simply waded ashore, entering through a nearby fishing village. The signal to attack was not long in coming.

An aerial view of FOB-4, located just southeast of Da Nang, shows the NVA POW camp in the foreground, and the main compound nearest Marble Mountain. To the left of the compound toward the beach is the recon barracks.

COURTESY JOHN STRYKER MEYER

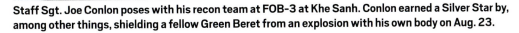

Staff Sgt. Joe Conlon poses with his recon team at FOB-3 at Khe Sanh. Conlon earned a Silver Star by, among other things, shielding a fellow Green Beret from an explosion with his own body on Aug. 23.

DISTINGUISHED SERVICE CROSS

STAFF SGT. PATRICK J. WATKINS

When it came, most of the compound occupants mistook the exploding satchel charges for routine incoming. In short order, the CCN communications bunker was taken out with a satchel charge, destroying telephones and radios. The Recon Company barracks was a prime target, too.

"Most of us simply rolled out of bed when the explosions and gunfire started and went to war," recalled Sgt. Watkins. "We didn't have time to get dressed." A consummate warrior and hardened combat veteran, Watkins was forced to use his pistol to kill NVA. "All I had was my old Colt .45, which was in my flight survival vest," he said. "Hell, I had never hit anything with a pistol before. Talk about miracle hits!"

He also found time to save American lives, particularly that of medic Bob Scully. Fellow SOG vet Staff Sgt. Joe Conlon submitted an affidavit supporting award of the Distinguished Service Cross (not actually presented until May 2014) to Watkins:

"Watkins threw himself on top of Scully to protect him from the blast [of a grenade] and was wounded … then picked Scully up and carried and passed him through heavy fire to the edge of the building … Though wounded multiple times, Staff Sgt. Watkins ignored his own painful injuries and continued the search for the wounded, and through indomitable courage and bravery, he rallied others to follow." Watkins modestly said of his DSC, "It's more of a recognition for what happened to all of us over there."

Conlon, finally awarded the Silver Star in October 2012, recalled, "That night was insane, surreal." Nonetheless, he performed life-saving acts of his own. As an explosion and fireball blasted out from a nearby building, he went to work. Immediately administering first aid, he shielded a fellow Green Beret with his own body. Stabilizing the wounded man, he secured the building from attack. Then Conlon fought his way outside to rescue more wounded Americans.

Sgt. 1st Class Luis J. Esparza did likewise. After killing an NVA in the motor pool, he

SILVER STAR

STAFF SGT. JOSEPH M. CONLON

SGT. 1ST CLASS LUIS J. ESPARZA

CAPT. CHUCK PFEIFER

> ## "The entire compound was now a swirling battleground, with dozens of small but deadly firefights in progress. It was difficult to tell the scantily clad Americans and indigenous personnel from the enemy." —JOHN STRYKER MEYER FROM *ON THE GROUND*

COURTESY LARRY TRIMBLE

The Recon Company hooches (barracks) were a primary NVA target. They became the scene of intense combat during the night, such as the one used by Larry Trimble.

flushed out two more to meet the same fate. Then he administered first aid to a critically wounded American. While carrying him, he was hit by shrapnel from grenades. Yet Esparza persisted in dragging the GI on a plank to a trench line. With the help of a medic, they got him to a hospital, says his Silver Star citation.

Hospital corpsman 3rd Class Henry V. Santo, though not stationed on the base and only two months in-country, selflessly came to the aid of the wounded, too. "That night was one of the most stressful experiences of my life," he said years later.

Fortunately, the compound also had some guardian angels above. An outpost on Marble Mountain overlooked all of the Da Nang compound. "Spike Team" Rattler provided an early warning system for FOB-4. Larry Trimble was the assistant leader of the nine-man team. The team saved lives by taking out an NVA mortar crew during the attack.

"We asked for continuous flares over Marble Mountain so we could observe any more mortars or enemy movement," Trimble said. "This worked out because we were able to stop any further enemy mortar fire from Marble Mountain into FOB-4 for the rest of the night."

WHEN CARNAGE PREVAILED

There was "nothing but carnage," Plaster wrote in his book. "In the light of burning buildings, American dead and wounded were sprawled everywhere, and everywhere it seemed, NVA sappers ran through the shadows."

Co-authors Meyer and John Peters described the scene in *On the Ground:* "The entire compound was now a swirling battleground, with dozens of small but deadly firefights in progress. It was difficult to tell the scantily clad Americans and indigenous personnel from the enemy. And there was no command coordination, just a lot of individuals struggling against uncertain and overwhelming odds."

But that did not stop Capt. Chuck Pfeifer, staff duty officer that night, who was blown out the door of his hooch by a grenade concussion. His Silver Star citation describes Pfeifer's actions in detail: After "rushing barefoot through a murderous crossfire to find adjacent buildings demolished and ablaze," he "assembled and led a small fire team methodically attacking and eliminating barracked enemy positions, exposing himself to enemy fire and ignoring his own wounds to rescue isolated groups of fellow soldiers. Firing his rifle and tossing more than 15 hand grenades with incredible accuracy."

Forward Operating Base 4, headquarters for Command and Control North, at Da Nang as it looked after the Aug. 23, 1968, attack. NVA sappers killed 16 SOG operatives—the largest single loss in U.S. Army Special Forces history.

By killing perhaps half the NVA in the Tactical Operations Center (TOC), Pfeifer allowed the Americans to recapture it. He also personally made sure no other sappers arose to wreak more havoc.

Meanwhile, 1st Lt. Robert Blatherwick saved a dozen men's lives by repeatedly rescuing the wounded with a medical jeep.

By 5:30 a.m., the bloodletting was largely complete and mopping up began. "In the pale dawn's light, skirmish lines of Americans advanced methodically through the compound, clearing each room, each roof, each crawl space to root out enemy holdouts," wrote Plaster. "They found sapper bodies in ones and twos everywhere. Each body had to be checked."

An AC-130 Spectre gunship hovered over CCN, dropping flares and shooting NVA in the wires and across the camp. At sunrise, a relief force arrived and eliminated communists attempting to escape.

Staff Sgt. Robert J. "Spider" Parks witnessed the aftermath. He related to author John Meyer the dreadful scene: "It was a sight I'll never forget. It looked like a hazy movie scene. There was a haze hanging over the camp—you could still smell the cordite from all the weapons fire. People were running around, some of them still dazed by the night's tragic events. There were still some sappers around in the camp and snipers firing down from Marble Mountain. The NVA fired on the ambulances leaving camp as well as the one pulling in. People in the camp got organized and linked up with the relief force Lt. Col. Roy Bahr brought in from Phu Bai."

The final body count was 38 NVA killed and nine captured, all of whom were wounded. The sapper attack, "calculated to disrupt SOG operations and release pressure on the Ho Chi Minh Trail," according to Viet Cong Gen. Dham Duc Nam, ultimately failed. SOG CCN was back in business in no time.

But the NVA had inflicted severe casualties on the SOG. Sixteen Green Berets lost their lives: Shrapnel killed eight, gunfire six and two succumbed to burns. Some 48 were wounded. This amounted to a casualty rate of 33%. In addition, at least 16 indigenous troops were KIA.

As elite warriors, SOG vets overcame their losses while never forgetting them. They went on to complete many more missions until deactivating their unit on March 12, 1973. By then, they were operating for a year under the cover of Strategic Technical Directorate Assistance Team 158.

When asked by a *Salt Lake City Tribune* reporter how he coped with so many deaths among fellow SOG operatives, Pat Watkins replied, "I had to recover bodies that had been in the jungles for days. But you've got to put that stuff in your kit bag and not worry about it." SOG losses, however, remain enshrined and honored in Army Special Forces history to this day. ✪

THE TOLL

U.S. KIA:
16

U.S. WIA:
48

BY JANIE DYHOUSE

'STORM OF STEEL': AP TRANG DAU

What occurred in the early morning hours of Sept. 6, 1968, in the village of Ap Trang Dau can only be described as "a living hell." The bloody battle there took place three miles east of Trang Bang in Hau Nghia province of III Corps Tactical Zone.

Just hours earlier, on Sept. 5, 96 men of A Co., 3rd Bn., 187th Inf. ("Rakkasans"), 101st Abn. Div., were flown into near the village, which was located close to Highway QL-1 some 26 miles north of Saigon.

Their orders were to assist B Co., 2nd Bn., 506th Inf., 101st Abn. Div., in cordoning off the village. Some believed high-ranking Viet Cong (VC) and North Vietnamese Army (NVA) officials were in the area, while intelligence reports claimed that two VC battalions were based there. The American intent was to secure the area and prevent the enemy from breaking through.

What awaited Alpha Company was almost unimaginable. Hitting the landing zone in the late afternoon of Sept. 5, the men were greeted by heavy enemy fire from the village. Some of the troops were wounded before the choppers even got to the ground, and one was killed.

The company spread out in the rice paddies fronting the village while taking fire. Capt. Kenneth B. Jenkins set up the company command post (CP) on the main road running through a field and into the village. Air and artillery support could not be used before or during the battle because there were too many U.S. units close to the village.

Along the far left front of the perimeter were 2nd Platoon members Spec. 4 Joseph Fuscone and Sgt. Joseph Nugent. Fuscone recalls setting up three-man defensive positions about 100 feet apart. 1st, 2nd, and 3rd platoons were placed as the front line to block any enemy retreat by way of the main road, while the 4th Platoon was in position to act as rear guard.

Due to heavy automatic weapons fire from the village, Nugent said his men were unable to move very far. And when they did move, they were not able to link up with any friendly units, as had been the original plan.

Members of 2nd Sqd., 2nd Plt., A Co., 3rd Bn., 187th Inf. Regt., 101st Abn. Div., pose for a photo in April 1968, near Song Be. A Company suffered a great loss months later when 27 of its own died in the Battle of Ap Trang Dau. Standing are Carl Lawson, Michael Kolarov (KIA) and "Phillips." Sitting are Jerry Towe, Anthony Montes (KIA), Joseph Fuscone, Mitchell Wnek, Joseph Nugent, "Baby Fat" Johnson and Ray Tysinger.

SEPTEMBER 1968

For 30 minutes in the early morning darkness of Sept. 6, 1968, the 187th Infantry's Alpha Company (96 men) fended off more than 600 communists, losing 28% of its men killed.

PHOTO COURTESY JOSEPH FUSCONE

Friends Spec. 4 Joseph Fuscone and Sgt. Joseph Nugent were together at Cu Chi one month before the deadly battle at Ap Trang Dau. Nugent earned the Silver Star for his actions.

> "He [Fuscone] had been shot through the lung. Before I could go any further, I had to shoot more of the VC who were coming toward us from the village."
>
> —SGT. JOSEPH NUGENT

The village of Ap Trang Dau was located between Trang Bang and Cu Chi, just off of Highway QL-1.

PHOTO COURTESY JOSEPH FUSCONE

Kneeling are William A. Gibbs (KIA), Ray Tysinger and Jeffery A. Davis (KIA). Behind them are Jeffrey A. Evans (KIA) and Joseph Fuscone.

After getting into position around nightfall, things seemed to settle down, Fuscone said. Not wanting to stick around until daybreak, the communists did try to break through the back side of the village. Elements of the 25th Infantry Division prevented their escape.

But around 2:15 a.m., things changed. The eerie calm quickly turned into a deadly storm of steel.

A 'MASSIVE HUMAN WAVE ATTACK'

"All hell broke loose," Nugent said. "We had been shot at off and on all night, but this was the most unbelievable volume of fire I had ever seen. They came out of the village in several waves. In the first wave, they had women and children in front of them."

Spec. 4 Bob Rummel of 3rd Platoon described the firefight as a "massive human wave attack." "A living hell began," he said. "There were so many VC and NVA coming that it was complete chaos. Had they wanted to, they could have killed us all. They just wanted to get out of there, and we just happened to be blocking their way."

During the up-to-30-minute battle, Sgt. 1st Class Thomas E. Warren noticed that several of his men holding a position about 82 yards on the far right flank were greatly outnumbered. He began firing his weapon and hurling grenades to draw enemy fire on himself, allowing the soldiers to get back with the main force. Later, harassed by sniper fire, Warren stood exposed in a rice paddy to guide in evacuation helicopters with a strobe light. Wounded several times, he was awarded the Distinguished Service Cross.

Meanwhile, Fuscone was positioned with four other men at the platoon CP, which was the last position on the left flank. They were all severely wounded, with Fuscone being the only one able to defend the position, despite his chest wound.

He radioed Nugent for help, telling him everyone was either wounded or dead. Before Nugent could get there, three NVA soldiers ran directly into Fuscone and his fellow wounded GIs. He told his buddies to lay still and play dead. Right before the enemy reached him, Fuscone threw a grenade and killed the communists. For his actions that night, Fuscone was awarded a Bronze Star for valor.

Due to heavy enemy fire, it took Nugent several tries to get to the CP, his squad "firing as fast as they could" to cover him. "When I got to the CP, I jumped over the dike and saw the bodies of my friends lying mangled and bleeding," Nugent said. "I went to Joe [Fuscone] first. He had been shot through the lung. Before I could go any further, I had to shoot more of the VC who were coming toward us from the village."

Human waves continued as hundreds of enemy troops fled the village, overrunning A Company's position. After about a half hour of intense fighting, it suddenly stopped. The only sounds were the cries of the wounded, Nugent said.

He made his way through the bodies trying to help those still clinging to life. "I did what I could for the wounded," he said. "I saw that many of our KIA had been shot at close range in the center of their foreheads." In fact, 23 of the Americans were shot at close range.

Jenkins and his men at the company CP also were killed, as the VC overran them, too.

AFTERMATH OF AP TRANG DAU

The 187th's C Company was on standby in nearby Cu Chi when it got word that A Company was taking heavy fire. The men hopped on choppers, fully expecting to be engaged at the landing zone.

To the surprise of C Company members like Spec. 4 Gary Foster of 3rd Platoon, there was no resistance. "At first light, as we went into position to where A Company was supposed to be, I could see bodies everywhere I looked," Foster said. "Then I was put on what I believe was the worst detail I have ever had to do: bagging the bodies of A Company's KIAs."

Foster said that during his "grisly task," the bodies were stiff and cold as they had lain there all night. One he vividly recalls, however, was folded in half beneath the poncho when he picked it up. The soldier's chest was gone, as if he had tried to smother a grenade, Foster says.

"A Company losses were losses to us," said Jon Lambie of C Company. "Many of us trained together in the States, and we knew each other personally."

Capt. James Bond, C Company commander, said his men spent the greater part of the morning separating the KIA from their gear and placing them in body bags to be evacuated. They also found a small wounded child and patched her up before getting her out of the field and to a hospital. "I don't know quite how to describe the situation," Bond said. "Like many things in Vietnam, it was somewhat of a paradox."

Members of A Company looked back to that small window of time and think the situation might have been avoided. "I asked myself, 'Where was the air and artillery support?'" former Spec. 4 Mitchell Wnek reminisced. "A lot of good men died that morning because we were overpowered. Air or artillery would have changed things for us."

Pfc. Jimmy Searle agreed. "I've often wondered what would have happened if they would have sent air strikes when Capt. Jenkins wanted them to," Searle said. "I have to think that some of those guys might still be alive today."

Nugent's bravery and quick thinking earned him the Silver Star. Fuscone credits him with saving his life. "Sgt. Nugent and his squad helped save the lives of a lot of men that night during and after the battle," Fuscone said. "In between fighting and tending to the wounded, Sgt. Nugent called for Medevac choppers and coordinated with the battalion to get much-needed support and help take command of the situation."

All told, 32 GIs were KIA and 42 WIA in the Battle of Ap Trang Dau. On Sept. 5, two members of the 506th Infantry were killed along with one man from Alpha Company. The remaining 29 died on Sept 6—27 from Alpha (including four attached medics), as well as one each from B Company (a clerk-typist) and E Company (a recon scout). Also, an infantryman from C Co., 1st Bn., 27th Inf.—part of the 25th Infantry Division's blocking force—lost his life. Gunfire caused 72% of the fatalities; shrapnel the remainder. Not surprisingly, being an airborne unit, more than 60% (20) of those killed were volunteers and 12 were draftees.

"Sept. 6: There isn't hardly a day that goes by when something doesn't trigger a thought about that day," said Ron Salme, who was shot three times and peppered with shrapnel at the village, and spent nearly six months recuperating in a hospital in Japan. ✪

DISTINGUISHED SERVICE CROSS

SGT. 1ST CLASS THOMAS E. WARREN

THE TOLL

U.S. KIA:
32

U.S. WIA:
42

BY ROBERT E. WIDENER   *OPERATION LANCASTER/TROUSDALE NORTH*

'DEADLY DILEMMA' AT LZ MARGO

An operation to trap two regiments of the NVA's 320th Division plunged men of the 2nd Battalion, 26th Marines, into a nightmarish mortar barrage on a barren hilltop on Sept. 16-17, 1968.

"**T**here was a sense of dread on Margo," remembers 1st Lt. Alan Green, 81mm Mortar Platoon leader of Battalion Landing Team (BLT), 2nd Battalion, 26th Marines. "We were just crowded on one hill with total exposure to our north for any indirect fire the NVA may have had. And they quickly demonstrated they had us right in their sights."

What began as an attempt to trap remnants of the 52nd and 48th NVA Regiments, 320th NVA Division, ended up cornering the Marines in one of the most deadly mortar barrages of the war.

Trousdale North, part of *Operation Lancaster,* was launched in August 1968. The 2/26, nicknamed the "Nomads," was to be a battalion-sized blocking force. They were to patrol north to the DMZ from near Mutter's Ridge in Quang Tri province and ambush NVA being driven toward them.

Most of the Leathernecks had undergone their baptism of fire during three months of fighting around Khe Sanh from January through April 1968 on Hills 558, 700 and 861A. The 2nd Battalion was bloodied on Hill 558 over April 6-7 when it sustained 29 KIA.

The unit reformed in July as a battalion landing team with reinforced rifle companies E, F, G and H. It also included a 4.2-inch mortar battery, engineer and tank platoons, and a 105mm artillery battery. Also attached was a platoon from E Co., 3rd Recon Bn.

But with *Trousdale North,* the battalion was reassigned to inland fighting as a "maneuver" unit, rotating thereafter under different regimental commands.

As H Company commander Capt. Charles Broughton lightheartedly put it, "We were a bastard battalion—we had no mommy or daddy."

PHOTO COURTESY KEN DEWEY

Maj. Jarvis Lynch and Capt. Ken Dewey wait before going ashore from the *USS Princeton* in early September 1968. Lynch would soon be faced with a dire decision on Margo.

MARGO: HARD CLAY AND ROCK

LZ Margo was the designated starting point for 2/26, which began landing there by helicopter on Sept. 13. The battalion's operations officer, Maj. Jarvis D. Lynch, later described Margo in his narrative, *The Dead Went Last,* as being shaped like a broken bowl: "A spring near the center of the zone fed a stream that had cut a deep draw, which meandered eastward and exited Margo between 2 and 4 o'clock."

As picturesque as this sounds, there was little to like about Margo. It was smaller than the maps indicated, making it difficult to assemble the nearly 1,000 Marines. Margo also sat at a lower elevation than the hills to the north. To top it all off, the soil was seemingly impenetrable—hard clay and rock, making it a struggle to dig fighting holes.

"Some foxholes weren't much more than indentations in the ground," said 1st Lt. Dale Wittler, 1st Platoon commander of E Company. "I couldn't dig more than six to eight inches."

Another drawback was Margo's history. It had formerly been a firebase, but unused for a time. It was suspected that the NVA had the site thoroughly reconnoitered. That much seemed likely based on the small-arms fire Marines took as the helicopters landed.

"It was a hot LZ," said Sgt. Larry McCartney of E Company. "Golf Company's machine guns were engaging enemy positions on the next hill that were firing on us as we disembarked."

Lynch summed it all up: "Not good … but not unusual."

Cpl. Joe Cooper, mortar forward observer, returned fire with an M-60 machine gun after spotting the source of the NVA mortars.

CHANGE IN ORDERS

All companies, with the exception of G Company, immediately headed out to sweep the ridgelines to the north. Pushing ahead in the nearly 100-degree heat, the Nomads worked through the double- and triple-canopy jungle that blanketed the landscape south of the DMZ.

Because of the lack of fighting there, little was known about the area. Marines soon discovered it was the NVA's backyard—bunkers, supply caches and "speed" trails all hidden within the forest. "We came across steps cut into the side of the hills reinforced with bamboo risers, and bamboo handrails," said McCartney.

Contact was light over the next two days despite reports of enemy activity in the area. Skirmishes did not evolve into larger fights. It was as though the enemy was more interested in keeping tabs on the Marines rather than engaging in a pitched battle.

The companies sustained two KIAs on Sept. 15. Cpl. Stanley R. Pettit of E Company was killed shortly after taking over point on a patrol. Right behind Pettit was Pfc. William Griffith who sustained a "sucking" chest wound in the fury of fire that followed. Despite being shot, he courageously fell on an enemy grenade. He lived to receive a Bronze Star for valor. Pfc. Douglas G. Impson of H Company also was killed during listening post duty.

The patrols confirmed beyond a doubt that a substantial number of enemy troops were in the area. Also causing alarm were discoveries of prepared, but empty, mortar positions. And NVA mortarmen had been sighted crossing the Cam Lo River, heading south of Margo.

Then about noon on Sept. 15, Lynch received orders for the companies to reverse direction and return to Margo by the next morning. A B-52 "arc light" bombing was scheduled for the area. "I was stunned," said Lynch, who was now faced with a deadly dilemma. "Comply with the order and risk NVA action, or move the companies toward Margo, retaining some semblance of tactical deployment north of the LZ and risk the arc light. Obedience would have a price, that much was obvious."

Despite a heated argument with the regiment's operations officer about the wisdom of returning to Margo, Lynch was told the orders would stand. The men would return to Margo.

CARNAGE AT THE WATERHOLE

E Company was the last unit to straggle back at about 2:30 p.m. on the 16th. Heatstroke had taken a toll and casualties were spread out near the waterhole, which by now had become crowded with men replenishing their canteens.

Meanwhile, at about 3 p.m., the battalion air liaison officer, Capt. Kenneth Dewey, along with Pfc. Dale Pack of E Company and Ron Smythe of G Company, both forward air controllers, gathered near the command post (CP). They watched the arc light bombing

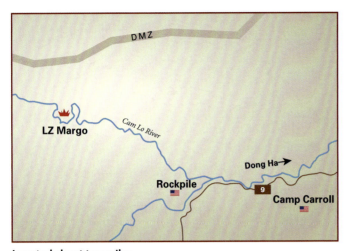

Located about two miles from the DMZ, LZ Margo was much smaller than the maps indicated, making it nearly impossible to accommodate the entire battalion.

> "I was lying in a hole and it was pure carnage— hearing blood-curdling screams. Finally I got hit."
>
> —PFC. STEVE HAISLEY, H COMPANY

proceed on schedule in the distance.

"A mile of bombs would go off," said Pack. "The sound roared through the jungle and you could feel the compression in the air as the bombs went off."

When it was over, Dewey suddenly noticed sunlight reflecting in a mirror from a hill to the north. Seconds later, the unmistakable sound of a mortar could be heard coming from the hills they had just patrolled.

An 82mm round landed short at the perimeter of Margo. Cpl. Pete Schroeder, squad leader and a grenadier in 2nd Plt., E Co., however, was not concerned. "We believed it was our own mortar crews registering fire for night defense," he said.

But Staff Sgt. James F. Doner of 2nd Plt., E Co., 3rd Recon Bn., which had dug in on the southern rim of Margo, knew it was a correction round and took off for the CP. He hadn't gotten far when he heard the "thump-thump" sound of volleys of mortar rounds being fired.

"They put about 20 rounds in the air and after a slight break, the second volley was in the air before the first even hit," he remembered.

The shelling concentrated first on the crowded waterhole. McCartney and Lance Cpl. Gary R. Daffin of 2nd Platoon were caught in the open. "We had only a small depression scooped out and Gary rolled into it," said McCartney. "I rolled in on top of him. We could hear the rounds walking right toward us."

Amid the explosions, the pair watched Lance Cpl. Clifton Spiller running toward the waterhole to aid Pfc. Devon Hunter and three other severely wounded Marines.

"Spiller picked up Hunter and started to leave the area when more rounds came in," said McCartney. "He dropped to the ground, covering Hunter with his body. A shell exploded close by, wounding him."

Daffin jumped up and bolted to help Spiller, telling McCartney to go for a corpsman. But as the two headed in opposite directions, a round landed between them. Daffin absorbed most of the explosion. McCartney was hit in the face, arms, legs and buttocks.

"Gary was dead before he hit the ground," said McCartney. "The metal came up underneath his helmet and partially decapitated him. A lot of what hit me was not shrapnel, but broken rock."

McCartney moved through the smoke over to the waterhole where wounded men were dead or dying. He recognized two of the dead—new 18-year-old replacements, Pfcs. Edward Cunningham and John M. Donohue. Each had barely been in Vietnam a week before Margo— seven and nine days, respectively.

Meanwhile, Schroeder was in his hole trying to "stretch his helmet over his body" when he heard Lance Cpl. Mecurio shouting from across the draw.

"He yelled for me to get out of my hole because the mortars were walking that way," said Schroeder. "I ran to the bottom of the draw and saw people staggering out. I got to the first fellow and helped him to a corpsman. I saw Mecurio knocked down about three times, but he got up and kept moving." When he returned to his hole later, Schroeder found that it had taken a direct hit. "Had nothing left. A bag of M-79 grenade rounds and everything was destroyed."

Pfc. Steve Haisley of H Company was on the north side of Margo. Rounds were exploding all around him. "I was lying in a hole and it was pure carnage—hearing blood-curdling screams," he remembered.

"Finally I got hit," he said. "It felt like a sledgehammer hitting my right arm." A chunk of shrapnel nearly severed his arm at the elbow. In shock, he stood straight up.

"The kid I was sharing the hole with yelled at me to get down," he said. "He said he had to go get a corpsman because I was hit really bad."

'BATTLEFIELD BAPTIST'

The command post and 81mm mortar pits also were prime targets. Mortar rounds were coming in from 360 degrees.

"The whole LZ erupted with explosions and all the guys could do was lay flat on the ground and hope for the best," Pack said. "I tried to get into Smythe's hole, but it wasn't deep enough for both of us."

So Pack ran toward a bomb crater about 40-50 yards away that was already occupied by several men. But before he got there, it took a direct hit. "The guys were blown up and backward," he said. "For a moment, it seemed like they were floating in the air."

Back at Smythe's hole, they pulled a 81mm crate filled with dirt over their backs as best they could.

2nd Lt. Corky Haisten, 3rd Plt., H Co., remembers watching the shells coming in. "You'd look up and could see the damn things turn over at the peak of their arcs," he said. "I watched five or six of them flip at a time as they started down on us. I became what they called a 'battlefield Baptist' and said a prayer."

Lt. Kent Wonders, an assistant to Lynch, ran to his hole that he had been able to deepen to two feet. But he was the last of four men arriving, leaving him six inches or more above ground. "During the thunderous explosions, my face was buried between the bodies of the Marines layered below me," he remembers. "The noise was so loud my ears rang for days afterward."

'12-ROUND BURSTS! 12-ROUND BURSTS!'

At the southern rim, James Doner was returning fire with an M-60, but the rounds were falling short. "I grabbed the legs and lifted the gun over my head for better elevation," he said. "Lance Cpl. Locke leaned back to sight while I moved the barrel where I wanted the fire to go and told him '12-round bursts, 12-round bursts!' "

The NVA now concentrated their fire on Doner's position. Soon about 25 rounds "knocked the hell out of the platoon," blowing Locke and Doner off their feet. Doner suffered an arm wound, but Locke was unconscious, his face shredded by shrapnel. The M-60 lay twisted in the mud.

Meanwhile, communication lines to Lt. Alan Green's eight mortars had been cut by the incoming rounds. Green grabbed a megaphone he had kept from his last trip on the USS *Princeton,* and stood at the top of the crater, exposed to the exploding shells.

Capt. John Cregan of E Company, who was nearby, remembers Green's next actions: "In the midst of mortars raining down on us there was Al Green shouting into a megaphone, 'All right you United States Marines! Get out of your holes and get on your tubes!' "

Men of 2nd Plt., E Co., 3rd Recon Bn., pose for a photo in Quang Tri before going to LZ Margo. Staff Sgt. James F. Doner is at right with arms crossed. Lance Cpl. Cavan Cox, front row center, was the first to come upon corpsman David L. Eisenbraun, who was KIA.

Lt. Kent Wonders stands just outside the CP prior to the attack on LZ Margo. When the mortar rounds began to fall, Wonders found that the fighting hole he had dug already had four Marines in it.

Lance Cpl. Eric Smith and 1st Lt. Alan Green served together on LZ Susan after the battle. Green used a megaphone to reach his mortarmen after communication lines were severed by mortar explosions.

Green remembers how proud he was of his men as he shouted coordinates and encouragement to them: "You would see a hand come up with a mortar round and drop it into a tube. Guys were running through the smoke and shrapnel to get ammunition. It was an incredible sight, but very frightening." For his actions, Green received a Bronze Star for valor.

Cpl. Lynn Joseph Cooper, a mortar forward observer (FO) who was manning an M-60 machine gun near the mortar pits, spotted one source of the NVA fire. According to Cpl. Bruce Pilch of the Mortar Platoon who was nearby, Cooper started yelling: "Sir, Sir, I can see them! I can see them! Can I fire?"

Cooper and his assistant, Larry Towne, returned fire as other M-60s could also be heard zeroing in on the NVA mortars. At one point, Cooper used bare hands to change the barrel that had gotten red hot from his continuous firing. He also received a Bronze Star for valor.

James Anton of E Company was nearby assisting an M-60 machine gunner until they ran out of ammunition. He took off between the explosions to retrieve more cans of ammo. But as he was passing below the mortar pits, a shell exploded right above him—a mortar tube rolled down the hill right at his feet.

"A guy above yelled at me to grab it," said Anton. The mortarman slid crates of mortar rounds down to him. Anton held the tube between his knees as the mortarman began dropping rounds into it. The machine gunner Anton had been helping shouted out adjustments for their fire.

"After a few more rounds, he started yelling, 'Pour it on them!'" Anton remembered. "I tried to hold it steady as we fired every round we had."

GROUND ATTACK: "NOSE-TO-NOSE"

Just as it had all started, light reflected once again from the distant hill. The shelling suddenly stopped. It had only been some 20 minutes since the first round hit, but it was enough time to transform Margo into a landscape of bloodied bodies. The Marines went about quickly tending to the wounded. "I had been counting mortar rounds the first few minutes, but stopped at 100," said Lynch. "In all, we probably took 400-500 rounds."

"They had fixed bayonets and were coming up the hill at us"

—CPL. DAVE HUNT, H COMPANY

Cpl. Dave Hunt of H Company was on the northwest perimeter of Margo when he suddenly noticed a line of NVA soldiers emerge from the tree lines. "They had fixed bayonets and were coming up the hill at us," said Hunt. "I was 22 years old and scared to death." The next thing he knew, he was "nose-to-nose" with an NVA soldier. "His bayonet cut my leg, but I killed him."

Hunt and other H Company men began to fire on the NVA. G Company riflemen crossed Margo to pitch in. Despite the attack's surprise, it was quickly crushed under volleys of Marine rifle fire.

A second mortar barrage began at 4:20 p.m., but did not last as long. "We didn't believe they would hit us again," said Schroeder, who was wounded in this second attack. "But there we were, picking up pieces and remnants of packs and rifles, when wham! Here it comes again."

Between attacks, medevac helicopters stayed busy shuttling out the wounded. One near catastrophe threatened the last helicopter that left just before dark. Dangerously overloaded, it dipped from view into the valley below. A few Marines rushed to the edge of Margo anticipating a crash. But the aircraft suddenly shot up in front of them, jettisoning fuel and lifting ever skyward.

PHOTO COURTESY BRUCE PILCH

At that moment, a single mortar round landed in the spot where the medevac had taken off. "They were telling us they could have stopped it at anytime," said Lynch.

WORSE THAN KHE SANH

E Company's ranks were so thinned it was rendered combat ineffective. Survivors remained behind the next day as the other companies patrolled northward. The NVA mortared Margo three more times on the 17th, inflicting more casualties. During an attack about 11:15 a.m., James Anton saw his sergeant, Juan Sanchez, mortally wounded after being caught out in the open. He had been looking for tree limbs to cover his fighting hole.

Survivors of 3rd Sqd., 2nd Plt., F Co., exhibit the classic '1,000-yard stare' while on patrol just 10 days after Margo.

Also among the dead that day was Navy Hospitalman David L. Eisenbraun, E Co., 3rd Recon Plt. The 20-year-old had been tending to Marine James Roach. Lance Cpl. Cavan Cox, also of E Company, had been looking for a corpsman when he came upon Eisenbraun slumped over Roach.

"I got there within a second of when he died," said Cox. "When they rolled him over, he breathed his last air. I know he took shrapnel in the back, and that Roach lived." Despite Eisenbraun's life-saving act, he received no posthumous medal for valor.

In all, 29 Leathernecks died on and near LZ Margo, 27 in the mortar attacks alone. Fourteen, or 48%, perished on Sept. 16; 12 on Sept. 17. Echo Company suffered the greatest loss with 11 KIA. H&S followed with nine killed and Hotel Company counted eight fatalities. Two Marines were KIA by gunfire on Sept. 15 and one on Sept. 18.

Every year, Hunt says he celebrates Sept. 16 as his second birthday. "It was the day I really should have died."

Like most who survived the attack, Haisley still feels the pain and sorrow: "There is not a day that goes by that I don't think about those guys. In fact, I have an LZ Margo tattoo."

For Schroeder, Margo was among the worse experiences he had in Vietnam. "When they pounded us that hard at Margo, there was no fear that can even come close to what that was like."

And according to Haisten's gunnery sergeant, Richard Porter, a Korean War veteran, "The incoming that day was worse than anything he experienced at Chosin."

Despite their horrific ordeal, there was some evidence that the "Nomads'" return fire had inflicted damage on the enemy. According to Maj. Lynch, a G Company patrol conducted during the following days found 18 graves near the spot where the mirror flashes had originated. Information left behind revealed that the NVA battalion commander, a veteran of the French Indochina War (1946-54), and much of his staff had been killed.

Because of Margo, Marine procedures changed regarding future arc light bombings. Thereafter, the tactical situation in the field would allow flexibility in determining safety margins. Charles Broughton probably summed up the LZ Margo ordeal best: "We got hurt worse at Margo than [during] all three months at Khe Sanh. We sat in one spot and got the crap pounded out of us." ✪

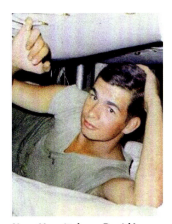

Navy Hospitalman David L. Eisenbraun was killed while protecting a Marine from a mortar barrage as he was giving aid.

THE TOLL

U.S. KIA:
29

U.S. WIA:
149

BRUTAL BATTLES OF VIETNAM
1969

CHU LAI
HILL 65
AP NHA MAT
IA DRANG VALLEY
KIM SON VALLEY
MY CANH
CHAU NGAI
DAU TIENG
LZ BIRD
SUOI TRE
KHE SANH
VINH HUY
RACH NUI
DAK TO
HAMBURGER HILL
CON THIEN
DONG SON
ONG THANH
TAM QUAN
THON THAM KHE
QUE SON VALLEY
HIEP DUC VALLEY
HOC MON
HILL 689
DAI DO
SAIGON
KHAM DUC
GO NOI ISLAND
AP TRANG DAU
RUSSELL AND NEVILLE
PLEI TRAP VALLEY
LIBERTY BRIDGE
HILL 996
FSB HENDERSON
CAMBODIA INCURSION
FSB RIPCORD
FSB MARY ANN

FEBRUARY 1969

BY JANIE DYHOUSE

HELL RAINS DOWN ON RUSSELL AND NEVILLE

In the early morning of Feb. 25, 1969, Marines on two remote fire support bases near the Laotian border came under heavy NVA attack, suffering a combined 43 killed in action in about three hours.

During the post-1969 Tet Offensive, Marines at Fire Support Bases Neville and Russell were attacked nearly simultaneously in the early morning hours of Feb. 25, 1969. North Vietnamese Army (NVA) sapper units numbering about 200 at each site, located five miles apart, penetrated the bases. The NVA's goal was to destroy the artillery pieces in the gun pits.

Pre-emptive air strikes on enemy positions in this region were not permitted because there was a no-bombing policy in effect due to the ongoing peace talks in Paris. When the bloodshed was over that day, neither firefight was given any publicity. Nor has it been the subject of much attention in the past five decades.

These are the stories of the men who fought at FSB Russell and FSB Neville on that fateful day.

FSB RUSSELL: 'DISTURBING AND UNSETTLING'

Having served with 3rd Plt., E Co., 2nd Bn., 4th Marines, Dennis Gardner remembers the first time he saw FSB Russell. "It was strange to view this cleared-off spot in the otherwise dense jungle," he said. "It had its own disturbing and unsettling appearance to me."

Just 10 miles from Laos in Quang Tri province, FSB Russell was situated on a rugged mountaintop within range of the Demilitarized Zone, which made it a frequent target for enemy mortar and ground attacks. It existed for just one year with its six-gun artillery battery continuously protected by about 300 Marines.

Russell was defended by platoons of E, F and K companies of the 2nd Bn., 4th Marines, 3rd Marine Div., as well as H and Mortar batteries of the 12th Marines and a detachment of the 1st Searchlight Battery, when it was hit by heavy mortar fire around 4 a.m.

That was quickly followed by a 200-man attack by elements of the 27th NVA Regiment, which had breached the base's northeast perimeter. Within minutes, the command post was decimated.

Assigned to 3rd Plt., E Co., Rich Woy, a Navy corpsman, recalls that he had just returned to his hooch when the base was attacked. "It was pitch black, but I could hear Lt. [William] Hunt whisper to us from the opening, 'Be quiet, there's gooks right outside the front door.' We could hear them speaking Vietnamese," Woy remembered.

Before Woy could act, a deafening explosion rocked the hooch. He pulled wounded Navy corpsman Bill Collins through a window and hid him in a concealed opening of another bunker. He made multiple trips up

Artillery guns were the main objective of the nearly simultaneous NVA attacks at both FSB Russell (above) and Neville. Each base was raided by about 200 enemy soldiers. The fire bases were five miles apart.

and down the hill, tending to the wounded.

"I was able to salvage only a few battle dressings, cravats and a few morphine syringes," Woy said. "After taking that up to the top, I remained there to help triage and load casualties on the arriving medevac choppers." (Woy earned a Silver Star for providing unrelenting medical aid that morning.)

Gardner recalls hearing the NVA coming up through the trash dump on the other side of the hill. "We fought them off until someone on the other side decided we weren't worth the cost," he said. "They broke off and moved away."

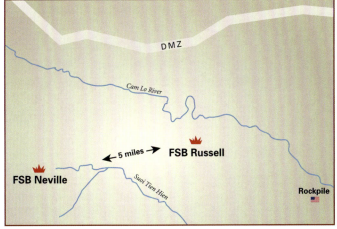

Situated on rugged mountain tops, FSB Russell and FSB Neville were only 5 miles apart.

He moved from the listening post because friendly fire was hitting all around, putting him and others in danger. "The ground shook and the night sky became brilliant with light from exploding rounds," Gardner recalled. "The noise was deafening, the battle was raging and the whole experience was both exhilarating and scary as hell. All we could do was hug the ground and ride it out."

Charles Davis was in a dark bunker when a satchel charge hit the door and blew up. He heard the NVA digging under the back wall, so he moved before they blew that wall, too.

Meanwhile, Sam Young, a section chief on the Gun 3 base piece, was immediately pinned down by enemy small-arms fire. A satchel charge hit a bunker wall near him, blasting Young

SILVER STAR

CPL. JEFFREY M. BARRON
(POSTHUMOUS)

PVT. MICHAEL A. HARVEY
(POSTHUMOUS)

2ND LT. WILLIAM H. HUNT
(POSTHUMOUS)

LANCE CPL. THOMAS McGRATH
(POSTHUMOUS)

HM2 WALTER P. SEEL, JR.
(POSTHUMOUS)

CAPT. ALBERT HILL

RICH WOY

NAVY CROSS

PFC. WILLIAM CASTILLO

MILITARY TIMES HALL OF VALOR

SGT. ALFRED P. LAPORTE, JR.

up the hill and over the parapet wall. "When I came to, I remember letting out a scream," he said. "I remember a loud ping as the satchel charge went off and what sounded like a thousand canaries chirping at the same time. My sight was gone except for a dim glow."

Young managed to find cover inside a bunker with two members of his crew who insisted on leaving to get a corpsman to treat him. The bunker was soon engulfed in flames after more satchel charges went off. He crawled out, calling for help along the way. "As I made my way across the parapet, I remember crawling over bodies, not sure if they were someone I knew or NVA," he said. He later found out that his two buddies who went for help were killed outside the bunker door.

When the battle was over, Gardner spent the day digging dead Marines out of collapsed bunkers, including the man whom Gardner had filled in for that night at the listening post.

"The Marines who were left were as stone-faced and somber as human beings could look," Gardner said. "One of the corpsman watched us come in, and he thought we were ghosts walking because no one could live through the hell that rained down upon us."

According to Ken Heins of H Battery, 10 of the 60 men in his unit were killed and up to 30 wounded. "As I remember, there were only about 12 of us left to operate the three upper guns," he said. "I remember going up to the top of the LZ in a daze, helping the wounded and loading the dead onto the helicopters."

Pfc. William Castillo aided the wounded, too. An ammo bearer in Echo Company, he rescued trapped Marines from demolished bunkers, provided vital mortar fire, led five men blinded by smoke to safety, repeatedly carried messages and carried casualties to an evacuation point. Castillo received the Navy Cross.

Capt. Albert Hill, commanding officer of E Company, has been described by the men who served under him as a "Marine's Marine," in part for his actions at FSB Russell. For his "skillful and proficient command" during the firefight, Hill was awarded a Silver Star.

Also awarded Silver Stars, posthumously, were 2nd Lt. William H. Hunt, platoon commander in E Company, and Pvt. Michael A. Harvey, a radio operator with H&S Company.

In all, 30 Americans were killed on the barren hilltop—20 members of the 4th Marines and 10 from H Battery. Of the 2nd Battalion dead, 12 belonged to H&S Company, including seven mortarmen, three anti-tank assault men and two Navy corpsmen. Artillery, mortars and rockets killed 40% of the men, gunfire 30% and hand grenades/satchel charges 27%. Some 77 were wounded.

NEVILLE: LIKE A 'HORROR MOVIE'

At FSB Neville, five miles west of Russell, the night looked like something "right out of a horror movie with fog drifting through the trees," according to Capt. John Knight, Jr., H

DA NANG COMPLEX PROVES A COSTLY DEFENSE

By Richard K. Kolb

In a virtually forgotten attack, NVA sappers took a deadly toll at 1st Marine Division sites in Da Nang on Feb. 23, 1969.

It was one of the deadliest actions of Vietnam, yet it remains one of the war's least documented. Amazingly, the official Marine Corps history dismisses it in one sentence: "On the northern slope of Hill 327, security elements for Headquarters, 26th Marines and 1st Marine Division, repulsed a nocturnal assault by satchel charge-equipped NVA sappers."

Hill 327 went by a variety of names—Division, Ridge and Freedom Hill among them. Located about 2½ miles west of Da Nang Air Base, the camp of the 1st Marine Division sat on a ridgeline at about 1,000 feet elevation. The camp harbored sensitive facilities (radar, for example) and was a ripe enemy target. An opportunity to strike came during the Tet Offensive of 1969.

Division Hill, as expected, was home mostly to logistical units and rear echelon elements. Included were the headquarters batteries of the 11th and 13th Marine regiments, as well as the HQ Company of the 26th Marines. Also there were motor transport, MP, service and communications companies. Musicians in the Marine band were there, too.

Early on Feb. 23, North Vietnamese Army (NVA) sappers hit division and

SILVER STAR

STAFF SGT. ROBERT M. LOUGH, JR. (POSTHUMOUS)

regimental command headquarters along with other targets. If the communists expected to meet anything other than fierce resistance at these base camp sites, they were sadly mistaken. The NVA may not have been aware of the adage, "Every Marine a rifleman."

Aggressively Tackling the Enemy

Staff Sgt. Robert M. Lough, Jr., of HQ Battalion, lived up to the Marine motto in every sense. Serving as a platoon sergeant of a reaction platoon, Lough arrived just in the nick of time to assist a beleaguered group of Marines. An air support radar team's position near the Division Command Post was being assaulted by 40 sappers firing machine guns and RPGs. Without hesitation, Lough aggressively went into action, directing the fire of his men until mortally wounded. He was awarded a posthumous Silver Star.

The bandsmen did their part, too. Cpl. James L. Kring was a "jazz man" in the 1st Marine Division Band. He and others were tasked with retaking guard posts Alpha 10 and 11. Kring was temporarily knocked out by the blast of a satchel charge. "The thunder of the battle was deafening," he recalled. "There were hundreds of explosions that night," he told the *Las Vegas Review-Journal* in 2012.

Three of Kring's fellow bandsmen—the first Marine musicians killed in action since WWII—died in defense of the Hill 327 complex. They were among the 30 Leathernecks killed fighting around 1st Marine Division sites that day. The dead included men from 11 units, ranging from mechanics to military policemen. But more than one-third were artillerymen. Destroying artillery pieces was a prime NVA objective. Gunfire (14), satchel charge explosions (10) and shrapnel (6) claimed the Marines' lives.

Not only was Hill 327 among the war's deadliest U.S. battles, but it was perhaps the single most lethal ground action for base camp units engaged in actual combat.

Company commander.

Three guns of G Btry., 3rd Bn., 12th Marines, and G Company, along with two platoons of H Co., 2nd Bn., 4th Marines were in place to defend the base.

Lt. Col. Joseph Hopkins, commanding officer of 2nd Battalion, described Neville as a "very rocky piece of ground" that often got overwhelmed by low-lying clouds, making it more difficult to navigate.

Harry Williams, communications chief for H Company, recalled Neville being about the size of a football field, with a sheer cliff on one side. He had only been on the hill about a week when the sappers made their way onto the base, via that steep cliff.

Outside the perimeter, about 200 soldiers from the 246th NVA Regiment threw grenades at the Marines from the south and east. Meanwhile, they tried to draw fire by making a great deal of noise with wooden sticks and metal banging against rocks. Somehow the enemy had automatic weapons set up inside the perimeter of the base.

"Enemy artillery, machine-gun fire and mortars pounded the hill," Sgt. Terry Webber said. "The earth trembled and the noise was deafening. I felt as if the world was ending that

"We listened for their voices and movement until they were close enough that we could hit them with our M-16s as if using a baseball bat."

—ROBERT CHATIGNY, 2ND PLATOON, GOLF COMPANY

FSB Neville was constructed on Hill 1103, offering a commanding view of the region. Some 200 NVA infiltrated the base in an attack on Feb. 25, 1969, that killed 13 Marines.

THE TOLL

(FSB Russell only)
U.S. KIA:
30

U.S. WIA:
77

foggy night."

According to Charles Garber, who served with H Company, the sappers first killed a two-man radio team. "It was apparent the sapper unit had conducted some very successful recon patrols on Neville to know the location of the radio team," he said.

The sappers crisscrossed the west side of the perimeter, killing anyone who got in their way. But the Marines were undeterred.

"We beat those sappers, who were supposed to be the worst thing the North Vietnamese had," recalled former Gunnery Sgt. John Timmermeyer. "We beat these people not with air, not with arty, not with any supporting arms. We beat them, and we beat them bad with weapons we had in our own company. We didn't have to have supporting arms. We did it without them."

Robert Chatigny remembers running out of M-16 ammo, but using the weapons just the same. "We listened for their voices and movement until they were close enough that we could hit them with our M-16s as if using a baseball bat," said Chatigny, who served with 2nd Plt., G Co.

When an enemy mortar round detonated in an 81mm mortar emplacement, H Company Weapons Platoon Sgt. Alfred P. LaPorte, Jr., took immediate action to extinguish the resulting blaze. He rescued two wounded Marines, and after seized another 81mm round near the command post. By throwing the sizzling hot round over an embankment, LaPorte saved numerous lives, according to his Navy Cross Citation.

After the battle, NVA bodies were found with satchel charges strapped to their backs, intending to kill themselves in an attempt to seize the hill. Their body count was 42. Maps, battle plans and opium were discovered on some of the bodies. Garber remembers the ground being so rocky they could not bury the enemy bodies, so battalion headquarters said to burn them.

The Marines lost 13 men on Neville and 29 wounded. Among the KIA were hospitalman corpsman 2nd Class Walter Phillip Seel, Jr., Cpl. Jeffrey M. Barron and Lance Cpl. Thomas McGrath, all of whom received Silver Stars posthumously. Ten of the KIA belonged to H Co., 2nd Bn., 4th Marines, and three to G Battery, 3rd Bn., 12th Marines. Shrapnel claimed 85% of their lives. All told, 43 Marines were KIA and 106 were WIA in about three hours of hellish fighting at both firebases. ✪

'INSIDE THE WIRE': SAPPERS ATTACK CU CHI AIRFIELD

BY KELLY VON LUNEN

The loss of life and equipment was great in one devastating raid in February 1969.

In the fourth deadliest single ground incident for an engineer unit in the Vietnam War, 10 men of the 554th Eng. Bn. (Construction), 79th Eng. Grp., were KIA over 2½ hours at Cu Chi Airfield.

Before dawn on Feb. 26, 1969, enemy sappers raided the 25th Infantry Division Headquarters Base Camp at Cu Chi, 20 miles northwest of Saigon.

With the base already on alert, one man slept in each of the 16 CH-47A Chinook helicopters to guard them. Rocket fire preceded the ground attack at 4 a.m.

Some 39 *Dac Cong* (VC special force) sappers, according to Tom Mangold and John Penycate in *The Tunnels of Cu Chi,* broke through the base's 10 outer rolls of concertina wire, sneaking into the perimeter. Their mission: to destroy Chinook helicopters of the 269th Combat Aviation Bn., 12th Combat Avn. Grp., 1st Avn. Bde.

Viet Cong special forces' sappers destroyed nine CH-47A Chinook helicopters in a morning raid at Cu Chi Airfield on Feb. 26, 1969, and killed 14 GIs.

"I was amazed to see that the dozens of trip flares we had put into our wire had been disabled by cutting the trip wire and wrapping the wire around the flare," remembered Ernest B. Milner of D Co., 554th Eng. Bn.

Michael Lynch was assigned to the 515th Engineer Platoon, attached to A Co., 554th Eng. Bn. He was awakened that morning by mortar rounds hitting inside the camp.

"We'd had these kind of attacks before," Lynch said. "It was nothing new. Then I heard someone yelling that the VC were trying to breach the fences surrounding the base camp. This

was something new."

Lynch got his rifle and ammo belt, and slowly made it to one of the doors on the side of the hooch. It was still dark outside, barely lit up from the flares on the bunker line. Then he heard someone yelling that the VC were in the A Company area.

"I could hear AK-47 fire close by," Lynch said. "I retreated back inside the hooch with my weapon trained on the door. Through the door I could see a body lying on the ground. It turned out to be Spec. 5 David Jackson who was killed by AK-47 fire during the night. Members of the 515th Engineer Platoon and A Company were never the same after that."

DEADLIEST HOSTILE ENGINEER LOSSES

KIA	DATE	UNITS	PLACE	CAUSE
15	1-3-69	D Co., 554th Eng. Bn.	Cu Chi Base Camp	Bomb Explosion (Mess Hall)
12	3-13-68	3 Cos., 937th Eng. Grp.	Hwy. 14, Pleiku City	Convoy Ambush
12	7-22-68	137th Eng. Co., 19th Eng. Bn.	Hwy. 1, Dai Duong	Convoy Ambush
10	2-26-69	3 Companies, 554th Eng. Bn.	Cu Chi Base Camp	Sapper Attack
10	5-12-70	937th Eng. Grp. & Eng. Cmd.	Plei Blang Yam	Helicopter Shoot-down
9	5-28-69	15th Eng. Co., 937th Eng. Grp.	Dak To Base Camp	Rocket Attack

A totally incinerated Chinook lies in ashes the morning after the attack.

Jim Murphy of C Co., 125th Signal Bn., 25th Inf. Div., was assigned to guard the motor pool at the time. He recalls running straight into an ambush.

"A rocket-propelled grenade (RPG) hit the lead vehicle with the duty officer and his driver," Murphy said. "We jumped out of our truck and hit the ground. In a scene reminiscent of the grand finale at a fireworks display, a barrage of RPG fire hit us."

Murphy saw Sgt. Alvin Fleming run into a group of the enemy. Fleming fought them single-handedly, breaking his M-16 over their heads. He received the Bronze Star for valor.

In the two-hour plus attack, 11 sappers were killed and another eight captured in the 554th's Hotel Sector alone. A

14 KIA AT CU CHI, BY UNIT

554th Eng. Bn. 10

HHC, 2nd Bn., 34th Armor 1

A Btry., 3rd Bn., 13th Arty 1

B Co., 65th Eng. Bn. 1

242nd Assault Support Helicopter Co. 1

maintenance officer captured one POW by himself.

"Capt. Mills Kitchen had stopped by the mess hall for a cup of coffee," recalls Maj. Jerry Headley of B Trp., 3rd Sqdn., 4th Cav. "As he headed to the squadron headquarters, an enemy soldier jumped out from between two barracks with his hands up. Capt. Kitchen, unarmed except for the cup of coffee, took the sapper to the headquarters where he was tied up and placed with other POWs."

Motor pool Sgt. Jack R. Hanover of C Co., 25th Medical Bn., 25th Inf. Div., saw soldiers pulling dead Vietnamese out of a bunker. "As we went around the bunker lines, we saw Viet Cong casualties lying on the ground," Hanover said. "Some of them had demolition charges pinned to their backs, RPG rounds and so forth."

Terry Schlossnagle, who was managing the trailer transfer point, also recalled "that some of the enemy dead had been booby-trapped."

A total of 14 U.S. servicemen were KIA, and at least 30 WIA. Some 71% of the KIAs were from the 554th Engineers alone: C Co. (four), A Co. (three) and D Co. (three).

Nine Chinook helicopters were completely destroyed and another three were severely damaged. "They ran down our flight line and threw satchel charges in most of our 16 Chinooks or hit them with RPGs at close range," remembered Gary Roush, a CH-47 pilot with the 242nd ASHC.

Some KIAs were not found until morning. "Troops manning the sector by the airstrip dozed off on watch and were found the next morning with their throats slit," Murphy said in *The Shifting Battlefields of Vietnam.* "Although I didn't know those guys, their fate has stayed with me to this day."

One specialist was sleeping aboard a Chinook helicopter when the sappers attacked. He was decapitated by an RPG. Two men of the 554th were killed en route to the showers, and another two were KIA when Bunker 66 was blown up by satchel charges. Overall, the airfield raid was mass confusion.

"That night there were no heroes and no cowards," Murphy said. "Just a bunch of ordinary guys caught up in a bad situation." ✪

BY JOHN F. BAUER   *OPERATION WAYNE GREY*

AMBUSH IN PLEI TRAP VALLEY

During *Operation Wayne Grey* in March 1969, a quickly forgotten battle came at a deadly price for A Co., 3rd Bn., 8th Inf., 4th Inf. Div.

T he Army's 4th Infantry Division began *Operation Wayne Grey* in early March 1969. Its mission was to prevent enemy movement in South Vietnam's Central Highlands, particularly in Kontum province near the Cambodian border.

Just northwest of Pleiku is the Plei Trap Valley—the site of a deadly ambush March 3. That engagement claimed the lives of 27% of the 86 men in Alpha Company. The stories of some who survived are told here with the hope that those who died will forever be remembered.

On the morning of March 3, A Company was dropped by helicopters into the valley to prepare for a night patrol. Regrettably, the 66th North Vietnamese Army (NVA) Regiment was ready and waiting for the GIs.

"We were undermanned and ill-prepared to enter a meat grinder," said 1st Lt. Felix Williams, who was the leader of 3rd Platoon. "What we did not know then was that we were out of artillery range."

As the men made their way along a ridgeline, they killed two NVA soldiers, and that's when the firefight began. A machine gun opened up at close range, killing one soldier and wounding another. Williams and his men took cover and returned fire, but more NVA joined in the fight.

"We were smack in a deadly crossfire, and guys began to drop all over," Williams said.

A medic tried to save the first wounded man who had been hit four or five times and had a sucking chest wound. The medic was killed, but the wounded soldier survived.

The company commander, Capt. Dennis Isom, was killed quickly and Williams was one of only two remaining officers.

"It was sheer chaos," said Williams, who took charge of A Company. "Dead

Members of A Company's 3rd Platoon enjoy cigars on Christmas Day, 1968. Second from left, front row, is Luis Ortiz, WIA. Holding the cigar box (far right) is Julio Leon. A number of these men were KIA, including Willie Hudson, standing next to the tree.

PHOTO COURTESY BILL FROMWILLER

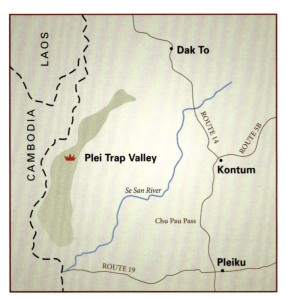

Capt. Dennis R. Isom (right) looks on with other officers prior to the operation in the Plei Trap Valley. Isom was later killed in action on March 3, 1969, in the ambush.

Plei Trap Valley was covered with triple canopy jungle, making an escape from the NVA ambush more arduous.

and wounded were everywhere. I had lost more than half of my platoon." (He was now responsible for the company's X-mode radio and code key.) Williams had done his utmost to save lives. Using hand grenades, he took out two NVA bunkers. After regrouping the company, Williams formed a second defensive line and was wounded in the subsequent assault. Then he coordinated artillery and air strikes only yards from his own position, states his Distinguished Service Cross citation.

For squad leader Julio Leon, it was "one of the scariest nights" of his life. "All I heard were people screaming and moaning in pain," he said. "We were way undermanned to have to face the 66th."

As night settled in on a nearby hill, Williams put the word out to pull back to the original night location. Once there, an ammo supply drop was made. But due to the triple-canopy jungle, only 20% of the ammo reached its intended target.

At daylight, Williams asked for volunteers to head back up the hill to retrieve the dead and wounded. Led by Sgt. Sam Jones, about 25 men set out to probe the area and recover casualties.

After going about 110 yards, they heard voices yelling, "Don't shoot! It's Bravo Company." Instead, it was the crafty NVA—posing as U.S. troops—who proceeded to open fire on the Americans.

Williams made the decision to get his men off the ridge, so he ordered them to pull back down the finger of the hill toward a dry creek bed. The weary troops carried their wounded buddies, while dodging enemy fire along the way.

"We only had one way off that steep hill," Leon said. "Some of the guys were just rolling to the bottom, losing everything they were carrying along the way."

A Red Bird (Cobra helicopter) pilot spotted the struggling GIs and opened fire on the more than 100 NVA troops following closely behind. He covered the Americans until Hueys (utility helicopters) arrived for evacuation.

"Guys with uniforms half gone, some without weapons, clambered aboard with wounded buddies," Williams said. "A couple died en route. I was the last man out."

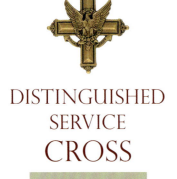

DISTINGUISHED SERVICE CROSS

1ST LT. FELIX WILLIAMS

SURVIVING ALONE FOR 10 DAYS

For squad leader Jones, the man originally tasked with heading back up the hill to retrieve the wounded, the evacuation didn't quite work as planned.

Before receiving Williams' order to retreat down the hill, he and his men were getting hammered with enemy grenades, as well as fire from both sides of the perimeter.

"The gooks were real close to coming through now," Jones recalled. "We kept firing away. Before we could get out, a B-40 rocket round hit nearby and killed a couple of guys next to me. I was stunned and disoriented."

When Jones regained consciousness, everyone was gone. He ran down the hill, but there was no one there. He realized he was going in the wrong direction, but decided to keep running, just the same.

For 10 days, Jones worked his way through the jungle with nothing more than one grenade, a compass, a pocket knife, a metal mirror and a plastic bag.

He tried to signal with the mirror to a pilot flying overhead, but instead caught the attention of an enemy sniper. He used the battery bag as a canteen, filling it up at night. He survived only on water, for fear of getting sick from eating foliage.

Jones followed the sound of where the U.S. artillery came from each day and finally found his way to Fire Base Mary Lou, about 16 miles from where the mission originated.

"Aside from losing 25 pounds, I was in good shape," Jones said.

He called home but the connection was so bad that his parents didn't first believe it was their son on the other end of the line. They put him to the test, asking him what color the family barn was. "Charcoal brown, Dad, charcoal brown," he responded. "Thank God, son," his grateful father replied.

'SCREAMING IN AGONY'

In the aftermath of the deadly battle, Williams' superiors threatened him with a court martial because he failed to return with the X-mode radio and code key. They further said that Williams had directly disobeyed orders on the hill. His men stepped forward on his behalf.

"We, the survivors of Alpha Company, were mad as hell when we found they were going to court martial Lt. Williams," said Emmett Myron Gwin, a squad leader with 3rd Platoon. "We got together and wrote a letter to division headquarters and the charges were dropped."

Gwin received the Silver Star for gallantry in action. That day, he killed a VC dressed only in loincloth and hiding in a tree sniping at him and his men. "I got off one round, but then my M-16 jammed," he said. "As a little bit of panic started to set in, I saw him sway back and forth in the branches. There was a hole in his chest, and head first he fell from the tree."

Medic John A. Holmes, III, also received a Silver Star for continuing to administer first aid, though wounded himself. Attached to A Company, Holmes carried two wounded GIs to the extraction point and was one of the last to leave.

In a letter to his parents a few days later, he aptly described the horrific scene: "They were in trees and bunkers. All I remember is people screaming in agony and bullets coming from all directions. I was the only able medic as two were killed and the third shot in both arms. After we left, the enemy went around and shot all the wounded in the back. We had to run about five miles before we could be picked up, and it was such a relief to get out of there."

Helicopter crew chief Ron Carey recalls extracting A Company following the battle: "I will never forget the smell of gun powder, burning, rotting jungle and the smell of death which hung over that hill."

When the battle in the Plei Trap Valley was over, 23 members of A Company were dead, including two medics from HQ Company and the forward artillery observer from C Btry., 6th Bn., 29th Arty. Nearly 75% of the men were draftees and the majority were killed by gunfire. Twelve posthumous Silver Stars—for 52% of all KIAs—were awarded.

At the time, the *New York Times* reported only: "The U.S. Command said today that 21 Americans had been killed in two days of intermittent fighting with a battalion of North Vietnamese regulars 31 miles west of Kontum City." To this day, Alpha's battle on March 3 remains buried in the war's history. ✪

Barry Horton (left) was 3rd Platoon's machine gunner. He was killed on March 3. With him are two other members, Dennis Fritz and Larry (last name unknown).

Pfc. John A. Holmes, III, a medic attached to A Company, received the Silver Star for braving a hail of enemy fire to help the wounded, despite being wounded himself.

THE TOLL

U.S. KIA:
23

BY KELLY VON LUNEN

SAPPERS TAKE A BEATING AT LIBERTY BRIDGE

The battery perimeter of Fire Support Base Phu Lac 6 was ringed with strands of triple concertina wire and tanglefoot, as well as 1,000 trip flares. Yet none of the flares were tripped prior to the March 19, 1969, attack on Phu Lac and the command post of the 1st Bn., 5th Marine Regt., both adjacent to Liberty Bridge (which spanned the Song Thu Bon River but was destroyed at the time), northeast of An Hoa and 14 miles southwest of Da Nang.

An estimated three companies of North Vietnamese Army (NVA) sappers hit Phu Lac with B-40 rockets, mortars, grenades and satchel charges about 2 a.m. One enemy company fired some 50 rocket and mortar rounds, and the other two attacked from the southwest. They breached the perimeter wire in several places, using AK-47 fire, grenades, Bangalore torpedoes and flamethrowers

The initial moments of the enemy assault were devastating to the Marines in the artillery positions. Once the surprise wore off, though, they fended off the attack with precision. Marines from D Btry., 2nd Bn., 11th Marines, went into action with a vengeance.

Combat was often hand-to-hand; the NVA flamed three bunkers, including that of Cpl. John Niedopytalski.

"When I looked out, all I saw were NVA running around our position," Niedopytalski said. "My hut was burned down by a flamethrower. I ran inside my ammo bunker. Three of my guys were in there. My guys ran out of the bunker and all were killed."

Through the course of the attack, Niedopytalski, section chief for D Battery, killed five sappers.

"We could see a group of enemy soldiers coming through the wire, so we lowered the muzzle of our howitzer and fired point-blank into them," Niedopytalski said. "I shot the first one as he jumped over the parapet. Then a Chicom grenade exploded

> "I don't know how long I was out, but when I came to, I realized that one of the sappers was using me as a shield while he fired into the other gun positions."
>
> – CPL. JOHN NIEDOPYTALSKI

On March 19, 1969, members of the 11th Marines (Artillery) at Phu Lac and 5th Marines at their command post a few hundred yards away administered a punishing blow to three attacking NVA companies.

MARCH 1969

PHOTO COURTESY KEN HEINS

A memorial service for the 12 members of D Battery, 2nd Battalion, 11th Marines, took place on March 24, 1969. The NVA paid dearly for the casualties they inflicted.

U.S. MARINE CORPS HISTORICAL CENTER PHOTO

An aerial view shows Liberty Bridge under reconstruction by Seabees of the 3rd Naval Construction Brigade. The 5th Marines compound at Phu Lac 6 guards the bridge's southern approach on the left.

USMC PHOTO BY HANK BERKOWITZ

Sgt. Jerry Locke and Pfc. Danny Mitchell stand next to one of the 105mm howitzers of the battery. The artillery pieces were used with lethal effect, firing beehive rounds—containing one-inch flechettes (see below)—point-blank into attacking sappers.

and I took a flesh wound in the shoulder and was knocked unconscious.

"I don't know how long I was out, but when I came to, I realized that one of the sappers was using me as a shield while he fired into the other gun positions. Still dazed from the grenade, I played possum until he moved off with three of his comrades. I picked up my rifle and prayed that there were some rounds still in it."

Niedopytalski had enough bullets to hit all four enemy soldiers in one burst. Then he crawled over the bunker, found a bag of grenades and started throwing them into the perimeter wire to keep any more sappers from coming through.

Capt. Wayne Babb, commanding officer of D Battery, spotted two NVA running with baskets of C-ration cans. He led a squad after the enemy, killing them. His Silver Star citation states that Babb completely disregarded his own safety when he learned that NVA had penetrated the perimeter defenses.

According to the citation: "He ignored the danger from exploding satchel charges and the heavy volume of enemy rocket grenade and small-arms fire as he boldly moved through the fire … Quickly organizing a reaction squad, he fearlessly led his men in an aggressive assault … personally killing two of the enemy and routing the others. Although painfully wounded, Capt. Babb steadfastly refused medical attention until he had completed the reorganization of the battery position and ensured that the serious Marine casualties were evacuated."

Years later, Babb would write in an account of the action: "In the midst of providing all-out fire support for the initially besieged company and Seabees on the north side, the cannoneers manning the howitzers were caught in the open and completely by surprise."

One D Battery artilleryman burst out of his tent, firing as he ran, and hitting three NVA. Finding two of his howitzer's crew dead, he scaled the gun's parapet and fired until he was killed by small-arms fire. Another Marine fired 300 pop-up flares for two hours during the attack, illuminating the battle area.

A tank crew, led by Sgt. Robert L. Lynch, claimed at least eight NVA dead. After seeing enemy soldiers attacking an artillery position, they cut them down with the tank's .30-caliber machine gun. 1st Lt. David Turner rounded up every Marine not actively engaged in fire support or close combat. With this impromptu quick reaction force, he went from bunker to bunker to destroy NVA.

Pfc. Robert K. Myer and Lance Cpl. Frank J. Rangel killed 20 NVA with their 105mm howitzer and M-16 rifles. They fired point-blank until NVA were on top of their position. Then Myer took out three NVA who were hiding behind the parapet. Rangel killed another five.

Pfc. James P. Murtha, attached to D Battery, remembered the "battle lasting about three hours of total chaos. I think we had 25 to 30 wounded."

1/5 COMMAND POST HIT

A few hundred yards distant, some 24 sappers penetrated the perimeter wire near the command post of the 1st Bn., 5th Marines. One gun crew killed nine of them inside their parapet. None of the attackers made it out alive.

Mike Stone was with Weapons Platoon (60mm mortars) of the 1st Battalion. "The fighting was intense," he said. "We were firing illumination, high-explosive and white phosphorous rounds at a rate that turned our tubes red hot."

NVA directly assaulted the mess hall. The mess sergeant, Gunnery Sgt. Floyd Keefe, saw enemy movement around the hall, so he left his bunker, told his men to cover him and rushed in. Keefe looked back and saw an NVA prepare to throw a grenade in the bunker; he shot him and continued to the mess hall. Another sapper wounded him with a grenade. When two of his men rushed to help, two NVA fired from the supply tent, killing Keefe and wounding one corpsman.

Lance Cpl. Donald R. Mitchell said that Keefe had told his men, "I'll defend my mess hall like Custer in his last stand." That he did.

Heroism was on display throughout the night's ordeal. Back at FSB Phu Lac 6, Navy corpsman David R. Ray, attached to D Battery, had been busy caring for wounded Marines when the NVA attacked. At one point, he was interrupted by two enemy soldiers who hit his position while he was bandaging a Marine. Ray killed one and wounded the other. He was wounded at the time, but kept working despite severe bleeding.

Ray died when he was hit by an enemy grenade. His body was covering that of a wounded Marine, who survived. Ray was awarded the Medal of Honor.

"Undaunted by the intense hostile fire, HM2 Ray moved from parapet to parapet, rendering emergency medical treatment to the wounded," his citation reads. "By his determined and persevering actions, courageous spirit and selfless devotion to the welfare of his Marine comrades, HM2 Ray served to inspire Battery D to heroic efforts in defeating the enemy."

Babb and Niedopytalski also were recognized with Silver Stars. Keefe earned the Silver Star posthumously.

D Btry., 2nd Bn., 11th Marines, suffered 12 KIA while defending Phu Lac; 1st Bn., 5th Marines, lost three men dead. Gunfire and shrapnel took an equal toll in lives.

Then-1st Lt. Mike Lipking co-piloted a CH-46 helicopter of Marine Medium Helicopter Squadron 165 on a medevac mission that night. "We continued to ferry the wounded to the field hospital throughout the night," he said. "Images of the pile of body parts at Liberty Bridge are something I try not to think about."

Yet 2nd Lt. Frank Satterfield of Delta Company recalled: "But the battle itself was extremely one-sided. We buried more than 70 NVA in a mass grave outside the concertina wire."

Lt. Gen. Robert E. Cushman, commanding general of III Marine Amphibious Force, commended the Marines following the battle: "The courage and resourcefulness and professional skill exercised by the defenders threw the enemy into confusion and successfully defeated his attack. The action typifies the best in our fighting tradition." ✪

MEDAL OF HONOR

HM2 DAVID ROBERT RAY
(POSTHUMOUS)

THE TOLL

U.S. KIA:
15

U.S. WIA:
30

BY JOSEPH L. GALLOWAY

TACKLING THE 'MOUNTAIN OF THE CROUCHING BEAST'

"You may not be able to read this. I am writing it in a hurry. I see death coming up the hill."

–FROM A LETTER HOME BY A 101ST AIRBORNE DIVISION TROOPER
FIGHTING ON HAMBURGER HILL IN MAY 1969

Between May 10-21, 1969, the 3rd Brigade (3rd Bn., 187th Inf.; 1st Bn., 506th Inf.; and 2nd Bn., 501st Inf.) of the 101st Airborne Division collided with the North Vietnamese Army's (NVA) elite 29th Regiment in a bitter struggle for one of the hills overlooking the A Shau Valley along the Laotian border.

On Vietnamese maps, the 3,000-foot peak was dubbed Dong Ap Bia, or Ap Bia Mountain. On U.S. maps, it was Hill 937. To the local Montagnard, it was "The Mountain of the Crouching Beast." Before the fighting was over, the grunts christened it Hamburger Hill—in comparison to such designations during the Korean War.

CLEANING OUT A SANCTUARY

On May 10, *Operation Apache Snow* was launched. It was an ambitious 10-battalion airborne/Marine/South Vietnamese sweep intended to clean out the A Shau and open it up with an all-weather highway that would permit allied operations even during the mountain monsoons.

Shortly after daybreak, Huey slicks began lifting Col. Joe Conmy's 3rd Brigade and two battalions of the Army of the Republic of Vietnam (ARVN) 1st Division into the A Shau. The 3rd Bn., 187th Airborne, was tasked with taking Hill 937. The *Rakkasans,* as they were nicknamed, were led by Lt. Col. Weldon Honeycutt, a Korean War veteran.

Soldiers of the 101st Airborne Division sort through the debris of the battle on Hamburger Hill in May 1969. It proved to be a turning point in the war.

From May 10–21, 1969, the 3rd Brigade of the 101st Airborne Division assaulted Ap Bia Mountain (Hill 937) in the A Shau Valley. To the American public, the battle would become known as "Hamburger Hill" for the sacrifice in lives.

MAY 1969

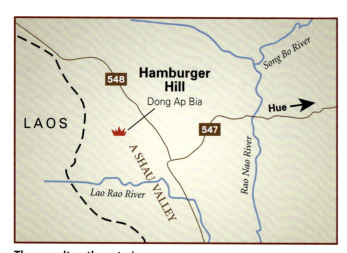

The assault on the notorious Hamburger Hill in I Corps' Thua Thien province in mid-May 1969 garnered immense media attention.

A and C companies were sent off on sweeps toward the Trung Pham River and mapped out a route up Ap Bia. B Company later headed up a steep, narrow trail into dim light of double- and then triple-canopy jungle, clogged with fallen trees, tangles of bamboo and vines.

Second Platoon led off, up and down the saddles until the enemy struck with a shower of rocket-propelled grenades (RPGs) and the flat crack of AK-47 rifles from the first line of bunkers and spider holes.

Artillery and the Air Force hammered at the jungle, but with darkness approaching, Honeycutt ordered Bravo Company's 107 men to dig in and wait for the morning.

'PRIDE OF HO CHI MINH'

The next morning, May 11, B Company's 1st Platoon took the lead. On point, Spec. 4 Phil Nelson gestured at the littered (including three NVA bodies) trail: "Something's wrong here, lieutenant." Sensing imminent danger, the advance slowed to a crawl.

Meanwhile, down below at battalion HQ, a clearly shaken Kit Carson scout (VC defector) translated the documents and letters taken off the three dead NVA.

"Those men we killed were members of the 29th NVA Regiment. It's called 'The Pride of Ho Chi Minh'… one of the best regiments in the entire North Vietnamese Army. Many, many soldiers everywhere. Hundreds of soldiers," said the scout. That unit had a reputation for being "big American killers."

When the advance resumed, 4th Platoon was leading. Pfc. Aaron Rosenstreich was on point, followed by Spec. 4 John McCarrell. After a pause to inspect a fat enemy commo wire running straight up the mountain, the company was moving again, under occasional sniper fire.

Then suddenly, an NVA soldier popped up in a spider hole and fired an AK burst into Rosenstreich's chest, even as another NVA jumped out of a bunker. He fired an RPG round that hit McCarrell in the chest, touching off a Claymore mine he was carrying.

The explosion blew Lt. Charles Denholm 10 feet into the air. Now machine-gun fire hosed down the trees and RPGs were exploding among the tree branches overhead, spewing shrapnel on the Americans below.

Denholm crawled to Rosenstreich and held

Now machine-gun fire hosed down the trees and RPGs were exploding among the tree branches overhead, spewing shrapnel on the Americans below.

him as he died. Other Americans, trying to maneuver against the hidden enemy, were dying. The survivors staggered back down the trail as B Company's forward observer called a 15-minute artillery barrage down. He also summoned two Cobra gunships as a follow-up, which tragically rocketed battalion HQ, killing two Americans and wounding 35.

Simultaneously, an NVA 120mm mortar across the border in Laos opened up on the headquarters LZ. Five NVA soldiers burst out of a draw to the south, charging the position until they were cut down by the stunned Americans.

ENDLESS ASSAULTS

Honeycutt's battered and disbelieving companies, however, would not let up. They took turns assaulting Ap Bia. They faced snipers tied in the treetops and other snipers dug into

TRAGIC SEQUENCE

Combat photographer Spec. 4 Rick Helton (insert left) of the 506th Signal Battalion attached to 2nd Plt., C Co., 187th Inf., captured the combat on Hill 937 during the first day of fighting. As members of the platoon wait below (above), one of their wounded is brought downhill by a trooper while another provides cover fire (top left).

Within minutes of these photos, an RPG landed in the middle of the group, killing several. A second rocket landed right in front of Helton and a few others, wounding Helton.

"We moved on to camp," he said. "Wounded and dead were brought in. I made a few shots of this, and then laid my camera down to help with loading soldiers onto the helicopters" (left).

1st Sgt. Donald Joubert (right), 3rd Bn., 187th Abn., 101 Abn. Div., takes a break from the fighting along with his men amid the desolation on Ap Bia Mountain. The *Rakkasans* alone sustained 39 KIA and nearly 300 WIA.

camouflaged spider holes.

Then there were the deep-dug fortified machine-gun bunkers. They were vulnerable only to a direct hit by one of the 1,000-pound bombs the Air Force was dropping, or a carefully aimed recoilless rifle round in a firing aperture. Worst of all were the RPGs: Every overhead burst took its toll on unprotected Americans, and the NVA were firing them by the hundreds.

It was not until the seventh day of battle that flak jackets were passed out, to provide some protection for those who could bear to wear them in the stifling 100-degree heat.

NVA were quick to maneuver against U.S. flanks once a company had been driven to the ground by the machine guns and had dead and wounded to care for. At the first sight of an American withdrawal, they poured out of bunkers and holes in hot pursuit.

REINFORCEMENTS ARRIVE

By the fourth day, Conmy ordered another battalion, the 1st Bn., 506th Inf., to join the attack. Its mission was to seal off the 29th Regiment's resupply routes to Laos and attack the mountain from the western slopes.

A combination of rugged terrain, high elephant grass and stiffening enemy resistance combined to prevent the "Currahees" from getting into position until late on May 17.

The next morning both battalions launched a coordinated assault. Mines, Claymores and RPGs took a heavy toll on Americans. But by afternoon, they were within easy reach of the summit and victory, when nature itself turned against them.

For a full week, U.S. artillery and bombs had lashed at the slopes and crest of the mountain, stripping it of all vegetation and literally pulverizing the earth. That sight stuck in many GIs' minds.

Pvt. Paul Clark, a forward observer with the 2nd Bn., 11th Arty, landed at Hill 937 on May 10 and spent five days operating there. "It was like some strange landscape," he recalled 30 years later, "like out of a movie: everything burnt, bent

1969: A DEADLY YEAR

U.S. deaths during the second deadliest year of the Vietnam War.

	HOSTILE	NON-HOSTILE
January	828	158
February	1,116	182
March	1,350	202
April	825	197
May	1,237	213
June	1,084	162
July	641	192
August	793	165
September	475	188
October	373	226
November	478	179
December	345	167
Total	**9,545**	**2,231**
Total Deaths		**11,776**

Source: Data Analysis Program Division, Defense Manpower Data Center, Office of the Secretary of Defense.

or twisted. It was very unnatural. Guys were just walking around like zombies. Some just sat and stared back."

Now came a monsoon deluge that turned it all into mud three feet deep in places. Mudslides and flash floods a foot deep roared down the slopes, carrying helpless Americans with them. Men clung to tree stumps and dug their toes and rifle butts into the goo to hang on. Victory was in sight but out of reach. They had been only 50 yards from the summit.

The 3/187th had that day, the eighth of the campaign, lost 15 killed and 64 wounded, and again was forced to withdraw. But it was not for lack of bravery. Spec. 4 Johnny Jackson, the 3rd Platoon machine gunner, led A Company's attack. Declaring, "I'm through with this retreating bullshit," he demonstrated incredible initiative, earning the Silver Star.

The 1/506th dug in for the night about half a mile from the crest. It had lost five KIA; and an artillery forward observer died, too, on May 18.

The high command now ordered two additional battalions, the 2/501st and the South Vietnamese 2nd Bn., 3rd Infantry, to reinforce the attack. On May 19, 2/501st was airlifted to the northeast slopes and 2/3rd ARVN to the east-southeast.

The 1/506th took advantage of the lull to move to within 220 yards of the crest.

Squad leader Arthur Wiknik, Jr., of A Co., 2/506th, landed by helicopter near the mountain on May 18 and participated in the final assault two days later. "The stench of decaying flesh, the shriveled NVA corpses, the silent body bags, and the massive destruction would be my lasting memory of that hill," he recalled. Wiknik later recorded his memories as chapter three of his book, *Nam Sense*.

Ten days of fighting completely denuded Hamburger Hill of all vegetation. Members of the 101st Airborne Division survey the damage after securing the hilltop.

PRESIDENTIAL UNIT CITATION

On the morning of May 20, a four-battalion attack was launched, and shortly before noon the first troops of 3/187th shot their way onto the summit. Then-Lt. Terrence M. Smith, a platoon leader with A Co., 2/506th (the only reinforcing company attached to 3/187th), led the assault of his unit that day.

"I feel my men and our company played a significant role," he wrote in a letter. "I fought with brave men who never faltered in a fierce battle. Please give them the credit they deserve." Temporarily blinded in the fight, he nevertheless continued to lead his men. He was awarded the Silver Star.

Samuel Zaffiri, author of *Hamburger Hill*, described the scene of desolation the GIs witnessed atop the hill: "They moved through an apocalyptic, surreal landscape. All that remained of the triple-canopy jungle were rows of jagged tree trunks surrounded by a muddy stew of splintered logs, bamboo, vines and tree branches.

"Scattered everywhere were pith helmets, pieces of clothing, bloody bandages, blankets, AK-47s, stick-handled grenades, and RPG and mortar rounds. NVA dead also littered the mountaintop, their sickening sweet odor mixing with the smells of urine, excrement, tree sap and cordite."

The 101st reported 630 enemy killed by count; U.S. trail-watchers operating across the line in Laos said they counted more than 1,200 NVA dead and wounded carried out. The 29th Regiment's 7th and 8th battalions, defending the mountain, were nearly wiped out.

DISTINGUISHED
SERVICE
CROSS

**1ST SGT.
DONALD L. JOUBERT**

**SPEC. 4 NICHOLAS
W. SCHOCH**

**1ST LT.
JERRY T. WALDEN**

THE
TOLL

U.S. KIA:
66

U.S. WIA:
372

NVA tenacity was clearly evident: some snipers chained or tied one leg to a tree. Cloth patches sewn on the front of their shirts read: "Kill Americans."

Some 66 Americans were KIA at Hamburger Hill. They included 39 men from the 3/187th, 23 from the 1/506th and three from the 326th Medical Battalion, when their helicopter was shot down. That crash claimed two lives on the ground, too. A forward observer from A Btry., 2nd Bn., 319th Arty, also was KIA. The hardest hit companies were Delta (14 KIA) and Charlie (13 KIA) of the 187th. By far, the single deadliest day was May 18—21 soldiers died.

Fifty percent of the deaths were caused by shrapnel; 30% by gunfire. Five fatalities and 53 of the wounded were due to "friendly fire." Draftees, by now forming the vast majority of rifle companies, accounted for 71% of the deaths; volunteers, 29%.

"Korea had Pork Chop Hill so they should call this one Hamburger Hill," James Thomas, a medic with 3/187th, said to a buddy. And that is the origin of the battle's name, according to Thomas.

"As the fight went on, Hamburger was simply the reference name of choice, picked up by every radio operator and others in the field for precise communication," remembered Carl Lindbeck of A Co., 1st Bn., 506th Inf. Ironically, the NVA called it the battle of *thit bam*— "the meat chopper."

On June 5, 1969, the last Americans were pulled off the mountain. Twelve days later, U.S. intelligence confirmed that some 1,000 NVA had reoccupied Ap Bia, probably the 29th Regiment.

New tactical limitations were imposed on commanders in the battle's aftermath. Political pronouncements made at the time still rankle many veterans. Sen. Ted Kennedy (D-Mass.), for example, called the war "immoral."`

"At least he could have said something about the valor of the troops involved and what they accomplished," said Robert Schmitz, 1st Platoon leader of A Co., 1/506th, years later. "They fought under some extremely difficult conditions and conducted themselves with honor as soldiers are supposed to do."

Indeed, eight of the KIAs alone received posthumous Silver Stars. Among those awarded the Distinguished Service Cross were 1st Lt. Jerry T. Walden, 1st Sgt. Donald L. Joubert and Spec. 4 Nicholas W. Schoch, all of the 187th.

Schoch of B Co., 3rd Bn., performed several incredible feats: While treating a wounded soldier, he killed an enemy sniper to save the GI's life; he performed a tracheotomy under fire; he grabbed a grenade, threw it in a bomb crater and then killed the NVA who had thrown it; and he retrieved an unconscious survivor of a downed and burning helicopter and carried him to safety through a barrage of sniper fire.

The courageous men of the 101st Airborne had done all that was asked of them, and more. Col. Joseph Conmy, commander of the 3rd Brigade, said: "No matter how tough the job is, the American soldier gets the job done. He might hate the hell out of it, but he never quits. ... On Hamburger Hill, they might have grumbled, but by God, they were there when the chips were down! They eventually went up that hill and took it!"

Conmy called it the toughest fight he had seen in three years in Vietnam. An infantry veteran of WWII and Korea (including the Chosin Reservoir), he commanded the 3rd Brigade from July 1968-July 1969. At Firebase Berchtesgaden in June, he was seriously WIA.

In token of its bravery and suffering, the 3rd Brigade was awarded a Presidential Unit Citation for its actions at Ap Bia Mountain. Also, a movie, *Hamburger Hill* (1987) was produced in honor of the GIs' sacrifices.

The recognition was well deserved. "I can attest that the NVA were tough, but we were tougher," said Carl Lindbeck with pride. "We fought our way through ambushes, spider holes, fortified bunkers, snipers and just plain tough enemy fighters. I recall picking up a pith helmet and our scout translated the writing on it as: *The A Shau Valley is a good place to die.*" ✪

'A HORRENDOUS BATTLE': NUI YON HILL

BY RICHARD K. KOLB

While all media remained fixated on Hamburger Hill, a similar but smaller-scale battle played out about four miles southwest of Tam Ky Airfield in Quang Tin province.

From May 12-15, 1969, a desperate struggle raged for control of Nui Yon Hill. On May 12, Communist troops overran the South Vietnamese regional forces camp there. Three Americans of Advisory Team 16 were killed. 1st Lt. Curtis Breedlove was awarded a posthumous Silver Star. "Although their remains were barely identifiable, it was evident that each of the Americans was shot in the head," said J. McCrary, a leader assigned to an ARVN unit during recapture of the hill.

That same day, C Trp., 1st Sqdn., 1st Cav (Armored Cavalry) made the initial assault. Then four companies of 3rd Bn., 21st Inf., 196th LIB, Americal Div., were flown in by helicopter. On the next day, Charlie Company air-assaulted into a hot landing zone. Hit on descent, the helicopters deposited the men for what turned out to be a furious two-day fight.

Some 89 men of the company encountered a much larger North Vietnamese force. The GIs were caught in ambushes as the enemy advanced. They had no idea what they were up against.

Casualties quickly mounted. Pfc. Daniel J. Shea, a medic with C Company who had been in Vietnam for only six weeks, immediately exposed himself to heavy fire. He carried four wounded soldiers to safety. While rescuing a fifth man, Shea was severely wounded. As he neared the perimeter, the Connecticut native was hit again. Shea received a posthumous Medal of Honor.

Recognition 48 Years Later

A fellow medic of C Company performed similar life-saving actions. He was credited with keeping alive 10 platoon members. Pfc. Jim McCloughan was hit in the back with shrapnel from an RPG while dragging two men into a trench line. Yet he stayed

MEDAL OF HONOR

MILITARY TIMES HALL OF VALOR

PFC. DANIEL J. SHEA
(POSTHUMOUS)

FAMILY PHOTO

Pfc. Jim McCloughan saved the lives of 10 men of C Co., 3rd Bn., 21st Inf., over May 13-14, 1969 during the fight for Nui Yon Hill. The secretary of the Army approved his recommended Medal of Honor in December 2016.

on. "I knew they were going to need me," he said. "I wasn't going to leave my men. Nope. I thought that would be my last day on Earth, though." Later, he took an AK-47 bullet to his right arm.

On Dec. 27, 2016, the then-secretary of the Army approved the recommendation for McCloughan's Medal of Honor. "This is not a James McCloughan award, it's an award for my men, for Charlie Company," the former medic told the *Detroit Free Press.* "We had a horrendous battle, a situation you will never forget. ... I wasn't going to leave my men, and they were going to protect me."

Like most genuine heroes, McCloughan remains modest. "There's a lot of people I couldn't save," he told a Michigan TV station. "I'm not a hero. I just did my job. I'm not a hero. There's a bunch of heroes there, a bunch of heroes. You know, any veteran will tell you [who] the real heroes [are], they're not here with us."

When a final tally was taken, C Company had lost 14 KIA and 43 wounded. Of the 14 dead, one had originally been taken prisoner. Spec. 4 Larry D. Aiken was badly wounded and captured. Rescued on July 10, 1969, in the only successful operation of its kind, he died 15 days later in the 91st Evac Hospital in Chu Lai. He had been in a coma from a head wound inflicted by his VC captors.

But Charlie Company's losses were only part of the casualty count. All told, 28 Americans died in the effort to hold and then retake Nui Yon Hill. A Company had two KIA; D Company, one. The 1st Cav Regiment sacrificed eight men—six in C Troop and two from A Troop. And the advisers, mentioned earlier, numbered three dead. Gunfire and shrapnel felled the men about equally. Sixteen were draftees and 12 were volunteers. As was the case throughout the war, they fought side-by-side valiantly. ✪

BY TIM DYHOUSE

'SCREAMING EAGLES' HOLD FIRM AT FIREBASE AIRBORNE

I n the fading light of dusk on May 12, 1969, Pfc. Dan McHugh peered down a steep ridge that marked the nearly impenetrable west side of Firebase Airborne. Almost a mile high, the firebase sat on a long ridge atop Dong Ngai Mountain in the A Shau Valley in Thua Thien province overlooking North Vietnamese Army (NVA) supply routes.

Less than two weeks earlier, U.S. troops had driven the NVA off the mountain in a series of firefights. GIs would learn later while interrogating a captured NVA soldier that the enemy had drawn up plans to overrun Firebase Airborne and kill every American on it.

What McHugh, of C Btry., 2nd Bn., 319th Arty, 101st Abn. Div., most likely witnessed in the early evening of May 12 was NVA troops massing for the attack. He says he saw a flash of light "like a match" on the valley floor and called an officer over for a look. The officer also saw the light and mentioned that no friendly forces were supposed to be down there.

> "It still bugs me. Nothing was done about it, and Capt. [Moulton] Freeman paid for it with his life."
>
> —DAN McHUGH, C BTRY., 2ND BN., 319TH ARTY

"It still bugs me," says McHugh. "Nothing was done about it, and Capt. [Moulton] Freeman [commander of C Battery] paid for it with his life."

'A ROADBLOCK FOR THE ENEMY'

Army engineers had constructed Firebase Airborne in a matter of days after GIs had secured the mountaintop earlier in the month. It occupied a relatively small area, some 82 feet wide by 656 feet long, with steep slopes on the west and northwest sides. A small knoll at the north end rose about 50 to 75 feet higher than the main compound. The northeast, east and south sides of the base had much more gradual slopes.

It was home to some 150 "Screaming Eagles" of the 101st Airborne Division. They comprised two companies, A and E (82 men), from 2nd Bn., 501st Inf. (the

A 101st Airborne Division infantryman watches a Chinook helicopter deliver howitzer ammunition to Firebase Airborne a few days before NVA sappers and infantrymen attacked the base during the early morning hours of May 13, 1969.

After a lethal two-hour sapper attack on May 13, 1969, 101st Airborne Division infantrymen and artillerymen held a small, strategic firebase towering over the enemy's supply routes in the A Shau Valley.

MAY 1969

PHOTO COURTESY MIKE KASID

PHOTO COURTESY MICHAEL HENDRICKS

A 105mm howitzer shows damage on its bottom side from a satchel charge explosion during the attack.

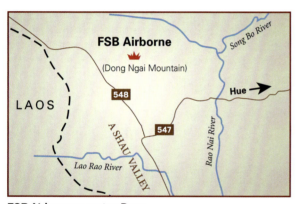

FSB Airborne was atop Dong Ngai Mountain in the "Valley of Death." The valley lived up to its reputation on May 13, 1969, claiming the lives of 27 Americans.

"Geronimos"); elements of B and C batteries from 2nd Bn., 319th Arty; and C Btry., 2nd Bn., 11th Arty.

The artillerymen operated 12 guns—105mm and 155mm howitzers—while the two infantry companies included a mortar platoon.

The June 9, 1969, edition of *The Screaming Eagle,* the 101st's newspaper, described the firebase as "a roadblock for the enemy," hindering the NVA's security and trafficking of its soldiers and supplies.

In response, Companies 3 and 4, 806th Bn., 6th NVA Regt., and the K12 Sapper Battalion (15 cells of 46 men) chose the early morning hours of May 13 to launch what 3rd Brigade commander Col. Joe Conmy would call "the worst result from a sapper attack that I have ever seen."

'CHARLIE WANTED THE 105s'

In the hours before the attack, NVA sappers, or special assault forces, many naked or dressed only in shorts, had silently cut through the concertina wire outlining the north end of the base. They also tied down strikers on trip flares in the wire with strips of bamboo. When the attack started at 3 a.m., many Americans were caught off guard or trying to catch some much-needed sleep.

"We were extremely tired," said Spec. 4 Clark Hunt, an assistant gunner with C Btry., 319th. "And I think the enemy knew that. I'm pretty sure they were watching us the whole time, looking for our weaknesses."

The area first hit was the knoll at the north end of the firebase, where E Company mortarmen manned 12 81mm and several 4.2-inch mortars. An AK-47 burst signaled the all-out attack, followed by rocket-propelled grenade (RPG) and mortar fire, as NVA infantrymen poured through six holes cut by the sappers in the perimeter wire.

"RPG and automatic weapons fire pounded our area," said Spec. 5 Michael J. Kasid, a fire direction controller for E Company. "The sky was filled with incoming green tracers and outgoing red tracers. Bright flashes from the RPGs were everywhere. Charlie wanted the 105mm howitzers [destroyed] and to get them, they had to knock out our mortars."

Pfc. Everett Ross, an ammo handler on Gun #5 with C Btry., 319th, was asleep when the attack started. Upon awakening, he ran toward a bunker. "I was the last one in," he said. "Sappers started tossing satchel charges in the bunker opening, and I took the brunt of one of the blasts."

Ross, who earned the Bronze Star for valor and Purple Heart that day, lost both legs in the explosion. "We did not have enough perimeter guards along the wire," Ross said. "The jungle vegetation was too close to our perimeter, and we didn't have enough concertina wire laid out. We were just another piece of equipment that was expendable."

Pfc. Michael Hendricks, also of C Battery, ran out of his hooch, which was near the 155mm howitzers positioned on higher ground. As he hit the dirt, another satchel charge landed right in front of his face. "I could see the fuse burning down and sizzling," he said. "A calm came over me, but then I heard a voice from God say 'Don't worry, it's not your time.' When the charge did not go off, a peace came over me that I cannot explain."

Hendricks and his sergeant loaded the #1 gun with firecracker rounds—golf ball-sized

"The sky was filled with incoming green tracers and outgoing red tracers. Bright flashes from the RPGs were everywhere."

—SPEC. 5 MICHAEL J. KASID, FIRE DIRECTION CONTROLLER FOR E COMPANY

Some two days after the battle, men are preparing to remove the artillery pieces from FSB Airborne. The 105mm howitzers were located on a lower slope of the firebase, and took the brunt of NVA attack. The 155mm guns were on a level which prevented the enemy from doing more damage.

bomblets that have a blast similar to an M-26 fragmentation grenade. They aimed at the perimeter where the NVA were advancing and began firing. "Someone set up an M-60 machine gun and were firing down the narrow trail leading up to the 155s to keep the sappers from getting to us," Hendricks recalled. With their access blocked, the enemy simply heaved their charges uphill toward the guns.

Besides the howitzers themselves, an initial NVA target was a CONEX container at the base of the knoll that U.S. officers used as a command post and fire-direction center. An RPG round destroyed it in the opening volley, killing all inside, including Capt. Moulton Freeman of C Battery.

Also awakened—and wounded—by the first satchel charge blasts was Pfc. Gary Enderlin of Gun #5. Lying next to Hunt, Enderlin remembers they had only one M-16 for protection.

"I told Clark to lay low while I went to get more ammo," Enderlin said. "On the way, I got shot through the forearm and dropped the gook who shot me."

Returning to the bunker as "RPGs and mortar rounds were flying everywhere," Enderlin says Clark had found a bandoleer with 200 rounds while he was gone.

DISTINGUISHED SERVICE CROSS

**SGT. 1ST CLASS
GEORGE W. PARKER**

"The satchel charges kept us down in our foxholes. If you came out, their infantry troops were waiting to shoot you."

—SGT. 1ST CLASS GEORGE W. PARKER

"Clark's hands were wounded, so he acted as my spotter," Enderlin said. "The gooks were coming up the hill, and we were picking them off. One of them threw a grenade at us, and Clark threw his body over mine. It was a dud, but I think Clark should have received some type of award. He truly went above and beyond."

VALOR ON THE KNOLL

Meanwhile, on the knoll, Sgt. 1st Class George Parker, a platoon sergeant in E Co., 2nd Bn., 501st Inf., and a veteran of WWII and Korea, remembers sappers "running around in g-strings throwing satchel charges" as enemy mortar rounds landed in his position.

"The satchel charges kept us down in our foxholes," he recalled. "If you came out, their infantry troops were waiting to shoot you. If the NVA had been able to gain control of the knoll, they could have shot right down the throats of our troops in the main compound."

As the Americans were pinned down in their bunkers, a steady stream of sappers and other NVA continued to squeeze through the holes in the perimeter wire. After an RPG knocked out one of the U.S. mortar emplacements, Parker, who by now was firing illumination rounds above the battle, ran to the mortar, replaced the weapon and turned it back on the enemy.

"Although a satchel charge thrown at his position momentarily stunned him, he continued his mission, often exposing himself to the enemy barrage to obtain resupplies of ammunition," Parker's Distinguished Service Cross citation noted. "On one of his trips to the munitions stockpile, he was attacked by four sappers armed with satchel charges. He eliminated them with a well-thrown grenade."

Hunt, who earned a Purple Heart at Firebase Airborne, says the illumination flares sporadically lit up the battlefield "like opening and closing your eyes." He adds that he thinks the flares "helped save us. It exposed the enemy and gave us something to shoot at."

Parker's actions helped rally the GIs, and the NVA attack let up somewhat on the north side of the base. But a barrage of some 20-30 RPG rounds signaled a fresh assault on the northeast perimeter. This time the Americans were ready.

"The more than 30 GIs manning the perimeter met the enemy troops with a blizzard of rifle and machine-gun fire," wrote Samuel Zaffiri in *Hamburger Hill*. "The wire was soon filled with dead sappers, and the NVA infantry waiting just outside the jungle retreated."

Rejuvenated, the 101st troopers launched a counterattack to oust the NVA who had taken over bunkers on the north end of the base.

'FIREBASE COVERED WITH DEAD'

All of the 105mm guns were disabled in the initial assault, and its artillerymen were unable to fire a single round in their defense. But several of the 155mm howitzers of C Battery (319th Atry) on the upper level of the base continued blasting away at the enemy during the attack despite receiving constant RPG and mortar fire. Other firebases nearby lent their support, too, and enemy mortars were soon silenced.

BEALLSVILLE'S DUBIOUS DISTINCTION

No town in the nation suffered a greater proportionate loss in the Vietnam War than this Ohio community.

Nestled in the Allegheny Mountain foot-hills is the tiny town of Beallsville, Ohio. Population 450, it is located astride the West Virginia border in rural Monroe County.

Beallsville has a unique and unwanted claim to fame. During the Vietnam War, it sustained the highest per capita deaths of any community in America. The town lost six men, computed at 90 times the national average.

In the spring of 1969, Beallsville made national headlines when Mayor Ben F. Gramlich requested that the four sons of Beallsville then serving in Vietnam be stationed elsewhere. Then-secretary of defense Melvin Laird refused the

KIA – VIETNAM

JACK PITTMAN
JULY 25, 1966

DUANE GREENLEE
AUG 25, 1966

CHARLES SCHNEGG
DEC. 4, 1967

RICHARD RUCKER
MAY 30, 1968

WM. ROBERT LUCAS
MAR 9, 1969

PHILLIP BRANDON
MAR 7, 1971

PHOTO BY LIZ GRAMLICH

request. At that time, the town had already sent 15 of its sons to Vietnam besides the four currently there. Among the four was the mayor's son.

All told, surrounding towns had given 35 men to the draft between 1965 and 1969. Of the six killed, four had been drafted. When Navy corpsman Robert Lucas was killed by a sniper in March

1969, the fifth from Beallsville, townspeople had reached the end of their tether.

A working class community, residents were justifiably bitter about college student exemptions that allowed so many others to escape service while their sons patriotically served. "Beallsville is more hawk than dove," Gramlich told the *New York Times* in 1969. "We just think we have given more than our share."

That May, a flagpole and a wall were erected at the entrance of Beallsville Cemetery in honor of these casualties. In 2004, the wall was rebuilt. Two years later, a marble slab engraved with the names of all six of Beallsville's sons was dedicated along with a walk of honor.

At 4 a.m., an AC-47 gunship (nicknamed Spooky) arrived over the firebase, and during the next hour the battle turned in the Americans' favor. Guided by strobe lights outlining the perimeter, the gunship circled the base, chewing up NVA still trying to get into the firebase. Those caught inside began fleeing toward holes in the wire, with U.S. troops in hot pursuit, killing as many as possible.

"We watched Spooky lay down his rain from the sky and that was awesome," said Lt. Phillip Jordan of B Btry., 319th, who earned the Bronze Star for valor on May 13. "Things got better after that, and I had to sit down because I was physically exhausted. We then made trip after trip bringing the wounded to the landing zone."

By 5:30 a.m., the battle was over. As the sun rose, it revealed a hellish scene.

"The firebase was covered from end-to-end with dead NVA and GIs," according to *Hamburger Hill*. "And everywhere there was debris—rifles, satchel charges and grenades, unexploded RPGs and mortar rounds, powder bags, belts of machine-gun ammo, M-16 magazines and piles of bloody bandages."

A total of 27 GIs were killed—13 from the 501st ("Alpha Avengers" lost 11 from its 1st Platoon and Echo Company, 2) and 14 from C Btry., 319th. Another 61 men were wounded. Shrapnel inflicted 78% of the fatalities; the cause of five deaths was "undefined." Two-thirds of the men were draftees; one-third volunteers.

Of the 113 NVA who directly attacked the base, 39 of their bodies were left behind, and the Americans captured two more (one of whom died).

The battle was over in less than two hours. "It seemed like it lasted three days," McHugh said. "They had orders to take the hill and kill everyone on it."

But the bravery of the Screaming Eagles, aided by some well-timed firepower from the air, saved Firebase Airborne. Its long-range guns would become a coveted asset later in the month in the fight for a nearby mountain, Dong Ap Bia, better known as Hamburger Hill. ✪

> ## "The firebase was covered from end-to-end with dead NVA and GIs."
> —FROM *HAMBURGER HILL* BY SAMUEL ZAFFIRI

THE TOLL

U.S. KIA:
27

U.S. WIA:
61

BY TIM DYHOUSE

BATTLES FLARE IN NORTHERN I CORPS

From the DMZ south to the Da Nang area, enemy activity persisted and the resulting firefights remained vicious in the latter half of this pivotal year.

Army and Marine units engaged in deadly firefights at places like Gio Linh, Phu An, Hill 154, Landing Zone (LZ) Sierra and the vicinity of Firebase Charlie between June and November 1969. Though seldom making headlines, these fights revealed the war's continuing intensity.

Here is a brief look at some of Vietnam's fiercest battles in the latter part of the war's second-deadliest year.

AMBUSH IN LEATHERNECK SQUARE

Late on the night of June 16, members of four companies (H&S, K, L and M) of the 3rd Bn., 3rd Marines, 3rd Marine Div., loaded onto trucks at Dong Ha destined for Gio Linh (one of the points on the rectangular area of operations known as Leatherneck Square), some seven miles northwest. The destination and the fact that they were traveling at night did not give the convoy occupants a secure feeling.

"Every time the Marines went into this area they had always run into trouble and were kicked out," said Jerry Eby, who served as a Navy corpsman with 2nd Plt., M Co. "These were very serious Marines on that truck ride."

After unloading the trucks and resting for a couple hours, the Marines set out on foot around sunrise. At 9:30 a.m. on June 17, an NVA company spread out among three-foot-high hedgerows some 30 yards apart, ambushed and decimated M Company's lead platoon.

"What was left of our point platoon was running and walking back to our position," Eby said. "Some Marines were dazed and had lost their weapons. Some were crying and yelling, 'They're all dead.' Some I had to inject with Thorazine, which is a sedative used to quiet them down and keep them from standing up or wandering away."

Yet courage shined through. 2nd Lt. Bruce Kolter saved the lives of two Marines at the cost of his own, earning the Silver Star. Pfc. Roger Rosenberger was awarded a posthumous Navy Cross. He went to the rescue of pinned down Marines, assaulting the enemy until mortally wounded.

A half-hour later and a little more than a mile south, L Company engaged the enemy in fortified positions on a small hill. Both firefights lasted throughout the morning, until the communists broke contact, leaving 20 dead behind.

At 2 p.m., a mile to the east of L Company's position, an NVA company launched a mortar-supported ground attack against the command post and elements of K Company. The Marines fought off the enemy, killing 37.

Meanwhile, a platoon from L Company on its way to help the command group engaged an NVA platoon in a bunker. As air strikes covered them, the Marines assaulted the position, killing eight.

"In the late afternoon, the firing slowed and then stopped," Eby said. "It was time to get our dead. As we stacked the bodies on the chopper, you could hear the air rushing out of their lungs under the weight."

Air strikes and artillery continued to pound the retreating NVA throughout the rest of the day. The Marines lost 20 KIA and 28 WIA, with half the dead from M Company.

"The Marines told me I did a good job for my first firefight and first day in the bush," Eby said. "But in the back of my mind, I knew I could have done more. I hoped I would not have to go through another day like that."

MARINES HIT HARD AT DMZ POSITIONS

Nearly two months later, the 2nd Bn., 3rd Marines also lost 22 KIA, northwest of LZ Sierra (Hill 461) located along the central portion of the demilitarized zone (DMZ).

Members of D Co., 1st Bn., 7th Marines, board amphibious tractors on their way to "The Arizona Territory"—the An Hoa Basin—in July 1969.

While hunkered down in a night defensive position west of Mutter's Ridge in the early morning hours of Aug. 10, the battalion's 81mm Mortar Platoon and E Company's 3rd Platoon were attacked by a reinforced company from the NVA 9th Regiment. Flinging satchel charges, throwing grenades and firing AK-47s, the enemy burst through a portion of the perimeter.

The Marines fought back viciously and drove the enemy out of their lines by sunrise, killing 17 NVA within the perimeter. In addition to their KIAs, 58 Marines were WIA.

About the same time a half-mile to the southwest, other NVA 9th Regiment troops attacked E Company's 1st Platoon. Artillery, air strikes and the Marines on the ground killed 19 NVA, while 1st Platoon lost six KIA and 17 wounded.

The pre-dawn attacks claimed 24 Leatherneck lives, including two from the 1st Battalion's Alpha Company. Overall, the 2nd Battalion's Echo Company (including four attached from H&S Company) suffered the greatest loss with 17 KIA. Six of the total KIAs received posthumous Silver Stars. This was the heaviest loss for Marines in the DMZ in some five months.

TWO-DAY BRAWL IN ARIZONA TERRITORY

Two days later, the 1st Bn., 7th Marines, 1st Marine Div., found itself thrust into a struggle over two days northeast of An Hoa in the large, broad plain called the An Hoa Basin, otherwise known as "The Arizona Territory."

At 4:15 a.m. on Aug. 12, an ambush squad from B Company and a listening post manned by D Company Marines opened fire on two dozen NVA threatening their location. The ensuing fight claimed the lives of eight men from Bravo.

"They were unable to withdraw to friendly lines, so one squad was directed to bring them back," said Hurbain J. Cote, a squad leader with 2nd Sqd., 2nd Plt., D Co. "Lance Cpl. Cornelius James Cashman, an M-60 machine gunner, accompanied the squad to the listening post. Once there, Cashman remained forward holding off the enemy attackers, firing his machine gun from the hip, killing, wounding and stopping the enemy."

Cote said Cashman, whose mother accepted his posthumous Silver Star 20 years later in 1989, was hit in the groin and died of his wounds. "I can still hear the cries of his pain," Cote said.

Cashman's bravery allowed his fellow Marines to pull back to a four-company (including

THE TOLL

Battle	U.S. KIA
Leatherneck Square	20
LZ Sierra	24
An Hoa	22
Hill 154	25
Cam Lo	15

Northern I Corps was the scene of bitter fighting in the summer and fall of 1969. But much of it never made the headlines back home.

COURTESY BOB DURAND

ABOVE: Gary Porterfield, Bob Durand and Jeff Provenzono.
BELOW: Bob Durand's squad of L Co., 3rd Bn., 3rd Marines. L Company lost 16 men on Hill 154 on Sept. 17, 1969.

A and C companies) night defensive position with each company on a separate hill. U.S. artillery prevented the enemy from massing against any one company during the rest of the night.

In the morning, battalion commander Lt. Col. John A. Dowd ordered C Company to track down the NVA. The Marines found them in a bunker complex near Phu An. At 1:30 p.m., D Company joined the fight, which lasted for several hours. The NVA who were not killed fled their bunkers. Nine Marines died in the firefight, two-thirds from Delta Company.

The next day, Aug. 13, aided by L Co., 3/7 Marines, and I Co., 3/5 Marines, the Americans engaged the enemy again around noon near Tan My (1). The battle lasted seven hours with only yards separating the two sides. Four Marines from I Company, along with Dowd, were killed. Lance Cpl. James A. Norris was among them. He earned a posthumous Navy Cross, as did Dowd.

"After adjusting fixed-wing air strikes and artillery fire on the enemy positions, Lt. Col. Dowd—who seemed to be completely without fear—was moving to an advantageous location from which to control the movement of his forces when he was mortally wounded by hostile machine-gun fire," read Dowd's citation.

1st Bn., 7th Marines lost a total of 17 men KIA over the two days of fighting, with B and D companies being hit the hardest. Including the five from 3/5, the total count was 22 Marines.

'THEY RIDDLED HIM WITH AK-47 FIRE'

The next month at the night defensive position at the base of Hill 154, northwest of The Rockpile below the DMZ, a reinforced NVA company attacked L Co., 3rd Bn., 3rd Marines, with rocket-propelled grenades, small arms and grenades shortly after midnight.

Around 2 a.m., on Sept. 17, according to Lance Cpl. Bob Durand of 3rd Platoon, a large explosion erupted some 30 yards to his right as he manned a fighting hole.

"Sappers had thrown a satchel charge almost right on top of one of our fighting holes," Durand said. "That was when our perimeter was breached. The NVA soldiers rushed in and took over one or two of our fighting holes."

Durand said the NVA started yelling "Corpsman, up!" Not knowing it was a trap, Hospitalman 3rd Class Scott Smith ran to help. Durand noted "they riddled him with AK-47 fire." Durand said he counted at least 15 entry wounds on Smith's dead body.

The two-hour fight was vicious, with L Company (including men attached from 1st Plt., B Co., 3rd Eng. Bn.) losing 16 Marines and Navy corpsmen KIA. Durand believes that most of the casualties were from 1st and 2nd platoons.

1st Lt. James P. Rigoulot reported that the battle area was littered with pieces of enemy weapons and body parts. "One machine-gun hole had 13 gooks stacked up in front of it," Rigoulot said. "That gun probably saved us from being overrun, they were right on us. The area was literally infested with them."

When I Co., 3rd Bn., 4th Marines arrived to set up a blocking force five miles southeast of Lang Cam, it took nine KIA and 25 WIA.

FORGOTTEN ON MUTTER'S RIDGE

In the summer of 1969, the Marines launched *Operation Idaho Canyon,* a series of offensive sweeps in northern Quang Tri province along the DMZ. Central to this operation was Mutter's Ridge, part of the Nui Cay Tre Ridge featuring Hills 461, 484 (Nui Cay Tre) and 400.

The name of the ridge was derived from the call sign of the commanding officer of the 3rd Bn., 4th Marines, which had fought a fierce battle there in the fall of 1966. Taking the ridge back then garnered significant media coverage.

Because the ridge controlled a key North Vietnamese Army (NVA) infiltration route from North to South, its possession was highly prized. Consequently, the 304th NVA Division, especially its 1st Regiment and 3rd Bn., 9th Regt., made repeated attempts to retake it in August and September 1969.

Like so many other battles waged in Vietnam after Hamburger Hill that May, the press and public paid little attention. Domestic cultural events seemed to take precedence now, captivating many Americans. Whether those events were rock concerts or deadly crime sprees.

Donald Elliott, who was on Hill 484 on Aug. 10, captured this sentiment when he said: "Although 24 Marines were killed and 58 wounded, they received little publicity. It happened at the time Charles Manson [instructed his followers] to kill those [nine] people [in California that summer] and the press thought that was more important to report than the Marines who had died in Vietnam on Mutter's Ridge."

NAVY CROSS

LT. COL. JOHN A. DOWD (POSTHUMOUS)

LANCE CPL. JAMES A. NORRIS (POSTHUMOUS)

PFC. ROGER D. ROSENBERGER (POSTHUMOUS)

NVA DETERMINED TO HOLD AT ALL COSTS

Some two months later, two Army battalions from the 5th Mechanized Infantry Division's 1st Brigade took on the NVA about four miles south of the DMZ near Cam Lo and southwest of Firebase Charlie 2.

Part of *Operation Fulton Square,* the battle started at 4:30 a.m. on Nov. 11, when Task Force 1-61 (A, B and C companies and the Scout Platoon of 1st Bn., 61st Inf., and D Co., 1st Bn., 11th Inf.) made contact with a reinforced battalion of the 27th NVA Regiment.

Fighting back with M-79 grenade launchers, small arms and Claymore mines, the Americans drove the estimated enemy platoon away.

Within three hours, however, elements of both battalions were in hot pursuit of a larger enemy force, which later broke off contact. "The battlefield had stretched for two kilometers [1.24 miles] and yielded 18 NVA KIA and two POWs (prisoners of war)," according to the after-action report.

The next day, Nov. 12, a helicopter monitoring a firefight was shot down. When a platoon went to help, it was "hit on all four sides by intense small-arms fire." Meanwhile, other platoons became engaged to the east.

A large force of NVA was dug into bunkers and bomb shelters, and U.S. commanders believed the enemy "was determined to hold the ground at all costs." Units air-assaulted into the area of operations were stopped cold, and command posts took direct fire.

As night approached, the Americans formed two night defensive positions. 1st Platoon of C/1/61 was still trapped in a draw despite several attempts to reach it throughout the day. "Every man in the platoon had been wounded at least once and three could not walk," the after-action report noted. Shortly after midnight on Nov. 13, seven volunteers crawled 800 yards through the enemy bunker complex to rescue 1st Platoon.

In the meantime, U.S. commanders correctly predicted that the NVA would launch an all-out sapper attack. "The enemy ground attack began at 3:30 a.m. with hand grenades, satchel charges, small-arms fire and automatic weapons from the north, northwest and west sides of the perimeter," reveals the post-battle report. After a stout six-hour defense, all enemy contact ceased. While this engagement forestalled an attack on the resettlement village of Cam Lo, it came at a price. GIs sustained 15 KIA: 10 men in the 61st Infantry and five from the 11th Infantry's Delta Company. ✪

NATIONAL GUARD'S DEADLIEST DAYS IN VIETNAM

BY RICHARD K. KOLB

The two National Guard artillery battalions that served in Vietnam in 1969 experienced the deadliest single-action losses of the war for citizen-soldier units. The homecoming for these casualties caused an outpouring of public emotion in Bardstown, Ky., and Manchester, N.H.

Infusion was the byword when it came to the National Guard during the Vietnam War. It was a policy designed to prevent too many men from the same hometown from dying in a single action from the same unit. However, in two instances, it was unable to avert fate.

The Army National Guard's single deadliest actions of the Vietnam War came in the summer of 1969. On June 19, C Battery, 2nd Battalion, 138th Field Artillery (Kentucky National Guard), was stationed at Firebase Tomahawk.

Perched atop a saddle-shaped hill astride Highway 1, 19 miles southeast of Hue, it was a prime enemy target. "This is a terrible place to be," recalled one officer when he first saw it. Besides the 70-man artillery battery—90% of whom originally hailed from the Bardstown area of Kentucky—the firebase was manned by the 18-man 1st Platoon of C Co., 2nd Bn., 501st Inf., 101st Abn. Div.

At 1:30 a.m., the 72nd Sapper Company of the North Vietnamese Army's (NVA) 4th Regiment attacked, quickly breaching the perimeter. "During the first 15 or 20 minutes, I didn't think we were gonna make it," Ronnie Hibbs remembered. It would be a tough night indeed for the citizen-soldiers.

"Seems like we fought for hours and hours," Reuben Simpson said, "but it really wasn't that long. When I went out at first light, I was amazed at what little was left. The whole hill was just about gone."

An estimated 150 enemy rocket-propelled grenades and satchel charges had destroyed three howitzers (and disabled one), an ammo storage area, nine bunkers, the mess hall, the dining tent, a maintenance area, four ammo carriers and three jeeps.

Of the 10 artillerymen killed, five were actually active-duty soldiers infused into the Kentucky battery. Of the 14 total

KIA, four died from gunfire, three from shrapnel and five succumbed to burns (three between June 23 and July 6). Four of the Guardsmen called Bardstown home; the other was from Carrollton. A total of 37 Guardsmen were wounded. The 101st platoon lost four KIA and 13 WIA.

Some 18 NVA sapper bodies were counted after base defenders repulsed the attack, including hand-to-hand combat.

Though Bardstown, population then 5,000, is sometimes referred to as suffering the highest per capita loss of the war (its surrounding area sustained 17 killed), that dubious distinction actually belongs to Beallsville, Ohio. With only 450 residents, it sacrificed six of its sons. (See page 325.)

Of Battery C's original 117 members, 85 were married. It enlisted seven sets of brothers, plus many cousins. Their fallen comrades, as well as other area residents killed, are honored by two monuments on the town's Courthouse Square.

"Bardstown would become a symbol of how deep into America the war had reached, and few, if any, communities in this land felt the impact of the war as did the people here," wrote Jim Wilson, author of *The Sons of Bardstown: 25 Years of Vietnam in an American Town.*

Manchester Mourns

Far to the northeast in New Hampshire, the 94,000 people of this mid-sized city may have taken exception to that statement. Manchester was home base to the 3rd Battalion, 197th Artillery (New Hampshire National Guard).

The battalion sent 506 soldiers to Vietnam, 80% of whom were married. Many of the men were of French-Canadian descent who attended the same schools and churches. Some lived on the same streets in the same West Side neighbor-

KENTUCKY

The five Kentucky National Guardsmen killed on June 19, 1969, at Firebase Tomahawk were 1st Sgt. Luther M. Chappel, Spec. 4 David B. Collins, Staff Sgt. James T. Moore, Spec. 4 Joseph R. McIlvoy and Spec. 4 Ronald E. Simpson.

NEW HAMPSHIRE

*Ranks include posthumous promotions.

Five New Hampshire National Guardsmen were killed on Aug. 26, 1969, when their vehicle hit a land mine. They were Sgt. Gaetan J. Beaudoin, Sgt. Guy A. Blanchette, Staff Sgt. Richard E. Genest, Sgt. 1st Class Richard P. Raymond and Sgt. Roger E. Robichaud.

hood. Some were not even U.S. citizens.

Once in Vietnam, 70% were "infused," or dispersed to regular Army units. No matter where they were stationed, actions on the homefront were felt keenly. CWO Albert Lahaie of Service Battery wrote in a letter published in the *Manchester Union Leader:* "We feel that the publicity at home has been focused so intensely on those who have not accepted their duty that by accepting ours, we have been forgotten."

On Aug. 26, five men of A Battery were on their way to regroup in Long Binh before heading home. About 32 miles from Saigon, their vehicle hit a 40-pound land mine on Highway 13, known as "Thunder Road."

"They were within sight of Lai Khe Base Camp," said Joe Comroe. "I was there and witnessed the explosion which blew the 5-ton truck they were riding in nearly 100 feet in the air."

When the men's bodies were returned home, 2,000 mourners turned out. The five flag-draped coffins were too much for family members to bear. (Four of the five were married.) "The moans and sobs of relatives were heard above the silence," according to the *New Hampshire Sunday News.* City officials called it the "saddest place, the saddest day in the city's history."

Veterans of the 197th have held various anniversary reunions. The deaths of those fellow unit members are never far from their thoughts. As Roy Hughes said, "Part of all of us is in those cemeteries in Manchester—and always will be." ✪

GLIMPSE OF GUARD IN VIETNAM

About 9,000 Army National Guard soldiers served in Vietnam as mobilized unit members, individual volunteers or reassignees. Some 97 members of the Guard (including nine airmen) died in Vietnam: 80 hostile and 17 non-hostile.

Eight intact Army NG units were sent to Vietnam, including the two artillery battalions mentioned and the 116th Combat Engineer Battalion (Idaho ARNG).

The only National Guard infantry unit in-country was Indiana's D Company (Ranger), 151st Infantry. Operating out of a base near Long Binh, D Company's 172 Guardsmen (plus 32 regulars) carried out long-range recon patrols. It suffered two KIA and 100 WIA during its 1969 tour.

A study done by National Guard historian John Listman shows that the Kansas National Guard lost the most men in Vietnam. Of its 30-era dead, 28 were killed and two died in training accidents stateside. Twenty of the dead were from the 137th Infantry.

The 133rd Infantry (Iowa) was next with 12 KIA, followed by the 299th Infantry (Hawaii) with 10 KIA. But keep in mind that all these Guardsmen died as individuals assigned to regular Army units in Vietnam.

An officer who volunteered from a Guard unit was posthumously awarded the Distinguished Service Cross: Lt. Harold L. McNeil, KIA, Aug. 12, 1964.

BY RICHARD K. KOLB   *OPERATION MONTGOMERY RENDEZVOUS*

TAKING HILL 996 AGAINST ALL ODDS

When three 101st Airborne Division infantry companies took
the communists head-on July 11, 1969, it went unnoticed and
was quickly forgotten in the press of "greater" events.

"No one will ever know what happened
here," Sgt. Gregory Denton, who
was killed 17 days later, said in the
aftermath of the battle for yet another
nondescript hilltop in Vietnam.
Nearly fifty years later, this fight
remained virtually unknown to all except those who
waged it. It is not even mentioned in such detailed
works as the *Vietnam Battle Chronology* or *Where We
Were in Vietnam*.

Mid-1969 heralded the second phase of the war for
U.S. ground troops. July was an especially pivotal
month. On July 7, with much fanfare, a battalion of
the 9th Infantry Division departed Saigon, signaling
the phased withdrawal of GIs from the war zone.
And in the wake of the adverse publicity surrounding
Hamburger Hill, the U.S. Army was ordered to avoid
headline-making battles.

In this instance, it succeeded masterfully. To be
sure, events conspired to conceal combat deemed
better left buried. Nine days after, this battle was
completely overshadowed by the Moon Landing.
Receiving virtually no media coverage, by then it was
already history. This would be the case, in the public
mind and much of the news media, for most of the
fighting over the next nine months.

ATTACKING WITHOUT FIRE SUPPORT

The reality on the ground, of course, was entirely
different. *Operation Montgomery Rendezvous* was
an obscure search and destroy mission designed
to rid the A Shau Valley of the North Vietnamese
Army (NVA), and perhaps thwart an enemy summer
offensive. The valley was the haunt of the 6th
Regiment; 6th Bn., 29th Regt.; and 9th Bn., 803rd
Regt.

Hill 996 was located in the A Shau Valley about
5½ miles southwest of A Luoi village in Thu Thien
province of I Corps. It also was 2½ miles southwest of
the by now much-maligned Hamburger Hill. In fact,
over perhaps eight hours on July 11, the U.S. units
involved lost about as many men as on any single day
of the 10-day struggle for Ap Bia Mountain.

Delta and Bravo companies of 1st Bn., 506th Inf.,
101st Abn. Div., backed by C Co., 2nd Bn., 506th
Inf., tackled Hill 996, in the same fashion as the
May action. It would be a direct assault, a tactic that
was supposed to be no longer employed. Besides the
"Currahees" (the unit's nickname), the Aero-Rifle
Platoon of the 2nd Sqdn., 17th Cavalry, participated.

When the rifle companies of the 506th saddled up
that morning, they faced terrible conditions. Very
steep and heavily vegetated, the hill was blanketed
by a heavy rain. To make matters worse, there was no

Infantrymen of the 101st Airborne Division prepare to move out in the A Shau Valley after being resupplied on June 14, 1969, during *Operation Apache Snow.* **A month later, three companies from the 1st and 2nd Bns., 506th Inf., fought on the valley's Hill 996.**

artillery preparation on the hill. Nor was artillery support, gunships or aerial rocket artillery provided to the advancing grunts.

"The NVA had the manpower, the terrain and the tactics," remembered Delta Company medic Richard "Doc" Daniels. "We had the firepower and the mobility—but not on this day." Moreover, he continued: "The early loss of our radio communications was unexpected and devastating."

That occurred because two battalion radio-telephone operators (RTOs) were killed and their radios destroyed. When Delta lost contact with one of its platoons, RTO Spec. 4 George H. Fry took the bull by the horns. About 12:30 p.m., he climbed a nearby ridge to communicate. Alone and unprotected, he held his ground relaying messages until mortally wounded. Fry received the Silver Star.

Delta Company was lured into an ambush with the bull's-eye in the middle of a U-shaped complex of NVA bunkers. Lt. Col. Arnold Hayward, battalion commander, led from the front. He, his headquarters group and Delta's 1st Platoon were caught in a saddle. Hit by intense fire from hillside bunkers concentrated on their flanks, they also had to contend with NVA coming up behind them.

Lt. Leonard Griffin, the artillery forward observer for D Company, was standing next to Hayward and his RTO, Cpl. Curtiss Fernhoff. "Suddenly, a burst of fire from an AK-47 hit the three of us," he recalled. "I was hit in the back of my left shoulder, breaking my upper arm

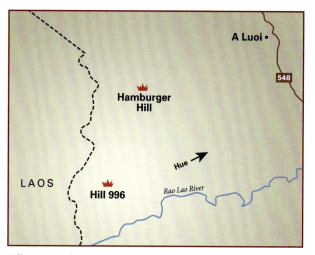

Hill 996 was located in the detested A Shau Valley of Thu Thien province in I Corps. It was 5½ miles southwest of A Luoi village. Throughout the latter part to the war, the valley was hotly contested, especially by the 101st Airborne Division.

with the bullet lodging in the joint." As Hayward and Fernhoff lay wounded next to him, he played dead. "Several hours later, the NVA came through, killing the unarmed wounded, and killed both Hayward and his RTO," Griffin said.

HEROISM UNRECOGNIZED BUT REMEMBERED

Delta remained in dire straits, but many men rose to the occasion. Claudie Fowler, age 25 with a wife and son, had plenty to lose yet he didn't hesitate to expose himself to enemy fire to rescue wounded. The camaraderie he inspired was typical of men in a tight-knit combat unit. Many attested to his selflessness.

"He died while performing one of the most heroic acts I ever saw," said Bill Farnie. "After helping 'Doc' Daniels move a badly wounded man to cover, he tried to reach another man who was wounded and stranded alone and get him to cover also." Salvador Gonzalez was in the 4th Platoon: "Claudie died helping others so they may live. That last courageous act cost Claudie his own life."

Brian Rapp, a machine gunner in 3rd Platoon, remembered: "I was severely wounded, my assistant machine gunner was knocked unconscious, and both of us were unable to move. Somehow, through the intense gunfire and grenades, Claudie got to me and pulled me down the hill to our medic and cover. If our country never honored him, it should have for he was a true hero." As is so often the case, Fowler was not awarded a medal for his bravery, according to public records.

SILVER STAR

SPEC. 4
GEORGE H. FRY
(POSTHUMOUS)

SOME OF THE 506th's KIAs

SGT. NORMAN H. BLOOMFIELD

PFC. MARK L. BRUNER

CPL. THOMAS P. FENUSH

CPL. CURTISS FERNHOFF

PFC. ALAN G. GEISSINGER

LT. COL. ARNOLD C. HAYWARD

PFC. BRADLEY W. KLUKAS

STAFF SGT. BYRON D. STEWART

KILLING: 'AN UGLY PART OF WAR'

At 6 p.m., Bravo Company moved up the hill to assist Delta. Among those infantrymen was Pfc. Gordon R. Roberts. He had enlisted at 17 only three days after graduating from high school. Nicknamed "Bird Dog" in Vietnam, he weighed only 123 pounds and stood 5 feet, 9 inches tall. Roberts was in-country three months by the time the battle occurred.

"The situation with my sister company seemed to be getting worse and worse," he said in a 2014 interview. "We got the order to air assault an unguarded ridgeline about a click, or one kilometer away. I was on point at the time, the four guys behind me were hit."

When his platoon became pinned down, Roberts charged ahead and silenced a two-man bunker. "There really wasn't any alternative to hitting that bunker," he recalled. Strapped with 600 rounds of ammo and six to 10 grenades, he continued his one-man assault on a second bunker, taking it out. Then he destroyed a third bunker with hand grenades. Although cut off from his platoon, Roberts assaulted yet a fourth enemy emplacement. Fighting through to elements of D Company, he assisted it in moving wounded men under fire to an evacuation area.

After taking a bunker, "you get adjusted," he told *The Cincinnati Enquirer* in 1997. "I really thought I was finished after the first one. You think it's the end of something." The last few bunkers contained three or four NVA per emplacement. "No one enjoys the thought of having to cause harm to anyone," he said. "But it's a factor of war that you don't want to live with. I felt like I was just doing my job. I was doing what I was taught to do. Closing with the enemy and destroying them. It just happens to be an ugly part of war."

Still, Roberts maintained a sense of humor. When asked how he was able to miraculously escape being wounded that day, he remarked, referring to his slight build, "I'd turn sideways and made the shot a little more difficult."

Roberts received the Medal of Honor in 1971 for protecting his fellow soldiers. In 2015, his image was among those that appeared on the commemorative postage stamps honoring Vietnam War Medal of Honor recipients.

'NO ONE GAVE UP, WE TOOK THE HILL'

Twenty men were KIA and 26 WIA on Hill 996. Fourteen of the KIA were from 1st Battalion and six from the 2nd Battalion's Charlie Company. Delta took the greatest hit, losing seven men. Headquarters Company had five—two RTOs, two medics and the colonel—and Bravo two. Gunfire and shrapnel claimed their lives about evenly. Draftees accounted for 13 (65%) of the fatalities; volunteers, seven (35%). This was reflective of the composition of an average line company in 1969.

It was a "very long and complex ordeal," Daniels, the medic, said, but "no one gave up, we took the hill." Because of the political climate then, recognition of his unit's accomplishment was not forthcoming. "Contrary to the stories circulating through America of U.S. soldiers in Vietnam being unwilling to fight, these men fought and did it against all odds," he stressed. "Nothing was ever mentioned about their sacrifices."

Despite the fact that U.S. policy and goals had clearly changed, that the war had entered a new phase, the vast majority of men were steadfast in their commitment to one another and to upholding their units' collective respect in the field.

Roberts' motivation for serving was not untypical. "The citizen-soldier concept was very strong" in Lebanon, Ohio, where he grew up, he said, "a very patriotic community, typical rural, southern Ohio." The passage of time did not dim that sentiment. "At the time the country was at war, and there were no second thoughts about your job as a citizen to serve," he said. Roberts understood fully the consequences of that service: "The amount of pain that you go through when you lose someone as close as a brother or more, it just defies description." ✪

MEDAL OF HONOR

CONGRESSIONAL MEDAL OF HONOR SOCIETY

PFC. GORDON R. ROBERTS

THE TOLL

U.S. KIA:
20

U.S. WIA:
26

LZ BECKY: A 'MOST INTENSE STAND-OFF'

BY RICHARD K. KOLB

The early mornings of Aug. 11–12, 1969, proved the mettle of a 1st Cavalry Division artillery battery and infantry battalion in the face of two full-blown sapper attacks.

"An eight-week 'lull' was shattered throughout the First Team's AO [area of operations] on August 12," J.D. Coleman wrote in *Air Cav.* "LZ [Landing Zone] Becky was the scene of what was perhaps the fiercest fighting."

When *Operation Kentucky Cougar*—essentially interdiction to back the South Vietnamese—was launched in the summer of 1969, the 2nd Bn., 8th Cav, 1st Cav Div., was sent to interdict the "Mustang Trail" and establish a base of operations. The base would exist for a mere three weeks, and be abandoned immediately after the attack.

Fire support for the 2nd Battalion was provided by the 155mm howitzers of a three-gun platoon (46 men) of A Btry., 1st Bn., 30th Artillery. Their nickname was "Hard Chargers." Also on hand was A Btry., 2nd Bn., 19th Arty (105mm Towed).

LZ Becky was positioned 2.5 miles from the village of Bo Tuc in Tay Ninh province, War Zone C, III Corps. At the closest point, it was only 4.3 miles from the Cambodian border. That area formed the lower tip of the Angel's Wing. It was called that because it was a wing-shaped border feature just north of the Parrot's Beak.

This was too close for comfort for the North Vietnamese Army (NVA) sheltered in its safe haven across the border. Dan Gillotti, historian for the 30th Artillery, explained why. "The NVA hated and feared the 155mm howitzers," he said. "They were wreaking havoc along the NVA's infiltration routes from their sanctuaries in Cambodia." This alone sealed Becky's fate as a prime target of Communist sappers.

'Glow of a Massed Firefight'

"The night was an unusually black one," wrote Donald Shacklette, a vet of B Battery who served two months after the fight, in a brief account. "The moon was in its dark phase on Aug. 11 and the sky was overcast. Visibility was less than 12 meters [13 yards] and the troopers of 2/8 Cav manning the bunkers could barely make out the first string of wire.

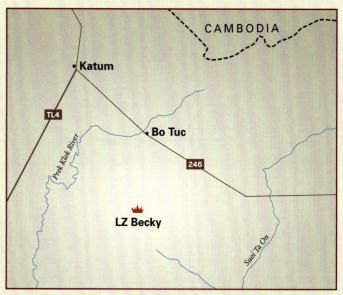

LZ Becky was situated only about four miles from the Cambodian border. With its 155mm howitzers, it invited Communist attack. The NVA saw the big guns as a direct threat to their sanctuaries. Some 22 GIs died in the Aug. 11–12, 1969, sapper attacks.

"It was a night that was made to order for the sappers assigned to the 95C Regiment. The barefoot sappers had only made their way through the outer string of wire when they were spotted." Orders had prevented the use of illumination flares, according to one vet.

Beginning at 3 a.m., 60mm and 82mm mortar rounds as well as rocket-propelled grenades (RPGs), smashed into the LZ. The ground assault by an NVA sapper company came next. It was all over in less than an hour. Seventeen sappers lay dead outside the wire. But six 8th Cav men lost their lives, too. Seven artillerymen also were wounded.

Almost exactly 24 hours later, at 4:10 a.m. on Aug. 12, the NVA struck again. Some 400 mortar and rocket rounds "repeatedly riveted holes in the surface of the LZ." Once the barrage destroyed an artillery ammo storage area, the sappers came from the north. "In the next 40 minutes, the landing zone was silhouetted with the flashing glow of a massed fire fight," is how Coleman described it.

Pfc. E. Tayloe Wise was with Blackfoot Platoon of Bravo Company. "As long as I live, I will never forget the obliteration of LZ Becky," he wrote in his memoir, *Eleven Bravo*. "It was 3:30 a.m. ... The world caved in, and the ensuing fury, which Charlie unleashed, was terrifying in its intensity.

"Exploding enemy mortar rounds were pelting almost every square foot of the LZ," he remembered. "Incoming rockets exploded everywhere, digging out five-foot craters in the landscape ... How any of us managed to survive is remarkable."

The NVA withdrew by daybreak, losing more than 100 men in an attempt to breach the perimeter. The American expense in stage two of the assault, however, was more costly. It claimed the lives of 16 GIs. The two attacks combined killed 22 of the LZ defenders and wounded 39. Shrapnel from exploding mortar and rocket rounds claimed

PHOTO COURTESY DAN GILLOTTI/WWW.HARDCHARGERS.COM

The three 155mm howitzers of the 30th Artillery were eventually knocked out of action. Nine "redlegs" perished in the carnage of LZ Becky on Aug. 12, 1969.

three-fourths of the men's lives.

All told, the 8th Cav had 13 KIA, seven of whom were in Echo Company. The 30th's A Battery counted nine KIA and 19 of the total wounded.

Among the "Hard Chargers" killed was Staff Sgt. Sam Abrams. Scheduled to go home in two days, he came in with the replacements. He insisted on going out to the LZ to be with his men. As chief of section, #3 Gun, he would be awarded a posthumous Silver Star for his courage. Likewise, Staff Sgt. George Snyder and Capt. Donald White inspired their men, keeping them engaged at the expense of their own lives.

Wise wrote that 750 NVA were reportedly poised for a mass attack, but that it was foiled by a "Mad Minute"—placing heavy fire around a defensive position at night to discourage enemy attacks. "We were damn proud of ourselves after this hell because we had survived—we had done our job," he wrote. Wise added, "I was proud to be a member of the First Team and to have served in it. It was a hell of an outfit, with a lot of fine individuals."

Much of that survival was owed to "Puff the Magic Dragon"—a C-47 armed with Vulcan machine guns mounted in the cargo doors—and Cobra gunships that tore into enemy ranks.

A gunship pilot flying overhead and providing support at LZ Becky later remarked: "It was the most intense stand-off attack on a fire base I've seen since the Cav moved to War Zone C."

SOME OF THE KIAs

STAFF SGT. SAMUEL ABRAMS, JR.

PFC. GREG A. BARKER

SPEC. 5 JEREMIAH M. HAYES

PFC. GARY L. HOSKINS

CAPT. DONALD H. WHITE

CPL. RICHARD J. ZISKO

THE TOLL

U.S. KIA: 22

U.S. WIA: 39

BY KEITH W. NOLAN

HIEP DUC: DEATH VALLEY

On July 30, 1969, President Richard Nixon visited Vietnam and instructed Gen. Creighton Abrams to avoid further American casualties in offensive operations. "Vietnamization"—the policy of turning the fighting over to the South Vietnamese Army—was officially announced that month. Earlier, on July 7, the first large U.S. infantry unit was withdrawn from the war zone.

It was now a whole new war—the third and final phase for the Americans. Abrams discontinued the former policy of applying "maximum pressure" on the enemy, replacing it with one of "protective reaction" for troops threatened with attack. It was fast becoming a war of "surprise firing devices," or booby traps. Once withdrawal began, it created an entirely different mindset for the fighting men left in its wake. The goal was no longer military victory. The effects on morale were predictable.

Yet the infantrymen on the ground persevered. In many ways, the grunts of the summer of 1969 were the same man-children who took Iwo Jima. The courage was the same, but it was a vastly different war they were fighting. They were proud, but they were products of their times. They just wanted to survive. And draftees performed no differently than volunteers.

After the war, Gen. Fred C. Weyand, successor to Abrams as U.S. commander in Vietnam, wrote: "Vietnam was a reaffirmation of the peculiar relationship between the American Army and the American people. The American Army really is a people's army in the sense that it belongs to the American people who take a jealous and proprietary interest in its involvement." Of course, these words were written when the draft theoretically affected every household in the land.

"When the Army is committed the American people are committed," Weyand continued, "when the American people lose their commitment it is futile to try to keep the Army committed." In short, GIs in Vietnam reflected the attitudes of the society they so loyally served.

Despite public pronouncements, however, the war's "protective reaction" phase did not begin immediately. Soldiers and Marines committed to the battle for Hiep Duc in August 1969 were in a fight for their lives.

While their counterculture contemporaries communed at the Woodstock "Festival of Life" Aug. 15-18, 1969, the soldiers and Marines at Hiep Duc were beginning an unforgettable struggle culminating in the loss of some 109 of their lives. But the media spotlight shined not on GIs' genuine sacrifices, but on the Woodstock goers.

For 13 days in late August 1969, men of the 196th Light Infantry Brigade and 7th Marines waged a life-and-death struggle centering on the resettlement village of Hiep Duc in the Que Son Mountains. It ranks among the war's deadliest battles, yet its participants have received scant public recognition.

AUGUST 1969

A machine-gun crew from G Co., 2nd Bn., 7th Marines, opens up on a fleeing enemy force during several days of fierce fighting east of Hiep Duc, August 1969.

PHOTO COURTESY CHARLES FINKBEINER

FSB West was built on Hill 445, dominating the southeast end of Hiep Duc Valley and overlooking the Song Chang River.

INTO THE VALLEY OF DEATH

Hiep Duc was located at the junction of the Song Lau and Song Tranh rivers. The village of 4,000 inhabitants with dirt streets and tin-roofed houses was the site of a resettlement center. It quickly became the focus of the Americans, who vowed to protect it, and the North Vietnamese Army (NVA) and Viet Cong (VC), which promised to destroy it.

"Hiep Duc village is one of those strange little nowhere places that suddenly finds itself in the limelight of the war," wrote an Army correspondent in *Stars and Stripes*. The Communist thrust to destroy Saigon's model pacification program ultimately failed, degenerating into an attempt to inflict maximum casualties on U.S. forces.

It was a battle that would envelop battalions from four regiments—1st, 21st, 31st and 46th—of the 196th Light Infantry Brigade, as well as two battalions of the 7th Marines. In addition, batteries from the 3rd Bn., 82nd Artillery, provided invaluable fire support from four firebases. Hiep Duc tested the mettle of all these men like few fights before or after.

Facing them were 1,500 Communist troops of the 3rd Regiment of the 2nd NVA Division and 1st Viet Cong Main Force Regiment.

On Aug. 17, at the French Hooch near An Lam (3), seven men of D Co., 4th Bn., 31st Inf., were KIA, initiating the grueling battle.

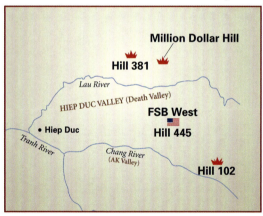

The fighting in Hiep Duc Valley was fierce during the last two weeks of August 1969. Men of the 196th LIB and 7th Marines displayed tenacity and courage.

On Aug. 18, an enemy force threatened the refugee center and D and B companies of 4th Bn., 31st Inf., based at LZ West, moved to help. LZ West sat atop Hill 445 (Nui Liet Kieh or the "Mountain of Black Leeches") about 5½ miles to the east. It overlooked Hiep Duc Valley ("Death Valley") to the north and the Song Chang River Valley ("AK Valley") to the south. Ambushed in AK Valley along the way, B and C companies lost seven KIA and 48 WIA.

The next day, the NVA shot down a UH-1D Huey of the 71st Assault Helicopter Company over Hill 102 inside NVA-occupied territory near An Lam (3), seven miles east of Hiep Duc. All eight GIs aboard (four crewmembers and four men of HHC, 3-21st) plus freelance photographer Oliver Noonan were killed. Casualties continued to mount for the 21st Infantry on the 20th when eight men of its A and B companies died in combat near the village of Thon Mot (4).

'GROUND TROOPS WERE SURROUNDED'

Retired Lt. Col. Robert Robeson was a co-pilot with the 236th Medical Detachment (Helicopter Ambulance) based at LZ Baldy. His crew flew 42 missions from Aug. 20-22, evacuating more than 150 wounded Americans from the Que Son Valley with two birds shot up.

Among the wounded was Pfc. Rocky Bleier, an M-79 grenadier with 1st Plt., C Co., 4th Bn., 31st Inf., who was hit Aug. 20, on "Million Dollar Hill" (Hill 102) just east of Hiep Duc. His platoon's mission that day was to recover bodies left behind by B Company.

Bleier would go on to win four Super Bowls with the Pittsburgh Steelers from 1974-80, but on that day, he was merely trying to survive the oppressive heat as he humped a 50-lb. rucksack, 60 grenades and other gear.

Bleier was wounded around 10:15 a.m., when his 25-man platoon walked into a 1st VC Regiment ambush. He was hit again about 3:10 p.m., and was airlifted out by Robeson's helicopter around 2 a.m. "Although I played a small part in the overall scheme of things, I am proud to have served there," Bleier said years later.

Robeson recalled, "We didn't know who we were carrying that night and it didn't matter. They were wounded Americans and it was our job to get them out of there. On a mission you never knew whose life you would be stepping into or who would be stepping into yours."

Robeson added that 15 of the missions—including the last on Aug. 22—were "insecure," meaning they had no gunship support.

"The ground troops were surrounded, low on ammunition and couldn't give us any covering fire," he said. "After our medic, Spec. 5 John Seebeth, was hit, the NVA shot out three of our four radios."

Aug. 22 also cost the lives of five men of 2nd Platoon of Alpha Company in the assault around Hill 202.

MARINES ENTER THE FIGHT

By now, the Army needed help and called on the Marines to relieve some of the pressure applied by the NVA. The 2nd Bn., 7th Marines, based at LZ Baldy some 35 miles north of Chu Lai, answered the call.

Marching west in more than 100-degree heat through Hiep Duc Valley, the battalion's F, G and H companies and command element zeroed in on Hill 381 just north of LZ West. The Army believed that NVA command posts of the units they were engaging were dug in along the hill.

Their first contact with the enemy came at around 11:00 p.m. on Aug. 22 when they ambushed an NVA party scouting their lines. The next afternoon, as the Marines struggled through head-high, razor-edged elephant grass, NVA snipers opened fire.

Soon, four Marines of Golf Company fell dead, and repeated attempts to retrieve their bodies failed. Napalm and bombs from U.S. aircraft and artillery from surrounding bases pounded the area, stripping the dense vegetation from a knoll where snipers hid. With little resistance, G and H companies took the knoll by noon on Aug. 24.

ONE BATTLE TOO MANY

Meanwhile, at about that same time, an incident occurred on Million Dollar Hill near Hiep Duc that garnered headlines, albeit sensationalized, around the world.

That day, Lt. Col. Robert Bacon, commander of 3rd Bn., 21st Inf., ordered weary GIs from A Company to retrieve the bodies still amid the wreckage of the helicopter shot down on Aug. 19. After five days of fighting, A Company was worn down. And though it was correctly assumed that the enemy had vacated bunkers defending the area, the surviving grunts were in no mood to press their luck.

So when A Company commander Lt. Eugene Shurtz asked his men what the delay was in getting moving, five told him they wanted more reinforcements.

Years later, Bacon said: "We were lucky to marshal one battalion's worth of artillery to support us. We operated in the Song Chang with no roads—and literally no reserves ... given areas to operate in that were two to three times greater than we could possibly clear."

One of the soldiers who supposedly balked at the mission refuted accusations advanced by journalists Horst Faas and Peter Arnett in a *New York Times* article. "We never at any time said we wouldn't go down the hill," Spec. 4 John Curtis told the *Pittsburgh Press* on Sept. 2, 1969. "When Lt. Shurtz gave us a direct order, we started moving."

Never mind that similar incidents had occurred numerous times during the "glory days" of WWII and Korea. Only a few understood that the young men in Alpha were simply soldiers in a company that had seen one battle too many.

Bacon, in a February 2006 letter to *Vietnam* magazine, wrote: "In spite of our dire

Pfc. Rocky Bleier was wounded in the thigh, and then again by a grenade on Aug. 20 on Million Dollar Hill. He recovered from his wounds and later became a running back for the Pittsburgh Steelers, leading the team to four Super Bowl wins.

"After our medic, Spec. 5 John Seebeth, was hit, the NVA shot out three of our four radios."

—ROBERT ROBESON, 236TH MEDICAL DETACHMENT

MEDAL OF HONOR

LANCE CPL. JOSE FRANCISCO JIMENEZ
(POSTHUMOUS)

Recovering Jimenez's body was a daunting prospect for his fellow Marines. Seven men initially volunteered for the task. Six were killed and nine more volunteers were wounded in the process.

situation, the soldiers fought extremely bravely. They fought on; to imply anything else is deceitful. I am so proud of them."

Also on Aug. 24, 2nd Plt., C Co., 4th Bn., 31st Inf., recovered the bodies of soldiers killed in the Aug. 18 ambush. In a letter home, platoon commander 2nd Lt. William Robinson noted how the task—amid a firefight—had a devastating effect on his men's morale. "The bodies were heavy and the smell sickening," he recalled. "I don't think I'll ever forget it."

Less than two miles to the east, on Aug. 25, 2nd Bn., 7th Marines lost 12 KIA and 60 WIA. The trouble started as F, G and H companies began to move west along the Song Lau River toward Hiep Duc. Around 1 p.m., elements of the 1st VC Regiment ambushed H Company. As the other two Marine companies came to help, they too were pinned down. The firefight lasted some eight hours.

On the 26th, mortar fire on the 2/7 command post killed four men of E and F companies. When their patrol was ambushed, two Marines of E Company and an attached two-man forward observer team from H Btry., 3rd Bn., 11th Marines (Artillery) died.

The next day, five GIs from C Co. and one from D Co., 4th Bn., 31st Inf., were killed in a matter of seconds near Million Dollar Hill when their platoon was hit by NVA machine-gun and small-arms fire. After nine days of combat, C Company was only able to muster 48 men. The following day it was ordered back to LZ West. On Aug. 28, Bravo Company lost four men assaulting a bunker.

Meanwhile, B and D companies from 1st Bn., 46th Inf., had been deemed no longer combat-effective. (However, records show no KIAs for the 46th during this battle.) Within days, the two companies were airlifted to LZ Professional.

MARINE HEROISM SHINES

On Aug. 27, 2-7 Marines largely left the Hiep Duc Valley and were replaced by I, K, L and M companies from 3rd Bn., 7th Marines. At 5 a.m. on Aug. 28, 3-7 Marines pushed out to complete the final link-up with 4th Bn., 31st Inf., that would essentially end the battle. But before they did, the Marines had to clear the enemy from Hill 381.

Lance Cpl. Bill Rolke, an M-79 grenadier with 2nd Sqd., 3rd Plt., K Co., remembers passing his fellow Marines from 2-7 as they trudged out of the valley.

"Most of the guys had bandages on their faces, arms and legs," he said. "They were literally walking wounded. They told us, 'we've never seen anything as bad as this.' It was a real creepy feeling walking into that valley."

NVA snipers and mortar rounds opened up on Rolke and his fellow Marines as they attempted to go up Hill 381.

"We ran out of body bags and had to use ponchos," Rolke said.

Rolke's fellow Marines from L Company encountered a harrowing sight as they advanced up Hill 381. They discovered the bodies of seven Vietnamese civilians lying side-by-side riddled with bullets, all shot in the head execution-style. There was an old man, a husband and wife, three children and a baby.

The Marines believed it to be the work of the NVA as revenge or a warning that the NVA withdrawal was only temporary. One Marine said he was revolted at the enemy's cruelty.

At 2 p.m., 2nd Plt., K Co., 3rd Bn., 7th Marines, received orders to take out an NVA 12.7mm anti-aircraft gun that was shooting at Marine F-4 Phantom jets supporting the grunts. As they advanced up Hill 381, the platoon had to hit the ground in shoulder-high elephant grass as the gun zeroed in on them.

Lance Cpl. Jose Francisco Jimenez "reacted by seizing the initiative and plunging forward toward the enemy positions," according to his Medal of Honor citation. In a matter of moments, Jimenez killed six enemy soldiers and silenced the machine gun. Seconds later, an AK-47 round hit him in the head, killing him instantly.

Recovering Jimenez's body was a daunting prospect for his fellow Marines. Seven men initially volunteered for the task. Six were killed and nine more volunteers were wounded in the process. Pfc. Dennis D. Davis and Cpl. Clarence H. St. Clair, Jr., each received a posthumous Navy Cross. Lt. Richard L. Jaehne also earned the Navy Cross. Lance Cpl. Johnny S. Bosser and Pfc. Edward A. Sherrod were posthumously awarded Silver Stars.

K Company's bravery was remarkable. Rifleman Davis raced across open terrain while severely wounded, taking out a machine gun before he died. Squad leader St. Clair crawled under intense cross fire, destroying a Communist emplacement while in pain before being mortally wounded. 2nd Lt. Jaehne crawled through a rice paddy to destroy a machine-gun nest, using his pistol to kill the last enemy gunner.

All told, 14 Leathernecks of K, L and M companies died that day—the worst single toll of the battle for the Marines.

By the end of the 29th of August, the Marines with three more KIA had basically finished their battle. The most intense combat had ended for the Army the day before. It was time now to assess the toll in lives and limbs.

'A SUCCESSFUL PRE-EMPTIVE BATTLE'

U.S. casualty figures for the Hiep Duc and Song Chang valleys are difficult to precisely ascertain, but it appears the Americal's 4th Bn., 31st Inf., suffered the most. Over 12 days, Aug. 17-28, the battalion lost 38 KIA and 204 WIA. It claimed 406 enemy killed and eight prisoners taken. The battalion, also known as the "Polar Bears," earned a U.S. Presidential Unit Citation for the defense of Hiep Duc and its "decisive defeat" of the enemy.

Meanwhile, the 21st Infantry sustained 23 KIA, the 1st Infantry had three dead, and two artillerymen of C Btry., 1st Bn., 82nd Arty, also were killed.

The 2nd Bn., 7th Marines had 30 KIA and 161 WIA over seven days (Aug. 23-29) of combat. The 3rd Bn., 7th Marines lost 14 KIA and at least 30 WIA, all on Aug. 28. Two forward observers of H Battery died in the fighting.

So a total of 116 Americans (70 soldiers and 46 Marines) were KIA between Aug. 17-29 in the valleys, including the four crewmen aboard the helicopter shot down on Aug. 18. Some 191 Marines were WIA and perhaps 300 Army personnel.

In the end, the Americans prevented the NVA from destroying the Hiep Duc Resettlement Village. Americal Maj. Gen. Lloyd Ramsey called it "a successful pre-emptive battle." But for the grunts on the ground, it was just another brutal battle in a grinding war that would last another three years. ✪

NAVY CROSS

PFC. DENNIS D. DAVIS
(POSTHUMOUS)

CPL. CLARENCE H. ST. CLAIR, JR.
(POSTHUMOUS)

LT. RICHARD L. JAEHNE

THE TOLL

U.S. KIA:
116

U.S. WIA:
491

BRUTAL BATTLES OF VIETNAM
1970

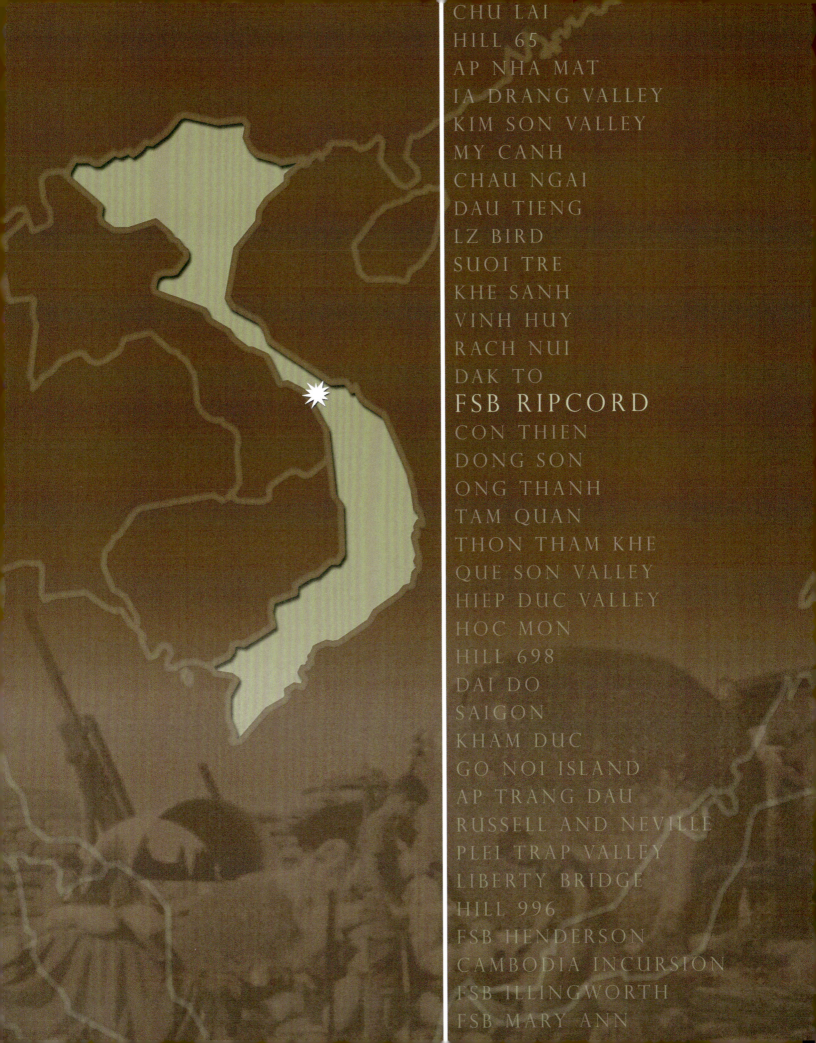

CHU LAI
HILL 65
AP NHA MAT
IA DRANG VALLEY
KIM SON VALLEY
MY CANH
CHAU NGAI
DAU TIENG
LZ BIRD
SUOI TRE
KHE SANH
VINH HUY
RACH NUI
DAK TO
FSB RIPCORD
CON THIEN
DONG SON
ONG THANH
TAM QUAN
THON THAM KHE
QUE SON VALLEY
HIEP DUC VALLEY
HOC MON
HILL 698
DAI DO
SAIGON
KHAM DUC
GO NOI ISLAND
AP TRANG DAU
RUSSELL AND NEVILLE
PLEI TRAP VALLEY
LIBERTY BRIDGE
HILL 996
FSB HENDERSON
CAMBODIA INCURSION
FSB ILLINGWORTH
FSB MARY ANN

BY TIM DYHOUSE

FIREBASE ILLINGWORTH ILLUMINATED IN A 'TITANIC ROAR'

April was the deadliest month of 1970 for U.S. troops in Vietnam with 730 deaths. On the first day alone, North Vietnamese Army (NVA) units shelled some 115 targets throughout the country and launched 13 ground assaults. April 1 turned out to be the single deadliest day of the year when 70 GIs perished.

At the center of that day's carnage stood Fire Support Base (FSB) Illingworth, where 36% of the Americans killed then died in a matter of two hours.

FSB Illingworth was a hastily constructed firebase built in a dry pond bed only five miles from the Cambodian border in Tay Ninh province. Its 219-yard-wide perimeter was protected by Claymore mines dug into a low earthen berm surrounding the base and a few bunkers. No concertina or barbed wire was in place.

One GI described it as a "hot, miserable little place." Another said it was "trouble waiting to happen." It was named for Cpl. John James Illingworth of A Co., 2nd Bn., 8th Cav, 1st Cav Div., who was killed March 14, 1970, near Tay Ninh City.

Defending the base were 215 men from the 1st Cavalry Division and attached units. They included C and E companies of the 2nd Bn., 8th Cav; elements of four field artillery batteries (I of the 29th, A-1-30th, A-2-32nd and B-1-77th) and two Air Defense Artillery batteries (B-5-2nd and D of the 71st). The 2nd Artillery provided dual 40mm anti-aircraft guns ("Dusters") augmented by D Battery's .50-caliber quad machine guns.

FSB Illingworth sat astride heavily trafficked NVA infiltration routes in the middle of an area GIs called the Dog's Head. Patrols disrupted Communist movement, and U.S. commanders were certain the NVA would attack. This would reveal their positions, allowing them to be bombed. Several veterans of the battle have used the word "bait" to describe the reason for the location.

"In the afternoon before the attack we could hear the enemy about a half-mile away in the tree line getting worked up for a fight," said Spec. 4 Ron Curry of A Btry., 1st Bn., 30th FA. "I wondered why we didn't shoot and wipe them out then. We were in enemy territory after all."

Artillerymen Spec. 4 David Mustain, Sgt. Paul V. Long and Spec. 4 Ralph Jones of A Btry., 2nd Bn., 32nd FA, clean a self-propelled 8-inch howitzer nicknamed "Aquarius" that was blown on its side during the battle April 1, 1970, at Fire Support Base Illingworth. This and another identical gun were positioned at Illingworth 10 days before.

A makeshift firebase close to the Cambodian border lured the NVA into an attack on April 1, 1970. Companies of the 8th Cav, 1st Cav Division, as well as parts of six field artillery batteries, persevered but the American victory came at a steep cost.

APRIL 1970

PHOTO COURTESY JOHN AHEARN

Survivors of the attack in the early hours of April 1, 1970, gather after the intense combat that claimed 25 Americans and wounded 54.

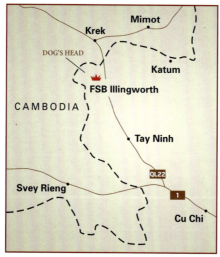

FSB Illingworth was located just five miles from the Cambodian border in the area referred to as the Dog's Head.

Anticipating an assault, Illingworth was reinforced on March 21 with two self-propelled 8-inch howitzers from A Btry., 2nd Bn., 32nd FA, and tons of ammunition for the big guns.

"From the first day on, we wanted to dig our ammo pits using our 8-inch howitzers as spades," said Ralph Jones of A Battery. "We were ordered not to, thereby allowing the enemy to view our ammo from the jungle line."

The decision to leave the ammo stacked above ground would have devastating consequences for the men at Illingworth.

'ALMOST IMAGINARY, LIKE A MOVIE'

At 2:18 a.m. on April 1, the first of 300 NVA mortar, rocket and recoilless rifle rounds began exploding in a 20-minute barrage inside Illingworth's perimeter.

The 32nd's Fire Direction Center (FDC) took a direct hit, killing three off-shift radiomen sleeping nearby. Likewise, the 77th's FDC was hit several times; that unit lost seven KIA.

"I directed over 1,000 rounds of artillery fire plus several air strikes and dozens of gunships," recalled then-Capt. John Ahearn, artillery liaison officer of the 1st Bn., 77th Arty, and fire coordinator for the 2nd Bn., 8th Cav. "Two things in particular stand out in my mind: that everyone was on 100% alert thus preventing us from being overrun and the courage of Cobra helicopter pilot Capt. Joe Hogg, who made possible communication from Illingworth during the desperate times of the battle."

Immediately thereafter, some 400 soldiers from the 272nd Main Force Regiment of the 9th VC/NVA Division charged the wire in a full frontal assault. They emerged like "ghosts through a mist," as a GI who was among only 77 infantrymen on the perimeter recalled.

"The dust was so dense you couldn't see 55 yards in front of you," said Sgt. Keith McKissick of Gun Sec. 241, 3rd Plt., I Btry., 29th FA, who earned a Silver Star. Still, combat was so close that the enemy was clearly visible. "Very rarely do you see the man who is trying to kill you," McKissick explained.

As the first wave of communists rushed the earthen wall, Spec. 4 Peter Lemon of Recon Plt., E Co., 2nd Bn., 8th Cav, moved to assist M-60 machine gunner Lou Vaca at the berm. The thick dust, Lemon says, caused Vaca's gun to jam and also obscured the onrushing NVA troops until they were only 50 feet from the Americans. "They were 40 or 50 across, wave after wave of them," said Lemon. "It was almost imaginary, like a movie, with all the dust and the flares."

Lemon was able to kill five NVA with his M-16 until it, too, malfunctioned. He then began throwing grenades at the attackers. Meanwhile, he says Vaca, who was trying to repair the machine gun, was shot three times in the stomach. Lemon describes the 18-20 men of Recon Platoon as "professional soldiers" who kept their nerve during the chaos.

"We knew we were going to get hit, and as they were coming at us, we were blowing off a lot of the Claymores," said the Medal of Honor recipient. "We were pretty calm. But I equate it to a prize fight. By the time the 10th round comes around and your opponent is still swinging, you say to yourself, 'This guy is pretty tough.'"

Lemon killed four more NVA advancing on the machine-gun position and then carried Vaca to the battalion aid station. Lemon was wounded a second time returning to Vaca's machine gun, where he found a group of NVA attempting to turn the gun on the Americans.

He drove them off with more grenades and killed an NVA soldier at the gun. Lemon repaired it and "placed effective fire upon the enemy," according to his Medal of Honor citation. Wounded a third time, he eventually collapsed from his wounds and exhaustion.

Two of Lemon's fellow E Company soldiers earned posthumous Distinguished Service Crosses during the firefight. Spec. 4 Casey O. Waller and Spec. 4 Brent Anthony Street tossed hand grenades at the enemy after their weapons jammed because of the overwhelming dust.

Both Street and Waller refused to withdraw when their grenade supply ran out and they resorted to hand-to-hand combat. Waller was killed by exploding ammunition and Street was eventually killed by a mortar round.

George Hobson, CO of Charlie Company, recalled the role of Silver Star recipient 1st Lt. Gregory Peters. "We were quite alone behind one of the 8-inch howitzers while directing

MEDAL OF HONOR

SPEC. 4 PETER C. LEMON

"They were 40 or 50 across, wave after wave of them."

—SPEC. 4 PETER C. LEMON

The morning light revealed the extent of the battle damage from the attack.

our combined efforts," he said. "When he lost his rifle, I gave him mine, and started throwing grenades while he used the rifle."

'THE EARTH SEEMED TO FAIL US'

The 8-inch howitzer crewmen, armed with M-16s, joined the infantrymen at the perimeter to fend off the waves of attackers. As Col. Morris J. Brady said, artillerymen "ignored the full fury of the NVA's fire to answer it with their own." Behind them, the stacks of howitzer ammo loomed ominously.

"I had never seen so many enemy in the open," said Spec. 4 Richard Whittier, a platoon radioman. "It is my profound belief that Illingworth wasn't overrun because these people stayed, probably in the knowledge of certain death and knowing that the 8-inch ammo dump was about to go up. They held their positions."

Some of the rounds in the initial enemy bombardment ignited crates of 8-inch artillery powder canisters and had spread to the shells themselves. The heat and the exploding canisters drove some of the Americans off the southwest portion of the perimeter.

At 3:18 a.m., a bunker containing about 190 rounds detonated with a tremendous blast, blowing a 20-foot-deep crater and knocking both 8-inch howitzers out of action.

In a "titanic roar," wrote author Keith Nolan, "it turned the whole base upside down." Nearly every defender was knocked flat and many were burned and deafened.

"Suddenly, the earth seemed to fail us," said Sgt. Stephen R. Richards, a squad leader with Mortar Plt., E Co. "[It was] the loudest explosion I have ever heard or felt and appeared to tear through everything on the landing zone. The sky was full of white phosphorus raining down on everything and everybody."

Lt. Col. Mike Conrad, commander of 2nd Battalion, said simply, "I thought the end of the world had come." Conrad received the Silver Star for his actions that day.

EXPLOSION BROKE THE ATTACK

An after-action report noted that the blast was followed by a complete lull of five to 10 minutes "in which everyone, friendly and enemy, attempted to recover from the stunning force of the explosion." As an "impenetrable pall of choking dust" settled, U.S. commanders rushed reinforcements to that portion of the berm—now gone— to resume defensive fire.

"I could hear the sound of the enemy's bullets as they passed my hand when I reached up to drop each mortar round," said Michael H. Russell, E Company's Mortar Platoon leader. "When the ammo went up, everyone went airborne for an instant. There were few complete NVA bodies outside the perimeter, but body parts were scattered everywhere."

"[It was] the loudest explosion I have ever heard or felt and appeared to tear through everything on the landing zone."

—SGT. STEPHEN R. RICHARDS, SQUAD LEADER, MORTAR PLATOON

SILVER STAR

1ST LT. CLEAVELAND F. BRIDGMAN (POSTHUMOUS)

PFC. BILLY P. CARLISLE (POSTHUMOUS)

LT. COL. MICHAEL J. CONRAD

PFC. NATHAN J. MANN (POSTHUMOUS)

PFC. ROGER J. McINERNY, JR. (POSTHUMOUS)

1ST LT. GREGORY J. PETERS

SGT. KEITH McKISSICK

The left flank was demolished and six GIs perished. Most of C Company's casualties were from a Chinook helicopter that had arrived earlier with replacements. At daylight, A Troop, 1st Squadron, 11th Armored Cav, arrived at the base's northeast corner of the clearing, firing its machine guns as it swept the perimeter. Two troopers were KIA.

Though sporadic fighting continued, the explosion "broke the back of the attack" as one GI said. By 5 a.m. the NVA had faded away, leaving 88 bodies behind.

Over three hours, some 3,372 artillery rounds were fired from three bases in support of the defenders.

The artillerymen at FSB Illingworth developed a deep affection for their infantry counterparts, with whom they shared front-line fighting positions.

"The courageous soldiers there fought against overwhelming odds," said Ralph Jones, whose unit, A Battery, earned a Valorous Unit Award for helping hold the perimeter. "All the men at Illingworth did things that went beyond what normal American soldiers are expected to do. We honored them with the Proud Americans Memorial Park in Fort Sill, Okla."

COURAGE APLENTY

A total of 25 Americans were KIA and 54 wounded at FSB Illingworth. Among the dead were 12 infantrymen, 10 artillerymen and two armored cavalrymen. C Company accounted for six KIA, four mortarmen (including the "friendly fire" fatality) died, as well as one member of A Company and two from HQ Company. Of the artillerymen killed, seven were with the 77th and three the 32nd. Virtually all died from shrapnel wounds. The ratio of draftee to volunteer was 60% to 40%. Besides the two posthumous DSCs, nine Silver Stars were awarded to the KIAs.

One other GI died due to "friendly fire." Bobby Barker, scheduled to leave Vietnam on March 31, had come to Illingworth to spend his last night with friends. Because he was leaving, Barker was unarmed and oblivious to the standing order to soldiers inside the FDC to shoot anyone who tried to enter. "Bobby didn't let them know who he was," Richards remembered. "He jumped into the FDC and got 20 rounds. When I saw him he was dead on a gurney."

Richards adds that the artillerymen and infantrymen at Illingworth performed courageously: "If every man on that LZ [landing zone] had not fought with every ounce of their strength, we would all have died."

No doubt about it, believes Russell: "Our success in defending FSB Illingworth was due to the heroic fighting spirit of all the soldiers who were there that night."

It's a sentiment that Lemon shares. "I had the opportunity to be next to some of the finest soldiers in the Army," he said. "Any one of my comrades could have received the award. If not for them, I would not be alive." ✪

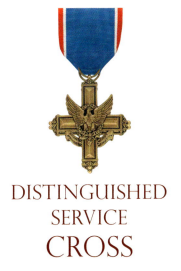

DISTINGUISHED SERVICE CROSS

SPEC. 4 CASEY O. WALLER (POSTHUMOUS)

SPEC. 4 BRENT ANTHONY STREET (POSTHUMOUS)

THE TOLL

U.S. KIA:
25

U.S. WIA:
54

BY CHARLES F. HAWKINS

HELL NIGHT at HENDERSON

The nighttime assault came with little warning. There was no drumroll of artillery to pave the way for teams of black-painted sappers, or give alarm to U.S. and South Vietnamese defenders of this rugged outcrop of mountain in northern I Corps.

Specially trained North Vietnamese Army (NVA) infiltrators, armed only with high-explosive satchel charges, were supported by infantry with rocket-propelled grenades, machine guns and AK-47 assault rifles. At least one Soviet-made flamethrower was part of their arsenal. Backing them up were NVA crews manning mortars and deadly effective recoilless rifles.

With uncanny stealth, the sappers closed within feet of thinly spread GI defensive positions before they were detected. Then they struck violently, breaching the perimeter and turning their attention to high-value targets—the tactical operations center (TOC), 105mm howitzers and a large amount of high-explosive ammunition.

Fire Base Henderson shuddered to the bark and bite of bursting satchel charges. Small-arms fire ripped across the hilltop and tracers stabbed the night sky—red for American, green for the North Vietnamese. Then, "a terrible explosion" roared across the mountaintop. Lt. Jim Knight recalled that "it was so deafening it drowned out all the other sounds of fighting." It was just past 5 a.m.

The great blast was a massive detonation of artillery ammunition. It lit up the pre-dawn sky with a vivid firestorm that consumed friend and foe alike. When it was over, more than a score of American soldiers of the 2nd Bn., 501st Inf. ("Geronimo"), 101st Abn. Div. (Airmobile), lay dead or missing.

Somewhat surprisingly, the story of the action at Henderson was shunted to page 17 by where the nation's largest newspaper had only this to report: "Early this morning [May 6, 1970], Fire Base Henderson, six miles southwest of Cam Lo near the demilitarized zone (DMZ), was attacked and 29 Americans were killed, 31 were wounded and two were reported missing. This was the largest American loss in a single action in more than a year." (These casualty figures were not correct.)

No doubt the events at Henderson were overshadowed by the tragedy at Kent State, and also by allied operations in the Cambodian incursion. Here's what happened

NVA sappers took advantage of the situation at Henderson and left a trail of destruction by targeting artillery pieces and the ammunition dump in a night attack. U.S. troopers fought back during the horrific firestorm, however, killing 29 of the enemy.

In a 45-minute melee at Firebase Henderson during *Operation Texas Star* on May 6, 1970, 25 men of the 101st Airborne Division lost their lives.

MAY 1970

PHOTO BY EDWARD CARLYLE

A wounded Sgt. 1st Class Edward J. Carlyle surveys the damage in the aftermath of the attack on Henderson, May 6, 1970.

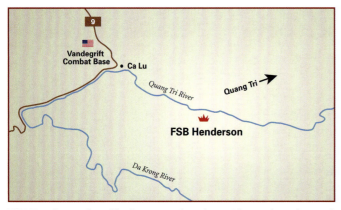

FSB Henderson faced higher ground on three sides and was located about seven miles southeast of Ca Lu.

south of Quang Tri River.

By early 1970, American troop withdrawals from Vietnam began affecting unit strength, including the 101st, although it was scheduled to be the last combat division to leave Vietnam. A full-strength airmobile rifle company could boast almost 140 soldiers, but most were operating at about 65% capacity, with a foxhole strength in the neighborhood of 80-90 infantrymen.

Adding to the challenges facing American commanders was the policy of "Vietnamization"—turning the conduct of the war over to the Army of the Republic of Vietnam (ARVN). This meant two things: first, U.S. troops increasingly assumed defensive postures on and around fire support bases; and second, combined operations of ARVN and U.S. forces were necessary to affect the transition.

Henderson typified the former and was an example of the latter. Of course, there also was the problem posed by the NVA, no small matter in itself.

HENDERSON: THE BUILDUP

In April, the 101st senior command and the 1st ARVN Division decided on a combined operation in the ARVN area of operations to interdict enemy forces moving south across the DMZ. The ARVN would retain tactical control and the 3rd Brigade of the 101st would reopen FSB Henderson to provide for ARVN and U.S. artillery support to ARVN ground units.

In addition to this division operation, brigade commander William Bradley said, "Third Brigade continued defensive missions with three fully committed infantry battalions 20 miles to the south." During the last few days of April, the allied buildup at Henderson began.

U.S. defenders, D Co., 1st Bn., 501st Inf., commanded by Capt. William Whitaker, arrived by helicopter. Whitaker and his men did not stay on Henderson very long, a bit more than a week, but in that time they noted some critical details. The rocky outcrop of mountain was big, larger than Whitaker's company could defend easily. In addition, "there was high ground on three sides," Whitaker remembered. There were also plenty of signs of enemy activity in the area.

Late on May 4, Bradley was ordered to return Whitaker's company to 2nd Brigade for other operations. Taking its place in defense were 84 troopers of A Co., 2nd Bn., 501st Inf., commanded by Capt. Jim Mitchell. The change was to take effect the following day.

Whitaker's outfit numbered about 120 men for field duty, an above-average strength for which he was grateful. By contrast, Mitchell's A Company from the 2nd Battalion was 30% less in strength. Whitaker wondered about the additional combat strength that Mitchell needed for defense.

When they departed Henderson, one of Whitaker's soldiers motioned to the incoming troopers and said, "Sir, they're all wearing new boots," a reference to replacements that Mitchell's company had recently received.

All told, 162 Americans were on the firebase. Among them were men of A and C companies, 2nd Bn., 501st Inf.; B Btry., 2nd Bn., 11th Arty; a squad of B Co., 326th

VALOR AT FSB MAUREEN

ON MAY 7, 1970, the day after Henderson, Pfc. Kenneth Michael Kays distinguished himself while serving as a medic with D Co., 1st. Bn., 506th Inf., 101st Abn. Div., at Fire Support Base Maureen (Hill 980) in the A Shau Valley. NVA sappers and infantry-men assaulted Company D's night defensive position, kill-ing seven members of 2nd Platoon. Kays had been in Vietnam for only two weeks.

Despite intense enemy fire and ground assault, Kays began moving toward the perimeter to assist his fallen buddies. He quickly became the target of concentrated enemy fire and explosive charges, one of which severed the lower portion of his left leg. After applying a tour-niquet to his leg, Kays moved to the fire-swept perimeter, administered medical aid to several wounded, and helped them to safety. In one instance, he used his own body as a shield against enemy fire.

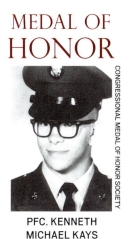

MEDAL OF HONOR

CONGRESSIONAL MEDAL OF HONOR SOCIETY

PFC. KENNETH MICHAEL KAYS

Engineers; a detachment of the 501st Signal Battalion; and a mortar platoon of E Company. The remainder of the 311 allied forces there were ARVN.

'HARD LUCK ALPHA'

Alpha Company had been on standdown to rest and refit after turning back a nighttime sapper attack against Firebase Granite barely a week earlier. The fight had been vicious and Jim Knight's 1st Platoon was in the thick of it. So, too, was Lt. Col. Otis Livingston, the battalion commander. "It was close," said Knight, "and Livingston was right there in a foxhole with the rest of us, firing a rifle at the attacking North Vietnamese." Livingston, years later, said, "I count my blessings every day, and thank God for the loyal and courageous troopers of 2nd Bn., 501st Inf."

Now, Alpha was back on another firebase, but this time it was detached from the 2nd Battalion. Nevertheless, seasoned veterans were prepared for what might lay ahead. Again, Knight's men would find themselves in the midst of heavy fighting.

Late on the afternoon of May 5, 17 reinforcements arrived at Henderson—Lt. Richard Hawley's battalion Reconnaissance Platoon had been summoned to man a critical portion of the perimeter.

Bradley had choppered in to Henderson that afternoon to make his command presence felt, and to ensure officers and men on the ground understood the importance of their defensive mission. Shortly after Bradley departed, a resupply Chinook hovered overhead to set down a sling-load of 105mm howitzer ammunition.

With darkness fast approaching, no one bothered to distribute the howitzer shells, fuses and powder bags under secure revetments. It would prove to be a costly and fatal oversight.

As daylight faded, they did what they could to prepare positions in the sector of the ARVN artillery battery. To their left was Knight's 1st Platoon, and behind them were six 105mm howitzers and a huge stockpile of ammunition.

AFTERMATH

About 5 a.m. on May 6, members of the 33rd NVA Sapper Battalion attacked Henderson from several directions. One assault sliced between Knight's 1st Platoon and Hawley's scouts. One of 1st Platoon's forward positions was cut off. Amazingly, two of the three defenders survived. Others were not so fortunate.

The sappers went for the howitzers and also the ARVN TOC on the hilltop. Medic Spec. 4 Dennis Hughes of B Btry., 2nd Bn., 11th Arty., was asleep alongside one of the wheels of a

Caught between enemy outside the wire and bursting shells behind, [Lt. Richard] Hawley's scouts were consumed by the massive firestorm. Foxholes became death traps.

PHOTO BY EDWARD CARLYLE

A sapper lies dead against a bunker wall with a grenade still clutched in his right hand. Twenty-nine communists were killed in the attack.

155mm howitzer when a satchel charge blew him into the air.

"When I came to my senses, I crawled over to help two guys, one of whom was on fire," he recalled. Despite his own wounds, Hughes tended to others as he moved through a trench system on the hill. His medical bag lost in the initial explosion, he cut strips from his uniform for dressings. Several times, he dashed under fire to pull the wounded to safety. His actions saved several lives, earning him a Silver Star.

High-explosive charges (or possibly the flamethrower) set off some of the artillery shells—sympathetic detonation did the rest. This was the "terrible explosion" that Knight reported.

Caught between enemy outside the wire and bursting shells behind, Hawley's scouts were consumed by the massive firestorm. Foxholes became death traps. Hawley and many of his soldiers died at their posts, or in the wire, preferring to take their chances against the enemy.

1st Sgt. Paul Pennington was one of several from B Battery who came to the aid of the scouts after radio contact went dead. "The first soldier we found was lying in a small bunker on an air mattress with his eyes open, rubbing his stomach," said Pennington. "His right leg was gone. We found another recon guy sprawled dead over a culvert position."

Jim Knight, exposed to murderous fire throughout the attack, was lucky. As the fighting began to wane, Knight spotted enemy soldiers walking away from the firebase. "They were illuminated by flares," he explained, "and were at sling arms, uncaring, as if we were all dead." Well-aimed fire by American riflemen dispelled that notion.

Most of the enemy fell back into the surrounding jungle before daylight, but NVA mortar and recoilless rifle crews kept firing throughout the day. One mortar round exploded as 3rd Brigade operations officer Maj. Tex Turner, and brigade Command Sgt. Maj. Raymond Long were heading for the TOC. The blast instantly killed Long, the last of the 25 Americans to die on Henderson.

E Company (Recon) counted the most fatalities with 10, followed by A Company with eight, HHC three and B Company one. B Battery lost three artillerymen. Draftees (14) and volunteers (11) were almost equal in numbers. Shrapnel accounted for virtually all of the KIA.

The dead included Spec. 4 Michael L. Antle, who was awarded a posthumous Silver Star. He had been in-country less than a month. At least 40 GIs were wounded. The enemy left 29 bodies behind during the 45-minute melee.

At Henderson, the enemy took timely advantage of an awkward situation, a changeover in defenders, and an unfortunate event, the massive explosion of artillery ammo. Nothing, however, can detract from the defenders' courage.

When "Hard Luck Alpha" took to the field again, there were fewer than 40 seasoned hands in its ranks. In the long summer ahead, they would continue to prove their mettle against the NVA. Each May, veterans of Henderson remember those who fell there, brave men who brought honor to themselves and their country. ✪

THE TOLL

U.S. KIA:
25

U.S. WIA:
40

BY AL HEMINGWAY

OPERATION ROCKCRUSHER

'PURE BLITZKRIEG': SACKING NVA SANCTUARIES IN CAMBODIA, 1970

The two–month sanctuary-busting excursion into Cambodia by 30,000 GIs during May and June 1970, may have prompted protest at home, but it ultimately saved American lives in Vietnam.

In his introduction to *Into Cambodia,* the late Keith Nolan, "the grunt's historian," offered it "in honor of those soldiers whom history has generally bypassed. Whereas the Cambodian incursion is remembered for the four dead at Kent State, in Cambodian jungles more forgotten men were dying at Rock Island East, Ph Tnaot, Landing Zone Phillips, Salty's Cache, and along the banks of the Rach Cai Bac."

Yet vets seldom express regrets. "Few who participated in the campaign, whether general or grunt," wrote J.D. Coleman in his 1991 book *Incursion,* "doubted that the decision to cross the border into Cambodia was both wise and just. The American soldiers who had withstood repeated blows from North Vietnamese regular army soldiers and then watched

AP PHOTO

A grunt of the 25th Infantry Division stands up to fire a burst at a nearby sniper position during a helicopter assault into Cambodia, northwest of Tay Ninh, on May 9, 1970.

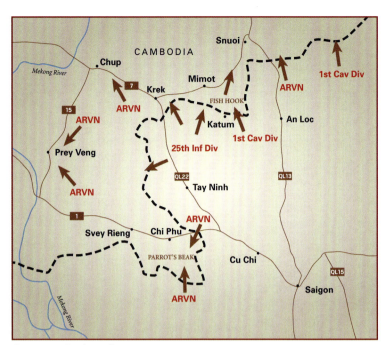

Operation Rockcrusher, the Cambodian incursion, penetrated multiple points along the Vietnamese-Cambodian border aimed at destroying NVA staging areas.

helplessly as they disappeared, wraithlike, into the sanctuaries of Cambodia had few reservations about the morality of the invasion. Even today, 20 years after the fact, former soldiers interviewed for this book were unequivocal when asked whether they would do it again. The answer, invariably, was 'Hell, yes.'"

By the spring of 1970 in South Vietnam, U.S. ground forces totaled nearly 385,000. However, many of those units were leaving or preparing to depart the war zone. The key word touted by the Nixon Administration was "Vietnamization," a term coined by Secretary of Defense Melvin Laird. Simply put, it meant turning the war over to the South Vietnamese military forces and stockpiling additional supplies for their future use in their fight against Communist aggression.

To prevent attacks on remaining U.S. troops in South Vietnam, and exert pressure on North Vietnam to enter serious negotiations in Paris, President Richard M. Nixon authorized a secret bombing campaign of Cambodia in 1969.

The aerial raids were designed to strike suspected North Vietnamese Army (NVA) supply depots along the border between the two countries. With the overthrow of Prince Norodom Sihanouk in March 1970 by Gen. Lon Nol, a supporter of the U.S., Nixon decided on a "limited" incursion into Cambodia to destroy the 14 major enemy bases there and the 50,000 NVA they harbored.

On hearing of the strike, many GIs were eager. For Warrant Officer Geoffrey Boehm, a 1st Cav Division helicopter pilot, it was a chance to avenge fallen buddies: "We had lost many men in combat assaults near the Cambodian border while the gooks would go back into Cambodia, sit there and laugh at us, so we were all together for going in."

Sgt. Michael Hackbarth, of H Trp., 2nd Sqdn., 11th ACR, who "had enlisted as a personal protest against the campus demonstrations" back in Wisconsin, said, "We agreed that finally we were doing something positive… There was a lot of elation… We were all happy."

For Scott Gauthier, a medic, the incursion "was going to make the war that much shorter."

TOTAL VICTORY

The Cambodia campaign is sometimes referred to by its codename, *Operation Rockcrusher,* even though it encompassed 10 distinct operations.

On April 29, 1970, *Operation Toan Thang #43,* meaning "Total Victory" in Vietnamese, was launched. Elements of the ARVN (Army of the Republic of South Vietnam) III and IV Corps initiated the cross-border attacks. Some 48,000 ARVN troops, accompanied by 100 U.S. advisers, ultimately streamed into Cambodia in an area dubbed the Parrot's Beak along Route 1.

Simultaneously, the 1st Cavalry Division, along with the 1st ARVN Airborne Division, entered the Fish Hook, a known NVA/VC (Viet Cong) supply and staging area. A senior U.S. officer told a reporter, "This Cambodian operation is pure blitzkrieg, like something from a World War II Panzer division's book of tactics."

In addition to destroying the supply depots, the two units were ordered to locate and eliminate Central Office for South Vietnam (COSVN) enemy fighters. COSVN numbered approximately 8,100 personnel who coordinated military affairs for all VC forces in South Vietnam.

Brig. Gen. Robert H. Shoemaker, 1st Cav Division deputy commander, headed the task force named after him. It also included elements of other units poised to enter Cambodia:

Spec. 4 Pete Zmitrovich, B Btry., 5th Bn., 42nd Arty, 23rd Arty Grp, 2nd Field Force, examines a captured weapons cache of 82mm mortars and 75mm recoilless rifles on May 16, 1970. The invasion of Cambodia netted the largest enemy arms caches of the Vietnam War.

the 4th, 9th and 25th Infantry divisions, 199th Light Infantry Brigade (LIB) and the 11th Armored Cavalry Regiment.

A total of 50,659 Americans ultimately participated in the campaign on both sides of the border, with 19,300 the peak inside of Cambodia. The 1st Cavalry Division committed the most troops—7,401—to the operation.

According to the plan, U.S. troops would penetrate the Fish Hook from the east, west and south while ARVN paratroopers would be heli-lifted into landing zones north of the area of operations. By doing this, the NVA/VC escape routes would be sealed off as the ARVNs proceeded south to link up with the Americans. Speed and surprise were critical to a successful operation.

On May 6, additional ARVN units poured across the Cambodian border at the Dog's Face, just north of the Parrot's Beak; northeast of the Fish Hook; and, just north of the city of Phouc Binh. Several days later other ARVN troops drove into the country along the Mekong River.

The ARVNs felt that securing the Parrot's Beak and the Fish Hook would drive the communists farther away from South Vietnam's III and IV Corps. Both of these tactical zones were strategically important to the South Vietnamese.

Numerous supply depots were uncovered, and tons of materiel was destroyed. Unfortunately, a slow start to the assault alerted the communists, who quickly fled deeper into the jungles of Cambodia to avoid battle. GIs would encounter the same problem.

Conditions in the field were harsh. "We are filthy, have various rashes and skin diseases, and other infections from the environment," wrote 1st Lt. Charles Giasson of HHC, 2nd Bn., 22nd Mech. Inf., 25th Div. "This is war, someone has to muck it out, fight, and suffer. Now I know what it is really like."

ARMS CACHES GALORE

As the ARVNs pushed deeper into Cambodia, *Task Force Shoemaker* was busy as well. At dawn on May 1, the assault began. Artillery lobbed nearly 2,500 rounds while fighter aircraft and the massive B-52s delivered the much-needed aerial support. Taken by surprise, the communists opted to run instead of fight. Helicopter gunships pounded enemy positions while NVA troops rapidly fled the allied juggernaut of tanks and armored personnel carriers (APCs).

PHOTO BY TIM DUBE

GIs of 2nd Plt., C Co., 2nd Bn., 5th Cav, 1st Cav Div., at LZ X-Ray in May 1970. Front Row: Roger Kiddy and Gary "Goldie" Howell. Standing: Platoon leader Richard Ferguson, Roger Lewis, Thomas "Peabody" Grover, David Resendez, Larry Fox, Tim Dube, Mike Combs and Capt. (Chaplain) Robert T. Comesky.

CONFISCATED ITEMS FROM "THE CITY," THE 7th NVA DIVISION'S SUPPLY DEPOT

1,282 individual weapons

202 crew-served weapons

2.2 million rounds of ammunition

58,000 pounds of plastic explosives

22 cases of anti-personnel mines

38 tons of rice and corn

While flying a treetop-level reconnaissance mission on May 2, Warrant Officer James Cyrus of B Trp., 1st Sqdn., 9th Air Cav, 1st Cav Div., made an important discovery. Spotting "well-camouflaged hooches, a bamboo-matted walkway, complete with street signs and rope banisters," he quickly marked it on his map. It turned out to be the huge supply depot of the 7th NVA Division dubbed "the City."

Charlie and Delta companies from the 1st Bn., 5th Cav, moved into the area to secure the valuable find. Accompanied by an NVA prisoner, the soldiers discovered 171 tons of enemy munitions, including: 1,282 individual weapons, 202 crew-served weapons, 2.2 million rounds of ammunition, 58,000 pounds of plastic explosives, 22 cases of anti-personnel mines and 38 tons of rice and corn. Also, 300 vehicles were found, including a Porsche and a Mercedes-Benz sports car. And that was just the beginning.

Though the general pattern was retreat, the NVA made a stand at Snuol between May 4-5. After two days of incessant bombardment, the 2nd and 3rd squadrons of the 11th ACR entered the town to find it reduced to rubble.

Fighting raged elsewhere, too. On May 5, six men of B Co., 2nd Bn., 47th Inf., 9th Div., were killed when their APC hit a mine, exploding ordnance aboard.

Next day, the second and third assault waves struck inside Cambodia, lasting between eight and 10 days. Units of the U.S. 25th Division went in under *Total Victory #44,* and 4th Division elements had as their banner *Binh Tay*—"Tame the West" in the Se Son Valley.

On May 7, troopers from D Co., 2nd Bn., 12th Cav, fought a bitter engagement with NVA regulars, costing the U.S. seven KIA and 20 WIA. In the end, the soldiers captured a massive supply area called "Rock Island East," named after an arsenal in Illinois.

The grunts unearthed 326 tons of ammunition and supplies, 932 individual weapons, 85 crew-served weapons, 469 122mm rockets, 4,002 B-40 rocket-propelled grenades, 20,886 mortar and recoilless rifle rounds, more than 7 million small-arms and machine-gun rounds, 1,734 hand grenades, three trucks and three jeeps.

Engineers of B Co., 588th Bn., 79th Eng. Grp., kept Highway 4 open to assure a free flow of all the captured booty. Indeed, engineers deserve credit for their overall role in Cambodia.

DYING ON BOTH SIDES OF BORDER

On May 10, the single deadliest American firefight of the invasion was fought. The 3rd Bn., 506th Inf., 101st Abn. Div., replaced a 4th Division battalion during Cambodia. Inserted into the Prek Drang base camp area, its B Company engaged in a pitched battle, fighting off two NVA companies. At the cost of eight KIA and 28 WIA, the men killed 47 enemy soldiers.

Dubbed the "Mother's Day Ambush," the company's 2nd Platoon took nearly 100% casualties in the battle that began at 3:15 p.m. Spec. 4 Richard Rios, a machine gunner, described what happened next in *Twelve Days in May,* written by Jerald Berry.

"My squad was the lead element of 2nd Platoon when we walked smack dab into a full enemy ambush," he recalled. "NVA regulars were in the trees, behind trees, underground, and on top of the ground. When we hit the ambush, all hell broke loose. We had to call in artillery on top of us to keep from being overrun. The 105 rounds were detonating at treetop level and shrapnel flew all over us, as well as the enemy. The NVA were that close to us. I had been in firefights before, but not this big, as long, or intense."

A Medal of Honor and two posthumous Silver Stars were awarded for heroism in this fight. Spec. 4 Leslie Sabo, an M-60 man, did not receive his posthumous medal until 2012. Repeatedly attacking and killing NVA, he took time to shield a wounded GI even after being wounded himself by a grenade. Then hit by small-arms fire and bleeding profusely, Sabo still stepped into the open to shoot an NVA firing at a medevac helicopter. While reloading ammo, he was killed.

"I went into Cambodia," said Don Balducci, "where we fought with the 4th Infantry Division and I am proud to have been part of the 506th's distinguished history. We were known as the 'Stand Alone' or 'Bastard' Battalion." The battalion's nickname was the Currahees—Cherokee for "We Stand Alone."

The only U.S. infantry battalion to go into the Parrot's Beak, where some of the heaviest combat of the invasion occurred, was the 6th Bn., 31st Inf., 3rd Bde. (Sep), 9th Inf. Div. It engaged the enemy at Chantrea and Ph Tnaot in the second week of May. For their screening operation, the Polar Bears earned the Valorous Unit Award (the equivalent of the Silver Star for an individual) and two unit members were awarded the Distinguished Service Cross (DSC).

Back in Vietnam, GIs also were dying in support of the operation. The 4th Division ferried troops from Pleiku to its forward base at Plei D'Jereng. When the NVA shot down a helicopter on the slope of Hill 275 on May 7, three crewmembers of the 61st Assault Helicopter Company, along with four grunts from A Co., 1st Bn., 12th Inf., 4th Div., died.

Five days later, May 12, .51-caliber anti-aircraft fire brought down another chopper near Plei Blang Yam on Route 509, killing 10 engineers of the 937th Engineer Group and Engineer Command.

An attack on a night defensive position, also on May 12, near Ph Romeas Hek, Cambodia, claimed the lives of six men of C Co., 1st Bn., 5th Inf., 25th ID. Among them was Spec. 4 Ardie R. Copas, awarded the DSC for his bravery.

Then on May 22, seven members of C Co., 2nd Bn., 22nd Inf., 25th ID, were KIA in a convoy ambush on Route 24 near Ph Ta Am village, Cambodia.

FRUSTRATION AND MORALE

Col. Morris Brady, commanding officer of the 1st Cav Division's artillery, saw the operation as the "answer to a soldier's prayer, as well as the end of long years of frustration and doubt: frustration at allowing a tough enemy, who struck us whenever he could, the advantage of a refuge from the retribution of our arms, and doubt of the leaders and national policy that require us to fight under such terms."

The reasons for the difficulty in maintaining high morale were numerous; an unsupportive

MEDAL OF HONOR

SPEC. 4 LESLIE H. SABO
(POSTHUMOUS)

CONGRESSIONAL MEDAL OF HONOR SOCIETY

AP WIDE WORLD PHOTO

Men of 3rd Sqdn., 4th Cav, 25th Inf. Div., unleash cannon, machine guns and M-16s on the enemy in the Mimot District during the invasion of Cambodia, May 1970.

home front not the least of them. Capt. David Kuter of C Co., 5th Bn., 12th Inf., 199th LIB, came to adopt his men's view of the protest movement: "I can't help but think that they are violent just for the sake of violence and with total disregard of those who are over here."

Keith Nolan captured this sentiment in *Into Cambodia:* "Lt. Pat Forster of the Dreadnaughts was furious that night as they sat reading the *Stars and Stripes* on their cots in their freshly dug position: Kent State dominated the front page. It enraged him that four students killed in what was essentially an accident were becoming martyrs.

"He could not get his mind off the eight GIs blown to pieces the day before, their deaths to be unrecognized and unremembered by all but their families: 'I had infinitely more admiration for the brave NVA we met in the field—not the liars in Hanoi like Le Duc Tho— than for anyone who demonstrated,' " he said.

Meanwhile, in Vietnam, Capt. Chuck Hawkins of the 101st Airborne Division wrote in a letter: "I am quite pleased with Cambodia and quite upset with student unrest at home. None of us here can understand it."

Gen. Creighton Abrams, U.S. commander in Vietnam, said: "They [GIs] have reacted well to attacking the enemy in his secure sanctuaries. American troops always feel better when they are on the offensive. Not only the soldiers, but also the leaders at all levels, have taken the initiative in getting the job done."

DEFENDING FIREBASES

Further into the operation, the NVA launched a series of attacks against the GIs' string of firebases.

At Firebase Brown on May 13, B and C companies of the 5th Bn., 12th Inf., 199th LIB, along with D Btry., 2nd Bn., 40th Arty, took on the NVA for two hours. Beehive rounds obliterated enemy ranks: 59 dead NVA were found in the wire. One "Redcatcher" mortarman was KIA and eight Americans WIA.

Ten days later, May 23, soldiers from the 5th Bn., 7th Cav, 1st Cav Div., and 199th LIB, repulsed the NVA at Hill 428 and made another discovery. Twelve-foot high supply bunkers honeycombed the hill. Tons of weapons, ammunition and food were found. Hill 428 was re-named "Shakey's Hill" in honor of Pfc. Chris Keffalos, who was killed in the original assault.

Tenacity was evident in all units. On June 14, at FSB David, men of the 1st Cav's 13th Signal

Battalion fought off an NVA attack, too. Sgt. Goldsworthy maintained communications throughout the assault, earning the Silver Star. Many of the signalmen were wounded.

On June 26, three days short of leaving Cambodia, three members of K Trp., 3rd Sqdn., 11th ACR, were KIA when the NVA shelled FSB Susan near Kdol Kraom. Two other troopers were KIA in unrelated incidents the same day. That squadron's L Troop was the last U.S. unit to leave Cambodia on June 29.

At their maximum penetration, GIs had advanced 19 miles into Cambodia. Some 30 U.S. gunboats reached 21.7 miles up the Mekong River as far as Neak Luong on May 8 as part of an effort to rescue refugees. U.S. advisers were attached to the South Vietnamese navy in what were called Riverine Assault Interdiction Detachments (Nos. 70-75).

In the largest allied operation in three years, GIs netted the war's biggest arms cache. Nixon called it "the most successful military operation of the entire Vietnam War." But like all offensives, there was a price to pay.

Official Army casualty figures for Americans actually killed and wounded *inside* Cambodia total 284 dead and 2,339 wounded. Broken down by month, the tally is: May—189 killed and 1,376 WIA; June—95 killed and 963 WIA. But if campaign-related casualties incurred in Vietnam are included, the number of deaths jumps to 382 for the two months.

SAVING LIVES

Congress repealed the Gulf of Tonkin Resolution and forced President Nixon to withdraw all U.S. forces from Cambodia by June 30 (ARVN troops remained longer). Nixon's claim that the Cambodian invasion helped save American lives fell on deaf ears at home. But his assertion was validated by the men in the field.

Joseph B. Anderson, Jr., commander of B Co., 2nd Bn., 5th Cav, 1st Cav Div., said, "As a guy who had to live or die by how well the enemy was equipped or fought, there was no doubt in my mind that the correlation was very great between us going into Cambodia and then not taking any more heat from the enemy. We'd wiped out all their supplies and demoralized them so greatly that they were not ready to fight."

Sgt. Paul Hodge, who had fought in Cambodia with B Co., 2nd Bn., 8th Cav, 1st Cav Div., told a *New York Times* correspondent, "I feel it was definitely worthwhile to do it. It kind of made me happy to capture weapons and ammunition that could be used against us."

Sgt. Martin Cacioppo, who entered Cambodia on May 15 with C Co., 4th Bn., 23rd Mech. Inf., 25th Inf. Div., could not understand the demonstrations at home against the incursion: "We had been told by intelligence that there were big enemy troop build-ups in Cambodia and that they could come across the border any time. So we really felt good, if you can describe it that way, about going across the border. I couldn't understand the protests. There were a lot of people who felt that way."

Helicopter pilot Geoffrey Boehm spoke for many of his fellow GIs when he commended the President's Cambodian decision in a letter to his hometown newspaper: "I have personally extracted or witnessed the destruction of thousands of weapons, medical supplies, and tons of rice, along with millions of ammunition rounds … We have definitely placed them [the enemy] in a bind and for every weapon and bullet we destroyed, these can no longer be

Spec. 4 Karl Potter (sitting), takes a break as Lt. Urban Kokenge checks orders in May.

M-60 machine gunner Spec. 4 Stanley Ciesielski and his assistant gunner, Spec. 4 Karl Potter, 3rd Plt., C Co., 2nd Bn., 35th Inf., 4th Inf. Div, take a break during the Cambodian campaign in May 1970. Ciesielski was killed in action a short time later on June 12.

DISTINGUISHED SERVICE CROSS

Bercaw, William E.	May 2	25th Inf. Div.
West, Thomas E.	May 2	1st Cav Div.
Bartley, K. Julius I.	May 6	4th Inf. Div.
Kiger, Dennis D.*	May 7	1st Cav Div.
Walker, Dennis K.	May 10	9th Inf. Div.
Wood, Daniel	May 10	9th Inf. Div.
Copas, Ardie R.*	May 12	25th Inf. Div.
West, Hugh M.	June 9	25th Inf. Div.
Burns, Edward D. *	June 22	1st Cav Div.
Comer, Billy R.	June 22	1st Cav Div.
Rowland, John R.	June 22	1st Cav Div.

*Note: Burns fell on a grenade.   *Posthumous*

VALOROUS UNIT AWARD

1st Cavalry Division: Fish Hook

5th Cavalry	8th Cavalry
7th Cavalry	12th Cavalry

9th Infantry Division

31st Infantry (6th Bn.)........................Parrot's Beak
47th Infantry (2nd Bn.) ....Fish Hook
60th Infantry (5th Bn.)..............................Fish Hook

11th ACR: Fish Hook

used to destroy our men."

Lt. Gen. Mike Davison, commander of II Field Force, said: "High during the incursion, morale stayed that way back in South Vietnam. U.S. troops were grateful for the chance to destroy the sanctuaries; they realized it meant far less danger in the months to come, the enemy lacking the means to endanger them as they left Southeast Asia."

In *Into Cambodia,* Nolan wrote: "After the 1968 Tet Offensive, Washington, faced with an enemy that had finally stood up to their firepower and been decimated, negated their advantage by stopping the bombing and placing their faith instead with negotiations.

"Likewise, after the 1970 Cambodian Incursion, Washington used the breathing space afforded them not to press on—not to cut the Ho Chi Minh Trail in Laos, to cross the DMZ (Demilitarized Zone), to shut down Haiphong and Hanoi—but to accelerate the withdrawals."

One infantry battalion operations officer said simply: "After Cambodia, you couldn't pick a fight. If only we had persisted, we would have won the war."

John Shaw wrote in *The Cambodian Campaign:* "Rather than being a minor operation, deserving only passing mention in the rush to focus on American campus protests and congressional outrage, the Cambodian incursion was as great a military victory as Tet 1968, made possible by political leaders seizing fleeting opportunities and armed forces carrying out a mission they were ready, willing and able to do."

Even famed adviser and war critic Lt. Col. John Paul Vann concurred, calling the incursion "the most favorable development, other than Tet [when the VC-NVA offensive was militarily defeated], that occurred in this war."

One vet of Cambodia leaves this advice for his fellow vets. "It's hard to be proud of something when the general public does not respect you or hold you in the same light as they do other veterans," said N. Dallas Tinsley, a vet of C Co., 1st Bn., 5th Inf., 25th Div. "[But] we need to break out of our shell and become publicly proud of the service that we did render."

Asked whether in retrospect after 40 years if the Cambodian operation was worthwhile, Robert A. Patterson—a former infantryman with D Co., 2nd Bn., 60th Inf., 9th ID—said, "My answer is a resounding yes! But when you do it, go all the way." ✪

THE TOLL

1st Cavalry Division	150
25th Infantry Division	84
11th Armored Cavalry Regiment	30
9th Infantry Division	28
4th Infantry Division	24
1st Aviation Brigade	18
199th LIB (5th Bn., 12th Inf.)	16
101st Abn. Div. (3rd Bn., 506th Inf.)	9
7th Air Force	7
20th Engineer Brigade	4
23rd Artillery Group	3
173rd Abn. (C Co., 75th Rangers)	2
MACV	2
USARV	2
Special Forces	2
II Field Forces	1

Total Killed..............................382

Source: *The Cambodia Campaign (Table 2, p. 158) by John W. Shaw.*

CAMBODIAN INVASION LONG OVERDUE, SAID VETS

Veterans of the Cambodian campaign were asked, "Do you feel that the destruction of the NVA sanctuaries in Cambodia relieved pressure on GIs in Vietnam and thus saved American lives prior to the U.S. withdrawal?" The overwhelming majority of them answered "Yes."

The Cambodian incursion was the most successful operation of the entire war. It was well worthwhile and did in fact save lots of American lives. Although what we accomplished was lost due to the publicity over the incident at Kent State University in Ohio.
—**James F. Meechan, 25th Scout Dog Plt., 1st Cav Div.**

Absolutely, it was worth it. In fact, if we had continued the campaign, I am quite sure we would have won the war. Unfortunately, the "NVA units" on U.S. college campuses rioted, Dick Nixon got scared, and we were extracted.
—**Richard J. Henry, Section Chief, A Bty., 1st Bn., 77th FA, 1st Cav Div.**

I think it was one of the best moves of this war, and I regret it didn't come before. It might and probably would have saved many GIs' lives. The only way this push could backfire is if … students destroyed our country from within. I am proud to be here for my country and possibly helping change the course of the war. Even though I wrote those words 47 years ago to my parents, I still hold to these sentiments today.
—**Mark J. Kelly, Infantryman, 1st Bn., 5th Inf., 25th Inf. Div.**

The Cambodian campaign effectively precluded any major North Vietnamese military operations for two years. Following this action, trying to find enemy activity in South Vietnam was next to impossible. It was like the war had ended, and they forgot to tell us.
—**Leonard Demaray, B Trp., 1st Sqdn., 9th Cav, 1st Cav Div.**

Cambodia was good for morale. It most definitely put a damper on NVA and VC activity during this period, and helped save some American lives later.
—**Karl Potter, RTO, 3rd Plt., C Co., 2nd Bn., 35th Inf., 4th ID**

President Nixon certainly made a courageous and long-before-needed decision. And those pitiful college kids! They don't even know what is going on. How uninformed they are. Nixon's decision will save lives in South Vietnam, promote Vietnamization and pacification, and get the American troops home sooner. I wrote those words from the field in 1970 and stand by them today.
—**Richard Hughes, Infantryman, C Co., 2nd Bn., 12th Cav, 1st Cav Div.**

PHOTO COURTESY RICHARD HUGHES

Cambodia was a good morale booster. The enemy was confused by our presence there. We were able to disrupt their supply lines and prevent a lot of weapons from getting into South Vietnam.
—**Paul Dell, Jr., Infantryman, B Co., 3rd Bn., 22nd Inf., 25th Inf. Div.**

I am sure the ordnance destroyed in Cambodia contributed to saving American lives.
—**Richard S. Wadleigh, 1st Cav Div.**

After studying the slowdown in the NVA operations tempo for months after the incursion, I am convinced that the campaign was long overdue, and was of great significance and benefit to U.S. troops.
—**Scott Smith, 8th Engineer Bn., 1st Cav Div./Sr. Adviser to 1st ARVN Cav Regt.**

Yes, I'm sure that we benefited as GIs in Vietnam, of which I became one again once we left Cambodia. Only being in there for 60 days, however, seemed to us to be another idea that was destined to provide temporary relief, but no permanent results.
Craig Fish, Infantryman, D Co., 2nd Bn., 12th Cav, 1st Cav Div.

I would hazard a guess that it didn't make much difference in III Corps. It may have well caused more casualties.
Buddy Bohager, Rifle Plt. Ldr., 1st Bn., 27th Inf., 25th ID

Cutting and/or eliminating all three major areas of supply unequivocally had a major effect on the NVA's ability to continue operations on any sustained level for the remainder of 1970 and probably into 1971.
John P. Monahan, A Co., 5th Bn., 7th Cav, 1st Cav Div.

I am sure everything we took out of Cambodia had a direct effect on the war. It is too bad our hands were tied and we could not have invaded Cambodia sooner!
—Richard A. Manor, Pathfinder, 11th Combat Avn. Bn.

The many bunker complexes, caches of weapons, and so many enemy soldiers that we destroyed in Cambodia relieved the pressure on American soldiers stationed in Vietnam. Without any doubt, we saved many, many lives prior to the U.S. withdrawal.
—Carlos DeLuna, Infantryman, D Co., 2nd Bn., 5th Cav, 1st CD

The Cambodian operation did relieve pressure on U.S. forces and save American lives prior to the U.S. withdrawal from Vietnam. When we invaded, my squad leader said, "I am voting for Nixon because he has guts!" I say, God bless Richard Nixon.
—Robert H. Baker, Mech Inf., 25th Inf. Div.

During the time GIs were in Cambodia and after they left, it was quiet around Tay Ninh. I am happy U.S. troops went in.
—Harry Renke, Artillery

I wholeheartedly believe the Cambodian incursion was a complete success. American lives were saved. The comparison of the threat level before and after was striking. I know that my life was safer in the months following the operation. Everyone in my unit felt we were finally accomplishing something, and we did.
—Mike Meadows, 31st Combat Eng. Bn., 20th Eng. Bde.

I do indeed believe the Cambodian campaign set back the Communist war effort by at least six months, and cost them a massive amount of war materiel.
—Al Sims, A Co., 2nd Bn., 27th Inf., 25th ID

This operation saved many lives of our fellow soldiers. So I was 100% behind the military decision to end the NVA sanctuaries in Cambodia.
—Donald C. Worley, Asst. Gunner, 1st Bn., 92nd FA, 4th ID

The cache sites found and exploited along with enemy captured went a long way toward saving GIs' lives for the rest of the war. And all of the "actionable intelligence" gathered was sent immediately to the field.
—Steve Gill, MACV J2 CMEC Field Teams

Our mission into Cambodia was very successful. By going into Cambodia and disrupting enemy supply lines and capturing their weapons and equipment, we saved many American soldiers' lives. It also allowed the policy of Vietnamization to go forward.
—Darriel R. Young, RTO, C Co., 1st Bn., 12th Cav, 1st Cav Div.

Did our Cambodian incursion save American lives? Damn right it did! Amazingly, afterward, when we left Cambodia, things were relatively quiet.
—John F. Moran, HQ Btry., 1st Bn., 77th FA, 1st CD

Leaving Cambodia off-limits made no sense. Overall, some NVA destruction was accomplished and we did save some U.S. lives. However, it seems too little too late for any real strategic success.
—Robert L. Pyle, Medic, 2nd Bn., 14th Inf., 25th Inf. Div.

Cambodia was the smartest operation of the whole war.
**—Howard Brown, APC Gunner, 1st Bn.,
16th Mech Inf./1st Field Force**

There is no doubt in my mind that the Cambodian incursion caused a lull in the action, thus saving innumerable American lives. After, the entire area along the Cambodian border became very quiet with very few rocket and mortar attacks, and little ground contact.
—Joseph W. Ward III, 60th Eng. Co.

Cambodia not only contributed to significant enemy loss of soldiers and supplies, but caused considerable disruption long after our departure. This in turn had to have prevented many American casualties.
—Richard R. Pane, 11th Armored Cavalry Regiment

Many thanks to Nixon for taking this politically unpopular action.
—John Boors, Civilian Sr. Police Advisor

BY CHARLES F. HAWKINS   *OPERATION TEXAS STAR*

RENDEZVOUS AT RIPCORD

For 23 days in July 1970, FSB Ripcord, defended by elements of the famed 101st Airborne Division, came under siege by a full NVA division. Yet it barely made the news at home, even though it was the last major U.S. ground battle fought in Vietnam.

Outside Arlington National Cemetery stands the 101st Airborne Division Memorial, its granite column topped with a bronze screaming eagle, the division symbol. Around its base are granite slabs inscribed with the place names of notable division actions in WWII, Vietnam and the Persian Gulf—St. Marie-du-Mont, Carentan, Eindhoven, Bastogne, Hue, Dak To, Dong Ap Bia, Ripcord. Ripcord. The name of this desolate Vietnamese mountaintop fire support base is virtually unknown except for a lucky few who survived its cauldron of fire in 1970. It is a story worth telling.

In 1970, the North Vietnamese Army (NVA) was still a potent force in I Corps. When the dry season began, the 101st and the Army of the Republic of Vietnam (ARVN) 1st Infantry Division started pushing west and north into the Nam Hoa Mountains beyond Hue. The NVA pushed back.

Initially, Ripcord was to provide support for an allied thrust into the A Shau Valley. Enemy action escalated at places such as Firebases Granite and Henderson, however, the A Shau plan was abandoned. American efforts then focused on defense and interdiction. The strategic initiative passed to the enemy, and Ripcord became the NVA's primary objective.

'CHEESEBURGER HILL'

Ripcord is the second highest mountain of the Coc Muen massif, a watershed and infiltration crossroads that dominates the northeastern A Shau. That March, the mission to seize the mountain peak and build

NATIONAL ARCHIVES PHOTO, #III-CC-70180

Fire Support Base Ripcord was situated atop a high mountain overlooking the A Shau Valley. It was designed to provide support for a new allied thrust, but was besieged for nearly a month in July 1970.

NATIONAL ARCHIVES PHOTO, #III-CC-70179

ABOVE: 155mm howitzers of A Btry., 2nd Bn., 11th Arty, 101st Abn. Div., in action on Fire Support Base Ripcord in July 1970. On the 18th, howitzers were shattered, spewing hot shells across the hill.
RIGHT: Ripcord's 3,041-foot elevation gave it a commanding view of the area.

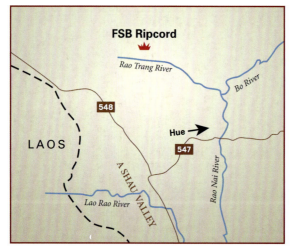

a firebase was given to Lt. Col. Andre Lucas' 2nd Bn., 506th Inf.—the "Best of the Currahees."

On March 12, an "exploratory insertion" by Alpha Company met withering fire as it tried to land. UH-1 Hueys skittered across the rocky mountaintop, discharging their human cargo without touching down. By late afternoon, it was clear that defenses could not be established. So Capt. Albert Burkhart moved his men east to a narrow wooded ridge that offered a chance to dig in. 2nd Lt. Dudley Davis became the first man killed trying to seize and hold Ripcord.

After a series of grim firefights, it was Bravo Company's turn, and it went in hot on April 1. Fighting was vicious in what came to be known as the April Fool's Day assault. B Company, too, pulled off Ripcord.

Lucas then committed his entire battalion to combat operations around the 3,041-foot-high mountain. On April 10, Charlie Company made a pre-dawn ground assault up the southern slope of Ripcord. Other than a preparatory artillery barrage, not a shot was fired.

The North Vietnamese had ceded the first phase of the battle.

As the remainder of the battalion sought the enemy, C Company began building defensive works that earned Ripcord the reputation as a premier firebase. Some of the soldiers called it "Cheeseburger Hill," a wry reference to the division action at Dong Ap Bia (Hamburger Hill) the year before, and the larger battle many expected was coming.

THE SIEGE

At 7:02 a.m. on July 1, a salvo of enemy mortar rounds crashed harmlessly into Ripcord's perimeter. Capt. Dave Rich's B Btry., 2nd Bn., 319th Artillery, and its 105mm howitzers quickly responded with counterbattery fire. This inauspicious event heralded the beginning of a 23-day siege.

That night on Hill 902, three miles south of Ripcord, two platoons of C Company were struck by a large force of NVA sappers and infantry. Spec. 4 Gary Steele remembers: "They started with satchel charges. I don't know how many, but they lit the night like the 4th of July back home." Steele, who was wounded five times, and his fellow Currahees didn't give up.

> ## "They started with satchel charges. I don't know how many, but they lit the night like the 4th of July back home."
>
> —SPEC. 4 GARY STEELE, CHARLIE COMPANY

"Those of us who were left," Steele recalled, "took the fight over, because now it was our turn." The eight men killed included Capt. Thomas Hewett, the commanding officer, and Pfc. Steve Harber was missing. It was a victory of sorts, but C Company was pulled off Hill 902 on July 2, and the key terrain was never reoccupied.

That day, the standoff attack by fire resumed. U.S. forces responded with a mix of artillery fire, Cobra gunship attacks and thundering air strikes by fighter jets. Soon the daily bomb tonnage doubled from five tons a day to 10, and then tripled to 30 tons. Many of the tenacious NVA chose to die in place.

With Hill 902 ceded to the enemy, Lucas and his boss, 3rd Brigade commander Col. Benjamin Harrison, turned their attention to the two remaining heights by Ripcord, Hill 1000, less than a mile west, and Hill 805, more than a mile southeast.

On July 6, Recon Team Bravo, led by Sgt. Robert Granberry, reported sounds of enemy activity on top of Hill 1000. The six-man team was then ordered to attack the enemy position, which it did, resulting in the loss of the entire team to wounding by enemy rocket propelled grenades (RPG) and small-arms fire. Delta Company, commanded by Capt. Rembert Rollison, was sent to their aid.

Next day, D Company assaulted Hill 1000, and again on July 8, supported by a platoon-sized C Company. Both days, the assaults gained ground, isolated and defeated enemy in underground bunkers, only to be beaten back. An under-strength platoon of C Company, led by 1st Lt. Jim Campbell, seized one of two knolls on Hill 1000 on July 8, but was recalled by Lucas in the late afternoon. Six men from the companies died in the assaults.

Fighting was brutal and close-in. Lucas even flew overhead in an observation helicopter, dropping cases of fragmentation and smoke grenades to his beleaguered Currahees, and adjusting fire. But the NVA fortifications were too numerous, too well-defended. Rollison's company strength fell to 40 men; the remnants of C and D companies were withdrawn.

Ripcord continued to take a daily pounding by enemy rockets, mortars and recoilless rifle fire. Capt. Ben Peters' B Company, now defending the perimeter, and Rich's artillerymen and those of A Btry., 2nd Bn., 11th Arty, bore the brunt of these attacks. Helicopters began to receive hits regularly. Some crashed. Others staggered over the jungle and back to the rear base at Camp Evans.

On July 10, A Company combat-assaulted from FSB O'Reilly to relieve pressure against

Four times Livingston's battalion attacked uphill against fierce opposition, and four times it was turned back by superior numbers of enemy troops.

—2ND BN., 501ST INF., ASSAULTING HILL 1000

Ripcord. Joining Alpha on the 12th in a two-pronged ground assault on Hill 805 was D Co. (Delta Raiders), 2nd Bn., 501st Inf., commanded by Capt. Christopher Straub and now under operational control of the 2/506th. After some minor skirmishes, Hill 805 was seized by Alpha and Delta. They dug in, expecting the worst.

At 10:30 that night, four enemy columns, led by black-painted sappers, slammed into the defenders on Hill 805. The Americans slammed back. The enemy was stopped in his tracks by U.S. artillery and mortar fire, shredded in a murderous crossfire of rifles, machine guns and grenade launchers, and turned away. Blood smeared the approaches to Hill 805, but it was NVA blood, not American.

Battered, but undeterred, the NVA continued their costly assaults against Hill 805 for four more nights. Delta Raiders stayed to defend the key hilltop, relieving some of the pressure on Ripcord and buying valuable time for its defenders. "It was costly," recalled Sgt. Ray Blackman, "but many of our wounded refused evacuation, preferring to stay to fight alongside their friends." Delta lost seven KIA on July 14. When they were finally withdrawn on July 17, Straub's company strength had been cut in half.

"It was costly, but many of our wounded refused evacuation, preferring to stay to fight alongside their friends."

—SGT. RAY BLACKMAN, DELTA RAIDERS

Meanwhile, the remainder of 2nd Bn., 501st Inf. (Geronimos), commanded by Lt. Col. Otis Livingston, air-assaulted near Hill 1000. Leading with his battalion scouts and following with A, B and C companies in echelon, Livingston led his battalion up the backside of this NVA-infested stronghold.

Four times Livingston's battalion attacked uphill against fierce opposition, and four times it was turned back by superior numbers of enemy troops.

Each time the Geronimos retaliated with fighter-bomber air strikes and Cobra rocket attacks. But it was no use. On the 17th, Livingston and his exhausted soldiers were withdrawn. Taking the place of the Geronimos was a single rifle company from the 1st Bn., 506th Inf.—D Company, commanded by Capt. Don Workman.

FIGHTING WITHDRAWAL

On July 18, disaster struck. A Chinook helicopter, ferrying a load of fuel to the firebase, was shot down and crashed onto the ammo dump. Burning fuel flowed into the bunkered facility. What the enemy could not achieve by ground attack was accomplished in seconds by a half-inch-sized bullet. The ammo dump exploded. Dave Rich's battery of howitzers was shattered; hot shells flew across the hill, spreading more destruction. The death knell for Ripcord had been sounded.

BRAVERY ABUNDANT

Besides the Medal of Honor awarded to Lt. Col. Andre C. Lucas, which as Col. Benjamin L. Harrison, 3rd Brigade commander, said was meant to be a "tribute to all the soldiers involved in Ripcord, a way to let the world know that something big and important had happened there." Battlefield courage at Ripcord was recognized by about 500 citations. The late Keith Nolan described many of these actions in his superb 2000 book, *Ripcord: Screaming Eagles Under Siege—Vietnam, 1970.*

Two Distinguished Service Crosses (DSC) were earned, by Capt. David F. Rich and Sgt. John W. Kreckel. Rich, commanding officer of B Btry., 2nd Bn., 319th FA, was wounded seven times in the battle, finally being evacuated. He had done four years in Vietnam by then and had already received the Silver Star. Kreckel earned his DSC posthumously for putting himself directly in the line of fire, saving the life of a fellow GI.

At least 43 Silver Stars (eight posthumous) recognized the heroism of GIs at Ripcord. A few earned two Silver Stars. Infantrymen, artillerymen and engineers

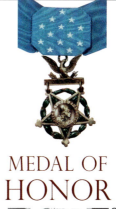

were among the recipients. Virtually every helicopter pilot involved in the evacuation got a Distinguished Flying Cross; every crew chief and door gunner earned the Air Medal for valor.

Unit performance was recognized, too. The Valorous Unit Award went to the 101st Aviation Group. Others no doubt deserved it.

Officers rated their men highly. 1st Lt. James H. Campbell said of the draftee infantrymen, "In a firefight, they were hellacious soldiers." Capt. Christopher C. Straub recalled, "They fought like tigers and showed how much they cared for each other." 2nd Lt. Sheldon C. Wintermute recounted: "They did an absolutely fantastic job. For all the stuff you read about bad morale in Vietnam, quite frankly, I never saw it."

As Nolan found, "There were moments of stunning courage," and "the men who did their best at Ripcord won a personal victory."

In 2012, Frederick Spaulding, A captain in 1970, was presented the DSC for taking four helicopters into Ripcord to direct fire and evacuate men.

MEDAL OF HONOR

LT. COL. ANDRE C. LUCAS
(POSTHUMOUS)

Two days later, Workman and D/1/506th air-assaulted east of Hill 805 to try to work up its reverse slope. It barely got off the landing zone before enemy mortars found the range. For two days, Workman and his men held on grimly in the face of nearly overwhelming odds. Rollison brought his company again to the rescue, followed by Capt. Ken Lamb and C Company. The three companies made a fighting withdrawal, but it cost the lives of Workman and nine of his men.

Meanwhile, from July 14 to 19, A Company penetrated enemy territory along a valley southeast of Ripcord. Contact was frequent, but one-sided, as A Company bloodied the enemy in a series of short, sharp firefights.

On the 20th, it discovered and tapped an NVA telephone wire. The wire tap revealed the presence of what was the NVA 324B Division and supporting elements of the 304B Division surrounding Ripcord, not the one or two regiments that had been suspected. This firsthand battlefield intelligence helped the acting division commander, Brig. Gen. Sidney Berry, make the difficult decision to withdraw from the Ripcord area of operations (AO).

In place of U.S. troops on the ground, Berry would employ massive firepower of artillery and air strikes against known enemy locations. Bombs dropped daily in the AO had reached 50 tons, but would triple in the next three days. Even so, tough fighting lay ahead.

A Company's (76 men) luck ran out July 22. Heading out of the valley for extraction, it ran headlong into an NVA battalion of 400 soldiers. "For a week," recalled Spec. 4 Jody Smith, "we owned that valley." But no longer. Alpha's daytime engagement was the longest and most costly of the siege. The NVA commander bet that he could overwhelm the Americans before they could bring their awesome firepower to bear. It was a bad bet, but not by much.

When it was over, when the last 250-pound bomb and napalm canister had been dropped, some on top of Alpha's position, when the last RPG had spent its explosive energy, the Currahees remained in control of their patch of jungle. The cost was high. More than 90% of Alpha's troops were either dead (13) or wounded (56). The NVA left 64 dead behind.

There was a final penalty. Lucas and his operations officer, Maj. Kenneth Tanner, were consumed by a barrage of 120mm mortar fire that struck Ripcord on July 23. Tanner was killed outright and Lucas was mortally wounded. Also killed was Pfc. Gus Allen. For his heroism during the siege, Lucas was posthumously awarded the Medal of Honor.

THE EXTRACTION

On July 23, A Company clung to its hard-won real estate and B Company secured Ripcord. Airlifts had been planned to extract the remainder of Lucas' Currahees in the face of stiff enemy resistance. Ripcord was first. At the same time, Rollison had gone again to assist a battered friend, and was helping A Company. They would leave last.

Throughout the day, jets had roared overhead, dropping 154 tons of bombs from 84 sorties. The effects of various sorts of ordnance were physically devastating. 1st Lt. Fred H. Edwards of B Co., 326th Eng. Bn., graphically described the scene on Ripcord. "Mortar rounds had exploded on virtually every square foot of the hill, charring it to a gray-black heap," he said. "It looked evil, malevolent. When the helicopter landed, it was like being dropped into an absolute hellhole."

Capt. Randolph House, commander of C Co., 158th Avn. Bn.—one of a number of assault helicopter companies involved in the battle—took control of air operations and the evacuation of the fire base. Disregarding enemy ground fire, he and his airmen plucked troopers off the firebase and then led the way into Alpha and Delta Company's location in the valley southeast of Ripcord. It was a near-run thing, but House's airmen pulled off the extraction of the last of the 2/506 defenders under the guns of enemy soldiers dug in on surrounding ridge lines.

Helicopters slipped around hills and hovered into Ripcord to pluck their precious cargo away from enemy shellfire. Ben Harrison called it the "greatest feat of airmanship in modern warfare." Finally, at 1:35 p.m., the last Huey climbed out of the valley southeast of Ripcord and sped toward Camp Evans.

Once the siege was ended and the withdrawal complete, it was time to take a final tally of the losses. They totaled 72 KIA, two accidental deaths (by a weapon and a falling tree) and 400 WIA. The 506th Infantry sustained 45 KIA while the 501st Infantry counted 16 KIA. Of the five artillerymen killed, four belonged to A Btry., 2nd Bn., 11th FA. The remaining six KIA hailed from five other units. Two-thirds of the men killed were draftees who "fought like tigers." The other third were volunteers who did likewise.

Ripcord wasn't a textbook battle; most combat operations aren't. But the evacuation from Ripcord was a successful withdrawal under fire, and the largest such airmobile operation of its kind in history. The NVA wanted a fight and the 101st obliged. A week afterward, the Currahees returned to the Nam Hoa Mountains. This time there were few enemy left to contest them.

Indeed, Doug Bonnot, who was in charge of a tactical signals intelligence team from the 265th Radio Research Company on Ripcord from mid-April to July 23, concluded that fighting around the firebase was a serious setback for the communists. It stymied "the NVA plan to move in force two infantry divisions plus supporting forces, including 103mm artillery, into the lowlands," he believes. ✪

More than 90% of Alpha's troops were either dead or wounded.

THE TOLL

U.S. KIA:
72

U.S. WIA:
400

BY JANIE DYHOUSE

OPERATION ELK CANYON I-II

HELICOPTER SHOOT-DOWN WAR'S DEADLIEST HOSTILE CRASH

Events at LZ Judy on Aug. 26, 1970, are forgotten but by a few. Yet, that's the day 31 men died when their Chinook was officially hit by a rocket-propelled grenade just shy of landing.

For Eric "Ric" Reid, Aug. 26, 1970, began like most days in Vietnam … at "0:dark-thirty." Flying with the 178th Assault Support Helicopter Company (ASHC), Reid was the pilot of a CH-47 Chinook (tail number 67-18445). Dan York was the aircraft commander and co-pilot, and Jole York, George Tifft and Hima McDougall filled out the crew.

As part of *Operation Elk Canyon I-II*, they were extracting elements of the 196th Light Infantry Brigade (LIB) from Kham Duc and transporting them 19 miles to Landing Zone (LZ) Judy.

On its last flight out of Kham Duc, the Chinook had a full load of troops, ammo cans and 81mm white phosphorus rounds.

With 25 grunts of the 2nd Bn., 1st Inf., 196th LIB, Americal Div., and two artillerymen from A Btry., 3rd Bn., 82nd Arty, on board, Reid remembers that final trip to LZ Judy as "routine."

PILOT SOLE SURVIVOR

"As we closed on LZ Judy, we were informed by the mission commander we were number seven for landing," Reid said. "It was like a major U.S. airport. We were actually in a holding pattern."

After watching the other six Chinooks land and discharge their troops and cargo, Reid's crew was cleared to land.

"About 200 yards out with approximately 150 feet of altitude, I heard a loud bang in the back of the aircraft," Reid said. "I was astonished to see the master caution light on as well as what appeared to be the majority of the caution panel lit like a Christmas tree."

PHOTO BY RAY TYNDALL

Soldiers from B Co., 1st Bn., 6th Inf., load onto a CH-47 helicopter of the 178th Assault Support Helicopter Company in September 1970. That same aviation unit lost the Chinook at LZ Judy on Aug. 26.

Reid said the aircraft was quickly losing altitude and started to turn to the right. He could see they were going right into the trees. "I locked my harness and watched fascinated as the aircraft settled into the trees," he said. "I remember thinking how much I would miss my wife and boys. I was knocked unconscious."

When Reid came to, he heard men moaning and the sound of crackling fire. Co-pilot York was dead, and Reid tried to get into the back to start pulling people out. The entry was blocked. While trying to get out of the burning Chinook, Reid lost his footing and hit the ground rolling downhill until he was stopped by two large boulders.

He freed himself and started up the slope when the aircraft exploded.

> # "I locked my harness and watched fascinated as the aircraft settled into the trees. I remember thinking how much I would miss my wife and boys."
>
> —ERIC REID, PILOT, 178TH ASSAULT SUPPORT HELICOPTER COMPANY

"One of the front landing gears landed not 10 feet from me," he said. "I knew the aircraft was lost. More importantly, my fellow crewmen and the troops that had trusted us to get them to LZ Judy safely were lost."

Reid was the sole survivor of the crash, but 31 others were killed and eight wounded, including one killed (from C Company) on the ground from debris. Reid thought there was one other survivor who was later flown to a hospital in Japan, but no one has ever been able to confirm this.

The final death tally broke down as follows: 18 men from Delta Company, five mortarmen from E Company, one each from A and C companies, the two artillerymen from A Battery and four crewmen from the 178th ASHC. The soldier from Charlie Company was killed on the ground by a rotor blade. The men ranged in age from 18 (three of the total) to 42. They were half volunteer and half draftee.

Retired Lt. Col. Richard Carvell, then-commander of the 1st Bn., 46th Inf., 196th LIB, was flying in a light observation helicopter not far behind Reid. While he never observed any enemy fire, he did see the Chinook go down. He said he was "following close enough to hear and see."

In his report of Sept. 1, 1970, Carvell wrote that the helicopter "allegedly" received ground fire. The after-action report states that the CH-47 "received enemy fire" while approaching LZ Judy.

"I don't know the exact truth of what brought us down," Reid said. "I only know that it did."

'NO DEFINITIVE' CAUSE OF CRASH

Greg Sanders was in the American Division Tactical Operations Center when the crash occurred, but did attend the Chinook crash briefing.

He said there was much speculation as to the cause. "The truth is, there is no definitive evidence one way or other as to the cause of the crash," Sanders said. "As with nearly all events, many eyewitnesses see things differently."

Sgt. Lynn Allen from Headquarters Company, an eyewitness, said, "I was filling sandbags and I saw a rocket-propelled grenade hit the right aft engine, causing the aircraft to instantly lose power and drop."

As commander of the 2nd Bn., 1st Inf., Al Coleman was overseeing the withdrawal of the security outposts at Kham Duc that day. Once everyone had been airlifted out, Coleman said he made one more pass over Kham Duc to make sure that the demolition guys had done their job.

"We were inbound for LZ Judy when I received a call that a CH-47 had crashed and that the LZ was closed," Coleman said. "We diverted to LZ Mary Ann, and I rejoined the battalion the next morning."

DEADLY HELICOPTER CRASHES DURING THE INDOCHINA WAR

DATE	LOCATION	CAUSE	DEATHS	HELICOPTER TYPE	MAJOR UNITS
1-8-68	Ba Long Airfield (near)	N	46	CH-53A	1st and 3rd Marine Divisions; Helicopter Squadron 463
11-28-71	Mom Kun Sac Mountain	N	34	CH-47C	A & HHC Cos., 1st Bn., 327th Inf., 101st Abn. Div.*
5-10-72	Bien Hoa City (near)	N	34	CH-47A	D Co., 2nd Bn., 8th Cav, 1st Cav Div.*
8-26-70	LZ Judy	H	31	CH-47B	D Co., 2nd Bn., 1st Inf., 196th LIB; A-3-82nd Arty; 178th ASHC*
2-28-68	Thon Khe ("Rockpile")	H	23	CH-46D	Helicopter Squadron 262; 7 other units
5-13-75	Thailand	N	23	CH-53A	Air Force 56th Security Police Sqdn.; 21st Special Ops. Sqdn.
5-4-66	Nhon Co (near)	N	21	CH-47A	2nd Bn., 502nd Inf., 101st Abn. Div.; 147th Avn. Co.
10-3-68	Phong Dien	N	20	CH-47	1st Cavalry Division
7-15-66	Song Ngan Valley	H	18	CH-46A	E Co., 2nd Bn., 1st Marines; 3rd Bn., 4th Marines*
11-18-70	Que Son Mountains	N	15	CH-46D	1st Marine Recon Bn; Helicopter Squadron 263
10-31-72	Ap Binh Ninh	H	15	CH-47C	18th Avn. Co. (Corps); C Trp., 16th Cav*
5-15-75	Koh Tang Island, Cambodia	H	14	CH-53C	2nd Bn., 9th Marines
6-6-68	LZ Loon	H	13	CH-46A	H&S Co. (including 9 of Mortar Plt.), 1st Bn., 4th Marines, 3rd Div.
3-12-70	FSB Rhode Island	N	13	UH-1D	B Co., 4th Bn., 9th Inf., 25th Div; 128th Assault Helicopter Co.
7-3-68	Elephant Valley, Phu Loc	H	13	CH-46A	1st Plt., B Co., 1st Recon Bn.; Helicopter Squadron 164

* = Additional units   **H**=Hostile   **N**=Non-Hostile

Sources: *Vietnam Helicopter Pilots Association, Gary Roush; Coffelt Database.*

While Coleman did not see the chopper hit the ground, the information he received, as well as a later visit to the crash site, led him to believe it was enemy gunfire that brought it down. Indeed, despite the official findings, many eyewitnesses insist it was AK-47 rifle fire that caused the crash.

The 178th ASHC (call sign Boxcars) commanding officer, Brian Foote, was flying in a Huey command and control ship a few minutes from the landing zone when the crash occurred. Foote also did not see the crash occur, but thought it was likely caused by a short burst from an AK-47.

He tells of losing an aircraft at LZ Siberia on Feb. 6, 1971. Unlike the crash at LZ Judy, Foote was able to retrieve many of the parts for evaluation. "Sometimes the cause is not always apparent to the observer," he said.

Bob Dolan was with D Co., 4th Bn., 31st Inf., 196th LIB, Americal Div., on LZ Judy that day. He was in a hole next to the helipad when the Chinook came around the hill on its approach. He said what he saw was a small burst of AK fire, less than a full magazine. "We humped down the hill shortly after and found that Reid survived," he said.

Roger Widdows, whose brother John of A Battery was killed on the chopper and who thoroughly investigated the crash, perhaps summed up the cause of the loss best. "The bird was raked with a burst of AK-47 fire followed by an RPG round that struck it on the port side, next to the rear engine. The secondary explosions from the ordnance carried on board is what brought her down," he found.

No matter the cause, the men who lost their lives are not forgotten by those who were there. Dan Hodge, a member of E Company attached to Delta, said, "I know I'll never forget that day and the friends that I lost. The day we hauled the body bags back up the hill was not a good one, either. With each bag we passed up the hill, you could see it in everyone's eyes [that they were] wondering which friend this one was." ✪

THE TOLL

U.S. KIA:
31

U.S. WIA:
8

DARING POW RAID
AT SON TAY

BY AL HEMINGWAY

On Nov. 21, 1970, top officials in Washington held their breath as a joint U.S. Army-Air Force rescue team attempted to free U.S. POWs from captivity in North Vietnam.

"We are going to rescue 70 American prisoners of war, maybe more, from a camp called Son Tay," announced Col. Arthur "Bull" Simons, combat veteran of World War II, Korea and Vietnam. "You are to let nothing interfere with this operation. Our mission is to rescue prisoners, not to take prisoners. If there's been a leak, we'll know it as soon as the second or third chopper sets down... We'll make them pay for every foot."

When Simons finished his speech, the room fell silent for a brief moment. Then every man applauded. The raid on Son Tay Prison Camp—deep within North Vietnam—was under way.

In May 1970, two POW camps were identified by the Interagency Prisoner of War Intelligence Committee (IPWIC). This committee, formed in 1967, was responsible for identifying POWs and the camps they were interned in and to veer bombing missions away from those areas.

The two camps were Ap Lo, about 30 miles west of Hanoi, and Son Tay, 23 miles from North Vietnam's capital, situated at the junction of the Song Con and Red Rivers. It was determined that Son Tay was being enlarged because of the increased activity at the camp. Intelligence also confirmed that 55 POWs were being confined at Son Tay. Photo reconnaissance discovered the letters SAR (Search and Rescue), apparently spelled out by the prisoner's laundry, and an arrow with the number 8, indicating the distance the men had to travel to the fields they worked in.

On May 25, IPWIC briefed Army Gen. Earle Wheeler, chairman of the Joint Chiefs of Staff (JCS), on a tentative plan to free the POWs at Son Tay. By 1970, the war was in its fifth year. Public support was waning, and a daring rescue of POWs would be a much-needed morale booster militarily; not to mention a political victory for President Richard M. Nixon who was under fire for his recent incursion into Cambodia.

Operation Polar Circle

Wheeler granted the request. Adm. Thomas H. Moorer, the new JCS chairman, sat in on the meeting. The first phase of the plan, dubbed *Operation Polar Circle,* was approved.

On June 10, a 15-man group, headed by Army Brig. Gen. Donald D. Blackburn, began the planning stage of the operation. Blackburn, no stranger to special operations, was the special assistant for Counterinsurgency and Special Activities. He conceived the idea for the raid and then appointed a panel.

Reconnaissance photos taken by SR-71 "Blackbirds" revealed that Son Tay "was active." The camp itself was in the open and surrounded by rice paddies. In close proximity was the 12th North Vietnamese Army (NVA) Regiment totaling approximately 12,000 troops. Also nearby was an artillery school, a supply depot and an air defense installation.

Five hundred yards south was another compound called the

Seated in the cabin of a C-130, Capt. Richard Meadows and his 14-man assault group "Blueboy" prepare for the coming raid during a training exercise in September 1970.

Surprise at Son Tay by Ronald Wong. On Nov. 21, 1970, the Army Special Forces pulled off a perfectly executed raid on the Son Tay POW Camp in North Vietnam. Not a single American was killed. But unknown to the would-be rescuers, the U.S. prisoners had been moved.

"secondary school," which was an administration center housing 45 guards. To make matters more difficult, Phuc Yen Air Base was only 20 miles northeast of Son Tay. It was evident that the raid would have to be executed swiftly. If not, the Communists could have planes in the air and a reactionary force at the camp within minutes.

Son Tay itself was small and was situated amid 40-foot trees to obstruct the view. Only one power and telephone line entered it. The POWs were kept in four large buildings in the main compound. Three observation towers and a seven-foot wall encompassed the camp. Because of its diminutive size, only one chopper could land within the walls. The remainder would have to touch down outside the compound.

Another problem the planning group had to consider was the weather. The heavy monsoon downpours prohibited the raid until late fall. Finally, November was selected because the moon would be high enough over the horizon for good visibility, but low enough to obscure the enemy's vision.

Operation Ivory Coast

With the planning stage completed, the next phase of the raid, called Ivory Coast, was ready to swing into action. Air Force Brig. Gen. Leroy J. "Roy" Manor, a stickler for organization, led the group. The National Security Agency (NSA) tracked the NVA air defense systems and artillery units nearby. Also, in addition to the Blackbirds, unmanned Buffalo Hunter "Drones" flew over the camp as well, although they had to cease flying because many feared that the NVA would spot them.

In July, an SR-71 photo recon mission depicted "less active than usual" activity in the camp. On Oct. 3, Son Tay showed very little signs of life. However, flights over Dong Hoi, an NVA port and base southeast of Son Tay, were picking up increased activity. The planners were scratching their heads. Had the POWs been moved? Had the NVA picked up signs that a raid was imminent?

In fact, the POWs had been relocated to Dong Hoi July 14, but not for the reasons the planners had anticipated. The Song Con River, where Son Tay was located, had begun to overflow its

As Donohue's chopper "floated" across Son Tay's main compound, the door gunners let loose 4,000 rounds a minute from their mini-guns. The observation tower in the northwest section of the camp erupted into flames. With that, Donohue set down at his "holding point" in a rice paddy just outside the prison.

As Maj. Herb Kalen tried to negotiate a landing inside the compound, he almost lost control of his chopper, call sign "Banana 1," that was carrying the assault group code-named "Blueboy." The 40-foot trees that surrounded Son Tay were, in actuality, much larger. "One tree," a pilot remembered, "must have been 150 feet tall . . . we tore into it like a big lawn mower. There was a tremendous vibration . . . and we were down."

Luckily, only one person was injured; a crew chief suffered a broken ankle. Regaining his composure, Special Forces Capt. Richard Meadows scurried from the downed aircraft and said in a calm voice through his bullhorn: "We're Americans. Keep your heads down. This is a rescue. Keep your heads down. We're Americans. Get on the floor. We'll be in your cells in a minute."

ABOVE: A North Vietnamese photo taken after the raid shows the wreckage of HH-3E that carried the Blueboy assault team, *Banana 1.* The helicopter was destroyed by the team before they were extracted.

RIGHT: An aerial view of the Son Tay prison camp show prisoner housing within the walled area.

banks. So because of the flooding problem, the prisoners were transported to Dong Hoi.

Operation Kingpin

Operation Kingpin, the final component of the raid, was approved by Nixon on Nov. 18. Next day, however, Adm. Moorer was notified that it was suspected that the POWs had been transferred. Unfortunately, the planners nixed the idea to move on Dong Hoi. Their reasoning was that the raiders had rehearsed on Son Tay all this time and changing to Dong Hoi at the last minute might cause catastrophic results.

On Nov. 21, 1970, at approximately 11:18 p.m., the Son Tay raiders, accompanied by C-130Es called Combat Talons, departed Udorn, Thailand, for the final phase of their mission. At the same time, the U.S. Navy began a huge carrier strike against North Vietnam to divert attention away from the raiding party.

As the group neared the prison, the two "Jolly Greens," dubbed "Apple 4" and "Apple 5," hovered at 1,500 feet to act as reserve flareships in the event the C-130s' flares did not ignite. Suddenly, Col. Frederic M. "Marty" Donohue's HH-53 helicopter, call sign "Apple 3," developed trouble. Without warning, a yellow trouble light appeared signaling transmission problems.

Donohue calmly informed his co-pilot, Capt. Tom Waldron, to "ignore the SOB." In a normal situation, Donohue would have landed. But this was no normal mission. "Apple 3" kept going.

Get on the floor. We'll be in your cells in a minute."

No one answered back, though.

The raiders sprung into action immediately. Automatic weapons ripped into the guards. Other NVA, attempting to flee, were cut down as they tried to make their way through the east wall. Fourteen men entered the prison to rescue the POWs. However, to their disappointment, none were found.

Furious Firefights

As the raiders were neutralizing the compound, Lt. Col. John Allison's helicopter, call sign "Apple 2," with the "Redwine" group aboard, was heading toward Son Tay's south wall. As his door gunners fired their mini-guns on the guard towers, Allison wondered where "Apple 1" was. Code-named "Greenleaf," it was carrying Simons. Allison put his HH-3 inside the compound and the Special Forces personnel streamed down the rear ramp.

Wasting no time, they blew the utility pole and set up a roadblock about 100 yards from the landing zone. A heated firefight ensued. Guards were "scurrying like mice" in an attempt to fire on the raiders. In the end, almost 50 NVA guards were killed at Son Tay.

"Apple 1," piloted by Lt. Col. Warner A. Britton, was having troubles of its own. The chopper had veered off the mark and was 450 meters south of the prison and had erroneously landed at the "secondary school." Simons knew it wasn't Son Tay. The

11 CROSSES

DISTINGUISHED SERVICE CROSS

Adderly, Tyrone J.	Sgt. 1st Class
Kemmer, Thomas J.	Master Sgt.
Meadows, Richard J.	Capt.
Powell, Thomas E.	Staff Sgt.
Simons, Arthur D.	Col.
Sydnor, Elliott P.	Lt. Col.

AIR FORCE CROSS

Allison, John V.	Lt. Col.
Britton, Warner A.	Lt. Col.
Donohue, Frederic M.	Maj.
Kalen, Herbert D.	Maj.
Wright, Leroy M.	Tech. Sgt.

DISTINGUISHED FLYING CROSS: 4
SILVER STAR: Army=50   Air Force=35

On Dec. 4, 1970, Secretary of Defense Melvin R. Laird presented Silver Stars to the Son Tay raiders at Ft. Bragg, N.C. Earlier, on Nov. 27, Col. Arthur Simons and Sgt. First Class Tyrone J. Adderly each received the Distinguished Service Cross at the White House.

structures and terrain were different and, to everyone's horror, it was no "secondary school"—it was a barracks filled with enemy soldiers—100 of whom were killed in five minutes.

As the chopper left, the raiders opened up with a barrage of automatic weapons. Capt. Udo Walther cut down four enemy soldiers and went from bay to bay riddling their rooms with his CAR-15. Realizing their error, the group radioed "Apple 1" to return and pick up the raiders from their dilemma. Simons, meanwhile, jumped into a trench to await the return of Britton when an NVA leaped in the hole next to him. Terrified and wearing only his underwear, the Vietnamese froze. Simons pumped six shells from his .357 Magnum handgun into the trooper's chest, killing him instantly.

Britton's chopper quickly returned when he received the radio transmission that Simon's group was in the wrong area. He flew back to Son Tay and deposited the remainder of the raiders there. Things were beginning to wind down. There was little resistance from the remaining guards. Meadows radioed to Lt. Col. Elliott P. "Bud" Sydnor, the head of the "Redwine" group on the raid, "negative items." There were no POWs. They had been on the ground exactly 27 minutes. The Son Tay Raid was over.

What Went Wrong?

Why had the raid on Son Tay failed? According to historian Dale Andrade: "The fact that initially the CIA, DIA and NSA would all be involved sounded like a good idea. But, in reality, they only muddied the waters of the planning and got in each other's way."

Another important factor was the seemingly never-ending poor weather. That's why the POWs had been relocated from Son Tay in the first place; because of the rapidly rising waters near the camp. Even Manor wrote in his after-action report that "five years of typhoons moved into the area of North Vietnam, South Vietnam and Laos" in the months just prior to the raid.

What most did not know was that a top-secret "weather modification" experiment named *Operation Popeye* was responsible for some of the inclement weather. (Col. Keith Grimes, an Air Force meteorologist, was on the raid.) Aircraft had been dropping "cloud-seeding paraphernalia" in the region, and the missions over Laos had doubled in 1970.

"Why didn't top officials in the CIA and Air Force tell the JCS and the *Ivory Coast Task Force* about *Operation Popeye?*" wrote Dale Andrade. "That gap in the knowledge of the planners could have endangered not only the lives of POWs in the area, but also the lives of the raiders."

After the raid, the NVA moved POWs from outlying POW camps to the Hanoi Hilton.

"What really stands out in my mind," remarked Special Forces Sgt. Terry Buckler, a member of the raiding party, "was the dedication the guys had. I was the youngest person on the raid, so I felt my life was unimportant. But the others had family. And they could have gotten off the mission at any time. But they stayed. That impressed me. These guys were willing to lay down their lives for their comrades. They were true professionals." ✪

BRUTAL BATTLES OF VIETNAM
1971

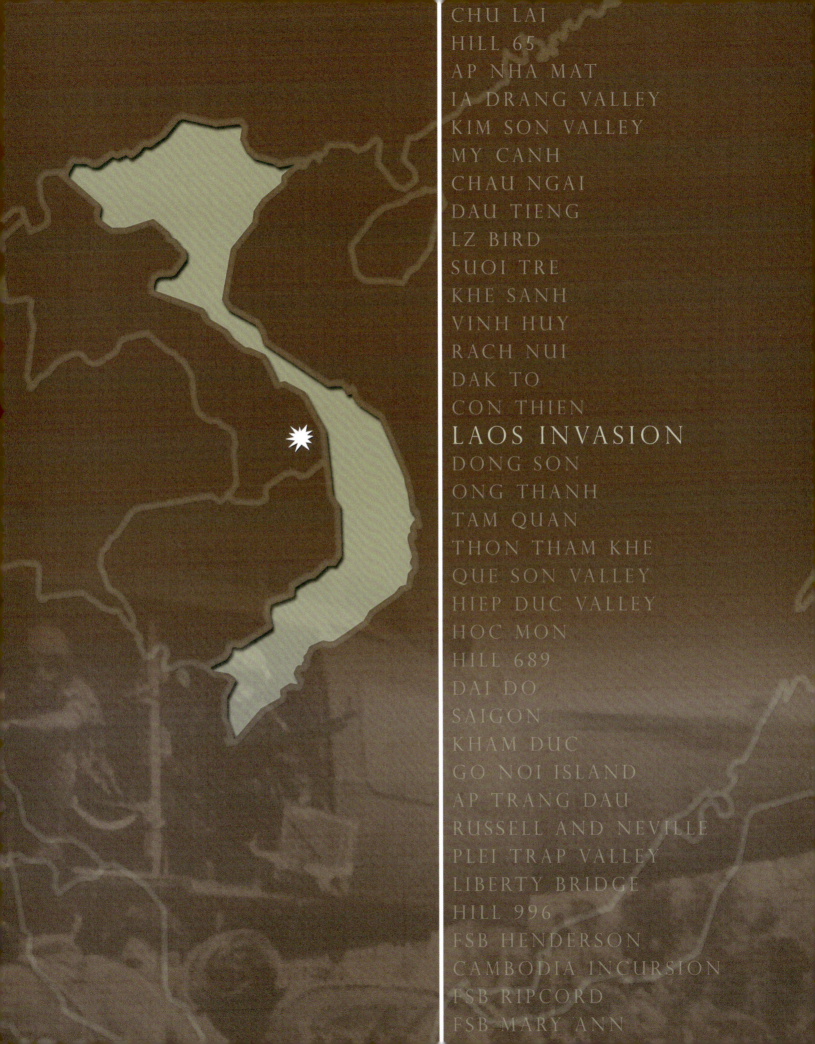

CHU LAI
HILL 65
AP NHA MAT
IA DRANG VALLEY
KIM SON VALLEY
MY CANH
CHAU NGAI
DAU TIENG
LZ BIRD
SUOI TRE
KHE SANH
VINH HUY
RACH NUI
DAK TO
CON THIEN
LAOS INVASION
DONG SON
ONG THANH
TAM QUAN
THON THAM KHE
QUE SON VALLEY
HIEP DUC VALLEY
HOC MON
HILL 689
DAI DO
SAIGON
KHAM DUC
GO NOI ISLAND
AP TRANG DAU
RUSSELL AND NEVILLE
PLEI TRAP VALLEY
LIBERTY BRIDGE
HILL 996
FSB HENDERSON
CAMBODIA INCURSION
FSB RIPCORD
FSB MARY ANN

BY RICHARD K. KOLB

HITTING THE HO CHI MINH TRAIL

"What kept them going, in spite of a pervasive sense that the war served no real purpose and the country didn't care," wrote battalion commander Lt. Col. William Hauser, "was a combination of pride, mutual interest and loyalty to good leadership."

These values did indeed motivate GIs serving in Vietnam in the 1970s, just as they had past generations of warriors. Morale then, as it has always been, was the key ingredient to unit cohesion. And members of combat units in the field fiercely held on to their morale.

On the surface, however, it may not have seemed so. Spec. 4 Mark Jury, an Army photographer who served in the war from 1969-70, about said it all when he made this observation:

"Often their opposition to the military had nothing to do with the moral aspects of Vietnam. It's just that they'd pick up a battered copy of *Life* magazine and see everybody else skinny-dipping at Woodstock, and that's a hell of a lot better than 'greasing gooks,' fighting malaria, and maybe going home in a plastic bag."

Yet the Laos operation was replete with sacrifice and genuine heroism. For those who served, place names like "the Rockpile," Lang Vei, Vandegrift, Khe Sanh, Lao Bao, Landing Zone (LZ) Lolo, LZ Hope and Ranger North would forever be imprinted on their minds.

CUTTING HANOI'S LAOTIAN LIFELINE

When asked in 1995 how the U.S. could have won the war, Bui Tin, a former North Vietnamese Army (NVA) general staff member, quickly replied: "Cut the Ho Chi Minh Trail inside Laos."

That's precisely what the Army of the Republic of Vietnam (ARVN) was sent to do in February and March 1971. Laos had served as a sanctuary and lifeline for the NVA for seven years, and it was time to sever Hanoi's umbilical cord.

The Ho Chi Minh Trail was actually 3,500 miles of roadways contained in a 30-mile corridor stretching the length of South Vietnam. All of its branches passed through the Tchepone area, 22 miles inside Laos. The most direct way to this dusty town was to head due west on old colonial Route 9, originating in Dong Ha.

ARVN's *Operation Lam Son 719's* intent was to drive a 15-mile-wide corridor to Tchepone with the objective of destroying NVA's base areas 604 and 611. This would, it was hoped, preempt any NVA offensives into South Vietnam.

No U.S. ground troops or advisers were allowed to accompany ARVN units across the Laotian border. Helicopter crews were the only exception. GIs on the ground had one essential mission: maintain Route 9 as a vital supply line to invading ARVN forces. That mission was dubbed *Operation Dewey Canyon II*.

Nearly 10,000 Americans participated directly in *Dewey Canyon II* and the helicopter aspects of *Lam Son 719*. These combined thrusts had many of the earmarks of a conventional WWII campaign. And it was one that required mobilizing the full range of Army assets then available in Vietnam.

'MAGNIFICENT TO BEHOLD'

Mobilized on South Vietnam's side of the border were the 101st Airborne Division; 1st Brigade, 5th Mechanized Infantry Division; 11th Infantry Brigade, Americal Division; elements of the 1st Aviation

In early 1971, GIs mounted a major operation in support of Saigon's incursion into Laos—a last offensive gasp to forestall the inevitable invasion of South Vietnam. This is the story of the GIs' role in operations *Dewey Canyon II/Lam Son 719*.

CORBIS PHOTO

Brigade; 223rd Combat Aviation Battalion; 108th Artillery Group; 45th Engineer Group; and two units (HMH-463 and HML-367) of the 1st Marine Air Wing.

In support, were the 5th Transportation, 801st Maintenance, 326th Medical and 426th Supply & Service battalions. A task force of the 834th Air Division, 7th Air Force, operated out of Quang Tri, and the Navy flew missions from carriers stationed in the Gulf of Tonkin.

U.S. helicopter crews and ARVN troops who actually entered Laos faced a formidable foe. Preparing for the invasion since October 1970, the NVA eventually fielded a modern, conventional force of 36,000 men. That figure included 10,000 members of *binh trams* (logistical units), as well as 5,000 allied Communist *Pathet Lao*. Two NVA armored regiments were equipped with Soviet T-34 tanks.

Arrayed against incoming choppers were 20 anti-aircraft battalions bristling with a deadly arsenal of 23mm, 37mm and 57mm guns. Standard 12.7mm machine guns were placed in multiple, mutual supporting positions. Crews endured the heaviest concentration of fire—WWII-style flak barrages—of the entire Vietnam War.

Every GI in the operation played a crucial role, whether he was a helicopter crewman, air

Two members of a helicopter recovery team at Firebase A Luoi turn their backs to dust whipped up as a Huey "slick" hoists a light observation helicopter, which had been shot down by NVA anti-aircraft fire. Although U.S. ground troops were forbidden from entering Laos, American pilots flew in support of *Lam Son 719*.

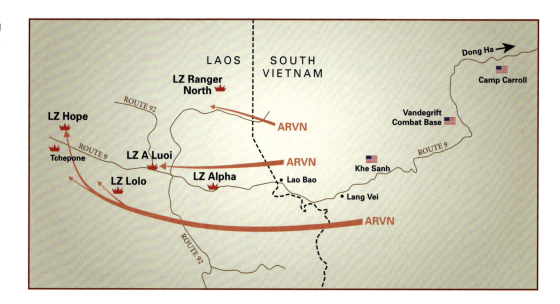

GIs manned bases from Dong Ha to Lao Bao on the Laotian border in supporting ARVN's thrust into the crossroads of the Ho Chi Minh Trail in February/March 1971.

Pfc. Thomas A. Love, a driver with the 529th Quartermaster Company, was wounded in action three miles east of Khe Sanh on March 6, 1971. He was one of 55 logistics GIs wounded while travelling perilous Route 9.

cavalryman, artillery gunner, grunt, Air Force or Navy pilot, Marine advisor, trucker or engineer. Operations had to be conducted in sync.

Securing Route 9 and constructing a secondary pioneer road—"Red Devil Highway" that paralleled the main road into Laos—was the first step. A Company, 7th Engineers, spearheaded the column along Route 9.

Combat engineers earned well-deserved praise from Lt. Gen. James Sutherland, Jr., commanding general of XXIV Corps. "One of the many parts of *Dewey Canyon II* and *Lam Son 719* which I continue to recall with professional pride and admiration was the performance of the 45th Engineer Group with its two battalions, the 14th and 27th," he said.

"It was the most outstanding performance that I had observed in my 34 years of service... the sight on D-Day was magnificent to behold—a steady stream of helicopters moving engineer equipment, culvert and bridge sections from the rear areas to the front."

Moving materiel along the route was a Herculean, risky venture. All told, 1,163 U.S. convoys made the journey. "The support of the operation was one of the major logistical feats of the war," wrote Lt. Gen. William J. McCaffrey, deputy commander of U.S. Army, Vietnam. "The equivalent of more than four divisions received supplies that travelled, for the most part, over a single road and into a single airhead."

Keith W. Nolan, in his superb account—*Into Laos*—aptly described the perilous conditions: "Through it all, the truckers kept hauling the supplies, enduring bad driving conditions every inch of the way, and occasional bouts with rockets, snipers and ambushes. They drove in all conditions around the clock, fighting sun glare and veils of dust in the day, and fog banks at night."

Thomas M. Roche was then an MP with the 23rd Military Police Company of the Americal Division. As a V-100 crew chief and driver, he escorted division units to Khe Sanh. "All along Route 9 we saw remnants of previous convoys," he recalled. "A truck-tractor cab was beside the road with a hole through the windshield about the size of a softball, and the area around it singed with extreme heat—courtesy of an RPG hit."

Thomas A. Love, a member of the 529th Quartermaster Company, drove a 2½-ton M-49C tank truck loaded with aviation fuel. Ambushed between Vandegrift and Khe Sanh on March 6, he was grazed in the head by an AK-47 round. "It felt like getting a knuckle sandwich from King Kong, and it bounced me two feet off the seat," he told a reporter.

Love was among many casualties sustained along Route 9. By operation's end, the Da Nang Support Command and the 504th MP Battalion had suffered 11 KIA, 55 WIA, 14 traffic

Grunts of the 1st Bde., 5th Mech. Inf. Div., take time out for some "C-rats" in February 1971. Route 9 and "Red Devil Highway" were the areas of operation for the 5th's men, 58 of whom died making them secure for the invasion of Laos.

Armored personnel carriers transport men of A Co., 1st Bn., 506th Inf. Regt., 101st Abn. Div., toward the Laotian border.

fatalities and 68 serious injuries.

This entire clearing operation ultimately cost 55 GIs KIA and 431 WIA over a period of about a week.

'TYRANNY OF TERRAIN'

To carry out *Dewey Canyon II,* a network of bases had to be established. Dong Ha served as the logistical hub. Within easy reach of NVA artillery, GIs there could see the big red Communist flag that flew just across the DMZ. Covering the eastern DMZ were firebases Charlie 2 and Alpha Four.

Vandegrift served as Forward Support Area-I and Khe Sanh as FSA-II. Both bases were subjected to 122mm rocket barrages, as well as sapper attacks. Nearby terrain features were occupied by grunts. The "Rockpile" was a piece of jungle-covered granite north of Vandegrift. Hill 400 was situated near Lang Vei. The valley between "Emerald City" and the Rockpile was nicknamed the "Punchbowl."

On the Laotian border itself, batteries of the 1st Bn., 44th Artillery, and 2nd Bn., 94th Artillery, for example, alternated duty at Lao Bao. During the operation, the two reinforced battalions of the 108th Artillery Group fired 208,962 rounds into Laos from such border positions and from Khe Sanh.

In the field, NVA infantrymen did not necessarily bring the greatest grief to the grunts. More often than not, it was the unforgiving hills, heat, stifling humidity, parasitic pests, jungle rot and immersion foot from constant sweating.

Nolan described the ordeal of the 3rd Bn., 187th Inf., 101st Airborne, northwest of Khe Sanh in March: "It was like being in an oven-hot green tunnel. Minute by minute, the landscape and sun were more of an enemy than any Vietnamese who might be lurking.

" 'Wait-a-minute' vines coiled around legs and canteen tops, thorns tore at arms and faces, jungle rot spread, clothes rotted in the humidity, mouths burned from thirst and bile, and leeches appeared seemingly from nowhere to attach themselves."

Exhaustion suffered in the boonies underscored Napoleon's dictum: "The first quality of a soldier is constancy in enduring fatigue and hardship. Courage is only the second. Poverty, privation and want are the school of the good soldier."

U.S. ARMY PHOTO

A U.S. Army UH-1D helicopter lands during *Lam Son 719* to take aboard a casualty. Helicopters played a pivotal role in ferrying and supplying ARVN troops in Laos. At least 140 U.S. choppers went down during the war's most intense helicopter operation.

Also there was a very real *armed* enemy. At a night defensive position on March 22, C Company sustained five KIA in close combat. The 3rd Battalion took out 48 NVA in firefights during the operation. But when it ended, the unit counted 19 helmets on rifles planted bayonet first in the earth at a solemn ceremony.

'ERNIE PYLE WOULD'VE LOVED 'EM'

Despite such losses and the constant battering by the elements, a comradeship of the bush was the glue that held prideful units together through thick and thin. The 101st fell into this category, according to many of its veterans.

Pfc. Bill Warren was a draftee who unhesitatingly expressed pride in being a "Screaming Eagle": "I would say morale was high and everyone had pride in the 101st. We never stayed in a safe position or faked coordinates. We never avoided contact and always fought our hardest when we encountered the enemy.

"As a matter of fact, we had a lot of men who were gung-ho and loved a good fight. I am still proud to this day that I served in this unit and with its gallant men."

Warren's feelings were shared by other GIs, too. Not surprisingly, members of P Co., 75th Inf. (Rangers), 5th Inf. Div., which fielded six-man teams for seven days at a time around Khe Sanh, Vandegrift and the Rockpile, were ingrained with a positive attitude.

Spec. 4 Henry E. Walters, Jr., was unequivocal in his views: "We never abandoned anyone in the field—dead or alive. If six went out, six came back—always. The leadership of P Company was superb; the morale, camaraderie, courage and dedication of our people were unqualified."

Some of the heaviest action for U.S. troops occurred during ARVN's withdrawal from Laos when the NVA was counterattacking. Fighting intensified on both sides of the border. Capt. Gerald Downey, commander of C Co., 2nd Bn., 1st Inf., 196th LIB, American Division, remembered:

"The guys from the 5th Mech and the other armored cav outfits were a brave and tough bunch of men. They fought their way up that road every day, sometimes several times a day, and each time they went they knew what to expect. They behaved in a way that would have made the original General Patton proud. If it had been World War II, someone would have written stories about them. Ernie Pyle would have loved 'em."

However, quite the contrary occurred. Lt. Col. Richard Meyer, commander of the 1st Bn., 77th Armor ("Steel Tigers"), 5th Mech, attempted to get correspondents, who could never measure up to Pyle, to take notice. "I had reporters seek out other units than mine because my troops were just doing their duty without any of the race and dope problems that made stateside headlines. They went looking for problems elsewhere."

FIGHTING ALONG THE 'YELLOW BRICK ROAD'

Five days into *Dewey Canyon II*, on Feb. 5, the first U.S. casualties were sustained. A Cobra of D Trp., 3rd Sqdn., 5th Cav, accidentally crashed northwest of Khe Sanh, killing both pilots. The following evening, A Btry., 1st Bn., 82nd Arty, American, near the Rockpile, was hit by 122mm rockets, killing one GI and wounding four. The first American blood of the operation had been spilled.

HEROISM ON DISPLAY: LAOS OPERATION, 1971

MEDAL OF HONOR

RECIPIENT	UNIT	DATE	LOCATION	MOS
Fitzmaurice, Spec. 4 Michael	D Trp., 2nd Sqdn., 17th Cav, 101st Div.	March 23	Khe Sanh	Infantryman

AIR FORCE CROSS

Carter, Capt. William R.	23rd Tac. Air Support Sqdn. (Thailand)	March 6-7	Laos	FAC*
Funderburk, Capt. Leonard J.	23rd Tac. Air Support Sqdn. (Thailand)	March 22	Laos	FAC*

DISTINGUISHED SERVICE CROSS

Barker, Maj. Jack L. (KIA)	B Co., 101st Avn. Bn., 101st Abn. Div.	Mar 20	FSB Brown, Laos	Helicopter Pilot
Bowers, Capt. Charles J.	1st Bn., 42nd Regt., 22nd ARVN Div.	Feb 27-Mar 5	Kontum Province	Senior Adviser
Chapman, Staff Sgt. Leslie A.	TF 1 Adv. Element, 5th SFG	Feb 16-18	FSB Thor, A Shau	Adviser
Fujii, Spec. 5 Dennis M.	237th Med. Det., 61st Med. Bn.	Feb 18-22	Laos, Ranger North	Crew Chief
Green, Chief WO Gerald D.	A Trp., 2nd Sqdn., 17th Cav, 101st Abn. Div..	Feb 18	Laos	Helicopter Pilot
Newman, Maj. James T.	C Trp., 2nd Sqdn.,17th Cav, 101st Abn. Div.	Feb 18	Laos	Helicopter Pilot
Pederson, Spec. 4 Roger A. (KIA)	3rd Sqdn., 5th Cav, 1st Bde., 5th Inf. Div.	Mar 29	Punch Bowl, Route 9	Medic

Spec. 4 Michael Fitzmaurice

| Capt. William R. Carter | Capt. Leonard J. Funderburk | Maj. Jack L. Barker | Spec. 5 Dennis M. Fujii | Maj. James T. Newman | Spec. 4 Roger A. Pederson |

NOTE: NOT ALL PHOTOS ARE AVAILABLE. PHOTOS COURTESY CONGRESSIONAL MEDAL OF HONOR SOCIETY, VIETNAM VETERANS HALL OF FACES, WWW.VETERANTRIBUTES.COM AND FAMILY SOURCES.

PRESIDENTIAL UNIT CITATION

UNIT	DATE	LOCATION	MISSION
158th Avn. Bn., 101st Avn. Grp.	Feb 8-Mar 24	Laos	Multitude of missions through barrages of enemy fire

VALOROUS UNIT AWARD

4th Bn., 77th Aerial Arty, 101st Abn. Div.	Feb 8-Apr 8	Laos	Deployed consistent aerial rocket artillery fire
14th Avn. Bn.	Feb 8-Apr 7	Laos	Assaults and extracted allied forces
101st Avn. Bn., 101st Abn. Div.	Mar 3-20	Laos	Battle for Tchepone
223rd Avn. Bn., 1st Avn. Bde.	Feb 8-Mar 24	Laos	52 combat assaults along Ho Chi Minh Trail
Trp. C, 7th Sqdn., 17th Cav	Feb 8-Mar 24	Laos	Assaults on Ho Chi Minh Trail
Trp. B, 7th Sqdn., 1st Cav	Feb 8-Mar 24	Laos	Assaults on Ho Chi Minh Trail

Note: *The air cav troops operated with the 223rd. *FAC = Forward Air Controller*

An unidentified helicopter pilot of C Trp., 2nd Sqdn., 17th Cav Regt., 101st Abn. Div., takes a break during *Lam Son 719*. The "Condors" played a pivotal role in providing life-saving air support for South Vietnamese forces.

That morning, gunships from the 2nd Sqdn., 17th Air Cav, confirmed six NVA KIA along the border. Casualties climbed on both sides as contacts intensified. The 4th Bn., 3rd Inf., Americal, occupied the Rockpile on Feb. 10. The hilltop hosting the command post was dubbed "Purple Heart Hill." The 4th's A Company went in with 122 men and left with 88 effectives. Battalion kills, though, totalled 122 NVA.

On Feb. 19, five men of 3rd Plt., D Co., 1st Bn., 11th Inf. Regt., were KIA in a firefight in the vicinity of Hill 819 after they were cut off from their company.

During a minesweeping operation on Red Devil Road near the Rockpile on Feb. 23, Spec. 4 Terry J. Johnson, a forward observer with 2nd Plt., C Trp., 3rd Sqdn., 5th Cav, had a close call. He told an Associated Press reporter, "That dink would have blown me away if he hadn't had a misfire. Instead, I cut him in half with my machine gun." For preventing his unit from being ambushed, Johnson earned a Silver Star.

As the operation drew down, the ground pounders achieved perhaps their greatest single victory on April 2. Off the Yellow Brick Road, a 20-man NVA unit was sighted. A Sheridan tank and 81mm-mortar crew quickly swung into action: the tank's 152mm main gun ripped the Communist patrol apart.

KHE SANH: RING OF FIRE

Meanwhile, NVA rockets and sappers had been taking a toll along Route 9. At a night position near Lang Ha (1) on March 14, an NVA barrage claimed the lives of five engineers of the 59th Eng. Co., 39th Eng. Bn.

Khe Sanh, famous for the 1968 siege, was hit hardest. The prospect of sappers penetrating the perimeter wire was not a pleasant one, but it became a reality.

Khe Sanh was defended by 650 troops—350 of them ground combat. On perimeter guard were men of the 2nd Squadron, 17th Cav, and 4th Battalion, 77th Aerial Rocket Regiment.

March 15 saw 200 122mm rocket rounds hit the base. A peak of 500 NVA artillery rounds hit it on March 19. Some 20 rounds an hour—all day long—rained in on the GIs.

Yet life had to go on. While repairing the airstrip on March 22, Staff Sgt. Donald Briggs of 1st Plt., A Co., 27th Engineer Bn., helped pull three men from a flaming helicopter. In return for his second- and third-degree burns, Briggs received the Soldier's Medal.

On March 23, 40 men of the 2nd Co., 15th NVA Engineer (Sapper) Battalion, breached the perimeter.

To meet them were 33 GIs of 3rd Plt. (an aero-rifle "Blues" outfit), D Trp., 2nd Sqdn., 17th Cav. The platoon's calling cards proclaimed them "The Grim Reapers of Death."

During the assault, either a satchel charge or an errant allied artillery flare hit the refuel/rearm point, igniting a 10,000-gallon fuel container and a store of 2.75-inch rockets.

"We fought them for four hours—Jesus, some of them were on the runway," Platoon Sgt. Terry Stallard said. "We killed 15 of them. The dinks had charcoal on their legs and faces. When they were throwing satchel charges into our bunkers they'd kind of start yelling." The "Blues" lost three KIA and 15 WIA.

That same night, Spec. 4 Michael J. Fitzmaurice of 3rd Plt., D Trp., 2nd Sqdn., 17th Cav,

101st Abn. Div., earned one of the six Medals of Honor awarded in 1971.

When the sappers entered the South Dakotan's trench, they dumped three satchels. He hurled two of the explosive charges from the bunker and then himself on top of the third, absorbing the blast through his flak jacket. Though suffering serious multiple wounds and partial loss of sight, he went on to engage the enemy single-handedly. "I never figured on living," Fitzmaurice recalled years after. "You just kept fighting."

"Fitzmaurice stumbled into the trench line, firing his M-16, gunning down two of the sappers," wrote Nolan in *Into Laos*. "He dropped the empty rifle, grabbed a machete, and stormed down the trench. He ran into three other sappers and hacked them all to death in furious hand-to-hand combat."

Having refused medical evacuation, Fitzmaurice spent 13 months at Fitzsimmons Army Hospital recovering from his wounds. His Medal of Honor was presented at the White House on Oct. 15, 1973. Fitzmaurice said some four decades later, "We were sent there to do a job. When we came home, people didn't think much of the war."

In the last two weeks of March, 1,150 NVA artillery rounds hit the dust-shrouded outpost. Six days later, Khe Sanh was once again abandoned.

On March 24, an OH-58 helicopter was shot down 14 miles northwest of Khe Sanh Airfield. When another Scout chopper came to its aid, it also was brought down. Five men of the Scout Plt., D Trp., 3rd Sqdn, 5th Cav, were KIA.

> ## "He dropped the empty rifle, grabbed a machete, and stormed down the trench. He ran into three other sappers and hacked them all to death in furious hand-to-hand combat."
>
> —DESCRIPTION OF MEDAL OF HONOR RECIPIENT SPEC. 4 MICHAEL J. FITZMAURICE'S ACTIONS

The next day, yet another selfless act of bravery was witnessed. A 12-man patrol from 1st Plt., B Trp., 1st Sqdn., 1st Cav, Americal Div., was ambushed on Hill 632, losing four KIA. During the melee, Staff Sgt. Manuel Puentes picked up a grenade to throw it away, but it exploded, killing him but saving the lives of several men.

In early April, Spec. 4 Leslie Liebowitz of the 3rd Plt., B Co., 1st Bn., 11th Inf., told a *New York Times* reporter: "We've been out here 60 days. We're just straight legs. The guys in the helicopters get all the attention. Most people don't even know we're here."

HUNTED BY THE ENEMY

While grunts were waging a ground war inside Vietnam, just over the border in Laos, U.S. helicopters were literally undergoing an ordeal by fire. "Missions were so bad," remembered pilot David Groen, "that crews taped 'chicken plates' [steel body armor] down to the chin bubble and on the floor to stop the bullets. Door gunners wore chest and back armor plates, and sat on pieces of armor."

Of the Americans directly supporting the invasion, 2,600, or 26%, were helicopter crews flying in hundreds of choppers. They flew nearly 46,000 sorties *inside* Laos, some 28% of the total flown during the operation. Marine birds flew additional missions. The war's largest helicopter assault involving 120 aircraft took place against LZ Hope and Tchepone. At LZ Lolo alone, 11 choppers were shot down.

Remarked one pilot: "In Vietnam, you have to hunt for the enemy. But in Laos, man, they hunt for you!" For the copter crews, at least three ops must have scarred their memories: Hope, Lolo and Ranger North all went down in the annals of helicopter warfare.

"During [ARVN] pickups in hot LZs, they would not provide covering fire, they simply kept their heads down."

—ROGER RILEY, A HUEY SLICK PILOT WITH A COMPANY ("GHOST RIDERS"), 158TH AVIATION BATTALION. RILEY WAS AWARDED A DISTINGUISHED FLYING CROSS.

At Firebase Ranger North in late February, the ARVN 39th Ranger Battalion was cut to pieces. The U.S. 158th Aviation Battalion flew around the clock supplying the Rangers and evacuating casualties. "Those helicopter pilots must have steel balls," said an airplane pilot.

An F-4 pilot, Air Force Capt. William Cathey of the 40th Tactical Fighter Squadron, described the frightening scene: "[Ranger North] looked like World War II must have. We put a napalm strike within 100 meters of [ARVN] troops. That was tight. We could see them in the trenches."

The 158th Aviation Battalion of the 101st Aviation Group symbolized the crews' courage. Its five companies and four assigned Transportation Corps detachments earned the prestigious Presidential Unit Citation for extraordinary heroism between Feb. 8 and March 24. Its A Company also led the massive flight of helicopters across the border.

Conducting combat assaults and resupply missions deep inside enemy territory along the Ho Chi Minh Trail, the battalion's "valorous aircrews flew mission after mission through barrages of enemy fire," according to the citation.

"Flying in Vietnam and Laos was vastly different for two reasons," remembers Roger Riley, a Huey slick pilot with A Co. (the "Ghost Riders"), 158th Avn. Bn. "In Laos, we were working with the ARVN, who may have been responsible for more American deaths than the NVA. This may sound harsh, but they completely fell apart. During pickups in hot LZs, they would not provide covering fire, they simply kept their heads down."

"Counter fire in Laos was far more intense than anything we normally encountered in Vietnam," he said. "We ran up against 23mm, 37mm and 57mm anti-aircraft fire, as well as tube artillery and even tanks. Sometimes pilots were caught on the ground and came under withering small-arms and mortar fire. There is no question that the NVA were a determined, tenacious, admirable foe. But the American crews flying during *Operation Lam Son 719* were more than a match for them."

Riley, who served in Vietnam from May 1970 through May 1971, was awarded the Distinguished Flying Cross for his heroism in Laos and at Firebase Ripcord the previous July.

On the ground, the astounding survival story of Spec. 5 Dennis M. Fujii stands out. The Distinguished Service Cross (for the six other DSC awardees see the chart on page 387) attests to his heroism. A crew chief aboard a helicopter ambulance of the 237th Medical Det., 61st Med. Bn., 67th Med. Grp., Fujii's bird was shot down during a rescue mission over Firebase Ranger North. He voluntarily remained behind rather than risk the lives of other helicopter crews. The only American on the battlefield, and disregarding his own wounds, he

TRAGEDY AT LZ LOLO

The image at right, taken on March 5, 1971, shows the sites where five helicopters were downed at LZ Lolo on March 3, as they dropped off ARVN troops. A CH-47 hovers over the scene in the upper right.

#1: *Chalk 2* of the 71st Assault Helicopter Co. (AHC), 145th Combat Avn. Bn., 1st Aviation Bde., was piloted by WO Gary Arne. Loss of tail rotor and hydraulics from enemy fire caused the aircraft to be skewered on a broken tree.

#2: *Chalk 4* of 71st AHC shoot-down. The crew chief was Will Fortenberry

#3: *Commanchero 39* of A Co., 101st Assault Helicopter Bn. (AHB), 101st Abn Div., was piloted by WO Robert Morris. It was forced to return to LZ Lolo after catching fire. The blaze was extinguished after landing.

#4: *Commanchero 14* of A Co., 101st AHB, 101st Abn Div. *(Chalk 18)*, piloted by CW2 John Gale and Capt. Gerald Crews. It took heavy fire during approach and caught fire.

#5: A "Lancer" of B Co., 158th AHB, 101st Abn Div., piloted by WO Manuel Catzoela and 1st Lt. Charles R. Anderson. The aircraft was hit by an RPG and burned.

Compiled by Mike Sloniker, Vietnam Helicopter Pilots Association

administered first aid to ARVN troops.

When his position was attacked, Fujii called in gunships for 17 hours while repelling the NVA with his rifle at close quarters. Finally rescued, he was shot down a second time and stranded for two more days at an ARVN Ranger base. His ordeal from Feb. 18-22 ended when he was ultimately lifted to safety in Phu Bai. He had directed helicopter and fixed-wing strikes over five days.

Six Huey pilots earned the Silver Star and six crewmen the Distinguished Flying Cross for attempting Fujii's rescue under heavy fire.

Spec. 4 Paul A. Lagenour, a door gunner aboard a UH-1C gunship, had another incredible experience. He was shot down on March 19 during a mission to FSB Alpha. Wounded, he directed air strikes and then evaded capture for 12 days until found by a U.S. armor patrol west of Khe Sanh.

Landing Zone Lolo, on March 3, was a death trap for helicopters. The LZ was pulverized, yet the NVA held on. "They [U.S.] put in five hours of airstrikes, and Cobras hit that hillside," remembered one pilot. "Then we went in and it sounded like a million people opened up on us." Nearly a dozen UH-1s were downed and 44 damaged in the hail of fire.

Three days later at LZ Hope near Tchepone, the war's largest helicopter combat assault occurred. Some 120 Hueys of the 223rd Combat Aviation Battalion, escorted by scores of gunships and tactical aircraft, flew 50 miles from Khe Sanh into Laos. While moving elements of the 1st ARVN Division, U.S. Army aviation survived the war's heaviest anti-aircraft fire. Yet, miraculously, only one Huey went down; 14 were hit.

In a March 15, 1971, article, *Newsweek* dramatically described the helicopter mission: "To the modern American cavalryman of the air, the plunge into Laos has been something like an old-time charge on horseback: admirably heroic, stunningly effective—and terribly costly."

Simon Dunstan, author of *Vietnam Choppers,* put the aviation war in proper perspective: "However equivocal the results of the ground campaign may have been, nothing can detract from the fortitude and professionalism displayed by the helicopter crewmen during *Lam Son 719.*" But the price was high to the bitter end: 75% of the choppers used to pick up the stranded ARVN sustained bullet damage.

NVA gunners brought down a total of 107 confirmed U.S. Army helicopters—including 53 Hueys and 26 Cobras. A prime example: NVA shot down a CH-47C on Feb. 15 near Ban Nalom on Highway 9. All six crew members of C Co., 159th ASHB, 101st, were killed. Five more were completely destroyed in accidents and 618 were damaged out of 659 deployed.

According to John Prados, in his book *The Hidden History of the Vietnam War* (1995), the official tally of hostile U.S. helicopter losses was 118 inside Laos and 22 in South Vietnam. (Seven fixed-wing aircraft with four pilots also were lost to enemy action.)

All told, 89 pilots and crew members were KIA along with 178 WIA. Helicopter crews constituted 35% of all American KIAs during the Laos operation.

"The magnitude of their [helicopter crews] sacrifices was unprecedented during the Vietnam War," Robert E. Jones wrote in *History of the 101st Airborne Division* (2005).

"Thanks to the courage of the crews aboard the choppers, it [Laos, 1971] may well rank as the finest hour in the history of U.S. Army aviation," wrote Earl Swift in *Where They Lay* (2003), an account of MIA searches.

FATIGUES ROTTED ON THEIR BACKS

ARVN's withdrawal from Laos was not a pretty sight. Marine Lt. Col. Robert Darron, flying in a forward air controller plane, recalled: "Route 9 was cluttered full of junk. Tanks and trucks and all kinds of things stretched about a mile." A week after ARVN's departure, the Ho Chi Minh Trail was in full operation. The campaign officially closed down April 6, 1971.

Saigon's gambit in Laos cost 253 Americans killed in action and 1,149 wounded. An additional 33 non-hostile U.S. deaths were associated with the campaign, too. (For a unit breakdown, see the chart at left.)

The grunts accepted their casualties stoically. Pfc. Michael DeAngelis, an assistant machine-gunner with B Co., 1st Bn., 61st Inf., 1st Bde., 5th Div., said it best in recounting his unit's experience: "They were out for 75 days and never got mail or clean clothes the whole time. Their fatigues were literally rotted on their backs and they were all caked with dirt and very pooped, too. They lost 15 men, six from my old platoon... there is now no one left from my old squad... What can I say to tell you how I feel right now?"

Like many other GIs, DeAngelis had gone to Vietnam believing in the cause. Yet others felt the lunge into Laos was the right move.

"In my opinion, the Cambodian operation and this operation [Laos] are the two most intelligent moves we have made since we have been in South Vietnam," Pfc. Clyde Baker wrote in a letter to President Nixon.

Believing at the time that it might end the war, he said in his unit that "everyone here is putting out 100%. I'm sorry for the lousy handwriting, but I'm writing this letter down inside a tank."

Ambassador to Vietnam Ellsworth Bunker summed up the American role best: "What we've done, *our* forces, on the ground and in the air has been magnificent. It's been a great performance." ✪

THE TOLL

LAOS OPERATION CASUALTIES FEB. 5-APRIL 3*

UNIT	KIA	WIA
101st Abn. Div.	85	261
5th Inf. Div., 1st Bde.	58	431
Americal Div., 11th Bde.	54	256
Other Support Forces	47	125
XXIV Corps Artillery	9	76
Total	**253**	**1,149**

*Actual beginning and ending dates that U.S. KIAs were sustained. An additional 19 GIs were killed in air accidents and 14 in road accidents. Helicopter pilot and crew losses accounted for 89 KIA and 178 WIA of the total.

Source: Into Laos (pp. 366-67) by Keith W. Nolan.

KIA: LAOS, 1961

BY RICHARD K. KOLB

Pictured here is a Douglas C-47 Skytrain similar to the SC-47 shot down on March 23, 1961.

American servicemen died in a forgotten theater of the Second Indochina War.

Laos hosted its own little war before Vietnam heated up for the Americans. It was a three-way civil war between Soviet-backed "neutralists," Communist Pathet Lao supported by North Vietnam, and the Royal Lao government aided by the CIA. Amidst this melee were deposited 107 Green Berets disguised as civilians in July 1959.

Special Air Force units also were secretly at work. On March 23, 1961, while flying over the strategic Plain of Jars, the *Rose Bowl* (SC-47 recon aircraft) was hit by 37mm anti-aircraft fire near Phonsavan. It was equipped with aerial photography and electronic surveillance gear.

Attached to the Defense Attaché's Office from the 314th Air Division based at Osan AB, Korea, the plane carried two Army officers on its way to Saigon. All six airmen and one of the soldiers died in the shoot-down four miles north of Phong Savan. (The burial site was found and four sets of remains recovered in July 1991, but three are still unaccounted for.) But assistant Army attaché Lawrence R. Bailey parachuted safely.

Captured by the Pathet Lao, Bailey recalled, "I was held in solitary confinement for 17 long, dark months in a 12-by-15 room." Bailey was released Aug. 12, 1962, along with two CIA Air America helicopter crewmen captured in May 1961 and a Green Beret POW.

On April 19, 1961, an official Military Assistance Advisory Group, eventually peaking at 666 men, was set up in the capital of Vientiane. Three days later, four members of Field Training Team 59 of B Co., 7th SFG, were lost in the Battle of Vang Vieng. Two men, Gerald M. Biber and John M. Bischoff, were killed in action at their armored car, one was captured and later released, and Capt. Walter Moon was executed in his prison quarters at La Houang on July 22, 1961.

Peace accords declared Laos neutral, and American advisers withdrew by Oct. 7, 1962. Quickly forgotten in the diplomatic shuffle were 10 Americans killed in an obscure campaign overshadowed by a far larger war. For those who served in the "Land of a Million Elephants," their compact conflict would rate an Armed Forces Expeditionary Medal. ✪

10 GIs Were Killed by the Pathet Lao in Laos, 1961

DATE	NAME	SERVICE	UNIT
Mar 23, 1961	Bankowski, Alfons A.*	Air Force	314th Air Division
Mar 23, 1961	Garside, Frederick T.	Air Force	314th Air Division
Mar 23, 1961	Magee, Ralph W.	Air Force	314th Air Division
Mar 23, 1961	Matteson, Glenn	Air Force	314th Air Division
Mar 23, 1961	Sampson, Leslie V.	Air Force	314th Air Division
Mar 23, 1961	Weston, Oscar B., Jr.*	Air Force	314th Air Division
Mar 23, 1961	Weitkamp, Edgar W.*	Army	Army Attaché Office
Apr 22, 1961	Biber, Gerald M.	Army	FTT #59, B Co., 7th SFG
Apr 22, 1961	Bischoff, John M.	Army	FTT #59, B Co., 7th SFG
Apr 22, 1961	Moon, Walter H. (5)	Army	FTT #59, B Co., 7th SFG

*Still unaccounted for.

Biber   **Bischoff**

Moon

BY AL HEMINGWAY

SIXTY MINUTES OF TERROR AT MARY ANN

"**M**ost of us didn't talk about it when we came home," said Ed Newton of Sawyer, Kan., and a veteran of the 46th Infantry. "In my opinion, the media blew it all out of proportion when they mentioned the drugs and sleeping on duty. It's time we set the record straight and tell the truth about Mary Ann." Indeed, it is.

In the early morning hours of March 28, 1971, an estimated 50 sappers from the 2nd Company, 409th Viet Cong (VC) Main Force Sapper Battalion, quietly neared their objective—Fire Support Base (FSB) Mary Ann—a remote outpost of the 198th Light Inf. Bde. (LIB), 23rd Inf. (Americal) Div., located in the western highlands of Quang Tin province in Military Region I of South Vietnam.

PRECARIOUS POSITION

Mary Ann's purpose was to provide a protective shield for Da Nang and other coastal hamlets. Also, it was a jumping-off point for operations designed to disrupt the flow of men and materiél coming down the Dak Rose Trail.

Erected on top of a ridge, it "occupied two camel humps with a shallow saddle in between." A series of ridges and hills enveloped the outpost on three sides, and thick jungle obscured the field of observation. Described as a "shantytown," 30 hooches, bunkers and other buildings were sprinkled over its interior. The base was 546 yards in length, 82 yards wide across its saddle and 136 yards wide at both ends.

Twenty-two bunkers, constructed from metal conex shipping boxes, were placed around the outer perimeter. Most of the headquarters buildings were situated on the southeast side of the base: the Battalion Tactical Operations Center (BTOC), company command post (CP), communications bunker, a sensor monitoring station, ammunition storage bunkers, three mess halls, artillery liaison center, battalion aid station and fuel storage area.

The northwest end of the camp held two 155mm howitzer parapets, the fire direction center and the artillery CP. Also, a quad .50-caliber machine gun team was placed along the perimeter together with a detachment from a searchlight unit.

One line company from the 198th LIB was rotated from the field to Mary Ann approximately every two weeks and was responsible for its security while there.

GIs arrive aboard a U.S. helicopter at Firebase Mary Ann. Situated atop a ridge, the base was hit by sappers on March 28, 1971.

Though the Vietnam War was winding down for the U.S. Army in 1971, the enemy attack on Fire Support Base Mary Ann in March claimed 30 American lives in one hour of no-quarters combat. The America's 1st Battalion, 46th Infantry, and attached units tied for the single largest U.S. hostile ground loss of the year.

MARCH 1971

PHOTO BY EDWARD MANSON, COURTESY OF GARY NOLLER

PHOTO COURTESY EDWARD MANSON

Men on Mary Ann examine the cache of weapons that was captured two weeks prior to the attack on March 28. It was thought that the VC were out to destroy C Company as a result.

ON THE PERIMETER

In all, 231 Americans and 21 South Vietnamese (ARVN) soldiers defended Mary Ann on that fateful night. Among them were the 75-man C Co., 1st Bn., 46th Inf.; an 18-man recon platoon; 34 medics, communications personnel, clerks and cooks from HQ Company; and an eight-man contingent from the 4.2-inch mortar platoon of E Company.

That crew was there assembling the remainder of the mortar ammo to take to LZ Mildred. (No heavy mortars were present that night on Mary Ann. Two mortars were sent to Chu Lai for repair, and the other two went to Mildred.)

There, too, were 81mm mortar crews from B and D companies; 20 men of 1st Plt., C Btry., 3rd Bn., 16th FA, manning two 155mm howitzers; and artillerymen from four other units. Finally, 22 grunts from A, B and D companies were in transit.

Mary Ann had been spared an all-out attack. With the war winding down, no one believed the VC would hit such an insignificant outpost. "There was a false sense of security at Mary Ann," said John Pastrick, an infantryman with C Co., 1st Bn., 46th Inf. "It was very lax all the time."

But on this fog-shrouded evening, 50 VC sappers, their bodies covered with charcoal and grease to make them more difficult targets in the darkness, quietly slipped through Mary Ann's perimeter. Crouching low in three- to six-man teams, they made their way through the base's unsuspecting defenders.

Lt. Col. William P. Doyle drew his .45 pistol and pumped a round into a sapper's chest just before another satchel charge was heaved at him.

STRUCK WITH A VENGEANCE

They wasted no time. Under the protective umbrella of a mortar barrage, sappers struck the vulnerable BTOC with a vengeance. Lt. Col. William P. Doyle, the battle-hardened battalion commander, was awakened when 82mm mortar shells landed with a resounding thud just outside his bunker.

To make matters worse, the sappers tossed CS (tear) gas into the BTOC. Choking and unable to see, Doyle was knocked down when a satchel charge exploded. Regaining his composure, he drew his .45 pistol and pumped a round into a sapper's chest just before another satchel charge was heaved at him.

The force of that explosion threw him to the ground, leaving him unconscious. Coming to, Doyle struggled to stand up, only to have a third explosion go off in the BTOC. As a result, Doyle was again knocked out. He eventually made his way out of the burning BTOC and linked up with Capt. Paul S. Spilberg, who had choppered into Mary Ann several days before with a three-man training team from Chu Lai.

Spilberg had written that he was "so proud of my men I could burst. When we were without food and it was cold and pouring down rain … there was good humor and the highest degree of cooperativeness. The grunts were clean in the jungle—no drugs." He earned his third Purple Heart on Mary Ann.

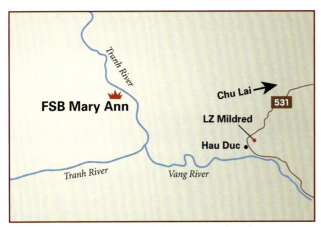

Overlooking the confluence of the Song Tranh and Song Vang River valleys, FSB Mary Ann was located about four miles northwest of Hau Duc.

Sgt. Johnny Watson's squad reinforces a position on the front of a bunker. The Song Tranh River in the background ran alongside Mary Ann, barring the enemy from attacking from that direction.

While the BTOC was being destroyed, C Company's CP also was being hit hard. Capt. Richard V. Knight, the company's popular commander, was killed outright. 1st Lt. Daniel J. Mack, executive officer, was struck in the right leg by an AK-47 round, shredding his calf muscles. He feigned death while a sapper ripped the watch off his wrist.

Spec. 4 Carl D. Carter, a radio operator, was buried under sandbags when a wall of the bunker collapsed on him. He went undetected as the VC sprayed the room with automatic weapons fire.

Not so lucky was Sgt. Ronald J. Becksted, an easygoing NCO, who was killed instantly as he tried to escape the CP. Spec. 4 Thomas Simmons also was gunned down, but survived.

Staff Sgt. John C. Calhoun was hit three times and was lying near Pfc. Michael S. Holloway, who was frantically trying to tie a tourniquet on Calhoun's leg. As enemy sappers approached, both faked death. Calhoun survived, but Holloway was killed. As the VC moved on, one let loose a burst and Calhoun was wounded two more times.

Mary Ann was struck with such ferocity that its defenders were unable to mount any type of counterattack. Many grunts, who were asleep in their hooches, were either shot trying to escape or buried alive when the satchel charges were hurled into their quarters.

MOUNTING RESISTANCE

A few soldiers managed to avoid the initial onslaught. Tripping over the body of a dead sapper in the confusion, Spec. 4 David Tarnay picked up his AK-47. As he carefully maneuvered about, he saw an enemy soldier in the wire attempting to leave. Tarnay took careful aim, killing him.

Sgt. Maj. Carl N. Prosser and Pfc. John A. Bruno killed another sapper trying to flee the area. When the VC returned fire, Prosser and Bruno manned the quad 50 (four .50-caliber machine guns mounted as one unit), while Spec. 6 Freddie Fillers, the chief cook, commandeered an M-60 machine gun. Between the two weapons, the trio let loose hundreds of rounds. At least three more sappers were cut down trying to make their way to safety.

A Night Hawk Huey gunship, with a starlight scope aboard, was the first aircraft on the scene. The chopper, flown by Capt. Norman Hayes, was from Trp. D, 1st Sqdn., 1st Cav. Hayes had to fly his helicopter at a higher altitude due to the thick smoke coming from the burning hooches at Mary Ann.

But the gunship did score some kills. "[We] … could actually see the VC in the wire … It

> ## "The firebase was a shambles with things burning all over the place ... There were many [soldiers] who were sitting around with rather dazed looks on their faces, and another group which was actively and energetically trying to pick up the pieces. There were no in-betweens." —MAJ. GEN. JAMES L. BALDWIN, WHO ARRIVED THE MORNING AFTER

The helicopter control shack was hit with a satchel charge that blew out one wall.

looked like they were trying to take people out of the wire … We engaged, and I know that anything we fired on ceased firing at us," said Hayes.

In the end, however, only 15 VC bodies were found. Evidence indicated the enemy dug a few hasty graves to bury their dead before withdrawing.

Unfortunately, by the time reinforcements arrived, the assault was over. It had lasted just an hour. The results were disastrous: 30 GIs killed and 82 wounded. The 46th Infantry lost 24 men, 80% of all KIAs. Its C Company (10 from 2nd Platoon alone) accounted for 19 with three in HQ Company and two in Alpha. The 1st Platoon of C Btry., 3rd Bn., 16th Arty, counted five dead and B Btry., 1st Bn., 14th Arty, one. Infantrymen were two-thirds of the dead. Ninety percent of the men were in their 20s; three 19. Draftees constituted 66% of those killed; volunteers 33%. Casualty records show all of the fatalities caused by shrapnel.

Fernando Sena got to the base a day after the attack. "What stuck in my mind most was the cross of about five feet high inscribed with the words, 'God is a Grunt,'" he said. "To me, it honored all the casualties."

Maj. Gen. James L. Baldwin, commanding general of the American Division, arrived on the scene at dawn. "The firebase was a shambles," he wrote in a letter home, "with things burning all over the place … There were many [soldiers] who were sitting around with rather dazed looks on their faces, and another group which was actively and energetically trying to pick up the pieces. There were no in-betweens."

INTELLIGENCE & NEGLIGENCE

The consequences of the attack were quickly felt. In the aftermath of an investigation, Baldwin and Col. William S. Hathaway, the 196th LIB commander, were relieved of duty. Both would retire soon afterward. A host of other officers were reprimanded, including the hard-driving Lt. Col. Doyle. He remained in the service until his retirement, but never received another promotion.

Many felt Baldwin's reprimand unjust. "It was a political thing," said Capt. John Strand, commanding officer (CO) of A Co., 1st Bn., 46th Inf. "Scapegoats were needed … What happened to Baldwin was wrong, but it's not hard for me to understand given how big organizations work."

Spec. 4 Ed Newton also felt "it was not right what they did to Baldwin. Hell, he was the division commander. It was a brigade and battalion problem. The day before we got hit they had us pull in all the sensors from around the perimeter.

"Kim, our Kit Carson scout, warned us we were infiltrated. He said the enemy was posing as ARVNs on the base. One ARVN officer even inquired about the easiest way to get off the firebase to fish. We thought that was strange and nobody told him. In fact, the night of the attack, we took fire from the ARVN position. When we returned fire, it stopped. Not one ARVN came out to help us. And the enemy left them alone. We tried to tell the officers what Kim had said, but they didn't listen to us. It was poor intelligence and gross negligence—plain and simple."

Allegations of drug use also have hovered over the performance of the GIs at Mary Ann.

Platoon Sgt. Bill Walker, who was in charge of bunkers 15 through 22, has a different view-point: "Everyone was awake when I made my rounds. There was no pot in my bunkers. And I know what pot smells like. One soldier, manning a bunker by the trash dump, was dozing. I stayed with him for a few minutes to make sure he was awake, then I returned to my bunker. Not two minutes later, everything hit the fan."

Sgt. Gary L. Noller, a battalion radio operator for the 46th Infantry, recalled: "The belief that the enemy would not waste its time attacking a force that was soon leaving anyway led to a false sense of security. And while drugs were present on Mary Ann, they were used only by a minority of soldiers."

WHY MARY ANN?

Why had the enemy made such a determined effort to overrun Mary Ann? It was late in the war, and Vietnamization was progressing steadily. GIs were being replaced by ARVN units.

Timothy Baldwin, son of Gen. Baldwin, who did extensive research on Mary Ann to clear his deceased father's name, may have found the answer: "The 1/46th was causing too much trouble from … Mary Ann." Just two weeks before the assault, the unit had unearthed a large enemy cache. Sgt. 1st Class Edward "Pop" Manson, platoon sergeant of the 4.2-inch Mortar Platoon, agrees: "Charlie was after Company C … they got the CO [Knight] in his bunker, too …"

Baldwin interviewed several Mary Ann VC veterans: They had no idea the Americans were about to abandon the firebase and turn it over to ARVN. "The VC," Baldwin wrote, "normally known for their superb intelligence-gathering, had failed on this issue."

That American courage was displayed on Mary Ann is indisputable. Silver Stars were awarded to Sgt. Elmer R. Head, Capt. Virtus A. Savage, senior medic Larry J. Vogelsang (a conscientious objector), Sgt. Ervin E. Powell, 1st Lt. Jerry W. Sams, Pfc. Paul G. Grooms, 1st Lt. Arthur D. Schmidt, Capt. Paul Spilberg and Spec. 4 David Tarnay. In one legendary exploit, 1st Lt. C. Barry McGee choked a sapper to death before being killed. He also received the Silver Star.

RECOGNIZING HARDSHIPS

In *Sappers in the Wire: The Life and Death of Firebase Mary Ann* (1995), the late author Keith W. Nolan counters many bogus claims. "Unfortunately, we historians got it wrong," he wrote.

"I do not mean to whitewash what happened at Firebase Mary Ann with such a remark, for the incident was a tragic disaster with much to teach today's soldiers about vigilance.

"What I do mean to say is that commentary which tars the 1/46th Infantry as a 'mob' … is grossly exaggerated. Most of the draftees on Mary Ann had already proven themselves in combat. And yet, however reluctantly, there were still soldiers like those in the 1/46th Infantry out fighting the war. Their hardships should be recognized.

"Author [Geoffrey] Perret got it right when he wrote that these troops who 'had faith in nothing much, least of all in men like [Presidents] Johnson and Nixon,' still 'served their country a lot better than it served them.'" ✪

SILVER STAR

PFC.
PAUL G. GROOMS

SGT. ELMER R. HEAD

1ST LT. C. BARRY McGEE

SGT.
ERVIN E. POWELL

1ST LT.
JERRY W. SAMS

CAPT.
VIRTUS A. SAVAGE

1ST LT. ARTHUR D.
SCHMIDT

CAPT.
PAUL SPILBERG

SPEC. 4
DAVID TARNAY

MEDIC LARRY J.
VOGELSANG

THE TOLL

U.S. KIA:
30

U.S. WIA:
82

APRIL '71 SEES FINAL DEADLIEST FIREFIGHTS FOR GIs IN VIETNAM

After May 1, 1971, U.S. ground units were no longer supposed to play a major offensive combat role in the war, relinquishing that responsibility to South Vietnamese forces. The historical record shows that was essentially the case. Only one firefight after this date claimed at least five American lives by small-arms fire in Vietnam.

NVA DEAL LETHAL BLOW NEAR LZ LIZ

BY KELLY VON LUNEN

Close to this Americal firebase on April 11, 1971, a platoon bravely attempted to rescue a downed helicopter crew, paying a severe price.

"The American command announced that North Vietnamese troops shot down an American helicopter 90 miles south of Da Nang Sunday, then ambushed an infantry force trying to reach the survivors," reported the *New York Times* on April 13, 1971. "The command said 11 Americans had been killed and eight wounded."

This short paragraph, buried at the bottom of a column on page 11, is all "America's newspaper of record" had to say about what turned out to be the fourth deadliest single firefight for Americans in Vietnam during 1971. Even a noble rescue attempt such as this at that stage of the war warranted no more coverage.

Yet for the men who experienced it, the 50-minute action on the afternoon of Easter Sunday (April 11), held immense meaning. Indeed, for the grunts of 3rd Plt., A Co., 1st Bn., 20th Inf., 11th LIB, Americal Div., it would create a memory lasting a lifetime.

Landing Zone (LZ) Liz was on the Nui Xuong, overlooking Song Tra Cau Delta, five miles northwest of Duc Pho. The LZ was headquarters for the 1st Battalion, 20th Infantry, and an obscure operation called *Finney Hill* was underway. Outside Liz, battalion units maintained a defensive position near Van Xuan in the Song Ve Valley. It had to be resupplied and personnel transported to and from by helicopter.

On that day, *Dolphin 21*, a slick from the 174th Assault Helicopter Company based at Duc Pho and piloted by Bob Chipley, had that duty. After picking up materiél and troops, he departed only to be hit by two M-79 grenade rounds (or an RPG). The chopper quickly crashed and burned.

"The ship landed firmly, fairly level and bounced," recalled Chipley. "Wayne [Spec. 4 Baggett, the crew chief] had a silver dollar-sized hole in his upper forehead. Chaplain Merle Brown was found near where the perimeter guard had been."

Lt. Tom Dolan, a B Company platoon leader who went in with the reaction force, later said, "It was unbelievable to me then, and now, that anyone got out of that aircraft alive."

As soon as the helicopter crashed, the landing zone came under intense enemy fire. Despite the concentration of fire and the bird being aflame, 3rd Platoon began evacuating the downed

Jon Melim (above) and Jack Begley (below) were among the 11 KIAs during the rescue beyond LZ Liz on April 11, 1971.

> ## "I always tried to forget the things that happened that day. It took only a few minutes and it was all over, 11 men KIA."
>
> —PFC. DEARL JORDAN, 81MM MORTAR SECTION, A COMPANY

chopper crew. As they did, it exploded five times in succession, killing one man and wounding four.

Within an hour, the communists broke off contact. In trying to save their fellow Americans, 3rd Platoon sacrificed a total of nine lives and sustained nine wounded. Including the helicopter crew chief and the 198th Infantry Brigade chaplain, the toll came to 11 Americans, making this the fourth highest GI death tally due to small-arms fire in 1971.

Pfc. Dearl Jordan, then with the 81mm Mortar Section of A Company, said in 2011: "I always tried to forget the things that happened that day. It took only a few minutes and it was all over, 11 men KIA. But I have never forgotten about my fellow soldiers who fell on Easter Sunday."

Operation Finney Hill still had one more blow to deal the hard-luck Americal. Less than two weeks later, on April 23, a booby trap planted about four miles from Duc Pho claimed eight more GIs—six from C Co., 4th Bn., 21st Inf., and two handlers from the 59th Infantry (Scout Dog) Platoon. Another 13 grunts were evacuated because of the seriousness of their wounds. ✪

U.S. KIA:
11

U.S. WIA:
9

NAM HOA: 'A FIGHT FOR LIFE'

BY KELLY VON LUNEN

Mid-April 1971 tested the 101st Airborne's "Delta Raiders" to the maximum. They would undergo an ordeal of fire in the notorious A Shau Valley.

It was the last offensive mission by a major American infantry unit in Vietnam. Consisting of search-and-destroy operations north of Route 547 (which led into the A Shau Valley) and on the high ground south of the Veghel Pass, the objective was to determine NVA movements east toward Firebase Bastogne.

When D Co. ("Delta Raiders"), 2nd Bn., 501st Inf. Regt., 101st Abn. Div., assumed that mission, it took on an added responsibility: recover the body of a GI earlier KIA and left behind by a sister company. For those 78 men, it would be an ordeal like none other.

Despite being severely wounded, Jim Zwit was among the lucky ones saved that day. He spent the following 18 months in the hospital undergoing some 20 operations.

ABOVE: D Co., 2nd Bn., 501st Inf., resupplies and updates its equipment inventory at FSB Bastogne in March 1971. Eight soldiers from Delta were KIA at Nam Hoa on April 15-16, 1971.

RIGHT: Firebase Veghel was the starting point for the operation near the Veghel Pass. The site consisted of two peaks with a saddle between them. It was located 17 miles southwest of Hue.

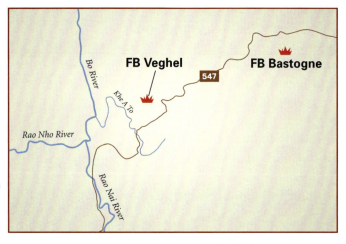

Firebase Veghel was situated along Route 547 at its intersection with Route 547A, southwest of Nam Hoa. Inserted into a hornet's nest, the Delta Raiders started taking fire in earnest around 7 p.m. on April 15. They had run into a tunnel complex occupied by a reinforced NVA company surrounding their position. Two men walking point for the 2nd Platoon went down in the first burst of fire. By the time ground contact had broken off around 8:30 p.m., D Company had taken six KIA and 10 seriously WIA.

Medevacs, called in immediately, were initially unable to land because of the triple-canopy jungle, despite numerous courageous attempts. The surrounded GIs would have to wait until daylight on April 16, so they could try again. The company had NVA to its front, rear and in between. Another GI was KIA and three more men were wounded in the meantime. Two wounded were finally flown out, one of whom died at Bastogne. Tragically, three of the men were killed by errant U.S. artillery rounds, including the two on April 16.

'AIR AMBULANCES' TO THE RESCUE

WO Fred Behrens piloted *Eagle Dustoff 913*, a ship of the Air Ambulance Platoon, 326th Medical Battalion, during the medevac missions. His co-pilot, 1st Lt. Stanley C. Marcieski, recalled, "Seventy-eight grunts of D Company had stumbled into 1,500 well-disciplined NVA regulars who were waiting in well-prepared, fortified positions. D Company was in a fight for its life."

Many of those lives were saved by the helicopter crews. "We were extracting wounded on top of an NVA regiment's underground bunker complex," Marcieski said. One of those saved was Jim Zwit. Severely wounded and not expected to live, after 20 operations and 18 months in the hospital, he survived to become a Chicago cop. All crew members of *Dustoff 913*

> **"As point man for the 3rd Platoon of Delta Raiders, I remember that firefight all too often. I wish I didn't. After we went to retrieve the bodies, the day went down hill from there. It was an ass kicker."**
>
> —HARRY BLASZKIEWICZ

received well-deserved Distinguished Flying Crosses.

Though unknown to the Raiders, a five-man recon team from E Co., 1st Bn., 502nd Inf., had been inserted on April 15 into the area near Dong Do Mountain, eight miles northwest of Ruong Ruong. All of the men were KIA.

Company D was finally and fully extracted by about 5 p.m. on April 16, to Firebase Birmingham. Their harrowing ordeal at Nam Hoa in the "Valley of Death" was over. The cost was eight dead Delta Raiders and 14 WIA. The bodies of two of their fellow grunts were not recovered until May 12, along with the A Company KIA. Combined, Delta and Echo companies lost 13 killed.

According to one account, "After April 16, the NVA seemed to disappear. For the rest of the month, little contact occurred anywhere in the Veghel-Bastogne area."

Said Zwit, "We did our duty in 1970-71 like those before us, and our KIAs should be equally remembered and honored." Zwit saw to that in 2011 when he and 14 other survivors were recognized by the Chicago White Sox at U.S. Cellular Field.

Note: Only one other firefight was fought in April that killed at least 5 GIs by gunfire. That was waged by F Trp., 2nd Sqdn., 11th ACR, while enroute to a night defensive position eight miles northeast of Trang Bang on the 17th.

U.S. KIA:
13

U.S. WIA:
14

TO THE RESCUE: RANGERS IN PERIL ON HILL 809

BY GARY LINDERER

One of the most daring rescues of the Vietnam War occurred in the A Shau Valley in April 1971.

On April 23, 1971, Capt. James Montano led a 24-man patrol from L Co., 75th Inf. (Ranger), 101st Airborne Div., onto the floor of the eastern rim of the A Shau Valley five miles north of A Sap. His mission: destroy a culvert in the dirt road that ran the valley's length. The culvert ran under the road channeling a stream, so it had to be blown in place. Two engineers were along for that task.

A six-man Ranger team, led by Sgt. Marvin Duren, was inserted that same day to act as a radio relay team for the Rangers operating in the valley below. The team consisted of Sgt. Fred Karnes, the senior radio operator; Sgt. Steve McAlpine, assistant team leader/medic; Spec. 4 Johnnie Sly; Pfc. James Champion and Spec. 4 Isaako Malo.

The 2nd Sqdn., 17th Cav, CO overrode L Company's Capt. David Ohle, and ordered the

Army Ranger Sgt. Marvin Duren was severely wounded at the outset of the ambush, but was airlifted to safety.

WO Fred Behrens (above and at right) alongside a minigun-equipped OH-6 helicopter at an earlier date. Behrens heroically returned twice to rescue the trapped Rangers, only to be wounded several times and forced to abandon his Huey.

helicopter pilot to insert Duren's team in a saddle farther up the ridgeline from the patrol. Depositing the men on Hill 809 overlooking Highway 548 was a fatal decision.

PINNED DOWN BY INTENSE FIRE

Before the Ranger patrol and radio relay team could link up and reach cover, small-arms fire erupted from NVA in well-camouflaged bunkers. The initial burst cut down Duren: hit twice in the right hip, once in the chest, and once in the stomach. He was hit several more times, taking rounds in the spleen, appendix, left lung, left arm and back.

Meanwhile, a Huey slick from B Trp., 2nd Sqdn., 17th Cav, piloted by Capt. Louis Speidel, departed for the valley. On board was Sgt. William Vodden, a Ranger team leader who volunteered to replace Duren.

Approaching the saddle, the chopper was hit, crashing into the hillside and rolling over twice before coming to rest upside down in the thick vegetation. Vodden had already cleared the aircraft. It was 4:25 p.m.

After retrieving door gunner Spec. 4 Brian Plahn, Vodden was hit by a burst of AK-47 fire that shattered the femur in his leg. He looked up to see a dust-off chopper drop into the LZ.

As Vodden watched helplessly, McAlpine and Sly rose from cover and began dragging Duren toward the waiting aircraft. Seeing the two Rangers struggling with the now-unconscious team leader, crew chief Spec. 5 Michael Brummer jumped from the dust-off and raced out into the LZ to help get Duren aboard.

WO Fred Behrens, 326th Medical Battalion, evacuated Duren and Plahn and then realized that another wounded man was left behind, so headed back to the valley.

Behrens brought the aircraft straight into the LZ and slammed it down in the clearing. Amid the swirling smoke and battle debris, McAlpine, Karnes, Malo, Sly and Champion quickly boarded the Huey. Vodden and Brummer were still on the ground.

Later, Behrens felt the dull pain of a round slam into his foot and another hit him in the upper body. A third round hit Brummer in the head, killing him instantly.

As Vodden watched helplessly, McAlpine and Sly rose from cover and began dragging Duren toward the waiting aircraft.

Behrens struggled to auto-rotate the craft back into the saddle because the chopper was hit in the turbine and lost power. The survivors spilled out both sides of the smoking helicopter, some heading for Vodden's position, the remainder for a bomb crater about 50 feet away from the crash site. Unable to keep up, Behrens limped away from the ship, collapsing into the first cover. It was 7:45 p.m.

GI BAIT FOR THE NVA

To everyone's surprise, the NVA remained in their bunkers during the night. That's because the enemy had decided to use the Rangers for bait. As long as there was anyone left alive in the saddle, the Americans would send more aircraft

Karnes, Sly and Capt. Roger Madison, the dust-off co-pilot, spent a sleepless night huddled in the bomb crater. At dawn, they tried to locate a radio by crawling on their hands and knees. An NVA sniper spotted Sly, killing him with a well-placed shot. But the radio was found.

An NVA battalion had been spotted moving up to reinforce the enemy on the hill. Madison spent the rest of the day directing airstrikes and gunship runs on the NVA positions surrounding them.

At 10:30 a.m. on April 24, Hueys from C Trp., 2nd Sqdn., 17th Cav inserted 77 "Blues" (Aero-Rifle Platoon) from D Troop into an LZ 1,000 feet northwest of the saddle. They walked head-on into an NVA ambush, suffering five KIA and 10 WIA. Gathering up their casualties, they fell back and set up a defensive perimeter.

B Co., 2nd Bn., 502nd Inf., and A Co., 1st Bn., 327th Inf., then air-assaulted into LZs down in the valley. Bravo Company secured the high ground and the next morning attacked south, helping secure the downed helicopter. Then it defended the perimeter until the wounded were evacuated.

Meanwhile, Karnes, Madison and McAlpine circled around enemy positions to the north, managing to link up with Delta Troop. Madison was evacuated with other wounded. Karnes and McAlpine spent their second night on the ground, this time inside the Cav perimeter.

Behrens, shot a third time, had taken his personal Thompson sub-machine gun with him when he abandoned his aircraft and managed to kill the NVA who had shot him.

Spec. 5 Robert Speer, Behrens's medic, was killed by small-arms fire when he came back to the saddle after trying to help the Cav pilots. Spec. 5 David Medina was killed by a strafing run from one of the supporting Cobra gunships. Both were with the 326th.

Vodden, Champion and the Cav crew chief Pfc. Clarence Allen were alone on the opposite side of the saddle. Champion attempted to escape, but a single shot followed by a burst of full automatic fire indicated he was cut down. He was never seen again.

During the night, co-pilot Capt. Bill Collum died. Now only Speidel was left alive in the wrecked 17th Cav aircraft.

At 6:35 p.m., Ohle landed at the Cav perimeter with four other Rangers, Sgts. Herb Owens, Dave Quigley, Dave Rothwell and Don Sellner. They had volunteered to try to reach those trapped.

MISSION COMPLETE

The next morning, April 25, the reaction forces were pulled out and an Arc Light (B-52 strike) was called in on the ridgeline. The five Rangers, plus Karnes and McAlpine who volunteered to lead them back to the LZ, moved out.

Quigley stumbled upon Behrens, seemingly dead, and got him on a medevac. Rothwell and Sellner located Allen; Vodden helped evacuate them. Owens and Quigley swept the ridgeline looking for Malo and Champion, but found no trace of them.

Speidel was evacuated with help from Bravo Company. He ultimately had both of his legs amputated and died 63 days later on Okinawa.

Later that afternoon, all U.S. forces were evacuated from the ridgeline. The final casualty count was 12 KIA—five D Troop, three of HQ & Support Co., 326th Bn., two B Troop, two L Company—and 20 WIA. One of the war's most daring rescues had been pulled off, but at a steep price for the men of the units involved. Isaako Malo was released from captivity on March 27, 1973. (He died Sept 10, 2014.) ✪

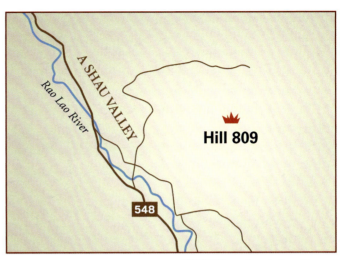

Hill 809 was located on the east rim of the A Shau Valley overlooking Highway 548. It was the scene of an heroic rescue effort, April 23-25, 1971.

Pfc. James A. Champion had earlier served with the 11th Armored Cav. Champion was presumed killed during the battle. His body was never recovered despite an extensive search.

U.S. KIA:
12

U.S. WIA:
20

BY RICHARD K. KOLB

DEADLY CLIMAX OF GROUND WAR ON FIREBASE CHARLIE 2

I t was our deadliest day in more than three years in Vietnam," said Society of the 5th Division (the Red Diamond Division of WWII fame) national historian Keith Short. "And it occurred on the 1st Brigade's last major mission—*Operation Montana Mustang* [April-July 1971]—in-country."

In the summer of 1971, U.S. forces turned over responsibility for the DMZ to the Army of the Republic of South Vietnam (ARVN). But before the change was complete, GIs there were struck by a tragedy that turned out to be one of the highest single-incident death tolls of the war.

"A single 122mm rocket made a direct hit on the sandbagged roof and in one screaming flash, [30] GIs were dead," is how the late author-historian Keith Nolan described it.

At a firebase known as Charlie 2, grunts of A Co., 1st Bn., 61st Inf. Regt., 1st Bde., 5th Inf. Div. (Mech), had come in for the night in May 1971. In this case, the bush would have been much safer.

The firebase, located four miles south of the DMZ among the rolling hills of Quang Tri province and three miles northeast of Cam Lo village, had been under frequent rocket attacks. Troops had almost grown accustomed to the incoming rounds, especially because the enemy's aim was often inaccurate.

"You could set your watch by the attacks," recalled supply Sgt. Bernard Gates of C Btry., 5th Bn., 4th Arty. "Every night at about 1700 hours [5 p.m.] the NVA would drop their rockets on us."

For three consecutive nights, the NVA had rained 122mm rockets on the base. At 102 pounds and 6$^1/5$ feet long, the projectiles have a range of 6½ miles. They were equipped with time-delayed fuses.

Six hours before the destructive round hit, just north of the base, two rocket sites and their NVA crews were reported. Gunships attacked them and grunts on the ground clashed with the regulars. During the encounter, two U.S. recon helicopters were shot down with three wounded.

Unfortunately, this did not deter another barrage on Charlie 2. Over a period of 15 to 20 minutes, 11 rockets landed within the perimeter.

At Charlie 2 around April 1971, Don Wilson, Darwin Olesen, Jerry Kemp, Robert Cadena and Mike Bodyl gather around an APC hit by a mine.

On May 21, 1971, 30 GIs of the 1st Brigade, 5th Mech, were killed in a single NVA rocket hit on a bunker atop a fire support base near the DMZ in Quang Tri province.

MAY 1971

"People were pinned by beams and dirt. Guys were screaming and scrambling to get out. It happened so fast—then other guys came over to pull people out." —SPEC. 4 WILLIAM BENTHIMER

PHOTO COURTESY JERRY KEMP

Bill Dodge, Ryan Riska, John Lacey, Jerry Garlinghouse, Andy Ramos and Terry Garrett at Quang Tri City airport, circa July 1970. Most were members of A Co., 1st Bn., 61st Inf. A Company lost 11 KIA in the rocket attack on Charlie 2 on May 21, 1971.

PHOTO COURTESY JERRIE OATMAN

Among those killed in the attack was Sgt. Leo Oatman, third from left. Other GIs in the photo were not identified.

On that May 21, evening rain clouds rolled in, concealing the NVA rocket launch site to the north. In the middle of evening chow, GIs had left the mess hall to take cover in a nearby club bunker, 16 by 32 feet.

Even though the bunker was covered by four layers of sandbags and three feet of dirt, the seventh rocket penetrated its protective barrier at 5:44 p.m. When the rocket struck, 65 to 70 GIs were inside.

'SCREAMING AND SCRAMBLING'

"There was a flash and a ringing noise and it knocked me down," said Spec. 4 William Benthimer, an APC driver. "People were pinned by beams and dirt. Guys were screaming and scrambling to get out. It happened so fast—then other guys came over to pull people out."

Gates helped in the rescue: "I volunteered to dig bodies out of the dilapidated bunker. I crawled into a hole to get those guys out. It was pretty messy. There were a lot of bodies in there. I didn't actually know how many until 25 years later.

"Chopper pilots flew in during the middle of the night to take out the bodies. They did one hell of a job. They all deserved medals for bravery."

Nearby units pitched in in other ways: "When Firebase Charlie 2 came under rocket attack, my platoon was setting up an NDP [night defensive position]," said Sgt. David Gahagan of 1st Plt., A Trp., 4th Sqdn., 12th Cav. "One of our track commanders spotted an explosion in and around the base. We radioed the Troop command post that rocket flashes were spotted about two kilometers away.

"We took our compass and shot an azimuth to the flashes and called in counter-battery fire from Alpha 4. The following morning we returned to Charlie 2 to resupply and refuel. We saw the bags containing the bodies of the soldiers killed in the bunker. An engineer unit was called in to assist in excavating the ruined bunker."

Some of the men felt it was an awful coincidence that local workers failed to come to work on May 21. "At the time of the attack, I was sitting outside our bunker and saw the rocket being shot out of the rocket tube toward the bunker," remembered Spec. 4 Charles Gray, a rifleman in B Company. "It was a small club near the mess hall. Because the NVA dropped rockets there at chow time, everyone went to the club bunker for cover.

PHOTO BY DAVID HUME KENNERLY / CORBIS

Cannon cockers protect their ears as they fire a self-propelled 175mm howitzer at suspected Communist positions on May 31, 1971, just 10 days after the attack.

"The rocket hit directly on top of the club bunker. What I could not figure out is why the Vietnamese who usually worked in the club did not show up for work that day."

RESCUING THE LIVING, RETRIEVING THE DEAD

By pure chance, a few of the GIs had just left the club before the rocket struck. Bill Dodge, then an infantryman with A Company, recalls: "I was in the mess hall when the rounds started. It had become pretty much a daily routine. The first sergeant came in and told everyone to go to the club for a drink until it stopped. I went to the club, then headed out and then shortly after ran back.

"I dug down into the rubble from the other side and we pulled several really badly wounded guys out and loaded them on Hueys. I remember yelling at the medics in the chopper because they were treating the injured so roughly.

"Guess there were so many that they were just trying to do the best that they could. They were throwing guys in like cordwood to haul them out. I remember digging until about 2:30 a.m. and sitting in the mud at the helipad. As usual, the mud was so deep and sticky that you couldn't even walk. There were so many dead. This was my worst night in Vietnam."

Firebase Charlie 2 was situated halfway between the Cam Lo River and the DMZ, just northwest of Dong Ha.

DIETER LUDWIG/CORBIS

In the aftermath of the rocket attack on Charlie 2, two GIs of the 5th Mech sit amongst a pile of helmets. With 30 KIA, it tied as the deadliest U.S. hostile loss of 1971 in a single action.

Spec. 4 Carl J. La Palme, an armor crewman in C Company, had a similar experience. "The first sergeant had ordered the men there because the club was above ground. I had just left it when the rocket landed there.

"I yelled out to my friend, 'Damn, that rocket hit the club.' Then I ran to the bunker. On the way, another GI ran right into me. His face was covered with blood. I took him back to my bunker and put him in my bunk, then ran back to the bunker and called a medic.

"By this time everyone was at the bunker. What we saw was shocking. The rocket had hit right in the middle of the club bunker, driving through the roof before exploding. It literally cut the tie rod beams that held up the roof.

"We started digging the men out of the bunker, using anything we had—shovels, our hands, anything. Confusion reigned: People were running around everywhere. It was about 6 p.m. now, and we started pulling the men out.

"I went to the place where the door used to be. A man was lying face-down in what I call the splits—his back was broken. I pulled him up by his collar and out of the doorway, then laid him on the ground out of the way. He was dead.

"Back in the bunker, I helped to get out the men who were still alive. When I got there, you could hear men praying and crying and screaming for someone to get them out of the fallen debris.

"We worked into the night rescuing the living and retrieving the dead. About midnight, we had the dead stacked on the helicopter pad waiting to be moved to Quang Tri City, brigade headquarters.

"Next day, CBS and NBC news arrived and took pictures of all the helmets and M-16s we had lined up. This was by far the most tragic time I spent in Vietnam."

TALLYING THE TOLL

Ten sub-units of the 1st Brigade sustained casualties in the bunker. The 61st Infantry was hit hardest, losing 14 men—47% of the 30 Americans KIA. A Company alone counted 11 killed; Headquarters Company, one; D Company, two; and brigade HHC, four.

The 7th Engineer Battalion's A Company also saw seven members perish in the rubble. A Company of the 77th Armor had one KIA, as did HQ Btry., 5th Bn., 4th Arty. Two batteries from the 26th and 65th Artillery, 108th Arty Group, probably there for fire direction control, each had a KIA, too. One grunt from the 11th Infantry died also.

Exactly 50% of those killed were infantrymen. Fatalities were split evenly between draftees and volunteers. Agewise, they ranged from 19 to 45 with 80% in their 20s.

Only the sapper attack on FSB Mary Ann the previous March equalled this toll in a single

SAGA OF FIREBASE 5

By May 1971, America's offensive ground war in Vietnam was over. Most U.S. actions were tied to South Vietnamese operations. Though GI participation in major combat became infrequent, those who did continued to display courage under fire.

There is no better example of this than the rescue attempt at Firebase 5 in the Central Highlands on May 25, 1971. Located north of Pleiku near Dak To in Kontum province, the ARVN base was under siege and completely surrounded by two NVA regiments. The day before, a chopper on an ammo resupply mission was downed by a mortar, killing two crewmen and stranding a wounded crew chief on the firebase.

The mission assigned the UH-1H of A Co., 227th Assault Helicopter Bn., 1st Cav Div. (then under the 1st Avn. Bde.): rescue him and two wounded ARVN. Knowing full well the strength of the NVA, the four-man medevac crew, call sign "Avengers," voluntarily flew through a hail of fire. The three wounded were picked up, but while leaving the base the bird was hit by fire and burst into flames, crashing into the jungle.

Adams **Curran** **Durand**

All four crew members were KIA: Maj. William E. Adams (pilot), Capt. John P. Curran (co-pilot), Spec. 4 Melvin C. Robinson (crew chief) and Spec. 4 Dennis Durand (door gunner). The wounded American (92nd AHC) and two ARVN also died. All told, Firebase 5 claimed seven GIs' lives in two days. The crew's remains were not recovered until July 1971.

Adams was awarded the Medal of Honor and the other three crewmen the Distinguished Service Cross (DSC). Adams is honored with a special helicopter memorial at his alma mater, Wentworth Military Academy in Lexington, Mo. Durand was on an extended tour. Robinson had been approved for a hardship discharge to care for his ailing grandmother.

Epilogue: Just a week later on Firebase 5, Chief Warrant Officer Peter Bradsell of B Trp., 7th Sqdn., 17th Cav, 1st Avn. Bde., volunteered to fly in a Vietnamese doctor. This was despite two previous shoot-downs and the base now being under siege for a week. Bradsell piloted his AH-1 Cobra, call sign "Undertaker," through intense mortar and rocket fire.

Grounded by an aircraft power failure, he assisted in base defense, directing air and artillery strikes. Continually exposing himself to enemy fire to care for the wounded, Bradsell inspired the garrison to victory. His ordeal lasted from May 31 until June 5, when the siege was lifted. He survived to receive a DSC.

---

ground incident during the war's last three years. Just one other single hostile action in the 1970s exceeded either toll. That was the helicopter shoot-down at LZ Judy on Aug. 28, 1970, which claimed 31 GIs' lives.

Besides the KIA, 33 soldiers were wounded.

John Estrada of A Co., 1st Bn., 61st Inf., was with the 5th Mech to the very end. Because he was on R&R on that fateful day, he narrowly missed the deadly strike. "Good friends of mine died on May 21," he says. "For many years, I buried those memories. During the unit's last few months in-country, the loss hung like a pall over our heads. But we maintained. Finally, within only the last few years did I come to terms with it and begin reconnecting with my fellow vets at reunions."

Less than two months after the rocket attack, on July 10, the last 500 members of the 5th's 1st Brigade departed Charlie 2. Two separate contingents of 50 American artillerymen and technicians each remained behind at Charlie 2 and Alpha 4 to monitor radar sensors and man a battery of 8-inch guns.

America's last days on the DMZ ended much as they had begun. From now on, the war in this no-man's land would be waged by ARVN. The 1st Brigade, 5th Division, left Vietnam on Aug. 27, 1971.

Though American infantry units remained on the ground for another year, never again would they sustain casualties even approaching those at Charlie 2. ✪

THE TOLL

U.S. KIA:
30

U.S. WIA:
33

LAST STAND OF RECON TEAM KANSAS

BY JOHN L. PLASTER

On Aug. 6, 1971, a handful of Americans of the shadowy Studies and Observation Group (SOG) pulled off one of the greatest combat feats of the Vietnam War. And behind enemy lines, the last Army Medal of Honor was earned.

The once bustling Khe Sanh Marine Base in South Vietnam's extreme northwest had been a ghost town for more than three years by the summer of 1971. It was, however, used briefly that February to support the South Vietnamese invasion of Laos. After that bloody debacle, they abandoned not just Khe Sanh, but the entire region, yielding immense areas to the NVA. Almost overnight, the North began extending the Ho Chi Minh Trail highways into South Vietnam.

In late July 1971, U.S. intelligence began tracking a large enemy force shifting across the DMZ a dozen miles east of Khe Sanh, threatening the coastal cities of Hue, Da Nang and Phu Bai where the last sizeable American ground units were based.

It was essential to learn what was happening near Khe Sanh, a mission assigned to a shadowy organization called "SOG." Created to conduct covert missions deep behind enemy lines in Laos, Cambodia and North Vietnam, the top-secret Studies and Observation Group had shifted most of its operations in-country in 1971 to cover the continuing U.S. withdrawal.

From among its clandestine assembly of Army Green Berets, Navy SEALs and U.S. Air Force Air commandos, the Khe Sanh mission eventually became a prisoner-snatch assigned to *Recon Team Kansas,* an 11-man Special Forces-led element, which included eight Montagnard tribesmen.

But how do you grab a prisoner in the midst of 10,000 or more NVA? Headed by an easygoing, lanky Midwesterner, 1st Lt. Loren Hagen, along with Sergeants Tony Andersen and Bruce Berg, the *RT Kansas* men had brainstormed through several scenarios until settling upon the best option: They would land conspicuously on an abandoned firebase—which obviously would draw some sort of NVA reaction—put up a short fight,

then extract by helicopter.

Except half of Hagen's men would stay hidden on the hill. When the NVA sent a squad up to see if the Americans had left behind sensors or bombing beacons—as SOG teams often did—the hidden men would ambush the NVA, seize a prisoner and come out.

In case a serious fight developed, Lt. Hagen reinforced his team with three more Green Beret volunteers: Staff Sgt. Oran Bingham and Sergeants Bill Queen and William Rimondi. Eight Montagnard tribesmen and six U.S. Special Forces troops brought the total to 14 men.

Beneath the hill, dismounting NVA soldiers formed up into platoons and companies, which their leaders marched through the darkness to their assigned attack positions, to wait for dawn.

Landing at last light on Aug. 6, 1971, Lt. Hagen surveyed the scrub brush and bomb craters below them and split his defense into three elements to cover three slopes. Immediately they went to work restoring the old firebase's two dilapidated bunkers and shallow trenches. The enemy must have seen them land, and Hagen reckoned to be ready.

Foreboding Night

It was well after dark when the SOG men noticed campfires on two facing ridgelines: unusual because the NVA normally masked itself. By midnight, enemy probers were at the base of the hill, firing provocatively from the north, south, east and west.

At 1 a.m., a U.S. Air Force AC-130 *Spectre* gunship arrived,

SOG *Recon Team Kansas,* with 1st. Lt. Hagen (3rd from right), was dropped into the Khe Sanh area on a reconnaissance "prisoner-snatch" mission in August 1971.

walking 40mm and 20mm fire around the hill nearly all night. Never once did the team fire their weapons, staying blanketed in darkness. Then at 3 a.m., the SOG men heard trucks and tail-gates dropping. This was odd, very odd.

Beneath the hill, dismounting NVA soldiers formed up into platoons and companies, which their leaders marched through the darkness to their assigned attack positions, to wait for dawn.

Just before sunrise it became forebodingly quiet. Then Lt. Hagen heard more trucks arriving.

Fifty miles away at a coastal airbase, a U.S. Air Force forward air controller (FAC) and a flight of helicopters was lifting away for the false extraction; they would be above *RT Kansas* in 30 minutes.

Encircled by the NVA

As darkness gave way to light, Lt. Hagen detected glimpses of NVA on one slope; then on another slope pith helmets appeared, bobbing in the fog. When his men reported NVA on the third slope, too, Hagen realized the hill was completely encircled by

NVA—but that would require a whole regiment, at least a thousand men.

The NVA regimental commander understood he had to dispatch the Americans quickly. They'd inadvertently landed almost within sight of the Hanoi High Command's most critical new venture, the first six-inch fuel pipeline laid across the DMZ.

It would be absolutely essential in a few months when entire tank battalions rolled through there for the war's largest offensive. Already the 304th NVA Division was massing there. Moreover, a regiment of the 308th Division was preparing for the 1972 Easter Offensive.

A fourth battalion moved into place; then, concealed in the ground fog, a fifth battalion arrived. Later, SOG's commander, Col. John Sadler, would learn an entire regiment had stormed the hill, supported by a second regiment. It was a mass assault by approximately 2,000 enemy infantrymen.

As the clearing ground fog disclosed that terrible truth, Lt. Hagen had no time for inspiring words, just serious soldier work; in those final moments he repositioned weapons while his

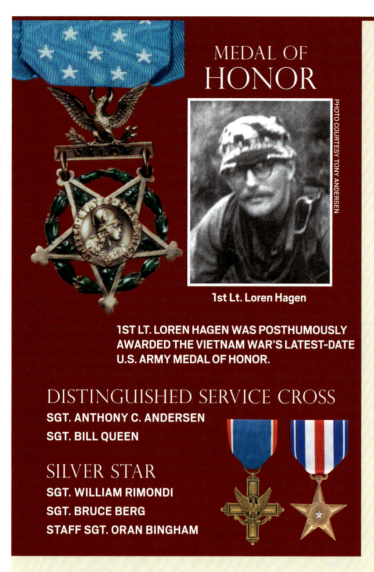

MEDAL OF HONOR

PHOTO COURTESY TONY ANDERSEN

1st Lt. Loren Hagen

1ST LT. LOREN HAGEN WAS POSTHUMOUSLY AWARDED THE VIETNAM WAR'S LATEST-DATE U.S. ARMY MEDAL OF HONOR.

DISTINGUISHED SERVICE CROSS
SGT. ANTHONY C. ANDERSEN
SGT. BILL QUEEN

SILVER STAR
SGT. WILLIAM RIMONDI
SGT. BRUCE BERG
STAFF SGT. ORAN BINGHAM

NVA troops mass-assaulted *RT Kansas* to conceal a fuel pipeline like the one shown here. It was being laid to support a new offensive by the NVA.

men readied grenades and stacked magazines. The Catholic Montagnards made the sign of the cross.

Then the NVA came.

Four KIA in Four Minutes

A well-aimed RPG rocket smashed into Bruce Berg's bunker, collapsing it and signaling the attack—fire went from nothing to 10,000 rounds per second. Andersen could see dozens of NVA rushing in lines up his slope, meeting them with his M-60 machine gun.

Hagen hollered that he was going to check Berg. And then he ran directly into a ferocious maelstrom, bullets ricocheting and slamming the earth in front of, behind, and beneath his dashing feet. He made it a dozen yards when fire from the other slope cut him down, killing him.

Then Oran Bingham left a bunker to reposition a Claymore and a bullet struck him in the head, apparently killing him. One Montagnard in a trench below Andersen fired several bursts then jumped up to pull back and fell into Andersen's lap, dead.

Four men had died in less than four minutes. It was up to Andersen, now the senior man.

Small arms fire rattled closer on all sides and grenades lobbed up from below the hillcrest where waves of NVA were scurrying behind small rises and rolling from bomb crater to bomb crater. Andersen dashed over the hill to look for Hagen, but couldn't see him anywhere—just 100 khaki-clad NVA almost at the top.

He fired one M-60 belt at NVA advancing up his own slope, then sped to the other approach and ran belt after belt on the 100 assaulting enemy. By then, grenades started coming from behind him as NVA closed in from his rear. Just a dozen yards away, beyond the curvature of the hill, enemy heads popped up, cracked a few shots, then dropped back down.

Still a dozen minutes away, the approaching Cobra gunships went to full throttle, leaving the slower Hueys behind.

Meanwhile, *RT Kansas* had just run out of hand grenades when a North Vietnamese grenade exploded beside Andersen's M-60, rendering it useless. He spun his CAR-15 off his back and kept shooting, then he tossed back another grenade, but it went off in front of him, nearly blinding him, yet he kept shooting. More shrapnel tore into him, then an AK round slammed through his webgear and lodged in his elbow, knocking him down. He stumbled back to his knees and kept firing.

The perimeter was pinched almost in half when Andersen grabbed his last two living Montagnards, circled below the nearest NVA and somehow managed to reach the survivors on the opposite side. He found Bingham, started to lift him, and saw he, too, was dead from a head wound. All around him he heard, "zzssss, zzssss, zzssss," as bullets flashed past his ears.

Last Stand

He dragged Bingham back to where Bill Queen lay, wounded. Only Rimondi wasn't yet hit and still fired furiously. Andersen put them in a back-to-back circle just off the hilltop where they would make their last stand. AK bullets had destroyed their team radio, another slug had shot Andersen's little survival radio out of his hand, so Rimondi tossed him another survival radio—their last.

Now the NVA were streaming, rolling over the crest like a tidal wave, their rattling AKs blending together into one never-ending burst. Andersen's men were firing not at NVA, but at hands wielding AKs over parapets and around bunkers. There was no place left to fall back. Andersen was shooting NVA little farther away than the length of his CAR-15 muzzle. The time it took to speed-change a magazine meant life or death.

From the air it looked like an ant mound, with moving figures everywhere. Cobra lead rolled in and sprinkled 20mm cannon shells around the surviving SOG men, and at last fighters arrived, adding napalm and Vulcan cannons to the melee. Then

> ## Andersen was shooting NVA little farther away than the length of his CAR-15 muzzle. The time it took to speed-change a magazine meant life or death.

at last the assault ebbed, turned, and the NVA fled for cover, just as the Hueys arrived.

Though wounded repeatedly, Andersen crawled out to fire his CAR-15 to cover the landing Hueys. With Rimondi's help, Andersen dragged as many teammates' bodies as he could to the first Huey, then helped the wounded Queen and others aboard the second.

Allied KIA Count: 64%

In one hellacious half-hour, nine of *Recon Team Kansas'* 14 men had been lost.

Lt. Hagen had died, along with Bingham; Berg was presumed dead; six Montagnards had died. Rimondi and Queen both suffered multiple frag wounds, Andersen had been struck by both small arms fire and shrapnel, and their other Montagnards, too, all had been wounded.

"It's amazing that any of us came through it with the amount of incoming that we were getting," Tony Andersen said years later. He attributes their survival to his deceased team leader,

---

FAMOUS LAST STANDS

- **Alamo:** 188 Americans stood against 3,000 Mexicans, a ratio of 16-to-1.
- **Custer's Last Stand:** 211 cavalrymen succumbed to 3,500 Sioux warriors, or 16.5-to-1.
- **1879 Battle of Rorke's Drift:** The most heralded action in British military history—resulting in 11 Victoria Crosses—occurred when 139 British troops withstood assaults by 4,000 Zulus, or 28-to-1.

Lt. Hagen's 14 men had held on despite being outnumbered 107-to-one, four times as disadvantageous as Rorke's Drift and seven times worse than the Alamo. It was one of the most remarkable feats of arms in American history.

Lt. Loren Hagen. "He epitomized what a Special Forces officer should be—attentive to detail, a lot of rehearsals, followed through on things," he explains. "We were ready. I think that was probably the only thing that kept us from being totally overrun. Everybody was alert and knew what was happening and was waiting."

As for Hagen's bravery, dashing into a wall of AK fire to try to save Bruce Berg, that didn't surprise Andersen, either. "Lt. Hagen was that kind of officer. He was a good man."

Against the loss of most of his teammates, Andersen learned, the U.S. Air Force counted 185 NVA dead on that hill—little *RT Kansas* had killed half a battalion and probably wounded twice that many NVA. But that gives Andersen little satisfaction compared to the loss of most of his team.

Perhaps Andersen's most difficult duty was carrying the bodies of his six Montagnard teammates—his "family" he called them—to their home village.

"As soon as they saw us driving up in the truck, they knew. Wailing and moaning started, and all the grieving." The villagers gathered in a circle around the headman's stilted longhouse. "Through one of the interpreters I tried to explain how proud we were of them, what good fighters they were, that they had died for a good cause."

That would be borne out a few months later when the intelligence generated by *RT Kansas'* spirited defense helped U.S. analysts read enemy intentions, enabling American airpower to counter the NVA's Easter Offensive.

And though details of this incredible fight would remain classified for decades, enough was disclosed that 1st Lt. Loren Hagen's family was presented the U.S. Army's latest-date Vietnam War Medal of Honor. Tony Andersen, who held together what remained of *RT Kansas* through those final mass assaults, and Bill Queen received the Distinguished Service Cross. Rimondi, Berg and Bingham were awarded Silver Stars.

Now we can appreciate the true significance of their noble stand. ✪

BRUTAL BATTLES OF VIETNAM
1972

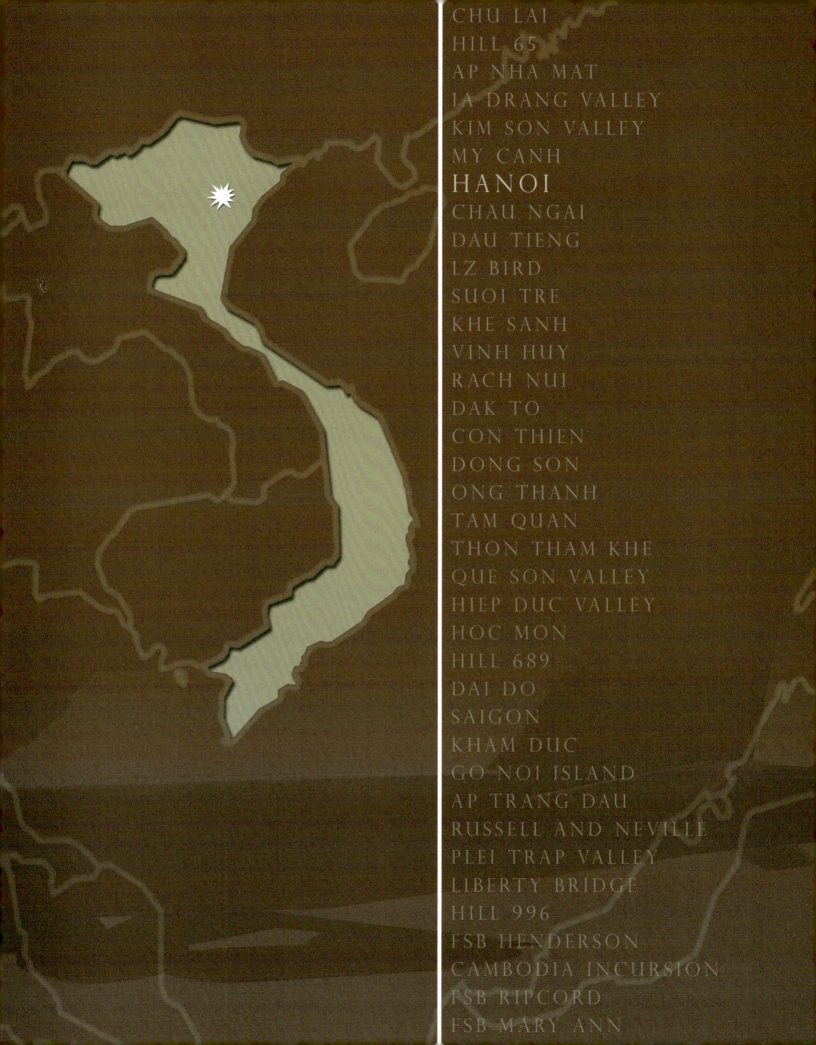

CHU LAI
HILL 65
AP NHA MAT
IA DRANG VALLEY
KIM SON VALLEY
MY CANH
HANOI
CHAU NGAI
DAU TIENG
LZ BIRD
SUOI TRE
KHE SANH
VINH HUY
RACH NUI
DAK TO
CON THIEN
DONG SON
ONG THANH
TAM QUAN
THON THAM KHE
QUE SON VALLEY
HIEP DUC VALLEY
HOC MON
HILL 689
DAI DO
SAIGON
KHAM DUC
GO NOI ISLAND
AP TRANG DAU
RUSSELL AND NEVILLE
PLEI TRAP VALLEY
LIBERTY BRIDGE
HILL 996
FSB HENDERSON
CAMBODIA INCURSION
FSB RIPCORD
FSB MARY ANN

1ST AVIATION BRIGADE SUFFERS ITS GREATEST AIR LOSS

Next to the Huey troop carrier, the CH-47 heavy-lift helicopter came to symbolize air mobility in Vietnam. The Army fielded 21 Chinook companies at peak strength. On Oct. 31, 1972, a CH-47 of the 1st Aviation Brigade sustained the unit's single largest personnel toll in a shoot-down.

"Copter Crash in Viet Kills 22 Americans" screamed the headline in the Nov. 2, 1972, issue of the *New York Daily News*. It was "the most catastrophic loss in the Group history," recorded the unit historian. Indeed, it was the single largest hostile U.S. casualty count of the year, as well as that of the 1st Aviation Brigade from the air in Vietnam during its seven years in the war.

Called "a second air force," the 1st—nicknamed the "Golden Hawk"—epitomized "the helicopter war." Formed in Vietnam in March 1966 and departing on March 28, 1973, it was there until the bitter end. The 1st commanded all non-divisional Army aviation assets in-country. Among its thousands of aircraft at peak strength were 311 CH-47 Chinook cargo helicopters.

One of these twin-rotor Boeing medium cargo handlers—affectionately known as the "Shithook" or "Forty-Seven"—would experience a cruel fate: a C model with tail number 69-17119. It belonged to the 18th Corps Aviation Company (CAC), 164th Combat Aviation Group (CAG), 1st Aviation Brigade.

Activated in June 1971, the 18th CAC was originally the aviation company for the Delta Regional Assistance Command (DRAC). It was attached to the 164th the following March as a separate unit. As the largest aviation company in Vietnam and indeed the Army, "Green Delta" boasted 50 aircraft and 500 men.

Attached and later assigned to the 164th was C Troop (Air) of the 16th Cavalry. Providing security for the group's operations, its motto was "Strike Hard." The 16th went by the call signs "Darkhorse" and "The Four Horsemen." Authorized strength numbered 266 air cavalrymen (infantrymen).

Both units were based at Can Tho, the center of all U.S. military operations in the Mekong River Delta. The capital of Phong Dinh province, the city was the largest population center in the Mekong. To the northeast was My Tho, capital of Dinh Tuong province. Both places harbored their share of Viet Cong. The Delta provinces also hosted 2,000 North Vietnamese regulars.

For self-defense, the Chinook was generally armed with a 7.62mm M-60 machine gun on a pintle (pivot pin) mount on each side of the helicopter. In reality, the M-60 was not much good against one of the newer weapons then being employed by the communists—the Strela (Russian for "arrow")-2 surface-to-air missile. It was known to Americans as the SA-7 Grail. Easily portable by one man and fired from the shoulder at low altitude, the high-explosive warhead was guided by passive infrared homing.

'A DOOMED CHINOOK'

Aboard the 69-17119 that Oct. 31, 1972, were 15 Americans: the five-man crew (pilot, co-pilot, flight engineer, crew chief and gunner), two avionic

The CH-47 Chinook helicopter (this is a model C) gained fame for its cargo-handling operations during the war. But it presented a tempting target for enemy troops.

Air cavalryman Delbert Wood and Chinook crew chief Richard Freeman were among the Americans killed in the Oct. 31 shoot-down and forgotten in the midst of the presidential campaign of 1972.

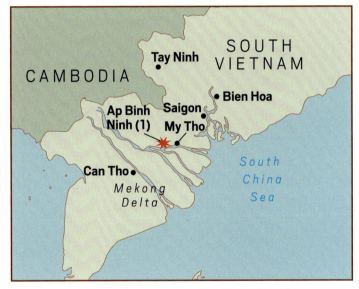

communications equipment repairmen from the 18th CAC, five C Troop cavalrymen, two advisers from DRAC headquarters and one personnel specialist from the 527th Personnel Service Company of the 1st Logistics Command.

The helicopter was on a courier run between Saigon and Can Tho; the members of C Troop were en route to their new assignment.

Near Ap Binh Ninh (1), 6.8 miles southwest of Dong Tam in Dinh Tuong province, a communist soldier fired an SA-7 missile, bringing down the Chinook into a flooded rice field. Of 43 known missile firings in the Delta, this was the only one to score a hit on a U.S.

Can Tho and My Tho were prime centers of military activity in the Mekong River Delta. A Chinook C, tail number 69-17119, was shot down into a flooded rice field near Ap Binh Ninh (1) not far from My Tho on Oct. 31, 1972.

A communist gunner like this one ended the lives of 15 Americans—12 of whom were members of the 1st Aviation Brigade—with a deadly Soviet-made SA-7 missile.

The 1st Aviation Brigade—the "Golden Hawk"—flew in Vietnam from March 1966 to March 1973, losing 1,057 men KIA.

aircraft. After this incident, the CH-47 underwent a major design change to protect against the SA-7s.

Despite the severity of the loss, it garnered only fleeting attention. Secret peace talks in Paris with a cease-fire rumored to be signed on Oct. 31 combined with the 1972 presidential campaign all-but obliterated news of the shoot-down.

As it turned out, initial news reports of 22 Americans killed were incorrect. But tragically, all 15 aboard died. Only the Feb. 10, 1965, ground attack on the Qui Nhon barracks of the 140th Transportation Detachment, which coincidentally claimed 22 members of that unit, surpassed the 12 men of the 1st (18th CAC and 16th Cav) killed in a single incident.

Those aboard were a varied group. They included nine regulars, four National Guard/Reserve members and two draftees. Their ages ranged from 19 to 31. Ten were single; five married. Four hailed from Michigan, three called California home, two were natives of Texas and the remainder had resided in six other states.

What little we know of their lives tells us they were sorely missed. More than three decades later, in 2005, 16th Cavalryman Delbert Wood from Phoenix would have his daughter, Tammy, write: "I wish I could have known you, but all I have are pictures. Grandma died a few years after you. I'm sure it was from a broken heart. I'm proud of you."

Only a few years earlier, Jan, the sister of crew chief Richard Freeman of Redondo Beach, Calif., said, "Not a day goes by that my younger brother is not thought about or missed." James Brown, another 16th infantryman, was only 17 when he enlisted in the Army in the summer of 1971 in San Angelo, Texas. He, fortunately, is permanently remembered along with fellow veterans on the Permian Basin Vietnam Veterans Memorial.

Patrick Finnegan, a 173rd Airborne Brigade vet of Vietnam, lost his brother Dennis that day, and spoke for many family members in 2012. "My goal is to put some flesh and blood on at least one of those forgotten names. Ironically, my brother was a passenger—an adviser. Dennis was on his third tour having been already wounded three times. He had arrived in early November 1971. He was on his way to Saigon; headed for home.

"Dennis left behind a widow and two young daughters. All the holidays since have not been holidays anymore. Dennis was one among 15 aboard a doomed Chinook that Oct. 31, and yet so much more." ✪

THE TOLL

U.S. KIA:
15

VIETNAM VETERANS MEMORIAL FUND/WALL OF FACES

FINAL KIA:

As fate would have it, the 18th CAC suffered the last U.S. KIA in Vietnam before America officially exited on March 29, 1973. On Feb. 16, Spec. 5 James L. Scroggins was mortally wounded when his unarmed CH-47C was shot down on a supply mission south of An Loc. He died of his wounds seven days later on Feb. 23.

BY AL HEMINGWAY   *OPERATION LINEBACKER II*

'INTO THE TEETH OF THE TIGER'

When the Paris peace talks collapsed in 1972, the mighty B-52s were unleashed in the largest bombing raid of the Vietnam War. It was called *Operation Linebacker II* and dubbed the "11-Day War."

In October 1972, Henry Kissinger, the chief U.S. negotiator at the Paris peace talks, publicly declared to the American people: "Peace is at hand." However, Kissinger's counterpart, Le Duc Tho, head negotiator for the North Vietnamese communists, relayed that peace was indeed at hand—under their terms—or there would be no peace at all.

Several weeks before Christmas in 1972, the North Vietnamese made good their threat when they walked out of the negotiations. Furious, President Richard M. Nixon quickly dispatched an ultimatum to Hanoi demanding it return to the bargaining table or else. The communists arrogantly refused. Unfortunately for Hanoi, Nixon was not bluffing. He had a bold plan to force Hanoi back to the talks.

LINEBACKER II COMMENCES

On Dec. 17, 1972, a message from the Joint Chiefs of Staff (JCS) was forwarded to all operational commanders in the 7th Air Force: "You are directed to commence at approximately 1200Z, 18 December 1972, a three-day maximum effort, repeat, maximum effort, of B52/TACAIR strikes in the Hanoi/Haiphong areas ...." *Operation Linebacker II*— the "11-Day War"—had begun.

This was the first time the B-52 Stratofortress was allowed to go "downtown" (pilots' nickname for Hanoi) during the Vietnam War. Before *Linebacker I* (May–October), the B-52s, or BUFs (Big Ugly Fellows) as they were called, were utilized primarily for ground support, hitting suspected enemy supply bases and supply routes in South Vietnam.

Pilots and crewmembers, for the most part, were excited about their new role and finally using the aircraft for its original purpose—that of a strategic bomber. Lt. Gen. Gerald W.

"HIGH ROAD TO HANOI" BY JACK FELLOWS / U.S. AIR FORCE ART PROGRAM

The Vietnam War's largest-scale bombing, dubbed *Operation Linebacker II,* occurred from Dec. 18-29, 1972 . The operation was so devastating to the communists that they were forced to negotiate in Paris.

Linebacker II targets included storage and supply complexes, railroad yards, transshipment points, repair facilities along the northwest and northeast rail lines, communication installations and MiG airstrips.

Some 140 planes, 80 from the 43rd Strategic Wing (SW), located at Andersen AFB on Guam, dubbed "The Rock," and another 60 from the 307th SW, situated at U-Tapao AFB, Thailand, along with aircraft from the 72nd SW (Provisional), were poised and ready to commence the operation.

B-52s normally fly in cells of three with the call sign for each cell designated a different color. Due to the massive scope of the bombing, 43 various shades had to be used. "They'd gone clear down to peppermint and bronze," laughed one pilot.

Within hours the operation was under way. Ground crews hustled to ready the big birds. Aircraft mechanics had to check the engines and do whatever it took to get the massive planes airborne to complete their missions. Crewmen loaded 750-lb. and 500-lb. bombs— 60,000 lbs. of additional ordnance in all.

Planners became increasingly concerned with the tough aerial defenses that the B-52s would encounter once they entered Hanoi's air space. The massive planes, already burdened with the extra weight from the bombs, would have a difficult time in maneuvering away from the SA-2 surface-to-air-missiles (SAMs) the communist gunners would be firing at them.

At an altitude of 30,000 feet, the BUFs would be flying at the SAMs optimum effective

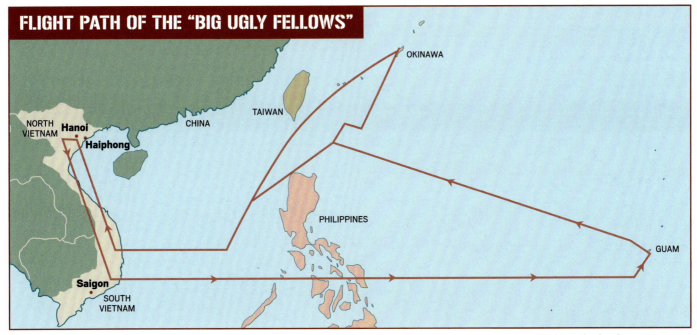

FLIGHT PATH OF THE "BIG UGLY FELLOWS"

OKINAWA

CHINA

TAIWAN

NORTH
VIETNAM   Hanoi

Haiphong

PHILIPPINES

GUAM

Saigon
SOUTH
VIETNAM

Flight paths for the B-52s
stretched an amazing distance
from Guam and Okinawa to
North Vietnam and South
Vietnam, then back. However,
during *Operation Linebacker
II,* no bombing missions
originated from Okinawa.
KC-135 refueling aircraft flew
from Kadena Air Base.

range. Also, they were ordered to fly an exact course to improve the accuracy of their bombing runs.

To counter this, the BUFs did have their own radar jamming equipment on board. To further assist them, EB-66 and EA-6 Electronic Counter Measures (ECM) aircraft flew with the B-52s to confuse the SAMs. As an added measure, F-4 Phantoms dropped chaff (strips of metallic foil) to jam enemy radar.

Another vital component of the air campaign was "Combat Lightning"—five specially outfitted KC-135s that provided communications support between the 7th Fleet and 7th and 8th Air Forces. "Crew members flew 24-hour support missions for 11 days," recalled former Air Force Master Sgt. Doug Maurstad.

BUFS GO DOWNTOWN

On Dec. 18, 1972, at 2:41 in the afternoon, 27 B-52s lifted off from Andersen AFB. Another 21 BUFs took off from U-Tapao and headed in an easterly direction to link up with the Guam-based planes. After this was accomplished, the 70-mile long string of BUFs began their flight to Hanoi.

F-111s, or Aardvarks, flew ahead of the B-52s and hit four MiG airstrips. Right behind them, F-4s sowed chaff corridors. However, a 100-knot wind blew the metal strips away prior to the arrival of the B-52s.

As the first cell of BUFs neared Hanoi, they were greeted with a salvo of 50 SAMs. One plane was damaged so badly from the flying shrapnel it was forced to abort its mission and fly back to base.

One pilot looked on in awe and remarked: "The valley [was] almost as bright as day."

Two SAMs found their mark and sent one B-52 crashing to the earth. Fortunately, three crewmen escaped injury when they successfully ejected before the 150,000-lb. fuel tanks erupted into a gigantic fireball. This was the first Stratofortress to be lost to hostile fire and only the second damaged in the entire Vietnam War to date. One pilot looked on in awe and remarked: "The valley [was] almost as bright as day."

At midnight, 30 more B-52s arrived over Hanoi. In all, 121 sorties were flown against the

A U.S. Air Force B-52G Stratofortress from the 72nd Strategic Wing waits beside the runway at Andersen Air Force Base, Guam, as another B-52 takes off for a bombing mission over North Vietnam during Operation Linebacker II on Dec. 15, 1972.

Kinh No and Yen Vien complexes, three MiG airfields, railroad repair facilities at Gia Lam and the Hanoi radio station. This temporarily put "Hanoi Hannah," the North Vietnamese "Tokyo Rose," off the air.

Another first was recorded that evening. Staff Sgt. Samuel Turner, a tail gunner on the *Brown 03*, downed a MiG-21 with a burst from his .50-caliber machine gun. He was the first tail gunner since the Korean War to do so.

Relatively few MiGs were airborne that night. The real threat to the B-52s were the SAMs. In all, it was estimated that more than 200 SAMs were launched against the big targets. Three BUFs were shot down with another two sustaining serious damage.

From his lonely berth in the rear of his plane, Tech. Sgt. Peter E. Whalen, the bombers' fire control operator, peered out. He described the scene later: "When the SAMs come up through the clouds, you can see a bright glow as the rocket fire reflects on the cloud. The clouds magnify the light and make the SAM look bigger than it really is."

U.S. AIR FORCE COMBAT DEATHS IN INDOCHINA

TYPE OF DUTY	KIA	% OF TOTAL A.F. KIA
Air (fixed wing)	1,445	83.0%
Ground	164	9.4%
Air (helicopter)	76	4.4%
Aboard aircraft (not crew members)	52	3.0%
Unknown	4	0.2%
Total	**1,741**	**100%**

Air Force deaths, including non-hostile, totaled 2,583. Of this total, 842 airmen died in accidents and from other causes. Air Force non-hostile deaths were 32.5% of that service's total fatalities in Vietnam. All told, Air Force hostile deaths equaled 3.6% of all American KIAs in the war. Air Force ground deaths, for instance, included 20 security policemen.

Source: *Defense Manpower Data Center.*

'EVERYONE WAS PROUD'

Despite the success of the first day, the pilots and crews started grumbling. The chaff support was woefully inadequate because of the strong prevailing winds. The sharp turns the pilots had to make were placing them directly into the 100-knot winds, causing the bombers to lose considerable speed, enabling the enemy radar to find weak spots in their jamming barriers.

Also, the B-52s had to utilize a single point for a post-target turn. By doing this, NVA gunners could zero in on the first wave of B-52s when they finished their laborious turning maneuver.

Ignoring the pilot's complaints, *Linebacker II* proceeded on schedule. On day two, 93% of the aircraft struck their targets with only one bomber receiving minor damage. However, Day 3 was different. Two of the G-model planes were hit while performing their post-target turn and sent earthbound. Also, a D-model was hit but managed to limp back to U-Tapao before it could finish its run.

POWS VS. PRESS

Anti-war protestors were quick to capitalize on the air campaign over North Vietnam. They coined the phrase "Christmas Bombings" and accused the U.S. of "carpet bombing" and inflicting indiscriminate destruction and casualties on the people of North Vietnam.

Sen. George McGovern (D-S.D.) said it was "the most murderous aerial bombardment in the history of the world" and "the most immoral action that this nation has ever committed in its national history."

One example used by left-wing activists was the bombing of Bach Mai hospital. Anti-war leaders reported that the medical facility was "razed to the ground." Soon, the media, notably *The New York Times* and *The Washington Post,* were quick to side with the anti-war protestors.

Nothing could have been further from the truth, but that didn't stop the press.

The hospital was not "razed to the ground" as some of anti-war activists had claimed. One wing of the building was hit when one of the BUFs inadvertently let loose its bombs early.

The carpet bombing claim was another lie concocted by the anti-war movement. In fact, it tried to persuade

Hanoi's mayor to tell the media that the city suffered over 10,000 killed because of *Linebacker II.* In an ironic twist, the city official refused, saying, "The government's credibility was at stake."

In all, 1,624 civilians lost their lives in two cities due to *Linebacker II.* This compares to the nearly 84,000 people killed in a single night during the bombing runs over Tokyo in March 1945.

In the final analysis, *Linebacker II* was a great U.S. victory. North Vietnam suffered material loss and psychological defeat.

POWs held at the Hanoi Hilton prison knew this firsthand. The guards were very quiet during the 11-day air campaign with " ...no joking, no laughing, no acts of defiance, or reprisal...," said one former prisoner.

Air Force Capt. Frank D. Lewis, a POW in Hanoi, later said, "I prayed for the men, the crews, and the aircraft they flew. To me they had become the hand of God that had reached out to bring me an inner peace and strength with which I could endure this cruel land."

Another POW, Air Force Col. Fred Cherry, recalled, "When the bombing stopped, we knew they didn't have any more missiles. And that the agreements

POWs Col. Fred Cherry and Col. Jon Reynolds both felt the bombings aided in drawing the war to a close.

were going to be signed."

U.S. Air Force Col. Jon A. Reynolds, held prisoner for many years, commented: "Some, perhaps most, will suggest that the negotiations did not result from the B-52 strikes. From my vantage point, however, the reason the North Vietnamese negotiated was obvious."

Nevertheless, airmen who waged the bombing campaign were especially castigated by the anti-war movement. Yet as President Ronald Reagan put it: "Who can doubt that the cause for which our men fought was just? It was, however imperfectly pursued, the cause of freedom." As CBS's Dan Rather even later admitted, "Those Americans may have gone to the wrong war, but they went for the right reasons."

SAC headquarters was troubled when word reached it that the BUFs had been lost. Regardless, the decision was made to press forward with the bombing. Despite the initial euphoria over the Bomb Damage Assessment (BDA) reports, some were distressed. "Many people in Washington were worried that the Air Force would fail," said Maj. Gen. Harry N. Cordes, SAC chief of staff.

Dec. 20 saw another six B-52s lost in aerial combat over North Vietnam's capital city. Morale hit rock bottom. There was a notable increase in sick call from the crews. Imaginary mechanical problems suddenly arose. And one officer even refused to fly. One pilot referred to the 70-mile stretch of BUFs as a "baby elephant walk."

Indeed, Dec. 20 proved to be the deadliest day of the operation with 17 airmen KIA—52% of total deaths in the aerial "11-Day War."

Continuing to neglect the pilots' concerns, 30 bombers headed toward Hanoi on Dec. 21. One pilot, flying in Blue Cell, said: "It looks like we'll walk on SAMs tonight." His premonition was correct. His aircraft was struck by two missiles, which caused one of the wings to catch fire.

Another BUF in Scarlet Cell fell victim when a SAM scored a direct hit. Capt. Robert E. Wolff later commented: "We had a formation approximately 70 miles long of one aircraft behind the other lumbering toward North Vietnam all using the same route, altitude and

One pilot flying in Blue Cell, said: "It looks like we'll walk on SAMs tonight."

AIR FORCE
CROSS

COL. JAMES R. MCCARTHY

CAPT. JOHN D. MIZE

heading. If 36 aircraft turned at a certain point to a certain heading, it does not require much of an educated guess to decide where to aim at number 37."

Although there was much vocal opposition to the strategy used during *Linebacker II*, the pilots and crews supported the bombing operation. "At last it seemed that we were going to attempt to end this war," said Wolff, "and everyone was proud to have some part in that operation."

'WHISPERING DEATH'

A 36-hour cease-fire was called on Christmas Eve. Planners immediately went to work to alter the strategy of the bombing runs. SAMs were the biggest obstacle to the vulnerable Stratofortresses and it was decided to eliminate as many SAM sites as possible.

To do this, the F-111 "Aardvark" was called upon. With its terrain-hugging capabilities, and its Mach 1 speed, it was virtually invisible to North Vietnamese Army (NVA) radar. Soon, the F-111s were flying an average of 24 times a night over Hanoi, releasing their 500- and 700-lb. snakeye ordnance. The NVA referred to it as the "whispering death."

Meanwhile, during the daylight hours, attack aircraft were pounding other important targets in the city. Railway lines, supply depots, and the Doumer and Canal Rapide bridges, were constantly bombed. Airmen flew almost 100 sorties daily, which prompted one pilot to say: "[The aircraft] were sitting nose to tail all the way out."

Additional safety measures were employed to protect the BUFs as much as possible. The number of support aircraft was increased substantially to 113 with the chaff being released in cloud-like formations to confuse the NVA gunners. Also, the BUFs were given different altitudes to enter Hanoi's air space and leave by diverse routes. The G-model B-52 was assigned lightly defended targets because of its inferior jamming equipment.

When these changes were implemented, morale quickly improved. Now, the pilots and crews felt they had a chance against the dreaded SAMs.

STRATEGY IS SUCCESSFUL

Dec. 26 saw the largest bombing raid of the Vietnam War. A meticulously planned and coordinated air assault was levied against Hanoi to bring the communists back to the bargaining table. The air armada consisted of 120 Stratofortresses with seven waves of the big birds hammering 10 different targets in the city within 15 minutes.

More than 100 support planes accompanied the BUFs. The Aardvarks strafed airstrips while U.S. Navy A-6 Intruders struck SAM batteries near Haiphong. The massive bombers diverged on Hanoi from northwest and southwest through Laos. The other cells, aimed at Haiphong and Thai Nguyen, flew in from the northeast and southeast.

The new tactics paid off. Some 4,000 tons of ordnance were released, destroying their targets. However, two B-52s were lost with six KIA to the barrage of SAMs. *Ebony 2* suddenly erupted into flames when it was hit by one of the projectiles. *Ash 1* crashed as it approached U-Tapao when it attempted to return to base after sustaining serious hits.

Salvos of SAMs blasted up to meet them. One returning pilot was asked how many missiles he had spotted: "Hundreds," he said.

Another pilot vividly described the way the missiles looked:

"Hold your hand at arm's length, fingers bunched and pointed toward your eyes," he said. "Now imagine that your fingertips are little points of light, and each one of those lights is a rocket motor on a missile. Now move your hand toward your face, fast, and spread your fingers. Those damned SAMs look like that going by."

Yet 43rd SW airborne mission commander Col. James R. McCarthy was awarded the Air Force Cross for leading his mission through "intense anti-aircraft fire and heavy salvos of surface-to-air missiles" on Dec. 26 "without sustaining a single loss."

Two days after Christmas, another 60 B-52s struck Hanoi. Capt. John D. Mize, a B-42 commander in the 307th SW, after seeing his aircraft severely damaged by SAMs on Dec. 27, "remained at his station to ensure that his crew had the best opportunity for safe egress over friendly territory," according to his Air Force Cross citation.

On the 28th and 29th, the mighty birds were on Hanoi's doorstep again with another bombing run. However, only a small number of SAMs greeted the attackers. It looked as if the NVA's aerial defenses were beginning to weaken. Right after that, the communists sent word that they wanted to resume the peace talks. *Linebacker II* was over.

Linebacker II lasted a mere 11 days, but in terms of firepower and destruction, it was awesome. In all, the B-52s flew over 700 sorties with tactical aircraft logging some 1,000 missions. A total of 15,000 tons of ordnance was dropped, destroying or crippling 1,600 military installations, 372 pieces of rolling stock, 80% of Hanoi's electric generating power, 25% of its petroleum supply and numerous airfields and roads.

The NVA also had eight MiGs shot down—two by B-52 tail gunners. Despite the magnitude of the bombing raids, civilian casualties were light: 1,318 deaths in Hanoi and 306 in Haiphong.

Linebacker II's complex tactics in combat "will eventually be recognized as one of the most outstanding feats of airmanship in strategic bombing operations in the history of aerial warfare," maintains retired Brig. Gen. James McCarthy.

The success of *Linebacker II* came at a high price, though. Some 15 B-52s and 11 tactical aircraft were lost with an additional nine BUF's damaged. Of the 98 Air Force crewmen shot down, 33 were KIA; 26 rescued; and 39 captured and subsequently released.

The breakdown for the total U.S. 37 KIA was 15 in the 72nd SW, 15 in the 307th SW, three in the 43rd SW and four naval aviators flying from the carriers *Saratoga, Ranger* and *Enterprise*.

The airmen killed have not been forgotten. On Guam at Andersen AFB in Arc Light Memorial Park they are forever remembered. On Dec. 8, 2012, the Linebacker II Memorial was dedicated at the Barksdale Global Power Museum on Barksdale AFB, La.

'THEY WERE AT YOUR MERCY'

In the end, it was the devastation of U.S. airpower that brought the communists back to the negotiations.

According to Vietnam War expert, the late Douglas Pike, "Hanoi officials experienced true, all-out strategic air war for the first time. It had a profound effect, causing them to reverse virtually overnight their bargaining position at the Paris talks."

Earl H. Tilford, author of *Crosswinds: The Air Force's Setup in Vietnam*, wrote that *Linebacker II* "had a psychological impact on Hanoi's leadership. That, coupled with the destruction of North Vietnam's air defense system, finally compelled a return to meaningful peace negotiations."

In *The Lessons of Vietnam,* British military authority Robert Thompson wrote: "In my view, on December 30, 1972, after eleven days of those B-52 attacks on the Hanoi area, you had won the war. It was over! They had fired 1,242 SAMs; they had none left, and what would come in overland from China would be a mere trickle. They and their whole rear base were at your mercy."

Historian George Herring concluded that "the U.S. position in South Vietnam was stronger at the end of 1972 than at any previous point in the war."

On Jan. 27, 1973, a month after *Linebacker II* ended, Le Duc Tho, and his negotiating team, signed the Paris Peace Accords. The communists paid Nixon the ultimate compliment: "Nixon proved to be extremely obstinate and reckless, and did things Johnson never dared to do." ✪

THE TOLL

U.S. KIA:
37

U.S. POW:
39

BRUTAL BATTLES OF VIETNAM
NAVY &
AIR FORCE

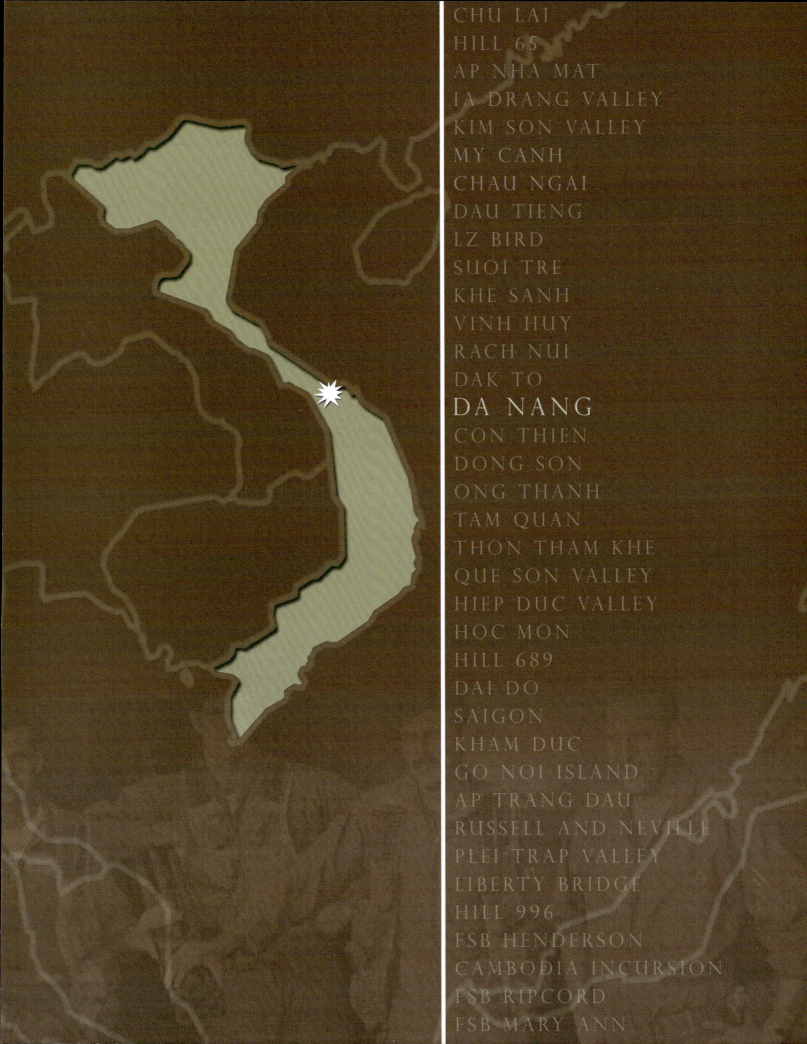

CHU LAI
HILL 65
AP NHA MAT
IA DRANG VALLEY
KIM SON VALLEY
MY CANH
CHAU NGAI
DAU TIENG
LZ BIRD
SUOI TRE
KHE SANH
VINH HUY
RACH NUI
DAK TO
DA NANG
CON THIEN
DONG SON
ONG THANH
TAM QUAN
THON THAM KHE
QUE SON VALLEY
HIEP DUC VALLEY
HOC MON
HILL 689
DAI DO
SAIGON
KHAM DUC
GO NOI ISLAND
AP TRANG DAU
RUSSELL AND NEVILLE
PLEI TRAP VALLEY
LIBERTY BRIDGE
HILL 996
FSB HENDERSON
CAMBODIA INCURSION
FSB RIPCORD
FSB MARY ANN

BY RICHARD K. KOLB

NAVY'S DEADLIEST ACTIONS IN VIETNAM

The U.S. Navy operated on the blue water ocean, along brown water inland waterways, in the air and on land during the Vietnam War. Along with carrier operations in the South China Sea, its best-known role was played on Vietnam's rivers and canals.

Riverine warfare required the services of the "Brown Water Navy" consisting of shallow-draft craft to combat the Viet Cong in the Mekong Delta.

The three Navy Task Forces (115, 116, 117) included the river patrol boat (PBR), fast patrol craft (PCF or swift boat), assault patrol boat (ASPB) providing destroyer and minesweeping functions, mechanized landing craft (LCM-6), monitor, armored troop carrier (ATC), command-and-communications boat (CCB) and the patrol air cushion vehicle (PACV).

Naval aviators also flew aerial reconnaissance missions and sailors served in several capacities on land as corpsmen, Seabees and SEALs.

DEADLY ROCKET ATTACK ON A LOADING RAMP

On Feb. 27, 1969, enemy 122mm rockets rained death on sailors working at the Da Nang naval facilities. The first rockets hit the covered storage area, killing three sailors of Supply Operations, Naval Support Activity (Da Nang).

Moored at the ramp were *LCU* (Landing Craft, Utility)-*1500* and the *YFU* (Harbor Utility Craft, Self-Propelled)-*78*. The LCU received a direct hit, detonating the ammo aboard. The explosion ignited a fire, which spread to the nearby YFU. Both ships were destroyed. The casualty toll was 22 KIA and 37 WIA. *LCU-1500* was hardest hit with 12 KIA, followed by the *YFU-78* with seven KIA.

Stanley Houlberg, Jr., was then assigned to the *YFU-74*. "I felt the initial explosion at least two miles away," he recalled. "The attack happened just after 11 p.m., and the fire and explosions lasted close to midnight. The third of three rockets hit the *1500* and both boats went up. The *78* probably had over 300 tons of black powder and projectiles on board; the 1500 about 200 tons."

Former Lt. Cmdr. John Schroll responded to the call for medical assistance from the naval station hospital. "The fury of the explosion was awful," he said. "We went across the bridge on foot. Because of the human devastation, we spent much of our effort identifying what was left of the remains. Walking along the ramp, I came upon a pair of

The U.S. Navy fought the war on the water, in the air and on the ground.
Its largest single hostile loss was 22 sailors in a 1969 rocket attack in Da Nang.

ABOVE: PCF-4 lost four sailors to a remote mine on Feb. 14, 1966, near Rach Gia. Swift boat sailors gained lasting fame for their exploits in Vietnam.

LEFT: A deadly rocket attack at the bridge ramp facility in Da Nang Harbor killed 22 U.S. sailors on Feb. 27, 1969. One landing craft alone lost a dozen men.

COURTESY U.S. NAVY SEABEE MUSEUM

Navy Seabees of Naval Mobile Construction Battalion 9 were hit on Hill 494 near Phu Bai on March 31, 1968. Six Seabees of Detail Echo died in one of the Navy's two single largest hostile losses in ground combat.

U.S. NAVY HOSTILE DEATHS IN THE VIETNAM WAR

AREA OF OPERATION	KIA	% OF NAVY KIA
Land	860[1]	53%
Air	429	27%
Fixed-Wing (351)		
Helicopter (78)		
Water	322[2]	20%
Total:	**1,611**	
Coast Guard	7	

[1] *Includes Navy corpsmen (638), Seabees (77), SEALs (34), naval gunfire spotters and advisers.*
[2] *Includes sailors on small boats on inland waters (riverine) and ships in open "blue" water.*
***Source:** Coffelt Database, 2017.*
Some 58 ship's crew were KIA aboard vessels at sea, according to the Defense Department.

Note: All told, Navy deaths numbered 2,569: 958 were non-hostile (37% of that service's total). Navy hostile deaths equaled 3.3% of all of American combat fatalities in the war.

combat boots with the feet still inside."

No other single enemy action caused a greater number of KIAs for American sailors in Vietnam.

MINES AND AMBUSHES TAKE A TOLL

Mines proved as deadly as rockets. The *USS Westchester County* sustained the highest hostile toll of any single U.S. ship in Vietnam. On Nov. 1, 1968, the *LST-1167* (Landing Ship, Tank) was rocked by two giant underwater explosions.

Viet Cong frogmen had attached limpet mines to the "Wesco's" hull. Part of the Mobile Riverine Base Alpha at My Tho, the ship lost 17 crewmembers, one sailor from River Assault Squadron 11, TF 117, five soldiers from the 9th Infantry Division and two South Vietnamese personnel.

A command-detonated mine sank the *YFU-62* on the Cua Viet River on Jan 16, 1969. The explosion killed eight men of the Literage Division of the Naval Support Activity.

A mine planted by a VC frogman took out the *YRBM* (Repair, Berthing and Messing Barge, Non-Self-Propelled)-*16* on Nov. 24, 1967, in the middle of the Ham Luong River closest to Ben Tre. Five sailors of River Division 52, TF 116, and two barge crewmen were KIA. Another 14 men were WIA.

On March 14, 1968, the Armored Troop Carrier 112-7 was leading a convoy between Cua Viet on the coast and the supply center at Dong Ha. "Tango 112-7" set off a 500-pound magnetic mine while minesweeping the Thach Han River. The boat flipped upside down and threw the crew overboard, killing six men of River Assault Squadron 11, TF 117.

Patrol Craft Fast Division 101, based at An Thoi, lost four men on the *PCF-4* of TF 115 to a remote mine explosion on Feb. 14, 1966. The vessel was patrolling the Baie De Cau River south of Rach Gia near the Gulf of Thailand.

Another swift boat, PCF-19, officially lost men to "friendly fire" from a U.S. Air Force plane on June 16, 1968, a half-mile off North Vietnam near the DMZ. But James Steffes, in *Swift Boat Down,* maintains that the four sailors of Coastal Division 12, TF 115, who were killed died as a result of hostile fire.

Over the course of the war, an estimated 3,500 "Swifties" served in Vietnam, with 52 being killed.

PBR-101, operating out of the River Section/Division 531 (TF 116) base at My Tho, was hit on May 24, 1967. Ambushed on the Ham Luong River, a VC 57mm recoilless rifle round killed four crewmembers.

Riverine warfare was a unique combat experience. "Sailors played a vital role in the Mekong Delta and elsewhere," said Albert Moore, who served aboard the *USS Benewah,* flagship of TF 117. "Though relatively few in number, riverine Navy personnel left their stamp on the war effort." Moore later founded the Mobile Riverine Force Association.

DEATH OVER THE SEA

Operation Market Time provided surveillance of the South Vietnamese coastline

'GHOST SQUADRON' DEFIES ODDS IN 'HARD AIR'

Two of the Navy's largest hostile losses in lives came not on the sea or ground, but in the air. The highly secretive Observation Squadron 67 (VO-67) was based at Nakhon Phanom Air Base in Thailand, and operated for only about eight months. Nicknamed the "Ghost Squadron," its veterans were sworn to secrecy and ordered never to reveal their missions.

Flying modified Neptunes, crew members dropped electronic sensors along the Ho Chi Minh Trail in Laos as part of the clandestine *Project Igloo White*. Because of the danger, the airspace over the Trail in Laos was called "The Hard Air." VO-67 had three planes shot down there with 20 KIA over 48 days.

On Jan. 11, 1968, a Neptune was hit near Phu Louang Mountain while descending through clouds and crashed

MR-6 of Observation Squadron 67 is identical to the modified Neptunes in the Air Forces' two largest hostile losses of the war.

into the north face of a sheer cliff around Ban Napoung. All nine crewmen were KIA. Then on Feb. 17, small-arms fire penetrated another "Ghost" aircraft in the vicinity of Ban Namm and it crashed

about two miles northwest of Muang Phine. Again, nine airmen died.

Ten days later, Feb. 27, there would have been a repeat outcome if not for the bravery of the aircraft's pilot. After being hit by 37mm anti-aircraft rounds, Capt. Paul L. Milius ordered the crew to bail out. He stayed at the controls to steady the flight. This allowed the crew to bail out, seven of whom survived. Milius received a posthumous Navy Cross. One other crewman died.

A full decade after its exploits were declassified, this unique squadron was awarded the Presidential Unit Citation in 2008.

and helped halt seaborne infiltration. Among the aircraft employed were P-3 Orions based in U-Tapao, Thailand, and Sangley Point, Philippines. The P-3s patrolled the Gulf of Siam.

On April 1, 1968, an unarmed P-3B from Patrol Squadron (VP) 26 was hit in the starboard wing by fire from a .50-caliber anti-aircraft gun. It was mounted on a landing craft manned by the *Khmer Rouge* (Cambodian communists) near Hon Doc Island.

"I saw the P-3 flying rather low and burning—it appeared the right wing was on fire," recalled Gunner's Mate 3rd Class Gary Goudie, who was aboard a patrolling swift boat that day. "The P-3 either exploded on impact or completely broke apart as the wreckage showed complete destruction and there were no survivors. It was rumored at the time that a Cambodian gunboat had shot the plane down."

An engine had caught fire and the plane crashed near the island of Hon Vang while attempting to land on Phu Quoc, less than 10 miles from the Cambodian coast.

"Suddenly, abruptly, the wing tore off between #3 and #4 engine, and the aircraft tumbled uncontrolled as it plunged into the sea," wrote VP-26 veteran A. Scott Wilson in his memoirs in 1996.

All 12 members of Crew One perished—the largest single hostile aviation loss for the Navy during the war. (Crew Eight of VP-26 was most likely lost due to autopilot problems, on Feb. 6, 1968. These 12 aviators also died in the Gulf of Siam. However, some vets believe an anti-aircraft round hit the plane's #5 tank.)

A P-3 Orion, similar to the one shown here, was downed by Cambodian Communist anti-aircraft gunfire on April 1, 1968, over the Gulf of Siam.

COMBAT ON THE GROUND

Navy in-country personnel peaked at 39,265 in October 1968. That number included

NAVY'S ONLY MEDAL OF HONOR HELICOPTER PILOT

U.S. NAVY PHOTO

On the night of June 18, 1968, Lt. (j.g.) Clyde Lassen became the only Navy helicopter pilot to receive the Medal of Honor during the Vietnam War. Lassen is shown at the controls with his crew and ground support personnel from HC-7 Detachment 4.

When a Navy F-4 Phantom jet was brought down by a SAM missile near Vinh on the night of June 18, 1968, the two-man crew found themselves surrounded by enemy forces.

Lt. (j.g.) Clyde Lassen maneuvered his UH-2 Seasprite during several rescue attempts guided by illumination flares. When the flares extinguished in one of two attempts, the chopper's blades struck a tree nearly causing a crash. In a third attempt in a rice paddy while under heavy enemy fire, Lassen had nearly landed when the flares once again went out.

Determined to save the pilots, Lassen turned on his landing lights and set down as his door gunners returned fire. The stranded aviators scrambled aboard and the Seasprite lifted off heading out to sea. Low on fuel, Lassen landed on the first ship he came across, the *USS Jouett,* with only five minutes of fuel left.

Aside from Lassen, co-pilot Clarence L. Cook received the Navy Cross. Aviation Machinist Mates Bruce B. Dallas and Donald N. West were each awarded the Silver Star.

gunboat crews, naval advisers, medical corpsmen, SEALs and Seabees.

Seabees suffered the second highest fatal hostile Navy casualties in one engagement on the ground (other than Navy corpsmen). Detail Echo, a 180-man detachment of Naval Mobile Construction Battalion 9, was assigned to develop a quarry on Hill 494. It was located between Phu Bai and Phu Loc in I Corps. Early on March 31, 1968, an enemy recoilless rifle round struck a berthing tent on the hill, wounding seven men. One died of massive head wounds while being medically evacuated.

Five hours later, two 82mm mortar rounds made direct hits on the No. 2 mortar emplacement. Five Seabees were killed instantly. (Five Seabees, of NMCB-74, also were KIA in an ambush along the Kinh Thot Not Canal on Dec. 31, 1970.) "It was like a nightmare," HM2 Thomas P. Kelly said. "The mortars shook the ground under us, and littered the air with smoke and debris. Everything seemed to move in slow motion, like in a bad dream."

SEAL teams operated primarily in the Rung Sat Special Zone, a thick mangrove swamp crisscrossed by rivers in the Mekong Delta. Their hunter-killer teams consisted of only three to seven men, so large-scale, single-battle casualties were not possible. Only on two occasions did a team lose up to three men in a hostile action. These were on April 7, 1967, in a river ambush and on May 17, 1969, when a mortar round hit their position at Kien Giang. In both cases, those killed were members of Detachment Golf, SEAL Team 1.

At least 32,238 Navy corpsmen served in Vietnam during the entire war. Some 638 were KIA and 4,563 WIA. Their single greatest daily loss was on July 2, 1967. Eight corpsmen of H&S Co., 1st Bn., 9th Marines, were KIA in an ambush on Route 561 northeast of Con Thien. Typically, 53 corpsmen were assigned to an infantry battalion, serving with rifle companies, one or two per platoon of about 40 men each. Four Medals of Honor, 30 Navy Crosses and 127 Silver Stars attest to their bravery in the heat of battle. ✪

BY SHANNON HANSON

'WESCO' MINED AT MY THO

Some 23 Americans (18 sailors and five soldiers) were killed when Viet Cong swimmers mined the hull of the *USS Westchester County* on Nov. 1, 1968. This was the U.S. Navy's greatest loss of life from a single ship as the result of enemy action in Vietnam.

In the fall of 1968, the *USS Westchester County* was in the middle of its fifth combat deployment to Vietnam, in support of Task Force 117, Mobile Riverine Force (MRF).

It was anchored midstream in the Tien Giang River, 3.7 miles southeast of My Tho. The "Wesco," a support/supply/barracks ship with a crew of 132, was serving as the temporary base for 175 soldiers of the 3rd Bn., 60th Inf., and 3rd Bn., 34th Arty, 9th Inf. Div., and 93 sailors of Navy River Assault Division 111.

As such, it was surrounded by the command ship *USS Benewah,* repair vessel *USS Askari,* two large barracks barges, three aluminum pontoon barges and various assault craft.

'TWISTED METAL, MANGLED BODIES'

In the early-morning hours of Nov. 1, the majority of the crew was asleep. Always on guard for a Viet Cong attack, picket boats circled the ships, dropping concussion grenades to ward off enemy swimmers.

But at 3:22 a.m., two mines—each containing an estimated 150-500 pounds of explosives—detonated on the starboard side of the ship, directly under the fuel and berthing compartments.

G.W. Frederickson, writing in the August 1998 issue of *Vietnam,* described the carnage: "In the crowded sleeping areas, the blasts rolled an entire deck upward and back, like the tongue of a shoe, leaving only a cramped crawl space jammed with twisted metal and mangled bodies between the deck and bulkhead."

One artilleryman remembered that night vividly. "I left the card game I was playing and

JAG PHOTO

Two large holes blown into the berthing and fuel compartments of the Wesco are clearly visible. Viet Cong swimmers mined the hull, and the resulting explosions claimed 23 American lives and wounded 22.

"Instead of grabbing my mattress to protect myself, I examined the room. The men I'd just passed who were sleeping were now dead."

—SPEC. 4 DONALD R. OUTEN

NAVY PHOTO

The USS *Westchester County* (LST 1167) underway sometime prior to 1967.

quietly made it to my bunk," said Donald R. Outen, then a specialist 4 aboard the ship. "I bent over to take my boots off, then there was this big explosion. I thought we'd been hit by B-40s [enemy rockets]. Instead of grabbing my mattress to protect myself, I examined the room. The men I'd just passed who were sleeping were now dead."

Within the ship, it was mayhem. Sailors jolted awake by the blast rushed to battle stations—most wearing only underwear or less—stopping to help any wounded they encountered along the way. Visibility was zero, as the lighting was knocked out, and clouds of steam and vaporized diesel fuel filled the air.

The deck of the sleeping area was blown upward, leaving sailors (many of them wounded) only a tight crawl space to escape. Below, in the Army quarters, river water rushed in through two gaping holes, each more than 20 feet in diameter.

COMPLETE CHAOS

"No one knew what was going on or what really happened," Outen said. "It was pitch black outside, and people were falling over each other because you couldn't see anything."

Robert Heiney, then a petty officer 2nd class, was working aboard one of the barracks barges (APL 30) moored 50-100 yards off the *Wesco* when the mines detonated.

"We felt the wave from the explosion," he said. "We soon joined the search for survivors who might be in the water. It was disorienting to see the night sky lit with illumination flares and spotlights from patrol boats and choppers. Soon the MRF ships were firing toward shore with their big guns, which added to the chaos."

It wasn't long before the ship began listing to starboard. Lt. Cmdr. John Branin knew that to save the *Wesco,* he had to correct the list. By using the ship's sophisticated ballasting system to pump out the ballast already held in internal tanks, he was able to offset the water that was flooding the ship through the holes created by the explosion.

Every senior petty officer was killed or wounded (their compartment was among the hardest-hit areas), so 22-year-old Petty Officer 2nd Class Rick Russell followed precise instructions and successfully righted the ship.

Meanwhile, below deck, Hospital Corpsman 1st Class John Sullivan, himself missing a large chunk of flesh from his leg, responded through the darkness to cries for help from the senior petty officers' quarters. He found two sailors pinned, one unconscious with a head injury and the other with a large metal hook through his arm. Sullivan was able to pry them out and helped evacuate them.

"We didn't obey a whole lot of first-aid rules on moving victims," Sullivan later said. "At the time, it was just a matter of getting them the hell out of there."

Only on his way to the bridge to see where else he was needed did Sullivan realize his leg was still bleeding and he had no clothes on. After donning pants and shoes, he continued to assist those in need, at one point giving first aid and support to two trapped men for more than an hour until they were freed.

A River Assault Division 111 barge alongside the *USS Westchester County* shows tremendous damage after the mining of the supply/barracks ship.

HAMPERED RESCUE EFFORTS

Once it was clear the *Wesco* was not under attack, men at their battle stations were ordered to assist with rescue operations. But the vaporized fuel in the air hampered their efforts.

According to a narrative by damage control officer Lt. (j.g.) Charles P. Vion, "Investigation was extremely difficult, as lights shone into the heavy vapors were useless until the atmosphere could be cleared."

Also of great concern were the more than 300 tons of explosives and ammunition stored on the tank deck—a flash fire that reached those could cause untold devastation. Rescuers couldn't use cutting torches to release those trapped by twisted metal until the vaporized fuel was cleared out. So they had to settle for chain falls, pry bars, come-alongs and screw jacks.

In daylight, recovery efforts and damage assessments could begin.

"Once the sun came up, teams were assigned to get the dead out," Outen said. "There was one 18-year-old kid who had just arrived the day before who I'd helped out. I saw them putting him in a body bag 12 hours later."

Branin chose to beach the ship to better assess the damage. The crew worked around the clock for 14 days making temporary repairs, after which they made the 2,500-mile trip back to Yokosuka, Japan, for dry-docking and repairs. Rough seas on the way there cracked and ruptured the temporary repairs, but the crew was ready, and they made it to Japan without major incident.

Retired Army explosives expert Capt. Robert Shelley called the mining of the *Westchester County* a "well-planned and executed enemy operation." He surmised that if the cargo had gone "high order," or exploded, it would have been equal to a small nuclear weapon. This would have destroyed the ship and could have immobilized or destroyed the entire Mobile Riverine Force. He credits the quick thinking and actions of the crew for averting that tragedy.

Crew members received 36 awards and commendations for their actions that day, including a Bronze Star for Lt. Cmdr. Branin and a Silver Star for corpsman Sullivan.

Although the day was still tragic—17 crewmen, one riverine sailor and five soldiers (of B Co., 3rd Bn., 60th Inf.), along with two South Vietnamese personnel, were KIA and 22 WIA—the crewmen prevailed, saving the *Wesco*. ✪

THE TOLL

U.S. KIA:
23
(18 sailors and five soldiers)

U.S. WIA:
22

BY TIM DYHOUSE

COMMANDO HUNTING OVER LAOS: SPECTRE GUNSHIPS IN ACTION

O n the early evening of March 28, 1972, at Ubon Royal Air Force Base in Thailand, U.S. Air Force Tech. Sgt. Sidney Terry received an unexpected order: He would be replaced on that night's AC-130 gunship mission by fellow airman Staff Sgt. Edwin Jack Pearce.

Terry, who had only been at Ubon for a couple months, says he didn't know Pearce that well but does recall that the staff sergeant had won quite a bit of money in a poker game earlier that day.

Scheduled for a "four or five hour" flight hunting enemy traffic on the Ho Chi Minh Trail in neighboring Laos, Pearce and the rest of the 14-man crew of the AC-130 gunship Spectre 13, nicknamed *Prometheus,* took off in the darkness at Ubon, where they were supposed to return in the morning.

"They never came back the next day," said an emotional Terry, a resident of Salina, Kan. "Rarely does a day go by that I don't think about that flight. To this day, it puts a lump in my throat because I'm here, and they're not."

All 14 men were killed when the *Prometheus* was shot down. It tied for the worst single loss of life suffered by Air Force gunships working the Ho Chi Minh Trail.

'AIRBORNE TANKS' PATROL OVER LAOS

During the later years of the Vietnam War, attacking enemy traffic on that route in a relatively slow moving AC-130 was indeed a hazardous, albeit necessary, duty.

Laos was officially a neutral country during the war, but its fractured coalition government and the aggressive Communist Pathet Lao made a mockery of that status. A separate agreement on Feb. 21, 1973, put a cease-fire in place there a month after Vietnam.

The Pathet Lao-controlled portions of Laos provided the North Vietnamese Army (NVA) a convenient supply route—the Ho Chi Minh Trail—running nearly the length of the country's southeastern panhandle. Winding through 1,700 square miles of steep, mountainous terrain, the trail featured at least four main offshoots into South Vietnam and continued southward into Cambodia.

AC-130E Gunship Serenade in the Moonlight by Charles Ball.
As dramatically depicted here, AC-130 aircraft wreaked havoc on NVA transports at night along the Ho Chi Minh Trail in Laos in the early '70s.

COURTESY AIR FORCE ART PROGRAM

Air Force AC-130 crews sustained 14 KIA in two separate shoot-downs in 1972, making them that service's largest hostile losses in single actions of the Vietnam War. Here is the story of the 16th Special Operations Squadron in the early 1970s as it interdicted Communist movement along the Ho Chi Minh Trail.

These massive belts of armor-piercing 20mm cannon shells represent the smallest caliber ammunition fired by the Air Force AC-130 gunship.

The U.S. Air Force—with help from the U.S. Navy, Marine Corps and Royal Laotian Air Force—targeted trucks, supply caches, storage bases, trail support structures and even the trail's geographic features. The overall air mission was known as *Operation Commando Hunt,* a series of seven campaigns from November 1968 through March 1972.

During the day, B-52s and fighters attacked the trail. At night, when most traffic moved on the route, the main workhorse was the AC-130 gunship. Known as an "airborne tank," the AC-130 was a converted cargo plane highly maneuverable at low speeds. It could spend hours orbiting at about 175 mph above a target while delivering a precisely placed stream of withering fire.

'FABULOUS FOUR-ENGINE FIGHTERS'

By 1972, its weapons system featured two Vulcan 20mm cannons, one 40mm Bofors cannon and a 105mm howitzer. This firepower made the gunship an extremely effective tank killer and the scourge of the enemy who ventured onto the Ho Chi Minh Trail.

The crews called themselves the "Fabulous Four-Engine Fighters" and the best "truck-killers" in Southeast Asia. Each man had a specific duty.

The pilots commanded the aircraft and were in charge of the crews, usually 11–16 men.

DEADLIEST AIR FORCE GUNSHIP LOSSES (6+) OF THE VIETNAM WAR

DATE	KILLED	AIRCRAFT	SQUADRON	COUNTRY	LOCATION
Mar 29, 1972	14	AC-130	16th	Laos	Muang Phine
Dec 21, 1972	14*	AC-130	16th	Laos	Ban Longam
Jun 18, 1972	12	AC-130	16th	Vietnam	A Luoi Village
Apr 22, 1970	10	AC-130	16th	Laos	Ban Tang Lou
Dec 17, 1965	9†	AC-47	4th	Vietnam	Ban Son Nut-Rang Phau
May 5, 1968	9	AC-47 (2)	4th	Vietnam	Pleiku Airfield
May 15, 1966	8‡	AC-47	4th	Laos	Ban Nampa Khon
Feb 15, 1968	8	AC-47	14th	Vietnam	Phan Rang
Sep 1, 1969	8	AC-47	4th	Vietnam	Bien Hoa (near)
Mar 13, 1966	7	AC-47	4th	Vietnam	A Ro
Jan 9, 1967	7§	AC-47	4th	Vietnam	Duc Pho
Mar 29, 1967	7	AC-47	4th	Vietnam	Hoi An
Apr 26, 1967	7	AC-47	4th	Vietnam	Cam Ranh Bay
Oct 3, 1967	7	AC-47	4th	Vietnam	Hue City
Dec 24, 1965	6	AC-47	4th	Laos	Ban Bac
Jun 3, 1966	6	AC-47	4th	Laos	Ban Pha Kat
Apr 28, 1970	6	AC-119	17th	Vietnam	Tan Son Nhut

Source: Vietnam Air Losses by Chris Hobson (Midland Pub., 2001).

* One was a pilot from the 497th Tactical Fighter Squadron, which escorted the 16th SOS.
† 5 members of 12th Civil Engineering Squadron
‡ 1 from 377th Combat Support Squadron
§ 1 from 606th Air Command Squadron
Note: Prior to 1969, the designation was 4th Air Commando Squadron (ACS).
The 16th Special Operations Squadron (SOS) began full-fledged operations mostly in 1969.

The 16th Special Operations Squadron's insignia.

LOSSES BY GUNSHIP TYPE

TYPE	NUMBER LOST	FATALITIES	PERCENT OF TOTAL DEATHS
AC-47	19	92	57.50 %
AC-130	6	52	32.50 %
AC-119*	5	16	10 %

*Only one AC-119 was lost to enemy action. On May 2, 1972, Stinger 41 of the 18th SOS was shot down over An Loc, sustaining 3 KIA.

Each flight carried four to five navigators, and in addition to plotting a flight's course, they also ran the gunships multiple night sensors.

Flight engineers readied the aircraft for inspections, kept systems running during missions and brought the various guns on line at the pilot's direction.

Illuminator operators (IOs) were in charge of the large light at the back of AC-130s used to illuminate Special Forces camps during close air-support missions. They spent most of their time lying flat on their bellies looking out over the open ramp calling out enemy anti-aircraft fire. As the NVA began to use surface-to-air missiles, the IOs used flares to divert them.

Gunners manned and maintained the guns and "shoveled brass" (cleaned up the expended shells that "flew everywhere" as the guns fired at a rate of 6,200 rounds per minute) after the missions. Each flight usually carried five or six gunners.

Photographers flew on every mission and took photos while over the targets. As they returned to base, they also helped gunners shovel brass. Once on the ground they turned over their film, which was processed and sent to Washington every day.

The first AC-130s began arriving in the war zone in 1967 and within a year, the Air Force

> ## "The SAMs [surface-to-air missiles] looked like headlights coming at you. They are air breathers. You could see through their intakes to their jet engines, glowing."
> —JOE ALBRIGHT, AN AC-130 GUNNER

U.S. AIR FORCE PHOTO

Master Sgt. Jacob E. Mercer and Sgt. Lonnie R. Blevins stand near the breech of a 105mm howitzer mounted in an AC-130 gunship, ready to reload.

had enough to form a squadron. On Oct. 30, 1968, it activated the 16th Special Operations Squadron—part of the 8th Tactical Fighter Wing—at Ubon Royal Thai Air Force Base, Thailand.

Over the next four years, the AC-130, more commonly known as the "Spectre" based on its squadron's call sign, would become the most deadly night-flying weapons system in Southeast Asia.

Equipped first with the AC-130A model gunship and later with the more advanced AC-130E/H models, Spectre aircrews flew the latest in the family of gunships, including the famous AC-47 Spooky, AC-119G Shadow and the AC-119K Stinger.

Nicknamed the "Great Laotian Truck Eater," the 16th SOS destroyed or damaged an average of 10,000 trucks per year on the Ho Chi Minh Trail. Additional roles included defense of hamlets and fire bases, supporting troops in contact with the enemy, escorting convoys and illuminating battlefields.

PLAYING A 'DEADLY GAME'

For AC-130 crews, those battlefields lay thousands of feet below in the thick jungles along the Ho Chi Minh Trail. The trail itself was actually a network of roads that totaled more than 2,700 miles in length. Richard L. Stevens, author of *The Trail: A History of the Ho Chi Minh Trail and the Role of Nature in the War in Viet Nam,* wrote that it was "a massive labyrinth of hundreds of paths, roads, rivers, streams, passes, caves and underground tunnels burrowing through mountains, forests and into the earth."

To get to those battlefields from Ubon, Spectre crews had to "cross the fence," or fly over the Mekong River, which formed the border with Laos, some 60 miles to the east. Crossing the fence signaled to the crews that they had entered hostile territory and to be alert for enemy gunners.

"Flying over the trail could scare the hell out of you," Joe Albright, an AC-130 gunner, told *Vietnam* magazine. "We played a deadly game. The triple A [anti-aircraft artillery fire], predominantly orange in color, looked like Roman candles. The 57mm never came up in a tracer; it would just explode out there.

"If a 57mm started walking in on your orbit, you would just leave the area and go someplace else. The SAMs [surface-to-air missiles] looked like headlights coming at you. They are air breathers. You could see through their intakes to their jet engines, glowing."

'SPECTRE SHUTTLE'

Supporting gunners like Albright were the ground crews at Ubon.

"Our job was to certify the other crews on the proper maintenance of the guns and flares, and also to help the gunners if they had problems," said Don C. Newton, who worked in the gun shop at Ubon from November 1971 to November 1972. "My crew helped install and get the first 105mm up and going. When I left, six of the 18 gunships there were armed with 105s."

Also based at Ubon were the "Night Owls" of the 497th Tactical Fighter Squadron, which provided F-4 fighters that accompanied the AC-130s on missions. Working together, the fighters and gunships were called the "Spectre Shuttle."

The fighters provided protection for the Spectres, which would drop ground flares to mark enemy gun emplacements that the F-4s would attack. They formed tight teams.

"The camaraderie and love of the hunt kept me coming back," Albright said of his four tours and 386 missions. "It was a high, literally."

DODGING ANTI-AIRCRAFT FIRE

While the inherent danger of flying missions in a Spectre gunship was thrilling for some airmen, it was potentially deadly for all. The large, relatively slow moving AC-130 was an inviting target for Communist gunners. In six shoot downs of 16th SOS aircraft between 1969-72, 52 U.S. airmen were KIA.

"When the 37mm was shot into the air, it looked like a glowing baseball," Pat Carpenter, a former Spectre gunner and current president of the Spectre Association, recounted to *Vietnam* magazine. "If you thought you could catch it, you were probably going to be hit. Lots of tracerless [ammunition] was fired at us. If you ran into 23mm, or the 'golden hose,' the best defense was to climb and become as small a silhouette as possible. It really lit up the sky and put a lot of rounds into the air quite rapidly, kind of like a shotgun blast or running into a sprinkler."

The first shoot down of an AC-130 occurred May 24, 1969, during a night mission over southern Laos. The aircraft was checking Routes 914 and 920 and was about to attack a truck convoy near the village of Ban Tanbok, about 20 miles southwest of the A Shau Valley.

As the plane orbited at 6,500 feet, two rounds of 37mm anti-aircraft fire ripped through the tail and fuselage, mortally wounding one crewman. As the pilot nursed the plane back to Ubon, he ordered most of the crew to bail out near the airfield before attempting to land.

As the plane slammed to the ground, the starboard wing was sheared off and the aircraft caught fire. The pilot was able to escape, but the flight engineer was not and died in the incident.

Less than a year later, on April 22, 1970, an AC-130—call sign Adlib 1 and called *War Lord*—and two fighters patrolled over Route 96A some 25 miles east of Saravan in southern Laos when the gunship took 37mm ground fire.

The flak caused the port wing to catch fire and one crewman managed to bail out. The other 10 airmen were killed in the crash near Ban Tang Lou.

WORST YEAR OF THE WAR FOR AC-130S

For nearly two years, AC-130 crewmen managed to avoid hostile fatalities, but that changed in

AC-130 gunships and EC-121 surveillance planes operated over Laos' perilous Ho Chi Minh Trail. Gunships were efficient at locating and destroying NVA trucks with deadly precision.

COURTESY DON NEWTON

Members of a gun shop crew at Ubon Royal Thai Air Force Base from 1971-72 take a break in front of two 40mm cannons. They are Ron Goings, Lyle Milliman, Don Newton and Mike Hamann.

1972 when 40 members lost their lives in shoot downs.

"It was clearly the worst year of the war for the AC-130 gunship," said Charles A. Berninger, a retired Air Force lieutenant colonel who flew 133 missions with the 16th SOS between February 1972 and January 1973. "Although the Vietnam War was supposedly winding down during 1972, the air war was still very active along the Ho Chi Minh Trail."

During Berninger's time at Ubon, the *Prometheus* went down March 29 over Laos. As the aircraft approached the town of Muang Phine, some 35 miles west of Khe Sanh, an SA-2 missile fired from a newly established SAM site in Laos struck the plane. The *Prometheus* burst into flames, crashed and exploded.

"It was in big orange flames," said former Lt. Col. Stephen J. Opitz, a fire control officer, recalling what a fellow co-pilot told him about the crash. "I guess it looked like the size of a football field just arching down the sky. They took a direct hit. They were loaded with fuel and it turned into a big orange ball."

Opitz, who earned the nickname "magnet ass" after surviving three SAM attacks, described the sound of a missile exploding overhead as "like a freight train and a thump." His Spectre 15 avoided a SAM attack in April 1972 around Tchepone, allowing the crew to continue hunting trucks, destroying two.

A search-and-rescue (SAR) task force found no survivors of the *Prometheus* crash. The Pathet Lao claimed it had shot down the plane.

The father of Staff Sgt. James Kenneth Caniford, who was killed on the *Prometheus,* told the *Frederick* (Maryland)-*News Post* about his feelings after his son's remains were identified in March 2008.

"When you're in MIA status, there is never any closure," Jim Caniford said. "That's the most difficult part. We will die without knowing what happened to our son. You have to comprehend the immensity of what this does in a family's life. The forgotten people in all of this are the wives, the brothers, the sisters."

PHOTO FROM WWW.SPECTRE-ASSOCIATION.ORG

Staff Sgt. James Kenneth Caniford was among the missing crewmen of the *Prometheus* that was shot down on March 29, 1972. His remains were eventually identified in March 2008.

'THE WHOLE WORLD WAS ORANGE'

Less than three months after the *Prometheus* went down, on June 18, 1972, another SAM found its mark. This time the missile was an SA-7, and it was the first time that type of missile had brought down a gunship of the 16th SOS.

The plane, Spectre 11, was patrolling near the A Shau Valley about 25 miles southwest of Hue. The missile hit the No. 3 engine, and the wing blew off moments later when a fuel tank exploded.

"At that point, the aircraft went into a flat spin, and I was immediately plastered up against the 40mm ammo rack," said former Capt. Gordon Bocher, who was serving as the fire control officer on the flight. "I could see other crewmembers plastered against the sides of the fuselage, too. That type of centrifugal force makes your body feel like it weighs about 2,000 pounds. There was really no hope of doing anything."

Bocher, of Stephens City, Va., says "everything was on fire and the whole world was blazing orange" inside the plane as it continued its death spiral toward the ground. Suddenly, Bocher says "everything went bright to black, as I guess I passed out. The next thing I knew, I wasn't hot anymore and I could see trees."

> ## "I could see other crewmembers plastered against the sides of the fuselage, too. That type of centrifugal force makes your body feel like it weighs about 2,000 pounds. There was really no hope of doing anything."
>
> —CAPT. GORDON BOCHER, FIRE CONTROL OFFICER ON SPECTRE 11 AFTER BEING HIT BY AN SA-7 MISSILE

He remembers pulling the ripcord on his parachute, which was open "only for about five seconds" before he hit the trees.

The plane had exploded "into about four pieces," Bocher says a fighter pilot told him. Bocher, 2nd Lt. Robert "Vic" Reid and Staff Sgt. Bill Patterson were the only crew members who were able to open their parachutes and survive the crash. A total of 12 airmen were killed.

"I'm alive today because I followed the pilot's orders," Bocher said. "Capt. Paul Gilbert's first priority was the safety of his crew, and he sacrificed his life so that we could get out. My son's middle name is 'Paul' in honor of Gilbert's heroism."

Bocher hid in a tangle of tree roots during the night, with an NVA patrol passing within "10 or 12 feet" of him about 2 a.m. "I even called in an airstrike on my own position," he said. "But the SAR guy told me to sit tight and keep my mouth shut."

Bocher, Reid and Patterson were all rescued by SAR helicopters—dodging intense enemy ground fire that delayed the extractions—the next day.

> ## "It was in big orange flames. ... I guess it looked like the size of a football field just arching down the sky."
>
> —FORMER LT. COL. STEPHEN J. OPITZ, A FIRE CONTROL OFFICER, RECALLING WHAT A FELLOW CO-PILOT TOLD HIM ABOUT THE CRASH OF PROMETHEUS

While he was trapped inside the plane, Bocher says "I knew I was dead, but I became very peaceful. I was with the people I wanted to be with. As far as I was concerned the 16th SOS was the best unit in Southeast Asia, and I was proud to serve with those men."

THOR GOES DOWN

Some six months later, the war's last hostile shoot down of an AC-130 happened. On Dec. 21, 1972, Spectre 17, nicknamed *Thor*, found three enemy trucks near Ban Laongam, 25 miles west of Saravan, Laos. As it was firing at targets from an altitude of 7,800 feet, it was hit by 37mm fire. The aircraft exploded—most likely a result of the flak hitting a fuel tank—and crashed in flames.

"I was the first person on the scene for the crashed Spectre 17," said H. Ownby, a forward air controller working under the call sign Raven 26. "I have dealt with the tragedy that night, the next day and all the years since then. There were three other Raven forward air controllers involved that night and the next day."

Of the 16 men onboard, 14 were killed, including a pilot from the 497th Tactical Fighter

Shown among this AC-130 crew just prior to a mission is Jerry Van Engen, third from the right in the back row. Van Engen was replaced at the last moment on the night of Dec. 21, 1972, when Spectre 17 was shot down over Laos, losing 14 men.

Van Engen (right) is with Robert Reid who parachuted safely from the Spectre 11 on June 18, 1972.

Squadron who was along for the ride. Two crewmen bailed out and were rescued within hours.

Jerry Van Engen was originally assigned to the flight, but was replaced by 1st Lt. Delmar Ernest Dickens, who was killed.

"That night will live in my memory for the rest of my life," said Van Engen, who served at Ubon from February 1972 to February 1973. "I do not know why I was spared and Delmar Dickens was taken when he replaced me on that flight."

HEROISM ON DISPLAY

Missiles and anti-aircraft fire were constant threats for AC-130 crews, but sometimes the airmen's heroism averted tragedy. The day after the *Prometheus* went down, March 30, 1972, Capt. Waylon O. Fulk was piloting Spectre 22 above Laos when he made a third pass over an enemy convoy that his gunners had shot up. A barrage of 37mm and 57mm fire hit the plane, ripping into the right wing and right side of the fuselage.

As he steered away from the ground fire, Fulk ordered his 14-man crew to prepare to bail out. He then notified other planes in the area and radar stations of his situation. After 13 men had parachuted out safely, Fulk, who had reported the jump site and engaged the autopilot to fly the plane away from enemy territory, joined his illuminator operator at the aircraft's cargo ramp.

Both men exited safely, and the next day all 15 crewmen were picked up—the largest and most successful mass crew rescue of the war. Fulk was awarded the Air Force Cross for his actions.

Without a doubt, the AC-130s flying out of Thailand were effective against the enemy. According to the NVA 377th Air Division history, "Just one hour when AC-130s did not operate over our choke-points was both precious and rare."

This was, after all, "the crucial struggle of the Vietnam War and one of the most significant encounters in history," said author Richard Stevens.

Jack S. Ballard, author of *Development and Employment of Fixed-Wing Gunships, 1962-72,* summed up the contributions of the flight crews best: "The gunship successes and failures were inseparable from the individuals involved—the indispensable human element."

A permanent reminder of that human sacrifice can be found in Memorial Air Park, Hurlburt Field, Fla. This special memorial reads: "In Memoriam 52 Spectres—16th Special Operations Wing." ✪

SAPPERS SACK SECRET RADAR SITE

BY KELLY VON LUNEN

On March 11, 1968, the U.S. Air Force sustained its greatest hostile ground loss of the Vietnam War at Lima Site 85, an isolated mountaintop in Laos. That unit's top-secret mission there remained classified until 1983.

A unique mission held top-secret until declassified 15 years later, Lima Site 85 holds a dubious distinction. Amidst the "shadow" war in Laos, the Air Force saw its largest single ground combat loss of the Vietnam War.

Not only was the program—code name "Heavy Green"—classified, but the participating airmen were "sheep-dipped." Because the U.S. military was not allowed in Laos, airmen were given cover as Lockheed employees while actually still serving in the Air Force.

Although American leaders foresaw an imminent North Vietnamese Army (NVA) attack on Site 85, they were reluctant to give up any advantage over the enemy sooner than necessary. In hesitating to get the airmen out, 12 American lives were lost on March 11, 1968.

"We may have pushed our luck one day too long in attempting to keep this facility [Site 85] in operation," said Laos Ambassador William Sullivan.

Sullivan's quote became the title of Timothy Castle's 1999 full-account book, *One Day Too Long: Top Secret Site 85 and the Bombing of North Vietnam.*

'We Knew Something Happened'

Phou Pha Thi ("Sacred Mountain") stands about 5,500 feet, a broad-based, ridged limestone formation that rises first gradually then suddenly and then nearly vertically, with a plateau on top. A cliff graced the western side. The mountain was chosen for Lima Site 85 for its location, less than 150 miles from Hanoi.

Nicknamed "Commando Club," Site 85

was part of the Air Force's Combat Skyspot radar bombing program. With these sites in the range of bombing targets, aircraft could hit them with a fair degree of accuracy even when visibility was limited due to bad weather.

Lt. Col. Gerald H. Clayton, commander of the 1043rd Radar Evaluation Squadron, headed the team of airmen from the 1st Combat Evaluation Group, a secret radar tracking unit based at Barksdale Air Force Base in Shreveport, La. Detachment 1—consisting of 16 airmen, one forward air controller and two CIA operatives—manned the site.

On Jan. 12, four enemy biplanes bombed Site 85. A CIA helicopter, an Air America UH-1, pursued the planes. Flight mechanic Glen Woods shot down the aircraft with an AK-47 from the helicopter. This is the only such recorded incident during the war. This and an attack yet to come remained a secret that many troops were suspicious of.

One Day Too Long by Keith Woodcock. **Flight mechanic Glen Woods fires an AK-47 from a CIA helicopter, an Air America UH-1, at an enemy biplane on Jan. 12, 1968. Four of the biplanes had bombed Lima Site 85. Woods' aim was true enough to down the aircraft.**

The Fall of Lima Site 85 by John Witt. **Witt's depiction of the events at the overrun top-secret radar position shows Air Force Chief Master Sgt. Richard Etchberger directing the rescue of fellow airmen. Etchberger was later mortally wounded. He received a posthumous Medal of Honor for the lives he saved.**

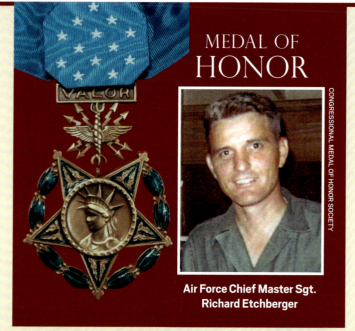

MEDAL OF
HONOR

**Air Force Chief Master Sgt.
Richard Etchberger**

Radio specialist Melvin A. Holland and cryptographic specialist Willis R. Hall were among the missing in action in the attack on Lima Site 85. They remain unaccounted for.

Diesel mechanic Willie Husband was rescued after successfully hiding from the enemy in the brush and rocks.

"Even when I was in Laos in 1969-70, we knew something happened but knew nothing else," said Eugene D. Rossel, who served with special operations on Project 404. "It was so classified that it was better for any inquirer to just mind his own business when it came to the fall of this site."

Against a decree by his superiors, Air Force Maj. Richard Secord armed the men working at and defending Site 85. He refused to see them remain defenseless.

"On my own authority, I drew 40 M-16s from USAF stock at Udorn," Secord wrote in his 1992 book, *Honored and Betrayed: Irangate, Covert Affairs, and the Secret War in Laos*, "plus a number of CIA-issue Browning autopistols and cases of hand grenades (and lots of ammo) and delivered it to the case officer on-site with instructions for him to give the 'civilians' a little refresher training in small-arms handling and marksmanship."

'No Way of Defending'

On the night of March 10, NVA Lt. Truong Muc led troops of the 41st Dac Cong (Sapper) Battalion and 93rd NVA Infantry Battalion in a ground attack on Site 85.

The enemy fired on the mountain from the north and east with mortar, artillery and rocket rounds, damaging living quarters, an antenna and a defensive gun position. Then 33 NVA sappers scaled the western side of the mountain and hid for three hours before attacking.

According to his Medal of Honor citation (upgraded from a DSC and awarded Sept. 21, 2010), Chief Master Sgt. Richard Etchberger was manning a defensive position when the base was overrun. The enemy was firing directly upon his location from higher ground.

With his entire group either dead or wounded, Etchberger continued to return fire thus denying NVA access to the ledge. He also continued to direct air strikes and call for air rescue on his emergency radio, enabling the air evacuation force to locate him and his men.

When the rescue team arrived, Etchberger deliberately exposed himself to enemy fire in order to place the three surviving, wounded airmen into rescue slings. After Etchberger was rescued, he was fatally wounded aboard the helicopter by enemy ground fire.

"His fierce defense, which culminated in the supreme sacrifice of his life, saved not only the lives of his three comrades but provided for the successful evacuation of the remaining survivors of the base," according to the citation.

Maj. Stanley Sliz was wounded, but survived on the rock overhang long enough to be rescued.

"The boy on my right died almost instantly," he said in

> ## "... We had no way of defending against it except when the grenades came bounding on in they would land in my proximity and I could just grab them and throw them down the hill."
>
> —MAJ. STANLEY SLIZ

Christopher Robbins' *The Ravens: The Men Who Flew in America's Secret War in Laos.* "The boy on my left had a broken leg from a bullet. ... There were at least half a dozen grenades tossed in through a small cavernous hole. ... We had no way of defending against it except when the grenades came bounding on in they would land in my proximity and I could just grab them and throw them down the hill."

Huey Marlow (actually an alias), working for the CIA, earned the Intelligence Cross for his actions leading a group of Laotians in a counterattack. His band destroyed an NVA machine-gun

JOE PANZA PHOTOS

Capts. Russ Cayler and Joe Panza piloted the rescue helicopter, "Jolly Green Giant 67," that hovered dangerously close to the radar site. They monitored the radio and scanned the cliffs for enemy forces.

nest on the summit of Phou Pha Thai and rescued four or five wounded troops on the ridge. They retreated back down the mountain, engaging in hand-to-hand combat all the way.

'Keep Asking Questions'

In all, 12 Americans were killed on the mountain (11 were never recovered, one was later recovered) as well as 42 Thais and Laotian Hmong troops below. Wounded Americans were rescued with the help of an Air America helicopter. On March 13, Capt. Donald E. Westbrook, 602nd Fighter Squadron, died when his plane was shot down as he returned to the site to search for survivors.

All KIA received Bronze Stars for valor in 1984.

MIA searches from December 1994 to January 1995 did not recover remains. A trip in March 2003, turned up remains of four unidentified troops. In October 2005, the remains of Tech. Sgt. Patrick L. Shannon were officially identified.

Tech. Sgt. James H. Calfee was one of the airmen killed in the attack but never recovered. (He was awarded the Silver Star in 2012.) Verna Yeamans, his sister, wrote a letter to President Lyndon B. Johnson seeking details of her brother's death and still seeks answers today.

"Don't give up," she wrote. "Keep looking, keep asking questions because there are still some answers there that we don't know."

Another family member of the fallen, Cory Etchberger, has also said that he didn't know the truth about his father's death and the surrounding mission until long after.

"I would say it wasn't until seven years ago that I really knew what had happened," he told the *The Kansas City Star* in 2005.

In recognition of the lives lost, the Skyspot Memorial at the Barksdale Global Power Museum at Barksdale Air Force Base in Shreveport, La., was dedicated Sept. 19, 2008.

John T. Correll aptly summed up the actions of the airmen on Lima Site 85 in *Air Force* magazine: "The courage and sacrifice of those who died on the mountaintop stood in counterpoint to the strategic indecision and changing political winds in Washington." ✪

WAR'S FACTS & FIGURES

Leathernecks of the 2nd Bn., 9th Marines, prepare to fire an 81mm mortar to suppress enemy fire while a Marine helicopter drops into the landing zone on Aug. 27, 1968. The LZ served as a night defensive position for the Marines as they conducted a search and clear mission southwest of Vandegrift Combat Base.

NATIONAL ARCHIVES PHOTO #127-GVB-264-A191952

COURAGE UNRIVALED

BY ROBERT E. WIDENER

During some eight years of America's war in Southeast Asia, the most highly decorated heroes earned **multiple awards** for valor. Five of them sacrificed their lives in doing so.

"**W**e are going to establish a perimeter right here, and you are going to fight or die," 1st Lt. Robert Howard told the men in his Army Special Forces platoon. Hopelessly surrounded by a large North Vietnamese Army (NVA) force after an ambush Dec. 30, 1968, Howard then did the unthinkable—he called in an airstrike on his own position.

That decision, plus others during the battle that day, earned Howard the Medal of Honor. Other awards he received during the Vietnam War place him clearly at the head of a list of 64 servicemen with **multiple high awards** for heroism (see chart on following pages).

Each man is ranked by the value of the highest multiple awards he received based on the military's order of precedence—the Medal of Honor, Distinguished Service Cross (DSC), Navy Cross or Air Force Cross, and Silver Star. *Military Times'* Hall of Valor has verified each man's awards.

The Medal of Honor, of course, receives the highest value and is placed at the top. The DSC, Navy Cross and Air Force Cross are equal in value and hold the second highest place. The third award, the Silver Star, is considered next.

Five men were killed in action: Lt. Col. Andre C. Lucas, Staff Sgt. John G. Gertsch, Capt. Riley L. Pitts, Maj. William W. Roush and 2nd Lt. Thomas E. Dobrinska.

Six men on the list were pilots who were shot down, captured and held as POWs. One of them, Rear Adm. James B. Stockdale, piloted one of four jet fighters on Aug. 5, 1964, during *Operation Pierce Arrow,* a prelude to the U.S. ground war in Vietnam.

All five Air Force aces of the war are on the list, too. Capt. Charles B. DeBellevue, 555th Tactical Fighter Squadron, leads that group with six air victories.

Here are more accounts of the brave men whose multiple acts of courage under fire should be remembered.

Robert L. Howard

George E. Day

James E. Williams

Patrick H. Brady

James B. Stockdale

Joe R. Hooper

Leo K. Thorsness

Jack H. Jacobs

Andre C. Lucas

'GREATEST HERO AMERICA NEVER KNEW'

1st Lt. Howard spent 54 months in combat during five tours in Vietnam, earning virtually every medal for valor the Army could possibly give. He was nominated for the Medal of Honor three times before it was finally awarded.

Howard also earned a DSC, Silver Star, four Bronze Stars and four Legions of Merit. In addition, he came home with eight Purple Hearts, though he was wounded 14 times. *D Magazine* (Dallas) writer David Feherty called him "the greatest hero America never knew."

Howard enlisted in the Army in 1956 at age 17, according to Peter Collier in *Medal of Honor: Portraits of Valor Beyond the Call of Duty*. A native of Opelika, Ala., his father and four uncles had been paratroopers in WWII. He followed in their footsteps by joining the 101st Airborne.

After his first tour in Vietnam in 1965, Howard transferred to the 5th Special Forces Group and spent six months in the States training at the Special Warfare Center. He returned to Vietnam in 1966 and spent most of his subsequent tours with the highly secretive Military Assistance Command, Vietnam—Studies and Observation Group (MACV-SOG). It conducted classified missions across the borders into Laos, Cambodia and North Vietnam.

Howard earned the Medal of Honor during a mission Dec. 28-30, 1968. His platoon of American and South Vietnamese special forces were searching for fellow Green Beret Robert Scherdin, reportedly missing in Laos.

After fending off an attack at their landing zone, they later stumbled into an ambush by 250 NVA soldiers. In that attack, a Claymore mine seriously wounded Howard and his lieutenant.

"When I came to, I was blown up in a crump on the ground, and my weapon was blown out of my hand," he related in a Medal of Honor Foundation interview.

Unable to walk because of shrapnel wounds, Howard began dragging his wounded officer down to a ravine as enemy rounds hit all around them. With a .45-caliber pistol, he killed several NVA soldiers who were charging at them with bayonets.

One bullet smashed into a magazine in Howard's ammo belt, hitting him with 15 to 20 rounds of exploding ammo that sent him tumbling down a hill. He was able to crawl back to his lieutenant and continue dragging him.

After finally reaching his men and getting a medic to administer aid to the officer, Howard formed a perimeter and called in the artillery strike.

"I remember fire landing right between my feet and ricochets hitting me in the face," he recalled. "That's how intense it was."

For the next 3½ hours, the NVA kept up the pressure on Howard's small force. Still unable to walk, he crawled from position to position directing his men and giving support. They were finally evacuated by helicopter.

Howard received his Medal of Honor on March 2, 1971. After the war, he attended college, eventually attaining two master's degrees—one in public administration and one in management.

Howard retired from the Army as a colonel in 1992 then worked 13 years at VA in Texas. A consummate supporter of America's veterans, he made five trips in the last three years of his life to visit troops in Afghanistan and Iraq.

After Howard died at 70 on Dec. 23, 2009, retired Maj. John L. Plaster and SOG historian wrote: "This great hero, a humble knight that was a paragon for all, belongs to history now."

'AN ARMFUL OF GRENADES'

Staff Sgt. Joe Hooper told his sister once that he got a "rush" during battle. He said "he could hear the adrenaline roaring in his bloodstream," according to authors Peter Maslowski and Don Winslow in *Looking for a Hero: Staff Sergeant Joe Ronnie Hooper and the Vietnam War*.

Gordon R. Roberts

Bennie G. Adkins

Sammy L. Davis

David C. Dolby

Bernard F. Fisher

James P. Fleming

Harold A. Fritz

John G. Gertsch

Lawrence Joel

NAME	SERVICE	BRANCH/MOS	MOH	DSC	NC	AFC	SS	TOTAL
1st Lt. Robert Lewis Howard	Army	Special Forces	1	1			1	3
Col. George Everett "Bud" Day (POW)	Air Force	Fighter Pilot	1			1	1	3
Petty Officer 1st Class James Elliott Williams	Navy	River Patrol Boat	1		1		1	3
Maj. Patrick Henry Brady	Army	Medical Corps Pilot	1	1				2
Rear Adm. James Bond Stockdale (POW)	Navy	Fighter Pilot	1				4	5
Staff Sgt. Joe Ronnie Hooper	Army	Infantry	1				2	3
Maj. Leo Keith Thorsness (POW)	Air Force	Fighter Pilot	1				2	3
Capt. Jack Howard Jacobs	Army	Infantry	1				2	3
Lt. Col. Andre Cavaro Lucas (KIA)	Army	Infantry	1				2	3
Sgt. Gordon Ray Roberts	Army	Infantry	1				2	3
Sgt. 1st Class Bennie G. Adkins	Army	Special Forces	1				1	2
Sgt. Sammy Lee Davis	Army	Artillery	1				1	2
Sgt. David Charles Dolby	Army	Infantry	1				1	2
Maj. Bernard Francis Fisher	Air Force	Fighter Pilot	1				1	2
Capt. James Phillip Fleming	Air Force	Helicopter Pilot	1				1	2
Capt. Harold Arthur Fritz	Army	Armor	1				1	2
Staff Sgt. John Gerry Gertsch (KIA)	Army	Infantry	1				1	2
Spc. 6th Class Lawrence Joel	Army	Medic	1				1	2
Capt. James Everett Livingston	Marine Corps	Infantry	1				1	2
Lt. Thomas Rolland Norris	Navy	SEAL	1				1	2
Capt. Riley Leroy Pitts (KIA)	Army	Infantry	1				1	2
Maj. Stephen Wesley Pless	Marine Corps	Helicopter Pilot	1				1	2
Capt. Ronald Eric Ray	Army	Infantry	1				1	2
Maj. Jay R. Vargas	Marine Corps	Infantry	1				1	2
Lt. Col. James Helms Kasler (POW)	Air Force	Fighter Pilot				3	1	4
Col. David Haskell Hackworth	Army	Infantry		2			7	9
Col. Henry Everett Emerson	Army	Infantry		2			4	6
Col. Thomas H. Tackaberry	Army	Infantry		2			3	5
Capt. Barry Richard McCaffrey	Army	Infantry		2			2	4
Col. George Smith Patton, IV	Army	Armor		2			1	3
Sgt. Adelbert F. Waldron	Army	Sniper		2			1	3
1st Lt. Joseph P. Donovan	Marine Corps	Medical Evac. Pilot			2		1	3

Indeed, the 29-year-old NCO earned a chest full of medals during his two tours in Vietnam, including the Medal of Honor, two Silver Stars and six Bronze Stars with "V" device. He also came home with eight Purple Hearts.

On the morning of Feb. 21, 1968, the adrenaline in Hooper's veins pumped profusely. A series of NVA bunkers along a riverbank stopped his squad from D Co., 2nd Bn., 501st Inf. Regt., 101st Abn. Div., just a few miles outside of Hue. Rockets, machine gun and small-arms fire from the well-concealed enemy emplacements kept his unit pinned down.

Telling his squad, "Follow me," Hooper led the attack in silencing the bunkers. Just as he helped the last of the wounded to safety, he was shot in the torso. Refusing medical treatment, he continued leading his men from one bunker to another, sometimes attacking single-handedly.

In one instance, he blew up three houses that concealed enemy snipers and then attacked a fourth that held three

DECORATED SERVICEMEN

NAME	SERVICE	BRANCH/MOS	MOH	DSC	NC	AFC	SS	TOTAL
Col. John Arthur Dramesi (POW)	Air Force	Fighter Pilot				2	1	3
Capt. Michael A. McDermott	Army	Infantry	2				1	3
Capt. Leland Thornton Kennedy	Air Force	Fighter Pilot				2	1	3
Brig. Gen. James Robinson Risner (POW)	Air Force	Fighter Pilot				2	1	3
Brig. Gen. John Russell Deane, Jr.	Army	Infantry		2				2
Brig. Gen. James Francis Hollingsworth	Army	Infantry		2				2
Maj. William Wakefield Roush (KIA)	Army	Infantry		2				2
1st Lt. Dennis C. Tomcik	Army	Infantry		2				2
Master Sgt. Jack Lewis Williams	Army	Special Forces		2				2
Capt. Martin L. Brandtner	Marine Corps	Infantry			2			2
Maj. Charles Edward Getz	Army	Infantry	1				6	7
Maj. John Charles Bahnsen, Jr.	Army	Aviation	1				5	6
Lt. Col. Robert Silber McGowan	Army	Infantry	1				4	5
Cmdr. James Benjamin Linder	Navy	Fighter-Bomber Pilot			1		4	5
Capt. Jeffrey S. Feinstein (Ace)	Air Force	Fighter Pilot				1	4	5
Capt. Richard Stephen Ritchie (Ace)	Air Force	Fighter Pilot				1	4	5
Col. Robert Michael White	Air Force	Fighter Pilot				1	4	5
Capt. Millard Arthur Peck	Army	Infantry	1				3	4
Lt. Col. Robert L. Schweitzer	Army	Armor	1				3	4
1st Lt. Gary Lynn Tucker	Army	Infantry	1				3	4
Capt. John Jay Barrett	Marine Corps	Helicopter Pilot			1		3	4
Capt. Charles Barbin DeBellevue (Ace)	Air Force	Fighter Pilot				1	3	4
Lt. Col. James Eugene McInerney, Jr.	Air Force	Fighter Pilot				1	3	4
Capt. Fred Shannon	Air Force	Fighter Pilot				1	3	4
Col. Jacksel Markham Broughton	Air Force	Fighter Pilot				1	2	3
Lt. Randall Harold Cunningham (Ace)	Navy	Fighter Pilot			1		2	3
Lt. (j.g.) William Patrick Driscoll (Ace)	Navy	Radar Intercept Officer			1		2	3
Col. Robin Olds	Air Force	Fighter Pilot				1	2	3
Maj. William P. Robinson	Air Force	Fighter Pilot				1	2	3
Capt. Dale E. Stovall	Air Force	Rescue Pilot				1	2	3
1st Lt. David A. Christian	Army	Infantry	1				2	3
2nd Lt. Thomas Earl Dobrinska (KIA)	Army	Infantry	1				2	3

MOH Medal of Honor
DSC Distinguished Service Cross
NC Navy Cross
AFC Air Force Cross
SS Silver Star

Note: Ranks are listed as they appear in the recipient's award citation.

---

enemy machine gunners.

When fire erupted from four more enemy locations, Hooper was wounded a second time. But according to Edward F. Murphy in *Vietnam Medal of Honor Heroes,* he was not about to stay down: "He gathered up an armful of grenades and raced down a small trench behind the bunkers, tossing grenades into each one as he passed it."

Hooper's tally when it was all over was impressive—12 NVA positions destroyed, most taken single-handedly. He also had personally killed some 22 of the enemy—stabbing one NVA officer with a bayonet. Suffering from bullet and grenade fragment wounds, he waited until the next day to be treated.

Army legend Col. David H. "Hardcore Hack" Hackworth served four tours in Vietnam, first deploying as a major in 1965. He had already made a name for himself during the Korean War, where he earned a battlefield commission to lieutenant and ended the war as a captain. He also earned three Silver Stars there.

During Vietnam in the Mekong Delta, he was especially noted for his command of the 4th Bn., 39th Inf. Regt., 9th Inf. Div. Simply known to his men as "Hack," he transformed the ragtag unit into a deadly fighting force in 10 weeks. It became known as the "Hardcore Battalion."

Hackwork employed his own hit-and-run guerilla tactics that were so effective the Viet Cong (VC) placed a bounty on his head. He also earned the admiration of his soldiers by leading from the front in battle. In one instance, he pulled men to safety as he rode the strut of a helicopter, all the while under fire.

Hackworth was the youngest colonel in Vietnam, having earned two DSCs and seven Silver Stars. Throughout his

"Slashing and blazing away at point-blank range, Fritz drove the NVA back into the jungle."

—EDWARD F. MURPHY, DESCRIBING 1st LT. HAROLD A. FRITZ'S ACT OF VALOR

military career, he earned some 90 awards.

Here are accounts of other notable heroes:

• **Capt. Riley L. Pitts** served with C Co., 2nd Bn., 27th Inf. Regt., 25th Inf. Div. Pitts was at the front of an assault on enemy positions at Ap Dong on Oct. 31, 1967. He threw a captured NVA grenade toward an enemy bunker, but it bounced off the dense foliage and landed right back at his men. Without hesitation, he threw himself on top of it, but it failed to explode.

Later, from an exposed position, he used a grenade launcher to pinpoint the position of NVA bunkers for his fire team until he was mortally wounded.

• **1st Lt. Harold A. Fritz** led the defense after a column of armored personnel carriers was attacked and surrounded near An Loc on Jan. 11, 1969. From the top of his burning vehicle, Fritz, who had been seriously wounded, directed men of A Trp., 1st Sqdn., 11th Armd. Cav, in the face of deadly enemy fire.

When the NVA threatened to overrun Fritz's position, he yelled to a small group of his men to follow him. He charged headlong into the body of the enemy armed only with a .45-caliber pistol and bayonet.

Edward F. Murphy described the scene: "Slashing and blazing away at point-blank range, Fritz drove the NVA back into the jungle."

A rescue column eventually arrived, routing the communists and saving Fritz and his survivors.

• **Capt. Barry R. McCaffrey** was a MACV adviser assigned to the South Vietnamese 2nd Airborne Task Force. On Oct. 6, 1966, he took command during a VC attack on the task force near Dong Ha after another Army adviser was killed. The other company commanders had been seriously wounded.

McCaffrey moved about the perimeter, organizing the South Vietnamese in repelling four human-wave attacks. During the 12-hour battle, he was wounded twice by mortar fragments. Only after all other wounded had been removed did he allow himself to be evacuated.

• **Sgt. Adelbert F. Waldron** is the second deadliest sniper in American history and the most decorated in the Vietnam War. His record of 109 confirmed kills stood until the Iraq War.

The 36-year-old had already served 12 years in the Navy before ending up with the Army's B Co., 3rd Bn., 60th Inf. Regt., 9th Inf. Div., from 1968-69. He is credited with an amazing nine kills from the same "hide" spot in one night.

LEATHERNECK HEROES

Capts. Jay R. Vargas and James E. Livingston each commanded companies of the 2nd Bn., 4th Marines, 3rd Marine Div., during a battle against the NVA's exalted 320th Division at Dai Do. On April 30, 1968, Vargas' G Company drove the enemy back into the village, sometimes with fierce hand-to-hand fighting. Vargas single-handedly took out three machine gun positions.

When the NVA counterattacked, Vargas ordered his men to dig up the bodies from fresh graves in the Dai Do cemetery, using the holes for cover. They withstood numerous attacks throughout the night of May 1.

"We didn't have much of a perimeter because these guys were coming in during the night and throwing grenades like they were newspapers," Vargas said, according to Larry

Barry McCaffrey George S. Patton, IV Adelbert Waldron Joseph P. Donovan John A. Dramesi Michael McDermott Leland T. Kennedy James R. Risner John R. Deane, Jr. James Hollingsworth

Smith in *Beyond Glory: Medal of Honor Heroes in their Own Words.* "But they didn't know where we were."

By the morning of May 2, some 300-400 NVA lay dead around their position.

With hardly a break, Vargas was ordered to renew the attack into nearby Dinh To. Livingston's E Company arrived to take the pressure off of what was left of Vargas' company. However, the NVA were pushed in such a corner that they had no option but to counterattack right back through Vargas' and Livingston's combined forces. Ammo on both sides was nearly depleted.

"We were in hand-to-hand combat at this stage— bayonets, helmets, rifle stocks, everything," Vargas said. "I saw Marines breaking stocks over guys' heads."

When Vargas' battalion commander, Lt. Col. William Weise, caught up to him, the battle was so intense that Weise took three rounds in the back. Vargas hauled the wounded commander through the fighting to a corpsman, firing his pistol as he went.

Vargas and Livingston each sustained three wounds over the course of the three-day battle that left 87 Marines dead and another 297 wounded. NVA dead were tallied at 1,568.

Here are more accounts of Marine heroism.

• **Maj. Stephen W. Pless,** Marine Obs. Sqdn. 6, Marine Aircraft Grp. 36, 1st MAW, earned the Medal of Honor on Aug. 19, 1967, near Duc Pho. When four trapped soldiers radioed for extraction, an Army rescue helicopter responded, but aborted the mission because the zone was too "hot" with enemy soldiers.

Pless, who was airborne in the area, picked up the call and responded, "I will take that mission."

When Pless arrived, some 50 VC were bayoneting and beating the wounded Americans. Pless attacked, firing machine guns and rockets. He came in so low that he flew right through the debris thrown up by the explosions he caused.

Pless used the helicopter as a shield as the crewmembers helped the wounded aboard. All the while, Pless kept the enemy pinned down with a steady stream of deadly fire.

The overloaded chopper headed out to sea but skimmed the water four times until Pless attained enough lift to make it back to Chu Lai.

Three of Pless's crewmembers also earned Navy Crosses for their roles in the rescue.

• **Capt. Martin L. Brandtner** earned the first of his two Navy Crosses when he became engaged in a grenade-throwing duel Sept. 3, 1968. His D Co., 1st Bn., 5th Marines, 1st Marine Div., became pinned down by enemy fire near

> ## "We were in hand-to-hand combat at this stage— bayonets, helmets, rifle stocks, everything.
> ## I saw Marines breaking stocks over guys' heads."
> —CAPT. JAY R. VARGAS

Lan Phouc. When enemy grenade shrapnel wounded Brandtner, he threw his own grenade, killing his opponent.

That act sparked an NVA grenade attack. According to *Leatherneck Magazine,* the battle intensified: "While directing his men's fire, Brandtner sprinted through their positions, scooping up enemy grenades and hurling them back toward the North Vietnamese."

One grenade landed near four of his men. He quickly flipped it aside and then pushed two Marines to the ground, protecting them from the blast with his body and flak jacket.

Brandtner rated a second Navy Cross just eight days later at My Binh while repulsing four attacks from a battalion-size NVA force.

RIVER BOAT FIGHTER

Navy Petty Officer 1st Class James E. Williams dropped out of high school in 1947 and enlisted in the Navy at 16. During the Korean War while serving aboard the *USS Douglas H. Fox,* he shuttled U.S. and South Korean raiders into combat from February to June 1952.

After Korea, Williams served off Cuba (1962) and the Dominican Republic (1965). Still, by March 1966 with the Vietnam War in full swing, he felt he had not adequately served his country.

William W. Roush

Dennis C. Tomcik

Jack L. Williams

Martin L. Brandtner

Charles E. Getz

John Bahnsen, Jr.

Robert McGowan

James B. Linder

Jeffrey S. Feinstein

So just 11 months shy of his retirement, Williams requested a transfer to the war zone, much to the angst of his family. The 36-year-old arrived in Vietnam in June 1966, assigned as boat commander of River Patrol Boat 105, River Section 531 of the My Tho Detachment.

On Oct. 31, 1966, in the Mekong Delta, Williams' two-boat patrol was in pursuit of an enemy sampan that ducked down a canal. Williams decided to go farther down the river and cut it off.

"I went around that corner at max speed to cut him off," Williams told *All Hands* magazine. "And lo and behold, I looked up and didn't see anything but boats and people and more boats and more people."

Williams had stumbled upon a large NVA force staging on the river in sampans and junks. He put down the throttle

"We had to just fight. There was no way out."

—PETTY OFFICER 1ST CLASS JAMES ELLIOTT WILLIAMS

and headed right toward them. The twin .50-caliber guns on Williams' boats blazed away as enemy machine gun fire and RPGs seemed to be coming at them from everywhere—ship and shore.

According to Thomas J. Cutler in *Brown Water, Black Berets,* Williams ran his boat right over three sampans. "The enemy was reduced to chaos as soldiers spilled into the canal from the stricken sampans, and still others were rolled into the water by the PBRs' wakes."

Williams' boats were no sooner clear of that gauntlet then they suddenly encountered a larger enemy group staging down another channel. He unhesitatingly attacked it, too.

"We had to just fight," he told *All Hands.* "There was no way out."

Helicopter gunships arrived, and together with Williams' boats, they turned the river into a mass of destroyed sampans, junks and enemy bodies. At the end of the three-hour battle, 65 NVA vessels had been destroyed and some 1,000 enemy reportedly killed.

By the time Williams ended his eight-month tour, he had been awarded every Navy medal for valor—the Medal of Honor, Navy Cross, Silver Star and two Bronze Stars with

"V" device. He also received two Purple Hearts. He returned home to his family in March 1967 as the most highly decorated *enlisted* man in the history of the Navy.

SAVING THE WOUNDED

Medevac helicopter pilot Maj. Patrick H. Brady compiled an incredible record in Vietnam in one year beginning in July 1967. Serving with the 54th Med. Det., 67th Med. Grp., 44th Med. Bde., he flew some 3,000 combat missions and is credited with rescuing more than 5,000 men.

Brady had already done a tour in Vietnam in 1964, and then two stints in the Dominican Republic (1965-66).

Brady's second mission on the morning of Jan. 6, 1968, sent him to the Hiep Duc Valley. The 198th Light Infantry Brigade had sustained 60 casualties in a firefight. Two dust-off choppers had already been shot down trying to reach them in a fog-shrouded section of the valley.

Brady found a hole in the fog, though, and despite heavy NVA fire from as close as 50 yards away set down to take on the wounded. He made three more such perilous trips back, saving 39 men.

At the end of the day, Brady had flown four missions in all, saving 51 soldiers. The feat required three separate Hueys due to the intense fire he took at times. He could barely fly one chopper because the controls had been so riddled by enemy fire. In fact, crewmen counted more than 400 bullet holes in the three aircraft.

Brady had little to say later about any of it other than, "I had a lot worse days."

Medic Spec. 6th Class Lawrence Joel was patrolling near Bien Hoa during *Operation Hump* in November 1965. The 37-year-old aidman for H&H Co., 1st Bn., 503rd Inf. Regt., 173rd Abn. Bde., had already been in the Army for 19 years, including service in the Korean War.

"Except for our platoon sergeant who'd been in Korea, none of us had seen combat," he told *Yankee Magazine.*

The Battle of Hill 65 on Nov. 8 changed all of that. A battalion-size enemy force ambushed Joel's unit, outnumbering them six to one. Joel was hit in the right calf while trying to reach some of the wounded. Undaunted, he gave himself a shot of morphine and pressed on.

Richard S. Ritchie

Robert M. White

Millard A. Peck

Robert L. Schweitzer

Gary L. Tucker

John J. Barrett

Charles B. DeBellevue

James McInerney, Jr.

Fred Shannon

Men in Joel's unit were amazed to see him rise to a kneeling position to hold up a plasma bag, seemingly unconcerned about the intense fire. After he got shot a second time, this time in the right thigh, he made a crude crutch from a stick and hobbled from casualty to casualty.

"I'd throw it [the crutch] to the ground, treat the soldier, then move on to the next one," he remembered. He exhausted his medic's kit after treating some 13 soldiers and then grabbed more supplies when an NVA counterattack wounded more men.

It wasn't until the battle was over some 24 hours later that Joel allowed himself to be evacuated. Some 49 Americans were killed and 83 wounded. Joel received the Medal of Honor for his actions that day, the first medic in Vietnam to be so honored.

CAPTIVE IN "THE FIERY FURNACE"

Among the 591 American POWs released after the war in 1973 were six men who earned multiple awards for valor. Most of them at one time or another were held at Hoa Lo Prison, which translates literally in English to "the fiery furnace." The Americans simply referred to it as the "Hanoi Hilton."

Air Force Maj. George E. "Bud" Day was shot down Aug. 26, 1967, while flying on a mission into North Vietnam. Day had already served in WWII and the Korean War, where he served two tours as a fighter-bomber pilot.

In Vietnam, he commanded a squadron of F-100s with Det. 1, 416th Tact. Fighter Sqdn., 37th Tact. Fighter Wing, based at Phu Cat Air Base. The "Misty Super Facs," as they were known, served as forward air controllers in selecting targets and calling in air strikes.

Day was initially captured 20 miles from the DMZ. He escaped his communist captors after five days despite a broken right arm and sprained knee he suffered when he ejected.

He evaded through the jungle between 11 and 15 days until he ran into an NVA patrol. Day was shot twice. At the time of his recapture, he had actually made it across the DMZ and was only two miles from the Marine base at Con Thien. He was the only American in the war to escape from North Vietnam.

Other Americans held at Hoa Lo were Navy Cmdr. James B. Stockdale, Maj. Leo Keith Thorsness, Maj. James H. Kasler, Col. John A. Dramesi and Lt. Col. James R. Risner. The North Vietnamese labeled all of them, including Day, as troublemakers and dealt more punishment to them than the other prisoners.

Stockdale was one of the primary organizers of prisoner resistance in the 7½ years he spent in captivity. He was shot down during a mission Sept. 9, 1965, as commander of Air Wing 16 from the *USS Oriskany*. When he ejected from his aircraft, he suffered breaks to his left leg and left shoulder and parachuted into the middle of a village. The locals surrounded and pummeled him until the NVA showed up.

As the highest-ranking Navy officer at Hoa Lo, Stockdale was routinely tortured. He spent a total of three years in solitary confinement, one of them in complete isolation. For two years, his legs were strapped in irons.

In 1969, when Stockdale suspected he was to be used in a propaganda film, he foiled his captors by cutting his scalp with a razor. When they put a hat on his head to cover the wounds, he bloodied his face by smashing it with a stool. Afterward, he kept his eyes swollen and bruises "freshened" with his fists.

When left alone in an interrogation room in September 1969, Stockdale slashed his wrists with broken glass to prevent revealing his POW conspirators under more torture. He nearly died.

"I had been through 13 different torture sessions," said Stockdale, according to author Edward F. Murphy. "I didn't want any more men to suffer as a result of my actions."

Relief for the POWs came when the Paris Peace Accords ended the U.S. war in January 1973. They were released beginning Feb. 12, 1973, as part of *Operation Homecoming.* ✪

Jacksel M. Broughton

Randall Cunningham

William P. Driscoll

Robin Olds

William P. Robinson

Dale E. Stovall

David A. Christian

Thomas E. Dobrinska

WAR'S DEADLIEST BATTLES

Death in Vietnam was dealt overwhelmingly in relatively small doses; small-unit actions characterized the combat. A 2017 analysis performed by the Coffelt Database showed 426 *individual* ground actions in which 11 or more Americans were KIA. In only 55 of these actions, were 30 or more GIs KIA. To keep comparisons consistent, generally battles of three or less days are listed separately from consecutive, multiple-day (a week or more) battles.

Ongoing operations are not included because they do not constitute distinct, identifiable, single engagements. Duration is most often roughly estimated. Rarely could the exact length of time during which deaths occurred be accurately pinpointed. Many times it was much shorter than indicated. Duration provides some context for the ferocity of the combat involved. About 13 battles counted 75 U.S. KIA or more: some lasting only minutes; one persisting for 2½ months.

Source: *Most of the raw numbers are courtesy of the Coffelt Database. The order and interpretation are the sole responsibility of the editor.*

BATTLE	KIA	DATES	DURATION
LZ Albany[1]	153	11-17-65	6 hours
Hill 875 (Dak To)[2]	131	11/18-23/67	6 days
Chau Ngai	101	3/4-6/66	3 days
"Marketplace" (Route 561)	92	7-2-67	1 day
Dai Do[3]	87	4/29 to 5/3/68	5 days
LZ X-Ray[4]	81	11/14-16/65	3 days
The Slopes (Hill 1338)	76	6-22-67	30 minutes
Vinh Huy	75	6/2-3/67	2 days
Ong Thanh	59	10-17-67	11 hours
Chu Lai[5]	56	8/18-20/65	3 days
C-123K Shootdown (Khe Sanh)	56	3-6-68	Minutes
Dong Son[6]	55	9-4-67	1 day
Dau Tieng	53	11/3-5/66	3 days
Firebase Gold[7]	52	3/19 & 21/67	4 hours
Hill 65	49	11-8-65	11 hours
Vinh Tuy Valley	49	3/21-23/66	3 days
Thon Tham Khe	49	12-27-67	1 day
Binh Son (1)	48	4/21-22/67	1 day +
Hoc Mon	48	3-2-68	8 minutes
Ap Bac (Rach Nui River)	47	6-19-67	1 day
Hill 861	45	4/24-26/67	3 days
Con Thien	46	5-8-67	3 hours
Bong Trang Woods[8]	45	8/25-26/66	1 day +
Hill 881S	45	4-30-67	1 day
Ap Nha Mat	43	12-5-65	Few hours
Hill 689	42	4-16-68	8 hours
LZ Eagle	41	5-26-67	5 hours
Hill 766/LZ Hereford[9]	40	5/16-18/66	3 days
Srok Dong	38	6/30 to 7/2-66	3 days
Hill 48	38	9-10-67	4 hours
Xa Cam My	37	4-11-66	7 hours
Xom Bo II/LZ X-Ray	37	6-17-67	8 hours
Thon Cam Son	37	7/29 & 30/67	1 day +

Battle	KIA	Date	Duration
Hill 823	37	11/12-13/67	2 days
My Canh[10]	36	2/6-7/66	2 days
Highway 506 Valley	36	12-17-66	1 day
Truong Son	36	3/20-21/67	2 days
Hill 110	35	5-10-67	1 day
Loc Ninh Rubber Plantation	34	6-11-66	9 hours
Cambodia Border	34	11-21-66	4 hours
Hill 881N[11]	34	5/2-3/67	2 days
Ia Pnon Valley	34	7-12-67	1.5 hours
Cam Vu	34	4-30-68	1 day
Mai Xai Thi West	32	3/1-2/68	2 days
Bai Lai River	32	4/4-5/68	2 days
Ap Trang Dau	32	9/5-6/68	1 day +
Trung Luong	31	6/20-22/66	3 days
Hill 158 (East of)	31	9-21-67	1 day
LZ Judy	31	8-26-70	Minutes
Chu Pong Massif	30	3-30-66	1 day
Plei Doc	30	5-18-67	1 day
LZ Hawk (Go Noi Island)	30	12/28-29/67	2 days
A-3 Strongpoint/Gio Linh Road	30	2-7-68	1 day
1st Marine Div. Complex (Hill 327)	30	2-23-69	1 day
Firebase Russell	30	2-25-69	3 hours
Firebase Mary Ann	30	3-28-71	1 hour
Firebase Charlie II	30	5-21-71	Minutes

MANY-DAY BATTLES

(Week or longer)

BATTLE	KIA	DATES	NO. OF DAYS
Hue	216	1/31 to 2/25-68	26
Khe Sanh	205	1/20 to 4/14-68	77
Que Son/Hiep Duc	182	1/2-8/68	7
Hiep Duc Valley	116	8/17-29/69	13
Go Noi Island	96	5/17-26/68	10
Cu Nghi/LZ 4[12]	74	1/26 to 2/1-66	7
Firebase Ripcord	72	7/1-23/70	24
Hamburger Hill	66	5/10-20/69	11
Hill 724	60	11/4-11/67	8
Tam Quan	59	12/6-15/67	9
Plei Doc	49	5/18-22/67	5
Kim Son Valley	40	2/17-23/66	7
Saigon (District 8)	39	5/5-12/68	8
Linebacker II	37	12/18-29/72	11

BAKER'S DOZEN DEADLIEST COMPANY KIA IN A SINGLE BATTLE

DATE	BATTLE	KIA	CO.	BN.	REGT.	DIV.
6-22-67	**The Slopes**	76	A	2nd	503rd	173rd Bde.
7-2-67	**Route 561**	52	B	1st	9th	3rd Marine
3-2-68	**Hoc Mon**	48	C	4th	9th	25th Inf.
11-17-65	**LZ Albany**	44	C	2nd	7th Cav	1st Cav
11-15-65	**LZ X-Ray**	39	C	1st	7th Cav	1st Cav
4-11-66	**Xa Cam My**	37	C	2nd	16th	1st Inf.
11-17-65	**LZ Albany**	35	A	2nd	7th Cav	1st Cav
11-21-66	**Cambodia Border**	34	C	1st	5th Cav	1st Cav
7-12-67	**Ia Pnon River**	34	B	1st	12th	4th Inf.
4-21-67	**Binh Son (1)**	31	F	2nd	1st	1st Marine
5-18-67	**Plei Doc**	30	B	1st	8th	4th Inf.
11-20-67	**Hill 875**	29	A	2nd	503rd	173rd Bde.
11-20-67	**Hill 875**	29	C	2nd	503rd	173rd Bde.

NOTE: *Attached Navy corpsmen or Army medics and artillery field observers are included when determinable.*

FOOTNOTES

1- *Battle of the Ia Drang Valley: LZ Albany + LZ X-Ray = 234 KIA. 85% of KIA at LZ X-Ray occurred on Nov. 15, 1965.*

2- *Dak To: 72 of KIA on Nov. 20 and 31 KIA on Nov. 19.*

3- *Dai Do: 51 of KIA on May 2.*

4- *LZ X-Ray: 69 of KIA on Nov. 15.*

5- *Chu Lai: 49 of KIA on Aug. 18.*

6- *Dong Son: Includes 18 KIA at Chau Lam.*

7- *FSB Gold: Includes 14 KIA from the March 19 helicopter shoot-down.*

8- *Bong Trang Woods: 39 of KIA on Aug. 25.*

9- *Hill 766: 29 of KIA on May 17.*

10- *My Canh: 30 of KIA on Feb. 7.*

11- *Hill 881 North: 29 of KIA on May 3.*

12- *Cu Nghi/LZ 4: 32 of KIA on Jan. 29.*

MAJOR U.S. UNIT DEATHS

Extracted from the Coffelt Database of Vietnam Casualties, April 28, 2017. **Copyright 2017.** *Provided by and used with the permission of The Coffelt Group.*

	Totals	Hostile	Non-Hostile	Percent DNH
SERVICES				
Army	**38,257**	31,005	7,252	18.96
Marine Corps	**14,856**	13,172	1,684	11.34
Air Force	**2,585**	1,732	853	33.00
Navy	**2,569**	1,611	958	37.29
Coast Guard	**8**	7	1	12.50
Totals:	**58,275**	47,527	10,748	18.44
MAJOR COMMANDS				
7th Air Force	**1,982**	1,390	592	29.87
Military Assistance Command Vietnam (MACV)	**1,270**	957	313	24.65
7th Fleet	**949**	386	563	59.33
U.S. Naval Forces Vietnam	**904**	568	336	37.17
13th Air Force	**431**	281	150	34.80
DIVISION-LEVEL COMMANDS				
1st Marine Division	**7,007**	6,394	613	8.75
3rd Marine Division	**6,862**	6,275	587	8.55
1st Cavalry Division	**5,370**	4,532	838	15.61
25th Infantry Division	**4,579**	4,233	346	7.56
American (23rd Infantry) Division	**3,922**	3,431	491	12.52
101st Airborne Division	**3,915**	3,345	570	14.56
1st Infantry Division	**3,078**	2,757	321	10.43
9th Infantry Division	**2,587**	2,345	242	9.35
4th Infantry Division	**2,536**	2,246	290	11.44
1st Logistical Command	**1,093**	324	769	70.36
BRIGADE-LEVEL COMMANDS				
1st Aviation Brigade	**2,065**	1,057	1,008	48.81
173rd Airborne Brigade	**1,729**	1,540	189	10.93
196th Infantry Brigade	**1,174**	1,067	107	9.11
11th Infantry Brigade	**1,133**	1,048	85	7.50
198th Infantry Brigade	**1,053**	956	97	9.21
199th Infantry Brigade	**744**	644	100	13.44
18th Engineer Brigade	**651**	376	275	42.24
1st Brigade, 5th Infantry Division	**515**	420	95	18.45
20th Engineer Brigade	**413**	214	199	48.18
1st Signal Brigade	**254**	98	156	61.42
3rd Brigade, 82nd Airborne Division	**226**	191	35	15.49
44th Medical Brigade	**196**	77	119	60.71
OTHER UNITS				
1st Marine Air Wing	**844**	534	310	36.73
11th Armored Cavalry	**728**	645	83	11.40
5th Special Forces Group	**714**	618	96	13.45

Percent DNH=
Died Non-Hostile

Note 1: *U.S. Navy personnel assigned to USMC units are included with the USMC unit's casualties.*
Note 2: *Deaths begin with the first U.S. non-hostile death in Saigon on June 8, 1956, and end with the 41 deaths associated with the SS Mayaguez/Koh Tang Island (Cambodia) incidents on May 13 & 15, 1975.*
Note 3: *The 11th, 196th and 198th infantry brigades were part of the American Division, but the 196th also operated separately.*

A GI'S COMBAT CHRONOLOGY 1959-1973

Few Americans identify the Vietnam War with specific battles. Because it lasted so long and was difficult to follow militarily, the war produced only a handful of well-known engagements. This timeline is designed to tell a more complete story of combat in Vietnam.

1959

Jul 8 — **First U.S. Military Hostile Deaths in Vietnam.** Maj. Dale Buis and Master Sgt. Chester Ovnand are shot while watching a movie at their MAAG compound in Bien Hoa.

1961

Dec 22 — **First American Killed in Battle.** Spec. 4 James T. Davis, a cryptologist with the ASA's 3rd RRU and serving with a South Vietnamese unit, is shot during an exchange of fire after his vehicle is ambushed on Highway 10 near Duc Hoa.

1962

Feb 2 — **First U.S. Aircraft Downed by Enemy Fire in South Vietnam.** 3 airmen of the 309th TCS, 464th TCW, are KIA when their C-123 Provider transport is shot down during a defoliant training mission between Bien Hoa and Vung Tau.

Feb 11 — **High KIA Tally.** 8 GIs—6 airmen of Det. 2A, 4400 CTTS, and 2 soldiers (MAAG)—are KIA when their Farm Gate SC-47 aircraft is shot down near Bao Loc during a leaflet-drop.

Feb 14 — **Authorization to Return Fire.** Officially granted for self-defense only.

1963

Oct 8 — **Single Largest U.S. Hostile Loss of Advisory Period.** Two

Marine helicopters of HMM-361 are downed during a search & rescue operation 20 miles SW of Ha Tan Airfield. KIA: 13.

1964

Aug 7 — **Gulf of Tonkin Resolution.** Congress authorizes the Johnson Administration "to take any measures necessary" to retaliate against North Vietnam for the naval incidents with Hanoi on Aug. 2. The GTR has been interpreted as a functional declaration of war.

Dec 31 — **Advisory Campaign.** From 1961 through 1964, 267 Americans are KIA and 1,531 WIA (783 hospitalized). Hostile ground deaths number 101—38% of the total. The remainder are killed in aircraft shoot-downs.

1965

Feb 10 — **Viet Cuong Hotel,** Bombing of. Qui Nhon. Unit: 140th Transportation Det. KIA: 23 (including 1 Green Beret). WIA: 21

Mar 8 — **First U.S. Infantry Units Arrive.** Leathernecks of the 1st and 3rd battalion landing teams, 9th Marine Regiment, land at Da Nang, signaling the beginning of America's ground war in Vietnam.

Apr 6 — **Authorization to go on the Offensive.** *National Security Action Memorandum 328* allows U.S. personnel to take the offensive to secure "enclaves" and to support the Army of the Republic of Vietnam (ARVN).

Apr 22 — **First Marine Infantry Unit Engagement with VC.** A patrol of the 3rd Marine Recon Bn. engages the Viet Cong for first time, at Binh Thai. No U.S. casualties.

Apr 24   **"Combat Area" Designation.** An executive order designates Vietnam as such, authorizing "hostile fire" pay for service there.

May 3–12   **First U.S. Army Ground Combat Unit Arrives.** 3,500 men of the 173rd Airborne Brigade is based at Bien Hoa.

Jun 8   **Direct Combat.** President authorizes use of U.S. troops in.

Jun 10   **Dong Xoai Special Forces Camp,** Battle for. 3.7 miles north of Dong Xoai. Units: Advisory Team 70, SF Det. A-342, Seabee Team 1104, 118th AHC & A Co., 82nd Avn. Bn. KIA: 19.

Jun 28–30   **First U.S. Offensive Operation.** Carried out by 3,000 troops of the 173rd Airborne Brigade in Zone D. KIA: 1; WIA: 9.

Jul 3   **Vietnam Service Medal.** Is authorized by *Presidential Executive Order 11231.*

Aug 18-20   **Chu Lai,** Battle of. An Cuong (2), Namyen & Hill 130. First major ground action (called *Operation Starlite*) fought only by U.S. troops. Units: 5,500 men of the 3rd, 4th and 7th Marines (L Co.). KIA: 56; WIA: 203. Aug. 18 (49 of KIA on).

Nov 6   **LZ Wing,** Battle of. West bank of Meur River, 7.4 miles west of Plei Me Airfield. Unit: 2nd Bn., 8th Cav, 1st Cav Div. KIA: 26; WIA: 53. C Company (17 of KIA).

Nov 8   **Hill 65,** Battle of. NE of Bien Hoa city. Unit: 1st Bn., 503rd Inf., 173rd Abn. Bde. KIA: 49. B Co. (20) and C Co. (18 of KIA). WIA: 83.

Nov 12   **Ap Bau Bang,** Battle of. 5 miles NE of Lai Khe Airfield. Units: A Co., 2nd Inf. 1st Div. & A Trp., 1st Sqdn., 4th Cav. KIA: 20; WIA: 39.

Nov 14-16   **LZ X-Ray,** Battle of. 3 miles east of Chu Prong Mtn. (Hill 732). Units: 1st Bn. & B Co., 2nd Bn., 7th Cav, 1st Cav Div. KIA: 81. C Co. (41 of the KIA). Nov. 15 (85% of KIA on). WIA: 129.

Nov 17   **LZ Albany,** Battle of. 4.3 miles NE of Chu Prong Mtn. (Hill 732). Deadliest single battle of the Vietnam War. Lasts 6 hours. Units: 2nd Bn., 7th Cav & 1st & 2nd Bns., 5th Cav. KIA: 153. 2nd Bn., 7th Cav (124, 82% of KIA). C Co. (44) & A Co. (35 of KIA). WIA: 121. 1st Cav Div. receives Presidential Unit Citation.

Dec 5   **Ap Nha Mat,** Battle of. Near Hill 36, NW of Ben Cat. Unit: 2nd Bn., 2nd Inf., 1st Div. KIA: 43. B Co. (21 of KIA). WIA: 119.

Dec 10-11   **Hill 407,** Engagement near. 5 miles SE of Que Son. Units: F Co., 2nd Bn., 1st Marines & E Co., 2nd Bn., 7th Marines. KIA: 20. 85% of KIA on Dec. 10.

1966

Jan 28-31   **Landing Zone 4,** Battle of. West of Phung Du. Units: 7th Cav (1st, 2nd Bns.) & 12th Cav (2nd), 1st Cav Div. KIA: 58. Jan. 29 (32 of KIA).

Feb 6-7   **My Canh,** Engagement near. SW of Tuy Hoa city. Units: Elements of 1st Bn., 327th Inf. & 2nd Bn., 502nd Inf., 101st Abn. Div. KIA: 36. B Co. (20 of KIA). 1st Bn., 327th, 83% (30) of KIA on Feb. 7.

Feb 17-23   **Kim Son Valley,** Running battle in. SW of Bong Son. Units: 5th Cav (1st & 2nd Bns.), 8th Cav (2nd), 12th Cav (1st), 1st Cav Div. KIA: 40. Feb. 18-19 (16 of KIA) & Feb. 23 (21 of KIA).

Mar 4   **My Phu,** Battle at. SW of Tuy Hoa. Units: A & B Cos., 1st Bn., 327th Inf., 101st Abn. Div. KIA: 20.

Mar 4-6   **Chau Ngai,** Battle of. 6.2 miles SW of Binh Son. Units: 2nd Bn., 7th Marines & 3rd Bn., 1st Marines. KIA: 101; WIA: 278.

Mar 21-23   **Vinh Tuy Valley,** Running battle in. Engagements at Xuan Hoa (1), Phoung Dinh (2), Phouc Loc (1) & Thach An Noi. Units: 3rd Bn., 1st Marines; 2nd Bn., 4th Marines; & 3rd Bn., 7th Marines. KIA: 49. (22 KIA at Xuan Hoa on March 21.)

Mar 30   **Chu Pong Massif,** Engagement in. SW of Plei Me. Units: A Co., 1st Bn., 12th Cav, 1st Cav Div. & A Trp., 1st Sqdn., 9th Cav Regt. KIA: 30. 10 of KIA are in a helicopter shoot-down.

Apr 11   **Xa Cam My,** Battle of. 6.8 miles NE of Binh Gia. Unit: C Co., 2nd Bn., 16th Inf., 1st Div. KIA: 37; WIA: 70.

May 16-18   **Hill 766,** Battle for. 4.3 miles NE of Vinh Thanh. Units: B Co., 2nd Bn., 8th Cav; elements of 1st & 2nd Bns., 12th Cav; 1st Bn. 5th Cav, 1st Cav Div. KIA: 40. B Co. (23 of KIA). May 17 (73% of KIA on). WIA: 110+.

May 28-29   **LZ 10-Alpha,** Engagement at. 8.6 miles NW of Duc Co Airfield. Units A & B Cos., 1st & 2nd Bns., 35th Inf., 25th Div. KIA: 20. Awarded Presidential Unit Citation for defense of LZ.

Jun 6   **Howard's Hill 488,** Defense of. 4.3 miles NE of Tien Phuoc. Unit: 1st Plt., C Co., 1st Marine Recon Bn. KIA: 11. Perhaps most highly decorated small unit in U.S. military history.

Jun 9-10   **Ngok Run Ridge,** Engagement on. NE of Dak To. Units: 2nd Bn., 502nd Inf. & 1st Bn., 327th Inf., 101st Abn. Div. KIA: 20. 85% of KIA on June 9.

Jun 11   **Loc Ninh Rubber Plantation,** Battle of. Unit: 2nd Bn. 28th Inf., 1st Div. KIA: 34. Recon Platoon (17 of KIA). WIA: 33.

Jun 20-22   **Trung Luong,** Battle of. 5 miles east of Dong Tre Airfield. Unit: 2nd Bn., 327th Inf., 101st Abn. Div. KIA: 31. June 20 (58% of KIA on). WIA: 155.

Jun 30-Jul 2   **Srok Dong,** Battle of. Highway QL-13, SW of Loc Ninh city. Units: 2nd Bn., 18th Inf. & 1st Sqdn., 4th Cav, 1st Div. KIA: 38; WIA: 94.

Jul 3   **Route 569,** Ambush on. 3.7 miles SW of Duc Co Airfield. Unit: B Co., 1st Bn., 35th Inf., 25th Div. KIA: 20 (most in 1st Platoon).

Jul 15   **CH-46A Helicopter,** Shoot-down of. Song Ngan Valley, 6 miles NW of Cam Lo. Units: 2nd Bn., 1st Marines & 3rd Bn., 4th Marines. KIA: 18.

Jul 24   **Razorback Ridge (Hill 362),** Ambush near. 7.4 miles west of Cam Lo. Units: I, K & L Cos., 3rd Bn., 5th Marines. KIA: 28; WIA: 82. I Company (19 of KIA).

Aug 8   **LZ Juliet,** Firefight near. Lasts 3 hours. 5.6 miles NE of Chu Prong Mtn. (Hill 732). Unit: A Co., 1st Bn., 7th Cav, 1st Cav Div. KIA: 25; WIA: 36.

Aug 25-26   **Bong Trang Woods,** Battle of. 5.6 miles NE of Ben Cat village. Units: Elements of 2nd Inf., 16th Inf., 26th Inf., & 4th Cav, 1st Div. KIA: 45. C Co. (15 of KIA). 1st Bn. 2nd Inf. Aug. 25 (87% of KIA on). WIA: 183.

Sep 16-18   **Cam Lo River Valley,** Engagement in. 3 miles NW of Thon Khe (The Rockpile). Units: B & D Cos., 1st Bn., 4th Marines. KIA: 25. Sept. 16 (16 of KIA on).

Nov 3-5   **Dau Tieng,** Battle of. 6.2 miles NW of Dau Tieng Base Camp. Units: 1st & 2nd Bns., 27th Inf.; 2nd Bn., 1st Inf; & 3rd Bn., 21st Inf. KIA: 53; WIA: 159.

THE UNITED STATES IN THE VIETNAM WAR, 1954–1973

1955–1960: EARLY ADVISORY PERIOD After the withdrawal of French forces, the United States assumed the mission of assisting the newly formed Republic of South Vietnam in organizing its armed forces. American advisors established training programs and schools and supplied U.S. arms and equipment to the newly formed Army of the Republic of Vietnam.

1961–1964: INTENSIFIED ADVISORY PERIOD In the early 1960's, the Kennedy Administration increased military aid and advisory support to South Vietnam in order to counter increasing levels of political subversion and military activity by Viet Cong (VC) insurgents. After a series of coups racked the Vietnamese government in 1963–1964, the enemy threat steadily escalated. While VC units struck at governmental and military installations, North Vietnam began active participation in the fighting by infiltrating elements of the North Vietnamese Army (NVA) along the Ho Chi Minh Trail. After attacks on U.S. Navy ships in the Gulf of Tonkin, President Johnson authorized the first retaliatory air strikes against North Vietnam.

1965–1967: AMERICAN INTERVENTION Increased enemy activity provoked the deployment of U.S. forces to insure the safety of U.S. advisors and installations. In July 1965, President Johnson committed U.S. forces to combat VC and NVA Main Force units who threatened the continued stability of the South. By the end of 1966 the enemy threat had been subdued to the point that American and South Vietnamese forces began limited offensive actions designed to disrupt enemy activities and to destroy enemy strongholds in rural areas. Throughout 1967, Allied forces expanded their offensive to strike enemy held zones in the Central Highlands and west of Saigon, destroying a number of strongholds and severely weakening enemy forces. By late 1967, American political and military leaders were confident that the war could be brought to a successful conclusion.

1968: THE TET OFFENSIVE During the final months of 1967, NVA and Viet Cong forces began to secretly mass for a large-scale offensive in the South. On the night of January 30, 1968, enemy regular forces violated the cease fire of the Tet Lunar New Year by striking at U.S. and Vietnamese military installations in the rural areas. Concurrently, Viet Cong units who had infiltrated into urban areas struck at virtually every major provincial and district capital across Vietnam, committing widespread acts of terrorism. Over the next month, U.S. and Vietnamese forces were able to restore stability and inflict tremendous losses of over 50,000 enemy killed and wounded. Lesser enemy attacks continued throughout the remainder of the year with VC and NVA forces failing to disrupt United States and South Vietnamese recovery and consolidation.

1969–1973: VIETNAMIZATION AND WITHDRAWAL In January 1969, peace negotiations began in Paris between the belligerents. In addition, the Nixon Administration announced that the South Vietnamese would once again assume the burden of the war effort, thereby allowing the gradual withdrawal of American combat troops. Through 1970, American forces continued to bear the brunt of the fighting while an intensified assistance program supplied over $3.1 billion in military materials to the South Vietnamese Armed Forces. In March, 1973, the last U.S. combat troops departed South Vietnam, leaving behind a more stable, democratic Vietnamese government and a much strengthened armed forces.

TIME LINE

Strength of U.S. Forces

French surrender at Dien Bien Phu, May 7	1954
U.S. aid to Diem begins	1955
Republic of Vietnam proclaimed, Oct. 26 / U.S. replaces French advisors, April 28	1956
Communists assemble armed force in South, Oct.	1957
	1958
Two Americans killed, July 8	1959
Armed struggles in Mekong Delta, Jan. 17	1960
Military Assistance Command Vietnam (MACV) organized, Feb. 8	1961
	1962
Kennedy assassinated, Nov. 22	1963
Tonkin Gulf Resolution, Aug. 7 / U.S. begins bombing, Dec. 14	1964
Operation Rolling Thunder, Feb. 28 / U.S. Marines land at Da Nang, March 9	1965
Demonstrations in Saigon, Hue, & Da Nang, March	1966
Antiwar demonstrations in U.S., April	1967
Tet Offensive, Jan. 30–31 / Bombing of North Vietnam halted, Oct. 31	1968
Peace talks begin, Jan. 25 / Secret B52 strikes in Cambodia	1969
Cambodian bases attacked, April / Tonkin Gulf Resolution repealed, June 24	1970
Invasion of Laos, Feb.–March / U.S. bombing resumes in North Vietnam, April 6	1971
Communist Easter Offensive	1972
Ceasefire signed, Jan. 27 / Last U.S. ground troops leave, March	1973
Vietnamese reconciliation talks break down, April–May	1974
Communist offensives in Cambodia & S. Vietnam, Jan.–April / South Vietnam surrenders, April 30	1975

THE VIETNAM WAR
1954–1973

- ◆ U.S. Base Area
- ◆ North Vietnamese Base
- ▇ Area of Confrontation
- ▇ Viet Cong Base Area
- ✦ Major Engagement
- ← Enemy Supply Route
- ▇ U.S. Bombing Target Area
- ← Enemy External Supply Route
- → U.S. Air Strikes
- --→ Route of Infiltration
- — Corps Tactical Zone Boundary

Map courtesy of the West Point Museum Collections, United States Military Academy

Nov 21   **Cambodian Border,** Clash on. 6.8 miles SW of Duc Co. Unit: C Co., 1st Bn., 5th Cav, 1st Cav Div. KIA: 34; WIA: 11.

Dec 17   **Highway 506 Valley,** Battle in. SW of Bong Son. Units: 1st Bn., 12th Cav & 1st Sqdn., 9th Cav, 1st Cav Div. KIA: 36. D Co. (18 of KIA). WIA: 81.

Dec 27   **LZ Bird,** Battle of. The Crow's Foot on Kim Son River, SW of Bong Son. Units: C Co., 1st Bn., 12th Cav; B Btry., 2nd Bn., 19th Arty; & C Btry., 6th Bn., 16th Arty, 1st Cav Div. KIA: 28; WIA: 67.

1967

Feb 16   **LZ 501,** Firefight near. Plei Trap Valley. Unit: C Co., 2nd Bn., 8th Inf., 4th Div. KIA: 23. Many of KIA in 1st Platoon alone.

Feb 22   **War's Only U.S. Conventional Combat Jump:** 845 paratroopers of the 2nd Bn., 503rd Inf. & Btry. A, 3rd Bn., 319th Arty of the 173rd Abn. Bde., parachute north of Katum during *Operation Junction City.* They sustain only 1 WIA and 11 minor injuries.

Feb 26   **Phu Hoa,** Attack on NDP near. 5.6 miles NE of Cu Chi. Units: A Co., 4th Bn., 9th Inf., 25th Div. & A Co., 65th Eng. Bn. KIA: 25 (20 in A Co., 9th Inf.)

Feb 27   **Navy Facilities,** Rocket attacks (two) on. Da Nang Harbor, north of Marble Mtn. Airfield. Units: LCU-1500 & YFU-78 of Assault Craft Unit 1 & Supply Operations. KIA: 22.

Feb 28   **Prek Klok,** Battle of. Off Rt. TL-4, SW of Katum Airfield. Unit: B Co., 1st Bn., 16th Inf., 1st Div. KIA: 26; WIA: 27.

Mar 19, 21   **FSB Gold,** Battle of. Suoi Tre. Units: 3rd Bn., 22nd Inf. & 2nd Bn., 77th Arty, 4th Div. KIA: 52 (including 14 in helicopter shoot-down, etc., on March 19). B Co. (20 of KIA). WIA: 187.

Mar 20-21   **Truong Son,** Engagements near. 2½ miles west of Tam Quan. Units: 5th (1st), 8th (1st) & 12th (2nd) Cav Regts., 1st Cav Div. KIA: 36. March 20 (22 of KIA) & March 21 (14 of KIA).

Mar 21   **One-Niner,** Battle of. Plei Trap Valley. NW of Duc Co. Units: Mostly C Co., 2nd Bn., 35th Inf., 25th Div. KIA: 25. C Co. (20 of KIA).

Mar 22   **Plei Duc,** Engagement in area of. West of Se San River. Units: A & B Cos., 1st Bn., 8th Inf., 4th Div. KIA: 27. A Company (21 of KIA).

Apr 8   **Hung Long,** Firefight near. An Lao Valley. 10 miles west of Tam Quan. Units: 1st & 5th Bns., 7th Cav, 1st Cav Div. KIA: 27.

Apr 21-22   **Binh Son (1),** Battle of. 3 miles SE of Que Son. Units: 2nd & 3rd Bns., 1st Marines. KIA: 48. F Co. (33 of KIA). WIA: 145.

Apr 24-26   **Hill 861,** Battle of. 4.3 miles NW of Khe Sanh Airfield. Units: 3rd Bn., 3rd Marines & 1st Bn., 9th Marines. KIA: 45. B Co. (23 of KIA), 9th Marines & K Co. (20), 3rd Marines.

Apr 30   **Hill 881 South,** Battle of. 5 miles NW of Khe Sanh Airfield. Units: 3rd Bns. of 3rd & 9th Marines. KIA: 45; WIA: 109. M Co., 3rd Marines (26 of KIA) & K Co., 9th Marines (18 of KIA).

May 2-3   **Hill 881 North,** Battle of. 5 miles NW of Khe Sanh Airfield. Unit: 2nd Bn., 3rd Marines. KIA: 34. May 3 (29 of KIA on). E Co. (22 of KIA).

May 8   **Con Thien,** Attack on. Lasts three hours. Units: A & B Cos., 1st Bn., 4th Marines. KIA: 46. WIA: 110.

May 9   **Hill 778,** Firefight at. 7.4 miles NW of Khe Sanh Airfield. Unit: F Co., 2nd Bn., 3rd Marines. KIA: 24.

May 10   **Hill 110,** Battle for. 1st Bns. of 3rd & 5th Marines. 2½ miles north of Que Son. KIA: 35; WIA 135. 3rd Marines (60% of KIA).

May 18-22   **Plei Doc,** Battle of. 8 miles NW of Duc Co. Unit: 1st Bn., 8th Inf., 4th Div. KIA: 49. May 18 (30 of KIA on) & May 20 (16 of KIA on). B Co. (30 of KIA).

May 20   **NVA Bunker Complex,** Assault on. 3 miles NW of Cam Lo village. Units: K & L Cos., 3rd Bn., 9th Marines. KIA: 25. K Co. (23 of KIA).

May 21   **Suoi Cat,** Ambush at. Highway QL-1. Unit: K Trp., 3rd Bn., 11th ACR. KIA: 18; WIA: 28.

May 26   **LZ Eagle,** Battle of. NE of Binh Son (1), 3 miles SE of Que Son. Unit: 3rd Bn., 5th Marines. KIA: 41; WIA: 82.

Jun 2-3   **Vinh Huy,** Engagements near. Nui Loc Son Basin, 5 miles SE of Que Son. Unit: 5th Marine Regt. KIA: 75; WIA: 139. F Co., 2nd Bn. (25 of KIA).

Jun 17   **Xom Bo (Second),** Battle of. North of Phuoc Vinh Airfield. Units: 1st Bn., 16th & 2nd Bn., 28th Inf., 1st Div. KIA: 37. 16th Inf. (70% of KIA). A Co. (15 of KIA). WIA: 150.

Jun 19   **Ap Bac,** Battle at. Can Giuoc District, 5.6 miles NE of Can Duoc, Mekong Delta. Units: 3rd & 4th Bns., 47th Inf., 9th Div. KIA: 47. 4th Bn. (87% of KIA). A Co. (27 of KIA). WIA: 150.

Jun 22   **Slopes,** Battle of the. Hill 1338, 4.3 miles SW of Dak To. Unit: A Co., 2nd Bn., 503rd Inf., 173rd Abn. Bde. KIA: 76; WIA: 23.

Jul 2   **Route 561,** Ambush on. 2 miles NE of Con Thien. Unit: 1st Bn., 9th Marines. KIA: 92. B Co. (52, 57%, of total KIA). WIA: 190.

Jul 10   **Hill 830,** Battle of. 7.4 miles south of Ben Het village. Units: 4th Bn., 503rd Inf., 173rd Abn. Bde and B Btry., 319th Arty. KIA: 26. WIA: 49.

Jul 12   **Ia Pnon River Valley,** Battle in. 7.4 miles south of Duc Co. Units: B & C Cos., 1st Bn., 12th Inf., 4th Div. KIA: 34 (all B Co.); WIA: 42; POWs: 7 (2 of whom DOW and are part of the 34 KIA).

Jul 19   **Boi Loi Woods,** Battle in. 6.8 miles NE of Trang Bang. Unit: A Co., 1st Bn., 27th Inf., 25th Div. KIA: 24; WIA: 32.

Jul 23   **Plei Ya Bo,** Firefight at. 4.3 miles south of Duc Co. Units: Mostly C Co., 3rd Bn., 8th Inf., 4th Div. KIA: 21; WIA: 53.

Jul 29   **Thon Cam Son,** Recon-in-Force into DMZ. 3 miles NW of Con Thien. Units: 2nd Bn., 9th Marines. KIA: 37 (including 4 from Medevac helicopter shoot-down on July 30). WIA: 251.

Sep 4   **Dong Son (1),** Battle for. SE of Que Son. Includes fighting at Chau Lam (1). Units: 1st & 3rd Bns., 5th Marines. KIA: 55; WIA: 104.

Sep 6   **Hill 43,** Battle of. Que Son Valley, 6.2 miles SW of Thang Binh. Units: I & K Cos., 3rd Bn., 5th Marines. KIA: 29; WIA: 109. I Co. (24 of KIA).

Sep 7   **The Churchyard,** Engagement in. 2 miles south of Con Thien. Unit: 3rd Bn., 26th Marines. KIA: 21; WIA: 70.

Sep 10   **Hill 48,** Battle of. 3.7 miles south of Con Thien. Unit: 3rd Bn., 26th Marines. KIA: 38. K Co. (17 of KIA). WIA: 192.

Sep 21   **Hill 158,** Battle near. 2 miles east of Con Thien. Units: F & G Cos., 2nd Bn., 4th Marines. KIA: 31 (includes 5 from H&S Co.).

Oct 14   **C-2 (Bastard's) Bridge,** Battle for. 5 miles north of Cam Lo village. Units: G Co., 2nd Bn., 4th Marines & H Btry., 3rd Bn., 12th Marines. KIA: 21.

Oct 17   **Ong Thanh,** Battle of. 6.8 miles SE of Minh Thanh Airfield. 11 hours of combat. Unit: 2nd Bn., 28th Inf., 1st Div. KIA: 59. D Co. (26 of KIA) & A Co. (21). WIA: 132.

Nov 4-11   **Hill 724,** Battle around. 7.4 miles SW of Dak To. Units: 8th & 12th Inf., 4th Div. KIA: 61. Nov. 11 (22 of KIA, 8th Inf.).

Nov 12-13   **Hill 823,** Battle of. 6.8 miles SW of Ben Het. Unit: 2nd Bn., 503rd Inf., 173rd Abn. Bde., KIA: 37. Nov 13 (B Co. 22 of KIA).

Nov 18–23   **Hill 875,** Battle of. Dak To. Units: 2nd & 4th Bns., 503rd Inf., 173rd Abn. Bde. KIA: 131. Nov. 20 (72 of KIA on): A Co. (29) and C Co. (29), 2nd Bn. WIA: 411.

Dec 6   **FSB Nashua,** Engagement around. 1.2 miles SE of firebase, 6.2 miles NE of Tan Uyen. Units: 7th Inf. (3rd), 12th Inf. (4th) & D Trp. 17th Cav, 199th LIB. KIA: 26; WIA: 92.

Dec 6–15   **Tam Quan,** Battle of. Includes engagements at My An (2) and Truong Lam (1). 4-5 miles south of Tam Quan city. Units: 12th Cav (1st Bn.), 8th Cav (1st & 2nd), 9th Cav and 50th Inf. (B, 1st). KIA: 59. Dec. 15 (22 of KIA). WIA: 250.

Dec 27   **Thon Tham Khe,** Battle of. 8 miles NE of Hai Lang. Unit: 3rd Bn., 1st Marines. KIA: 49. L Co. (27 of KIA). WIA: 86.

Dec 28-29   **LZ Hawk,** Battle of. Bao An Dong, Go Noi Island. Units: 2nd Bn., 3rd Marines & 3rd Bn., 5th Marines. KIA: 30. E Co (20 of KIA). WIA: 40.

1968

Jan 1-2   **Firebase Burt (Soui Cut),** Attack on. NE of Tay Ninh. Units: 2nd & 3rd Bns., 22nd Inf., 25th Div. KIA: 23; WIA: 152. 3rd Bn. sustains 74% of KIA.

Jan 7   **Xuan Que (1),** Firefight at. 3.7 miles SW of Que Son. Units: 2nd Bn., 12th Cav, 1st Cav Div. KIA: 24 (including 7 in helicopter shoot-down).

Jan 10   **Cai Be District,** Engagement in. Dinh Tuong province in Mekong Delta. Units: A & C Cos., 3rd Bn. 60th Inf., 9th Div. & B Btry., 3rd Bn., 34th Arty. KIA: 20; WIA: 50.

Jan 20– Apr 14   **Khe Sanh,** Battle of. 6,683 men of the 26th Marines; 1st Bn., 9th Marines; and two batteries of the 13th Marines, come under siege by several NVA divisions for 77 days. KIA: 205; WIA: 852.

Jan 30– Feb 26   **Tet Offensive.** In the war's largest offensive, 88,000 Communist troops attack 105 cities and towns throughout South Vietnam. A total of 81,000 lives are lost, including 3,895 U.S. KIA and 14,300 civilians. Political turning point of the war.

Jan 30– Feb 7   **Saigon,** Battle of. Some 11,000 U.S. and ARVN forces dislodge 1,000 VC from the capital city during a week of intense fighting.

Jan 30   **Tuy Hoa North Airfield & Cemetery Hill,** Attack on. NW of Tuy Hoa city. Units: 503rd Inf., 173rd Abn. Bde.; batteries of 32nd & 319th Arty. KIA: 23.

Jan 31   **Highest Daily KIA Count for U.S. Forces:** 246 KIA.

Jan 31   **Saigon,** Defense of. U.S. Embassy, BOQ-3 and Phu Loi Racetrack. Units: 716th MP Bn. (A, C & 527th Cos.) and 52nd Inf. (C & D Cos.) only. KIA: 27; WIA: 44.

Feb   **Hue,** Battle of. The Citadel, Thon Que Chu, Thon Lieu. Units: 1st & 5th Marines; 1st Cav & 101st Abn. Divs. Marines: 147 KIA; WIA: 857. Army: 69 KIA; WIA: 507.

Feb 7   **A-3 Strongpoint/Gio Linh Road,** Battle along. 1.2 miles SW of Gio Linh village. Unit: 3rd Bn., 3rd Marines. KIA: 30. K Co. (25 of KIA). WIA: 35.

Feb 7   **Lang Vei Special Forces Camp,** Siege of. 5 miles SW of Khe Sanh Airfield. Units: Det. A, 5th SFG & Det. B-16 (Mobile Strike Force Co.). KIA: 10. 3 POWs. 1 Medal of Honor & 8 Silver Stars.

Feb 8   **Alpha I Outpost,** Attack on. Hill 64, 2 miles west of Khe Sanh Airfield. Unit: A Co., 1st Bn., 9th Marines. KIA: 27.

Feb 8   **Lo Giang (1),** Engagement near. 3.1 miles SE of Da Nang AB. Unit: A Co., 1st Bn., 6th Inf., 198th IB, Americal Div. KIA: 19.

Feb 10–17   **Second Highest Weekly U.S. Casualties:** 543 KIA; 2,547 WIA.

Feb 25   **Khe Sanh "Ghost Patrol,"** Less than 1 mile south of base. Unit: 3rd Plt., B Co., 1st Bn., 26th Marines. KIA: 28; WIA: 17.

Feb 25   **FSB Jaeger,** Attack on. 8.6 miles east of Cai Lay. 4½ hours. Units: 5th Bn., 60th Inf., 9th Div. & B Co., 15th Eng. Bn. KIA: 22; WIA: 70.

Feb 28   **CH-46D Helicopter,** Shoot-down of. 4.3 miles SW of Thon Khe (Rockpile). Units: HMM-262 (10 of KIA) & 7 other units. KIA: 23.

Mar 1-2   **Mai Xai Thi West,** Battle of. 4.3 miles NE of Dong Ha. Units: 3rd Bn., 1st Marines & 1st Plt., 1st Armored Amphibious Co., 11th Marines. KIA: 32. March 1 (nearly 75% of KIA on). 3rd Bn. (28 of KIA)—19 from M Co. WIA: 81.

Mar 2   **Hoc Man,** Ambush at. Route 248 Bridge, Quoi Xuah Hamlet, 6.8 miles NW of Tan Son Nhut Air Base. Unit: C Co., 4th Bn., 9th Inf., 25th Div. In an 8-minute burst of VC fire, this single company (150 men) is decimated. KIA: 48; WIA: 28.

Mar 6   **C-123K,** Shoot-down of. 5 miles east of Khe Sanh Combat Base. Units: Six. KIA: 56. 26th Marines (46 of KIA). Its 1st Bn. (27 of KIA).

Mar 11   **Lima 85 Radar Site,** Overrunning of. Phou Pha Thi Mountain, Laos. Units: Air Force 1043rd Radar Evaluation Squadron. KIA: 13.

Apr 4-5   **Bai Lai River,** Multiple engagements on south bank of. 3 miles NE of Ben Tre city. Units: 3rd & 4th Bns., 47th Inf., 9th Div. & Navy Riverine Squadron 9. KIA: 32. 63% of KIA on April 4.

Apr 6-7   **Hill 558,** Firefight near. 2½ miles NW of Khe Sanh Airfield. Unit: 2nd Bn., 26th Marines. KIA: 29. G Co. (15 of KIA). Apr 7 (66% of KIA on).

Apr 13   **Canal 7,** Firefight along. 4.3 miles east of Hue Citadel. Unit: 1st Bn., 27th Marines. KIA: 27. A & B Cos. (each 10 KIA).

Apr 16   **Hill 689,** Battle at. 3 miles west of Khe Sanh. Unit: 1st Bn., 9th Marines. KIA: 42. C Co. (20 of KIA). WIA: 32.

Apr 29–May 3   **Dai Do,** Battle of. North bank of Cua Viet River, 2½ miles NE of Dong Ha. Units: 2nd Bn., 4th Marines & 1st Bn., 3rd Marines. KIA: 87; WIA: 297. May 2 (51 of KIA). 4th Marines (76% of KIA). F Co. (22 of KIA).

Apr 30   **Cam Vu,** Battle of. 3 miles NE of Cam Lo. Units: 1st & 3rd Bns., 9th Marines. KIA: 34. L Co. (15 of KIA). WIA: 94.

May 5-6   **An Bao,** Battle at. 7.4 miles north of Phu My city. Units: 1st Bn., 50th Inf. (attached to 173rd Abn. Bde.); B Co., 1st Bn., 69th Armor; & 335th Assault Helicopter Co. KIA: 22. May 5 (18 of KIA). 73% of KIA from 50th Infantry.

May 3–10 **Highest U.S. Weekly Hostile Casualty Toll of War:** 562 KIA.

May 5-12 **Saigon (District 8),** Engagements. Units: 31st (6th Bn.), 39th (3rd), 47th (2nd) & 60th (5th) Inf. Regts. KIA: 39. May 9-10 (21 of KIA).

May 2, 6 **Nhi Ha,** Engagements at. 4.3 miles north of Cua Viet River. Units: 3rd Bn., 21st Inf., 196th LIB. KIA: 24. A Co. (12 of KIA) & C Co. (11). WIA: 130.

May 10 **Ngok Tavak,** Attack on. 5 miles SW of Kham Duc. Units: D Btry., 2nd Bn., 13th Marines & Det. A-105, 5th SFG. KIA: 16. D Btry. (13 of KIA).

May 11-12 **Kham Duc,** Withdrawal from. SW of Hiep Duc. 2nd Bn., 1st Inf., 196th LIB, Americal Div. & 774th TAS. KIA: 26. 1st Inf. (19 of KIA). 5 crew (774th) in C-130 shoot-down. May 12 (22 of KIA).

May 13 **Nui Ba Den (Black Virgin Mtn.),** Attack on. 6.8 miles NE of Tay Ninh city. Mostly Signal units, especially the 125th Signal Bn. KIA: 22. Signal members 77% of KIA. 1 POW.

May 17-26 **Goi Noi Island,** Engagements on. Le Bac (1), Phu Dong (2) and Liberty Bridge. Units: 27th Marines. KIA: 96; WIA: 300. May 17 (28 of KIA). I Co. (20 of KIA).

May 22-23 **Hill 158,** Firefight near. 2 miles east of Con Thien. Units: 1st Bn., 4th Marines & 3rd Bn., 3rd Marines. KIA: 26. B Co. (13 of KIA). May 22 (81% of KIA on).

May 31 **Highway QL-9,** Engagements near. 2½ miles SE of Khe Sanh. Units: 1st Bn., 1st Marines & 2nd Bn., 3rd Marines. KIA: 27. B Co. (13 of KIA).

Jun 6 **LZ Loon,** Attack on. 5 miles SE of Khe Sanh Airfield. Unit: 1st Bn., 4th Marines. KIA: 26. H&S Co. (50% of KIA), especially Mortar Platoon (9 KIA). On June 5, C Co. of 1/4 has 10 KIA from 130mm artillery fire on its position near LZ Loon.

Jun 7 **Cu Ban (3),** Firefight at. 1.2 miles SW of Liberty Bridge. Unit: 1st Bn., 26th Marines. KIA: 25. A Co. (17 of KIA).

Jul 3 **CH-46A Helicopter,** Shoot-down of. Elephant Valley, 8.6 miles south of Phu Loc. Units: 1st Plt., B Co., 1st Recon Bn. & HMM-164. KIA: 13.

Aug 23 **FOB-4 Compound,** Attack on. Base of Marble Mountain, Da Nang. Units: CCN, Studies & Observation Group (SOG). KIA: 16. Largest single hostile loss in Army Special Forces history.

Aug 25 **Highway QL-22 Convoy,** Ambush on. Near Ap Nhi & Ben Cui Rubber Plantation. Nine units—including 4 transportation companies (particularly of 48th Trans. Grp.)—sustain dead. KIA: 19 (11 in convoy; 8 in 25th Inf. Div. reaction force). POW: 3.

Sep 5-6 **Ap Trang Dau,** Battle of. 3 miles east of Trang Bang. Units: Mostly A Co., 3rd Bn., 187th Inf., 101st Abn. Div. KIA: 32. Sep 6 (91% of KIA on).

Sep 15-18 **LZ Margo,** Attack on. West of Mutter's Ridge on the Cam Lo River. Unit: 2nd Bn., 26th Marines. KIA: 29; WIA: 149.

Oct 14 **Mandatory Second Tours.** Army and Marine Corps announce that 24,000 men will be sent back to Vietnam involuntarily.

Nov 1 **U.S. Navy's Worst Ship Loss to Enemy Action:** *USS Westchester County (LST-1167).* Mined while anchored in Tieng Giang River 3.7 miles SE of My Tho. KIA: 18 sailors (17 crew + 1 of Riverine Squadron 11). Also, 5 men of B Co., 3rd Bn., 60th Inf., 9th Div., aboard are KIA. WIA: 22.

Dec 3 **LZ Eleanor,** Combat assault on. SE of Loc Ninh Airfield.

5-hour fight by 116 men. Unit: D Co., 2nd Bn., 7th Cav, 1st Cav Div. KIA: 23; WIA: 52.

Dec 31 **Peak U.S. annual combat deaths:** 14,933.

1969

Jan 3 **554th Engineer Battalion Mess Hall,** Attack on. Cu Chi Base Camp. Unit: Delta Company. KIA: 15. Camp also hit Feb. 26, losing 14 KIA from 8 units.

Jan 13 **War's Largest Amphibious Assault:** 2,500 Marines (7th Fleet Amphibious Force) land on Batangan Peninsula in *Operation Bold Mariner.*

Feb 21-22 **Route 922,** Firefight along. Da Krong River Valley. Unit: 1st Bn., 9th Marines. KIA: 20. A Co. (14 of KIA). WIA: 72.

Feb 23 **1st Marine Division Complex Around Hill 327,** Attacks on. Da Nang. Units: 11 (those that sustained KIA). Artillery batteries hit the hardest. KIA: 30. Gunfire (47%), satchel charges (33%) and shrapnel (20%) account for the deaths.

Feb 23 **Patrol Base Diamond I,** Attack on. 5 miles SW of Go Dau Ha. Units: Mostly C Co., 2nd Bn., 27th Inf., 25th ID. KIA: 18.

Feb 25 **FSB Russell,** Attack on. 8.6 miles NW of Ca Lu Airfield. Units: 2nd Bn. (H&S and E), 4th Marines & H Btry., 3rd Bn., 12th Marines. KIA: 30; WIA: 77. H Btry. (9 of KIA). Meanwhile, **FSB Neville** is hit, with 13 KIA (H Co. 10 of KIA).

Mar 3 **Plei Trap Valley,** Battle in. Along western edge of Central Highlands. Unit: A Co., 3rd Bn., 8th Inf., 4th Div. KIA: 23.

Marc 19 **Phu Lac (6),** Sapper attack on FSB & CP. Liberty Bridge, 4.3 miles NE of An Hoa Airfield. Units: D Btry., 2nd Bn., 11th Marines & 1st Bn. (D and H&S), 5th Marines. KIA: 15 (12 in D Btry.).

Apr 30 **Peak U.S. troop strength in Vietnam:** 543,482.

May 10–21 **Hamburger Hill,** Battle of. Ap Bia Mtn. (Hill 937), A Shau Valley. Units: 3rd Bn., 187th Inf. & 1st Bn., 506th Inf., 101st Abn. Div. KIA: 66; WIA: 372. 187th (39 of KIA) & 506th (23 of KIA). May 18 single worst day—21 KIA.

May 12-14 **Nui Yon Hill/Regional Forces Camp,** Attack on. 3.7 miles SW of Tam Ky Airfield. Units: 3rd Bn., 21st Inf., 196th LIB; 1st Sqdn., 1st Cav Regt. & Advisory Team 16. KIA: 28. C Co. (15 of KIA).

May 13 **FSB Airborne,** Attack on. 4.3 miles NW of A Luoi village. Lasts 90 minutes. Units: A & E Cos., 1st Bn., 501st Inf., 101st Abn. Div. & C Btry., 2nd Bn., 319th Arty. KIA: 27; WIA: 62. C Btry. (14 of KIA).

Jun 11 **LZ East,** Sapper attack on. 4.3 miles northeast of Tien Phuoc. Units: 3rd Bn., 21st Inf., 196th LIB & B Btry., 3rd Bn., 82nd Arty. KIA: 16; WIA: 33. 50% of KIA are artillerymen.

Jun 17 **Leatherneck Square Area,** Firefight in. 2 miles SW of Gio Linh village. Unit: 3rd Bn., 3rd Marines. KIA: 20; WIA: 28. M Co. (10 of KIA).

Jun 19 **FSB Tomahawk,** Attack on. Hill 132, 2 miles NE of Phu Loc. Units: C Btry., 2nd Bn., 138th Arty (Kentucky ANG) & 1st Plt., C Co., 2nd Bn, 501st Inf., 101st. KIA: 14 (including 5 National Guard).

Jul 7 **Phased Withdrawal of U.S. Troops Begins:** 3rd Bn., 60th Inf., 9th Inf. Div., leaves Saigon.

Jul 11 Hill 996, Battle of. 5.6 miles SE of A Luoi village. D & B Cos.,1st Bn. & C Co., 2nd Bn., 506th Inf., 101st Abn. Div. KIA: 20; WIA: 26.

Aug 10 LZ Sierra, Attack on. NDP on Mutter's Ridge (Hill 184). Units: 1st (A) & 2nd Bns. (E and H&S), 3rd Marines. KIA: 24.

Aug 11-12 LZ Becky, Sapper attacks (2) on. 2½ miles SW of Bo Tuc. Units: 2nd Bn., 8th Cav & A Btry., 1st Bn., 30th Arty, 1st Cav. KIA: 22; WIA: 39. A Btry. (10 of KIA) and 2nd Bn. (12). Aug. 12 (16 of KIA).

Aug 12–13 An Hoa Airfield, Engagements near. NDP, Phu An & Tan My (1). Units: 1st Bn., 7th Marines and 3rd Bn., 5th Marines. KIA: 22; WIA: 100.

Aug 17–29 Hiep Duc, Battle of. Units: Army—1st, 21st and 31st Inf., American Div. Marines—2nd & 3rd Bns., 7th Marines. KIA: 116; WIA: 491.

Sep 17–18 Hill 154, Attack on NDP at. Cam Lo River Valley, 8 miles NW of Ca Lu. Units: L Co., 3rd Bn., 3rd Marines & 3rd Eng. Bn. (B). KIA: 16; WIA: 47. I Co., 3rd Bn., 4th Marines: 9 KIA; 25 WIA.

1970

Jan 6 FSB Ross, Night attack on: 1.2 miles west of Que Son. Units: Mostly 1st Bn., 7th Marines. KIA: 15; WIA: 63.

Feb 11 FSB Rifle, Attack on. 10 miles south of Phu Bai Airfield. Units: B & E Cos., 2nd Bn., 502nd Inf., 101st Abn. Div. & HQ Btry., 2nd Bn., 320th Arty. KIA: 11.

Feb 12 Dong Son (1), Ambush near. Ly Ly River, 2½ miles SE of Que Son. Units: B & C Cos., 1st Bn., 7th Marines. KIA: 14; WIA: 13.

Feb 14 Bau Tam Ung, Engagement near. 7.4 miles NW of Nui Ba Den Mountain. Units: C Co., 2nd Bn., 8th Cav, 1st Cav Div. & 11th ACR. KIA: 11; WIA: 30.

Feb 20 Hill 43, 2 engagements near. 5.6 miles east of Que Son. Units: A Co., 2nd Bn., 1st Inf., 196th LIB & F Trp., 17th Cav. KIA: 15; WIA: 29.

Mar 20 FSB Granite, Attack on. West of Hue. Units: C & E Cos., 1st Bn., 506th Inf., 101st Abn. Div. & B Co., 326th Eng. Bn. KIA: 11; WIA: 31.

Mar 29 FSB Jay, Attack on. 5 miles SW of Thien Ngon Airfield. Units: A Co., 2nd Bn. 7th Cav, 1st Cav Div.; B Btry., 2nd Bn., 12th Arty; and B Btry., 2nd Bn., 19th Arty. KIA: 14; WIA: 53.

Apr 1–2 Spring Offensive. Communists shell 115 locations and launch 13 ground assaults throughout Vietnam.

Apr 1 FSB Illingworth, Attack on. Highway LTL-20, 3.7 miles SW of Thien Ngon Airfield. Units: 2nd Bn., 8th Cav, 1st Cav Div.; A Btry., 2nd Bn., 32nd Arty; and Trp. A, 1st Bn., 11th ACR. KIA: 25; WIA: 54.

Apr 2 Renegade Woods, Firefight in. 6.8 miles NW of Go Dau Ha. Units: 2nd Bn., 27th Inf., 25th Div. and F Co., 75th Rangers. KIA: 12; WIA: 35.

Apr 2-30 Dak Seang Special Forces Camp, Siege of. U.S. Air Units: 483rd TAW, 52nd AB, 37th ARRS & 17th Cav. KIA: 25.

Apr 15 Hill 238, Booby trap. 3.7 miles south of Duc Pho. Booby-trapped 105mm shell and secondary explosions. Units: C Cos. of both 4th Bns. of 3rd and 21st Inf., 11th LIB. KIA: 15; WIA: 32.

Apr 22 War Lord, Shoot-down of. AC-130 gunship is downed by

37mm fire. Near Ban Tang Lou, Laos. Unit: 16th SOS. KIA: 10.

May 1– Jun 30 Cambodia Campaign. Clearance of NVA sanctuaries in the Fish Hook and Parrot's Beak. Captures war's largest arms cache. Snuol is leveled. 30 U.S. gun boats penetrate 21.7 miles up the Mekong River as far as Neak Luong. Units: 30,000 U.S. troops from the 4th, 9th, 25th and 1st Cavalry divisions, 11th ACR; 3rd Bn., 506th Inf., 101st; 5th Bn., 12th Inf., 199th LIB; and 1st Avn. Bde. KIA: 382 KIA; 1,689 WIA.

May 6 FSB Henderson, Sapper attack on. 7 miles SE of Ca Lu. Units: A & E Cos., 2nd Bn., 501st Inf., 101st Abn. Div. & B Btry., 2nd Bn., 11th Arty. KIA: 25; WIA: 40.

May 12 Plei Blang Yam, Helicopter shoot-down near. Downed by .51-caliber anti-aircraft fire. On Route 509, 8.6 miles west of Pleiku. Units: 937th Eng. Grp. & Eng. Cmd. KIA: 10.

Apr 22 AC-130 Gunship, Shoot-down of. Saravan, Laos. Unit: 16th SOS. KIA: 10.

Jul 1-23 FSB Ripcord, Battle for. A Shau Valley. Units: 2nd Bn., 506th & 2nd Bn., 501st Inf., 101st Abn. Div. KIA: 72; WIA: 400. Over July 21-22, single worst day—19 KIA. 506th Inf. (45 of KIA) and 501st (18).

Aug 26 LZ Judy, CH-47B Shoot-down at. SW of Hiep Duc. Worst U.S. hostile helicopter loss of war. Shot down by RPG while removing troops from Kham Duc. Units: D Co., 2nd Bn., 1st Inf., 196th LIB; A Btry., 3rd Bn., 82nd Arty; & 178th ASHC. KIA: 31. D Co. (17 of KIA). WIA: 8.

Sep 20 DMZ Helicopter Shoot-down and Recovery. 2 miles north of Hill 158 (Con Thien). Units: Team 1-8, P Co., 75th Rangers; C Co., 158th Assault Helicopter Company; and A Co., 1st Bn., 61st Inf., 5th Mech. KIA: 11; WIA: 11. 9 of KIA in crash.

Nov 21 Son Tay POW Camp Raid. In an attempt to free 55 U.S. POWs held in North Vietnam, a team of 50 Special Forces land 23 miles west of Hanoi. The POWs had been removed but the team kills foreign advisers and guards in 40 minutes of combat. All team members return safely.

1971

Feb 1– Apr 6 Laos Campaign. *Operation Dewey Canyon II.* U.S. support for *Operation Lam Son 719:* the invasion of Laos to assault the Ho Chi Minh Trail. Units: 10,000 GIs from the 1st Bde., 5th ID; 11th Bde., American; 101st Combat Aviation Grp.; 223rd CAB; 108th Artillery Group & 45th Engineer Grp. U.S.: 253 KIA; 1,149 WIA. Highest KIA: 101st (85), 5th Mech (58) & American (54). 107 helicopters downed; 618 damaged; and 5 planes destroyed.

Mar 28 FSB Mary Ann, Sapper attack on. 4.3 miles NW of Hau Duc. 1-hr. battle. Units: C Co., 1st Bn., 46th Inf., 198th Inf. Bde., American Div. & C Btry., 3rd Bn., 16th Arty. KIA: 30; WIA: 82. C Co. (20 of KIA).

Apr 11 Van Xuan, Assault on NDP near. Song Ve Valley, south of Quang Ngai. Units: A Co., 1st Bn., 20th Inf., 11th LIB, American Div. KIA: 11 (9 from A Co. & 2 in 174th AHC helicopter shoot-down).

Apr 15-16 Last U.S. Offensive Ground Action. Nam Hoa, 2½ miles SE of LZ Veghel. Units: D Co., 2nd Bn., 501st Inf., 101st Abn. Div. & E Co., 1st Bn., 502nd Inf. KIA: 13.

Apr 23-24   Hill 809, Rescue at. A Shau Valley, 5 miles north of A Sap. Units: B & D Trps., 17th Cav; HQ Co., 326th Medical Bn.; & L Co., 75th Rangers, 101st Abn. Div. KIA: 12.

May 1   Offensive U.S. Ground Combat Ends. American ground troops are no longer supposed to play a major ground combat role, relinquishing that responsibility to the South Vietnamese.

May 21   FSB Charlie 2, Rocket strike on. 3 miles NE of Cam Lo village. 122mm rocket hits club bunker. Major units hit: 1st Bn., 61st Inf., 1st Bde., 5th Mech & A Co., 7th Engineers. KIA: 30; WIA: 33. 61st Inf. (14 of KIA).

Jun 14   Last Most Deadly U.S. Firefight. Engagement near FSB Furr, 3.7 miles north of Xuan Loc Airfield. Units: Mostly D Co., 2nd Bn., 5th Cav, 1st Cav Div. KIA: 7 (4 by gunfire).

Jun 26   Last Marine Combat Unit Departs Vietnam. 3rd Marine Amphibious Brigade leaves from Da Nang.

Jul 8–9   DMZ Troop Turnover Complete. Last 500 members of the 1st Bde., 5th Inf. Div., turn over fire bases Alpha 4 and Charlie 2 to the South Vietnamese. Two separate contingents of 50 U.S. artillerymen each remain at both bases to monitor radar equipment and operate artillery.

Nov 12   "Defensive Role." U.S. ground troops officially begin.

1972

Mar 29   Spectre 13 (Prometheus), Shoot-down of. AC-130 gunship downed by SA-2 missile over Muang Phine, Laos (8 miles SW of Tchepone). Unit: 16th SOS. KIA: 14.

Mar 30   Easter/Spring Offensive. NVA crash across the DMZ.

Apr 2-16   Rescue of Bat 21. EB-66C (Bat 21) aircraft is shot down by an SA-2 missile 2 miles NE of Cam Lo village. 5 crewmen are KIA, and 8 GIs die in the rescue effort.

Apr–Jul 11   Siege of An Loc. In support of the ARVN, 31 Americans are KIA: 13 of Det. 1, 374th TAW; 7 Cobra pilots of F Btry., 79th ARA; 8 advisers of AT-51 and TRAC; and 3 of the 18th SOS. Units are awarded the Presidential Unit Citation.

Jun 9   Last U.S. Infantrymen KIA in Vietnam. By an explosive device at Tan Uyen. Unit: Team 76, H Co., 75th Rangers. KIA: 2 (Sgt. Elvis Osborne and Spec. 4 Jeffrey Maurer).

Jun 18   Spectre 11, Shoot-down of. AC-130 gunship downed by SA-7 missile 2½ miles SW of A Luoi village. Unit: 16th SOS. KIA: 12.

Aug 11   U.S. Infantry War Ends: D Co., 3rd Bn., 21st Inf., Task Force Gimlet, completes the last mission from Aug. 8-10. Fire Team Bravo, 2nd Squad, 3rd Platoon, is the last to board a helicopter and leave the field. 3 WIA from booby traps—Spec. 4 James McVicar is the last grunt WIA. The 3rd Battalion is deactivated Aug. 11.

Aug 12   C-130E Transport, Shoot-down of. Hit during take-off from Soc Tang in the Mekong Delta. Units: 50th TAS, MACV AT-14 and Navy Det. Soc Trang. KIA: 14.

Oct 12   Last Green Beret KIA in Vietnam. Sgt. Fred Mick, a medic, is killed by gunfire in a convoy ambush on the Ben Hoa Highway from Long Hai. Unit: 3rd Plt., Det. 22, TF Madden, B Co., 2nd SF Bn., 1st SFG. Advising Cambodians when KIA.

Oct 31   Chinook CH-47C, Shoot-down of. By SA-7 missile. Near Ap Binh Ninh (1), 6.8 miles SW of Dong Tam in Mekong Delta.

Units: 18th Avn. Co. (Corps) & C Trp., 16th Cav. KIA: 15

Dec 18–29   *Operation Linebacker II* ("Christmas Bombing"). In the most concentrated air offensive of the war, U.S. aircraft drop 40,000 tons of bombs over Hanoi and Haiphong. Participating strategic bomber wings: 72nd, 307th and 43rd. KIA: 37 (27 on Dec. 21). WIA: 39.

Dec 19   USS Goldsborough, Shelling of. Hit by NVA counter-battery fire during a gunfire mission. KIA: 3; WIA: 5.

Dec 21   Spectre 17 (Thor), Shoot-down of. AC-130 gunship downed by 37mm fire 10 miles west of Ban Longam, Laos. Unit: 16th SOS. KIA: 14.

1973

Jan 8   Last Group U.S. Hostile Loss in Vietnam. UH-1H helicopter is shot down by a SA-7 missile 3.1 miles SE of Dong Ha Airfield. Units: 62nd Avn. Co. and MACV advisers. KIA: 6.

Jan 27   Last U.S. Soldier KIA Before Vietnam Truce: Lt. Col. William B. Nolde of Advisory Team 47 is killed by artillery fire at An Loc, 11 hours before the cease-fire.

Jan 27   End of U.S. War in Vietnam. Paris Peace Accords mandate *total* withdrawal of U.S. troops from South Vietnam within 60 days. At the time of the armistice, Saigon controls about 75% of South Vietnam's territory and 85% of its population. ARVN is well-equipped and S.V.'s air force is the world's fourth largest. 1.1 million South Vietnamese are under arms.

Feb 5   Air Campaign in Laos. EC-47Q (*Baron 52*), Shoot-down of. 13.6 miles south of Ban Alan, Laos. Units: 361st TEW Sqdn., 56th SOW and Det. 3, 6994th Security Sqdn. KIA: 8 (4 in each unit).

Feb 12–27   Operation Homecoming. First 142 of 587 U.S. POWs are returned. Virtually all of last known 67 POWs are released March 29.

Feb 16   Last U.S. KIA Pre-Withdrawal from Vietnam: Spec. 5 James L. Scroggins is mortally wounded when his CH-47C helicopter of the 18th Aviation Company is shot down on a supply mission south of An Loc. He dies Feb. 23.

Mar 29   Last GIs Depart Vietnam. Only a Defense Attaché Office remains. 209 uniformed Americans remain behind—159 Marine Security Guards at the U.S. Embassy in Saigon and consulates and 50 military attachés.

Jun 16   Last KIA of Cambodia Air Campaign. (U.S. air support continued there after U.S. troop departure from Vietnam.) On Route 19, 21.7 miles SE of Phum Colapouk Mtn. KIA: 2—Capt. Samuel Cornelius of the 336th Tactical Fighter Squadron (TFS) and Capt. John Smallwood of the 58th TFS.

Editor's Note: 989 men from the 4th and 9th Marines covered the 18-hour evacuation of the U.S. Embassy in Saigon on April 29-30, 1975. Two Marine embassy Security Guards were killed in a rocket attack. On May 7, 1975, the Vietnam Era officially ended, and on May 15, 18 Marines, Navy corpsmen and airmen were killed by Khmer Rouge (Cambodian Communists) during the *SS Mayaguez* incident 60 miles off the Cambodian coast on Koh (island) Tang in the Gulf of Thailand. Another 23 U.S. airmen died in Thailand in a related accidental helicopter crash on May 13.

VIETNAM TROOPS: A PROFILE

SOURCE: CONGRESSIONAL RECORD, OCT. 1, 1982

Compiled by Richard K. Kolb, Volunteer Chairman, Vietnam Veterans Leadership Program of Houston
Updated May 2017 as required

IN UNIFORM AND IN-COUNTRY

- Vietnam vets: 9.7% of males of their generation.
- 9,087,000 military personnel served on active duty during the Vietnam era (Aug. 5, 1964—May 7, 1975).
- 8,744,000 personnel were on active duty during the U.S. war years (Aug. 5, 1964—March 28, 1973).
- 3,403,100 (including 514,300 offshore) personnel served in the Southeast Asia Theater (Vietnam, Laos, Cambodia, Thailand and sailors in adjacent South China Sea waters).
- 2,594,000 personnel served within the borders of South Vietnam (Jan. 1, 1965—March 28, 1973).
- 50,000 U.S. troops served in Vietnam between 1960-64.
- 7,484 women (83.5% were nurses) served in-country.
- Peak troop strength in Vietnam: 543,482 (April 30, 1969).

CASUALTIES

- Total deaths: 58,275.
  Hostile: 47,528. Non-hostile: 10,747 (18%).
- 8 nurses died—1 was KIA.
- Married men killed: 17,215.
- 61% of the men killed were 21 years old or younger.
- Highest state death rate: West Virginia—84.1 per 100,000 males (national average in 1970: 58.9).
- Army Combat Arms Hostile Deaths: Infantry, 70%; Aviation/Helicopter, 6%; Field Artillery, 4%; Medical Service, 3%; Armor, 2%; and Combat Engineers, 2%. These branches account for 87% of Army hostile deaths.
- Wounded: 303,704—153,329 hospitalized + 150,375 wounded who required no hospital care.
- Severely disabled: 75,000—23,214 100% disabled; 5,283 lost limbs; 1,081 sustained multiple amputations.
- Amputation or crippling wounds to the lower extremities were 300% higher than in WWII and 70% higher than in Korea. Multiple amputations occurred at a rate of 18.4% compared to 5.7% in WWII.
- Prisoners of War: Captured: 778. Died in captivity: 117.

DRAFTEES VS. VOLUNTEERS

- 25% (648,500) of total forces in-country were draftees. (66% of U.S. armed forces in WWII were drafted.)
- Draftee deaths: 17,692. Hostile: 15,485 (32.5% of all hostile deaths); Non-hostile: 2,207. (Included are a total of 683 Marine deaths.)

- Reservist deaths: 5,771. Hostile: 4,350; Non-hostile: 1,421. National Guard deaths: 97. Hostile: 80; Non-hostile: 17.

RACE AND ETHNIC BACKGROUND

- 88.4% of the men who actually served in Vietnam were Caucasian (includes Hispanics); 10.6% (275,000) were black; 1% belonged to other races.
- 86.1% of the men who died in Vietnam were Caucasian; 12.4% (7,265) were black; 1.5% other races/not reported.
- 170,000 Hispanics served in Vietnam; 3,070 (5.2% of total) died there.
- 86.8% of the men who were killed as a result of hostile action were Caucasian; 12.1% (5,741) were black; 1.1% belonged to other races or not reported.
- 14.1% (1,524) of non-combat deaths were among blacks.
- 34% of blacks who enlisted volunteered for combat arms.
- Overall, blacks suffered 12.4% of the deaths in Vietnam at a time when the percentage of black males of military age was 13.5% of the total population.
- Religion of dead: Protestant—64.4%; Catholic—28.9%; other/none—6.7%.

SOCIO-ECONOMIC STATUS

- 76% of the men sent to Vietnam were from lower middle/working class backgrounds.
- Three-fourths had family incomes above the poverty level; 50% were from middle-income backgrounds.
- Some 23% of Vietnam vets had fathers with professional, managerial or technical occupations.
- 79% of the men who served in Vietnam had a high school education or better when they entered the military service. (63% of Korean War vets and only 45% of WWII vets had completed high school upon separation.)

AGE & HONORABLE SERVICE

- Average age of the Vietnam War GI: 22.
- 97% of Vietnam-era veterans were honorably discharged.

PRIDE IN SERVICE

- 91% of Vietnam War veterans and 90% of those who saw heavy combat are proud to have served.
- 66% of Vietnam vets said they would serve again if called.

Note: Views on serving were polled in the 1980s.

FURTHER READING

Only full-length books and book chapters on specific battles are listed here. For general background information, reference works also are provided. Book listings appear in the same order as the battles in the narrative. Many battles, however, have never received book-length coverage. Most of this book's contents were pieced together from numerous newspaper and magazine articles, as well as first-person accounts collected and interviews conducted over many years.

GENERAL REFERENCES

Clodfelter, Michael. Vietnam in Military Statistics: *A History of the Indochina Wars, 1772-1991*. Jefferson, N.C.: McFarland & Company, 1995.

Ebert, James R. *A Life in a Year: The American Infantryman in Vietnam, 1965-1972*. Novato, Calif.: Presidio Press, 1993.

Hobson, Chris. *Vietnam Air Losses: U.S. Air Force, Navy and Marine Corps Fixed-Wing Aircraft Losses in Southeast Asia, 1961-1973*. Hinckley, England: Midland Publishing, 2001.

Kelley, Michael P. *Where We Were: A Comprehensive Guide to the Firebases, Military Installations and Naval Vessels of the Vietnam War, 1945-1975*. Central Point, Ore.: Hellgate Press, 2002.

Reinberg, Linda. *In the Field: The Language of the Vietnam War*. N.Y.: Facts on File, 1991.

Sigler, David B. *Vietnam Battle Chronology: U.S. Army and Marine Corps Combat Operations, 1965-1973*. Jefferson, N.C.: McFarland & Company, 1992.

Stanton, Shelby L. *Vietnam Order of Battle: U.S. Army and Allied Ground Forces In Vietnam*. Washington, D.C.: U.S. News Books, 1981.

DONG XOAI (June 10, 1965)

Booth, James W. *Returning Fire in the Beginning* (pp. 287-312). Bloomington, Ind.: Author House, 2011.

CHU LAI (Aug. 18-21, 1965)

Henderson, Charles W. Chapter 11: "Starlite" in *Marshalling the Faithful: The Marines First Year in Vietnam*. N.Y.: Berkley Books, 1993.

Lehrack, Otto J. *The First Battle: Operation Starlite and the Beginning of the Blood Debt in Vietnam*. Havertown, Pa.: Casemate, 2004.

Wilkins, Warren. Chapter 5: "Van Tuong" in *Grab Their Belts to Fight Them: The Viet Cong's Big-Unit War Against the U.S., 1965-1966*. Annapolis, Md.: Naval Institute Press, 2011.

IA DRANG VALLEY (November 1965)

Alley, J. Lyles. *The Ghosts in the Green Grass: The Journey of the Second Battalion, 7th Cavalry in the Hell of the Ia Drang Valley in 1965*. Signal Mountain, Tenn.: Codi Publishing, 2015.

Galloway, Joe and Harold Moore. *We Were Soldiers Once … and Young: Ia Drang, the Battle That Changed the War in Vietnam*. N.Y.: Random House, 1992.

HILL 65 (Nov. 8, 1965)

Conetto, Al. *The Hump: The 1st Battalion, 503rd Infantry in the First Major Battle of the Vietnam War*. Jefferson, N.C.: McFarland & Company, 2015.

MY CANH (Feb. 6-7, 1966)

Bowers, Curt. *Forward Edge of the Battle Area*. Kansas City, Mo.: Beacon Hill Press, 1987.

Hackworth, David. Chapter 15: "The Year of the Horse" (pp. 500-09) in *About Face*. N.Y.: Simon & Schuster, 1989.

CHAU NGAI (March 5-6, 1966)

Lee, Alex. Chapter 13: "Operation Utah" (pp. 241-77) in *Utter's Battalion: 2/7 Marines in Vietnam, 1965-66*. N.Y.: Ballantine Books, 2000.

VINH HUY VALLEY (March 21-23, 1966)

Wilkins, Warren. Chapter 11: "Winter-Spring Battles: Region 5" in *Grab Their Belts to Fight Them*. Annapolis, Md.: Naval Institute Press, 2011.

COURTENAY RUBBER PLANTATION/XA CAM MY (April 11, 1966)

Wilson, George. Chapter 1: "Legacy" (pp. 2-42) in *Mud Soldiers*. N.Y.: Scribner's 1989.

HILL 766 and LZ HERFORD (May 17 and 21, 1966)

Marshall, S.L.A. Chapters: "Almost Hill 766" and "Men Facing Death" in *Battles in the Monsoon*. N.Y.: William Morrow & Co., 1967.

LOC NINH RUBBER PLANTATION (June 11, 1966)

Kurtz, Richard. Chapters 13-16 in *Then A Soldier*. Lynchburg, Va.: Warwick House Pub., 2011.

SIEGE of HILL 488 (June 13, 1966)

Hildreth, Ray and Charles W. Sasser. *Hill 488*. N.Y.: Simon & Schuster, 2003.

TRUNG LUONG (June 20-22, 1966)

Marshall, S.L.A. *The Fields of Bamboo: Dong Tre, Trung Luong and Hoa Hui*. N.Y.: Dial, 1971.

'VALLEY of a THOUSAND GHOSTS' (Nov. 21, 1966)

Marshall, S.L.A. "Ordeal by Ambush" (pp. 175-208) in *West to Cambodia*. N.Y.: Cowles, 1968.

DAU TIENG (Nov. 3-5, 1966)

Marshall, S.L.A. *Ambush: The Battle of Dau Tieng*. N.Y.: Cowles Book Co., 1969.

LZ BIRD (Dec. 27, 1966)

Marshall, S.L.A. *Bird: The Christmastide Battle*. N.Y.: Cowles, 1968.

BINH SON (April 21, 1967)

Lehrack, Otto J. Chapter 2: "Bald Eagle" in *Road of 10,000 Pains*. Minneapolis: Zenith Press, 2010.

HILL 110 (May 10, 1967)

Lehrack, Otto J. Chapter 7: "Union I: The Battle for Hill 110" (pp. 57-76) in *Road of 10,000 Pains*. Minneapolis: Zenith Press, 2010.

LZ EAGLE (May 26, 1967)

Lehrack, Otto J. Chapter 10: "Union II: The Enemy Strikes Back" (pp. 102-115) in *Road of 10,000 Pains*. Zenith Press, 2010.

HILL FIGHTS (April 30-May 12, 1967)

Murphy, Edward F. *The Hill Fights: The First Battle of Khe Sanh*. N.Y.: Presidio Press, 2003.

Maras, Robert and Charles W. Sasser. *Blood in the Hills: The Story of Khe Sanh, the Most Savage Fight of the Vietnam War*. Guilford, Conn.: Lyons Press, 2017.

'NINE DAYS in MAY' (May 18-22, 1967)

Wilkins, Warren K. *Nine Days in May: The Battles of the 4th Infantry Division on the Cambodian Border*. Norman: Oklahoma University Press, 2017.

VINH HUY (June 2-3, 1967)

Lehrack, Otto J. Chapter 18: "The Second Battle at Vinh Huy" (pp. 217-29) in *Road of 10,000 Pains*. Zenith Press, 2010.

XOM BO II (June 17, 1967)

Hearne, David. *June 17, 1967, Battle of Xom Bo II*. Lumberton, Texas: Subterfuge Publishing, 2016.

RIVERINE WARFARE/AP BAC (June 19, 1967)

Weist, Andrew. Chapter 5: "The Day Everything Changed" in *The Boys of '67: Charlie Company's War in Vietnam*. N.Y.: Osprey Publishing, 2013.

'THE SLOPES' (June 22, 1967)

Murphy, Edward F. Chapter 4: "Battle of the Slopes" in *Dak To: The 173rd Airborne Brigade in South Vietnam's Central Highlands, June-November 1967*. Novato, Calif.: Presidio Press, 1993.

MAYHEM in the 'MARKETPLACE' (July 2, 1967)

Coan, James P. Chapter 8: "Buffalo" (pp. 109-136) in *Con Thien: The Hill of Angels*. Tuscaloosa, Ala.: University of Alabama Press, 2004.

Nolan, Keith W. *Operation Buffalo: USMC Fight for the DMZ*. Novato, Calif.: Presidio Press, 1991.

DONG SON (Sept. 6, 1967)

Lehrack, Otto J. Chapter 15: "Operation Swift" in *Road of 10,000 Pains*. Minneapolis: Zenith Press, 2010.

Mode, Daniel L. "Semper Fidelis" in *The Grunt Padre* (Father Vincent Capodanno): Vietnam, 1966-1967. Oak Lawn, Ill.: CMJ Marian Publishers, 2000.

'THE CHURCHYARD' and HILL 48 (Sept. 7 and 10, 1967)

Coan, James P. Chapter 11: "Into the Valley of Death" (pp. 182-211) in *Con Thien: The Hill of Angels*. U. of Ala. Pr., 2004

Hammel, Eric. Part I: "The Churchyard" in *Ambush Valley*. Novato, Calif.: Presidio Press, 1990.

ONG THANH (Oct. 17, 1967)

Maraniss, David. *They Marched Into Sunlight: War and Peace, Vietnam and America, October 1967*. N.Y.: Simon & Schuster, 2003.

Shelton, James E. *The Beast Was Out There: The 28th Infantry Black Lions and the Battle of Ong Thanh, Vietnam October 1967*. Chicago: Cantigny First Division Association, 2002.

DAK TO/HILL 875 (Nov. 20, 1967)

Eggleston, Michael A. Chapter 3: "Dak To" (pp. 45-98) in *Dak To and the Border Battles of Vietnam, 1967-1968*. Jefferson, N.C.: McFarland & Company, 2017.

Murphy, Edward F. *Dak To*. Novato, Calif.: Presidio Press, 1993.

FIREBASE NASHUA (Dec. 6, 1967)

Tonsetic, Robert L. Chapter 3: "The Bloodiest Day" and Chapter 4: "Victory at Night" in *Days of Valor: An Inside Account of the Bloodiest Six Months of the Vietnam War*. Drexel Hill, Pa.: Casemate, 2006.

THON THAM KHE (Dec. 27, 1967)

Young, Paul R. *First Recon—Second To None: A Marine Reconnaissance Battalion, 1967-1968*. N.Y.: Ballantine Books, 1992.

QUE SON and HIEP DUC VALLEYS (Jan. 3-10, 1968)

Humphries, James F. *Through the Valley: Vietnam 1967-1968*. Boulder, Colo.: Lynne Reinner Publishers, 2000.

CEMETERY HILL (Jan. 30, 1968)

Arthurs, Ted G. "Cemetery Hill" (pp. 42-59) in *Land With No Sun*. Mechanicsburg, Pa.: Stackpole Books, 2006.

MPs BATTLE in SAIGON (Jan. 31, 1968)

Irzyk, Albin F. *Unsung Heroes, Saving Saigon*. Raleigh, N.C.: Ivy House Publishing Group, 2008.

Nolan, Keith. *The Battle for Saigon, Tet 1968*. Novato, Calif.: Presidio Press, 2002.

HUE (February 1968)

Bowden, Mark. *Hue 1968: A Turning Point in the American War in Vietnam*. N.Y: Atlantic Monthly Press, 2017.

Hammel, Eric. *Fire in the Streets: The Battle for Hue, Tet 1968*. Chicago: Contemporary Books, 1991.

Krohn, Charles A. *The Lost Battalion: Controversy and Casualties in the Battle of Hue*. Westport, Conn.: Praeger, 1993.

Nolan, Keith. *Battle for Hue: Tet 1968*. Novato, Calif.: Presidio Press, 1983.

Smith, George W. *The Siege at Hue*. N.Y.: Ballantine, 1999.

Warr, Nicholas. *Phase Line Green: The Battle for Hue, 1968*. Annapolis, Md.: Naval Institute Press, 1997.

KHE SANH (February–April 1968)

Archer, Michael. *A Patch of Ground: Khe Sanh Remembered*. Central Point, Ore.: Hellgate Press, 2004.

Brinkley, Douglas and Ronald J. Drez. *Voices of Courage: The Battle for Khe Sanh, Vietnam*. N.Y.: Bulfinch Press, 2005.

Clarke, Bruce B.G. *Expendable Warriors: The Battle of Khe Sanh and the Vietnam War*. Westport, Conn.: Praeger, 2007.

Ewing, Michael. *The Illustrated History of Khe Sanh*. N.Y.: Bantam Books, 1987.

Hammel, Eric M. *Khe Sanh: Siege in the Clouds*. N.Y.: Crown Publishers, 1989.

Jones, Gregg. *Last Stand at Khe Sanh: The U.S. Marines' Finest Hour in Vietnam*. Boston: Da Capo Press, 2014.

Pisor, Robert. *The End of the Line: The Siege of Khe Sanh.* N.Y.: W.W. Norton, 1982.

Prados, John and Ray W. Stubbe. *Valley of Decision: The Siege of Khe Sanh.* Boston: Houghton Mifflin, 1991.

Stubbe, Ray W. *Battalion of Kings: A Tribute to Our Fallen Brothers Who Died Because of the Battlefield of Khe Sanh.* Wauwatosa, Wis.: Khe Sanh Veterans, 2008.

LANG VEI SPECIAL FORCES CAMP (Feb. 7, 1968)

Phillips, William R. *Night of the Silver Stars: The Battle of Lang Vei.* Annapolis, Md.: Naval Institute Press, 1997.

HOC MON (March 2, 1968)

James, Larry D. *Unfortunate Sons: A True Story of Young Men and War.* Washington, D.C.: Cambridge Dent Publishers, 2005.

DAI DO (April 30-May 2, 1968)

Nolan, Keith. *The Magnificent Bastards: The Joint Army-Marine Defense of Dong Ha, 1968.* Novato, Calif.: Presidio Press, 1994.

NHI HA (May 2 & 6, 1968)

Humphries, James F. Chapter 25: "Nhi Ha Village in *Through the Valley.* Boulder, Colo.: Lynne Reinner Publishers, 2000.

GO NOI ISLAND (May 16-24, 1968)

Simonsen, Robert. *Every Marine: 1968 Vietnam, A Battle for Go Noi Island.* Westminster, Md.: Heritage Books, 2004.

KHAM DUC (May 11-12, 1967)

Davies, Bruce. *The Battle at Ngok Tavak: A Bloody Defeat in South Vietnam, 1968.* Lubbock: Texas Tech University Press, 2009.

SAIGON (May 8-12, 1968)

Nolan, Keith W. *House to House: Playing the Enemy's Game in Saigon, May 1968.* Osceola, Wis.: Zenith Press, 2006.

FOB-4/CCN NORTH/SOG (Aug. 23, 1968)

Meyer, John S. and John E. Peters. Chapter 7: "Cry Havoc" in *On the Ground: The Secret War in Vietnam.* Levin Pub. Co., 2007.

Plaster, John L. Part II: "Recon" (pp. 74-81) in *Secret Commandos: Behind Enemy Lines With the Elite Warriors of SOG.* N.Y.: Simon & Schuster, 2004.

PLEI TRAP VALLEY (March 3-4, 1969)

Carey, Ronald. *The War Above the Trees: Operation Wayne Grey.* Bloomington, Ind.: Trafford Publishing, 2004.

FIREBASE AIRBORNE (May 13, 1969)

Zaffiri, Samuel. Chapter 11: "Sideshow at Firebase Airborne" in *Hamburger Hill.* Novato, Calif.: Presidio Press, 1988.

NUI YON HILL (May 12-15, 1969)

Pozdol, Thomas. *Tam Ky: The Battle for Nui Yon Hill.* Lincoln, Neb.: iUniverse, 2009.

HAMBURGER HILL (May 11-20, 1969)

Boccia, Frank. *The Crouching Beast: A U.S. Army Lieutenant's Account of the Battle for Hamburger Hill.* Jefferson, N.C.: McFarland & Company, 2013.

DiCongsiglio, John. *Vietnam—The Bloodbath at Hamburger Hill.* Danbury, Conn.: Scholastic Library Publishing, 2009.

Zaffiri, Samuel. *Hamburger Hill: The Brutal Battle for Dong Ap Bia, May 11-20, 1969.* Novato, Calif.: Presidio Press, 1988.

FIREBASE TOMAHAWK (June 19, 1969)

Trowbridge, John M. *Kentucky Thunder in Vietnam.* Frankfort, Ky.: Kentucky National Guard, 2010.

Wilson, James. *The Sons of Bardstown: 25 Years of Vietnam in an American Town.* N.Y.: Crown, 1994.

HIEP DUC VALLEY (Aug. 17-29, 1969)

Nolan, Keith W. *Death Valley: The Summer Offensive, I Corps, August 1969.* Novato, Calif.: Presidio Press, 1987.

FIREBASE ILLINGWORTH (April 1, 1970)

Keith, Philip. *Fire Base Illingworth: The Epic True Story of Remarkable Courage Against Staggering Odds.* N.Y.: St. Martin's Press, 2013.

CAMBODIA INCURSION (May-June 1970)

Berry, Jerald W. *Twelve Days in May: The Untold Story of the Northern Thrust Into Cambodia by the 4th Infantry Division.* Bloomington, Ind.: Xlibis, 2010.

Coleman, J.D. *Incursion: From America's Chokehold on the NVA's Lifelines to the Sacking of the Cambodian Sanctuaries.* N.Y.: St. Martin's Press, 1991.

Morgan, Paul. *The Parrot's Beak: U.S. Operations in Cambodia.* Central Point, Ore.: Hellgate, Press, 2000.

Nolan, Keith W. *Into Cambodia: Spring Campaign, Summer Offensive, 1970.* Novato, Calif.: Presidio Press, 1990.

Poole, Eric. *Company of Heroes: A Forgotten Medal of Honor and Bravo Company's War in Vietnam.* N.Y.: Osprey Publishing, 2015.

Shaw, John M. *The Cambodian Campaign: The 1970 Offensive and America's Vietnam War.* Lawrence: University Press of Kansas, 2005.

FIREBASE RIPCORD (July 2-23, 1970)

Harrison, Benjamin L. *Hell on a Hill Top: America's Last Major Battle in Vietnam.* Lincoln, Neb.: iUniverse, Inc., 2004.

Nolan, Keith W. Ripcord: *Screaming Eagles Under Siege, Vietnam 1970.* Novato, Calif. Presidio Press, 2000.

SON TAY RAID (Nov. 21, 1970)

Gargus, John. *The Son Tay Raid: American POWs in Vietnam War Were Not Forgotten.* College Station: Texas A&M Press, 2007.

Guenon, William A. *Secret and Dangerous: Night of the Son Tay POW Raid.* East Lowell, Mass.: Wagon Wing Press, 2005.

Schemer, Benjamin F. *The Raid: The Son Tay Prison Rescue Mission.* N.Y.: Harper & Row, 1976.

LAOS INVASION (February–April 1971)

Nolan, Keith W. *Into Laos: The Story of Dewey Canyon II/Lam Son 719, Vietnam, 1971.* Novato, Calif.: Presidio Press, 1986.

Sander, Robert D. *Invasion of Laos, 1971: Lam Son 719.* Norman: University of Oklahoma Press, 2014.

Willbanks, James H. *A Raid Too Far: Operation Lam Son 719 and Vietnamization in Laos.* College Station: Texas A&M University Press, 2014.

FIREBASE MARY ANN (March 28, 1971)

Nolan, Keith W. *Sappers in the Wire: The Life and Death of Firebase Mary Ann.* College Station: Texas A&M University Press, 1995.

DECEMBER 1972 BOMBING CAMPAIGN (Dec. 18-29, 1972)

Eschmann, Karl J. *Linebacker: The Untold Story of the Air Raids Over North Vietnam.* N.Y.: Ivy Books/Ballantine, 1989.

Michel, Marshall L. *The Eleven Days of Christmas: America's Last Vietnam Battle.* San Francisco: Encounter Books, 2002.

LIMA SITE 85 (March 11, 1968)

Castle, Timothy. *One Day Too Long: Top Secret Site 85 and the Bombing of North Vietnam.* N.Y.: Columbia University Press, 2000.

AIR FORCE GUNSHIPS over the HO CHI MINH TRAIL

Head, William P. Chapters 6-9 in *Night Hunters: The AC-130s and Their Role in U.S. Airpower.* College Station: Texas A&M University Press, 2014.

CAPSULE BIOS OF
CONTRIBUTING WRITERS

RICHARD K. KOLB: Publisher and editor-in-chief of *VFW* magazine for 27 years (1989-2016), Kolb conceived the idea for *Brutal Battles of Vietnam,* selected and edited all of its contents and wrote 40 of the chapters. He partially authored and edited *Faces of Victory* (a two-volume history of WWII), *Battles of the Korean War: Americans Engage in Deadly Combat, 1950-1953, Cold War Clashes: Confronting Communism, 1945-1991* and *Combat Action: Cambodia to the Balkans, 1975-1991.* Kolb served in Vietnam with the 4th Infantry and 101st Airborne divisions during 1970-71 in the Central Highlands and I Corps as an artillery RTO.

ROBERT WIDENER: For 27½ years, Widener designed *VFW* magazine as art director. An accomplished graphic artist, his work has been recognized by numerous national awards. Besides designing the entire book, he wrote the chapters on *Courage Unrivaled* (America's most highly decorated Vietnam warriors) and LZ Margo. He also compiled the Index, constructed the battle maps, obtained each of the 700 photos and coordinated all production aspects of publishing the book.

VFW MAGAZINE STAFF (present and former)**: Tim Dyhouse** has been senior editor for 22 years and **Janie Dyhouse,** associate editor, has been on the staff for 19 years. **Kelly Gibson, Kelly Von Lunen** and **Shannon Hanson** were all senior writers for the magazine.

AL HEMINGWAY: Author of *Our War Was Different: U.S. Marine Combined Action Platoons in Vietnam,* Hemingway served in Vietnam with the 3rd Marine Division during 1969. He has written extensively on Vietnam, and contributed 15 of the chapters.

SUSAN KATZ KEATING: Keating wrote *Prisoners of Hope: Exploiting the POW/MIA Myth in America.* A journalist specializing in national security, she writes for *Time* and *People* magazines, as well as the Army National Guard's *GX* magazine and *Soldier of Fortune,* including articles on recent wars. She wrote three of the chapters.

KEITH W. NOLAN: Before his untimely death at age 44 in 2009, Nolan was (and still is) the "dean" of Vietnam combat historians. The author of some dozen books on Vietnam, he focused exclusively on the grunt's ground view of the war. He wrote two of the chapters.

CHARLES HAWKINS: Hawkins was a platoon leader in C Co., and later company commander of A Co., 2nd Bn., 506th Inf., 101st Airborne Div. He was wounded four times during the siege of Firebase Ripcord. He wrote two chapters.

CHARLES W. SASSER: Co-author of *Hill 488,* Sasser is author, co-author or contributing author of 60 books, most recently *Blood in the Hills: The Story of Khe Sanh (2017).* He served in the Army Special Forces (1965-66, 1972-1983).

JOHN L. PLASTER: A three-tour vet of the elite Studies and Observation Group in Vietnam, former Green Beret Plaster wrote *SOG: The Secret Wars of America's Commandos in Vietnam,* among other books on Vietnam.

JOE GALLOWAY: A renowned war correspondent, Galloway is best known for co-authoring *We Were Soldiers Once ... And Young* (on the Battle of the Ia Drang Valley). He currently serves as a consultant to the Vietnam War 50th Anniversary Commemoration project run out of the Secretary of Defense's office.

LARRY JAMES: A radio journalist, James wrote the book on Hoc Mon entitled *Unfortunate Sons: A True Story of Young Men and War.* He served with the 9th Infantry Regt.

JOHN F. BAUER: A platoon leader in D Co., 3rd Bn., 8th Inf., 4th Div., Bauer's unit arrived in the immediate aftermath of the 1969 battle in the Plei Trap Valley.

GARY LINDERER: A LRRP veteran of the 101st Airborne Division, Linderer has written extensively about the Rangers in Vietnam. He was elected to the U.S. Army Ranger Hall of Fame in 2016.

INDEX

Units and names of individuals are referenced when they first appear in a particular battle and may be mentioned later.